FROM POPULAR FRONT
TO COLD WAR

FROM POPULAR FRONT TO COLD WAR

The Interracial Left and the
International Workers Order,
1930–1945

Edited by Elissa Sampson
and Robert M. Zecker

ILR PRESS
CORNELL UNIVERSITY PRESS
Ithaca and London

Support for the publication of this book was provided by the Hull Memorial Publication Fund of Cornell University.

Copyright © 2025 by Cornell University

All rights reserved. Except for brief quotations in a review, this book, or parts thereof, must not be reproduced in any form without permission in writing from the publisher. For information, address Cornell University Press, Sage House, 512 East State Street, Ithaca, New York 14850. Visit our website at cornellpress.cornell.edu.

First published 2025 by Cornell University Press

Librarians: A CIP catalog record for this book is available from the Library of Congress.

ISBN 9781501785160 (hardcover)
ISBN 9781501785177 (paperback)
ISBN 9781501785184 (pdf)
ISBN 9781501785191 (epub)

To the members of the IWO and their descendants, and to new heirs

Declaration of Principles

(Adopted at the Third National Convention of the IWO, May 1935)

THE International Workers Order is a workers' fraternal organization. It provides its members with sick, disability and death benefits, as well as with medical aid and other forms of help. It accepts members irrespective of sex, nationality, color, creed or political beliefs.

Workers' fraternal mutual benefits serve the purpose of meeting the problems of the economic insecurity of the workers. But they cannot solve the problem. The I.W.O. therefore considers it its duty as a workers' organization to aid all other of the workers' efforts to liquidate their economic insecurity.

—Manual of the International Workers Order, 1936

Contents

Acknowledgments ix
Abbreviations xi
Note on Transliteration xiii

Introduction: Race and Ethnicity in the US Left
Robert M. Zecker and Elissa Sampson 1

Part I **Beginnings: Yiddish-Speaking Immigrants and Class Solidarity**

1. *Achdus*: Forging Jewish Unity in Wartime Platforms
   Elissa Sampson 23

2. "Why Must You Have Your Own University?" Yiddish Adult Education and the Communist Movement in the United States   *Dylan Kaufman-Obstler* 50

3. Portrait of a Radical: June Gordon, the Emma Lazarus Clubs, and Communist Jewish Women's Activism, 1920–1970   *Jennifer Young* 72

Part II **A Radical Urban Black Belt: Tackling Race, Colonialism, and Internationalism**

4. Du Bois's Cold War Revisions: The Color Line and the Jewish Problem, from Galicia to Dougherty County   *Ben Ratskoff* 99

5. Langston Hughes and the International Workers Order
   Matthew Calihman 122

6. Staging the Interracial Left: Paul Robeson, Black Artistry, and the International Workers Order   *Felicia Bevel* 145

7. Fighting for Black Rights Through the Fraternal Arena: Louise Thompson Patterson in the International Workers Order   *Elissa Sampson and Robert M. Zecker* 172

Part III **A Left Diaspora: Internationalism and Radicalism**

    8. *Di progressive*: YKUF in Argentina and South America
        Nerina Visacovsky   205

    9. A Constellation of One's Own: Canadian Jewish Communists and Their Mass Organizations   *Henry Srebrnik*   229

    10. "Dancing at Two Weddings": Radical Jewish Artists and Their Relationship to Yiddishkeit, from the Popular Front to the Postwar Era   *Lauren B. Strauss*   251

    11. "We'll Stay Here 'til the Fascist Tomb Is Made": The IWO and the International Brigades   *Annabel Gottfried Cohen*   276

Part IV **Endings: Persecution and Legacies—The Shift from the Old to the New Left**

    12. "A Fraternal Order Sentenced to Death": The Legal Persecution of the International Workers Order
        Robert M. Zecker   309

    13. From Many Roots, One Tree: Jews and the Origins of Multiethnic Communism in the United States, 1921–1972   *Paul C. Mishler*   333

    Coda: "The Melting Pot Has a Scorched Base"   *Paul Buhle*   354

Appendix   363
Contributors   365
Index   369

Acknowledgments

The editors and the publisher would like to thank the following institutions and individuals for their kind permission to use the illustrations in this book:

Abraham Lincoln Brigade Archives, Tamiment Library and Robert F. Wagner Labor Archives, New York University, New York, New York. Henceforth: Courtesy of ALBA and Fay (Florence) Itzkowitz

Beinecke Rare Book and Manuscript Library, Yale University, New Haven, Connecticut

Chicago American Left, Ephemera Collection, 1894–2008, AIS.2007.11, University of Pittsburgh, Pittsburgh, Pennsylvania

Division of Rare and Manuscript Collections, Cornell University Library, Ithaca, New York

IWO Collection, International Workers Order (IWO) Records #5276, Kheel Center for Labor-Management Documentation & Archives, Catherwood Library, Cornell University, Ithaca, New York. Henceforth: Courtesy of the Kheel Center. Digitized Kheel Center IWO documents can be found at https://digital.library.cornell.edu/collections/iwo-jpfo

Louise Thompson Patterson Papers, Stuart A. Rose Manuscript, Archives, & Rare Book Library, Emory University, Atlanta, Georgia, with the permission of MaryLouise Patterson

Spanish Refugee Relief Association Records (SRRAR), Rare Book and Manuscript Library, Columbia University, New York, New York

Abbreviations

ACIZ	Asociación Cultural Israelita Zhitlovsky (Zhitlovsky Jewish Cultural Association)
ACPFB	American Committee for Protection of Foreign Born
ACWA	Amalgamated Clothing Workers of America
ALBA	Abraham Lincoln Brigades Archives
AMIA	Asociación Mutual Israelita Argentina (Argentine Jewish Mutual Association)
Ambijan	American Committee for the Settlement of Jews in Birobidzhan
AR	Arbeter Ring (Workmen's Circle, Workers Circle)
ARTEF	Arbeter Teater Farband (Workers' Theatre Association)
ASA	Associação Sholem Aleikhem (Sholem Aleichem Association)
ASC	American Slav Congress
BIBSA	Biblioteca Israelita Brasileira Sholem Aleikhem (Brazilian Sholem Aleichem Jewish Library)
Bund	Algemeyner Yidisher Arbeter Bund in Rusland, Poyln un Lite (General Union of Jewish Workers in Russia, Poland, and Lithuania)
CAA	Council on African Affairs
CAWS	American Committee of Jewish Writers, Artists and Scientists
CI	Communist International
CP	Communist Party of Canada
CPI	Communist Party of Israel
CPUSA	Communist Party of the United States of America
CRC	Civil Rights Congress
DAIA	Delegación de Asociaciones Israelitas Argentinas (Delegation of Jewish Argentinian Associations)
DP	Displaced Persons
DW	*Daily Worker*
ELF	Emma Lazarus Federation
FAP	Federal Art Project
FBI	Federal Bureau of Investigation
FEPC	Fair Employment Practices Committee
FNB	Foreign Nationalities Branch of the Office of Strategic Services

FOC	Finnish Organization of Canada
GOSET	Moscow State Jewish Theater
HUAC	House Committee on Un-American Activities
ICIB	Instituto Cultural Israelita Brasileiro (Brazilian Jewish Cultural Institution)
ICOR	Yidishe Kolonizatsye Organizatsye in Ratn-Farband (Organization for Jewish Colonization in Russia)
ICUF	Idisher Cultur Farband (Yiddish Cultural Association)
IFT	Idisher Folk Teater (Yiddish Folk Theater)
ILD	International Labor Defense
ILGWU	International Ladies' Garment Workers' Union
INS	Immigration and Naturalization Service
IRS	Internal Revenue Service
IWO	International Workers Order
JAC	Jewish Anti-Fascist Committee
JDC	Joint Distribution Committee
JPFO	Jewish Peoples Fraternal Order
JVP	Jewish Voice for Peace
KKL	Keren Kayemet LeIsrael (The Jewish National Fund, also known as the JNF)
LPP	Labor-Progressive Party
NAACP	National Association for the Advancement of Colored People
NNC	National Negro Congress
OPFA	Organización Popular Contra el Fascismo y el Antisemitismo (Popular Organization Against Fascism and Antisemitism)
PLO	Palestine Liberation Organization
SWS	Slovak Workers Society
TAIB	Theater de la Casa do Povo (Theater of the People's House)
UJPO	United Jewish People's Order
ULFTA	Ukrainian Labour Farmer Temple Association
UN	United Nations
USHMM	United States Holocaust Memorial Museum
WPA	Works Progress Administration
Yevsektsiya	Jewish Section of the Comintern or the Communist Party
YIVO	Yidisher Visnshaftlekher Institut (YIVO Institute for Jewish Research)
YKUF	Yidisher Kultur Farband (Yiddish Cultural Association)

Note on Transliteration

YIVO (Yidisher Visnshaftlekher Institut or YIVO Institute for Jewish Research) standards of transliteration have mainly been used when providing terms, titles, and names from Yiddish into English. We have tried to be consistent where possible, while respecting authors' wishes. Notably, exceptions can be seen in the case of personal names and to some extent for pre-YIVO transliterations. When Yiddish-speaking immigrants chose their own English names, they often used popularly accepted transliterations or adopted English names as part of a process of immigrant acculturation. Typically they arrived in the United States before the YIVO standards were promulgated, and did not employ YIVO's system to determine the spelling of their names or those of many other words. Hence, in rendering names we have used the names that the immigrants themselves used. Thus, Itche Goldberg is rendered as "Itche," since that is how he spelled his name in English, while Pesach Novick used Paul as his English first name. Other examples abound. We see something similar although not identical in Latin America, where they did not use the YIVO system of transliteration. An English translation is provided for transliterated terms and publications.

Twentieth-century Yiddish itself does not necessarily use a fully phonetic orthography. Yiddish, a fusion language spelled with Hebrew letters, includes Germanic, Slavic, Semitic, and Romance components. Words and expressions of Hebrew or Aramaic origin are spelled as they are in the source language. Thus, the history of the Yiddish language is reflected in its variable orthography. Notable here is that aside from differences based on regional dialects, most IWO Yiddish writers and publications did not use the Soviet "simplified" system, which discouraged the retention of Hebrew or Aramaic spellings. While Yiddish orthography may well reflect ideology, in the case of the International Workers Order's confiscated archives housed at Cornell University's Kheel Center, it does not necessarily do so.

FROM POPULAR FRONT
TO COLD WAR

Introduction

RACE AND ETHNICITY IN THE US LEFT

Robert M. Zecker and Elissa Sampson

**O, yes,
I say it plain,
America never was America to me,
And yet I swear this oath—
America will be!**

—Langston Hughes, "Let America Be America Again" (1936)

The words that Langston Hughes penned, later published by the International Workers Order (IWO) in his 1938 volume of poetry, *A New Song*, encapsulate the ethos of the IWO, which was founded on the interracial, multiethnic activism of Jewish and other immigrants, at its best. From 1930 to 1954, this leftist fraternal society championed civil rights, racial justice, the provision of affordable health care and life insurance to working people, and advocacy of progressive social programs. The IWO also was instrumental in organizing and supporting industrial unions within the Congress of Industrial Organizations (CIO) that improved the life chances of its members. This volume highlights the IWO and its sixteen "language divisions," especially that of its founding section for Yiddish-speaking members, eventually known as the Jewish Peoples Fraternal Order (JPFO), as well as the vital actions of the Order's Black leadership within what became its Douglass-Lincoln Society.

The IWO, which had its heyday in the 1930s and '40s, was pioneering in its understanding of the importance of what we now call intersectionality, seeing the battle against racism, antisemitism, and anti-immigrant xenophobia as all of a piece and campaigning to ameliorate the class-based hurdles that working people—especially women—faced in an unregulated, capitalist America. Indeed, African American IWO officer Louise Thompson, who became a vice president in 1940, had in 1936 already used the phrase "triple oppression" to condemn the special wounds capitalism inflicted on Black women.[1] The minutes of IWO meetings held by Jewish, Slovak, Polish, and Italian lodges are replete with notices of campaigns to end Jim Crow segregation, defend victims of racialized justice such as the Scottsboro defendants or Rosa Lee Ingram, and press Congress to enact anti-lynching legislation or integrate the armed forces.

Although the IWO was an immigrant-founded fraternal benefits society that offered members a social safety net by providing needed low-cost insurance for workers, including disability benefits, the Order also pushed for lasting federal improvements to workers' safety. It lobbied for federal unemployment insurance and old-age pensions, promoting these measures years before Social Security became law, and also for a guaranteed annual income and government-funded universal health care. (We are still waiting on these measures.) The Order also established low-cost health clinics, including birth-control clinics, that were open evenings to accommodate working mothers. Given its focus, the IWO might serve as a useful early multiethnic model of intersectional, pathbreaking, militant activism around inequities of race *and* class that can help bridge the false dichotomy between them and allow us to exit the cul-de-sac of dubious arguments where "identity politics" comes into conflict with supposedly more genuine issues of class.

The IWO was initially comprised of "national" sections of Jewish and other immigrants whose communities had been "stranded" in the United States after the gates of immigration were purposely closed to "New Immigrants" and Asians in 1924 with the passage of the Johnson-Reed Act. The IWO termed its constituent societies "national sections" even though some sections, such as the Jewish and Carpatho-Russian societies, did not have nations of their own or fit the Marxist definition of a nation. Likewise, the IWO and other Communist-inflected organizations struggled accurately to define a "Black nation," eventually forming a Black Douglass-Lincoln Society following World War II. At a time when the Socialist movement had already divided on many issues, including World War I and the Bolshevik Revolution, there was a receptive audience among Yiddish-speaking immigrants, American Blacks, and other groups for new fraternal societies. The IWO was born in 1930 out of a decade-long split within the Yiddish-speaking Arbeter Ring (Workmen's Circle) that reflected the policies of the Communist Party of the United States of America (CPUSA) and the Comintern's Third Period.

During the late 1920s and early 1930s, with the onset of the Great Depression, the CPUSA (the Party) became convinced that capitalism's internal contradictions, especially the country's gaping economic inequality and the increasing immiseration of industrial and agrarian workers, portended the fall of the capitalist system. Consequently, the Party pursued a policy of "Bolshevization" in which it eschewed preexisting unions and educational institutions, as well as relatively small ethnic fraternal societies, and instead established or encouraged new institutions under Party control or within its broader orbit. Yet, the CPUSA was at best ambivalent about its own language sections and about the value of loosely associated fraternal orders, both of which were popular with immigrants. Immigrant workers attracted to the CPUSA often were more comfortable meeting in the Party's language sections such as the Slovak Workers Society or the Greek, Jewish, Polish, and other language sections. Party leaders, though, wanting to deflect criticism of the Party as a completely "foreign," un-American affair, often stressed that workers should assimilate into the Anglo-American majority to be effective advocates of the class struggle. This was especially the case in the "Third Period" of the late 1920s and early '30s, and by 1930 the language sections had been discouraged. The IWO was a good fit for poorer, racialized "New Immigrants," such as eastern European Jews and southern Italians, who were legally but not socially accepted as white and had good reason to fear discrimination and hatred. Slavs fell into this category as well: immigration restrictionist sociologist Edward Alsworth Ross in 1914 asserted that "a Pole could live in dirt that would kill a white man."[2]

It was within this milieu that, in 1930, the International Workers Order was born. In valorizing Soviet life while fighting US antisemitism and "Jim Crow," the founders of the IWO committed to activism that, they believed, benefited all American workers. Moreover, unlike its mainly Communist-led leadership, the vast majority of the members of this mutual benefit fraternal society were not connected to the Communist Party; most, though, were pro-Soviet and comfortable with the IWO's mix of benefits and political and cultural activities, both within and across their own national language ethnic sections.[3] Ideological diversity within the IWO as well as the Party grew after 1935, however, when the CPUSA reversed course and entered the "Popular Front" era, in which it recognized the threat of fascism as necessitating the broadest possible coalition of progressive allies. Party members now worked with an array of progressive groups in CIO unions, civil rights organizations, and the IWO. By the mid-1930s, militant Marxist rhetoric grew rarer in Order publications and speeches, replaced with praise for President Roosevelt's New Deal and celebrations of industrial unionism in the CIO as the fulfillment of America's democratic promise. In this Popular Front moment, the IWO's progressive, multiethnic Americanism proved attractive to workers of various political stripes: estimates are that of its 188,000 members, only about 10 percent belonged to the CPUSA.[4] When Nazi Germany invaded the Soviet Union in June 1941 after the Molotov-Ribbentrop Pact ruptured, the CPUSA saw the value of foreign-language groups as a means to obtain support for World War II. More importantly, the IWO's sections understood this immediately and rose to the occasion.

The IWO's white ethnic members worked, too, with African American Order members and organizers such as Louise Thompson and Edward Nelson, who carved out a space for progressive Black nationalism in Order spaces such as South Chicago's Du Sable Community Center even as they forged alliances with progressive white ethnics on racial and class justice campaigns. The Order's Cervantes Society, under the leadership of Afro–Puerto Rican Communist Jesús Colón, similarly enabled Puerto Ricans, Mexicans, Cubans, and others to develop a source of Latino/a autonomy and pride (as when annual gala Cervantes balls in the Bronx crowned the society's queen in a rebuke to the denigration of Latinos/as by most white Americans) while still working in tandem with other progressive ethnic communities in the IWO.[5]

These examples bring to the fore questions regarding forging solidarity and unity with "white progressives" while shaping shared interracial as well as distinctively Black and Latino/a communal space, institutions, and politics. Questions of ethno-racial autonomy within interracial unity as negotiated by the IWO remain relevant for progressives in the twenty-first century, as racial justice movements such as the contemporary Movement for Black Lives advocate for equity in a perilously polarized moment. The Order's framework of diversity within unity and its insistence on tying the fight against Jim Crow to the fight against antisemitism and anti-immigrant sentiment encouraged solidarity among racial and racialized groups, offering a vital ideological ancestor to today's progressive movement. These understandings were hard-won and contentious, as well as deeply welcome, as the chapters in this book show.

Early Ethnic and Interethnic Organizations

Why was the IWO so critical to its members' lives? And why does its brief, quarter-century existence still offer a compelling model of interracial, intersectional organizing? The Order was founded in 1930 by five thousand pro-Soviet members of the Socialist-oriented Arbeter Ring (Workmen's Circle), a fraternal benefit mutual-aid society that, as its Socialist orientation suggests, also championed unions and working people's rights. The Yiddish-speaking members of the Workmen's Circle's *linke* (left), though, believed the Circle insufficiently supportive of the Soviet Union and founded the IWO in 1930. These left-wing Yiddishists subsequently turned themselves into the IWO's Jewish-American Section—in 1944 renamed the Jewish Peoples Fraternal Order (JPFO)—after first successfully inviting leftist Slovak, Russian, Hungarian, and other autonomous immigrant fraternal benefit societies to join their organization under a now broader IWO umbrella that included interracial general lodges. Officers of the IWO eventually included such fellow travelers as Vito Marcantonio, congressman for an East Harlem district that was primarily Italian and Puerto Rican, and artist and writer Rockwell Kent. Throughout its ideological permutations, the IWO remained ethnically and racially diverse and expansive in its geographical reach.[6]

Organizing the IWO

The IWO's leadership was elected at national conventions every five years, where elected lodge delegates also debated and passed resolutions setting Order policy on insurance, civil rights, economic issues, member recruitment, and the IWO's organizational structure. Such resolutions often called on the federal government to take such steps as ending segregation, enacting federal anti-lynching laws, passing the Social Security Act, or offering protection from discrimination to Black and immigrant Americans through organizations such as the Fair Employment Practices Committee (FEPC). The New York City national headquarters administered the Order's insurance and health-care programs. Although the CPUSA interfered through appointing officers such as Communist Max Bedacht, who was for thirteen years the IWO's general secretary, in many respects the IWO's sixteen "national" societies retained great autonomy since they were fully represented on its general executive board, which met monthly. By 1947, the Order's sixteen lodge-based ethnic-group language federations encompassed interracial English-language branches, general lodges that were unaffiliated with a particular section, and a Spanish-speaking Cervantes Society that welcomed Puerto Rican, Cuban, Mexican, Guatemalan, and other Latino/a members; total Order membership grew to 188,000.[7]

While less numerous, Chinese, Japanese, Cape Verdean, Arab, and Black Muslim lodges were also part of the IWO. On the Pacific Coast, white ethnic members belonged to interracial lodges with Japanese and Chinese as well as Mexican members in areas such as Los Angeles's Boyle Heights. Consequently, during World War II, some Order lodges in Oakland, California, forcefully denounced the wartime internment of Japanese Americans. In Congress, Representative Marcantonio of the Order's Garibaldi Society similarly called for the end of the relocation camps, while also introducing bills for the integration of the armed forces and major-league baseball.[8]

Although this volume primarily focuses on Jewish and African American members of the IWO and the less well-known aspects of that broader story, it is important to note that the Order's other "language federations" were also vibrant social and cultural organizations. In coal and steel towns of the Midwest, Slovak and Polish lodges offered cultural programs, social services, and medical care to members, providing an array of bands, sports teams, and entertainment centers that were some of the first independent worker-controlled organizations in hitherto company-dominated towns. The commitment to cultural work, racial justice, and working-class justice that we will see in the chapters devoted to the JPFO was mirrored in the Slavic, Italian, Greek, and other white ethnic components of the Order. Articles in the Order's national magazine, *Fraternal Outlook*—some published in Yiddish, Spanish, Polish, and other languages—explained to the various national society members the importance of the Order's campaigns for racial and economic justice. National societies urged their members to sign petitions and letters to congressmen or attend rallies supporting measures such as the proposed federal anti-lynching bill, and many members enthusiastically participated. In this way the Order coordinated social justice campaigns in its decentralized, ethnically based organization.[9]

The cultural and political work of Communist and other left-leaning Poles, Slovaks, and Italians to build multicultural solidarity with African American and Puerto Rican activists has largely gone unremarked in histories of this period, overshadowed by the better-documented phenomenon of southern and eastern European whites engaged in "crabgrass-roots politics" by sometimes violently resisting neighborhood integration.[10] However, these Italian and Slavic white ethnic groups were a vital component of the IWO, working with African Americans and Puerto Ricans in fighting for racial equality and with Jews in combatting antisemitism. While not foregrounded in this volume, their interracial and interethnic activism was important and is a field that future research should address. To be sure, white ethnics in the IWO were always a small if vocal subset of their communities, but their activism around economic justice in anti-eviction fights and in campaigns for union recognition and for equality for Americans of all races during open-housing battles, for example, often successfully mobilized neighbors beyond the IWO's immediate ideological orbit, indicating that another, multicultural world was possible. Indeed, the government's destruction of the IWO and other interracial, leftist organizations arguably forestalled support for the enactment of Black voting and civil rights for two long decades.

Prior to joining the IWO, other leftist ethnic fraternal members, such as the Yiddish leftists in the Workmen's Circle, had broken from the American Socialist Party, and after the Russian Revolution of 1917 aligned with the new, pro-Soviet Workers (Communist) Party (later the CPUSA). The Slovak Workers Society (SWS), whose Socialist roots went back to 1906, also split with the Socialist Party. After the split its newspaper, *Rovnosť ľudu* (Equality for the people), championed anti-colonialism, civil rights for African Americans, and justice for all working people, while lauding the Soviet Union as the beacon of a dawning revolutionary nirvana. Peter Shipka, who had been active in the Newark, New Jersey, area chapter of the SWS since the 1910s, would in the early 1930s back his society's amalgamation into the IWO. Shipka would then serve as the Order's national treasurer for much of its life. Other organizations—the American Russian Fraternal Society founded in 1920 and the Hungarian Workingmen's Sick and Benefit Society that dated to 1900, as well as preexisting leftist Croatian and Finnish fraternal societies—likewise joined the Order. The Finnish case, though, suggests the difficulty in achieving unity within diversity, for they jealously guarded their autonomy, particularly control of preexisting social halls and the editorial policy of their leftist newspaper, *Työmies* (Worker). They would not fully merge into the IWO until the early 1940s.[11]

With World War II, the IWO seemed to be welcomed into the broad-tent, Popular Front, win-the-war coalition. Croats, Ukrainians, Slovaks, Carpatho-Russians, and other Slavs in the Order in 1942 joined a broad-based, pro-Allied, Soviet-backing American Slav Congress (ASC), an organization that, at least until the Cold War's onset, united Slavic organizations across the ideological spectrum. This "congress" of preexisting Slavic organizations, including the IWO's affiliates, lobbied for U.S. support of its Soviet ally, but also advocated enactment of Roosevelt's Four Freedoms with a guaranteed living wage, universal healthcare, and robust industrial unions. By war's end, twenty years after the Johnson-Reed Act had slowed immigration to a trickle, many such members were second-generation, American-born white ethnics, who retained sympathies with their parents' homelands while also demanding that America extend full equality to all her sons and daughters of all races; their whiteness did not develop in a reactionary manner. The ASC would later fracture as it continued its postwar social-democratic lobbying in alliance with the Progressive Party, but IWO affiliates such as the SWS stuck with the Congress until the end.[12]

It was no exaggeration when the IWO recruited new members with the selling point, "No Jim Crow in the IWO!" In 1940s America, with ethnic meeting halls and recreational sites de facto racially segregated, including in Northern cities such as Chicago or Philadelphia, the IWO was a uniquely interracial fraternal society where one found African Americans (whether Baptist or Muslim), Polish Catholics, Puerto Ricans, and eastern European Jews (typically secular) meeting together, joining common singing or theater groups, amicably playing baseball or basketball together, and marching arm in arm in campaigns to enact anti-lynching bills, desegregate the armed forces, secure the right to form a workplace union, or celebrate May Day. The IWO's Slovak Workers Society's newspaper in 1936, for example, lauded the campaign to enact an anti-lynching bill, praising in particular the efforts of a young Ella Baker in this cause. Baker would later be a key aide to Dr. Martin Luther King Jr. in the Southern Christian Leadership Conference (SCLC).[13] And Slovaks in the IWO participated alongside Black activists in 1930s "swim ins" at Chicago's segregated beaches, prefiguring the later 1960s integration campaigns of the Congress of Racial Equality (CORE).[14]

Mutual Aid and Civil Rights

The Order's primary mission was the provision of quality insurance, accident, sickness, death, and burial benefits to its members, as well as providing health services such as dental and optical; its general medical clinics were tasked with breaking even and making no profit. In these matters the Order equaled or exceeded America's plethora of immigrant ethnic fraternal societies by offering extensive, nondiscriminatory, low-cost benefits; unlike commercial insurers, it did not refuse or charge coal miners or Black members higher prices. For immigrant and Black families, the shame of not being able to afford to bury the dead and the consequences of not being provided for was very real. These may now seem minor matters, but prior to Social Security and other New Deal reforms, the minimal protection afforded by fraternal societies was all that kept workers from falling into destitution.

Its Socialist roots, however, meant that insurance benefits—important as these were in industrial America—were only the beginning of the IWO's activism. From its founding, the Order combined mutual aid and insurance benefits with a social justice, pro-labor platform. A wartime brochure for union members that is explicit about its nondiscriminatory insurance policies crucial to immigrants and Black people promotes IWO insurance rates as an added, needed bonus. It explains: "It has Negroes and White, Jews and gentiles in its ranks. They all help each other. The IWO is the only interracial fraternal organization in the USA."[15] The IWO's leaders as well as its more active lodge members saw it as their mission to push America in a more social-democratic direction. As necessary as the safety-net services the IWO provided to its members were, the Order saw these as bandages on the many wounds inflicted by free-market capitalism. Nonetheless, the Order fell apart legally and otherwise once its insurance certificate became a casualty of the Cold War (see chapter 13).

It became particularly apparent that industrial society needed a systemic overhaul during the Great Depression, when general prosperity seemed impossible to achieve; the Order in this period lobbied lawmakers for the enactment of stronger unemployment insurance, a guaranteed annual income, and universal health care, which were most forcefully enunciated in the IWO's 1940 social-democratic platform, "Our Plan for Plenty." National IWO conventions passed resolutions on these matters and societies such as the SWS and the Italian American Garibaldi Society sent letters to local lodges urging members to sign petitions and write letters to congressmen calling for the introduction of measures such as the Social Security Act. While some IWO officials, such as Max Bedacht and Louise Thompson Patterson, were up front about their CPUSA membership, non-Party members were somewhat indifferent to questions of the leaders' "Red" affiliation at the height of the Great Depression, looking instead to tangible relief from economic misery. This the Order provided, with lodges also often leading the way as well as working with others in anti-eviction campaigns and local consumer boycotts against exploitative businessmen and merchants.[16]

Although economic justice was important to the IWO's mission, racial justice was also a primary focus of its activities, and its literature connected the fight against anti-Black racism to the fight against antisemitism and anti-immigrant and anti-labor movements. A 1944 wartime formulation from IWO vice president Vito Marcantonio stated bluntly:

> This war has challenged not only the military might of America but the moral fiber of the nation.... The destruction of Fascism's regiments and military weapons must be accompanied with an eradication of Fascism's ideology everywhere in the world. Anti-Semitism, anti-Negro, race supremacy, white supremacy, anti-labor and all other similar undemocratic growths must be cut out of the world by a united people everywhere. America must lead the way in this crusade for a better world based on the principles of equality and justice.[17]

As early as 1931 Slovak, Latvian, Russian, Hungarian, and Irish lodges, as well as the Jewish American Section, were orchestrating civil rights campaigns, such as their efforts on behalf of the Scottsboro defendants—nine African American young men on Alabama's death row after their speedy conviction on trumped-up rape charges.[18] Later, the IWO helped "hold the line" in defending Paul Robeson at a 1949 concert in Peekskill, New York. The Order battled segregation and housing discrimination, too, as when the Polish section's newspaper, *Głos Ludowy* (People's voice) decried the white rioters assaulting Black renters seeking to move into Detroit's Sojourner Truth housing project.[19] It would similarly orchestrate a campaign to combat the whites-only policy at New York's Stuyvesant Town and Parkchester housing complexes, which were owned by the Metropolitan Life Insurance Company.[20]

The IWO extended its intersectional approach to opposing racial and ethnic oppression through the anti-racist, multilingual pedagogy practiced in its network of workers' schools, children's schools, and summer camps. In these spaces, bands, theater groups, choirs, and other cultural activities were utilized to advance social and racial justice and were also key to reinforcing and celebrating the idea that immigrant cultures were worthy of inclusion in Anglo-Saxon America's civilizational landscape. Ukrainian dance troupes, Jewish mandolin groups, Black theater groups, and Italian folk theaters, among other IWO organizations, performed important valorization work at a time when anti-immigrant and racist venom permeated mainstream American cultural discourse.

The Order's boast of "No Jim Crow in the IWO" was carried through internally, too, and the gendered glass ceiling was likewise breached. In 1940, it elected a Black female vice president, the future founder of Sojourners for Truth and Justice, Louise Thompson Patterson, who was in charge of its Chicago-based recruiting efforts. In 1939 the IWO tasked Clara Lemlich Shavelson—who in 1909 had led the first women's garment action, known as the "Strike of the 20,000"—with founding its Women's City Committees, which under the Jewish American Section's auspices worked with housewives to publish newsletters that alerted members to consumer actions combating the high cost of food and held classes addressing childcare and other issues. In New England, Jewish and Portuguese women in the IWO Women's Committees engaged in anti-eviction campaigns and consumer boycotts.[21] The Slovaks' society, too, was headed for ten years by a woman, Helen Vrábel. At a time when "mainstream" America relegated women to subordinate places, these progressives were comfortable discussing the needs of women, especially immigrant and non-white women, in organizations headed by women; the IWO actively recruited them as potential members and included them in leadership ranks. By 1937, too, the IWO was establishing birth-control clinics at its Union Square headquarters, as well as other programs to ameliorate the special burdens working women and homemakers faced.

The Demise of the IWO

The state, whether the Federal Bureau of Investigation, local police "Red squads," HUAC, the Office of Strategic Service's Foreign Nationalities Branch, courts, or other agencies, provided the best "recording secretaries" of the American left. Even though these government agencies worked tirelessly to expose the supposed Communist menace that leftist organizations ostensibly posed to the United States, the Freedom of Information Act records of these agencies' surveillance inadvertently, and ironically, offer a treasure trove of information on the tireless campaigning these groups engaged in to achieve racial equality and social justice for working-class Americans.[22] New York State's Department of Insurance did scholars an enormous (if unintentional) favor when it commandeered the International Workers Order's records, correspondence, and financial records as it pursued liquidation proceedings against this left-leaning mutual-benefit fraternal society. After the IWO was dismembered by state diktat in early 1954, these materials were deposited in Cornell University's Kheel Center for Labor Management, where they now offer an invaluable window into the Order's activism on behalf of African Americans, Latinos/as, and Jewish and other "New Immigrant" workers facing the scourge of antisemitism and anti-immigrant vitriol in the

1930s, 1940s, and 1950s. The Order's record of tireless work on union campaigns on behalf of the CIO and lobbying to enact needed social legislation is likewise demonstrated in these confiscated archives.

Largely because of its commitment to interracial organizing and union activism, the IWO was targeted by government "Red" hunters beginning in 1947, culminating in its legal dissolution in 1954. The suppression of left-leaning dissent—including the denaturalization of immigrants and their threatened deportation—demonstrates just how narrow the parameters for critiques of racism, class inequities, or America's militarized foreign policy were. This suppression has had enduring effects on the United States and this book has some sobering lessons for our time. The suppression of dissent narrowed the degree of progress on economic justice and racial civil rights in America for decades afterward, and the story of the IWO's demise has relevance for twenty-first-century America, when another permanent emergency has narrowed the range of critiques of government policy and the unequal racial and economic status quo. Contemporary targeting of #BlackLivesMatter and other activists for government surveillance, mass deportations, and anti-immigrant hysteria—these and other militarized state repressions of dissent would have been familiar to IWO members.

Plan for the Book

The IWO's unusual, historically bounded unity in left-wing diversity is reflected in this book's chapters, which demonstrate how that diversity was deliberately and usefully harnessed in the IWO's cultural programming, labor union campaigns, and anti-racism actions. Perhaps the Order's shining moment of "unity in diversity" came with its support of the Allies during World War II, as seen in Elissa Sampson's chapter (chapter 1) on the Order's Jewish American Section winning a seat at the table of the broader American Jewish community in the win-the-war campaign, which was tied to its support of the Soviet-based Jewish Anti-Fascist Committee. While that campaign focused on working primarily with mainstream Jewish organizations in a wartime context, within the IWO multiple admixtures of cultural programs were created in and across its sections, and in its public cultural programs. Across the IWO's history, the diverse cultural expressions it sponsored, such as Ukrainian dance troupes, Harlem's Suitcase Theatre, Paul Robeson concerts, and Yiddish poetry journals were celebrated by Order members and audiences as contributors to a broader, progressive coalition in multiethnic, interracial America. During the 1930s and '40s—when a segregationist Mississippi senator was still able to read anti-Italian and antisemitic diatribes into the *Congressional Record* and dismiss a Brooklyn IWO member as a "Dago" (slurs that were called out by Congressman Marcantonio)—the Order unflinchingly stressed the American bona fides of Black, Jewish, Italian, and other white ethnic members.[23] This is powerfully demonstrated in Felicia Bevel's chapter 6 on IWO member Paul Robeson's performances of "Ballad for Americans" and other songs at interracial venues such as the IWO's Camp Wo-Chi-Ca ("Workers' Children Camp"). Matt Calihman's chapter 5, too, explores celebrating the humanity of all working people as central to the struggle against Jim Crow in Langston Hughes's chapbook of poems published by the Order and in his work with the Order's Harlem Suitcase Theatre highlighting the especially pernicious racism that barred the achievement of full citizenship for Black people. These chapters foreground the tensions between the goals of multiracial, international solidarity, Communist politics, and attention to particular racial or ethnic oppressions.

Louise Thompson Patterson, a Black Communist and vice president of the Order, negotiated these tensions, too, in her work organizing the IWO within the Black community while also working with Croatian, Ukrainian, and other white ethnic leftists in coal and steel communities. Elissa Sampson's and Robert Zecker's chapter 7 explores the challenges Patterson faced when charting a Black nationalist path within the multiethnic, interracial Order. The IWO also provided an arena for advocating within pro-Soviet circles for Black "space" as seen in community centers and cultural programs that linked Black international and US struggles. This was most strongly seen, perhaps, in the petition presented to the United Nations in 1951 by IWO members Paul Robeson and William L. Patterson (spouse of Louise Thompson Patterson), "We Charge Genocide." This legal jeremiad condemned the segregation, violence, and discrimination faced by African Americans but linked their fate to enduring colonial oppression in an Africa dominated by European powers. The IWO had already condemned postwar imperialism in venues such as the 1946 Win the Peace Conference, chaired by Robeson, which demanded independence for African and Asian colonies.[24]

Women in the Jewish American Section, too, sought to make common cause with other marginalized groups, particularly African Americans. Jennifer Young (in chapter 3) explores the career of June Gordon, who engaged in organizing strikes in a variety of interracial, labor, and women-based venues and organizations, while focusing on educational work in the Soviet Union and the United States before joining the IWO. She then led its Emma Lazarus Division of Jewish women, an organization that continued battling for racial justice into the 1970s.

It was not always easy to balance a pan-ethnic commitment to working-class solidarity with concern for one's own community's special needs, as seen in the chapters by Dylan Kaufman-Obstler and Lauren Strauss. The CPUSA workers schools as well as the educational programs offered by the IWO presented a working-class pedagogy of a universalistic, Marxist bent, but immigrants who yearned to preserve progressive, Yiddish-based schooling were central to founding the Jewish Workers University, as Kaufman-Obstler notes in chapter 2. The Jewish Workers University "boasted of a distinctly working-class body," but it did so in a distinctly Yiddish milieu, while the CPUSA's *Daily Worker* columns covered the more ecumenical (or Marxist-ecumenical!) workers schools. The Jewish Workers University also sought to lionize distinctly Jewish progressive icons at a time when the broader workers schools, and the CPUSA, were embracing an "Americanism for the twentieth century" that claimed Thomas Jefferson, Sam Adams, Abraham Lincoln, and Tom Paine as forerunners of the Communist movement and namesakes of workers schools. Other Order societies, such as the Slovaks and the Latino/a Cervantes Society, similarly retained their own ethnic-based schools in places such as Youngstown, Ohio, and East Harlem.[25] The embrace of ethnic particularism and progressive universalism that sometimes ran through the IWO and the Old Left in general was a paradox that created certain tensions. Strauss documents (in chapter 10) that progressive Jewish artists often put pen and brush to work on behalf of working-class causes, but that with the horrors of the Holocaust becoming ever more tragically apparent during and immediately following World War II, secular artists such as William Gropper and Minna Harkavy increasingly turned to Jewish sources for inspiration and commemoration.

The chapters in this book provide a window into the politics and culture of many of the ethnic groups in the IWO, particularly the Yiddish-speaking immigrant left, including into questions of antisemitism and how they played out in the pre- and postwar periods. In chapter 4 Ben Ratskoff notes that W. E. B. Du Bois revisited his earlier "color line" thesis in a nuanced response to Jewish leftists concerning race and the Nazi genocide after his 1949 visit to the ruins of the Warsaw Ghetto, an encounter that triggered a circuitous rethinking of his initial understandings of race and difference described in accounts of his prior European journeys. An older Du Bois revised his notions of race, contextualizing and making connections between racism, antisemitism, and xenophobia at a moment in which his politics had moved farther left and touched IWO circles. These broader linkages between racism, antisemitism, and xenophobia in the American context had always been central to the Order's interethnic, multiracial model.

The book also offers a transnational, comparative turn in the study of the immigrant left, with chapters examining the related but distinct histories of Communist Jewish organizations in Canada, ably documented by Henry Srebrnik in chapter 9, and of Yiddish-speaking workers' educational centers in Buenos Aires, Argentina, as examined by Nerina Visacovsky in chapter 8. In Canada Communist Jewish organizations at times allied with the IWO, even as they worked to address the needs and platforms most central to leftist communities in Toronto, Winnipeg, and other cities. The Canadian campaign also included support for the establishment of Birobidzhan in the Soviet Far East as an answer to the "Jewish Question." In Buenos Aires and other South American cities, as Visacovsky shows, educational centers designed to serve Yiddish-speaking workers engaged in transnational collaboration with the Order's Jewish section and other groups in establishing the Yidisher Kultur Farband (YKUF), a Popular Front attempt to bring together Yiddish artists and writers worldwide just before World War II.

One thread seen in the volume is that many chapters refute an older erroneous historiography that portrays Communists and fellow travelers as cynical outsiders using their bona fides and skills to sway their communities. Rather, the progressivism of the IWO and its international circuits fell within a broad range of responses from communities that were reacting to systems that appeared broken, whether in the United States, Canada, or Argentina. Many Jewish Communists were committed to creating a secular Yiddish workers' culture; they were not simply Jews who were Communist. It was possible for Jewish, Black, Slavic, and Italian IWO members to express a naturalized cultural identity *within* their working-class communities. This quotidian progressivism has received insufficient attention from historians.

As migrants from many lands, progressives in the immigrant left and their offspring were often internationalist in outlook and attuned to mutual assistance networks including through a diasporic, internationalist lens. Perhaps the Order's internationalist perspective is most strongly demonstrated in Annabel Cohen's examination in chapter 11 of the IWO's many members who volunteered for the International Brigades fighting in Spain on behalf of the anti-fascist Loyalist government. In 1936, many IWO officials belonged to the Party and were not reticent about publicizing their membership (General Secretary Max Bedacht, for one, ran as the CPUSA candidate for the US Senate in New York); thus it is not surprising that the Order backed Moscow's support for Madrid's anti-fascist war. Still, it is estimated that only 10 percent of IWO members were in the Party, and progressives in the Order of whatever political stripe were vocal in their commitment to the Abraham Lincoln Brigade, whose members fought and died in the struggle against Francisco Franco and his Nazi and Italian fascist supporters. While International Brigade veterans would soon be demonized by conservative politicians as "premature anti-fascists," Cohen documents the complexity of the lives and identities of those Order members who fought in Spain or provided financial and material aid to this international anti-fascist cause. Ambivalence as well as enthusiasm can be seen in dealing with the Party's foreign-policy stances: deeply committed to fighting fascism in Spain and Italy, Gino Bardi and others in the IWO's Italian section remained consistently anti-fascist in their writings and speeches despite the CPUSA's abrupt turn to neutrality toward Hitler in August 1939 when the Molotov-Ribbentrop Pact was signed.

While progressive causes such as Loyalist Spain, Ethiopia, and battles for racial justice, seemed just and even "all American" to Order members basking in their seemingly secure place in Franklin Roosevelt's win-the-war coalition, Red-baiting of the IWO and other Communist-affiliated organizations always lay under the surface, even during the years of the IWO's seeming legitimacy. Robert Zecker's chapter 12 demonstrates that as early as the 1930s, the Department of Justice, the House Un-American Activities Committee, and departments of insurance in several states were investigating the Order for allegedly subversive, Communist activities. A more persistent Cold War anti-Red campaign by President Harry S Truman's Justice Department began shortly after the Second World War and led to the organization's state-ordered demise in 1954.

The state, however, could not fully extinguish the fire that motivated ex-IWO members to campaign for racial and economic justice. Paul Mishler (in chapter 13) and Paul Buhle (in the volume's coda) both demonstrate the enduring progressivism of "Old Left" Jewish activists that allowed them to recover aspects of a usable past from their collective memory of activism in the IWO and other organizations. Sometimes the IWO served as an institutional base, or as an impetus or inspiration for its heirs, whether the New Left in the 1960s or contemporary activists. The JPFO's Camp Kinderland has just celebrated its centennial; *Jewish Currents* (formerly *Jewish Life*) has taken off into an online world that the Old Left could not have imagined.

Legacies of the IWO

Radicalism and left-wing organizing endured in other ethnic components of the former IWO, too. The Polonia Society's newspaper, *Głos Ludowy*, survived the dismemberment of the Order and continued to demand enactment of civil rights legislation and full equality for African Americans until it went out of business in 1979. The Polish American politician Stanley Nowak, who had headed the Michigan IWO, and ex-Order member Conrad Komorowski continued editorializing on the need to grant independence to African colonies such as Algeria and Rhodesia/Zimbabwe, celebrated Black students' 1960 lunch counter sit-ins, and took Attorney General Robert Kennedy to task over his inaction in investigating the murder of Black civil rights workers in segregated Mississippi. Ed Falkowski, who had recruited CIO members into the Polonia Society in the 1930s, as late as 1972 wrote a column in *Głos Ludowy* championing African American civil rights and condemning US imperial adventures in places such as Vietnam, which were lonely editorial stances in the Polish American community. Falkowski wrote an article in 1972 titled "Racism Seeks to Invade Academic Circles" that condemned the genetic theories of white supremacist William Shockley.[26]

The former summer camp of the IWO's American Russian Fraternal Society, Arow Farm, likewise survived the Order's liquidation, and as late as 1979 hosted a fundraising picnic for the CPUSA's newspaper, the *Daily World*.[27] The Finnish section's leftist newspaper, *Työmies*, continued publishing Socialist content out of Superior, Wisconsin, until 1998. Sol Rotenberg, who had been an Order official in Philadelphia, was treasurer of the Delaware Valley Committee for Democratic Rights in 1963 when he hosted Elizabeth Gurley Flynn's talk, "The McCarran Act and American Liberties," at his home.[28] Veterans of the SWS-IWO were recalled in eulogies at their 1970s funerals as unrepentant leftists who still wrote for the Communist newspaper *Ľudové noviny* (People's news) and engaged in interracial community organizing in Newark, New Jersey, until their demise. In Chicago, former Slovak IWO mainstay Frank Scheibenreif was likewise lauded for penning articles in *Ľudové noviny* and directing a progressive Slovak radio hour, as well as serving as its announcer, until 1983. In that year, too, Fred Fine, who had organized cultural events for the Order at Chicago venues such as the Ukrainian People's Auditorium and the Polonia Society's Chopin Cultural Center, was appointed city director of cultural affairs by Chicago's first Black mayor, Harold Washington. Although Fine's appointment received considerable pushback from a more conservative Polish and eastern European community than the one that had formerly thrived at the Chopin Center, this IWO veteran was confirmed and served the progressive Washington administration for four years—continuing the kind of interracial cultural work he had engaged in for the IWO in North Side Chicago forty years previously.[29]

In Detroit, the helpful members of that city's police intelligence section (formerly known as the "Red Squad") scrupulously noted in 1973 that the Michigan Communist Party would be hosting an "International Bazaar for Peace and Freedom" at 18491 Muirland Street. In 1936, an equally thorough Detroit police "Red Squad" had listed the same address as an IWO hall. The progressive roots of aging Old Leftists continued to run deep decades after the Order's demise, even if the organizational density of such leftist activism had been destroyed in the postwar Red Scare.[30]

Today's activists involved with the Black Lives Matter movement, embroiled in battles against white nationalist antisemitism and racism, and agitating against restrictions on voting rights, anti-immigrant violence, and xenophobia, as well as those combating a new Gilded Age that features gaping chasms of economic inequality, might find both solace and inspiration in the ways that the Old Left effectively tackled these dilemmas with creativity and vigor. This book is the product of an online conference on the IWO that was attended by more than six hundred people, some with direct ties to the organization and others who were learning about it for the first time. As we consider the import of that history in the present, we should appreciate the progressive achievements and activist energy of the IWO and other leftists, even as we critically evaluate their shortcomings and acknowledge that Stalinism does not taste better with time. The complicated yet often successful politics of diverse cultural production that marked the IWO's life before it was shut down in the Cold War are noteworthy when interrogating how it navigated the various contested and sometimes contradictory or even apologetic policies and struggles of its day.

NOTES

1. Louise Thompson, "Toward a Brighter Dawn," *The Woman Today* 1, no. 14 (April 1936).
2. Edward Alsworth Ross, *The Old World in the New: The Significance of Past and Present Immigration to the American People* (Century, 1914).
3. Some of these national sections do not map neatly onto a map of nation-states. Moreover, standard Marxist definitions of a nation do not necessarily apply here; linguistic and ethnic affinities as well as self-identification are in play, with the IWO encompassing an American Russian Fraternal Society; Rusyn, Lemko Carpatho-Rusyn (Ruthenian) lodges; and Hispanic, Jewish, and Slovak (not then a separate nation-state) national sections. Some Jews joined the Romanian and most especially Hungarian sections. Marxist terminology and doctrine use the strict four-point definition of a nation formulated by Lenin and updated by Stalin, which meant that Jews did not qualify as one: see the chapters by Jennifer Young and Elissa Sampson and Robert Zecker, which touch on the Black Belt resolutions regarding the status of Black people in the United States as an "oppressed nation."
4. "IWO Challenges Constitutionality of Attorney General Clark's Report; Plans Legal Action," puts the IWO membership at 188,000 members. Press release, December 5, 1947, International Workers Order Collection, folder 13, Tamiment Library and Robert F. Wagner Labor Archives, New York University, New York, New York (hereafter IWO, NYU).
5. Program of the Coronation of First Queen of the Children's Spanish Section of the IWO, April 26, 1941, Jesús Colón Papers, box 19, folder 17, Hunter College Institute for Puerto Rican Studies, Hunter College, New York, New York (henceforth Colón, Hunter); "Plan General: La IWO y el Problema Nacional" [General plan: The IWO and the national problem], [1941–45?], box 20, folder 5, Colón, Hunter; "La Srta. Lydia Romero, coronada Lydia Primera, Reina de la Victoria de la Sociedad Fraternal Cervantes, Sección hispana de la I. W. O. en un grandioso Baile de Coronación, el sábado 26 de Mayo del 1945, en los salones del Hunt Point Palace" [The senorita Lydia Romero, crowned Lydia I, victorious queen of the Cervantes Fraternal Society, Hispanic Section of the IWO at the Grand Coronation Ball, Saturday, May 26, 1945], box 32, folder 23, Colón, Hunter.
6. Robert M. Zecker, *"A Road to Peace and Freedom": The International Workers Order and the Struggle for Economic Justice and Civil Rights, 1930–1954* (Temple University Press, 2018), 19–54.
7. Zecker, *"A Road to Peace and Freedom,"* 34–54.
8. Zecker, *"A Road to Peace and Freedom,"* 121, 127–32.
9. "In Appreciation of Negro History Week: 'Democracy and the Negro People,'" flyer, February 9, 1947, International Workers Order and Jewish Peoples Fraternal Order Collection, box 49, folder 16, file 3, Kheel Center for Labor-Management Documentation and

Archives, Catherwood Library, Cornell University, Ithaca, New York (hereafter Kheel), https://digital.library.cornell.edu/catalog/ss:19043803.

   A poster with the following quote was sent from the IWO national office to all societies to distribute to branches: "THE UNBREAKABLE UNITY of Negro and white is the burning need of these decisive days when the peoples' ranks must be solidly formed for the winning of democracy, security and lasting peace, and for the defeat of Jim Crow and anti-Semitism, to end lynching and all forms of discrimination." The next year, an even more elaborate campaign was launched, with a foldout in *Fraternal Order* containing an editorial that stated: "Our whole Order must learn this fundamental truth. Our whole Order must learn from Negro History Week that democratic America cannot endure while 15,000,000 people live under the most undemocratic conditions of segregation, Jim Crow, lynch terror and second class citizenship. We of the nationality groups in America must especially learn these truths.

   What should we do?

   1. Back up and support the historic petition of the National Association for the Advancement of Colored People to the United Nations for redress of grievances of the American Negro.
   2. Work for the abolition of Jim Crow; the passage of a Federal Fair Employment Practices Act; the rigid enforcement of the 13th, 14th and 15th amendments to the Constitution; outlawing of racist propaganda and discriminatory practices.
   3. Enlist in the fight to end restrictive covenants.
   4. Support these bills: Anti-lynch Bill—HR 3488, S 1352; FEPC-S 984; Anti-Poll Tax-HR 29; Outlaw Race Hate Literature—HR 2848; Abolish Un-American Committee—HR 46."

National Negro History Week brochure, February 9, 1948, box 48, folder 1, file 1, Kheel. The editorial was from the IWO national office; the foldout was written partially by Herbert Aptheker and featured W. E. B. Du Bois's work.

   10. Thomas J. Sugrue, "Crabgrass-Roots Politics: Race, Rights, and the Reaction Against Liberalism in the Urban North, 1940–1964," *The Journal of American History* 82, no. 2 (September 1995): 551–78; Sugrue, *The Origins of the Urban Crisis: Race and Inequality in Postwar Detroit* (Princeton University Press, 1996).

   11. Al Gedicks, "The Social Origin of Radicalism Among Finnish Immigrants in Midwest Mining Communities," *Review of Radical Political Economics* 8, no. 3 (1976): 1–31; Paul Mishler, "Red Finns, Red Jews: Ethnic Variations in Communist Political Culture during the 1920s and 1930s," *YIVO Annual* 22 (1995): 131–54.

   12. Robert Szymczak, "From Popular Front to Communist Front: The American Slav Congress in War and Cold War, 1941–1951" (PhD diss., Lancaster University, 2006).

   13. "Harlem Asks Federal Penalty for Lynching," *Ľudový denník*, March 6, 1936, 6.

   14. "The IWO Stands for Racial Equality!," *Denník Rovnosť ľudu*, July 27, 1934, 4.

   15. *The Best Insurance Protection for Your Family*, brochure, January, 1947, box 48, folder 7, Kheel. This blue and white membership foldout brochure includes insurance rates with the callout, "How Much Will it Cost for the Insurance that You Need?" The IWO brochure states, "It has Negroes and White, Jews and gentiles in its ranks. They all help each other. The IWO is the only interracial fraternal organization in the USA."

   16. "Meat Strikers Will Rally," *Daily Worker*, June 14, 1935; Annelise Orleck, *Common Sense and a Little Fire: Women and Working-Class Politics in the United States, 1900–1965*, 2nd ed. (University of North Carolina Press, 2017).

   17. "Greetings from the Hon. Vito Marcantonio" (June 1944), in *Our People: The Jew in America*, ed. I. Goldberg et al. (Cooperative Book League of the Jewish American Section, I.W.O., 1944).

18. Minutes of CPUSA Language Department meeting, May 11, 1931, Communist Party USA files, reel 177, delo 2332, Library of Congress, Washington, District of Columbia (henceforth CPUSA, LC); letter from Charles Dirba of the Lettish [Latvian] Bureau to the Language Department, May 6, 1931, reel 177, delo 2336, CPUSA, LC; letter from Czecho Slovakian Bureau to Comrade John Mackovich, May 7, 1931, reel 177, delo 2336, CPUSA, LC; letter from Mackovich of the Czechoslovak Bureau to Central Committee, CPUSA, May 6, 1932, reel 214, delo 2766, CPUSA, LC; minutes of the Tenth Convention of the Russian Mutual Aid Society of America, held in Chicago, June 17–23, at the Ukrainian Workers Home, 2547 West Chicago Avenue, Chicago, 1933, International Workers Order (IWO) Records #5276, box 12, folder 4, Kheel; letter from Emil Gardos of Cleveland to Earl Browder, June 29, 1932, reel 214, delo 2752, CPUSA, LC.

19. Ed Falkowski, "On the Polish American Front—How United is Polonia?," *Głos Ludowy*, April 11, 1942, 5; "Stop Discrimination!," *Głos Ludowy*, June 13, 1942, 5; "Żadanie Federalnej Inwestygacji Piątej Kolumny w Detroit" [We invite a federal investigation of the fifth column in Detroit], *Głos Ludowy*, July 4, 1942, 2; "'Krwawy Pondelok' w Detroit" [Bloody riot in Detroit], June 26, 1943, 1, 6.

20. Max Taber, "Stuyvesant Town for Whites Only," *The Jewish Fraternalist*, February–March 1950, 6–7, box 46, Kheel. On November 16, 1951, *Morgn Frayhayt* ran a story about Stuyvesant Town's attempt to evict seven tenants who were members of Local 65 of the Distributing, Previewing, and Office Workers Union for picketing the Jim Crow policies of the Metropolitan Life Insurance Company (the owner of Stuyvesant Town and Parkchester). The JPFO defended the picketers and white IWO members invited Black members to move into their apartments in Parkchester (*Morgn Frayhayt*, November 16, 1951, IWO Supplemental Records #5940 [hereafter IWO supplemental], box 2, Kheel). Meanwhile, the ultraconservative *New York Journal-American* lionized Stuyvesant Town, built due to the state's use of eminent domain, which privatized it while rendering it affordable, as superior to public housing projects that were costly and faced completion delays. "Built by Private Enterprise . . . BEGUN IN 1945 . . . Tenants Will Move in Soon. Government Building Project . . . BEGUN IN 1943 . . . Work Barely Started," *New York Journal-American*, June 5, 1947, 15.

21. Orleck, *Common Sense*.

22. William J. Maxwell, *F. B. Eyes: How J. Edgar Hoover's Ghostreaders Framed African American Literature* (Princeton University Press, 2017); Mary Helen Washington, *The Other Blacklist: The African American Literary and Cultural Left of the 1950s* (Columbia University Press, 2014).

23. Letter from Senator Theodore G. Bilbo of Mississippi to Josephine Picolo, IWO member of Brooklyn, July 1, 1945, Vito Marcantonio Papers, box 46, New York Public Library, New York, New York (hereafter Marcantonio Papers); letter from Picolo to Congressman Vito Marcantonio, July 18, 1945, box 46, Marcantonio Papers; letter from Marcantonio to Bilbo, July 21, 1945, box 46, Marcantonio Papers; "Vito Demands Apology on 'Dago' Note," *New York Daily News*, July 24, 1945; letter from Bilbo to Marcantonio, July 24, 1945, box 46, Marcantonio Papers; letter from Marcantonio to Picolo, July 24, 1945, box 46, Marcantonio Papers; letter from Marcantonio to Bilbo, July 25, 1945, box 46, Marcantonio Papers; report of Max Bedacht, general secretary, to the general council meeting of the International Workers Order, September 7–8, 1946, folder 13, IWO, NYU; minutes of general council meeting, September 15–16, 1945, 7–8, folder 12, IWO, NYU. In this last meeting Albert Kahn of the JPFO and Morris Shafritz of Philadelphia both spoke of the need to work to remove Bilbo. Letter from the National Committee to Combat Anti-Semitism and the JPFO (with petition on Senator Theodore Bilbo, Representative John Rankin, and others "spreading the dangerous seeds of anti-Semitism and other forms of hate propaganda in Congress"), November 12, 1945, box 30, folder 6, Kheel; letter from

George Starr of the JPFO to "Dear Brothers and Sisters," November 18, 1946, box 30, folder 7, Kheel; letter from Nathan Shaffer of the New York County Jewish Peoples Fraternal Order, IWO, to Congressman Vito Marcantonio, August 30, 1945, box 48, Marcantonio Papers; letter from Sol Rotenberg to Sam Milgrom regarding the resolution against Senator Theodore Bilbo passed at an IWO community meeting at Bok Vocational School, Eighth and Mifflin Streets, Philadelphia, December 6, 1945, box 8, folder 10, Kheel.

24. *Five Things You Can Do to Win the Peace* (Win the Peace Conference, 1946), box 46, Kheel; "Declaration of Principles" of the Win the Peace Conference (resolutions on Latin America, Puerto Rico, the Philippines, Indonesia, India, and Africa), April 6, 1946, box 22, folder 24, Kheel.

25. Maria Hojsa, "Ženský Obzor—Nebezpečie Militarizmu Medzi Školskú Mladéžou" [Women's perspective—the danger of militarism among school youth], *Rovnosť ludu*, May 30, 1924, 4; plan and tentative budget for Casa de Puerto Rico, 1947, box 15, folder 6, Colón, Hunter.

26. Ed Falkowski, "Racism Seeks to Invade Academic Circles," *Głos Ludowy*, July 15, 1972, 10, box 3, folder 3-12, Don Binkowski Papers, Wayne State University, Detroit, Michigan (henceforth Binkowski); interoffice memorandum of the Detroit Police "Red Squad," surveillance of farewell banquet for Gus Polites, CPUSA member, deported to Greece, January 18, 1963, box 1, folder 1-11, Binkowski. Conrad Komorowski was chairman of the banquet and Stanley Nowak attended. Robert M. Zecker, "'Nothing Less Than Full Freedom': Radical Immigrant Newspapers Champion Black Civil Rights," *American Communist History* 20, no. 3–4 (2021): 165–88; Zecker, "'Suppressed by Swords and Lead': Radical Polish and Slovak Newspapers Combat Colonialism," *Journal of Transnational American Studies* 15, no. 1 (2024): 33–69.

27. Letter, "To All Clubs and Press Directors," August 9, 1979, TAM 132, box 229, folder 4, Communist Party USA Collection, Wagner Tamiment Library, New York University (hereafter CPUSA, NYU). The letter concerned the annual *Daily World* picnic to be held at Arow Park, September 9, 1979. Arow Park in Monroe, New York, had formerly been owned by the American Russian Fraternal Society of the IWO.

28. Invitation to hear Elizabeth Gurley Flynn speak, flyer of the Delaware Valley Committee for Democratic Rights, June 8, 1963, box 297, folder 1, CPUSA, NYU.

29. Typescript eulogy for Joseph Lednicky (Slovak former IWO member), April 10, 1978, Lillian Donalek Papers, box 1, folder 7, Chicago History Museum, Chicago, Illinois (henceforth Donalek, CHM); "Hundreds in N. J. at Rites for Lednicky, CP Activist," *Daily World*, April 14, 1978, 11; memorial obituary for Ján Mackovič (Slovak former IWO member and former editor of *Ľudový denník*), *Ľudové noviny*, May 6, 1977, 3, box 1, folder 8, Donalek, CHM; *Ľudové noviny*, May 6, 1977, 3, typescript eulogy for Mackovič, printed on third anniversary of his 1974 death, box 1, folder 8, Donalek, CHM; typescript eulogy for Frank Scheibenreif (Slovak former member of the IWO and director and announcer until 1983 of Chicago's Slovak Radio Hour), April 23, 1993, box 1, folder 9, Donalek, CHM; biography of Fred Fine, n.d., box 1, folder 5, Donalek, CHM; Sneed and Lavin, "Clout City," *Chicago Tribune*, n.d.; Michael Arndt, "Ethnic Community Fumes Over Ex-Communist's Nomination," *Chicago Tribune*, n.d.; Jim Strong, "Ex-Communist Clears a Hurdle," *Chicago Tribune*, November 10, 1984, 5; Richard Christansen, "Chicago's Arts Custodian Driven—With Gentility," *Chicago Tribune*, January 24, 1985, 8. On the Chopin Cultural Center, see *IWO Bowling Bulletin*, October 23, 1949 and November 27, 1949, box 1, folder 2, Donalek, CHM; Glenn Jeffers, "Fred Fine, 89," *Chicago Tribune*, February 12, 2004.

30. Report of Detroit Police Intelligence Section, March 8, 1973, box 2, folder 2-55, Binkowski (reporting on the "International Bazaar for Peace and Freedom" at 18491 Muirland Street, Detroit); "The Communist Party in Detroit," report of Detroit Police, October 21, 1936 (includes an IWO hall at this same address), box 2, folder 2-55, Binkowski.

Part I
BEGINNINGS
Yiddish-Speaking Immigrants and Class Solidarity

"Immigrants One, Immigrants All," was a slogan embraced by IWO members who navigated the tensions of shaping and celebrating particular ethnic cultures while committing to universalist campaigns for radical working-class movements. Institutions such as the Jewish Workers University encapsulated in their very name the prongs of this dilemma. June Gordon and other IWO activists formed a Jewish women's division that moved beyond its members' own ethnic community in advocating for racial and gender equality, while during World War II the imperative of wartime unity spurred the IWO's Jewish American Section to build unlikely alliances with important mainstream Jewish organizations in a win-the-war campaign.

1

ACHDUS
Forging Jewish Unity in Wartime Platforms

Elissa Sampson

During World War II, the Jewish-American Section of the International Workers Order (IWO) provided deep support for wartime cultural work in the hope of building a broadly anti-racist culture that would simultaneously tackle fascism, antisemitism, and Jim Crow.[1] One pamphlet proclaimed, "In this global war against fascism, the music, songs, drama, dances of the people are mighty weapons. Let's use them for victory."[2] Even so, these unwelcome, presumed Jewish Communists needed a very different sort of political armor to be able actively to participate in support for both US and Soviet wartime efforts in the fight against fascism along with other Jewish organizations in a unity platform.

Given its prior, acrimonious dealings with American Jewish organizations, most particularly with Socialists, the Jewish-American Section's participation in a "Jewish unity" platform was not easily achieved. Its leaders, although not its members, typically belonged to the Communist Party (CPUSA); its activities, including its visible involvement in leftist causes and interracial campaigns, made it an unlikely political partner for mainstream Jewish organizations. From its very beginnings the organization's leadership claimed it as the sole rightful heir to an older Jewish leftist ideology of secular *Yidishe Kultur* (Yiddish culture) while consistently portraying Soviet policy as supportive of Jewish life. It achieved a hard-fought acceptance into mainstream Jewish politics in the war years, which was reflected in its 1944 change in name to the Jewish Peoples Fraternal Order (JPFO). This more neutral and independent moniker was an indication of its desire to participate in Jewish national organizational communal life. The nomenclature signaled its broad claim to being the legitimate secular inheritor of Jewish tradition through representing leftist popular Jewish fraternal life, and was also prompted by the realization that its aims would be better met by judiciously deemphasizing the part of its name that referenced the IWO.

Wartime Soviet policy promoting Jewish unity required a major shift in the newly minted JPFO's orientation in its dealings with other Jewish groups. In order to participate in the American Jewish Conference, a brand-new wartime umbrella group that sought to bring together mainstream American Jewish organizations, it first needed to prove that it was a Jewish organization per se.[3] In order to do so, the JPFO worked to gain acceptance among other Jewish organizations in forging a unity platform. This included taking a leading role in the organization of the Soviet Union's Jewish Anti-Fascist Committee tour of the United States in 1943 and assuming, somewhat improbably, a leadership role in unified Jewish efforts to gain wartime support for a fight led by the United States, Great Britain, and the Soviet Union.

Archival Sources

We have an unusual window into that world and that particular moment of acceptance, courtesy of New York State's Insurance Department, which deposited the IWO's confiscated papers at Cornell University's Kheel Center after it shut down the organization in 1954. The Kheel Center's holdings of documents in English, Yiddish, and other languages reveal a complex and negotiated leftist Yiddishist politics that includes cultural production as well as alliance-forging among Black, Latino/a, Slavic, Italian, and other leftists. They also show the increasing drive for Jewish organizational unity that developed primarily during the Popular Front and war years. Concert flyers, fundraising materials, exhibits for Negro History Week, journals, volumes of poetry, songs and books for Yiddish schools and camps, material from war bond drives, and literary works, along with items from antisemitism, anti-lynching, and anti-poll tax campaigns, show the broad range of cultural/political activities engaged in by IWO members and by those fellow travelers who worked with the JPFO. Most notably, perhaps, is the anti-lynching song "Strange Fruit," first published as the poem "Bitter Fruit" in 1937 by Lewis Allen (Abel Meeropol), a CPUSA member who would later adopt the children of Julius and Ethel Rosenberg after their conviction and execution on conspiracy to commit espionage charges. (The Meeropols sent the children to an IWO camp.) After Meeropol, his wife Anne Shaffer, and the singer Laura Duncan set the poem to music and performed it in 1938, and Billie Holiday began to sing it in 1939, it was published in the IWO's magazine *Fraternal Outlook*.[4]

As a resource, Cornell's IWO archives, in combination with other collections, reveal much about structures of power and of forgetting, not least by offering a window into how mainstream US Jewish organizations worked with the JPFO as part of the war unity effort. Given the general dislike of the August 1939 Molotov-Ribbentrop Pact and its support by Communists, this broadening of cooperation is discernable after Hitler attacked the Soviet Union in June 1941 in Operation Barbarossa. Documents pertaining to Jewish fellow travelers, artists, and intellectuals such as Albert Einstein, Sholem Asch, B. Z. Goldberg, and Marc Chagall speak to the wide support commanded by the Soviet Union during the war. Artists such as Paul Robeson and Langston Hughes, who had already worked with the IWO during the Popular Front period, redoubled their efforts after the invasion of Ethiopia, the Spanish Civil War, and Operation Barbarossa. Writers such as Howard Fast joined the CPUSA, viewing the Soviet Union as the "last man standing" in the fight against Hitler. Others who were part of the IWO's leadership included Louise Thompson Patterson, Clara Lemlich Shavelson, Congressman Vito Marcantonio, and artist Rockwell Kent. These documents show how leftist political activism intersected with popular culture, including through the participation of well-known Black, Italian, Anglo-American, and Jewish artists and public figures in marshaling public support, most especially for wartime fundraising.[5]

The Jewish-American Section of the IWO grudgingly won acceptance and participation in newly opened Jewish organizational spheres in 1943 when it was admitted due to grassroots support for its inclusion at a point in which winning the war was seen to be of paramount importance. Its activities demonstrate the significance of a US-based Jewish fraternal organization that was able to articulate its advocacy for Soviet policies and simultaneously for Jewish life and for America itself, a position that increasingly made sense during World War II. But in the war's aftermath, its ability to continue to do so became increasingly constrained on both sides of the Iron Curtain. By 1946, the beginning of Cold War repression had overlapped with Stalin's suppression of the Jewish Anti-Fascist Committee (JAC, JAFC) and murder of most of its members; the JPFO had helped bring JAC speakers to the United States on a 1943 wartime fundraising tour. Despite the JPFO's extraordinary support for the war in tandem with mainstream groups, after the war those organizations wasted no time in distancing themselves from the Yiddish-speaking Communists about whom they had previously expressed qualms.

Given the obvious difficulties these leftists faced in retaining alliances with non-Communist fellow ethnics following the war, it is perhaps not surprising that the vibrancy of the Jewish, Italian, and other leftist groups within the IWO has been largely forgotten. While the erstwhile importance and popularity of the Yiddish-speaking immigrant left, *di linke*, is often underestimated, its bilingual archive offers insight into the everyday activities of a Soviet-oriented Jewish immigrant organization and how it successfully cooperated with other Jewish groups during the war. Similarly, records of the IWO's other language sections such as the Polonia Society indicate that during the war they cooperated with their former ideological adversaries in broad-based, "win-the-war' coalitions as part of the American Slav Congress (ASC).[6] The IWO archives are indeed a resource for scholars and activists who attend today to issues that the older left effectively tackled with vigor: expressing interracial solidarity while fighting antisemitism and racism and protesting anti-immigrant actions, as well as providing comprehensive health care and other insurance for precarious workers. But they are also a resource in understanding the necessarily complicated politics of attempts at unity. As we consider the import of that history in the present, we can appreciate *di linke*'s progressive achievements and drive to activism, while we attend to and critically evaluate its ideological shortcomings.

Di Linke

Di linke's original five thousand Yiddish-speaking members, after breaking off from the Socialist-oriented Arbeter Ring (Workmen's Circle), founded the International Workers Order (IWO) in 1930. It subsequently turned itself into the IWO's Jewish (later its Jewish-American) Section when it invited other groups such as leftist immigrant Slovak, Russian, and Hungarian fraternal benefit groups to join its organization. By the time it was renamed the Jewish Peoples Fraternal Order in 1944, the IWO's largest section had grown to encompass almost fifty thousand members with three hundred lodges in more than sixty communities; at its height the broader IWO boasted 188,000 members. While the well-established B'nai B'rith, a Jewish cultural lodge-based association initially created by German-speaking Jews, was larger, the JPFO's membership meant that it was one of the largest US lodge-based Jewish fraternal organizations.

For eastern European immigrants, radicalization was often part of the American experience: for many "greenhorns," or newcomers, organizing Yiddish-speaking unions, strikes, and tenant leagues became a way of life. The initial eastern European Jewish urban immigrant experience was typically one that included working in New York's garment trade, often in sweatshops, and living in overcrowded tenements.[7] Before World War I, New York's impoverished Lower East Side was the world's largest Jewish city and the most densely populated place on the planet. While Yiddish theater and publishing blossomed, tragedies such as the Triangle Shirtwaist Fire of 1911, in which 146 garment workers, mainly young women, perished due to locked fire doors, were not viewed as accidents, but as inherent in a system of labor that valued immigrant lives less than the goods that they produced. Turbulent Socialist politics famously flourished in the wake of mass immigration and labor unions benefited from achieving a critical mass of organized workers. So did landsmanshaften (hometown benefit societies) and fraternal societies, which served as critical safety nets, reinforcing immigrant ties even as they helped Americanize immigrants.

Jewish immigrants enthusiastically greeted the overthrow of the Russian tsar in early 1917. Russia's Bolshevik Revolution later that year enlarged the ruptures over Soviet Russia, Bundism, Socialism, and Communism in Jewish leftist circles and in the American left generally. A decade of splits (1920–30) consumed the Jewish Socialist Federation (JSF) as well as the Socialist-oriented Arbeter Ring, a labor fraternal benefit society that offered funeral and other insurance, ran a publishing house, and organized Yiddish culture schools and summer camps. Jewish Communists became a known part of the Yiddish left and eventually founded their own institutions.

Later, during the 1940s war years, the IWO's commitments to fighting Jim Crow, pushing for the integration of the armed forces, working toward building interracial sports leagues and theater and music troupes, and, in the JPFO, a Yiddish after-school system, did not diminish; if anything, those commitments grew in scope and were strengthened, as was its work promoting Russian War Relief, an organization that helped the Soviet Union through the provision of material and political support. However, its work during the war with other groups far outside of the Order's ideological circles was novel. For the Jewish Section it was a departure from earlier Yiddish Popular Front politics, when it had successfully worked to pull together YKUF (Yidisher Kultur Farband, the Yiddish Cultural Association) as a Yiddish leftist umbrella organization formed primarily of American and European-based writers in Paris in 1937.[8] This was a much farther stretch.

Arguably one of the most interesting aspects of the JPFO's history concerns its connections to mainstream Jewish organizations in the promotion of a politics of wartime Jewish unity articulated in the context of a unity (*achdus*) that called for brotherhood in language replete with religious resonance and complexity.[9] Historically, Jewish communities were enjoined to overcome differences and to pull together under that demanding rubric when threatened, or when dissent challenged those running communal institutions. In this case, due to the genocidal exigencies of World War II, a Jewish Soviet-oriented US fraternal order answered the call for *achdus* issued by the Jewish Anti-Fascist Committee (JAC), the Soviet Yiddish group that published the journal *Eynikayt* (Unity), which issued a plea in 1942 for Jews worldwide to assist the Soviet war effort through a united Jewish front.

It was American, Yiddish-speaking Jewish Communists who lobbied for *achdus*, hoping that major US Jewish organizations would offer unprecedented cooperation by admitting them into their ranks during the war. Materials from the archives show how a famous JAC tour, in conjunction with a well-organized campaign designed to promote inclusion into a Jewish umbrella organization, helped propel the JPFO's eventual entry into the American Jewish Conference's Executive Committee after it was initially denied admission on the grounds that it was not an exclusively Jewish national organization.

This dilemma arose from a Yiddish-speaking fraternal organization initially positioning itself to expand so as to create a new entity that indeed was not a uniquely Jewish national organization. In 1930 *di linke* created a Soviet-oriented US immigrant fraternal society whose fusion of left-wing Yiddishist and American Jewish politics often made for surprising agency vis-à-vis top-down CPUSA politics at a time in which the CPUSA had already started discouraging its language sections. When the original IWO purposely and rapidly expanded by inviting in other immigrant fraternal societies as well as Black and Latino/a members, this Yiddish-speaking organization remade itself into yet another IWO "national" section. Unsurprisingly, its initial existence as a "national" Yiddishist immigrant group in a fraternal order was a source of unease for some Party leaders. Although *di linke* had started the Jewish Workers University in 1926, the unease was apparent since the Party did not view Jews as a national minority whose culture should be recognized and promoted per se.[10]

Soviet Sympathies

Di linke offered a controversial answer to questions about the Jewish future. It saw the fusion of workers' and Jewish rights, championed by the Soviet Union, as a way to bridge Jewish and universal human sympathies. *Di linke* was grounded in an identity that viewed being a worker and a Jew as a natural pairing: its Yiddish activist politics represented a way of being Jewish. An intense debate among the left concerning the broader meaning of the Russian Revolution's turn to Bolshevik politics, as well as its meaning to Jews per se, transpired during World War I and its aftermath. When terrible violence took place in Ukraine during the Russian Civil War, Jews were mainly defended by the Red Army, and by the early 1920s, there was a flourishing of the Yiddish arts in the new Soviet Union. Tempering that knowledge was the awareness that the Bolsheviks rejected the Jewish Labor Bund's articulation of Jewish cultural autonomy. The defense of Jewish religious life per se was not a concern of the left.

It was in this context that *di linke* claimed the mantle of secular Yiddishism, a movement that started in late nineteenth-century Europe. Although "Yiddish-land" lacked a national homeland, Yiddish as a language cut across the map of Europe. *Di linke*'s emphasis on fostering *Yidishe Kultur* was consistent with an overall leftist focus on harnessing *Kultur-Arbet* (cultural work) for overtly political ends in its ARTEF (Arbeter Teater Farband or Workers' Theatre Association) group, musical choirs and orchestras, and publishing house. Its stress on alignment with Soviet policy meant that ideological aspects of an earlier universalism as well as of a Jewish particularism often became subservient to defending and promoting the best interests of the USSR, or at the least, presenting it sympathetically to a Jewish public.

That tension between the Party line and Jewish particularist tendencies is palpable in the pages of *Morgn Frayhayt* (Morning freedom), which started in New York in 1922 as a Yiddish, Communist-affiliated newspaper published by former Bundists Moissaye Olgin and Shakne Epshtein in opposition to the Socialist *Forverts* (Forward) edited by Abraham Cahan. By 1923, *di linke*'s answer to the "Jewish Question," meaning how Jewish difference, nationalism, and antisemitism would be addressed, was tied to that of the Comintern and the Party. This made for some uncomfortable editorial choices. As Lauren Strauss discusses in this book, the *Frayhayt*'s 1929 coverage of deadly riots in Hebron followed the Party line, causing the paper to lose prized writers (and readers) even though it held onto Moshe Nadir, who later published with the IWO. In the 1930s, the paper's unwavering support for Stalin during the Great Purge made editorial attention to the antisemitic (and anti-Yiddishist) aspects of Soviet state policy impossible. Nevertheless, after the founding of the IWO in 1930, the paper's editors worked directly with its top leadership, even though the IWO officially viewed Jews as a national minority whose language and distinctive history should be promoted for its own sake (see Dylan Kaufman-Obstler's chapter on the Jewish Workers University).

By September 1939, a sharp contradiction had emerged with *di linke*'s impassioned defense of the Molotov-Ribbentrop Pact. This agreement guaranteed Soviet neutrality when Germany conquered much of Poland, thus consigning it to the Nazi war machine as the USSR grabbed the rest. The Jewish-American Section's leadership echoed the Party line that the nonaggression pact was necessary to protect the Soviet Union. When Jews from Poland's east found themselves living behind Soviet lines, the Jewish-American Section promoted the dubious claim that the USSR saved two million Jews from the jaws of Hitler. It also followed the Party line in its denials regarding the deaths of Henryk Erlich (1942) and Wiktor Alter (1943), Bundists who escaped Nazi-conquered Poland in 1939 only to be imprisoned and die in the Soviet Union.[11]

Nonetheless, at certain points the Nazi genocide—and the refusal of Soviet-led Communism to acknowledge its particular anti-Jewish valence—put the Jewish-American Section of the IWO somewhat, if not completely, at odds with Communist Party policy and leaders who often denied the specificity of antisemitism, including the Nazi variety.[12] Members and leaders sometimes exercised autonomy when loyalties and priorities did not perfectly align. The archives reflect tensions and choices, often defensively crafted in response to the criticism of Soviet politics offered by the Yiddish press and by other leftists. In 1939 Jewish IWO members issued a Yiddish pamphlet condemning the Soviet Union's signing of the nonaggression pact. Signatories of "Der Stalin-Hitler Opmakh un der Internatsyonaler Arbeter Ordn" (The Stalin-Hitler Pact and the International Workers Order) addressed "all Order members and Leftist Jewish workers" in condemning the pact. Jewish IWO members opposed to the pact joined with *Frayhayt* staff members, creating a League Against Fascism and Dictatorship, and vowed to stay in the Order and fight policies they found odious. From Newark, New Jersey, a report came that Jewish, Polish, and Slovak members similarly denounced the leadership's support of the pact. Finns, Italians, and Ukrainians likewise had no love for their Order's abrupt turnaround.[13] Yet once the United States and Soviet Union were both engaged in the fight against Nazism, all was forgiven, and on December 28, 1942, when the Jewish-American Section organized a rally in Madison Square Garden to protest the killing by Nazis of two million Jews, mainstream speakers reinforced the message that American Jews were indeed their brothers' keepers.[14]

Wartime Unity

Less than two years after the nonaggression pact was signed, on June 22, 1941, Hitler attacked the Soviet Union and began to target its Jews. The Jewish-American Section of the IWO responded immediately; its wholehearted support for the war effort marks its political apogee, as its goals aligned fully in defense of the USSR and of Jews and against the Nazi threat. With the US entry into the war after Pearl Harbor, the Jewish-American Section expanded its mobilization from its earlier focus on raising funds for Soviet tanks and medical aid to encompass large-scale Jewish community fundraising for US war bonds and troops. This was true of the IWO generally: organizationally, all of its sections worked to organize wartime support within as well as outside their "national communities." Notably, in doing so the Order continued to advocate and loudly agitate for the racial integration of the US Armed Forces and the end of Jim Crow, and championed African American contributions to America's war effort.

By 1942, Stalin was officially seeking overseas support from Jews and authorizing the Moscow and Kuibyshev-based Jewish Anti-Fascist Committee, which had officially been founded in April of that year, to obtain financial and political aid for Soviet troops and civilians.[15] Obtaining such support meant pressuring the West to open a second front and that would require organizing and travel. A Jewish unity platform was needed that could influence US public opinion so that the "Jewish Street" and its organizations would speak with one official voice in backing Soviet priorities. With far less fanfare, Stalin also authorized other committees to reach out to their diasporas for support of the Soviet Union. Out of such directives, the pro-Soviet, win-the-war American Slav Congress was born: the pressure for unity in the name of wartime support was not unique to Jews. (As with the JAC, calls for wartime unity made for strange bedfellows: the ASC leadership included Russian Orthodox priests; a Republican Polish American judge from Pittsburgh; Leo Krzycki, a Polish American Socialist and labor leader; and Communist officers in the IWO's Polish, Slovak, and Ukrainian societies.) The JAC, along with four other anti-fascist committees, had Stalin's explicit permission to raise funds for the Soviet war effort, document Nazi atrocities, and encourage support for an Allied second front.[16]

Within the IWO, its Polish, Serbian, and Croatian sections, among others, were also active in their ethnic communities in drumming up support for the second front and other Soviet priorities. Nonetheless, while this stress on wartime unity was widely seen in Soviet-oriented circles, it should not be understood as uniquely pro-Soviet; in IWO circles, support for the war was explicitly understood as support for the United States and for President Franklin D. Roosevelt (FDR), and as a profound expression of American patriotism. The JPFO's new wartime focus meant that it continued its existing work with other leftist organizations and other IWO sections that were also tasked, although in different ways, with prioritizing the war effort. One notable example entailed the efforts of the IWO's Italian Garibaldi Society in reaching out to the pro-Mussolini Sons of Italy fraternal society to pull together an Italian American war unity platform, a gesture that was more fully welcomed once Mussolini's imminent downfall and Allied success were seen as inevitable. Nonetheless, because of the JPFO's direct involvement with the JAC, and given the reality of antisemitism and anti-Communism in a genocidal context, the stakes were far higher in attempting to create "Jewish unity." Jewish life was under siege; its future, hanging in the balance, necessarily depended on Soviet military success.

These escalating shifts in wartime conditions encouraged the Jewish-American Section of the IWO to respond rapidly to the JAC's call to create a "Jewish unity" front to support the war effort by attempting to join the American Jewish Conference, a new wartime umbrella group. Its campaign over the course of nine months to win mainstream acceptance—Jewish and otherwise—underscores its flexible accommodation of the requirements for official participation in a Jewish unity platform. Wartime Soviet policy promoting "Jewish unity" required a major shift in orientation; the Jewish-American Section of the IWO first had to prove itself to be a Jewish organization per se in order to participate in the American Jewish Conference, which was busy convening its new umbrella group for its own wartime reasons. All of which brings us back to the Jewish Anti-Fascist Committee (JAC).

The Jewish Anti-Fascist Committee

A call for help and Jewish unity was first broadcast in Yiddish from Moscow on August 24, 1941, followed by another broadcast to "Jews throughout the world" on April 7, 1942, arguably the founding date of the JAC. Two dozen Jewish cultural figures led by Shloyme Mikhoels issued an international radio appeal in Yiddish to Jews worldwide to unite in the struggle against Nazi Germany and to support buying tanks for the Allies.[17] They also published an extremely rare booklet of Yiddish poetry from Moscow in the summer of 1941, *From the Homeland in Battle* (Farn Haymland in Shlakht).[18] On May 24, 1942, the Jewish-American Section of the IWO mobilized a coalition to broadcast an American Jewish radio response to the JAC's appeal, which included Einstein, Nachum Goldman, and other prominent Jewish figures.[19] The Jewish Council for Russian War Relief published a Yiddish booklet with a transcript of that short-wave response, which committed to assisting Soviet Jews at a time of literal siege, battle, and death (see figure 1.1).

The historian Shimon Redlich has written that "in the various appeals and approaches to non-Soviet Jewry, the JAC always emphasized some basic themes: the national unity of the Jews, the common struggle against the Nazis, the Jewish heroism in its historical perspective, and the contribution of the Jewish people to world culture. Jewish suffering and martyrdom were particularly stressed. Such . . . names as Bar Kokhba and Judah Halevi were common in the vocabulary of the JAC." Redlich goes on to note the usage of "such phrases as: 'On the soil of Israel such men as Judah Maccabee and Bar Kokhba raised the flag of revolt fighting the precursors of Hitler and Mussolini. . . . It was there that our great Judah Halevi [from Spain] created his last poems, poems of unlimited affection for the land and for its eternal people.'"[20]

This language is reflected in the work of William Gropper, the IWO/JPFO's famous artist and cartoonist (see Lauren Strauss's chapter regarding Gropper's work). The images he drew for wartime fundraising of donated tanks bedecked

FIGURE 1.1. "Yiddish Radio Broadcast to the Jews of the Soviet Union," May 24, 1942. The cover has a modernist graphic of a radio microphone accompanied by words indicating that it is an NBC short-wave transcript. Courtesy of the Kheel Center.

with famous Jewish names, including those of Bar Kokhba and Judah Maccabee, invoke two improbable Communist heroes given their association with Jewish national revolts. Likewise improbable is the affixing of Hayim Solomon's name to an American Jewish tank, given that he is best known as a financier of the American Revolution. (In a similar vein, the IWO's Polonia Society resurrected the aristocratic Casimir Pulaski and Tadeusz Kosciuszko as proletarian-nationalist icons, and the Party venerated Thomas Jefferson while still condemning African American oppression.) It is also unclear what might be implied philosophically in the posthumous mustering of Baruch Spinoza to the battlefield to illustrate support for Soviet Jews in 1942. The resounding unifying message from these disparate Jewish names inscribed across the collapsing of time and geography agrees that if there is to be any Jewish future at all, it must be defended militarily by the Soviet Union. Yet as with all JAC calls to diasporic unity, it also whispers in Yiddish the signaling of a Jewish nation.

A year later, *di linke* helped organize the successful North American leg of the fundraising tour by JAC figures in support of the Soviet war effort, a tour that Stalin had explicitly authorized. On June 17, 1943, Shloyme Mikhoels and Colonel Itzik Fefer came to the United States and stayed for more than four months, raising $16 million. Prior to the war, Mikhoels was the Soviet Union's most famous Yiddish actor and the director of GOSET, the Moscow State Jewish Theater. Fefer was a poet known for his straightforward and often propagandistic style; he also had ties to the Russian secret police, the NKVD. Leaders of the Jewish-American Section of the IWO served on the executive boards of the two groups instrumental in organizing the tour: the American Committee of Jewish Writers, Artists and Scientists (CAWS) headed by Einstein, Sholem Asch, and B. Z. Goldberg, and the Jewish Council for Russian War Relief. The tour also took Mikhoels and Fefer to Mexico, Argentina, Canada, and England.

On July 8, 1943, at New York's Polo Grounds, approximately forty-seven thousand people welcomed Mikhoels and Fefer to a "family reunion" of Soviet and American Jews—the world's two largest Jewish populations—separated for more than twenty years by the politics of world war, revolution, and immigration quotas.[21] Official greeters included Mayor Fiorello LaGuardia, Rabbi Stephen S. Wise, Einstein, Asch, and actor Eddie Cantor, as well as representatives from the Joint Distribution Committee (JDC), B'nai B'rith, and the World Jewish Congress. The well-attended Polo Grounds event was a success despite opposition by Socialists aligned primarily with the *Forverts*, as well as by organizations such as the American Jewish Committee, which feared that overt Jewish support for Communists would feed antisemitic perceptions that World War II was a "Jewish War."

Fefer's Polo Grounds speech reinforced the link between Jewish unity and support for the Soviet Union. "Unity is the surest guarantee for victory," he asserted. "He who speaks against the unity of our people aids our enemies. He who speaks against the Soviet Union acts against the interests of our people."[22] Fefer's remarks made clear that the fate of Soviet Jews, and of all Jews, depended on Soviet victory; the call for unity and support in effect demanded that American Jewish organizations paper over existing differences regarding the Soviet Union.

The tour also enhanced the credentials of the Jewish-American Section of the IWO in its campaign for mainstream acceptance and boosted its standing in Jewish leftist circles. In this context, the value of Yiddish was reinforced as a tie between the "two great branches of the Jewish world." In August 1943, Fefer came to visit the JPFO's Camp Kinderland, where children performed for him in Yiddish to the acclaim of many (see figure 1.2). A photo printed in *Morgn Frayhayt* shows a CAWS reception at the Soviet Consulate for Mikhoels and Fefer featuring luminaries such as Einstein and Sholem Asch along with Jewish-American Section head Rubin Saltzman and other leadership figures, including

FIGURE 1.2. August 1943 photo of Itzik Fefer at Camp Kinderland. *Left to right*: S. Davidovitch (a camp director); Edith Segal (Kinderland's dance director); Fefer (in suit and tie); an assistant of A. Cohen; and Cohen himself. The Yiddish word *Kinderland* is handwritten on the bottom right. Courtesy of the Kheel Center.

George Starr, Gedalya Sandler, Itche Goldberg, A. Grossfeld, Joseph Men, as well as Chaim Zhitlowsky's widow, Nora. IWO member Paul Robeson also met with Mikhoels and Einstein at the consulate.

In January 1943, when the American Jewish Conference was first being organized, the Jewish-American Section's leadership started a campaign to be admitted to its first plenary meeting as a national Jewish organization, which involved an extensive correspondence between its leadership and that of the major Jewish organizations who dominated the Conference's executive committee. A brief summary of the many ways to say "no" would include a January 20, 1943, telegram sent to the Jewish-American Section by B'nai B'rith, whose head was chairing what was to be the newly convened American Jewish Conference. It read: "Regarding your telegram, we are inviting only Jewish membership organizations, not affiliates of general organizations." It would also include a letter sent on June 14, 1943, by Jesse Calmenson, explaining that "action previously taken by the Executive Committee, after careful consideration, was reaffirmed and ratified for the reason previously given, that the organization nationally is not exclusively Jewish and that the Jewish American Section is a part of a non-sectarian organization."[23]

FIGURE 1.3. 1942 poster: What is the American Jewish Conference? Courtesy of the Kheel Center.

When letters and telegrams did not suffice, the IWO's Jewish-American Section vigorously began to promote large-scale petition campaigns and meetings in major cities, demanding democracy and accountability in elections for conference delegates.[24] Bilingual posters made the case that an excluded Jewish group thought that broad-based communal input was urgent (see figure 1.3). The question posed in public forums was who should represent all of America's Jews at a time when the war effort demanded Jewish unity. In fact, petitions for the Jewish-American Section's admission to the conference were provided to attendees of the Polo Grounds rally, who could see for themselves that many conference leaders attended the rally. If Rabbi Wise from the American Jewish Congress could welcome Soviet Jewish Communists at the Polo Grounds, surely he could welcome American Jewish Communists as well.

On August 30, 1943, after nine months of campaigning to be recognized as a national Jewish group that could be admitted to the conference, the Jewish-American Section was given the green light in a telegram inviting it to attend—at the last minute—a general committee meeting at the Waldorf Astoria Hotel in

New York City.²⁵ Its work, including at the Polo Grounds, had paid off handsomely and the larger Jewish political arena indeed became more permeable to its presence.²⁶ In January 1944, the Jewish-American Section was officially invited to join the Interim Committee, which made most of the conference's decisions. This shift in the prevailing winds was not merely in support of the war, whose Jewish stakes were becoming increasingly apparent; the conference explicitly and quite unrealistically wanted a voice at the table in shaping the postwar situation. Tragically, it did not particularly concern itself with rescue efforts.

Correspondence with the dominant organizations in the American Jewish Conference documents the Jewish-American Section's lengthy, contested, but ultimately successful grassroots wartime campaign to convince establishment groups such as B'nai B'rith, the Zionist Organization of America, and the American Jewish Congress to accept it as a Jewish organization worthy of admission to its new umbrella group. The sticking point was its relation to the IWO, and by implication, to the CPUSA. This begs the question: How did the Jewish-American Section of the IWO manage to demonstrate a national Jewish fraternal organization's independence in regard to the IWO?

A June 3, 1943, letter from IWO national secretary Max Bedacht to the National Executive Committee of the American Jewish Conference urged reconsideration of their decision that the Jewish-American Section of the IWO was not "a national Jewish membership organization." The letter explained that the various national group sections within the IWO exercised "full autonomy," each with its own national committee, and only shared an administrative benefits structure:

> The national group sections through their national committees have full autonomy for their civic activities. They themselves decide on their policies in this field of action, and they themselves bear responsibility for putting these policies into action. They themselves determine the character of the cultural life of their lodges and are responsible for serving the needs of their own people. . . .
>
> . . . Each national group retains freedom of action for adapting its fraternal and cultural life and its civic actions to the desires, the life and the needs of their respective people.²⁷

Given that it does not accurately describe either Bedacht's views or the IWO's organizational structure, the letter's very existence argues for the view that the Jewish-American Section was deeply interested in reaping the perceived benefits of Jewish unity through organizational participation with mainstream Jewish groups.²⁸ It is hard to imagine that this letter could have been sent without support from those at the very top who wanted this unity campaign to succeed. For those within the organization that would shortly become known as the JPFO, growing awareness of the Holocaust made support for the Soviets imperative, and such wartime support allowed Jewish and other IWO members to embrace, not merely burnish, their American patriotism. The irreconcilable had become reconcilable, however briefly.

The organizational name shift went as planned: the Jewish-American Section of the IWO became the Jewish Peoples Fraternal Order (JPFO), a change that was adopted on July 4, 1944, at the IWO's national convention at Madison Square Garden. While eleven sections chose not to do so, three others—Polonia (Poland), Garibaldi (Italian), and Cervantes (Sección Hispana)—also chose new names that stressed national connections and dropped the IWO reference so as to broaden their appeal within their communities. Protocol topics at the convention included the Declaration of Independence, democracy, World War II, Social Security, the JPFO's funding of four Air Force bombers with $1 million in war bonds, Nazi genocide against Jews, universal health care, "Negro rights," the welcoming of English-speaking lodges, support for the Teheran Conference's agreement on Allied nations' cooperation, and an envisioned social-democratic postwar economy and society. Wartime unity continued to be strongly encouraged, as the Order pledged "first and foremost" to work for "winning of the war." In an IWO resolution passed on July 2, 1944, in conjunction with other groups, the Order also pledged support of politicians committed to halting racial and religious discrimination and to work for "the rescinding of all discriminatory laws and practices against people because of their race or nationality, and the outlawing of all fascist efforts to set one part of the American people against another because of race, national origin, or religious beliefs."[29]

Conference Dancing: Zionism as a Partner

Upon the Jewish-American Section's acceptance into the conference, its leadership began to think that the previously unachievable goal of creating a cohesive cultural and political alignment of Yiddishist or Anglophone Jewishness with both American and pro-Soviet identification was realizable and envisioned it as permanent, as seen in the correspondence between Saltzman and Rabbi Wise of the American Jewish Congress. The future JPFO intensified Jewish organizational support for the war and for the long-delayed launching of a second front, but it did so by proposing and agreeing to Jewish unity resolutions and platforms with mainstream organizations that were also explicitly devoted to the promotion of Zionism. In response to the JAC's call to prioritize Jewish unity, the anti-Zionist, Yiddishist JPFO undertook work that actively supported the Jewish *Yishuv* (settlement) in British Mandate Palestine.

In a 1943 letter to B'nai B'rith, the section's founder Rubin Saltzman amicably described the American Jewish Conference's purpose as "to help achieve common agreement on the post-war status of the Jews and a program for Palestine."[30] By the end of the war, the newly minted JPFO had already mobilized with major Jewish organizations to support coordinated large-scale campaigns urging President Harry Truman to vote for the partition of Mandate Palestine in the United Nations in order to establish a Jewish state. This stance only aligns partially with Soviet policy regarding Palestine and its postwar protest against British imperialism since the Soviet Union only officially supported the UN resolution on partition on November 29, 1947.

The JPFO's rank and file were aware of popular support for Zionist causes. Despite the *Frayhayt*'s relatively uninhibited sniping at Zionism, at a time when almost every American Jewish organization was raising money first for Jewish resettlement in Mandate Palestine and then in Israel, the JPFO often acted like most other Jewish organizations. In other words, the anti-Zionist JPFO accommodated its political goals to take into account Zionist priorities: It geared its postwar charitable activities so that support for homeless Jewish refugees in displaced persons camps and for the rebuilding of Jewish life in Poland, Romania, Belgium, and France would also encompass the *Yishuv* in Palestine. As part of its fundraising for postwar "rehabilitation efforts," the JPFO carefully chose to support the pre-state *Yishuv* and Israel solely through donations to children's medical aid. Funding went to build a children's tuberculosis wing at Hadassah Hospital, buy ambulances, and establish a kindergarten and children's clinic. It should be noted that much of the pro-Soviet left saw the emergence of the State of Israel as aligned with Socialism and as a potential ally to the Soviet Union; the JPFO was not unique in that regard. Nonetheless, just before Soviet official support for partition had been obtained, its officially anti-Zionist stance became the lever that the liberal American Jewish Congress pulled to expel JPFO Communists from the communal fold.[31]

Unity Is Internal

Although Yiddish was foundational to the JPFO's work, a generational shift took place as its push for Jewish unity became internal to the organization and it began to encourage and support a new generation's explicitly Jewish identity. While a discernable shift to English on the part of native-born offspring was positioned as a response to the wartime need for internal unity, the JPFO's leadership was aware of and had actively debated why it had not been halted by the existence of a strong, successful *shule* (Yiddish after-school program) system run in tandem with its Camp Kinderland. The problem of second-generation members shunning foreign-language branches was similarly identified by Slovaks and others in the IWO. But as executive board member George Starr proudly reported in 1944, the JPFO's English-speaking lodges participated for the first time at its sixth convention, which immediately followed the IWO's annual meeting:

> As a result of the war, there has been an awakening and deepening of the national consciousness . . . especially of the Jewish people. . . . The terrible fate our fellow-Jews met at the hands of Hitler and the pernicious antisemitism of Hitler's American followers, the native fascists, shook them into a realization of their Jewishness. . . . It is imperative for the American Jews to maintain their Jewish identity, and that the nurturing of a Jewish consciousness will in turn strengthen the overall American democratic tradition. . . . The organization of English-speaking lodges [is] to join side by side with the already existing Yiddish-speaking lodges, to advance the best interest of the Jewish people.
> . . .We find that for the first time American-born Jews are thinking of the role of Jewish culture in their lives. The whole problem of what constitutes a Jewish cultural program in our lodges has now come to the fore.
> One thing is certain—the fight against anti-Semitism does not represent a comprehensive program for our English-speaking lodges. We have already stated that the combatment of anti-Semitism is not a specific Jewish problem, but the responsibility of the whole community. . . . We must understand however, that stemming the tide of anti-Semitism does not meet the cultural needs of Jewish men and women.
> It is true that many Jews have become aware of their Jewishness because of the sting of discrimination and anti-Semitism. We have the opportunity and the responsibility of transforming their reactions into profound political understanding and action in [sic] behalf of the needs of Jewry. The way to this transformation is found in understanding our proud and ancient heritage—our culture.[32]

The JPFO increasingly grappled with seeing itself as Jewish American and tackling the new set of dilemmas that entailed, but by the IWO's 1940 convention, African American vice president Louise Thompson Patterson was already touching upon the critical role of English lodges in fostering interracial work that also fought antisemitism and supported immigrants. She argued that "our English lodges must see that their task is not confined only to the cementing of the unity of the native-born Negro and white peoples of our community but that our lodges again can play a key role in coordinating the activities of all our various national group lodges in such communities so that we tackle as one Order the fight against anti-Semitic, anti-Negro, anti-alien propaganda and legislation."[33]

Even as it welcomed an American-born generation, the JPFO's pursuit of a Jewish unity agenda also prompted a wartime recalibration of its relationship to the IWO and CPUSA. Part of this recalibration involved finally agreeing with the CPUSA's message that English needed to be accommodated. Nonetheless, the increased autonomy necessary for wartime support contributed to an unease concerning the JPFO's existence as the main "national" section of an immigrant fraternal order that recommitted itself to the propagation of Jewish culture in the wake of Nazi genocide.

Cold War Blues

The JPFO's unceasing support for the war and for FDR as commander-in-chief entailed numerous campaigns, often in coalition with other Jewish groups as well as with wider pro-Soviet circles. One welcome result was that an increasing broader recognition of its role ensued. A dependable ally for large-scale fundraising for war bonds and military equipment, it could also organize mass rallies, clothing drives, letter-writing campaigns, get-out-the-vote programs for FDR, concerts, Soviet relief drives, and support for soldiers and veterans.

Senator James E. Murray (D-MT) addressed JPFO members at their 1944 convention in a striking example of recognition of their wartime activities:

> Let us not fail to recognize the tremendous contribution made by Russia [whose] . . . heroic armies . . . are progressively destroying the so-called invincible German Forces. . . . It is particularly gratifying and encouraging to our American citizens to know that you are here tonight commemorating the fulfillment of your pledge to purchase one million dollars' worth of war bonds to provide four giant bombers for our gallant fighting forces of the air. . . . As the descendants of a long-suffering people—the Jewish people—you are making this sacrifice cheerfully because you know better than most of us the significance of the present world upheaval. . . . You will make possible in the future, . . . to avenge the Nazi murderers . . . where Hitler's legions have perpetrated their unspeakable crimes upon defenseless peoples. . . . As a fraternal benefit society with a membership close to two hundred thousand, you have made notable contributions to the cause of American National unity.[34]

Murray, a fervent New Dealer from a Western state, thought it worthwhile as part of the war effort to address the IWO/JPFO convention by acknowledging the

Soviet Union as an ally and by addressing Nazi genocide. As Frank Capra's 1943 US military film, *The Battle of Russia*, shows, hailing the Soviet Union as a crucial wartime ally was not unique to Murray.

Yet as the war ended, antisemitism in the Soviet Union, further fueled by Stalin's paranoia, began to combine with the Cold War blues at home. The JPFO's involvement in 1946 in the JAC's *Black Book* project of documenting Nazi crimes against Jews exemplified the contradictions of garnering support for Soviet policies as its work in the Soviet Union unraveled; Stalin's shutting down of the Soviet part of the *Black Book* project was a prelude to his subsequent suppression of the Jewish Anti-Fascist Committee and murder of most of its members.

Much to the surprise of the JPFO's leadership, its troubled pro-Soviet legacy came home to roost precisely as the memory of its full-fledged mobilization in support of America's role in World War II faded with the onset of the Cold War. As mainstream Jewish organizations increasingly joined the fight against Communism—an ideology that they did not want to have associated with Jews—their work with the JPFO became problematic. Once the Cold War began, the JPFO remained intent on retaining the goodwill of those American Jewish organizations it had worked with, now busy officially distancing themselves from any association with perceived Communists. In response to formal questions, the JPFO continued to attest to its support for the *Yishuv* and then for Israel even as its commitment to doing so was sharply questioned by the conference's constituent organizations. Unsurprisingly, the JPFO's official anti-Zionist ideology was used as the reason for its expulsion from the American Jewish Conference, which in any event had started to fall apart as its constituent mainstream organizations such as the American Jewish Congress gained further clout outside of its confines.

After the war, the JPFO continued to raise funds primarily to aid Jewish refugees and orphans, mostly in Poland but also in France, Belgium, and Mandate Palestine. Letters from Marc Chagall show his continued participation in a JPFO project to raise funds for a Jewish orphanage in Andrésy, France. The JPFO advocated for the right of Jewish refugees to stay in Europe if they preferred, or to settle elsewhere, including by obtaining visas for the United States in its "Let My People In" campaign for those in displaced persons camps, or through transport to Mandate Palestine.[35] Arguably, this was their most principled stand, and they encountered real political difficulty in advocating for a variety of choices.

The Cold War years had a chilling effect on the activities of the IWO, particularly once it was placed on Attorney General Tom Clark's "Red List" (a blacklist of subversive organizations that marked the beginning of the postwar Red Scare) in December 1947.[36] The American Jewish Committee, whose 1947 *Year Book* had listed the JPFO as a national Jewish organization, strategically began to align itself with Cold War perspectives and by 1951 had published a study on Soviet treatment of Jews with the stated goal of arousing "public opinion with the hope of cutting Russia off from its allies and the neutral nations."[37] By 1948, Jewish umbrella organizations that had worked with the JPFO had expelled it as part of an anti-Communist purge; the convergence of its legal woes with those of the Rosenbergs, IWO members accused of conspiracy to commit nuclear espionage, accelerated this push.[38] Unsurprisingly, the IWO and JPFO rapidly lost members. In the end, a fiscally conservative, successful leftist fraternal mutual benefit society lost its ability to provide insurance due to the New York Insurance Department's claim that its politics posed a "moral hazard," as Robert Zecker's chapter amply demonstrates.

The JPFO's refusal to acknowledge the possibility that antisemitism existed in the Soviet Union increasingly constrained and distorted its responses at a point where members began to leave, partly in response to Cold War pressures. Mikhoels was assassinated on Stalin's orders in January 1948. On August 12, 1952, after arrests in 1948 and 1949 were followed by false confessions, imprisonment, torture, and a trial, almost all of the remaining JAC members accused of espionage and treason were killed in Moscow's Lubyanka Prison in what is now known as the Night of the Murdered Poets. Three years after Stalin's death, on April 4, 1956, Hersh Smolar published an article in the Warsaw *Folks-Shtime* (People's voice) about the suppression of Soviet Jewish culture. The article was reprinted in *Morgn Frayhayt* on April 11 and then appeared in the English-language magazine *Jewish Life*, which was connected to the JPFO. Three years after the belated revelations about Stalin, the magazine was relaunched as *Jewish Currents*, although the JPFO had already been shut down.

Given the complex history of Stalinism (the Great Purge, the Holodomor, the Molotov-Ribbentrop Pact, the Doctors' Plot, and the liquidation of the Jewish Anti-Fascist Committee) and of the Cold War itself, it is hardly surprising that despite its critical, visible role in creating a progressive Jewish voice on issues of national and international import, the IWO/JPFO's historical importance and popularity is commonly ignored, underestimated, or even effaced. Nonetheless, especially given the availability of newly digitized resources, enough time has passed to reassess its legacy and provide a more nuanced understanding of the contributions of that controversial past.

At a moment of growing interest in understanding intersectionality and racial solidarity in fighting for progressive causes, this history also brings us back to how internal and external unity efforts worked, and the insights they may offer, including for contemporary cultural identity politics. Excising *di linke* from this larger, messy narrative continues the legacy of a Cold War that no one won. While agency and angst can both be glimpsed at unexpected points in the story of the JPFO, it is beyond doubt that in forming and joining an immigrant Yiddish fraternal organization, there was no evasion of Jewish identity. Its founders saw themselves as profoundly and naturally Jewish; being a Jewish Communist offered a way of being Jewish without betraying working-class interests and alliances. Their Americanization as immigrants was mediated through adherence to a beloved immigrant fraternal organization that promoted Yiddish culture even as it offered solidarity with others such as Hispanics, African Americans, Italians, and Poles, who were equally comfortable celebrating their ethnic cultures and working-class unity. We can learn from the failures and successes of that tightrope dance even as we mourn its misplaced allegiances.

NOTES

1. The IWO manifested its anti-racist work through its support of anti-lynching and anti–poll tax campaigns, its advocacy for the integration of the armed forces, and its fight against discrimination and promotion of Black employment, be it in sports, housing, unions, or any other arena, including the hiring of Black labor in its own ranks and leadership. Distinctive to the IWO was its formulation of the close ties between antisemitism, Jim Crow, and anti-immigrant sentiment; for the IWO, a unified fight against these forces was central to becoming American and to defining what a better America should be. While its work as an interracial fraternity was certainly not devoid of contention, its leadership in anti-racist work was integral to the IWO's self-understanding. See the Sampson and Zecker chapter, "Fighting for Black Rights Through the Fraternal Arena."

2. Maxine Wood, *Call to a Cultural Conference*, IWO New York District pamphlet, 1942, International Workers Order (IWO) Records #5276, box 49, folder 6, Kheel Center for Labor-Management Documentation and Archives, Catherwood Library, Cornell University, Ithaca, New York (hereafter Kheel), https://digital.library.cornell.edu/catalog/ss:19043101. Langston Hughes served as keynote speaker for the conference.

3. The American Jewish Conference's convening is regarded as important by historian James Loeffler, who writes: "When the first session convened in late August 1943 at the Waldorf Astoria Hotel in New York City, the 501 delegates included 378 directly elected and 123 chosen by 64 Jewish membership organizations. The formal platform of the American Jewish Conference adopted at the first session was summarized in its credo: 'The American Jewish Conference is the representative body of American Jews, organized democratically for the specific purpose of planning the immediate rescue of European Jewry, taking action upon Jewish postwar problems in Europe and implementing the right of the Jewish people with regard to Palestine.'" Loeffler, "Nationalism Without a Nation: On the Invisibility of American Jewish Politics," *Jewish Quarterly Review* 105, no. 3 (Summer 2015): 386.

4. Emanuel Levin, "Strange Fruit on Southern Trees," *Fraternal Outlook*, March 1939, 4–5, Kheel.

5. Michael Denning, *The Cultural Front: The Laboring of American Culture in the Twentieth Century* (Verso, 2011). The artist Rockwell Kent, who was IWO president, made much of his colonial New England forebears during his 1948 Progressive Party campaign for Congress. IWO vice president John Middleton, too, highlighted his "old stock" roots.

6. Office of Strategic Services report on the American Slav Congress, May 2, 1942, Don Binkowski Papers, box 1, folder 1–22, Walter P. Reuther Library, Wayne State University, Detroit, Michigan (hereafter Binkowski); "70,000 members of the IWO," advertisement,

American Slav Congress conference program, Detroit, Michigan, April 1942, box 5, folder 5–29, Binkowski; OSS/Foreign Nationalities Branch report on the Polish American Left, June 16, 1944, box 2, folder 2-53, Binkowski.

7. Annelise Orleck, *Common Sense and a Little Fire: Women and Working-Class Politics in the United States, 1900–1965*, 2nd ed. (University of North Carolina Press, 2017).

8. On the eve of World War II, the JPFO's leadership worked with Yiddish Communists to organize those in the Yiddish arts under a sympathetic Popular Front umbrella. At the Alveltlekher Yidisher Kultur Kongres (World Jewish Culture Congress) in 1937 in Paris (also known as the First World Yiddish Congress), an agreement was brokered to found YKUF (Yidisher Kultur Farband or the Yiddish Cultural Organization) as a new political, cultural, and arts organization to bring together some of the most esteemed Yiddish writers in the Americas and in Europe. See Nerina Visacovsky's chapter in this book for Latin American participation in YKUF.

At the Congress, the *Frayhayt*'s then-editor Moissaye Olgin enthusiastically noted the miraculous growth of Yiddish culture, describing culture itself as an armament for the people of the Soviet Union and the United States that could develop political and national consciousness. See the speech "Kultur un Folk" [Culture and people] by Olgin at the YKUF founding conference in Paris, September 17, 1937. The reprint or adaptation of the talk is printed in Moissaye J. Olgin, *Kultur un Folk* (Idishn kooperativn folks-farlag fun Internatsyonaln arbeter ordn, 1939), https://digital.library.cornell.edu/catalog/ss:19043019.

See Annette Aronowicz, "Haim Sloves, the Jewish People, and a Jewish Communist's Allegiances," *Jewish Social Studies* 9, no. 1 (Autumn 2002): 48. Aronowicz describes the Congress's Paris organizer, Haim Slovès, as someone for whom at that time "there seemed to be a perfect consonance between the communist and the Jewish sides of their allegiance. All of Sloves's militant activities attested to what one might call a symbiosis" (97). The 1938 correspondence between the Jewish-American Section's general secretary Rubin Saltzman and Haim Slovès on YKUF's founding and its financial and political underpinnings shows its deep connections to the American group's Soviet-oriented leadership. Henri Slovès to YKUF directorate about report on trip, November 1938, box 53, folder 7, Kheel, https://digital.library.cornell.edu/catalog/ss:20604618.

9. *Achdus* comes from the Hebrew component of Yiddish and invokes brotherhood, an appropriate fraternal gesture, as well as unity. I have chosen to use it rather than the more common *Eynikayt* since that was the name of the Soviet Yiddish-language publication of the Jewish Anti-Fascist Committee.

10. The question of what constitutes a nation is central to Marxist theory as seen in Joseph Stalin's *Marxism and the National Question*, Marxists Internet Archive, 1913, https://www.marxists.org/reference/archive/stalin/works/1913/03a.htm. It "is a historically constituted, stable community of people, formed on the basis of a common language, territory, economic life, and psychological make-up manifested in a common culture." According to this definition, Jews did not qualify as a nation given the lack of geographic contiguity. Yiddishland had no designated territory per se, and the Bund had advocated for "national" cultural autonomy. This debate preceded the 1917 Bolshevik Revolution and was augmented by the 1903 split in which the Bund had temporarily sided with the Bolsheviks' opponents, the Social Democratic Mensheviks.

11. Paul (Pesach) Novick, *Der emes vegn Erlich-Alter* [The truth about Erlich-Alter], box 45a, folder 5, Kheel, https://digital.library.cornell.edu/catalog/ss:21072623.

12. Antony Polonsky, "Jews and Communism in the Soviet Union and Poland," in *Jews and Leftist Politics: Judaism, Israel, Antisemitism, and Gender*, ed. Jack Jacobs (Cambridge University Press, 2017), 147–68.

13. Lucy Davidowitz, "History of the Jewish People's Fraternal Order," November 1950, IWO Collection, folder 8, Tamiment Library and Robert F. Wagner Labor Archives, New

York University, New York, New York; Brother Landy, "A Special Problem," from minutes of the Fifth Annual Convention of the IWO New Jersey District, Newark, November 30–December 1, 1940, 2–3, box 8, folder 3, Kheel; questionnaires sent to IWO national office from Albert Steinberg of Denver (April 16, 1941), Sylvia Linna of the Bronx (April 14, 1941), A. Prisiaznuk of Edwardsville, Pennsylvania (April 24, 1941), box 18, folder 13, Kheel.

14. "Halt the Bloody Atrocities of Hitlerism!," leaflet, box 45, folder 1, Kheel, https://digital.library.cornell.edu/catalog/ss:21072659. The leaflet was issued under the name "The Jewish People's Committee" with a tagline at the bottom indicating that it was distributed by the City Central Committee and the Jewish-American Section of the International Workers Order. As seen in the same folder, the December 28, 1942, rally was advertised in diverse Yiddish newspapers, including *Der Tog* (Day), *Der Morgn Journal* (Morning journal), and *Di Morgn Frayhayt* (Morning freedom). Speakers included Rabbi Joseph H. Lookstein of the Rabbinical Council of America, Congressman Emmanuel Celler (D-Brooklyn), and Michael Quill of the Transit Workers Union.

15. Erlich and Alter had proposed an earlier version of such a committee; the politics of their death and its connection to the later founding of the Jewish Anti-Fascist Committee show a complicated Stalinist landscape that involved the NKVD. Shimon Redlich, *Propaganda and Nationalism in Wartime Russia: The Jewish Anti-Fascist Committee in the USSR, 1941–1948* (East European Quarterly, 1982); Redlich, *War, Holocaust and Stalinism: A Documented Study of the Jewish Anti-Fascist Committee in the USSR*, New History of Russia 1 (Routledge, 2016); Redlich, "The Jewish Antifascist Committee in the Soviet Union," *Jewish Social Studies* 31, no. 1 (1969): 30–31, https://www.jstor.org/stable/4466454.

16. Joshua Rubenstein, "Jewish Anti-Fascist Committee," *The YIVO Encyclopedia of Jews in Eastern Europe*, accessed May 15, 2016, https://yivoencyclopedia.org/article.aspx/Jewish_Anti-Fascist_Committee.

17. In addition to Shloyme Mikhoels and Itzik Fefer, its members included Peretz Markish, Dovid Bergelson, Ilya Ehrenburg, Vasily Grossman, General Iakob Kreizer, and Lina Shtern, who called on "our Jewish brethren throughout the world" to aid the Soviet Union. Other members were Salomon Lozovsky, Shakne Epshtein, Salomon Bergman, Aaron Katz, Boris Shimeliovich, Joseph Yuzefovich, Leib Kvitko, Dovid Hofshteyn, Benjamin Zuskin, Ilya Vatenberg, Izi Kharik, Lev Strongin, Emilia Teumim, Leon Talmy, Pinkhes Kahanovitsh ("Der Nister"), Iosef Yuzefovich, Aron Kushnirov, Shmuel Halkin, and Khayke Vatenberg-Ostrowskaya. See Madeleine Cohen's resource kit documents, "The Night of the Murdered Poets," Yiddish Book Center, accessed May 18, 2025, https://www.yiddishbookcenter.org/educational-programs/resources-teachers/resource-kits-teachers/soviet-jewish-experience/night.

18. Jewish Anti-Fascist Committee, *Farn haymland in shlakht* [From the homeland in battle] (Moscow, 1941), box 47, folder 16, Kheel, https://digital.library.cornell.edu/catalog/ss:19043040. The Jewish Anti-Fascist Committee published a wartime poetry booklet from Moscow in the summer of 1941, which is among the rarest of the Kheel archival holdings. The booklet was presumably printed between July 1941 and the Nazi invasion of Moscow in October; on October 15, Stalin ordered the evacuation of the Communist Party, the General Staff, and various civil government offices from Moscow to Kuibyshev (Samara). The archives show the head of the Jewish-American Section of the IWO, Rubin Saltzman, sending a telegram to Mikhoels in Kuibyshev on October 21, 1942. See box 29, folder 5, file 7, Kheel, https://digital.library.cornell.edu/catalog/ss:20631971.

19. Stanley Isaacs et al., *Radio brodkest tsu di Yidn fun Soviet Rusland* [Radio broadcast to the Jews of Soviet Russia], box 45a, folder 9, Kheel, https://digital.library.cornell.edu/catalog/ss:21072647. The Jewish Council for Russian War Relief, Inc., was part of Russian War

Relief. The historically significant Yiddish booklet from the May 24, 1942, New York City transmission contains speeches from prominent American Jewish leaders in politics, education, philanthropy, and religion, including Labor Zionists. The response starts with "Dear Brothers"; participants included Stanley Isaacs, Abraham Goldberg, and Israel Goldstein.

20. Shimon Redlich, "The Jewish Antifascist Committee in the Soviet Union," *Jewish Social Studies* 31, no. 1 (1969): 30–31, https://www.jstor.org/stable/4466454.

21. In 2020 an impression of that day could still be felt when Milton Leitenberg described a highlight of his childhood: as a member of the JPFO's *shule* children's chorus directed by Moshe (Maurice) Rauch, he was positioned only a few feet away from Shloyme Mikhoels during his speech since the chorus's performance preceded Mikhoels's fundraising appeal. Jewish Studies Program, "Di Linke Conference Session 6: First Panel; The Art of Resistance; Second Panel; Memories and Reflections," 2 hr. 19 min., posted April 30, 2021, Cornell Video, 2:14, https://vod.video.cornell.edu/media/Di+Linke+Conference+Session+6%3A+First+Panel%3B+The+Art+of+Resistance%3B+Second+Panel%3B+Memories++Reflections/1_5qqbqcgx/380519982.

22. Itzik Fefer, "The Jews of Russia: Excerpts from Speeches Delivered at the Rally of 47,000 New York Jews to Welcome the Soviet Jewish Anti-Fascist Delegation," *American Hebrew: The National Weekly of Jewish Affairs*, July 16, 1943, 8–9.

23. Telegram from Maurice Bisgyer of B'nai B'rith to Rubin Saltzman, Jewish-American Section of the IWO, January 20, 1943, box 42, folder 4, Kheel, https://digital.library.cornell.edu/catalog/ss:21072298. Also see Jesse B. Calmenson to Rubin Saltzman about the decision preventing IWO participation in the conference, June 14, 1943, box 42, folder 4, Kheel, https://digital.library.cornell.edu/catalog/ss:21072322.

24. Massachusetts Jewish-American Section, IWO, "Vos iz di Yidishe Asembli?/What Is the American Jewish Conference?," flyer, for Dorchester, Boston, June 10, 1943, box 42, folder 4, Kheel, https://digital.library.cornell.edu/catalog/ss:21072321. More than fifty-four thousand petition signatures were gathered by the campaign.

25. Telegram from Meyer W. Weisgel, secretariat member of the American Jewish Conference, to Rubin Saltzman, August 30, 1943, box 42, folder 4, Kheel, https://digital.library.cornell.edu/catalog/ss:21072340.

26. See Loeffler, "Nationalism Without a Nation," 387n59: "The Jewish Labor Committee also withdrew to protest the decision to admit the Jewish People's Fraternal Order of the International Workers Organization, a Communist group." "Background: Jewish Labor Committee, 1945," American Jewish Conference Papers, I-67, box 1, folder 4, American Jewish Historical Society.

27. Letter from Rubin Saltzman and Max Bedacht to the American Jewish Conference, describing the IWO national section structure as fully autonomous, June 3, 1943, box 42, folder 4, Kheel, https://digital.library.cornell.edu/catalog/ss:21072319.

28. See Roger Keeran, "National Groups and the Popular Front: The Case of the International Workers Order," *Journal of American Ethnic History* 14, no. 3 (Spring 1995), for a description of Bedacht's increasingly persistent out-of-sync views on the IWO's national (ethnic) groups and on fraternalism more broadly. "While most Communists within the IWO developed and promoted the new [Popular Front] approach toward national groups, the Order's leader, though a leading Communist, resisted the implications of the new line for national groups" (Keeran, 38). "Bedacht continued to insist that the IWO must recruit English-speaking workers, whatever their national origins, to the English Section" (39). Ironically, Bedacht was an immigrant from Germany. He was eventually pushed out of the IWO, belatedly resigning in 1947.

29. IWO, "Sixth Convention Resolution Number One: The Main Task Before Our Order," July 2, 1944, 2–3, box 49, folder 6, Kheel, https://digital.library.cornell.edu/catalog/ss:19043806.

30. Letter from Rubin Saltzman to Henry Monsky about request for participation in the American Jewish Conference, January 1943, 1, box 42, folder 4, Kheel, https://digital.library.cornell.edu/catalog/ss:21072300.

31. On November 29, 1947, the United Nations General Assembly voted to partition Palestine, adopting Resolution 181; on May 14, 1947, Andrei Gromyko had signaled that Soviet support for partition was on the table. Earlier, on April 23, 1947, the American Jewish Congress's executive director, David Petegovsky, had sent identical letters to Rubin Saltzman and to Jewish Labor Council head William Lovner (who worked with Ben Gold, the head of the CIO-affiliated Furrier's Union), pointedly asking, "What is the official position of your organization with regard to the establishment of a Jewish state in Palestine?" He also asked: "Does your organization support the demand for the immediate abrogation of all restrictions on land purchased by Jews in Palestine?" and "Does your organization support the demand for the entry of 100,000 Jews to Palestine immediately?" Letter from David Petegovsky to Rubin Saltzman, April 23, 1947, box 42, folder 11, file 11, Kheel, https://digital.library.cornell.edu/catalog/ss:21072482. Letter from David Petegovsky to William Lovner, April 23, 1947, International Fur and Leather Workers Union Records #5676, box 7, 72-D-1, folder 9, Kheel; letter from David Petegovsky to Rubin Saltzman, April 23, 1947, IWO Records #5276, box 67, folder 1, Kheel, https://digital.library.cornell.edu/catalog/ss:21072935.

32. George Starr, Committee on English-Speaking Work report, "Protokol fun der zekster natsionaler konvenshun fun dem Yidishn Fraternaler Folks-Ordn" [Protocol of the Sixth National Convention of the Jewish Peoples Fraternal Order of the I.W.O.], copy 1, 1944, 81, 83, box 27, folder 2, Kheel, https://digital.library.cornell.edu/catalog/ss:20631854.

33. Louise Thompson, "Report on the English Section," Fifth National Convention, IWO, June 8–14, 1940, 20–21, box 3, folder 2, Kheel.

34. James E. Murray, "Address by the Honorable James E. Murray, United States Senator, Before Sixth Annual Convention to the Jewish-American Section, IWO," July 4, 1944, 3–4, box 27a, folder 2, Kheel, https://digital.library.cornell.edu/catalog/ss:20631858.

35. On January 5, 1946, the JPFO organized a "Free the Jews from the European Concentration Camps" rally at the Manhattan Center asking for US visas for war refugees in DP camps. The rally was part of its "Let My People In" campaign. National Coordinating Committee for the Admission of 100,000 Homeless Jews into the United States, "Free the Jews from the European Concentration Camps!," postcard, January 1, 1947, box 45, folder 5, Kheel, https://digital.library.cornell.edu/catalog/ss:21072721. The address on the flyer is that of the American Federation of Polish Jews, with whom the JPFO worked during the war.

36. Arthur J. Sabin, *Red Scare in Court: New York Versus the International Workers Order* (University of Pennsylvania Press, 1993). Sabin focused his energies on the Kheel Center's IWO case files (#5940) to ensure that a solid legal history of the IWO's battle with New York State's Insurance Department would be written.

37. Even as late as 1947, the *American Jewish Year Book*'s list of Jewish national organizations blandly describes the JPFO as "a fraternal benefit society, chartered by the Department of Insurance of the State of New York. Provides life insurance, sick benefits and medical services. Promotes civic, educational and social activities of interest to English-speaking and Yiddish-speaking Jewish men and women." "Jewish National Organizations: The United States," in *The American Jewish Year Book* 50 (1948–49), 584, https://www.jstor.org/stable/23603372.

Also see American Jewish Committee, "Jews in the Soviet Union," 1951, and "Jews in the Soviet Satellites," 1953, as quoted by Alan Mittleman et al. in *Jewish Polity and American Civil Society: Communal Agencies and Religious Movements in the American*

Public Square (Rowman & Littlefield, 2002), 48. Also see Naomi Cohen, *Not Free to Desist: The American Jewish Committee, 1906–1966* (Jewish Publication Society, 1972), 499n94.

38. The Rosenbergs were executed in June 1953. The IWO/JPFO insisted that the Rosenbergs were victims of antisemitism, maintaining that antisemitism was a known US phenomenon absent from (and legally forbidden in) the Soviet Union.

2

"WHY MUST YOU HAVE YOUR OWN UNIVERSITY?"

Yiddish Adult Education and the Communist Movement in the United States

Dylan Kaufman-Obstler

The Jewish Workers University (Der idisher arbeter universitet) is an all-but-forgotten institution of the Jewish left. Founded in New York in 1926, it was created to educate Jewish working-class adults to become activists in the labor movement and Communist Party, literate in Yiddish language and literature, and prepared to train the next generation of Jewish youth in Communist ideals. At its debut in 1926, the Jewish Workers University was assigned an esteemed purpose in the Communist movement as its leaders proclaimed it as "the educator of the international worker activist," "a center" where Jews would concentrate their energies on "freeing the working class from capitalist rule," and an institution that would "give us worker intellectuals" who would elevate Jews' ideological commitments to Communism.[1] While its rhetorical emphasis reflected the shifting stances of the Communist Party USA (CPUSA) and the Party's ambivalent relationship to national identity, from its very beginnings the Jewish Workers University was a consistent incubator for the maintenance, creation, and propagation of Yiddish culture.

The Jewish Workers University was just one institution within a larger project by Yiddish Communists to build a cohesive cultural world. Jewish adults attended the Jewish Workers University to become union activists and Yiddish teachers while their children joined strike picket lines on Yiddish school field trips. Families spent their summers at the Yiddish Communist summer camp, Kinderland, where children held dance performances honoring Lenin. They read the Yiddish Communist daily newspaper, *Morgn Frayhayt* (Morning freedom), and sang workers' songs in Yiddish Communist choirs. They built a housing cooperative in the Bronx. With other ethnic groups, such as Slovaks, Poles, Hungarians, Ukrainians, and Italians, they would create an integrated, multicultural fraternal organization, the International Workers Order (IWO), to serve as the organizational apparatus for their cultural work.

The project of Yiddish Communist education and culture, of which the Jewish Workers University was a part, was critical to building a base for the Communist movement in the United States. Jewish immigrants, many of whom participated in the labor movement and Socialist organizing and had their origins in what was formerly the Russian Empire, were a crucial recruiting ground for the Party. Their membership numbers in the Party were significant and the extent of their cultural institution-building within the Communist movement, often in the form of auxiliary organizations, was unparalleled in any other ethnic group. The questions, debates, and activities that took place in the realm of Yiddish Communist culture were not only important to the Jewish participants but also mattered for how the rank and file of the Communist movement operated in the United States.[2]

Yiddish Communist education, however, was a paradoxical endeavor. While it was a central vehicle for the preservation of Yiddish language and secular Jewish culture, its activists had to fit their Yiddish work into a movement that ultimately sought, by its ideological philosophy, to dissolve national differences. As Communists in an organization that demanded doctrinal compliance, these Jewish activists shifted their language concerning the meaning of Yiddish education according to the phase the Party was in. Yiddish Communist writings during the periods of Bolshevization (1924–28) and the Comintern's Third Period (1928–34), for instance, emphasized the internationalist aspects of their work and downplayed references to specifically Jewish themes. Writings by Yiddish Communists at the time dismissed "Yiddishism" (that is, the idea of preserving Yiddish for its own sake) in favor of emphasizing the language as a tool to organize Jewish immigrants and communicate Communist doctrine. Yiddish Communist rhetoric on Yiddish culture and Jewish themes changed noticeably after the introduction of the Popular Front in 1935, as the Party shifted to a more cooperative mode. The outbreak of World War II encouraged celebrations of Jewish culture and ethnicity among Communists, informed by their fight against fascism and the violent antisemitism of Hitler's regime. This shift in rhetoric before and after the Popular Front has led some scholars to describe Yiddish Communists as changing their approach to increase support for Yiddish, which was seemingly absent before.[3]

As much as Yiddish Communists adapted their rhetoric to reflect the different positions of the Party, however, they were in fact consistent in their commitment to Yiddish. Through building institutions such as the Jewish Workers University, they attempted to ensure a future for Yiddish language and culture. The history of the Jewish Workers University, beginning in the 1920s, is evidence of their unwavering belief that building Yiddish culture was foundational to their work in the Communist movement in all of its phases, not just during the Popular Front. Yiddish Communists, while maintaining a justification for their Yiddish work in the Communist movement, sidestepped the assimilatory pressures coming from the American branch of the Communist Party, and in so doing, ultimately built a significant base for the Party that identified with the Communist movement politically and culturally.

The Roots of Yiddish Cultural Activism and Education in the United States

Although the Jewish Workers University was a project tethered to the Communist movement, the challenge it raised of balancing the Jewish national question and Marxist internationalism had been a continuous problem for leftist Jewish immigrants. The leaders of the Yiddish Communist movement had contended with the issue of Yiddish culture in an internationalist movement even before they had become Communists, as many of them had been politicized in the revolutionary climate in Russia as participants in the Jewish Labor Bund. Bundists had worked out a program of advocating for Yiddish cultural autonomy while condemning nationalism, as well as a program of "neutralism," which acknowledged a Yiddish community in the present while not advancing an explicitly Yiddish preservationist agenda.[4] The leaders of the Jewish Workers University, many of whom had previously been participants in the Bund or other Jewish nationalist movements at the turn of the century, were deeply invested in Yiddish culture-building as part of the movement to build Socialism, and made theoretical arguments about the importance of non-assimilationism, much like the Bundists had, that purported to explain why internationalism and Yiddish culture were not contradictory but complementary.

To understand the importance of cultural work for Yiddish Communists, therefore, one must examine their activities in the years before they became Communists as well as the reasons they became Communists in the first place. Many Jews in the Communist movement were committed to Yiddish not just as a language but also as a secular culture and a vehicle for Socialism, and the possibility of its flourishing in the Soviet Union was part of what made Communism attractive. When they arrived in the United States, many before the revolution and before "Communism" existed, they advocated for creating Yiddish schools against the desires of an older generation of Jewish Socialists who were more interested in facilitating Americanization among Jewish immigrants.

Many of those who became Communists were part of a cohort of Yiddish culturalists who struggled against these Jewish cosmopolitan Socialists, believing that assimilation was the opposite of what they should try to achieve. As Rubin Saltzman recalled, it was "the progressive element," that is, those who would become part of the pro-Soviet faction known as *di linke* (the left), who emerged from the Jewish Socialist fraternal order the Arbeter Ring (Workmen's Circle) and "who fought for these [Yiddish] schools."[5] Saltzman was an early advocate for Yiddish schools in the Arbeter Ring and part of the pro-Soviet faction; he would later become the general secretary of its Communist-affiliated rival fraternal society, the International Workers Order (IWO), and then the head of its Yiddish-speaking Jewish Section. Deeply affected by new possibilities for remaking their former home that came with the overthrow of the tsar and the revolution, Yiddish culturalists who would become part of the *linke* saw a great opportunity for expanding Yiddish cultural work in not just what would become the Soviet Union but in the United States as well.

The Russian Revolution was initially broadly celebrated by Socialists, especially Jews who had lived under tsarist rule, but factionalism between the more moderate reformists and a radicalized left wing grew in its immediate aftermath.[6] As early as 1921, when the Bolsheviks suppressed the Kronstadt Uprising, many Socialists became disenchanted with the Soviet Union. The divisions between the *linke* and their counterpart, which they called *di rekhte* (the right), would take several years to intensify, but would eventually reconfigure the Jewish labor movement. Mirroring a split in the Socialist movement that resulted in a left wing that created a separate Communist movement, the *linke* split off to form their own Yiddish cultural and educational institutions. The *linke* were not synonymous with the Jewish section of the Communist Party, but were a more fluid group largely reflective of the newer generation of immigrants for whom Communist influence dominated. In the 1920s, the *linke* agitated against their *rekhte* rivals in the Arbeter Ring's Jewish Socialist fraternal organization, competing with it for control of the organization. As the lines between the Socialists and Communists hardened and the Communists grew more aggressive in their tactics for organizational influence, the *linke* escalated its efforts to control its own sphere of Yiddish life.

The *linke* took an especially provocative step in their feud with the *rekhte* when they dramatically separated from the Arbeter Ring to build their own, separate Yiddish school movement in the late 1920s. In 1926, the *linke* took control of seventeen of the twenty-four Yiddish Socialist children's schools of the Arbeter Ring, renaming the schools the "Umpartayishe arbeter ring shuln" (Nonpartisan Arbeter Ring schools) and defying the procedures of the Arbeter Ring Educational Committee. In the following months, the *linke* started a housing cooperative in the Bronx with a Yiddish kindergarten, *shule* (Yiddish after-school program), and library, and opened the Jewish Workers University. In 1929, *linke* activists were expelled from the Arbeter Ring after they refused to pay dues as a final protest tactic.

This split in the Yiddish schools created a fourth branch of Yiddish secular education in the United States, adding to the ranks of the Socialist Arbeter Ring, the Labor Zionists of Linke Poale Tsiyon with their national radical schools, and the Yiddishist, politically unaffiliated Sholem Aleichem schools. The *linke*'s schools now operated within their own Communist-dominated educational environment and competed for primacy in the realm of Yiddish education. When these same *linke* activists created the IWO in 1930, these schools would come under its leadership and would eventually, for a period, become the largest of the Yiddish secular school networks in the United States, serving a reported eight thousand students nationally in a single year.[7]

The Jewish Workers University During Bolshevization

The Jewish Workers University opened as the *linke* was transitioning strategically into a competing movement within the Jewish Socialist sphere. Within its first year, the Jewish Workers University had between 250 and 300 students and 35 teachers. It offered a large number of evening classes to Yiddish-speaking adults in the left-labor movement, including courses on Yiddish composition and literature, Jewish history, economic development, the cooperative movement, trade unionism, and other central Jewish and Communist subjects. Its full course roster offered six class hours a week on Communism; five class hours a week on English and Yiddish language; thirteen hours a week on "general sciences" (including history and Marxist theory); four hours a week on trade unionism; and two hours a week on literature ("Jewish, General, and American," according to the Jewish Workers University course roster).[8] It was designed to be either a two- or three-year program, with the third year for those in the Yiddish teacher training program who would go on to teach in the Yiddish children's schools. Prospective teachers in their third year took courses such as History, Philosophy of History, Historical Materialism, Methods, and Psychology. In addition to holding classes at its own campus at 126 East Sixteenth Street near Union Square (later at 108 East Fourteenth Street), the Jewish Workers University also held classes in Brooklyn and the Bronx, New Jersey, and Philadelphia, and would eventually expand across the country to the Midwest and West Coast.[9]

The foundation of the Jewish Workers University was an unlikely event in the context of the Americanizing aims of the Party at the time. Beginning in

1924, under the direction of Stalin, the Communist movement began a program of Bolshevization, during which the American Party attempted to dismantle its language federations in an effort at centralization. While the Communist Party did not eradicate the language federations until 1925, there was increased pressure for immigrants to move into the English-language spheres of Party work rather than separate according to nationality and language. Language federation members resisted this drive, though, demonstrating the salience of ethnicity for those engaged in the class struggle. The period of Bolshevization was a remarkably productive one in Yiddish Communist institution building. When the Jewish Workers University began in 1926, Yiddish Communists also began a Yiddish periodical, *Der hamer* (Hammer), and founded "the Coops," the United Workers Cooperative Colony, a housing cooperative on Allerton Avenue in the Bronx, which would house a Yiddish library and after-school program, including a kindergarten.[10] At a moment in which Yiddish Communists felt great pressure from the Party to Americanize, they in fact increased their efforts to do *more* in Yiddish, with the justification that Yiddish was necessary as a language to communicate Communist ideas to Jewish immigrants and that there were significant Yiddish cultural efforts in the Soviet Union.

The Jewish Workers University, as a project of adult education, was influenced by a movement for adult worker education in the United States and Europe. In the first two decades of the twentieth century, unions, Socialists, and then later Communists created institutions to educate the working class in the United States to serve the larger projects of labor activism. These included the Finnish Work People's College of Duluth, Minnesota, established in 1903; the Rand School of Social Science developed by the Socialist Party in 1906, and the International Ladies' Garment Workers' Union's Workers University established in 1918.

In the Soviet Union, the movement for workers' universities catalyzed at the conclusion of the Civil War in 1919 when the Bolsheviks sought to craft a new academic and cultural order. The idea of people's universities had begun earlier, in 1905. These "folks universities" functioned outside of the imperial system in order to provide access to women and the broader masses. Revolutionaries saw these universities as a way of "democratizing" education, but they also criticized them for not being political enough. This tension between the goals of "enlightenment" of the masses and their politicization became a central conundrum in Communist education, which on the one hand sought to impart Communist theory, yet also was committed to the practical matters of labor organizing.[11]

During the period of Bolshevization, Communists were committed to increasing the ideological understanding and commitment of Party members and adult education was a key avenue for that work. Building on the labor movement for higher education in the United States as well as the Bolshevik program for higher education in the Soviet Union, the Communist Party created the New York Workers School in 1923. Delivering an address at the school in 1924, then–assistant executive secretary of the Workers (Communist) Party, James P. Cannon, gave a speech called "The Bolshevization of the Party," in which he described the crucial responsibility that institutions such as the Workers School had in advancing a new approach to education and moving away from what Cannon called a previous "class of 'educators' who reduced education to the study of books."[12] Rather, he claimed, education "must be partisan . . . a weapon in the hands of the party for implanting the party ideology in the minds of the students who attend its classes."[13]

The Workers School, as a tool of Bolshevization, fulfilled the Communist vision of educating constituents on the Party's ideology and having its own educational program distinct from that of the Socialists. Bertram Wolfe, who was the former publicity director of the Socialist Rand School for Social Science, headed the New York Workers School as its director at its founding. In 1926, giving a report on workers' education at the third conference of the Workers Party of America (renamed the Communist Party USA after 1928), Wolfe explained the meaning of worker education in the Communist movement. Reprinted in *Der hamer* in Yiddish, Wolfe's "What Is Worker Education" made the argument that the working classes needed to direct their own institutions. "One must look at worker education as an instrument," Wolfe claimed, "that should organize the working class politics and industry, and that should develop its consciousness for its own needs and goals."[14] The Workers School was therefore a key component of efforts to create a new educational program for workers that would make them ideological Communists and effective activists.

To many inside and outside of the Communist movement, the Jewish Workers University simply looked like the Yiddish-speaking version of the New York Workers School. The two schools even shared an address at one point at 108 East 14th Street. Abraham Markoff, a later director of the Workers School, would write in 1937 about an address "which leads educational activity among the Jewish workers who cannot easily orient themselves in the English language, does good work. . . . We, who lead the same work on a larger scale, through the Workers School, are aware of the many difficulties this institution faces."[15] Markoff, in proclaiming that the two schools did the same work and that the Jewish Workers University's raison d'être was to overcome the language barrier, presented the Jewish Workers University as a partner institution with the same aims but serving a different population.[16] Markoff's characterization of the Jewish Workers University suggests its public role was to be an organizing tool and instrument of acculturation for Jewish Communists. Even into the Yiddish-friendly era of the Popular Front, when Markoff gave his remarks, the

Jewish Workers University was presented as a place for Jewish immigrants to assimilate and Americanize, even as they were (overtly) working to Yiddishize the American-born generation.

The Jewish Workers University, in terms of its structure and political ethos, indeed had attributes that were similar to the Workers School. One aspect that the Jewish Workers University prided itself on was student-led governance and the "working-class character" of the institution. In its first spring celebration in 1927, the director of the Jewish Workers University, Jacob Mindel, proudly proclaimed, "The students are not only students, they are also the managers of the university."[17] It also boasted a distinctly working-class student body. As a writer in the *Frayhayt* described the students: "They are workers. The majority are in the needle industries. 55 percent work in clothing factories."[18] Additionally, the university populated its board with members of unions and cooperatives and members of the Jewish section of the Workers Party. It was clear that the founders of the Jewish Workers University desired a Communist learning community that was truly an institution of the working class.

Although the Jewish Workers University opened three years after the Workers School, Yiddish Communist leaders had laid out their plan for an educational institution open to workers several months before the Workers School launched.[19] In a report addressed to "all the Jewish worker clubs, the *Frayhayt* association, and cooperative and culture organizations," the Jewish section of the Workers (Communist) Party announced its interest in a specifically Jewish adult school, saying, "The Jewish worker in America should have its own culture center and university, that should serve its interests."[20] Minutes from 1923 further show that they attempted to create a Party school for members of the Jewish Socialist Federation and Jewish members of the Young Workers League on Monday evenings.[21]

Yiddish Communists in the Bolshevization period would describe their work by contrasting their efforts for proletarian culture-building in Yiddish versus Yiddishism. In an unsigned editorial in the Communist monthly *Der hamer*, the Jewish Communist position on Yiddish in the Party is laid out in the following terms: "The assimilator (English nationalist) says: a maximum English; The Yiddishist (Jewish nationalist) says: a maximum Yiddish. The Communist says: a maximum class consciousness, organization, battle-readiness, courage, clarity of goals—utilization of the best tool in a given situation."[22] Building from previous arguments about how Yiddish could be used for Communist ends, the argument claimed that Yiddish was the "best tool" for their purpose. This concept was repeated in all levels of Yiddish Communist cultural work, including in descriptions of the purpose of the Jewish Workers University: Yiddish was necessary as long as it was helpful for building the Communist movement.

Despite their insistence that their work in Yiddish was shaped by a practical need to communicate with Yiddish-speaking immigrants, Yiddish Communists were not, in practice, just mirroring the program of the Workers School for a Jewish audience. Before embarking on building their own adult school, the founders of the Jewish Workers University initially tried to take over the Sholem Aleichem Institute's People's University, which trained Yiddish teachers, where a number of the *linke*, such as Moissaye Olgin, the *Frayhayt*'s editor, were serving as faculty. In a letter from the secretary of the Jewish Section of the Workers Party Culture Committee from 1924, comrades were invited to come to a meeting to discuss "the question of taking over the 'folks universitet' [People's University] in our hands."[23] But this "takeover" ultimately did not materialize, as demonstrated by their decision to leave the People's University to the Sholem Aleichem Institute and instead build their own *linke*-controlled adult school in the form of the Jewish Workers University.[24]

The *linke*, in a show of competitiveness, sought to recruit students from the other Yiddish adult schools. According to the *linke* founders of the Jewish Workers University, the teacher education at the Arbeter Ring and the Sholem Aleichem Institute did not adequately serve the Jewish worker since they lacked an appropriate class character. Jewish workers therefore needed a university as "a center where [they] will get what they need for their education."[25] What workers needed, they believed, was a greater emphasis on the theories of Marxism-Leninism as taught by organizers within the Communist movement. For these reasons, the education committee of the Jewish section of the Workers Party began the project of establishing a university, calling a conference to create an initial plan.

The Jewish Workers University crafted its plans with primarily the Yiddish educational sphere in mind, a dimension of its work that stood apart from the Workers School. Many of the Jewish Workers University's first teachers, including Moissaye Olgin, Kalman Marmor, and Moyshe Katz, had been teachers at the Sholem Aleichem Institute and Arbeter Ring's adult education programs, and could model their vision based on their experience of teaching in those venues. Kalman Marmor, who would become a primary figure in Yiddish Communist cultural work, had previously written glowingly in *Frayhayt* about the first graduation of the teachers course in the Arbeter Ring, where he was an instructor. Marmor stated that one of the principal problems in Yiddish education was a lack of teachers, a problem that its teachers course was built to solve. This commitment to educating more Yiddish teachers would influence the program he would help build at the Jewish Workers University.

The force with which the *linke* pursued its competition with the Arbeter Ring and the Sholem Aleichem Institute suggests that they were intently focused on maintaining the Jewish identity of their institution. The Jewish Workers University sought to cultivate a different kind of Jewish experience, one that rejected both Jewish traditionalism and the Socialist institutions of the past. In an article on the accomplishments of the Jewish Workers University from its first graduation in 1927, faculty member Shakne Epshtein described how earlier attempts to create a Jewish Workers School in the Arbeter Ring had faced difficulties because of the organization's "petty bourgeois spirit" and the "unsystematic character of the courses."[26] In contrast, their vision at the Jewish Workers University was, in the words of Epshtein, "not to prepare one academically, but to offer practical service to the working class."[27] While, as another faculty member wrote, American society "lack[s] the worker intellectuals that played an important role in Europe," the Jewish Workers University would deliver such a new cohort.[28] The Jewish Workers University was meant to be not solely academic but also trained intellectuals to build their movement.

The students of the Jewish Workers University in its first years appeared to be more concerned about the university's position as a rival to the other Yiddish adult schools than about the meaning of their institution to the Party. As a second-year student wrote in their 1927 graduation program, "There are people who ask us: Why must you have your own university? Why work to build your own when in New York there are two of these schools, like the [Scholem Aleichem Institute's] Jewish Teachers' Seminary and the Arbeter Ring teachers' course?"[29] It is telling that the student was not responding to a question about why they were not part of the Workers School. The point he wanted to emphasize, rather, was why they were not part of the other Yiddish schools and why their institution was different. Students for this reason also focused on contrasting their experience to those in the other Yiddish schools. As one student wrote, "One looks over to the building on the other side of the street, and thinks: There one learns also, but what a difference! It is a tense atmosphere . . . whereas for us it is warm, friendly, [and] vibrant."[30] Students also championed the school as being a uniquely working-class institution that had dedicated teachers and a clear focus, whereas the other Yiddish schools, they claimed, treated the workers movement as a "stepchild."[31]

The Jewish Workers University, as a rival to the "Yiddishists" as well as an instrument of the Party's organizing work, needed to maintain these two faces at once: one for the Jewish Street and one for the larger Communist sphere. In the 1920s, the aim of the Jewish Workers University was as much to produce ideological Communists as it was to train Yiddish teachers for children in Yiddish schools. For these activists, these were mutually reinforcing commitments. However, the environment of Bolshevization meant that the latter goal was less publicly visible, for it suggested a commitment to the future of Yiddish that fit uncomfortably with the aims of the Party. Writings from the period show only glimpses of the full extent of the university's work in Yiddish education:

University leaders knew they had to speak about their work using the correct terms so as to remain aligned with the aims of the Party even as they competed for students in the realm of Yiddish education. It would not be until the Popular Front that the importance of training Yiddish teachers and imparting Yiddish to the first American-born generation was spoken about explicitly as a foundational goal of the Jewish Workers University. Therefore, as much as the work of Yiddish Communists reflects the periodization of Party doctrine, their commitment to Yiddish also transcends it, revealing the long history of how their work in Yiddish was central to their political identities and activism.

The Jewish Workers University and the Popular Front

The curriculum of the Jewish Workers University did not change significantly once the Popular Front began, but the way Yiddish Communists spoke publicly about Yiddish education did. The political climate of the Popular Front led to a sea change in Communist practices that affected the Jewish sphere and beyond. The mid-1930s were an especially active period for the Jewish Communist movement, as the Great Depression provided new opportunities for Communists to point out the failings of capitalism. In these years, the Yiddish Communist movement grew impressively, helped by the creation of the IWO in 1930 as the new home for Yiddish Communist cultural activity; the IWO took on the organizational sponsorship of the *linke* Yiddish schools and invested in their expansion. By 1934, the IWO had twenty thousand members in its Jewish section alone and was trying to expand its work in its youth section and English section in an effort to make the Order a "mass organization." At the same time, it continued expanding its fraternal umbrella through incorporating other pro-Soviet ethnic societies such as Slovak and Hungarian associations into its new IWO language sections. The IWO forged an interethnic fraternal world and with the deliberate recruitment of Black and Hispanic members, became an interracial champion of working-class people.[32]

When the Communist International endorsed the Popular Front as a coalition designed to fight against fascism in 1935, the entire Party transformed its orientation, moderating its position and seeking to work collaboratively with Socialists and even liberals. The revolutionary rhetoric of the earlier period, which used terms such as "proletarian," was replaced by more moderate-sounding and inclusive terms such as "progressive," even if the Communists continued to represent the leftmost pole of American politics. Words such as "progressive" were still indications of one's Communism, but reflected the new direction of the Party during the Popular Front, which did not fixate on class divisions as much as it strove to find common cause as part of a wider left.

The Popular Front as an anti-fascist movement was especially significant for Jews in the United States and internationally. The increase in anti-Jewish sentiment and violence in the 1930s that accompanied the rise of Nazism further reinforced Jewish Communists' belief that they could conduct their political struggle as Jews and also led them to take antisemitism seriously as one of the principal aspects of their anti-fascist work. America's potential role in opposing fascism, coupled with the idea that all Jews had a stake in combating fascism, created a sense in the Popular Front that emphasizing Jewishness was a political act that could form the basis of alliances with other Jewish groups. It became natural for the Yiddish schools to be not only unapologetic in their use of Yiddish and Jewish content, but also confident about how they were advancing the Party's aim to build a broad movement under the banner of anti-fascism. Their orientation toward unity was helpful for those working in Yiddish culture, as they understood that cultural survival was dependent on all the different Yiddish institutions working together.

While much of its initial program had stayed the same since its 1926 founding, the Jewish Workers University had refined its program and methodology over the years. It added "Order Courses," designed to train activists in organization and mass movement–building for the IWO and its Jewish Section and to train them in "not only the economic functions . . . but also [the] political, societal, and cultural functions" of fraternal organizations.[33] It also divided its student body into three tracks: those who needed to receive a more foundational education in basic Yiddish literacy, those whose primary interest was to become organizers in the labor movement, and those who were in training to teach Yiddish.

More significant than programmatic changes, however, were the ways in which its leaders explained the purpose of the Jewish Workers University. In the Bolshevization period, the university's founders quietly emphasized teacher training even as the university openly celebrated its relationship to the Workers School; during the Popular Front, the founders spoke plainly about their emphasis on Yiddish teacher training. For instance, Kalman Marmor, who became the director of the Jewish Workers University during the Popular Front era, clearly explained in a 1937 address that when the *linke* separated out its children's schools in 1926, it had a central purpose: to develop Yiddish teachers for their schools. So important was replenishing Yiddish teachers with the correct politics and adequate Yiddish education, he said, that during "the first years of the Jewish Workers University, the concentration was on the teachers' courses."[34] Marmor's remark about the focus on creating new teachers shows just how central this project was to the founders of the Jewish Workers University. While he and the other founders did not hide the teacher training component of the Jewish Workers University in the 1920s, his comments nonetheless reveal that their priority for the institution was not to educate Yiddish-speaking adults who were unable to learn activism and ideology in English. They concentrated on the teachers' courses because they were seeking to build their Yiddish children's school network and grow their Yiddish cultural movement.

Furthermore, in a telling statement from the Popular Front period, Yiddish pedagogue and editor Itche Goldberg, who taught Yiddish high school graduates at the Jewish Workers University, asserted that the university had always been conceived of in relation to the Yiddish children's schools (*shules*). He wrote: "There is no coincidence—that the schools and the university are the same age. . . . Our schools have a problem of new teachers."[35] Goldberg, who ran the *shule* system, claimed that from its beginning the Jewish Workers University existed to serve the Yiddish school movement and build a future Yiddish-speaking generation. Goldberg argued that the importance and attraction of the Jewish Workers University was its Jewish character rather than its Communist ideology. He continued, "Why do the youth come to the Jewish Workers University? Is it maybe to continue their Marxist education? Is it to deepen their knowledge in political economy, in Marxism, for which they have received merely an introduction in *mitl shul* [high school]? No."[36] The real reason, he said, was that these youth "come there to initiate the development of a proletarian Yiddish speaking intelligentsia in America."[37] Goldberg's comments tell us much about the perceived role of the Jewish Workers University and the interests of its students at that stage. Unlike in the Third Period, during the Popular Front he and the other faculty needed to emphasize that their work was not just about a Communist education. What made their pedagogy distinctive was their educational goal of creating a sustainable secular Yiddish intelligentsia and culture that would live on in subsequent generations. According to Goldberg, this was always, in fact, the main purpose of the Jewish Workers University. For, as he pointed out, they could have gone to the Workers School if they simply wanted a Marxist education. The shifting atmosphere of the Popular Front permitted Goldberg to state the interest of the IWO's Jewish Section in developing a lasting Yiddish cultural movement in explicit terms.

Indeed, many of the features of the Jewish Workers University that the Yiddish Communists began emphasizing in the Popular Front period had in fact been there from its beginning in the 1920s. The issue of Yiddish culture and Jewish identity had always been central to student experience. A retrospective student testimonial from one of the earliest classes of students at the Jewish Workers University describes a deep commitment to Yiddish culture as the driving force for student enrollment. This student had a background common to many of the

Yiddish school activists; in coming to the United States from Vilna he was already deeply influenced by what he called the "the national factor" in Jewish experience.[38] He described the experience of being in an early teacher training cohort at the Jewish Workers University in the following terms: "We came to the Jewish Workers University as a group of students with two ideological orientations. One orientation was expressed by the nationalist influence, what the [teachers'] seminary offered us. The second orientation was our own passion to connect with the working masses and to find a solution for the Jewish question through the working class."[39] This student's description shows how their commitment to Jewish national issues, in this student's words, to "find a solution for the Jewish question," was the dominant factor in their participation and the primary motivation determining students' participation in a Communist institution to study Yiddish. Testimonials such as this underscore the distinctions between the purpose of the Jewish Workers University and the Workers School; the draw of the Jewish Workers University was its identity-building opportunities, not just communication in the Yiddish language. We can sense the seriousness and importance of this endeavor for the community the university created through its adult students, who attended the university after long workdays (see figures 2.1–2.6).

A paradox of the Popular Front period was that as Yiddish Communists began more openly to embrace their commitment to Yiddish culture as a project of its own, they witnessed the maturation of a Jewish generation that spoke little Yiddish. By the mid- to late 1930s the youth that had been in the Yiddish children's schools were in their twenties, the age at which they would enter the Jewish Workers University. Despite the best efforts of the Yiddish educational system that they had created, the Yiddish language skills of this new generation were not deemed strong enough to carry the mantle forward. This raised the stakes for leadership at the Jewish Workers University, for if their Yiddish schools were going to continue, they needed a younger generation with the ability to teach Yiddish.

The Popular Front was thus both the apex of the Yiddish Communist movement and the beginning of its decline. In the early Popular Front years, the IWO reported that they had an enrollment of between seven and eight thousand students in their schools. This number, however, would begin to decrease at the onset of World War II, likely due to the changing demographics of the American-born generation, although it was not helped by the era of the Hitler-Stalin non-aggression pact (1939–41), during which Yiddish Communists found themselves again pitted against what had been their tenuously rebuilt alliances.[40]

To rebuild the movement they saw slipping away, Yiddish Communists focused on engaging youth in their Yiddish cultural, political, and educational work more broadly including at Camp Kinderland, but there were few as committed

FIGURE 2.1. Faculty of the Jewish Workers University in 1937. In the front row, third from the left, sits Kalman Marmor, who was the director of the Jewish Workers University at the time. *Tsen yor: Yidisher arbeter universitet* (New York, 1937), 3. Courtesy of the Kheel Center.

FIGURE 2.2. "Student-rat fun i. a. universitet." Image of the student council of the Jewish Workers University, 1937. In contrast to the faculty, the student council is about half women. *Tsen yor: Yidisher arbeter universitet* (New York, 1937), 50. Courtesy of the Kheel Center.

קלאס פון מיטל שול גראדואירטע, איצטיקע סטודענטן אין א. א. אוניווערסיטעט. לערער, א. גאלדבערג

FIGURE 2.3. Itche Goldberg teaching the *mitl shul* graduates at the Jewish Workers University, 1937. *Tsen yor: Yidisher arbeter universitet* (New York, 1937), 41. Courtesy of the Kheel Center.

FIGURE 2.4. Jewish Workers University chorus, demonstrating its cultural work in addition to academic subjects. *Tsen yor: Yidisher arbeter universitet* (New York, 1937), 22. Courtesy of the Kheel Center.

א װינקל אין ביבליאטעק, צימער פון א. א. אוניווערזיטעט

FIGURE 2.5. The Jewish Workers University library. *Tsen yor: Yidisher arbeter universitet* (New York, 1937), 48. Courtesy of the Kheel Center.

סעריע לעקציעס איבער דער אינטערנאציאנאלער לאגע מיט כּיטע גינא מעדעם (די ערשטע רעכטס)

FIGURE 2.6. A packed lecture hall for a series of lectures on "the international situation" by Gina Medem, an activist for the Organization for Jewish Colonization in Russia (ICOR), correspondent for the Communist-affiliated magazine *New Masses*, and regular writer and lecturer for *linke* Yiddish publications. *Tsen yor: Yidisher arbeter universitet* (New York, 1937), 27. Courtesy of the Kheel Center.

to Yiddish as they were. Indeed, American-born Jewish young adults during the Popular Front period demonstrated a strong sense of Jewish identity, but unlike the immigrant generation, this identity primarily existed outside of the Yiddish sphere. Itche Goldberg, in an effort to engage the American-born youth, invited a few graduates to speak on their relationship to Yiddish. Overwhelmingly, the graduates made clear that Yiddish was not central to their Jewish identities, for it was simply not part of their daily lives nor their sense of political purpose. As a twenty-year-old student, Ruth Rozetski, who graduated from the IWO *shules* in 1935 wrote, "In daily life I speak English; in college I learn in English; with friends I speak mostly in English. With Yiddish I use it merely when I find myself in Yiddish speaking spaces, and also with students of the Jewish Workers University. I cannot say that I live in Yiddish. But I want the Yiddish language to live and develop."[41] Rozetski describes a distinct generational change, in which English operated as the primary language. As a result, there were two realms of Jewish activity, one in English and one in the "Yiddish-speaking spaces" such as at the Jewish Workers University. While Rozetski and others of her generation wanted Yiddish to continue, it was not a dominant part of their lives. During World War II, the IWO's Slovak Workers Society (SWS) similarly lamented the declining enrollment among the second generation at SWS institutions such as its own workers schools. The role of such places became less practical and more preservationist.

Due to demographic and political change, the Jewish Workers University failed to survive as its own institution through the end of World War II. In 1941 it was renamed Der yidisher lern-institut (The Jewish Educational Institute) and continued its activity in this form until 1943. This name change was one of several that happened in the Jewish Communist movement, such as when the Jewish Section of the IWO became the Jewish Peoples Fraternal Order (JPFO) during the war, or the earlier change in the name of Goldberg's Yiddish Communist journal from *Proletarishe dertsiung* (Proletarian education) to *Heym un dertsiung* (Home and education). Likewise, in late 1943, the Workers School became the Jefferson School of Social Science, taking on a number of courses, such as Yiddish language and political economy, that had been taught at the Jewish Workers University.

Despite the fact that Communists could now openly celebrate Jewish identity and cultural work, it no longer made sense to have a separate Yiddish institution such as the Jewish Workers University. The Jefferson School for a time had a whole Jewish Studies division, again reflecting the desire to organize Jews while bridging the English- and Yiddish-speaking worlds. As its course roster from 1944 shows, it had courses in English on "The National Question and the Jewish People," courses in Yiddish on political economy, and Hebrew language courses.[42] The IWO also continued with *hekhere kursn* (higher courses) for graduates of the children's school so they could continue their studies in Yiddish literature, culture, and teacher training; Hebrew was also taught as well as American Jewish history. A few of the early leaders of the Yiddish schools and Jewish Workers University, such as Rubin Saltzman and Itche Goldberg, who believed in the need for a distinct Jewish adult school, were instrumental in setting up a new School of Jewish Studies in 1945, which was intended to "fill the great need for knowledge and unity in the Jewish Community" and was focused on the study of Jewish history and culture.[43] But the original version of Yiddish adult education as it existed in the Jewish Workers University did not continue into the postwar period, mainly due to the changing demographics and needs of the American Jewish community.

The Jewish Workers University was hardly just Communism dressed in Yiddish: It was set up to ensure a future for Yiddish language and culture for the next generation and to develop teachers who could be cultural leaders for a movement. This aim of the Jewish Workers University had always been apparent, but during the Popular Front its activists could discuss more comfortably aloud what they had been working on all along. Without denying that the Popular Front period changed the orientation of the Yiddish Communist movement so that it embraced Jewish national culture unapologetically, we can also see that there was continuity in Yiddish Communist educational work in terms of how its cultural mission was prioritized, although it was obscured by the Party rhetoric that characterized and distinguished earlier phases of Communism from the Popular Front. These continuities tell a deeper story of Yiddish education than of Communism in a Yiddish key. Rather, they show a long-term and consistent project among Yiddish Communists of building Yiddish culture in the United States that was at once informed by the various fluctuations in Communist Party history yet at the same time constant in its purpose.

The tension Yiddish Communists grappled with between particularism (Jewish or Yiddish identity) and universalism (a broader movement of the international working class) was not only central to the history of Communism but also arguably to the wider left of the early twentieth century. The left as a whole was similarly dominated by an intellectual climate among Marxists who believed that identity should be surrendered for a more universalist aim. The institutions that served to grow the left, such as the Jewish Workers University, show us a complex and dynamic example of particularism driving their political activism, all the while under the banner of a universalist vision that reached far beyond the Jewish community.

For Yiddish Communists, Communist ideals and priorities stemming from their Jewish identities went together. As much as their work to build the Jewish Workers University centered on Yiddish, it was also never only about Yiddish, but how Yiddish was integral to their political commitments. It was the balance of their particularism and universalism that was always the project; there was never one without the other. This recognition of the importance of both further fueled their work for interethnic solidarity. These activists were part of the lifeblood of the left in the early twentieth century, working to declare a space where Yiddish work and the pursuit of social justice were mutually reinforcing. For if they did not, they feared they would lose the part of themselves that inspired them to become activists in the first place, and with it, a future for Jews as central participants in the left.

NOTES

1. Dylan Kaufman-Obstler, "Language for a Revolution: Yiddish Schools in the United States and the Making of Jewish Proletarian Culture" (PhD diss., University of Wisconsin–Madison, 2021). Translations from the original Yiddish are mine. See M. Epstein, "Der arbeter universitet vet undz geben an arbeter inteligents" [The Jewish Workers University will give us worker intellectuals], in *Ershter friling yontef* [First spring holiday] (Idisher Arbeter Univerzitet, 1927).

2. Henry Felix Srebrnik claims that 15 percent of the Communist Party was Jewish in the 1920s and this figure would grow, by some estimates, to 50 percent in the 1930s to 1940s. Srebrnik, *Dreams of Nationhood: American Jewish Communists and the Soviet Birobidzhan Project, 1924–1951* (Academic Studies Press, 2010), 3.

3. Naomi Prawer Kadar, *Raising Secular Jews: Yiddish Schools and Their Periodicals for American Children, 1917–1950* (Brandeis University Press, 2016).

4. Tony Michels, *A Fire in Their Hearts: Yiddish Socialists in New York* (Harvard University Press, 2005), 170.

5. Rubin Saltzman, *Farrat in arbeter ring* [Struggle in the Workmen's Circle] (Kooperativn folks-farlang, 1940), 6.

6. Tony Michels, "The Russian Revolution in New York, 1917–1919," *Journal of Contemporary History* 54, no. 4 (2017): 960–61.

7. Kadar, *Raising Secular Jews*, 135.

8. "Idisher arbeter universitet" [Jewish Workers University], in *Ershter friling yontef*.

9. Kadar, *Raising Secular Jews*. Documents from 1927 show the address as 126 East Sixteenth Street, whereas documents from 1928 to 1930 show 108 East Fourteenth Street. United States Territorialist Collection, RG 117, box 79, folder 79.3, YIVO Institute for Jewish Research, New York, New York; Kalman Marmor, "Undzer kultur tetikayt in der mitlvest" [Our cultural activities in the Midwest], *Der funk* 3, no. 3 (July 1932): 17–18.

10. Like the *linke*, or the IWO and its Jewish Section, for that matter, the Communist influence dominated the Coops. However, not all, or even most, of the Coops residents were Party members.

11. Michael David-Fox, *Revolution of the Mind: Higher Learning Among the Bolsheviks, 1918–1929* (Cornell University Press, 2016).

12. James P. Cannon, "The Bolshevisation of the Party" (October 5, 1924) in *James P. Cannon and the Early Years of American Communism: Selected Writings and Speeches, 1920–1928* (Spartacist, 1992), https://www.marxists.org/archive/cannon/works/1924/bolsh.htm. This language was paralleled in the New York and Chicago workers schools as well.

13. See Cannon, "Bolshevisation."

14. Bertram Wolfe, "Vos iz arbeter bildung?" [What is workers' education?], *Der hamer* 1, no. 2 (April 1926): 55.

15. A. Markoff, "Fun der 'verkers skool' tsum yidishn arbeter universitet" [From the workers' school to the Jewish Workers University], in *Tsen yor: Yidisher arbeter universitet* [Ten years: Jewish Workers University] (New York, 1937), 28, International Workers Order (IWO) Records #5276, box 6, folder 47, file 2, Kheel Center for Labor-Management Documentation and Archives, Catherwood Library, Cornell University, Ithaca, New York (henceforth Kheel), https://digital.library.cornell.edu/catalog/ss:19042997.

16. On a smaller scale, similar ethnically defined workers' schools flourished for Slovaks in places such as Youngstown, Ohio, and for Spanish-speaking migrants in East Harlem.

17. Y. Mindel, "Der yidisher arbeter universitet" [The Jewish Workers University], in *Ershter friling yontef*.

18. P. Shvartsman, "Tsvey yor yidisher arbeter universitet" [Two years of the Jewish Workers University], *Frayhayt*, May 31, 1928, 3.

19. Minutes from the meeting of the Culture and Publishing Committee, January 7, 1923, Kalman Marmor Papers, RG 205 MK 495, folder 441, YIVO.

20. Report from Jewish Section of the Workers Party, "Studye ale mitglider fun der yidisher federatsiye vorkers partay" [Study of members of the Jewish Section of the Workers Party], August 6, 1922, Kalman Marmor Papers, folder 441, YIVO.

21. Minutes from the meeting of the Culture and Publishing Committee, January 7, 1923, Kalman Marmor Papers, folder 441, YIVO.

22. "Di arbet fun di yidishe komunistn in amerike" [The work of Jewish Communists in America], *Der hamer* 3, no. 12 (December 1927): 25.

23. Minutes from the meeting of the Culture and Publishing Committee, January 7, 1923.

24. A similar battle within the Workmen's Circle (Arbeter Ring) would occur in 1929, with the *linke* activists leaving to form the International Workers Order in 1930.

25. Minutes from the meeting of the Culture and Publishing Committee, January 7, 1923.

26. S. Epshtein, "Dos ingste kind fun der linker arbeter bavegung" [The first child from the left workers movement], in *Ershter friling yontef*.

27. See Epshtein, "Dos ingste kind."

28. M. Epstein, "Der arbeter universitet vet undz geben an arbeter inteligents"[The Jewish Workers University will give us worker intellectuals], in *Ershter friling yontef*.

29. Moris Payzer, "Undzer proletarishe shul" [Our proletarian shule], in *Ershter friling yontef*.

30. P. Shvartsman, "Tsvey yor yidisher arbeter universitet," [Ten years of the Jewish Workers University], in *Frayhayt*, May 31, 1928, 3.

31. Epshtein, "Dos ingste kind."

32. R. Saltzman, "20 toyznt mitglider in der yidishe sektsiye" [Twenty thousand members in the Jewish Section], *Morgn Frayhayt*, November 10, 1934, 3.

33. "Organizational Course of the IWO: Jewish Workers University, New York, 1939–1940," RG 1311, box 1, folder 15, YIVO.

34. Kalman Marmor, "Bildung far masn, firer, un lerer" [Education for the masses, leaders, and teachers], in *Tsen yor*, 8.

35. Itche Goldberg, "Di ordn shuln un der abeter universitet" [The Order's schools and the Jewish Workers University], in *Tsen yor*, 40.

36. Goldberg, "Di ordn shuln."

37. Goldberg, "Di ordn shuln."

38. S. Horvat, "Mit tsen yor tusrik" [Ten years ago], in *Tsen yor*, 49–51.

39. Horvat, "Mit tsen yor tusrik," 49–51.

40. Paul Buhle, "Jews and American Communism: The Cultural Question," *Radical History Review* 23 (Spring 1980): 26. Buhle argues that while a number of leaders left as a result of the pact, the *shule* enrollments actually went up due in part to an increasing awareness of antisemitism.

41. Ruth Rozetski, "Di tsukunft fun der yidisher shprakh" [The future of the Yiddish language], *Heym un dertsiyung* [Home and education] 5, no. 5 (April 1939): 6, YIVO.

42. Pamphlet from the Jefferson School of Social Science for winter term, February to April, 1944, Bund Archive, RG1400, folder 34, YIVO.

43. School of Jewish Studies, *Winter Term* (New York, 1946), Printed Ephemera of Organizations Collection, PE036, box 88, Tamiment Library and Robert F. Wagner Labor Archives, New York University, New York, New York. Hershl Hartman notes that "the School for Jewish Studies [was] CPUSA-affiliated as was its contemporary Jefferson School for Social Science. SJS was headed by Khayim [Chaim] Suller [who was] also on the staff of the *Morgn Frayhayt*," Kinderland, and the *shule*. Hartman also mentions that SJS was a night school and had an extension program in Brownsville, where he taught. Hershl Hartman, email message to editor, July 21, 2021, forwarded to author.

3

PORTRAIT OF A RADICAL

June Gordon, the Emma Lazarus Clubs, and Communist Jewish Women's Activism, 1920–1970

Jennifer Young

On Tuesday, July 24, 1945, a group of women gathered at the Statue of Liberty to celebrate the birthday of the poet Emma Lazarus, whose poem "The New Colossus" adorns the statue's base. The women, who brought picnic lunches to eat with their families and flower garlands to bedeck the statue, were all members of the Emma Lazarus Clubs. They sought both to honor the poet and to claim connection with a fellow American Jewish woman who spoke out on behalf of the Jewish people, immigrants, and victims of injustice. Lazarus's poem, which included the famous lines "Give me your tired, your poor, your huddled masses yearning to breathe free," transfigured the statue from a tribute to republicanism into the iconic "Mother of Exiles," a symbol of maternal strength echoing biblical matriarchs who welcomed and aided the stranger in their midst. The women of the Emma Lazarus Clubs adapted and molded the ideas of this wealthy Sephardic poet and her symbolic creation to suit their need for a politically progressive Jewish American heroine.

The women had been gathering yearly for the previous five years, but this year had added significance. Germany had surrendered to the Allies just two months earlier. Closer to home, the Emma Lazarus Clubs had just celebrated their first anniversary. Officially known as the Emma Lazarus Division of Jewish Women's Clubs, "the Emmas," as they called themselves, were a part of the Jewish Peoples Fraternal Order (JPFO), which itself was the founding section of the multiethnic International Workers Order (IWO). While the Emma Lazarus Clubs were new, they had already made a major impact. In 1945 the clubs were composed of hundreds of local neighborhood and city chapters, totaling thousands of members across the country. Both Louise Waterman Wise, the prominent American Jewish philanthropist and cofounder of the international Jewish women's organization Hadassah, and former first lady Eleanor Roosevelt sent remarks to be delivered at the ceremony.[1] Mrs. Roosevelt's message underscored the importance of mutual cooperation. She wrote: "I think the celebration of [Emma Lazarus's] birthday [by the Emma Lazarus Clubs] will remind us all that it is through tolerance and fellowship that we remain a strong nation."[2]

In her speech at the statue, June Gordon, national president of the Emma Lazarus Clubs, highlighted the fact that antisemitism and race hatred had not gone away, even though the war in Europe was over. She declared that it was urgent to "rally the nation's effort to uproot Nazi ideas that persist and plague our own land."[3] The leaders of the Emma Lazarus Clubs believed that antisemitism was a threat to Jews not only overseas but also at home in America. In their analysis, antisemitism could not be addressed on its own but had to be understood as a system of oppression inextricably linked to racism, sexism, and economic oppression. They dedicated themselves to working to combat these pernicious forces as Jews, as women, and as "builders of unity" between Black and white Americans.[4] In so doing, they believed, they were working to defeat the fascist forces that also affected their own lives and communities. If the enemy of Jews and Black people is the same, they reasoned, then that made the two groups kin.[5]

Even though the Emma Lazarus Clubs were newly founded, its leaders drew on more than twenty years' worth of previous women's activism on the Communist left. Most club members were born in eastern Europe at the turn of the twentieth century and had immigrated to the United States as children. Forced by economic pressure to leave school in their early teens, they began working in garment factories, enduring long hours, poor working conditions, and low pay. This experience politicized them and they began to join unions, stand on picket lines, and organize union chapters in their workplaces. In the 1920s and 1930s, many found themselves doing unwaged labor as parents and caregivers, so they turned their focus from the industrial workplace to the home front, organizing around "women's issues" such as housing conditions, overcrowded schools, food, and the high cost of living. As these women's political activism deepened during the Great Depression, some gravitated toward the Communist Party of the United States (CPUSA), where they could connect their local struggles with those on an international scale.

In the postwar years, many of these same women continued their work with the Emma Lazarus Clubs, speaking out against racism and antisemitism and for peace and nuclear disarmament, since they believed that only true solidarity between marginalized groups could create systemic social and economic change. This work, which continued through the 1980s, was grounded in personal and political alliances established in the early 1920s that rested on the foundation of charismatic leaders well-trained within the Communist movement and a membership base with decades of experience in grassroots organizing work among working-class and Black women. In the Cold War era, with the dissolution of Popular Front organizations focused on multiracial and interethnic alliances, the Emma Lazarus Clubs continued to build relationships with and support Black activists based on long-standing personal and professional relationships.

White Jewish women recognized their own privilege relative to Black women, even as they faced similar threats as targets of political repression. Ultimately, the women who had started in the IWO's Emma Lazarus Division continued to speak out on behalf of others despite possible risk to themselves; they avoided the Cold War shutdown of the IWO through incorporating in 1951 as the legally independent Emma Lazarus Federation (ELF). These women remained committed to the notion that marginalized groups needed to work together in order to achieve true equality. They believed, in the words of Emma Lazarus herself, that "until we are all free, we are none of us free."[6]

June Gordon: A Life in the Struggle

In order to understand the role that the Emma Lazarus Clubs played in postwar American Jewish women's lives, we must first examine the woman who shaped the organization for almost three decades. For the sake of clarity and continuity, I will refer to her primarily as June Gordon, the name she used for the second half of her life, but in her early years, she was known by a number of other names and aliases, most often as Sonia Croll and then June Croll. She became June Gordon around 1940 and continued using that name until her death in 1967.

June Gordon was born Sheyne-Mirl Croll in 1901 in Odessa, Russia, and immigrated to Montreal with her parents and two sisters in 1903. June's father, Hyman Croll, worked as a barber, eventually opening his own barber shop. Just before Passover 1909, Hyman Croll contracted pneumonia and died, leaving his widow with the shop's debt as well as five children under ten years old. Just after Hyman's death, the family suffered another blow: the death of June's youngest sibling, still an infant.

The pressure to keep the remnants of the Croll family together fell on June's mother, Bessie, as well as on June, the eldest child. Bessie tried to keep the family business solvent, but ultimately had to sell the shop and seek an income in Montreal's garment industry. In 1913, ten-year-old June went to work in a men's clothing shop and was employed at the lowest level and the least-skilled job, pulling bastings. Later that year, Bessie became a finisher in the same shop. In 1914, the workers in June and Bessie's shop called a strike and June and her mother walked off the job together. Her mother began to attend trade union meetings and brought June along with her. The strike was lost, and June took a job as a parcel girl at a department store. Unable to return to school, she found political and intellectual engagement within the labor movement and took part in the activities at the Baron de Hirsch Settlement House, a community hub in which a number of immigrant aid and Jewish cultural groups ran courses and activities.

The adult June Gordon later remarked that she "began having suffragette ideas" when she was thirteen, around the start of World War I, when the fight for women's suffrage gained traction as women took jobs in war industries and organized national campaigns to support the war effort.[7] June's political coming of age was not limited to suffrage, however; the Russian Revolution helped to place her on the political path she would follow for the rest of her life. Working clandestinely, a group of activists set up the Canadian Communist Party in summer 1921 in "a very good barn in Guelph" with "only one cow."[8] Later that summer, the Third World Congress of the Communist International called on Communists to engage in uniting the working class as a whole. In 1922, political leaders founded the legal Workers' Party of Canada, (by 1924 it had become the Communist Party of Canada). In February 1923, June attended the second annual convention of the Workers' Party of Canada in Toronto.

In February 1922, the year she turned twenty-one, June left Montreal and moved to New York. She studied at the Rand School of Social Science, likely inspired by her comrade Annie Buller, a Montreal Jewish radical who had studied there in 1919 before returning to Montreal to found the Montreal Labor College in 1920. (Buller, who joined the Workers' Party in early 1922, would become a lifelong Communist and later a member of the United Jewish People's Order [UJPO], the Canadian branch of the IWO.) The Rand School, located on East Fifteenth Street, was founded in 1906 and offered a wide range of courses related to the history of Socialism and its practical application. Perhaps it was here that June met the man who would become her first husband, Carl Reeve (1900–1980), a prominent Communist Party operative. Gordon met Reeve in July 1922 and by her later account they fell in love immediately; by the summer of 1923, Gordon and Reeve had been assigned Communist Party posts in Chicago.

Chicago was a beacon to young Communists. The Party's headquarters were located there until 1927, and Chicago Party membership in the early 1920s averaged around 2,400 members who were organized into neighborhood and trade union groups. Appointed as the head of the technical staff of the Communist Party central office, June Gordon was now in the midst of the action. Another element of June's life uniquely positioned her within arm's reach of Communist Party leadership: her mother-in-law. Carl Reeve's mother was Ella Reeve Bloor

(1862–1951), known universally as "Mother Bloor," commonly regarded as Communist "royalty." Bloor was a white woman born to the middle class who migrated politically from temperance to suffrage to Socialism and then to Communism. She participated in the formation of the Communist Party in 1919 and became a member of the Central Committee of the Communist Party (CPUSA), serving as the chair of the Party's National Women's Commission. She was "the most visible, nationally recognized woman organizer in the Communist Party."[9] Although Carl and June separated in 1929, for the rest of her life June Gordon would be referred to in the press and by casual acquaintances as "Mother Bloor's daughter-in-law."[10]

As June developed her own identity and position within the CPUSA, her mother-in-law's reputation preceded her, particularly in Chicago. Bloor was one of the very few Party women whose activism included an analysis of gender. In comparison to their comprehensive analysis of race and class, the CPUSA spent relatively little time on the "Woman Question": feminism per se was seen as antithetical to Party theory and interests because the suffrage movement was so closely associated with the bourgeois middle class. The Party believed that gender inequality would be "solved" by the eventual Communist revolution. Despite the Communist Party's tepid interest in "women's issues," it nevertheless needed good organizers and strong leaders and therefore opened its ranks to Mother Bloor. She helped lay the foundations for an alternative current within the Party by introducing women's organizing around community issues that affected women's daily lives. "In contrast to masculine models of Marxist class politics," the historian Kathleen Brown remarked, "Bloor offered an organizing practice which emphasized family and community as central elements in the creation of class consciousness and the bringing about of a communist revolution."[11] Bloor argued instead for women, home, and community as essential to the underpinnings of a mass movement for class consciousness and class struggle. This women-focused class consciousness would prove integral to the later establishment and success of the Emma Lazarus Clubs.

June's Communist education was only just beginning. In the fall of 1925, she and Carl Reeve were given a new assignment, this one in Moscow. Gordon was assigned to study at the "Eastern school," also known as KUTV, while Reeve was assigned to the nearby Lenin School for political leaders. KUTV, an acronym for Kommunisticheskii Universitet Trudiashchikhsia Vostoka (the Communist university for the toilers of the east) was established in 1921 to train students primarily from African and Asian countries, although it also accepted Black and some white American students from the working class. The school's "normal course" or twenty-month curriculum included detailed study of Marxist theories of dialectical and historical materialism, as well as political analysis of capitalism, colonialism, and imperialism. The curriculum also included a "special course," in which students learned to prepare for political work necessitating secret identities, including codes and cryptography, developing pseudonyms and false passports, and how to set up an apartment for underground work.[12]

KUTV and its environs were disturbingly cold, inside and out, and the students ate an unremitting amount of unseasoned kasha. They found the sanitary conditions challenging, and suffered from bedbugs even though they slept on boards. Even more serious, the Black students faced racism from white American and Canadian fellow students, as well as from the Soviet citizens they encountered in daily life. The everyday problems of building a Socialist state were therefore clearly evident. Even in the Soviet Union, it seemed, racism could not disappear at will, nor could even adequate amounts of food or hot water be allowed to every citizen.

Three aspects of her time at KUTV shaped the future of June Gordon's activism: receiving a formal education on colonialism and racism; the shift in Communist policy toward the "Black Belt thesis," which would bring a new cadre of Black leadership into the Party; and meeting the Black comrade who would become her lifelong friend, Maude White.

Maude White arrived in Moscow in December 1927, clad in a sealskin coat and silk stockings, shaking with cold in the minus thirty-five-degree Celsius weather. White was born around 1904 to a working-class family in McKeesport, Pennsylvania that was one of the very few Black families in town. Her high school teacher, Eleanor Goldsmith, was a Communist, and took White to a Communist meeting in Pittsburgh where Communist orator Scott Nearing spoke. White was impressed that the audience was integrated and that members spoke against Negro oppression. Jumping at an opportunity to leave town, White moved to Chicago to live with a sister and began speaking at open-air Communist meetings. As a promising young activist, White was offered a spot at KUTV.

Changes in Communist policy in the late 1920s created exciting new opportunities for young Black activists committed to effecting change back home in the United States. In the summer of 1928, at the Sixth World Congress of the Communist International in Moscow, Party leaders and activists officially put forward the position on the "Negro Question" titled the "Black Belt thesis" after the concentration of Black Americans in the geographically contiguous regions of the Deep South. Under this framework, the Comintern called for African American self-determination (in a 1928 resolution) and explicitly noted that Black Americans constituted an "oppressed nation" (a 1930 resolution). Because of the need for large numbers of workers to produce the cotton harvest on plantations, Black workers did indeed constitute a majority in these regions. Maude White served on the Comintern's Negro Subcommission, which put forth a resolution that explicated the role of the Black "peasantry" in the South and proclaimed that it was the "duty of the Communist Party of the U.S.A. to mobilize and rally the broad masses of the white workers against black oppression."[13] Many Black Communists felt the Sixth Congress was a major turning point for the Communist position on race in America since it led to the establishment of the National Negro Department, as well as of district and section Negro committees. Black men and women were then appointed to a number of prominent positions, including to the Central Committee of the CPUSA.

The Comintern's Sixth Congress in 1928 also formally ushered in the "Third Period," in which, according to the prevailing political theory, revolution was imminent. The Communist Party in the United States prepared for economic collapse and increasing political radicalization. Participation in political reform movements and mainstream unions was now set aside in favor of establishing separate revolutionary organizations and radical unions. All these changes would profoundly influence Gordon's and White's political trajectories.

It is evident from the work Gordon produced in this period that her studies at KUTV focused on the role of women, and Black women in particular. In a 1926 article (written under the name Sonia Croll) she argues: "As powerful an imperialist country as America is today . . . it nevertheless provides a vast and fertile field for work among women," most of whom are "foreign-born, [or] Negro men and women" and [American-born, white] women, most of whom live barely above the subsistence level."[14] "Women are the 'slaves of slaves,'" she writes, quoting without attribution from a 1905 speech by the Black anarchist Lucy Parsons, who was born enslaved. Parsons did not specifically refer to Black women in her speech, since she preferred to emphasize the strong distinction between women and men's economic exploitation under capitalism. In her article, Gordon turns this quotation around, arguing that the economic exploitation of Black women is the worst form of oppression. Capitalism further divides white and Black women by utilizing "race prejudice cultivated by the bosses," she writes, in order to maintain the cheapest labor for the "meanest" work. "When [Black] women and white women work in the same factory or mill, the [Black] women are given the most unpleasant, the most undesirable and poorly paid work," she writes, and are often "shamefully abused" by white men.[15]

Gordon returned to the United States at the end of 1928, but her time in Moscow had clearly left an imprint. Over the next several years, Gordon focused entirely on her role as a textile organizer of women workers. Now a well-trained operative, she would soon become a seasoned organizer, traveling relentlessly across the Northeast from strike to strike. Her return from Russia did not pass unnoticed by the federal government. In a Bureau of Investigation (BOI) memo forwarded to J. Edgar Hoover in March 1928, Gordon (identified as Sonia Croll) was noted as "being trained for special work [i.e., Communism or communistic spying] in England or America."[16] The report also stated that Gordon's home address was on Saint Dominique Street in Montreal, that she was recording secretary for the Workers' Party, and that she gave lectures on Marxism at the Montreal Labor College. Although BOI agents were erroneously convinced that Sonia Croll was the same woman caught spying in Britain for the German Communist Party in 1927, they had developed sufficient intelligence to mark Gordon as a highly trained Communist operative, if not a spy.

Regardless of what the BOI may have thought, Gordon likely returned to New York from Moscow and immediately became an organizer with the National Textile Workers Union, a Communist-led union founded in New England in 1928. She served multiple roles in Communist organizations in the area, including as the business agent for the Dressmakers' Local of the Needle Trades Workers Industrial Union in Philadelphia and secretary of the Lehigh Valley International Labor Defense. After its formation in September 1929, she also became an active member of the Trade Union Unity League, the industrial union umbrella organization founded by the Communist Party.

The onset of the economic crisis sparking the Great Depression in the fall of 1929 would only serve to underscore the deep divisions between those who wished to protect capitalism and those who worked for its downfall. In June 1930, June Gordon was appointed head of the Women's Department of the Needle Trades Workers Industrial Union. *Working Woman* magazine declared that her appointment heralded positive changes in the industry, including a concerted effort to recruit women into the union "on the basis of full pay for equal work, and no discrimination against Negroes."[17] Although union organizing among Black women was still emergent among Party unions, a new key player soon arrived on the scene when Maude White returned from Moscow in 1930. "Since I was a Negro woman Communist just returned from the Soviet Union, I was put right up in the front ranks," she recalled later. She plunged into the hectic activities of the time, writing leaflets and articles and taking part in demonstrations.[18]

Gordon continued to travel nonstop throughout New England on behalf of textile workers' strikes. On August 1, 1932, she was arrested in Lawrence, Massachusetts, along with three other Communists, after police broke up a meeting of more than three hundred people. Unlike her other past arrests, this time she was charged with being an enemy alien and threatened with deportation. Her warrant stated that her place of birth was undetermined. Released on bail, she went back to work as an organizer. When summoned to an immigration hearing, Gordon stated confidently that she was not an alien at all. Rather, the reason the government could not find a record of her birth in the United States was that she had been born in San Francisco and her birth records had been destroyed in the

San Francisco earthquake of 1906. This startling and daring fabrication relied on the fact that a fire in San Francisco's Hall of Records, sparked by the earthquake, destroyed all the city's public birth and marriage records. If someone claimed to have been born in San Francisco before April 1906, there was now no way to disprove it. This accident of fate had created a legal loophole that had already been well utilized by Chinese immigrants, otherwise restricted through the 1882 Chinese Exclusion Act, to claim citizenship.[19]

In a twist of fate, June Gordon's deportation case soon reached the highest echelons of power. When Franklin Delano Roosevelt took office in March 1933, he appointed Frances Perkins as secretary of labor, making her the first female cabinet member. Perkins inherited a slew of deportation case files from the outgoing secretary, including June Gordon's. In early July 1933, the commissioner general of immigration, Daniel MacCormack, wrote to Perkins with concern regarding the Gordon/Croll case, stating: "This is the woman who was arrested as a Communist although there was no evidence she was an alien." He explained that he had warned his staff against "carelessness in the instigation of warrant proceedings," specifically citing Gordon's case as "most unfortunate," because there was a distinct absence of evidence proving that she was, in fact, an alien.[20]

Only a few days later, Perkins announced the elimination of "case fixing and terrorization of aliens," declaring that "hereafter the deportation laws will be enforced with due regard to human values."[21] Throughout her time in office, Perkins withstood considerable pressure to pursue particular individuals in high-profile cases, most famously in the case of Australian-born labor leader Harry Bridges in the late 1930s. Bolesław Gebert, later leader of the IWO's Polish section, likewise had a 1931 deportation order stemming from his strike activity for the Communist National Miners Union that was deferred throughout the Roosevelt administration. It seems this approach had its origins in the Croll case. Ultimately, Immigration Bureau investigators failed in their attempt to disprove June's claim of nativity. In August 1933, she received official notice of the cancellation of her deportation.

It was around this time that June Gordon met the man who would be her partner for the rest of her life, Eugene Gordon. In 1935, June gave birth to the couple's son, Eugene Gordon Jr. The couple may have been living in Maude White's apartment in Boston at the time.[22] Eugene Gordon, born in 1891, was raised in New Orleans and on his grandfather's farm in Hawkinsville, Georgia. Eugene's father had been taken to Liberia by his grandfather immediately after Lincoln's 1863 Emancipation Proclamation had freed the enslaved; Eugene's father remained in Africa and Europe until he was thirty. Eugene attended Howard University before settling in Boston, where he worked as a journalist for the *Boston Daily*

Post, one of the few Black journalists on a white-owned paper. It was here that he developed his radical politics.

Eugene Gordon dedicated a significant portion of his political and journalistic work to assessing the conditions of Black women under capitalism. In the May 1934 issue of *Working Woman* magazine (a Communist Party–funded publication that served as the public mouthpiece for the United Council of Working Class Women), Eugene Gordon wrote, "Negro women are held at the bottom of the economic structure in the United States both by the conditions which hold Negro men there and by the additional fact of their sex. As women they are restricted to certain fields of ill-paid labor, and as Negroes they are made to take the meanest and lowest paid jobs in these fields."[23]

The assertion of Black women's double oppression was further problematized in the same publication by the IWO's vice president, Louise Thompson (later Patterson), who published a landmark essay on Black women, "Toward a Brighter Dawn," in April 1936. Thompson argued that "Negro women are the most exploited group in America," and put forth the idea that Black women were "triply exploited . . . as workers, as women, and as Negroes."[24] These ideas would play an important role in the Emma Lazarus Club's policy and activism on racial issues in the postwar era. In 1941, June had begun a clerical job with the IWO using the name June Gordon, the name she used for the rest of her life. She then took on the role of national secretary of the Jewish American Section's women's groups, the immediate precursor to the Emma Lazarus Clubs.

Jewish Communist Women's Community Organizing

The political and institutional history of the Emma Lazarus Clubs stemmed from the founding of the United Council of Working Class Women (UCWCW), which was established in 1924 and merged with the International Workers Order in 1939. The United Council of Working Class Women held its first meeting in December 1923, when a coalition of local trade unions, Socialist groups, and women's organizations held a convention to create a new working-class women's organization to be founded and directed by working-class women themselves (and led by a prominent Communist Party member, Kate Gitlow, mother of the Party's general secretary). Women affiliated with the Council understood that the problems of their own particular households were similar to those of other women and thus could be linked together to be addressed through far-reaching systemic change.[25]

In 1931, Rose Nelson became a member of the executive board of the United Council and then executive secretary. She began to envision a broader scope for the organization, one in which millions of American housewives could be organized together to create social change. Rose Nelson (who became Rose Raynes after marrying Alex Raynes in 1962) was born Reyzl Nemerovsky in Ukraine in 1903 and immigrated to the United States with her family ten years later. She left school at fifteen to support her family, became a hat trimmer, and joined Local 43 of the millinery union. She became a strong and effective organizer and helped expand the organization to include sixty-one councils spread throughout New York, Connecticut, and New Jersey. Under Nelson, the councils honed their ability to effectively organize women into local, neighborhood, and city-wide units.

Council women were extremely effective organizers; they would select an apartment building and visit women in every single apartment, giving them information about the council. The organizer would have the whole building elect a delegate to the United Councils conference, who would draft a report for mobilizing the women of the building. The new council members would then select local campaigns to get involved in, from school overcrowding to tenement safety conditions, and choose various methods to address the issue, from attending local council meetings to picketing or holding baby carriage parades.

In May 1933, the United Council held their tenth annual conference in New York. At the banquet dinner, Communist leader (and June Gordon's former mother-in-law) Ella "Mother" Bloor was the keynote speaker. Council leaders took note of the fact that the organization now boasted many American-born young women, white as well as Black. The likelihood, however, is that the majority of members were Yiddish-speaking eastern European Jewish immigrants. The Yiddish Communist daily newspaper *Morgn Frayhayt* (Morning freedom) had its own delegate at the conference and the United Council had raised $1,900 for *Frayhayt* in the previous year, showing the United Council's continuing close relationship with immigrant Yiddish-speaking Communists.[26]

Working hand in hand with the Unemployed Councils (an initiative of the CPUSA designed to mobilize unemployed workers), United Council leaders prided themselves on their ability to win gains for working-class women as the Great Depression deepened, from fighting for increases in welfare from the Home Relief Bureau and leading rent strikes and consumer boycotts to mobilizing neighborhood women to stand in picket lines. They spoke frequently about the need to bring more Black women into their organization but acknowledged that there were significant issues obstructing Black women's participation, cautioning, "We must be patient and persistent in organizing Negro workers for they have been fooled so many times that they are now suspicious until we prove our sincerity to them."[27] This comment suggests that white women had not been reliable allies for Black women and that racism played a role in Black women's reluctance to work with white women.

In early 1935, council leaders expressed the fact that living conditions for working-class housewives were becoming unbearable, but also saw that Black women's living conditions were even worse. Black women could not rent safe apartments and were stuck in unsafe and overcrowded conditions. It was harder for them to get factory jobs and receive union wages, benefits, and job protection. Instead, they were forced to work in domestic labor, where they received even lower wages than whites for hours of heavy work. Not least, they were discriminated against by the government when they applied for home relief. Sensing perhaps both an injustice and an opportunity for community organizing that would strengthen their own organization, council leaders declared again that white women should organize and unite forces with Black women to fight for better conditions.

Faced with the mounting economic despair of their members, the council began planning its biggest action yet—a boycott on the high price of meat that would become a nationwide phenomenon. Organizers held an Eastern conference in New York and a Western conference in Cleveland to prepare for a national boycott of meat to protest high consumer prices. New York began its strike first, in May. The council's primary aim was to achieve a reduction in the cost of meat to twenty-four cents a pound. To do that, they had to get the attention of the meat wholesalers, part of a notorious trust that controlled prices across the country. The women reached out to local kosher butchers in Brighton Beach and Coney Island, Brooklyn, and planned a weeklong boycott, echoing the Lower East Side's more well-known kosher meat boycott of 1902. On May 22, 1935, butchers tacked signs to their doors, "Closed in sympathy with the strikers," and headed out to the picket lines outside their shops, alongside the women. Butchers who would not agree to close were physically shut down by the protesters. With butcher shops closed, meat wholesalers were stuck with hundreds of pounds of meat, representing huge losses. The strike spread to Williamsburg and Brownsville, Brooklyn, and then to Black neighborhoods in Sheepshead Bay, Brooklyn, and Harlem.

Bonita Williams, a British West Indies–born Communist leader in Harlem, created and chaired the Harlem chapter of the United Action Committee Against the High Cost of Living, part of the United Council's strike committee. In early June, Williams and her colleagues negotiated a strike agreement with eighty Harlem butchers for a four-day shutdown of all neighborhood meat markets to draw attention to the cause and force wholesalers to reduce prices. In tandem with this Harlem housewives organized a mass campaign, picketing in front of butcher shops and urging shoppers to boycott meat until the prices came down 25 percent. The committee also demanded "a better grade of meat, honest weight, and sanitation."²⁸ The butchers who participated in the shutdown also provided trucks to transport "a flying squadron of pickets" to forcibly close any stores that remained open. Williams led a march down 125th Street with hundreds of women protesting the high price of meat. After a week, one hundred butcher shops agreed to a 28-percent cut in retail prices, one of the most significant victories of the entire campaign.

The 1935 New York strike lasted for one month. Officials from the retail kosher meat authority estimated that 3,000 of 4,500 kosher butcher shops in the city had closed or were forcibly shut down during the strike. After relentless daily picketing, demonstrations, open-air meetings, and indoor mass meetings, the women won a reduction of four to five cents a pound in more than a thousand stores throughout the city. The New York leadership then helped set up councils in nearly every major city. The strike in New York paved the way for strikes in Chicago, Saint Louis, Kansas City, Philadelphia, Boston, Paterson, and Los Angeles. On June 20, a dozen housewives from Chicago and New York, including Rose Nelson, traveled to Washington to demand a congressional inquiry into a monopoly in food prices and an immediate reduction of the price of meat. After the meeting, Rose Nelson called government officials "deluded," saying that they were searching high and low for a reason for high meat prices other than the most obvious one: the money of working-class people was being used to line the pockets of the meat packers' trust.

Buoyed by their boycott success and a boost in membership, and likely influenced by the Communist Party's Popular Front, the United Council embraced a more populist persona in the summer of 1935 and changed its name to the Progressive Women's Council. The new name highlighted the role of women as activists while underplaying the class aspects of the struggle for better housing conditions, lower rent, and lower food prices. It also suggested that their goals included further expanding their membership. Council leaders stated that they believed they could do still more to "reach the broad masses of housewives, and Negro women, who are the most exploited, and are as yet represented only in small numbers in the Councils."²⁹ But mass growth in the councils proved to be impossible, in part because the CPUSA abruptly changed its policy on the "Woman Question," and discontinued the United Council's primary means of mass communication, *Working Woman* magazine. In 1938, Rose Nelson, Clara Lemlich Shavelson, and other leaders of the original United Council were transferred from their leadership roles within the renamed Progressive Women's Council and given jobs within the Party.

The council held its last convention in January 1939 and in May of that year it officially merged with the International Workers Order. The IWO's New York City Committee Women's Department was now headed by Yiddish-speaking Lemlich Shavelson, and Rose Nelson became director of the IWO Women's

Section, transferring the council's membership roster of 4,500 women into various IWO lodges. June Gordon also became an official women's organizer for the IWO/JPFO at this time. All three, especially Lemlich Shavelson, worked with mothers, organizing homemakers as working activists whose training included attending free courses and producing Yiddish newsletters. Together, the three women would form the backbone of women's organizing within the IWO's Jewish Women's Section, which in 1944 became the Emma Lazarus Division of the JPFO.

The Emma Lazarus Clubs and Postwar Politics

Women's activism within the progressive movement transformed dramatically during World War II. As thousands of the men in the Communist movement fought overseas, women moved into leadership positions. In the IWO, Louise Thompson was already a vice president, and Helen Vrábel headed the Slovak Workers Society: by 1943, more than thirty thousand women made up half of the CPUSA's membership. When the United States entered World War II, June's role at the IWO expanded. She began leading the Front Line Fighters Fund, raising money for the war effort, and, in a more maternalist mode, headed up women's knitting circles to produce socks for US soldiers overseas. In 1943, she became national secretary of the Jewish American Division of Women's Groups, which shortly thereafter became the Emma Lazarus Division.

The Emmas carried over their activism into the postwar era, especially as employment opportunities began shrinking and even progressive men assumed that women would resume their positions within the private sphere. Growing out of the IWO's mobilization of women as a progressive, anti-fascist force supporting the American war effort in the workplace and at home, the Emmas proclaimed their mission as a "cultural and civic organization for women . . . dedicated to advance the interests of the Jewish people and the country as a whole." They added that the struggle for labor and the Jewish struggle were, in essence, inextricable: "We believe that the struggle for Jewish freedom everywhere—in the U.S.A., Europe and Palestine—can be won only if the Jewish people travel together with labor and all progressive forces."[30] Their stated objectives listed protecting the freedom of Jews in all lands, promoting the "progressive currents in Jewish culture and traditions . . . to foster understanding and harmonious community life between Jews and non-Jews, Negro and white Americans," and working for democracy through the labor movement "and [with] all others who take action against discrimination [and for] lasting peace."[31] Membership in the Emmas was open to any Jewish women willing to pursue these goals.

Although during her first two decades of activism she seemingly never acknowledged herself publicly as a Jew, under June Gordon's postwar leadership the Emma Lazarus Clubs became an organization grounded in Jewish language, culture, and, as June called it, "self-knowledge." The Emmas, as part of the JPFO, adopted a Jewish war orphanage in Andrésy, France, and were deeply involved in European relief work. While internally some members disagreed over the amount of support the clubs should extend to Communism and the Soviet Union, the organization as a whole maintained a commitment to world peace and coexistence with the USSR. In keeping with their attention to Jewish cultural identity, the Emmas' bylaws stipulated that the national board required two recording secretaries, one Yiddish and one English.

In the announcement for their first national conference in 1947, June Gordon made explicit the connections between the fight for women's rights and the fight for ethnic culture against increasing xenophobia:

> The opinion that [a] woman's place is in the home, like the theory of the melting pot, must be discarded as another hoax which serves only those who seek to paralyze the healthy, progressive forces in the struggle for a better life. Just as the fine-sounding theory of the melting pot covered attempts at assimilationism, so the catchphrase woman's place is in the home really serves to keep women from broadening their viewpoint and their participation in the social and cultural affairs in the world outside their homes. It is a catchphrase to keep women backward, at the mercy of the profiteers, the racemongers and all anti-social elements who, like the Nazis, really have the greatest contempt for home and family life and seek to destroy it.[32]

As American Jews in the IWO struggled to understand their place in the post-Holocaust world, they pledged to continue the wartime work they had undertaken to recruit more Black membership and to pay special attention to the issues affecting the Black community. By the fall of 1949, two widely reported incidents underscored the fact that many Americans on both the left and the right regarded the Black and Jewish situations as linked. These incidents added impetus to the IWO's plans in nationally organizing both Black lodges and Black-Jewish unity. In September, after twenty thousand people gathered in Peekskill, New York, to hear an outdoor concert featuring Paul Robeson, the audience, which included IWO members, faced a hostile, rock-throwing crowd while exiting the concert grounds. Rumors abounded of crosses burning on the hillsides; protesters threw rocks and shouted racial slurs and threats against Jews and Blacks. In response, union members as well as IWO and JPFO members actively supported and defended Robeson at a second Peekskill concert. In a second incident that

November, a Jewish unionist and IWO member invited Black colleagues to his home on Chicago's South Side. White neighbors, worried that the family was planning on selling their house to Blacks, instigated a weeklong "reign of terror." Crowds of up to ten thousand people gathered on the streets, yelling political and racial slurs.[33]

However, it was a different incident, reminiscent of the Scottsboro case of the 1930s, that mobilized the progressive left to decry institutional racism in the United States and in the South in particular. In November 1947, Rosa Lee Ingram, a sharecropper who lived in a rural part of central Georgia, was accused of killing her white neighbor, a fellow sharecropper. "He was a sharecropper, just like us, but, because he was white, he tried to boss us," she recalled later.[34] John Stratford seemed to take pleasure in harassing the Ingram family. On the fatal day, Stratford became angry when some of the Ingram family's livestock wandered onto his property. A struggle ensued and Stratford aimed his rifle at Mrs. Ingram. One of her sons intervened and struck Stratford with his own gun. He fell down, dead; Mrs. Ingram and four of her sons were charged with murder. The Schley County Grand Jury was composed entirely of white people, despite the fact that the majority of the county was Black. They indicted all five Ingrams on January 22, 1948. Authorities denied them the right to contact an attorney until the day of the trial, January 26. The next day, Judge W. M. Harper pronounced the verdict: Mrs. Ingram and her sons Wallace and Sammie were sentenced to death by electric chair, their execution to take place in exactly one month. Attorney Dykes won a stay of execution on a motion for a new trial before the same judge. The judge granted a stay and reduced the death sentences to life in prison, but refused to take any further action.

Black women's organizations immediately began campaigning for the Ingrams' freedom. In March 1949, the Civil Rights Congress helped found the National Committee to Free the Ingram Family. Its leader was Maude White (now known as Maude White Katz), June's former comrade from her studies in the Soviet Union. Prominent Black women activists, including Claudia Jones, Eslanda Robeson, and Shirley Graham Du Bois also joined the organizing committee. The Communist-led Civil Rights Congress, as well as the National Association for the Advancement of Colored People (NAACP), launched legal defense and support campaigns on behalf of Rosa Lee Ingram. The IWO also immediately got involved, founding the Ingram Children's Education and Welfare Fund; June Gordon served on the board of trustees. Additionally, the IWO sponsored a speaking tour featuring James Ingram, Mrs. Ingram's twelve-year-old son, who spoke on his mother's behalf. The IWO raised funds to send two of Mrs. Ingram's children to IWO-run camps, Camp Kinderland and Camp Wo-Chi-Ca.

Claudia Jones, a prominent Black feminist intellectual within the Communist Party, traveled to Washington, DC, in June 1949 as the official Party delegate of the National Committee to Free the Ingram Family. Jones saw the Ingram case as lying at the heart of the problem of white supremacy and bourgeois liberal hypocrisy. No other case highlights the problems Black women face today as dramatically as that of Mrs. Rosa Lee Ingram, she declared, as it illustrates the "landless, Jim Crow, oppressed status of the Negro family in America."[35]

The government's Cold War crackdown on the IWO and on all progressives, especially immigrants, had a profound impact on Black and Jewish women's organizing. In 1950, both Rose Nelson and Claudia Jones were arrested as foreign subversives under the terms of the newly passed Subversive Activities Control Act, also known as the McCarran Act. FBI agents charged them as aliens affiliated with the Communist Party. Jones and Nelson were taken to Ellis Island, where they were held with fourteen others arrested under the same law, in a sweep that would test the government's authority to carry out a law so controversial that President Truman himself had vetoed it—although Congress immediately overrode the president's veto. After twenty-five days, the detainees were finally released on bail. With fundraising help and legal defense from the American Committee for Protection of Foreign Born, an immigrants' rights activist group, the "McCarran 17" were granted a reprieve; the US District Court held that their arrests were illegal. They now had to wait in suspense for Immigration and Naturalization Service hearings as well as the legal challenges being mounted against the constitutionality of the McCarran Act.

In March 1951, Rose Nelson officially received a deportation order from the United States; she immediately registered an appeal. Rose's case became the first McCarran Act deportation hearing to be reviewed by the Board of Immigration Appeals. In May 1951, Rose and her legal team traveled to Washington to plead her case. The appeal was denied and a final administrative order of deportation was issued. Because the Soviet Union refused to admit her, and no other country would take her, she spent the rest of her life in the United States, officially a citizen of no nation.

At Claudia Jones's December 1950 hearing she was also found deportable under the terms of the McCarran Act. FBI informants testified that they knew her to have served as a Party official. Several months later, she suffered her first heart attack; she was only thirty-six years old. In 1955, she was sent to spend a year and a day in federal prison at Alderson, West Virginia. She was then deported to the United Kingdom, where she joined the Communist Party of Great Britain and became a well-known organizer in the African-Caribbean community. She died of a heart attack in 1964, at the age of forty-nine. Other IWO officials faced similar deportations. Bolesław Gebert's deportation order was taken out of mothballs and he voluntarily returned to his native Poland. Henry Podolski and Peter Harisiades of the IWO's Polish and Greek sections fought their deportations, to no avail.

In 1950, the IWO began to fight the lengthy court battles against the State of New York that would lead to its dissolution in 1954. In 1951, the Emma Lazarus Division formally separated from the IWO and reconstituted itself legally as an independent entity, the Emma Lazarus Federation of Jewish Women's Clubs (ELF). The following year, IWO vice president Louise Thompson Patterson and Maude White Katz cofounded a new political association of progressive Black women, Sojourners for Truth and Justice (STJ). According to its statement of purpose, the STJ was "the first all Negro women's organization with the unalterable purpose of winning complete and equal rights for American Negro citizens residing within the United States or anywhere else in the world."[36]

The organizers of Sojourners knew that the complicated and sensitive work needed to free the Ingrams, as in the Scottsboro case, required many allies. In March 1952, one hundred members of the Sojourners gathered together in Harlem's YMCA for their Eastern Seaboard conference. They were joined by fifty members of the Emma Lazarus Federation for a special "Unity Lunch" where the women pledged to work together on joint campaigns to combat racism. Invoking Sojourner Truth, Ernestine Rose, Harriet Tubman, and Emma Lazarus as symbols of Negro-Jewish solidarity, they promised each other "to walk in dignity and struggle together" and proclaimed the "alliance of Negro and Jewish women for equality, security and peace." "We hold that none of us can feel secure," they stated, "until the country is cleansed of white supremacy and all the evils that flow therefrom."[37] Louise Thompson Patterson, now executive secretary of the Sojourners, stood next to June Gordon to convene the proceedings; June presented the Sojourners with a check for $200, and made a pledge to provide $50 per month for the duration of the campaign.

Announcing their partnership with the Sojourners in the first issue of ELF's publication *The Lamp*, Jennie Truchman wrote, "The Emma Lazarus Federation has taken a stand before in condemning genocidal actions against the Negro people, through legislation, by sending delegations into the south to protest murders and jailings, yet we have never united formally with a Negro women's organization. But these actions have been sporadic. For some time now federation leadership has been discussing ways and means which would enable us to contribute to the basic need—the need to eliminate the whole system of Negro oppression—Negro Ghettoes, the whole system of Genocide."[38]

The materials produced by the Emma Lazarus Clubs in the early 1950s reflected this emphasis on structural inequality. In the early 1950s, ELF produced a booklet (likely authored by Truchman) titled, "Racism—Enemy of the Jewish

People," intended for use at local club events for "Brotherhood Month" and "Negro History Week." The booklet declared that "in the U.S., the fight against anti-Semitism cannot be placed on the same level as the fight against oppression and inequality of Negro people." On the contrary, "Negro people suffer forms of oppression much deeper than any other group. There can be no comparison in the degree of discrimination faced by Negro people in housing, political life, education, jobs, and business."[39] In the section titled, "Racism and white supremacy among Jewish people," the text addressed the issue of Black women employed in domestic service by directly utilizing the ideas of Louise Thompson Patterson and Claudia Jones. "Negro women suffer triple oppression," the text stated, "as women, as women-workers, and as Negroes."[40]

Jennie Truchman, along with fellow ELF member Anna Newman, traveled to Georgia from New York City alongside twenty-one other white and Black delegates in December 1953 to plead with Georgia's governor to grant parole to Rosa Lee Ingram. Truchman later recalled, "The thought that kept racing through my head was that as a Jewish woman I had a deep kinship with Mrs. Ingram, that I had a responsibility to help get her free. The enemy of the Jew and the Negro is the same, though the Negro is far more intensely the object of that enmity."[41]

Related political analysis pushed forward the idea that whites, especially Jews, would make significant gains by supporting Black equality. In March 1958, June's husband Eugene Gordon penned an article for *The Lamp* arguing that Black and white Americans had common economic needs that should bind them together. "Whereas brotherhood ... is generally regarded as a situation resulting from 'helping' Negroes win their constitutional rights," he wrote, "it is, instead, a situation resulting from whites' helping Negroes win and make secure the constitutional rights of both whites and non-whites. The reason is that the primary interests of both are jeopardized. This fact is especially significant when the whites are Jews, whose history of persecution ... parallels Negroes' history."[42] Eugene Gordon, with his more intimate understanding of Jewish history and antisemitism due to his close contact with his wife June and other Emma Lazarus members, was well placed to make this argument.

At a meeting preparing for the third convention, in November 1958, ELF leaders announced their "deep sense of responsibility to intensify our efforts alongside the Negro people in their efforts and leadership to overcome the organized drive of the white supremacists who are both anti-Negro and anti-Semitic. . . . We will show financial, moral, and civic support and cooperation with national and Southern Negro leadership."[43] ELF leaders listed initiatives in which their clubs were currently engaged, such as lobbying the government for laws to end employment discrimination, a national law to end housing discrimination, ending poll taxes, enacting a national law against lynching, and forming a federal Civil Rights Commission that would have the power to prosecute crimes motivated by racism. ELF also pledged continued financial support to the "Youth March for Integrated Schools Committee," a campaign led by A. Philip Randolph and Martin Luther King Jr., among others. ELF had already contributed to the NAACP, the Montgomery Improvement Association, and the prayer pilgrimage to Washington in 1957. New York City clubs participated in city council hearings that led to the passing of a citywide fair housing ordinance outlawing segregation in private housing, supported a city hospital for the predominantly Black Brooklyn Bedford-Stuyvesant neighborhood, and helped in the fight to desegregate city schools. Marking Mother's Day 1960, ELF launched nationwide picket lines at Woolworth's stores, dedicating the day to the mothers of the Black youth involved in pro-integration sit-ins across the South. ELF published and distributed twenty thousand pamphlets at the demonstrations.

In August 1963, ELF participated in the March on Washington for Jobs and Freedom. They considered it their duty to "render leadership" among white women and the Jewish community, and affirmed that ELF's support of the Black freedom struggle had been an "integral part of our work all through the years."[44] A large contingent of Emmas from New York marched behind an ELF banner, and large groups from Los Angeles and Chicago, as well as smaller groups from communities such as Newark, participated. As the women marched, they saw a group of neo-Nazis, supporters of Lincoln Rockwell, founder of the American Nazi Party. Two young Episcopalian ministers sprinted up to them, as did another Black marcher, so that the Emmas presented a united front, an idealized vision of an alternate America. June Gordon remained at the forefront of marching and organizing during those years.

As the Emmas continued to work for a better society, they also continued to face the consequences of a government that targeted anyone involved in the Communist movement. J. Edgar Hoover had been amassing information on June Gordon for many years. The FBI kept tabs on ELF's phone and mail, and followed June Gordon and her family, including her ex-husband, Carl Reeve, and her sisters and their husbands. Someone identified her 1936 passport photo as the same as a woman born in Russia in 1901, not San Francisco. Now that the government was able to prove that she had lied about possessing birthright citizenship, they were able to prove that she had entered the country illegally in 1928. June was once again under a deportation order. Her appeal was dismissed by the Board of Immigration Appeals in October 1960. As in the 1950 case of Rose Nelson, the government was hampered by the fact that they could not find a country to deport her to—the Soviet Union would not admit her. June became part of a larger case led by prominent attorney Blanch Freedman, who continued the fight to keep June and others in the country.[45]

In the early morning of January 6, 1967, June Gordon was stricken by a cerebral hemorrhage and died the following day in the hospital. In notes for her eulogy, her husband Eugene revealed something of what it had meant to him to live with June, and with the Emmas, as an African American man in a large extended family of Jewish women. He struggled to articulate how it felt to live with his own personal grief, while relating it to "the griefs, just as personal and profound, that others experience."[46] Eugene and June shared the experience of belonging to communities coming to terms with profound hatred and loss, whether in the Holocaust or in the Jim Crow United States. They both experienced what it was like to live as subjects of the state, rather than as full citizens. Thus, Eugene indicated in his graveside words that grieving a loved one, such an intensely personal experience, was in itself a kind of political act. Paying tribute to his wife, Eugene acknowledged his understanding of the fundamental message of her life's work: the lives of ordinary people are inherently political, not lived in isolation but in constant resonance with others. In choosing an inscription for June's gravestone, Eugene and the Emmas chose the phrase that had so often passed from June's lips: "Until we are all free, we are none of us free."

In 1970, marking the fiftieth anniversary of winning the ballot and the sixtieth anniversary of International Women's Day, the women of ELF rededicated themselves to ending the "immoral war" in Vietnam, striking for equal pay for equal work, helping promote Black and other minority women to leadership in unions and community organizations, ending racism and antisemitism, ending male supremacy, and working for "a fuller life in a better world."[47]

The Emmas also continued their solidarity work with African American women. In 1971, after Black feminist activist Angela Davis was charged with murder and conspiracy for her alleged role in a failed prison escape, the Emmas immediately began fundraising for her defense campaign, due in part to the fact that Louise Thompson Patterson was the nationwide coordinator. Davis's case reminded the Emmas of countless other frame-ups they'd fought in the 1950s and 60s, especially that of Rosa Lee Ingram. Long-standing political relationships and friendships across racial lines helped give the Emmas an ever-fresh sense of injustice, a reason to get up in the morning and hit the picket lines. The Emmas, the vast majority of whom were by this time in their mid-sixties or older, were receptive to many of the changes transforming leftist politics and so continued a tradition they had helped create in the 1920s, drawing strength from their own communities while building alliances with others in the fight for a more open and equal America.

NOTES

1. Louise Waterman Wise was the spouse of Rabbi Stephen S. Wise who worked in coalitions with the JPFO during World War II.
2. Flyer for outing for Emma Lazarus Division, 1945, International Workers Order (IWO) Records #5276, box 28, folder 5, Kheel Center for Labor-Management Documentation and Archives, Catherwood Library, Cornell University, Ithaca, New York. Henceforth Kheel.
3. Flyer for outing for Emma Lazarus Division.
4. Sadie Doroshkin, from the Brownsville chapter of the JPFO, general executive board minutes, IWO, February 12–13, 1944, box 1, folder 1, Kheel.
5. See, for example, Jennie Truchman, "Negro and Jewish Women on Freedom's Road," *The Lamp* 1, no. 1 (May 1952). *The Lamp* was the journal of the Emma Lazarus Foundation. Emma Lazarus Federation of Jewish Women's Clubs Records, MS-583, box 8, folder 5, The Jacob Rader Marcus Archives of the American Jewish Archives, Cincinnati, Ohio.
6. Emma Lazarus, excerpt from "An Epistle to the Hebrews," in *An Epistle to the Hebrews*, ed. Morris U. Schappes (Jewish Historical Society of New York, 1987), 30. (As cited in Joyce Antler, *The Journey Home*.)
7. Testimony of June Croll, 1960, 88, American Committee for Protection of Foreign Born files, June Croll Gordon file, mixed materials 86, folder 11, Labadie Library, University of Michigan, Ann Arbor, Michigan (hereafter Croll).
8. Ian Easterbrook, "'A Very Good Barn in Guelph': The Founding of the Communist Party of Canada in 1921," in *Wellington County History* (Wellington County Historical Society, 1995), 8:20–34.
9. Kathleen A. Brown, "The 'Savagely Fathered and Un-Mothered World' of the Communist Party, U.S.A.: Feminism, Maternalism, and 'Mother Bloor,'" *Feminist Studies* 25, no. 3 (Autumn 1999): 537.
10. In later testimony related to her 1960 deportation proceedings, Gordon stated that she and Reeve had drifted apart. They were certainly physically far apart, since Reeve was sent by the Party to Gastonia, North Carolina, and June was tied to Party work in the textile industry of the Northeast. See, for example, "Deportation Plea Lost: Appeal by Daughter-in-Law of Mother Bloor Is Rejected," *New York Times*, October 26, 1960, 43.
11. Brown, "'Savagely Fathered,'" 570.
12. Holger Weiss, "The Making of an African Bolshevik: Bankole Awoonor Renner in Moscow, 1925–1928," *Ghana Studies* 9 (January 2006): 204. See also Irina Filatova, "Indoctrination or Scholarship? Education of Africans at the Communist University of the Toilers of the East in the Soviet Union, 1923–1937," *Paedagogica Historica* 35, no. 1 (1999): 41–66. June Gordon did in fact assume a pseudonym, Doris Parks, when she worked with the Communist-led National Miners Union in Harlan, Kentucky, in 1932.
13. Walter T. Howard, *Black Communists Speak on Scottsboro: A Documentary History* (Temple University Press, 2007), 159.
14. Sonia Croll, "Work Among Women in America," *International Press Correspondence*, vol. 6, no. 53, July 22, 1926, 884.
15. Croll, "Work Among Women," 884.
16. Memo from Robert F. Kelley, chief, Division of Eastern European Affairs, Department of State, forwarded to J. Edgar Hoover, Bureau of Investigation, Department of Justice, "Letters Concerning Sonia Croll, A Jewess," March 8, 1928, Natalie Grant Wraga Papers, Recently Declassified Government Records, Hoover Institution Library and Archives, Stanford University, Palo Alto, California.
17. "Women's Department Established in the Needle Trades," *Working Woman*, July 1930, 5.

18. Oral history interview, Maude White Katz, Oral History of the American Left series, box 4, cassette 130, Tamiment Library and Robert F. Wagner Labor Archives, New York University, New York, New York.

19. Huping Ling and Allan Austin, *Asian American History and Culture: An Encyclopedia* (Routledge, 2015), 229.

20. Memorandum from Colonel MacCormack to Perkins re: arrest of June Croll, July 5, 1933, Frances Perkins Papers, 1928–1955, series 3, box 1, folder 27, Correspondence and Memorandum, 1928–1955, Linda Lear Center for Special Collections and Archives, Connecticut College, New London, Connecticut.

21. "Our Woman Secretary Takes It On the Chin," *Boston Globe*, July 16, 1933, Croll.

22. This is recorded as the observation of an informant in Eugene Gordon's FBI file. I am grateful to Daniel Candee for sending me this document. Federal Bureau of Investigation case file, subject: Eugene Ferdinand Gordon, granted via Freedom of Information Act to Verner T. Mitchell, University of Memphis. See Daniel Candee, "A Pair Against Opression: June Croll, Eugene Gordon, Communism and the Forging of American Anti-Racism" (master's thesis, University of Chicago, August 2022), 68.

23. Eugene Gordon, "Unconquered Spirit: The Negro Women's Battle Under 'Freedom,'" *Working Woman*, May 1935, 8.

24. Louise Thompson, "Toward a Brighter Dawn," *Woman Today* (formerly *Working Woman*), April 1936, 14.

25. Gitlow, a Russian Jewish immigrant, like some earlier Communist Party founders, left the CPUSA in 1930, as did her well-known son, Ben Gitlow.

26. Clara Bodian, "Conference Plans the Struggle," *Working Woman*, June 1933, 7.

27. Bodian, "Conference Plans the Struggle," 7.

28. "Meat Strikers Will Rally," *Daily Worker*, June 14, 1935.

29. Dora Rich, "A Thousand New Members," *Working Woman*, December 1935, 4. Rich went on to work for the Jewish Women's Section of the New York City Committee, IWO/JPFO, joining Clara Lemlich Shavelson in efforts aimed at organizing homemakers and other women, and then later on worked for the JPFO's Emma Lazarus Division.

30. Founding statement, Emma Lazarus Division of Jewish Women's Clubs, Emma Lazarus Federation of Jewish Women's Clubs Records, MS-583, box 1, folder 1, American Jewish Archives, Hebrew Union College, Cincinnati, Ohio (hereafter Emma Lazarus Federation).

31. Founding statement, Emma Lazarus Division.

32. June Gordon, "First National Convention of the Emma Lazarus Division," *The Jewish Fraternalist*, June 1947.

33. Helmut Lorsch, "Rabbi Berman Denounces Outbreaks of Racial Riots Here," *The Sentinel*, November 17, 1949. See also George Starr, "The Need for Negro-Jewish Unity," *The Jewish Fraternalist*, February–March 1950.

34. Harry Raymond, *The Ingrams Shall Not Die*, pamphlet published by the *Daily Worker* in March 1948. American Left Ephemera Collection, 1875–2015, AIS.2007.11, Archives and Special Collections, University of Pittsburgh Library System, Pittsburgh, Pennsylvania.

35. Claudia Jones, "An End to the Neglect of the Problems of the Negro Woman," *Political Affairs*, June 1949.

36. Summary proceedings, Eastern Seaboard Conference, March 1952, Louise Thompson Patterson Papers, Sojourners for Truth and Justice subject file, box 12, folder 17, manuscript collection no. 869, Stuart A. Rose Manuscript, Archives and Rare Book Library, Emory University, Atlanta, Georgia.

37. Summary proceedings.

38. Truchman, "Negro and Jewish Women."

39. "Racism: Enemy of the Jewish People," typed manuscript, Emma Lazarus Division of Jewish Women's Clubs, box 9, folder 12, Emma Lazarus Federation.

40. "Racism: Enemy of the Jewish People."

41. Jennie Truchman, "Pilgrimage to Atlanta," *Jewish Life*, February 1954.

42. Eugene Gordon, "Common Economic Needs—Sound Basis For Brotherhood," *The Lamp*, March 1958, 1.

43. Preconvention notes, November 1958, Emma Lazarus Division of Jewish Women's Clubs, box 6, folder 5, Emma Lazarus Federation.

44. Report on the Fifth National Convention, September 1964, Emma Lazarus Division of Jewish Women's Clubs, box 6, folder 7, Emma Lazarus Federation.

45. "Re: Dymytryshyn et al. v. Esperdy," Blanch Freedman draft memorandum calling a meeting of all plaintiffs, January 6th, 1967. Eugene Gordon papers, b.1 f.10, Sc MG 117, Schomburg Center for Research in Black Culture, Manuscripts, Archives and Rare Books Division, New York Public Library, New York, New York (henceforth Schomburg).

46. Personal papers pertaining to June Gordon's death, Eugene Gordon Papers, box 1 folder 11, MG 117, Schomburg.

47. "Fifty Years of Women's Suffrage," souvenir journal, August 1970, Emma Lazarus Federation of Jewish Women's Clubs, Los Angeles, California, box 1, folder 7, Emma Lazarus Jewish Women's Clubs of Los Angeles Records, 1945–1980, Southern California Library for Social Studies and Research, University of Southern California Digital Library, Los Angeles, California.

Part II
A RADICAL URBAN BLACK BELT
Tackling Race, Colonialism, and Internationalism

"No Jim Crow in the IWO" was the defiant slogan of this uniquely interracial fraternal organization, and for twenty-four progressive years it lived up to this goal. Black artists and intellectuals found a home for their liberationist practice, with Langston Hughes and Paul Robeson producing work in IWO venues. The Order, as the IWO was referred to by its members, also advanced the career of Black Communist Louise Thompson Patterson. As IWO vice president, Patterson balanced the need to create an explicitly Black radical space for her social justice campaigns with her work with racialized immigrant Jewish, Slavic, Italian, and more conventionally white American IWO comrades.

4

DU BOIS'S COLD WAR REVISIONS
The Color Line and the Jewish Problem, from Galicia to Dougherty County

Ben Ratskoff

On April 16, 1952, Dr. W. E. B. Du Bois delivered a speech at the "Tribute to the Warsaw Ghetto Fighters" event organized by *Jewish Life* magazine, a monthly that had been connected with the Jewish Peoples Fraternal Order (JPFO) since 1946. This speech came at a precarious time for both the invited speaker and the inviting organization. On February 9, 1951, the US government had indicted Du Bois as an "unregistered foreign agent," alleging his anti-war Peace Information Center was illegally receiving orders from Moscow.[1] As a result, many of Du Bois's friends and supporters—including leadership of the National Association for the Advancement of Colored People (NAACP)—began to distance themselves from, or even publicly denounce, the octogenarian.[2] By this time, the JPFO—the Jewish section of the International Workers Order (IWO)—was nearly defunct, and the IWO was facing its own legal troubles: a New York court in June 1951 granted the state's request to dissolve the organization, a ruling the IWO appealed until its dissolution in 1954. Du Bois had been invited to speak at the tribute by *Jewish Life*'s managing editor Louis Harap. In a February letter, Harap noted the plan to include Black participants in the concert portion of the event and asked Du Bois to speak "on the significance of the ghetto fight for the Negro people of the United States today in relation to cooperation with their allies, the Jewish people and the common people of America."[3]

The invitation itself is not surprising; Du Bois had maintained a relationship with the JPFO since after the war, at least, and had given a speech for them as recently as 1950. When Du Bois was indicted in 1951, lawyer Vito Marcantonio, former congressman and then IWO vice president and Garibaldi Society leader, traveled to Washington to successfully take up Du Bois's defense. Du Bois was aware of the IWO's connections to his world, not least through the IWO's support of the American Labor Party (ALP), on whose ticket Du Bois ran in a failed bid to become a US senator from New York in 1950 alongside Marcantonio—then a seven-term congressman from East Harlem. Du Bois's companion and then spouse, writer and organizer Shirley Graham, was in 1951 a cofounder of the radical Black women's civil rights organization Sojourners for Truth and Justice along with Louise Thompson Patterson; Patterson was compelled to testify in a New York court in 1951 in the context of the IWO's shutdown since she had worked for the IWO for fifteen years and was a national vice president.[4]

Du Bois's speech was published in the May 1952 issue of *Jewish Life* as an essay titled "The Negro and the Warsaw Ghetto." This essay was structured as a travelogue of Du Bois's successive visits to Poland over nearly sixty years, culminating with his 1949 visit to the remains of the Warsaw Ghetto and Nathan Rapoport's memorial to the Warsaw Ghetto Uprising, erected in 1948.[5] These visits, Du Bois reflected, transformed his understanding of "the race problem" by putting pressure on his color line thesis, which had framed "race prejudice" primarily as "color prejudice."[6] For these visits revealed to Du Bois how, unlike in his previous understanding, race "cut across lines of color and physique and belief and status."[7] The cumulative discovery of familiar patterns of marginalization, segregation, and violence in the central and eastern European borderlands forced him to reevaluate the color line's scope as the primary or even exclusive frame for understanding the "Negro problem." Du Bois explained, "The problem of slavery, emancipation, and caste in the United States was no longer in my mind a separate and unique thing as I had so long conceived it." The result, Du Bois asserted, was an "enlarged" conception that did not supplant but rather refined his color line thesis.[8]

The color line thesis refers to Du Bois's epochal evaluation that hierarchically ordered perceptions and doctrines of human difference, coded primarily onto the physical body as skin pigmentation and hair texture, would function as the fundamental antagonism of the twentieth century. First articulated before the American Negro Academy in 1899 and again in his closing address to the first Pan-African Conference in London in 1900, Du Bois argued, "the problem of the twentieth century is the problem of the color line, the question as to how far differences of race, which show themselves chiefly in the color of the skin and the texture of the hair, will hereafter be made the basis of denying to over half the world the right of sharing to their utmost ability the opportunities and privileges of modern civilization."[9] As Nahum Dimitri Chandler summarizes it, "Du Bois was concerned with a certain idiom and practice" of proscribing human freedom, a form of "proscriptive distinction" produced out of the historical relations of

Atlantic slavery and modern imperialism.[10] Given this genealogy, Du Bois's formulation prioritized a light/dark, or white/Black, value scale as the fundamental axis of global racialization. Lewis Gordon notes that Du Bois's "problem of the color line" was "born from the divide of black and white" but also "serves as a blueprint for the ongoing division of humankind."[11]

The "Negro and the Warsaw Ghetto" is frequently cited as a model for comparison and solidarity, not least because of its self-critical admission that the color line may have expository limits. One claim as to its meaning can be seen at the United States Holocaust Memorial Museum, which includes the text in their "Experiencing History" digital teaching and learning platform of primary sources, part of the "Black Americans and World War II" collection. The website frames the essay as Du Bois's description of "the impact that viewing the ghetto ruins had on his thinking," arguing that Du Bois "abandoned his previous belief that antisemitism and white racism differed in their origins, and he moved towards a new 'unitary theory of prejudice' that understood both as forms of scapegoating and aggression."[12] This summary, which reduces Du Bois's comparative thought to a singular "theory of prejudice," lacks any mention of the first half of Du Bois's essay, which detailed his previous trips to Poland in 1893 and 1937, and overstates the development of Du Bois's thought in the wake of his visit to the Warsaw Ghetto ruins in 1949.[13]

Du Bois's claim to have revised the color line thesis in light of his gradual awareness of the "Jewish problem" has rarely received focused critical interrogation, nor have the essay's accounts of his nineteenth-century travels been studied.[14] Although Du Bois's recollection of his postwar visit raises important questions about the Holocaust's relationship to slavery and colonialism and the potential parallels between Black and Jewish ghettoization, his direct comments in the essay on the "Jewish problem" are quite limited and vague.[15] It would be a mistake, too, to characterize Du Bois's revision in 1952 as a sudden pivot from local to global concerns. In his first public articulation of the color line thesis at the American Negro Academy in 1899, Du Bois announced his purpose to "consider . . . the problem of the color line not simply as a national and personal question but rather in its larger world aspect."[16] This global framing explicitly included consideration of the "furious racial prejudice" exhibited during the contemporaneous Dreyfus Affair and the national "race conflict[s]" between Germans, Hungarians, Czechs, Jews, and Poles in the Austro-Hungarian Empire. A global perspective is one of the few constants across the many decades of Du Bois's writings.[17] Precisely how and why Du Bois's confrontation with the "Jewish problem" as early as 1893 compelled a revision of his color line thesis and a rearticulation of a global perspective in 1952 remains largely unexamined.

A close reading of this revision and of the role played by his earlier travels through the imperial borderlands of central and eastern Europe, as well as an exploration of the other revisions he made in this historical moment, shows how Du Bois, addressing a left Jewish audience during the Cold War Red Scare, developed a historicized conception of the color line by considering his personal relation to the regions from which many JPFO members—and IWO members more broadly—had immigrated. The far earlier travel recollected by Du Bois triangulated the color line with both Polish and Jewish minority problems, navigating the complex historical contingencies that had brought a Black American university student to the multinational regions of East Prussia and the Austro-Hungarian Empire. Not so incidentally, these regions included many of the national groups whose working-class immigrant sectors would unify under the banner of "interethnic solidarity" in the IWO—Poles, Slovaks, Hungarians, Jews, and others. The 1952 essay announcing his "enlarged view" was followed a year later by another revision: the literal reworking of references to Jews in Du Bois's most canonical text, *The Souls of Black Folk* (1903).[18] This sequence of rewritings suggests a broader revisionary process amid the Cold War Red Scare in which Du Bois was compelled to reconsider and refine his understanding of antisemitism and Jews and their relation to the color line.[19]

Du Bois on Travel and Comparison

In Du Bois's reflection on the significance of the Warsaw Ghetto Uprising for Black Americans and especially for their relationship to Jewish "allies" in the United States, Du Bois recounted his visits to Poland over some sixty years.[20] He introduced his reflection with a blunt assertion of sustained international travel and firsthand observation—"I have been to Poland three times"—before detouring readers to his student years in Berlin.[21] There, as Du Bois narrates, a Polish fellow student exposed him not to the negative treatment and representation of Jews, as one might have expected from the essay's context, but to German and Austrian imperial repression of the Polish minority.

It is worth dwelling on Du Bois's chosen literary form of the travelogue. Michael Rothberg notes that Du Bois's self-representation as a traveler in the May 1952 essay had special significance given the US government's indictment of him as an "unregistered foreign agent" a year earlier in 1951 and the related denial of his request for passport renewal as recently as February 1952.[22] At the same time, Du Bois's travelogue is unsurprising given his consistent foregrounding of transnational travel as a key mechanism through which he developed his understanding of race and the color line and especially their operation between local, national, and global contexts.[23] In the 1952 essay, Du Bois underscored the importance of transnational travel and interaction for his awareness of "the Jewish problem of the modern world and something of its history" and his "more complete understanding of the Negro problem," both in the United States and globally.[24] The relation between the Jewish problem and the color line could not be grasped and articulated from a detached, distant national viewpoint. For Du Bois, such an approach would misrepresent anti-Jewish discrimination in central and eastern Europe as the mirror image of the color line in the US South, expanding the specific situation of Black Americans rather than situating the two in a dynamic, global context.

Notably, Du Bois had resisted a simplistic, analogical internationalism two decades earlier in the context of the Scottsboro Nine's defense by the Communist Party of the United States (CPUSA). Then a critic of the CPUSA (although an admirer of the Soviet Union), Du Bois advocated for the legal defense organized and led by the NAACP—an organization he had helped found in 1909.[25] His "bright-eyed optimism" about Bolshevism in Russia was matched with a sober suspicion of white labor's unwillingness to break its racial solidarity with white elites in the United States.[26] In his "Postscript" column for the September 1931 issue of the NAACP magazine, *The Crisis*, Du Bois offered an "Editorial Critique of the Relation of the American Negro to Russian and American Communism," attempting to reconfigure Black American racialization in international and relational terms.[27] Du Bois argued pragmatically that the CPUSA's aggressive militancy would only inflame Southern white judges and, most urgently, enlist Black workers as "shock troops" of the revolution, all but ensuring their (and the Scottsboro defendants') death.[28] However, Du Bois also criticized what in his view was the sloppy application of Marxist mantras, promulgated from Moscow, onto the US South, generating a "ludicrous misapprehension" of white supremacy. In other words, Comintern theories of class exploitation, peasant uprisings, and proletarian internationalism could not easily or accurately assimilate what he called the "American situation." Still, in his early writings Du Bois was already making frequent references to Europe as a "figure of comparison, remark, and reference," including analogies in *Souls* between the situation of Black Americans and various European peasantries.[29]

But Du Bois in this 1931 column rejected an analogy to Jewish emancipation in the Russian Empire and Soviet Union. Du Bois argued that Black "emancipation will not come, as among the Jews, from an internal readjustment and ousting of exploiters; rather it will come from a wholesale emancipation from the grip of the white exploiters without."[30] Du Bois's criticism of the analogy functioned to defang both the CPUSA's antagonism toward middle-class Black leadership and its idealization of white labor's interracial interests. Du Bois's characterization of Jewish emancipation as the normative foil to Black emancipation in the United States framed the former as an internal class struggle against an exploitative Jewish bourgeoisie, and thus a "foreign" model of minority emancipation more suited to Communist doctrine. He suggested that the global application of this model flattened local and national specificity, demonstrating "the error into which long-distance interpretation, unsupported by real knowledge, may fall."[31] By "real knowledge," Du Bois implied the kind of immersive intimacy and firsthand observation gained through sustained travel, correctives that could foreground the specific political economies and ideological formations that gave minority problems their shape while not foreclosing a necessarily international perspective.

Du Bois's criticism of Communist "misapprehension" in the context of the Scottsboro case anticipated his approach to the "Jewish problem" in his 1952 essay for *Jewish Life*. In that essay, Du Bois did not depart from the assumed commensurability of Black and Jewish ghettoization (and its implications for organized revolt or collective solidarity), as one might have expected given the essay's solicitation for a Warsaw Ghetto Uprising tribute. Du Bois rather presented his encounter with the "Jewish problem" as a series of insights and reorientations accumulated through the course of multiple journeys in the central and eastern European borderlands.[32] This revisionary process reconfigured the color line in comparative relation to an expansive set of racializing idioms and autobiographical examples, beginning with his confrontation with German-Polish antagonism in the late nineteenth century. Du Bois commenced not with the visit to the ghetto ruins but his interaction with racialized minority problems in the imperial age of European nationalisms.

Du Bois underscored that of all his visits to Poland his "view of the Warsaw ghetto" was particularly critical to his "more complete understanding of the Negro problem," helping him "emerge from a certain social provincialism" that characterized the color line as "separate and unique."[33] But in his comments on visiting postwar Warsaw, Du Bois only alluded to the color line as a contrast to the German destruction of the city amid and following the Warsaw Uprising of 1944, led by the underground Polish Home Army: "I have seen something of human upheaval in this world: the scream and shots of a race riot in Atlanta; the marching of the Ku Klux Klan; the threat of courts and police; the neglect and destruction of human habitation; but nothing in my wildest imagination was equal to what I saw in Warsaw in 1949. . . . There had been complete, planned and utter destruction."[34] As for the prior visit to Poland in 1937, Du Bois said almost nothing, dwelling instead on a curious conversation in Berlin with a German ambivalent about Nazi rule. A more extensive record of this visit to Germany and Poland, including his then interpretation of Nazi antisemitism, can be found in the columns he wrote in correspondence for the *Pittsburgh Courier*.[35] The surprising minimization of this 1937 visit in the 1952 essay draws further attention to Du Bois's lopsided focus on the first visit. Indeed, it was his first visit to Poland in 1893 that received an extended reflection in the essay, and this reflection was the most detailed and illustrative of Du Bois's evolving conception of race. Furthermore, the chronicle of this first visit included a critical experience that had hitherto been unmentioned in Du Bois's recollections of his time in Europe as a student, an experience he describes as already potentially expanding his conception of "race."[36]

The First Visit

Du Bois's introductory description that "the first time" he went to Poland was as "a student at the University of Berlin" referred straightforwardly to the visit made during summer vacation. But it also indicated Du Bois's indirect path from the color line to the "Jewish problem." When Du Bois was a young student in 1893, an independent Polish state did not exist and the borderland regions of the German and Austro-Hungarian empires were home to millions of Poles and Jews. Mapping German imperial power while complicating his conception of "race problems," Du Bois's detour to the university highlighted the transnational movements producing an encounter in Berlin between a Black American abroad and a conservative Polish student from an influential family of the Kraków intelligentsia.[37] The geographic detour through Berlin and the conceptual detour through the Polish problem also demonstrated the imperial dislocations entangling multiple minority groups and dislocated the "Jewish problem" itself from a fixed position of direct comparison. And the rhetorical move from abstract Poland ("I have been to Poland three times") to historical German Reich called attention to the historicity of national borders and consequent contingency of minority "problems."

Overall, Du Bois's travelogue did not arrange a trio of direct comparisons between the oppression of Polish, Jewish, and Black people. Rather, it revealed complex sets of interlocking minority problems at contingent sites of racialization: the overlapping of German, Polish, and Jewish minority problems across the imperial borderlands of central and eastern Europe, the dichotomy of national ("Aryan") revolution and intensified Jewish exclusion in the Third Reich, and the contradiction between dystopic, postwar destruction and utopian, Socialist rebirth in the Republic of Poland. Du Bois did not measure the color line against the "Jewish problem" as much as he historicized and triangulated oppressed minority groups across local, national, and global and international scales, outlining their convergences, homologies, asymmetries, and interactions across space and time.

The Polish schoolmate described by Du Bois was Stanisław Estreicher. Estreicher would critically bookend Du Bois's 1952 travelogue; Du Bois alluded near the conclusion of his essay to Estreicher's 1939 murder in the Sachsenhausen concentration camp.[38] At its start, however, Du Bois wrote, "The first time [I visited Poland] was 59 years ago, when I was a student at the University of Berlin. I had been talking to my schoolmate, Stanislaus Ritter von Estreicher. I had been telling him of the race problem in America, which seemed to me at the time the only race problem and the greatest social problem of the world. He brushed it aside. He said, 'You know nothing, really, about real race problems.'"[39] Estreicher's hyperbolic reaction seems to assert a competitive logic, provincializing Du Bois's personal experience and minimizing its global relevance. But Estreicher also stretched Du Bois's conception of the color line by referring him to seemingly incommensurate problems of nationalism and imperialism in central and eastern Europe's borderlands.

Estreicher described "the problem of the Poles and particularly of that part of them who were included in the German empire; of their limited education; of the refusal to let them speak their own language; of the few careers that they were allowed to follow; of the continued insult to their culture and family life."[40] (Some of these problems were ones with which the Jewish, Slovak, Polish, and other immigrant members of the IWO, far poorer than Estreicher, would also have been familiar.) Du Bois explained, "Race problems at the time were to me purely problems of color, and principally of slavery in the United States and near-slavery in Africa." Estreicher challenged this narrow conception through his discussion of intra-European minority policies and racial discourses.

The "problem of the Poles . . . in the German empire" revealed to Du Bois a system of underdevelopment, cultural repression, and discrimination whose political structure did not derive from chattel slavery and whose racial idiom did not appear definitively organized by an epidermal value hierarchy. The imperial dislocation of Polish people, the racial shape of the German drive to the east, and the Germanization policies of Polish Prussia had no evident correspondence within the problem of the color line, as Du Bois understood it.[41] Du Bois "was astonished," and this led him to promise to visit Estreicher at his home in Kraków (then in the Austro-Hungarian Empire, which imposed its own restrictions on its Slavic subjects) during summer vacation. In Du Bois's retelling, radical difference and incommensurability prompted curiosity, not closure, and transnational travel promised an opportunity to acquire "real knowledge." The essay as a whole was framed by this momentous confrontation with the German racialization of Poles, yet the precise relation between Du Bois's "problems of color" and Estreicher's "problem of the Poles" remained, at this juncture, unclear.

The subsequent paragraph, in which Du Bois reported his "discovery" of the "Jewish problem," ostensibly detailed his summer visit to Estreicher in Poland in 1893, but it was in fact dominated by Du Bois's surprising "new experience with a new race problem" while en route, an experience that would become a sort of primal scene for Du Bois's comparative understanding of race: "On the way" to Kraków, Du Bois was apparently mistaken by his cab driver for a Jew.[42] It is notable that Du Bois presented an experience here rather than information received in dialogue (as with Estreicher) or from reading. Experience is the critical term Du Bois had used in *Souls* to describe his simultaneously personal and historical sense of racialization: "Being a problem is a strange experience."[43] One might suggest that the autobiographical example of Du Bois's misidentification by the cab driver invokes and supplements the infamous scene of "revelation" at the New England schoolhouse when a classmate refused Du Bois's visiting card. At that moment, Du Bois said, it "dawned upon me with a certain suddenness that I was different from the others."[44] Unlike Du Bois the child's self-conscious realization of racial difference, the cab driver's mistake disarticulated Du Bois from the racial identity imposed on him by the color line in New England while assimilating him to local Galician codes governing relations between groups. In the process, the problem of the color line was both delimited and redeployed.

As Du Bois narrated in the 1952 essay, the cab driver "looked at me and asked if I wanted to stop '*unter die Juden*.'"[45] Du Bois "was a little puzzled, but told him 'Yes.' So we went to a little Jewish hotel on a small, out of the way street. There I realized another problem of race or religion, I did not know which, which had to do with the treatment and segregation of large numbers of human beings."[46] The experiential nature of Du Bois's realization here, and its exemplary function in his comparative analysis, underscores how for him the personal and the global intersect.

Du Bois did not encounter the "Jewish problem" as a foreign observer or listener, nor did the segregation and marginalization of Jews present an additional, faraway problem with no apparent correspondence to his own. Du Bois provisionally experienced himself within the "Jewish problem." As Du Bois wrote, the cab driver "looked at me," his gaze interpellating Du Bois's body and steering its movements accordingly. While the cab driver's gaze re-sorted Du Bois from Blackness to Jewishness, it also signaled a continuity between the problem of the color line and the "Jewish problem." The intersection of the personal and global in this experience pointed to a puzzling new convergence of anti-Black and anti-Jewish signifiers, a kind of Jewish Blackness, which materialized from the cab driver's gaze and subsequent decoding of Du Bois's body. The color line was thus not entirely irrelevant to central and eastern European "race problems," as Estreicher had suggested.[47]

This encounter inserted the "Jewish problem" into Du Bois's literal and conceptual "visit" to Poland, and in so doing revealed a shared repertoire of visual codes and social practices that twisted the color line beyond the context or legacy of chattel slavery. Du Bois concluded, "I went on to Krakow [sic], becoming more and more aware of two problems of human groups, and then came back to the university, not a little puzzled as to my own race problem and its place in the world."[48] The central and eastern European patterns of anti-Jewish oppression that he "discovered" modified the hitherto unique status of the Black American situation and at the same time activated the color line within Europe's internal empires. Du Bois enlarged his conception of the color line to account for a renewed exemplarity of corporeal darkness *and also* the incommensurable specificity of central and eastern European visual hierarchies of human difference.[49]

Du Bois retold this story in the posthumously published autobiography, *A Soliloquy on Viewing My Life from the Last Decade of Its First Century* (1968). This version contained considerably more detail about how Du Bois's trek across the borderlands exposed him to uncanny dynamics of nationalism and marginalization. Furthermore, this autobiography elaborated on Du Bois's experience with the cab driver. Du Bois clarified that he departed from Vienna for Budapest and then ultimately across the Tatra Mountains on foot and into Galicia. In his retelling of the impetus for the journey, Du Bois presented a less competitive response from the student Estreicher: "While at Berlin, I found myself once explaining to a schoolmate, Stanislaus Ritter von Estreicher, the race problem in America. He was not as impressed as I thought he should be. He said: 'I understand only too well; but you should see the race antagonism in my home. Come to Krakow [sic] and see the clash of German and Pole!'"[50] Here, Estreicher responded to Du Bois with empathetic identification and made a more boldly racial representation of a binary antagonism between Germans and Poles in Galicia. As in the *Jewish Life* essay, Estreicher was silent on the problem of the Jewish minority. Du Bois continued, "I promised that I would visit him when near. So now I travelled alone into Hungary, with the object of turning north through Slovenia and over the Tatra mountains into Poland. It was a journey with a hint of adventure and with a far-off likeness to my American South."[51]

This attribution to the multinational borderlands of a "far-off likeness to my American South" bears further analysis. Du Bois's American South, at that young age, was the post-Reconstruction South to which he had journeyed while enrolling at Fisk University in 1885. This South, Du Bois wrote, was "a region where the world was split into white and black halves, and where the darker half was held back by race prejudice and legal bonds, as well as by deep ignorance and dire poverty. But facing this was not a lost group, but at Fisk a microcosm of a world and a civilization in potentiality. . . . A new loyalty and allegiance replaced my

Americanism: henceforward I was a Negro."[52] Though Du Bois did not elaborate further on the synchronic "likeness" between the "far-off" regions, the parallel suggested spatialized segregation and immiseration while raising the problem of nationalism and its subaltern doubles.[53] Both resource-rich regions were peripherally dependent on centers of industrial capital as the fortunes of landowning aristocrats declined; moreover, both witnessed the development of powerful, nationalist resentments toward industrial and imperial power perceived as foreign. In his autobiography, Du Bois wrote of his central and eastern European travels, "In Budapest I was struck by the hostility to German Austria. . . . The Hungarians were asserting their desire for independence."[54] Just as the move from North to South tilted his identity toward the segregated Black side of American society, travel from Berlin to Kraków implicated Du Bois in the local and multinational landscape of ethnic hostility and nationalist aspiration: however briefly, he was assumed to be a Galitzianer Jew.

When Du Bois described the experience with the cab driver in the autobiography, he provided a more forthright interpretation of the racial dynamics than he did in the *Jewish Life* essay, extending the color line to describe Europe's internal hierarchies. He wrote of his train travel across "Hungary": "My dark face elicited none of the curiosity which it had in blonde north Germany, for there were too many dark Gypsies and other brunettes. I was several times mistaken for a Jew; arriving one night in a town of north Slovenia [sic], the driver of a rickety cab whispered in my ear, 'Unter die Juden?' I stared and then said yes. I stayed in a little Jewish inn."[55] Here Du Bois provided a richer description of European physical diversity, noting his comfortable assimilation to the southeastern social landscape but also his consequent mistaken identification within it. He also multiplied the experience reported in *Jewish Life* by recalling that it occurred "several times" en route from Budapest to Kraków. In doing so, Du Bois transformed the chance encounter in that essay into an iterative process, one that repeatedly decoded his specific, Black American body according to anti-Jewish contexts and ideologies in Austria-Hungary. The "Jewish problem" appeared to cohere within the problem of the color line at the same time that racialization was rendered a false measure of identity. The seeming overlap between his "own" problem and the racialization of Jews (and Roma and others) demonstrated that the problem of the color line, pace Estreicher, did in fact have direct relevance in central and eastern Europe, ordering social relations between various minoritized groups.

This intriguing experience with the cab driver has been remarked upon by scholars seeking to demonstrate noncompetitive study and comparison of Black and Jewish racialization or a certain worldly basis for solidarity in Du Bois. Most notably, Paul Gilroy's *The Black Atlantic* mentions it when discussing the influence of the "Jewish problem" on the development of Pan-Africanism.[56] Harold

Brackman frames the experience as anomalous in the young Du Bois's otherwise limited understanding of antisemitism.[57] For Rothberg, the experience reveals the "necessary misunderstanding" that produces comparative insights and also "allegoriz[es] his position of enunciation in 'The Negro and the Warsaw Ghetto,'" addressing Jews from within the pages of *Jewish Life*.[58] Chandler understands it as opening a "new sense of possible companionship" and giving shape to a "fantastic sense of an illimitable collectivity."[59]

It is unclear, though, how much Du Bois's reading of the experience adequately accounted for local histories, behaviors, and social structures. Du Bois interpreted an assumption behind the cab driver's suggestion of the Jewish inn: the assumption that Du Bois was a Jew. This interpretation read the cab driver's suggestion as the social enforcement of some kind of segregation. While entirely plausible, this interpretation reflects the logic of the color line in the US South, where the binary segregation of social space extended to public accommodations. Jews, however, had historically functioned as innkeepers in Galicia, due to the lease system of Polish noble estates; and it is possible the Jewish inn in this unnamed village was a legacy of this history even though, by the time of Du Bois's travels, the decline of the Polish nobility had diminished the number of Jewish innkeepers.[60] It is thus possible the cab driver did not mean to interpellate Du Bois as a Jew by directing him to a Jewish inn. He might have straightforwardly proposed a lodging establishment to a traveler in need, according to local history and idiom.

While certainly destabilizing Du Bois's impression of some kind of Jewish Blackness in Galicia, this supplementary interpretation emphasizes how Du Bois's "discovery" of the "Jewish problem" passed through subjective experience, essential but imperfect. Together, his interpretation and the supplementary one above represent the experience not as an epiphany providing comparative closure but a question mark, an ongoing inquiry into the color line's global relevance and relation to intersecting but not identical patterns of social marginalization. The multiple versions of the story, along with its ambiguous meaning, emphasize the ongoing process of revision necessary for comparisons elaborated across time and space and suggest a more cautious approach to claims of Jewish Blackness in central and eastern Europe.

Furthermore, by sketching the potential convergence of anti-Black and anti-Jewish signifiers, Du Bois drew attention to his own specific intimacy with the "Jewish problem." As with the color line in the US South, the "Jewish problem" signaled a minority problem veiled in the discourses of national empires. In Galicia, Du Bois was unexpectedly, briefly brought behind the Polish veil, recognizing a conceptual traffic between the color line and the "Jewish problem." Ultimately, Du Bois reconfigured the color line only in an oblique relation to

Estreicher's Polish minority problem, a relation mediated by the problem of Polish and Slovak marginalization of Jews. Estreicher's "problem of the Poles" had initially delimited Du Bois's understanding of race and the color line and this problem was itself now delimited by Du Bois's experience of the Polish or Slovak cab driver who interpellated him as a native Jew. Minority problems were not directly comparable because they were themselves overlapping and hierarchically structured. Du Bois would remark later in the 1952 essay, "How much [Estreicher] realized that behind the Polish problem lay the Jewish problem and that all were one crime against civilization, I do not know."[61] Solidarity urgently required a self-critical form of comparison.

Revising *Souls*

This first visit to Poland is the only one of Du Bois's three visits that occurred before he wrote *The Souls of Black Folk*. This chronology is especially striking: what is described as "a new experience with a new race problem" in the 1952 essay apparently preceded both his most famous formulation of "the strange meaning of being black here in the dawning of the Twentieth Century" and affirmation that "the problem of the Twentieth Century is the problem of the color-line" in the 1903 *Souls*.[62] His 1893 experience in Galicia might have theoretically informed the essays that make up *Souls* since it ostensibly occurred before their composition.[63] Yet Du Bois only disclosed the 1893 experience with the cab driver in 1952, marking its belated interpretation in his public thought. While Du Bois's time as a student in Berlin certainly informed the arguments published in *Souls*, a modification and enlargement of the color line conception is not evident—on the contrary, *Souls* remains the most cited source for Du Bois's *original* formulation of the problem of the color line rather than an exhibit of its revision.

For Europe remained something of an exception to the global color line in Du Bois's early writings. He stated in *Souls* that "being a problem is a strange experience,—peculiar even for one who has never been anything else, save perhaps in babyhood and in Europe."[64] Du Bois's 1899 address to the American Negro Academy provided a global illustration of "the race problem in space" that ended with "the one part of the world where we have not visited in our quest of the color line—Europe."[65] He continued, "There are three significant things in Europe of to-day which must attract us: the Jew and Socialist in France, the Expansion of Germany and Russia, and the race troubles of Austria. None of these bring us directly upon the question of color; and yet nearly all touch it indirectly." All three of these topics correlate to Du Bois's interaction with Estreicher and his travel across the borderlands: nationalist antisemitism (here referring to the Dreyfus

Affair), German imperialism, and minority problems in Austria-Hungary. These topics are positioned on the periphery of Du Bois's conception of the color line, as, he argued, they only "touch [questions of color] indirectly."[66]

It is noteworthy that Du Bois described how "puzzling" he found the "outcome" of the "curious and complicated race conflict between Germans, Hungarians, Czechs, Jews and Poles," which Chandler explains as the German and Hungarian suppression of minority groups and their resistance to this suppression.[67] This language confirms Du Bois's recollection in the 1952 essay of the puzzling impact his travels in the borderlands had on him, although by 1952 Du Bois had clarified that this puzzlement was directed toward the color line: "I . . . came back to the university, not a little puzzled as to my own race problem and its place in the world."[68] Du Bois's disjointed and protracted recollection of events suggests that the experience in Galicia was not immediately meaningful. Only after central and eastern European antisemitism was marshaled by a regime of mass murder and after Cold War hysteria instigated the persecution of Communists in the United States was Du Bois compelled to revise his conception of the color line.

This revisionary process ultimately extended to *Souls*, one year after the 1952 essay was published. In February 1953, Du Bois wrote to Herbert Aptheker expressing his desire to make five minor revisions to the text of *Souls*. These revisions were included in the 1953 jubilee edition published by Blue Heron Press, a press that published texts likely to be targeted by McCarthyism.[69] All five of Du Bois's requested revisions addressed references to Jews in the Black Belt. As editors Henry Louis Gates Jr. and Terri Hume Oliver point out in the 1999 critical edition of *Souls*, there were modifications made to eight references to Jews.[70] While the original references were undoubtedly stigmatizing and likely reflected the language of his native informants, they can also be considered part of Du Bois's attempt to situate the history and present of the Black Belt in a global context, not only through analogy to European regions but also by tracing transnational migration to the United States. These were not the only references to Jews in *Souls*; positive depictions of biblical figures—including Jesus as a "dark and pierced Jew"—are also evident.[71]

Du Bois's modifications in 1953 for the most part translated representations of avaricious Jewish capitalists in the post-Reconstruction South into more sociologically abstract representations of "foreigners," "immigrants," and "American[s]."[72] The original 1903 edition read, "The Jew is the heir of the slave-baron in Dougherty. . . . Here and there are tales of projects for money-getting, born in the swift days of Reconstruction . . . nearly all failed, and the Jew fell heir."[73] The 1953 modifications for the jubilee edition swapped out the Jewish carpetbaggers for generic immigrants and foreigners: "Immigrants are heirs of the slave-baron in

Dougherty.... Here and there are tales of projects for money-getting, ... most failed, and foreigners fell heir."[74] Du Bois's revision of the color line at the *Jewish Life* tribute and his decision a year later to revise *Souls* raise questions about the correlation between Du Bois's "enlarged view" of the color line and the erasure of references to Jews in the post-Reconstruction South.[75]

The 1952 essay was not the original impetus for revising the passages in *Souls*. When he wrote to Aptheker, Du Bois explained that after having had the opportunity to reread *Souls* for "the first time in years," he found "five incidental references to Jews. I recall that years ago Jacob Schiff wrote me criticizing these references and that I denied any thought of race or religious prejudice and promised to go over the passages in future editions. The editions however succeeded each other without any consultation with me, and evidently the matter slipped my mind."[76] Frankfurt-born Jewish railroad investor, military financier, and liberal philanthropist Jacob Schiff had funded the formation of the NAACP and sat on its inaugural board. A Reconstruction-era immigrant to the United States, Schiff had grown up on Frankfurt's Judengasse, one of the once-gated "ghettos" Du Bois had visited in Europe and evoked in his writing.

In the 1952 essay, Du Bois linked the Judengasse and Warsaw Ghetto in a historical pattern of segregation and immiseration, although his experience of the former largely contrasted with the latter: "One afternoon, I was taken out to the former [Warsaw] ghetto. I knew all too little of its story although I had visited ghettos in parts of Europe, particularly in Frankfort [sic], Germany. Here there was not much to see. There was complete and total waste, and a monument."[77] In a 1936 column for the *Pittsburgh Courier*—sent as correspondence from Du Bois's second visit to Poland—Du Bois alluded to Schiff by name: "I have seen the old Juden-gasse in Frankfort [sic], where the Rothschils [sic], Schiffs and other great capitalists were caged up of nights in narrow quarters, lest they contaminate Christians; and where they laid the foundations of wealth and power, despite insult and oppression."[78] Although Nazi ghettoization differed sharply from the late medieval and early modern segregation of Jews, the link drawn by Du Bois between Schiff's marginalized birthplace and the Nazi biopolitical governance of space in occupied Poland makes the return to Schiff's criticism in 1953 all the more poignant.[79] Du Bois actually vacillated on the question of revising *Souls*. After his initial letter, he wrote, "Even unconscious repetition of current folklore such as the concept of Jews as more guilty of exploitation than others had helped the Hitlers of the world.... But [eliminating the references] I finally realized would be historically inaccurate. I have therefore with some regret let the passages stand as written believing that other references to Jews in this very book and my evident personal indebtedness to Jewish culture will absolve me from blame and unfairness."[80]

While Du Bois ultimately did make the revisions for the 1953 edition, his comments here reveal both an awareness of how representations of Jewish exploitation functioned politically and a concern with the text's historicity. The revisions of *Souls* displaced the generalizations that conflated Jews with exploitation by foregrounding instead the role of immigration in the dissolution of the plantocracy and the reproduction of the Black Belt. Du Bois's revisions were still somewhat inaccurate and might have rankled Jewish, Polish, or Italian IWO members or other readers: with few exceptions, immigrants did not control the industries of the New South. In the chapter "Of the Sons of Master and Man" there is also one revision that reframes anti-Black exploitation from an immigrant vocation to a homegrown Americanism. The 1903 edition reads, "I have seen, in the Black Belt of Georgia, an ignorant, honest Negro buy and pay for a farm in installments three separate times, and then in the face of law and decency the enterprising Russian Jew who sold it to him pocketed money and deed and left the black man landless"; in the 1953 edition, "enterprising Russian Jew" became "enterprising American."[81]

Critically, this revision de-ethnicized the capitalist exploiters of Black people, depicting the reproduction of the color line as a national heritage rather than an ethnically Jewish trait. Such a move revealed not simply critical attention to how antisemitic stereotypes distorted the source of economic suffering, but also a revised understanding of the color line's historical and spatial contingency, such that Russian Jewish migrants became (white) Americans in the Black Belt—similar to how Du Bois's Black American identity was delimited when he "became" a Jew in Galicia. Alongside the other changes highlighting generic immigrants, one can conclude that Du Bois, as in the essay, modified but did not displace his understanding of the global framework shaping the post-Reconstruction Black Belt. In his letter to Aptheker, Du Bois admitted, "As I re-read these words today, I see that . . . harm might come if they were allowed to stand as they are. First of all, I am not at all sure that the foreign exploiters to whom I referred in my study of the Black Belt, were in fact Jews. I took the word of my informants, and I am now wondering if in fact Russian Jews in any number were in Georgia at the time. But even if they were, what I was condemning was the exploitation and not the race nor religion."[82] Du Bois here cast doubt on his ethnographic knowledge, circumscribed by the biases of those to whom he had access, and he espoused a Marxist emphasis on practice over identity without erasing the specificity of the migrant role.

Erasing the Jewish descriptor of exploitation, Du Bois instead implied its generic whiteness and Americanness, opting for a political vocabulary that triangulated emancipated Blacks with native Southern whites and European immigrants. The revision accounted for multiple idioms of racialization and modulated them carefully. When writing the first edition of *Souls*, which was superficially evocative of European Jewish migration to the Black Belt, Du Bois had not yet brought the "Jewish problem" to bear on his conception of the color line in the historicized and contingent ways outlined in the "Negro and the Warsaw Ghetto" essay. They remained only indirectly linked, as Du Bois described in his 1899 address. Only once he arrived at his understanding of the color line's historically contingent convergences in central and eastern Europe—his "becoming" a Jew— did he account for a revised conception not simply of antisemitism but also of its dynamic and contingent relation to the problem of the color line. This growing conception led him to erase Jewishness from the jubilee edition almost entirely. If some of the capitalist exploiters were indeed *Jewish* immigrants, characterizing them as such obfuscated their functionally operative whiteness or Americanness in the post-Reconstruction South. Moreover, it suggested a timeless association between Jews and foreign exploitation that would contribute to nativist forms of antisemitism targeting his Jewish Communist peers and interlocuters in the 1950s, including Aptheker as well as IWO members Ethel and Julius Rosenberg. He wrote to Aptheker, "I did not, when writing, realize that by stressing the name of the group instead of what some members of the /_group_/ [sic] may have done, I was unjustly maligning people in exactly the same way my folk were then and are now falsely accused."[83]

By the time of Du Bois's revisions, anti-immigrant hysteria was rampant. IWO members such as the Polonia Society's Henry Podolski and the American Hellenic Brotherhood's Peter Harisiades had been deported as politically undesirable aliens, as were some of those Du Bois was more likely to know from local political circles, such as IWO member Michael Salerno, editor of the Italian Communist newspaper *L'Unita del Popolo* (Unity of the people). Jamaica-born Communist Claudia Jones, a friend of his wife Shirley Graham Du Bois, was already imprisoned, and would soon be deported, too.[84] As George Bornstein notes, the substitution of terms such as "immigrant" and "foreigner" "carry their problems of their own in both his time and ours and could be seen as fueling either xenophobia or resistance to immigration."[85] However, the timing overlaps with the US State Department indicting Du Bois as an "unregistered foreign agent" for the Soviet Union in 1951, one month before the Rosenbergs were convicted of espionage.[86] In 1952, the State Department confiscated his passport; this was shortly after he signed the "We Charge Genocide" petition that William Patterson and Paul Robeson submitted to the United Nations.[87] The State Department had ensnared Du Bois in its own nativist crosshairs, a nativist anti-Communism. While the substitution of terms such as "immigrant" and "foreigner" in 1953 might reflect too great an emphasis on protecting against particular ethnic discrimination at the expense of protecting against nativism itself, it can also be interpreted with reference to Du Bois's own targeting as a Black "foreign agent."[88]

The 1952 essay may not have led directly to Du Bois's subsequent reworking of *Souls*, but in tandem these works suggest the Cold War Red Scare was an extraordinary revisionary moment. What had once appeared as discrete and incommensurable "race problems" became a shifting series of sites of convergence, from the discursive convergence of epidermal darkness to the political convergence of nativist anti-Communism. The revisions might indicate the influence of the elderly Du Bois's Cold War interlocutors and a certain gratitude toward those who remained at or rallied to his side. His abandonment by Black middle-class leadership struck a direct blow to another of his earliest theses: that of the Talented Tenth.[89] In contrast, some of the working class, including a number of large trade unions, the IWO, the ALP, and the Communist-affiliated Jefferson School of Social Science where he taught, were unwavering in their support.

Du Bois had long been skeptical of Socialism's viability in the United States, largely due to his suspicion of white labor. However, when persecuted by the US government and isolated from a number of friends and colleagues, "standing resolutely by his side were communists."[90] It is thus likely that the political landscape of the postwar United States and the particular persecution he suffered within it provoked a wide-ranging reevaluation of his arguments on race and class. It is not surprising that this broader reevaluation, including of the Talented Tenth thesis, appeared in the "Negro and the Warsaw Ghetto" essay. Du Bois concluded that text by warning, "Negroes are dividing by social classes, and selling their souls to those who want war and colonialism, in order to become part of the ruling plutarchy, and encourage their sons to kill 'Gooks.' Among Jews there is the same dichotomy and inner strife, which forgets the bravery of the Warsaw ghetto and the bones of the thousands of dead who still lie buried in that dust. All this should lead both these groups and others to reassess and reformulate the problems of our day."[91] This text, along with the revisions Du Bois made to *Souls*, offer a critical contribution to the reassessment and reformulation of these problems as the Cold War began to reshape the globe.

NOTES

1. Charisse Burden-Stelly and Gerald Horne, *W.E.B. Du Bois: A Life in American History* (ABC-CLIO, 2019), 172.

2. Burden-Stelly and Horne, *Du Bois*, 173.

3. Letter from *Jewish Life* to W. E. B. Du Bois, February 13, 1952, W. E. B. Du Bois Papers, mums312-b137-i103, MS 312, Special Collections and University Archives, University of Massachusetts Amherst Libraries, University of Massachusetts, Amherst, Massachusetts, https://credo.library.umass.edu/view/full/mums312-b137-i103. Henceforth, Du Bois Papers. The letter refers to a "concert-meeting."

4. See Gerald Horne, *Black & Red: W.E.B. Du Bois and the Afro-American Response to the Cold War, 1944–1963* (State University of New York Press, 1986), 283; Burden-Stelly and Horne, *Du Bois*, 175. See Erik S. McDuffie, *Sojourning for Freedom: Black Women,*

American Communism, and the Making of Black Left Feminism (Duke University Press, 2011), 139. For Thompson Patterson's testimony, see transcript: *Court of Appeals of the State of New York in the Matter of the Application of the People of the State of New York, by Alfred J. Bohlinger, Superintendent of Insurance of the State of New York, Petitioner-Respondent, for an Order Directing Him to Take Possession of the Property and to Liquidate the Business, and Dissolving the Corporate Existence, of the International Workers Order, Inc., Respondent-Appellant,* 1951, 3767, https://catalog.hathitrust.org/Record/005663863.

5. The monument, funded by donations, including from the JPFO, was built by sculptor Nathan Rapoport on the site of the Warsaw Ghetto to mark the fifth anniversary of the Ghetto Uprising. The JPFO sent a delegate to attend the monument's unveiling. See Rubin Saltzman to Joel Lazebnik about donations, October 1947, International Workers Order (IWO) Records #5276, box 53, folder 18, Kheel Center for Labor-Management Documentation and Archives, Catherwood Library, Cornell University, Ithaca, New York (henceforth Kheel), https://digital.library.cornell.edu/catalog/ss:19043927; Central Committee of Jews in Poland (CKŻP, Centralny Komitet Żydów w Polsce), Regarding the monument to Ghetto heroes, April 1947, box 45, folder 7, Kheel, https://digital.library.cornell.edu/catalog/ss:21072801; outline notes for two talks (early 1948), box 53, folder 25, Kheel, https://digital.library.cornell.edu/catalog/ss:19043952.

6. Du Bois, "The Negro and the Warsaw Ghetto," *Jewish Life: A Progressive Monthly* 6, no. 7 (May 1952): 14.

7. Du Bois, "The Negro and the Warsaw Ghetto," 15.

8. Du Bois, "The Negro and the Warsaw Ghetto," 15.

9. Pan-African Association, "To the Nations of the World," [1900?], mums312-b004-i321, MS 312, Du Bois Papers, https://credo.library.umass.edu/view/full/mums312-b004-i321.

10. Nahum Dimitri Chandler, *"Beyond This Narrow Now" Or, Delimitations, of W. E. B. Du Bois* (Duke University Press, 2022), 9–10.

11. Lewis Gordon, *Existentia Africana: Understanding Africana Existential Thought* (Routledge, 2000), 63.

12. United States Holocaust Memorial Museum, "W. E. B. Du Bois: 'The Negro and the Warsaw Ghetto,'" Black Americans and World War II, Experiencing History: Holocaust Sources in Context, accessed December 7, 2023, https://perspectives.ushmm.org/item/w-e-b-du-bois-the-negro-and-the-warsaw-ghetto. The speech has no reference to scapegoating per se. See Harold Brackman, "'A Calamity Almost Beyond Comprehension': Nazi Anti-Semitism and the Holocaust in the Thought of W. E. B. Du Bois," *American Jewish History* 88, no. 1 (March 2000): 86.

13. Holocaust Memorial Museum, "W. E. B. Du Bois."

14. Du Bois uses the term "Jewish problem" four times in his essay. One exception to the lack of attention to Du Bois's claim to have modified his conception of the color line is found in Michael Rothberg's close reading, which asserts that "Du Bois can serve as a model of multidirectional memory because of the way his writings on Jews, race, and genocide hold together commonality and difference in a revised version of double consciousness." See Rothberg, *Multidirectional Memory: Remembering the Holocaust in the Age of Decolonization* (Stanford University Press, 2009), 112. Also see 116, 121.

15. Du Bois, "The Negro and the Warsaw Ghetto," 14.

16. Du Bois, "The Present Outlook for the Dark Races of Mankind," in *The Problem of the Color Line at the Turn of the Twentieth Century: The Essential Early Essays*, ed. Nahum Dimitri Chandler (Fordham University Press, 2015), 111, 118–19.

17. See Robin D. G. Kelley, "'But a Local Phase of a World Problem': Black History's Global Vision, 1883–1950," in "The Nation and Beyond: Transnational Perspectives on United States History," special issue, *The Journal of American History* 86, no. 3 (December

1999): 1045–77. Chandler insists that the global perspective exhibited in Du Bois's color line thesis was "developed initially from Du Bois's attempt to understand the specific African American situation" and was formulated "during the half dozen years before the publication of his most famous book [*The Souls of Black Folk* in 1903]." Chandler, *"Beyond This Narrow Now,"* 13–14.

18. Du Bois, "The Negro and the Warsaw Ghetto," 15; W. E. B. Du Bois, *The Souls of Black Folk*, ed. Henry Louis Gates Jr. and Terri Hume Oliver (W. W. Norton, 1999).

19. For Du Bois's rethinking of race in the context of the "Jewish Question," see, too, Asaf Angermann, "Du Bois, Marx, and the Jewish Question Reconsidered," *Critical Philosophy of Race* 12, no. 1 (2024): 53.

20. Letter from *Jewish Life* to W. E. B. Du Bois, February 13, 1952.

21. Du Bois, "The Negro and the Warsaw Ghetto," 14.

22. Rothberg, *Multidirectional Memory*, 117; Horne, *Black & Red*, 115.

23. Indeed, the unpublished essay "The Afro-American" (circa 1894/1895), written following Du Bois's return from his two-year study period in Germany, contains some of the earliest sketches of "the problem of the color line" and opens with a "scene . . . of the Negro abroad, beyond the borders of his natal habitation in a local, regional, or national sense." See Chandler, *"Beyond This Narrow Now,"* 53, 61.

24. Du Bois, "The Negro and the Warsaw Ghetto," 14, 15.

25. Burden-Stelly and Horne, *Du Bois*, 59.

26. Burden-Stelly and Horne, *Du Bois*, 109–10.

27. W. E. B. Du Bois, "Contents for September 1931," *The Crisis* 38, no. 9 (September 1931): 293.

28. W. E. B. Du Bois, "Postscript," *The Crisis* 38, no. 9 (September 1931): 315.

29. Chandler, *"Beyond This Narrow Now,"* 38.

30. Du Bois, "Postscript," 314.

31. Du Bois, "Postscript," 315.

32. Du Bois, "The Negro and the Warsaw Ghetto," 15.

33. Du Bois, "The Negro and the Warsaw Ghetto," 15.

34. Du Bois, "The Negro and the Warsaw Ghetto," 15.

35. While these columns on the whole demonstrated ambivalence about German nationalism, including in its fascist variety, Du Bois was unequivocal that "there is a campaign of race prejudice carried on, openly, continuously and determinedly against all non-Nordic races, but specifically against the Jew, which surpasses in vindictive cruelty and public insult anything I have ever seen; and I have seen much." See Du Bois, "Forum of Fact and Opinion: Germany," *The Pittsburgh Courier*, December 5, 1936.

36. Chandler, *"Beyond This Narrow Now,"* 15.

37. Du Bois, "The Negro and the Warsaw Ghetto," 14.

38. On Stanisław Estreicher's end, see Jan Tomasz Gross, *Polish Society Under the German Occupation: The Generalgouvernement, 1939–1944* (Princeton University Press, 1979), 128.

39. Du Bois, "The Negro and the Warsaw Ghetto," 14.

40. Du Bois, "The Negro and the Warsaw Ghetto," 14.

41. For a comparative discussion of German colonialism in Polish Prussia and African and South Pacific colonies, see Sebastian Conrad, "Internal Colonialism in Germany: Culture Wars, Germanification of the Soil, and the Global Market Imaginary," in *German Colonialism in a Global Age*, ed. Bradley Naranch and Geoff Eley (Duke University Press, 2015), 246–64.

42. Du Bois, "The Negro and the Warsaw Ghetto," 14.

43. Du Bois, *Souls*, 10.

44. Du Bois, *Souls*, 10.

45. Du Bois, "The Negro and the Warsaw Ghetto," 14.
46. Du Bois, "The Negro and the Warsaw Ghetto," 14.
47. Du Bois, "The Negro and the Warsaw Ghetto," 14.
48. Du Bois, "The Negro and the Warsaw Ghetto," 14.
49. Du Bois suggests "puzzlement might be an appropriate rhetorical and political strategy for the apprehension of the simultaneously global and local dimensions of intersecting histories." Rothberg, *Multidirectional Memory*, 121.
50. W. E. B. Du Bois, *The Autobiography of W.E.B. DuBois: A Soliloquy on Viewing My Life from the Last Decade of Its First Century* (International Publishers, 1968), 163.
51. Du Bois, *The Autobiography*, 163. Du Bois's reference to Slovenia, which he then repeated when describing the location of the Jewish inn, seems inaccurate; it is more likely that Du Bois meant Slovakia, located between Budapest and the Tatra Mountains (then governed by the Austro-Hungarian Empire).
52. Du Bois, *The Autobiography*, 98.
53. Du Bois, *The Autobiography*, 163.
54. Du Bois, *The Autobiography*, 164.
55. Du Bois, *The Autobiography*, 163–64.
56. Paul Gilroy, *The Black Atlantic: Modernity and Double Consciousness* (Harvard University Press, 1993), 211–12.
57. Brackman, "'A Calamity,'" 55.
58. Rothberg, *Multidirectional Memory*, 121, 120.
59. Chandler, *"Beyond This Narrow Now,"* 41.
60. Historian of Hapsburg central Europe Daniel Unowsky notes that in the larger towns of Western Galicia in 1898, "75 percent or more of the taverns, inns, and restaurants; clothing, furniture, and shoe stores; bakeries; and artisan shops . . . were owned or administered by Jews" and "more than 80 percent of all people who worked in the production and sale of alcohol were Jews." See Unowsky, *The Plunder: The 1898 Anti-Jewish Riots in Habsburg Galicia* (Stanford University Press, 2018).
61. Du Bois, "The Negro and the Warsaw Ghetto," 15.
62. Du Bois, " The Negro and the Warsaw Ghetto," 14; Du Bois, *Souls*, 5.
63. Indeed, Chandler demonstrates the influence Du Bois's European travels had on some of his earliest formulations and notes that the first chapter of *Souls*, "penned in late spring or early summer of 1897, is perhaps his earliest published retrospective reference to his experience as a student in Europe." James M. Thomas likewise argues that Du Bois's engagement with German discourses of antisemitism while a student in Berlin shaped his conception of double consciousness. Chandler, *"Beyond This Narrow Now,"* 39; James M. Thomas, *The Souls of Jewish Folk: W. E. B. Du Bois, Anti-Semitism, and the Color Line* (University of Georgia Press, 2023).
64. Du Bois, *Souls*, 10. Time spent in Europe is here linked to natality, a space enabling a rebirth. Remarking on the figure of Europe that runs through the essays making up *Souls*, Chandler argues, "Du Bois's main preoccupations here are otherwise than with Europe as such. . . . Europe is on the periphery of his principal thetic concerns. . . . Thus it is also the case that it is in later autobiographical references and texts strewn across his long career that Du Bois elaborates upon the time and experience of this first trip to Europe and to Germany." Chandler, *"Beyond This Narrow Now,"* 39, 41.
65. Du Bois, "Present Outlook," 118–19.
66. Du Bois, "Present Outlook," 118.
67. Du Bois, "Present Outlook," 119, 134n26.
68. Du Bois, "The Negro and the Warsaw Ghetto," 14.
69. See Henry Louis Gates Jr. and Terri Hume Oliver, "Note on the Text," in Du Bois, *Souls of Black Folk*, xxxix.

70. Gates and Oliver, "Note on the Text," xxxix–xli. The majority were in the chapters "On the Black Belt" and "Of the Sons of Masters and Men," with one additional reference modified in the chapter "Of the Faith of the Fathers."
71. Du Bois, *Souls*, 142.
72. Gates and Oliver, "Note on the Text," xli.
73. Du Bois, *Souls*, 83–84.
74. See Gates and Oliver, "Note on the Text," xli. Du Bois, *Souls*, 83–84.
75. Du Bois, "The Negro and the Warsaw Ghetto," 15.
76. Letter from W. E. B. Du Bois to Herbert Aptheker, February 27, 1953, mums312-b284-i097, MS 312, Du Bois Papers, http://credo.library.umass.edu/view/full/mums312-b284-i097. Others also protested Du Bois's language in the decades following the original publication, including Rabbi Stephen Wise and historian Morris U. Schappes, a JPFO leader who was an editor of *Jewish Life* and its successor publication *Jewish Currents*. See Jonathan S. Kahn, "There Are No Clean Souls: The Promises and Perils of Political Theology in *The Souls of Black Folk*," in *Race and Political Theology*, ed. Vincent Lloyd (Stanford University Press, 2012), 123.
77. On the ruins of the Warsaw Ghetto, Du Bois paradoxically asserted, "And the monument brought back again the problem of race and religion, which so long had been my own particular and separate problem." Du Bois, "The Negro and the Warsaw Ghetto," 15.
78. Du Bois, "Forum of Fact and Opinion: Race Prejudice in Germany," *The Pittsburgh Courier*, December 19, 1936.
79. On the opportunistic use of the word "ghetto" by the Nazis, see Mitchell Duneier, *Ghetto: The Invention of a Place, the History of an Idea* (Farrar, Straus and Giroux, 2017), 15–25. Rothberg argues that Du Bois's essay "reveals how racial thinking as well as racial violence emerge simultaneously with the production of 'biopolitical' space." See Rothberg, *Multidirectional Memory*, 115.
80. Quoted in Kahn, "There Are No Clean Souls," 124.
81. Du Bois, *Souls*, 109; Gates and Oliver, "Note on the Text," xli.
82. Du Bois to Aptheker, February 27, 1953.
83. Du Bois to Aptheker, February 27, 1953.
84. Robert M. Zecker, *"A Road to Peace and Freedom": The International Workers Order and the Struggle for Economic Justice and Civil Rights, 1930–1954* (Temple University Press, 2018), 241–44. See also "Red Editor Is Deported," *New York Times*, November 24, 1950. On Jones, see Charisse Burden-Stelly, "Claudia Jones, the Long Durée of McCarthyism, and the Threat of US Fascism, *The Journal of Intersectionality* 3, no. 1 (Summer 2019): 46–66.
85. George Bornstein, "W. E. B. Du Bois and the Jews: Ethics, Editing, and the Souls of Black Folk," *Textual Cultures: Texts, Contexts, Interpretation* 1, no. 1 (Spring 2006): 66. In Jonathan S. Kahn's analysis, a nativist resentment led Du Bois to traffic "in anti-Semitic stereotypes as a way of protesting the manner in which Jews are, indeed, becoming white in late nineteenth- and early twentieth-century America" while restricting the "rights and riches" of its native Black citizens; and he concludes that, through his revisions, "Du Bois only reinforces the nativist sentiment of these few passages. In an attempt to fix the anti-semitism of *Souls*, Du Bois reinscribes not only what is plausibly the text's original nativist tics but the very sort of American theological exceptionalism he tries to disrupt." Kahn, "There Are No Clean Souls," 127–28.
86. Burden-Stelly and Horne, *Du Bois*, 172.
87. See letter from United States Dept. of State Passport Division to W. E. B. Du Bois, February 12, 1952, Du Bois Papers, mums312-b138-i244, https://credo.library.umass.edu/view/full/mums312-b138-i244. Regarding the "We Charge Genocide" petition, its authors, lawyers William Patterson and Paul Robeson, were deeply connected to the IWO; see chapters by Sampson and Zecker and by Bevel.

88. Burden-Stelly and Horne, *Du Bois*, 172.

89. Burden-Stelly and Horne explain, "Du Bois was taken aback when those he had touted—the Talented Tenth—generally headed for the exits when they were asked to support him. Thus imploded one of his earliest theses, that the touting of this well-educated sliver of the population would be the savior for Black Americans." Burden-Stelly and Horne, *Du Bois*, 173.

90. Burden-Stelly and Horne, *Du Bois*, 188.

91. Du Bois, "The Negro and the Warsaw Ghetto," 15.

5

LANGSTON HUGHES AND THE INTERNATIONAL WORKERS ORDER

Matthew Calihman

At a March 24, 1953, closed-door hearing before Joseph McCarthy's Senate Permanent Subcommittee on Investigations, Langston Hughes (1901–67) struggled to speak authentically about his radical left writings of the 1930s and 1940s while also denying the committee's accusation that he had studiously followed "the Communist Party line."[1] The committee members and their counsel, Roy Cohn, attempted throughout to direct Hughes's testimony with leading yes-or-no questions, but Hughes eventually maneuvered the body into a position in which it was obliged to hear some of his account. After reminding the committee of its commitment to individual rights ("I would much rather preserve my reputation and freedom than to save time"), he proceeded to recall several of his formative experiences as a Black American born at the beginning of the twentieth century. It is noteworthy but not surprising that as someone who had made his way in life as a writer and a speaker, Hughes recounted episodes about cultural and educational institutions and intellectual labor. He had been barred, he remembered, from the Jim Crow movie theater in Lawrence, Kansas, during his years living there as a child. He had learned that his father had studied law but that Oklahoma Territory, where he then resided, had denied him the opportunity to take the bar exam. Hughes himself had been admitted to a previously all-white school in Topeka, Kansas, but was subject to his teacher's anti-Black speech. He had been admitted to Columbia University as well, but his housing reservation had gone missing, and he had joined the student newspaper staff, though only to be assigned a beat—society news—to which a Black reporter could obviously obtain little access.

But his experience at Cleveland's Central High School had been different: "I went to a high school in a very poor neighborhood and we were very poor people. My friends and associates were very poor children and many of them were of European parentage or some of them had been brought here in steerage themselves from Europe, and many of these students . . . began to tell me about Eugene Debs, and about the new nation and the new republic. Some of them brought [Debs's publications] to school. I became interested in whatever I could read that Debs had written or spoken about."[2] Hughes thus located one of the origins of his radical literary expression in an embracing interracial, multiethnic working-class intellectual community committed to Socialism. Of course, there was much more that he could have said that day. He might have told the Committee, as he did the readers of the National Association for the Advancement of Colored People's *Crisis* later that spring, about his family's "long history of participation in social struggle—from my grandfather who went to prison for helping slaves to freedom and another relative who died with John Brown at Harper's Ferry to my great uncle, John M. Langston, only Negro representative in Congress from Virginia following the Reconstruction, and who had supported Abraham Lincoln in his recruiting Negro troops, and spoken for freedom on the same platform with [William Lloyd] Garrison and [Wendell] Phillips."[3] Or, if Hughes had been speaking under very different circumstances, he might have talked unguardedly about the two decades that he had spent in the Communist movement. Instead, he traced his interest in social struggle back to his youth. His experience at Central High School had prompted him to search the Socialist tradition for "some kind of way of thinking about this whole problem of myself, segregated, poor, colored, and how I can adjust to this whole problem of helping to build America when sometimes I can not [sic] even get into a school or a lecture or a concert or in the south [sic] go to the library and get a book out."[4]

Among Hughes's later efforts to work through this problem were his collaborations during the late 1930s and early 1940s with the International Workers Order (IWO). A mutual-benefit fraternal society, the IWO was one of the many Communist-affiliated organizations with which he was identified during this period. Through his close friend Louise Thompson Patterson (1901–99), an IWO official, Hughes became involved in the Order's cultural work.[5] He published books and single poems under the IWO imprint, led a Harlem theater company sponsored by the Order, and contributed to IWO educational events. Animating all these endeavors were his and the Order's shared commitments to working-class interracialism; full citizenship for Black Americans; anti-fascist struggle; economic security; and, as an ultimate goal, Socialism. Hughes and the IWO also shared a commitment to a left cultural pluralism: a recognition that distinct ethnic communities persisted in America; that the members of these communities lived their cultural heritages, including their usable radical pasts; and that many American laborers needed to be engaged as members of ethnic communities, members of a larger American national community, and members of the working class.

The IWO had been organized largely along ethnic-linguistic lines since its founding in 1930, but it and other radical left and progressive organizations placed even greater emphasis on ethnicity during the long Popular Front period that began in the mid-1930s and extended through the late 1940s. Ethnicity was more important at this time even though the Order recognized that with post–World War I immigration restrictions in place, the percentage of foreign-born people in the US workforce was declining. As Roger Keeran writes, "The depression was frustrating economic mobility and assimilation." Furthermore, "the rise of fascism was heightening the awareness of national oppression and was increasing national group identification."[6] To be sure, not all of Hughes's writings of the 1930s and 1940s represent ethnicity per se (for example, Black/African Americans, Italian Americans, and Jewish Americans), as distinct from race (for example, Black people and white people). Sometimes the labor solidarity that Hughes envisioned was more generally interracial or global. Yet, like Patterson and many others in the IWO, when he looked at American workers, he often saw not only class and race but also ethnicity.

As Hughes informed the McCarthy committee, he had told the story of his Central High School days in his autobiography, *The Big Sea* (1940), which appeared in the middle of his years-long involvement with the IWO. While almost silent concerning his radical work of the preceding decade, the book reveals his yearning for interracial, multiethnic, revolutionary working-class solidarity. If he was wary, even in 1940, of publishing an autobiography that identified him with the present-day Communist movement, he was ready, as he would be in 1953, to identify himself with its beginnings in the late 1910s. During his time at Central, "it was very nearly entirely a foreign-born school, with a few native white and colored American students mixed in." In speaking of "foreign-born" students, he referred to "children of foreign-born parents. Although some of the students themselves had been born in Poland or Russia, Hungary or Italy. And most were Catholic or Jewish."[7] Hughes had many Jewish friends, and his best friend was Polish. "These children of foreign-born parents," he recalled, "were more democratic than native white Americans, and less anti-Negro." What made them so was their relative proximity to "foreign" nations and their immersion in European Socialist cultures that were regarded as doubly alien amid the nativism and anti-radicalism that prevailed during World War I and the postwar period. His friends were "almost all interested in more than basketball and the glee club."[8] They lent him radical left-wing novels and literary magazines and took him to hear Debs, who would soon be convicted of violating the 1918 Sedition Act and sentenced to a ten-year prison term. "And when the Russian Revolution broke out," Hughes wrote, "our school almost held a celebration." After being called to the principal's office to declare their loyalty to the United States, Hughes and a number of his schoolmates became members of Central's Americanism Club, of which he was elected president. But this organization was short lived, because, he said, "we were never quite clear about what we were supposed to do. Or why. Except that none of us wanted Eugene Debs locked up."[9] Now conscious of radical working-class movements, Hughes glimpsed new social vistas: "From the students I learnt that Europe was not so far away, and that when Lenin took power in Russia, something happened in the slums of Woodlawn Avenue that the teachers couldn't tell us about, and that our principal didn't want us to know. From the students I learnt, too, that lots of painful words can be flung at people that aren't *n*----- [anti-Black slur]. *K*--- [anti-Jewish slur] was one; *s*---- [anti-Italian and anti-Latino/a slur], and *h*---- [anti-central European and anti-eastern European slur], others."[10] Here Hughes offered an urban regionalist portrait of international Socialism, rendering it as a neighborhood cross-ethnic politics. His Central High School experiences disclosed both the possibility of a left solidarity that defied racialism, white supremacy, and nativism and the possibility of a future world beyond racial capitalism.

However, Hughes also discovered that this same capitalism threatened the solidarity that was meant to challenge it. The white ethnics with whom he grew up—"scorned though they might be by the pure Americans—all had it on [Black people] in one thing. Summer time came and they could get jobs quickly. For even during the war, when help was badly needed, lots of employers would *not* hire Negroes."[11] Hughes would return to these discoveries throughout the 1930s and 1940s. In his IWO projects he identified with an interracial, multiethnic, radical working-class movement, but he also refused to generalize away Black Americans' particular circumstances under US capitalism, circumstances that also shaped Black experiences in the movement.

Hughes first became associated with the IWO in the late 1930s, a decade after his friendship and collaboration with Patterson had begun. Raised mainly in the US West and educated at the University of California, Berkeley, Patterson spent a few years in her twenties teaching at historically Black institutions in the South and then moved to New York to take a position in the Department of Social Relations at the Congregational Education Society. She and Hughes met at Hampton University in 1928, where she then taught and which he visited on one of his many reading tours, and the two began what would become a lifelong friendship. He had by then established himself as a Black literary celebrity with the publication of two volumes of poetry, *The Weary Blues* (1926) and *Fine Clothes* to the Jew (1927). During the same decade, Hughes had begun publishing in such radical left magazines as the Workers (Communist) Party–affiliated *Workers Monthly* and *New Masses*, and during the early Depression years both he and Patterson drew very close to the Party. In 1932, they were among the twenty-two Black Americans who traveled to the Soviet Union to make *Black and White*, a film about Black workers in the United States. The film was never made, but the would-be cast members were treated to months-long tours of the USSR, with Hughes and Patterson taking special interest in the lives of national minority peoples under Soviet modernity.[12]

After returning to the United States, Patterson worked for several months as an organizer for the Communist Party–affiliated National Committee for the Defense of Political Prisoners (NCDPP), which was best known for its advocacy on behalf of the Scottsboro defendants, a cause that engaged her and Hughes throughout much of the decade. The defense of the young Alabama men wrongly accused of rape had already been embraced by the IWO's many language societies. In 1933, Patterson joined the staff of the IWO, and around the same time she became a member of the Communist Party (CPUSA) as well. She remained on the IWO staff until 1948, holding several high-level leadership positions, including vice president. When the Order was liquidated by court order in 1954, Patterson still held this position. Much of her IWO work focused on organizing Black lodges and building Black membership in interracial English-speaking lodges, though she cooperated toward these ends with the members and officials of the IWO's other ethnic-linguistic sections. She later recalled that the members of these sections readily accepted leadership from a Black woman.[13] Patterson also served on the editorial board of the IWO's magazine, *New Order/Fraternal Outlook*, and wrote for it.

While Hughes never joined the CPUSA, he published widely in such Party- or Comintern-affiliated magazines as *The New Masses*, *Anvil*, *Negro Worker*, and *International Literature* throughout the 1930s. He was also publicly identified with Party-affiliated organizations such as the John Reed Club, the League of American Writers, the NCDPP, the League of Struggle for Negro Rights, and the IWO. In 1937, Hughes and Patterson would visit Spain, he to cover the Spanish Civil War for the *Baltimore Afro-American* and other publications and she to represent the IWO in a delegation from the North American Committee to Aid Spanish Democracy. As Annabel Cohen's chapter in this book makes clear, IWO members committed to the anti-fascist struggle in Spain with dollars, medical donations, and blood spilled on Spanish battlefields.

Although Patterson was not an artist, she was involved in Hughes's creative work, and it figured in her organizing. For about a year, starting in late 1929, Hughes and Patterson shared a patron, the wealthy white heiress Charlotte

Osgood Mason, who paid him to write (so long as she approved of what he was writing) and her to serve as a secretary to Hughes and to Zora Neale Hurston, another recipient of Mason's support. Patterson, who had many other artist friends, also became a builder of cultural institutions. One was the Vanguard Club, the political forum that she and sculptor Augusta Savage ran in Harlem. Then, too, there was an aesthetic dimension to Patterson's organizing work. According to her biographer, Keith Gilyard, Patterson "often enhanced her lectures with [Hughes's] poetry and sought a broader audience for it."[14] In the fall of 1937, as she campaigned to persuade the IWO to publish *A New Song*, a chapbook of Hughes's radical verse, she told him that she had the manuscript with her as she traveled, and she promised, "I shall use the poems in my talks."[15]

Beginning in the 1920s, Hughes found some success in mainstream cultural institutions, and by the late 1930s, he was a major figure on the literary left. Yet he still struggled under Jim Crow to earn a living as a writer and often felt as if he worked in exile. A member of the League of Professional Groups for Foster and Ford (the CPUSA's presidential and vice-presidential candidates in 1932), Hughes was one of the signatories to its *Culture and the Crisis: An Open Letter to the Writers, Artists, Teachers, Physicians, Engineers, Scientists and Other Professional Workers of America* (1932). This pamphlet was a crucial early effort not only to rally such workers to the side of industrial laborers but also, as Michael Denning has argued, to "theorize the social and political significance of modern mental labor" and, more specifically, the cultural front in the revolutionary struggle.[16] The crisis that the letter probed, one born of the Depression-era crisis of capitalism itself, was the mass unemployment of intellectual workers in the United States. Dismissing the objection that "there are too many doctors, teachers, artists, writers and the like," the authors contended that "this country has never yet been able to provide its population with a sufficiently large body of trained intellectuals and professionals to satisfy its cultural needs."[17] But even though *Culture and the Crisis* took a definite stand against Jim Crow, just as the CPUSA did in other contexts, the pamphlet failed to address the special problem confronting the Black intelligentsia, a group of workers rendered inessential at the convergence of anti-intellectualism and racism.

Hughes, however, took up this problem in many of his writings, including "Democracy and Me," his address at the 1939 meeting of the CPUSA-affiliated League of American Writers. Even with the specter of fascism hanging over the world, Hughes complained, Americans had not yet moved to achieve an interracial cultural democracy (nor an interracial democracy of any other kind). Publishing, like other types of work, remained part of a racial capitalist economy: "The market for Negro writers . . . is definitely limited as long as we write about ourselves. And the more truthfully we write about ourselves, the more limited our market becomes."[18] A year later, in *The Big Sea*, Hughes charted the short history of the 1920s vogue in Black cultural expression. The "market" for his writing seems to have become more limited in the early 1930s, when it often pictured revolutionary struggle. By 1934, Knopf had brought out five of Hughes's books, but when he sent the firm a collection of his recent radical lyrics in that year, Blanche Knopf told him that the "moment" was not right for him to "publish a book of poems—I think that you have become much more important than this poetry is and that the publication of such a book now would tend to hurt your name rather than help it."[19]

Nor was this kind of obstacle the only sort that Hughes faced. Complicating his predicament and that of other Black writers, he said in "Democracy and Me," was their exclusion from most of the mental work on which many of their white counterparts relied to subsidize their creativity: "Magazine offices, daily newspapers, publishers' offices are as tightly closed to us in America as if we were pure non-Aryans in Berlin."[20] In many US towns Black writers were not invited to address white audiences, and in places where Black writers had such engagements, vigilant doormen and elevator operators sometimes stood in the way. The movie industry was likewise Jim-Crowed, as were movies themselves. "Of course, Negro novelists do not sell their novels to motion pictures," Hughes wrote. "No motion picture studio in America, in all the history of motion pictures, has yet dared make one single picture using any of the fundamental dramatic values of Negro life—not one. . . . On the screen we are servants, clowns, or fools. Comedy relief. . . . Such Negro material as is used by the studios is very rarely written by Negroes." "Hollywood insofar as Negroes are concerned," he concluded, "might just as well be controlled by Hitler."[21] Hughes further suggested that, like American writers of northwestern European descent and Protestant background, white ethnic writers had greater access to these kinds of professional opportunities than did Black writers. Lecturing, for example, was a much more dependable "source of income for many Nordic and non-Nordic writers who are white" than it was for Black writers.[22]

With these observations, Hughes rendered a portrait of Black people's marginal relation to the "cultural apparatus" that the left-wing American sociologist C. Wright Mills began to theorize in the late 1930s and whose conceptual origins Denning traces back to the *Culture and the Crisis* group. By "cultural apparatus," Mills meant "all the organizations and *milieux* in which artistic, intellectual and scientific work goes on" and "the means by which such work is made available to circles, publics, and masses."[23] Hughes did not conclude, as Mills eventually would, that artistic, intellectual, scientific, and communications institutions were fast becoming the only source of radical social alternatives, but he challenged the League of American Writers to lead the desegregation of these organizations.

"Democracy and Me" thus anticipated Hughes's complaint, at his 1953 Senate hearing, about the difficulty of "helping to build America" while being barred from schools, libraries, and concert halls.

It is therefore not surprising that Hughes found a home in the IWO. Atypically for 1930s America, the Order was committed to democratic cultural pluralism as a basis for working-class solidarity. As Robert Zecker writes, the organization hoped to model for the United States "a multiethnic, politically progressive and racially inclusive nation of nations."[24] In an unpublished interview conducted in 1984, Patterson described the Order's federal structure: "When I came into the IWO in 1933, it was already international in the sense of the ethnic groups it represented. Though it was a united organization, each group was separate with its own leadership. . . . They found that when they joined together and pooled their assets, they could have a stronger organization."[25] Among these shared assets were of course the IWO's life insurance, sick benefits, disability protection, and burial plans, along with the medical and dental services and birth-control centers that the organization provided in larger cities. The affordability and quality of IWO insurance distinguished the Order from for-profit carriers, which often denied coverage to Black people or offered them meager coverage for higher premiums. Another shared resource was a large nationwide organization that could be mobilized for a variety of progressive causes—for example, the Scottsboro defense, fighting Jim Crow, social security legislation, the Congress of Industrial Organizations, the Spanish republic, and decolonization in Africa and Asia. The IWO also sustained a cultural infrastructure of publications, theater and dance collectives, vocal and orchestral groups, lecture programs, workers' schools, lending libraries, sports teams, and summer camps. Some of these cultural institutions were identified with particular ethnic societies, but their members came together in citywide and national IWO events.[26]

Although the IWO that Patterson joined in 1933 was overwhelmingly an organization of European immigrants and children of European immigrants, she and others did much both to build the Order's Black membership and to establish community centers, cultural institutions, and programs for Black lodges, while Jesús Colón and other Latino/a activists built the Order's Cervantes Society. Some of the IWO's European ethnic group societies had previously been independent working-class fraternal orders, but its Black and Spanish-speaking lodges had to be created. In her 1951 testimony on behalf of the Order in *Bohlinger v. International Workers Order*, Patterson explained that "the work among the Negro people was started from scratch, because what we believed in more than anything else was that we wanted to have an interracial society representative of as many sections and segments of America as there are people in it."[27] Campaigns to organize Black and interracial lodges involved the national IWO leadership, leaders of its various ethnic societies, and many rank-and-file members. Patterson recalled that when she and other Black members were organizing Harlem's Solidarity Lodge 691 in the mid-1930s, "members of other lodges, Jewish lodges, Ukrainian lodges, Hungarian or what have you . . . came with us."[28]

The founding of Lodge 691's Harlem Suitcase Theatre (HST), for which Hughes served as executive director, was likewise a contribution to the IWO's pluralist project. In her unpublished memoirs, Patterson wrote that "every [ethnic] unit [in the IWO] had its own form of culture. The Ukrainian section had Ukrainian dances. The Russians, for one thing, had balalaika dances. The Jewish group might have a choir or a chorus. . . . The idea was that each group would have this opportunity to express its own cultural background. So we were very happy to have this theater group as a part of our activity and got our players mainly from the youth in our lodge."[29] The aim of initiatives such as the HST, Patterson told the *Bohlinger* court, was "to bring into the orbit of the International Workers Order the cultural life, the fraternal tradition of the Negro people."[30] When she began to pitch the idea of the Order's publication of a book of Hughes's radical verse, she framed the project in similar terms: "I believe that the publication of this volume of your poems can be used as a means of bringing Negro culture to the masses of people and I cannot tell you how enthusiastic I am about the whole idea."[31]

Hughes, for his part, had sought such an opportunity for years, at least since Knopf responded coolly to his radical poems. In his reply, he asked her to release his manuscript so that he could publish it "in a form available to a working class audience, that is, in a cheap edition." He wanted to send the manuscript to "the [CPUSA's] International Publishers or some others who cater to a workers public and who will distribute it through workers' bookshops, unions, etc. throughout the country."[32] The IWO's National Education Department undertook this project, printing ten thousand copies of *A New Song* (1938), Hughes's largest English-language edition so far, and selling the booklet for fifteen cents.[33] *New Order*'s April 1938 issue, which was dedicated to the IWO's upcoming national convention, included the title poem and a full-page back-cover advertisement recommending *A New Song* to the organization's 150,000 members and offering discount prices to branches placing bulk orders.[34] The collection included an introduction by Mike Gold, the author of the Lower East Side novel *Jews Without Money* (1930), a member of the *New Masses* editorial board, and one of the Communist Party's leading literary critics. He placed Hughes in a Whitmanian tradition of American democratic poetry and found it "altogether fitting that the International Workers Order, a fraternal society serving the American people of all races and nationalities, should have chosen this poet as its first author in a series of literary pamphlets for the people."[35] Hughes was in fact a stalwart defender of Whitman, especially his encompassing vision of the American people and his prophecy of an expanding world democracy. In the introduction to *I Hear the People Singing: Selected Poems of Walt Whitman* (1946), a juvenile-audience anthology published by the Communist Party's International Publishers, Hughes wrote that Whitman's "all-embracing words lock arms with workers and farmers, Negroes and whites, Asiatics and Europeans, serfs, and free men, beaming democracy to all." "The good gray poet of democracy," Hughes told his young readers, "is one of literature's great faith-holders in human freedom. Speaking simply for people everywhere and most of all for the believers in our basic American dream, he is constantly growing in stature as the twentieth century advances and edition after edition of his poems appears."[36]

But Hughes also attempted to hold America to Whitman's word, his assurances about the breadth of the nation's embrace, and Hughes took the same kind of stance toward the Communist movement. Many of the poems in *A New Song* are about making space in the movement for Black working-class radicalism. If the "darker brother" of Hughes's "I, Too" (1925), an early dialogue with Whitman, envisions joining the US national community—tomorrow he will "sit at the table / When company comes"—the speakers in *A New Song* see themselves in an emerging proletarian fraternity.[37] In "Sister Johnson Marches," a Black American woman becomes visible in the workers' struggle without leaving the Black world. First published in 1937 in the CPUSA-affiliated magazine *Fight Against War and Fascism*, the poem is a vernacular dialogue between the eponymous speaker, who is marching in a May Day parade, and another Black woman, an onlooker. To this interlocutor Sister Johnson confides her joy in taking part in this demonstration of working-class solidarity. She also rejoices in the knowledge that "we owns de land!" in the world that she and the other marchers are heralding.[38] Robert Shulman argues that "in tone and content 'Sister Johnson Marches' exemplifies the ideals of the IWO and the non-revolutionary side of the Popular Front."[39] Like many American and international left-wing organizations in the half-century following the 1886 Haymarket affair, the IWO and its ethnic societies indeed embraced May Day as a workers' holiday. According to Donna Haverty-Stacke, labor's May Day reached the height of its popularity in the United States during the Popular Front era, when parades in New York and other cities drew many thousands of workers, including "colorful contingents from the IWO."[40] May Day celebrants, who also appear in *A New Song*'s "Chant for May Day," assembled for a wide range of progressive and radical aims, including "non-revolutionary" ones. Yet nothing could be more revolutionary, at least in proletarian writing, than the collective ownership on which Sister Johnson sets her sights. Her Black vernacular radical voice sounds from within the May Day masses.

Biographer Arnold Rampersad shows that by the end of Hughes's high school years, during which he wrote poems and short stories (publishing some in his school's literary magazine), he was already recognizable as both a writer of social conscience and a Black folk bard.[41] Rampersad tends, though, to overdistinguish between these creative selves, and he understates considerably the depth of Hughes's later, two-decade commitment to the Communist left. By contrast, Barbara Foley regards Hughes as first a poet of class struggle. She reminds us that his earliest radical left publications appeared in the mid-1920s: "In Hughes's *Workers Monthly* poems [published between 1924 and 1927], the voice of the New Negro was virtually indistinguishable from that of the class-conscious proletarian of any race or nation. Clearly the figure usually seen as the first folk troubadour of the Harlem Renaissance did not need to wait for the Great Depression to write pro-communist poetry foregrounding the class contradiction."[42] However, what Foley deprecates as "culturalism" had likewise appeared in Hughes's work by this time, even though, by her account, the left radicalism of the early Harlem Renaissance gave way to an emergent cultural pluralism: "A minority discourse in the aftermath of 1919, cultural pluralism would war for hegemony through the decades to come; as multiculturalism, it would attain the status of dominant ideology by century's end. From the outset, however, it was always an opposition loyal to American democratic capitalism, whose 'other'—cosmopolitan communism—was unthinkable." The Black literary left that formed around 1919, Foley argues, was deradicalized by a pluralism that understood the United States as "a nation untroubled by internal [i.e., class] schisms."[43] Defining pluralism/"culturalism" as a type of nationalism, she rejects it as class collaboration (insistence on the naturalness and rightness of the class character of capitalist society).[44] But, as we have already begun to see in *A New Song*, the radical Hughes was both a pluralist and a Communist.

"Let America Be America Again," by far the best-remembered poem in *A New Song*, makes space for Black workers in not only the Communist movement but also the national community. A Popular Front epic about a coming radical social reconstruction of the United States, the poem identifies an interracial, multi-ethnic working class as the American people and envisions the nation as a cultural democracy and a workers' society. As in "Sister Johnson Marches," Hughes deploys a call-and-response form. The poem's first speaker yearns for a lost American golden age of true republicanism and limitless economic opportunity:

> Let America be America again.
> Let it be the dream it used to be.
> Let it be the pioneer on the plain
> Seeking a home where he himself is free.

This voice twice more appeals for the restoration of "America," nearly silencing the second speaker, who cannot find such a nation in the past. The second speaker can only interject single-sentence dissents like "America never was America to me," each enclosed in parentheses and printed as a separate strophe. The first speaker does not reply, but a third voice, this one rendered in italics, asks the second speaker, "*Say who are you that mumbles in the dark? / And who are you that draws your veil across the stars?*"[45] Now heard, the second speaker dilates, offering a Whitmanesque catalogue of themselves and seizing authorship of America, along with the remainder of the poem. This speaker's voice, rising from centuries of American life, is that of Black people, poor white people, Indigenous people, immigrants, farmers, industrial workers, and young people. A similar polyphony structures John Latouche's lyrics for the equally Whitmanesque "Ballad for Americans" (1939), the Popular Front anthem debuted by another IWO member, Paul Robeson, and performed at many Order events. Like "Ballad," "Let America Be America Again" evokes the histories of the various segments of the Popular Front coalition and gives voice to their social needs, and in so doing the poem registers some of the differences among these groups. In one inevitably complicated sentence, Hughes narrates the migration histories of several European American groups as well as that of Black Americans:

> O, I'm the man who sailed those early seas
> In search of what I meant to be my home—
> For I'm the one who left dark Ireland's shore,
> And Poland's plain, and England's grassy lea,
> And torn from Black Africa's strand I came
> To build a "homeland of the free."[46]

Whereas the European migrants are unquestionably the subjects of their migrations ("I'm the man who sailed," "I'm the one who left"), the Black migrants are only equivocally so ("torn from Black Africa's strand I came"). In another crucial passage, Hughes relies on the anaphora so closely identified with Whitman's democratic poetry, but the passage's content finally upsets the running analogy that the form is meant to sustain:

> I am the farmer, bondsman to the soil.
> I am the worker sold to the machine.
> I am the Negro, servant to you all.[47]

Here, as in the previously quoted passage, Hughes refuses to write racism out of the past and present of the American working class and the US national community. And yet this poem is committed to both of these social formations, which are united in the future that the poem desires.

In recent decades, several scholars have argued that "Let America Be America Again," unlike many of Hughes's other 1930s poems, retreats from Marxist revolutionary politics. Such arguments often draw too stark a distinction between the Comintern's Third Period and Popular Front stances. Anthony Dawahare writes that "the publication of 'Let America' signifies that by 1938 Hughes, influenced by Popular Front politics (which, aside from advocating a 'peoples' nationalism, no longer advocated socialist revolution and the class-based politics of the Third Period) was moving away from his radical beliefs."[48] But, as "Let America" itself shows, the Popular Front neither simply substituted nation for class nor gave up hope of Socialist revolution. It is true that the first published version of "Let America," which appeared in *Esquire* in 1936, was much less radical than the 1938 *New Song* version that Dawahare and I discuss. *Esquire* bought only half of Hughes's manuscript, taking a pass on its final five strophes, the last of which calls on an interracial, multiethnic American working class to remake the nation by establishing collective ownership of its means of production.[49]

> We, the people, must redeem
> The land, the mines, the plants, the rivers,
> The mountains and the endless plain—
> All, all the stretch of these great green states—
> And make America again![50]

A New Song's version of the poem included these lines, and this longer "Let America Be America Again" was soon collected in *Negro Caravan* (1941), a major African American literary anthology that went through several editions in the half-century following its initial publication. This version of the poem sought at once a cultural democracy and a workers' society, all the while acknowledging Black people's particular histories and present-day circumstances as Americans, workers, and revolutionaries.

At the time of *A New Song*'s publication, Hughes was also involved more directly in the IWO's organizing efforts. In late 1937, the Order had sent Patterson on a lecture tour to speak about the Spanish Civil War, and early the next year Hughes was dispatched to address the same topic. One flyer announced that "Mr. Hughes has just returned from an extended stay in Spain. He visited the battlefields, interviewed Negro soldiers [in the International Brigades] and Moorish prisoners [Moroccan colonial subjects serving in Franco's army], and witnessed the barbarous destruction wrought by Franco's fascist army of intervention." Titled "A Poet Looks at a Troubled World" or "A Negro Poet Looks at the World," Hughes's presentation included some of his Spanish Civil War poems and surely drew on his war reporting.[51]

Recognizing that cultural projects like these lecture tours were the "inner life of the lodges," Patterson called on Hughes and others to help sustain this life at Lodge 691 and in the surrounding community.[52] The lodge hall at 317 West 125th Street was home to the branch's Harlem Community Center. In the spring of 1938, the lodge hosted a multi-week Seminar in Negro History. Hughes, a brochure announced, would present "A Poet Looks at a Troubled World." The Black Communist journalist, critic, and fiction writer Eugene Gordon would lecture on national minorities in the USSR, where he had spent several years on the staff of the *Moscow Daily News*.[53] Max Yergan, a CPUSA member and the executive director of the new anti-colonialist International Committee on African Affairs (later the Council on African Affairs), would explain how "A Negro Views the Tokio-Rome-Berlin Axis." James W. Ford, the Black CPUSA official and vice presidential candidate, would interpret the ongoing struggle for anti-lynching legislation. The series also included a lecture by the historian Carter G. Woodson, who had founded the Association for the Study of Negro Life and History in 1915 and inaugurated the observance of Negro History Week in 1926. A swing "dansante" followed each seminar lecture, and the lodge held an annual ball at Harlem's Savoy Ballroom.[54]

Hughes's most ambitious IWO project was probably the Harlem Suitcase Theatre. He cofounded the theater with Patterson in early 1938 and served as its executive director until June 1939, when he resigned because other creative projects were drawing him away from New York.[55] Years earlier, during his long visit to the USSR, he had encountered Soviet avant-garde theater and met with two of its leaders, Vsevolod Meyerhold and Nikolay Okhlopkov. Hughes began then to yearn for a theater of his own, and his experiences in Spain in 1937 only deepened his desire for the kinds of social agency that seem possible on the stage. Shortly after his return to the United States in January 1938, he once again told Patterson that he wanted a theater, and she soon arranged for IWO sponsorship of HST and for its use of the Harlem lodge hall, which could accommodate two hundred seats.[56] (To remain in compliance with city regulations, the theater moved in 1939 from the IWO hall to a few temporary locations and then to a more permanent space at the 135th Street branch of the New York Public Library.)[57] HST initially had forty-seven members, many of whom were also Lodge 691 fraternalists.[58] Most were not professional theater workers, though the group included such prominent or later-prominent persons as the poets Gwendolyn Bennett and Waring Cuney; the Harlem teacher, writer, actor, and Negro Experimental Theater founder Dorothy Peterson; and the actor Robert Earl Jones. A small number of white people, including Harlem IWO member Ernest Goldstein, were members of the company.[59] The theater launched several careers, most notably Jones's. HST survived for two seasons, from 1938 to 1939, performing two or three times each week.⁶⁰ Its innovative in-the-round productions used no scenery, no curtain, simple lighting, and no more props than could be carried in a suitcase.

HST's main offering was Hughes's one-act play *Don't You Want to Be Free?: A Poetry Play, From Slavery Through the Blues to Now—and Then Some!, with Singing, Music, and Dancing* (1938). The author described it as "an impressionistic play endeavoring to capture within the space of an hour the entire scope of Negro history from Africa to America."⁶¹ *Don't You Want to Be Free* debuted on April 21, 1938, and the group performed it 135 times (a long run for a Harlem production), often on a program with other plays.⁶² During HST's second season, the theater supplemented it with short skits authored by Hughes: *Colonel Tom's Cabin*; *The Em-Fuehrer Jones*; *Hurrah, America! (Jersey City Justice)* (cowritten with Louis Douglas); *Limitations of Life: A Satire on the Movie Imitation of Life*; *Scarlet Sister Barry*; and *Young As We Is* (all 1938). Charging an admission price of thirty-five cents, the company sought a mass audience of "students, teachers, artists, members of labor unions, tourist groups, members of college sororities, and church groups."⁶³

In a December 1938 profile in *Opportunity*, the organ of the National Urban League, Edward Lawson reported that the Harlem performances attracted such groups and people "from every walk of life, from laborer to businessman, from housemaid to housewife." There had "rarely been a vacant seat since the first performance." Lawson further estimated that "the audience is about 75 percent Negro and 25 percent white—much better, from the point of view of Negro theatre, than the [Harlem Federal Theatre Project's] record of something like 70 percent white patronage last year."⁶⁴ With perhaps a hint of skepticism, he acknowledged that the company's financial support came from "labor groups who just now are striving to build up a 'people's theatre' in America." But HST had given Harlem "a theatre that is thoroughly its own, geared to present the type of material its people can appreciate and enjoy, and operated with no thought in mind but to reflect, as honestly and sincerely as the exigencies of stagecraft permit, the thinking and the dreaming of the group that it intends to serve."⁶⁵ Writing in the same magazine, the Black critic-philosopher Alain Locke, an early theorist of cultural pluralism, lauded HST's effort to create "a people's theatre with an intimate reaction of the audience to the materials familiar to it."⁶⁶ And *Don't You Want to Be Free* would soon become an important work in the African American theatrical repertory: Among the many subsequent productions in which the cultural legacy of HST and the IWO endured was the Black radical Free Southern Theater's 1975 staging of the play.⁶⁷

The kind of praise that Lawson and Locke offered *Don't You Want to Be Free* must have been gratifying for Hughes, Patterson, and their colleagues. Their aim was "to fill a long-felt need in [the Harlem] Community for a permanent repertory group presenting plays dealing with the lives, problems, and hopes of the Negro people in their relation to the American Scene."[68] Patterson later often remembered that, in addition to arranging IWO sponsorship for the theater, she had contributed to the development of its signature play. When Hughes wondered what the company would perform, she asked, "Why don't you string a lot of your poems together and make a play out of them?"[69] Hughes soon returned with a script that interpolated many of his published poems, along with fragments of Black vernacular music, in a modernist montage epic of Black American history. The play's single-act structure and recurring characters express the coherence and continuity of its various historical episodes, as does its reliance upon what Hughes called "a rapid moving-picture technique of one scene flowing directly into another."[70] The play's scenes are also bound together under the signs of racial violence and the depersonalization of Black labor: The play's setting is a *"bare stage, except for a lynch rope and an auction block."* On this stage, the figure whom Hughes had called "the Negro, servant to you all," claims for an hour the prerogative to revisit three centuries of Black life on "the American Scene." Breaking the fourth wall in the play's first speech, the Young Man hails a Black "you"—and a white one, if they, too, are listening: "Now I'll tell you what this show is about. It's about me, except that it's not just about me standing here talking to you—but it's about me yesterday, and about me tomorrow. . . . This show is about what it means to be colored in America." Then, issuing an imperative that he will repeat throughout the play," the Young Man says, "Listen: . . ." *Don't You Want to Be Free* calls on "you" to listen to the play's mimetic action and to Hughes's poetry, which often evokes Black music, as well as to the play's actual music, performed by the cast (and, in the HST productions, by pianist Carroll Tate). As the play's full title informs us, *Don't You Want to Be Free* plots Black social history in a history of Black music. The first poem heard is Hughes's "Negro" (1922), whose speaker has been "a slave," "a worker," "a victim," and, at the same time, "a singer," and the opening group of poems is followed by the chants of enslaved people and by Black sacred music.[71] As James Smethurst puts it, the play "suggests that Black popular and folk art and forms encode within them an account and interpretation of historical events." Encoded in *Don't You Want to Be Free* is "a history of interracial struggle against oppression, linking racial or [Black] national oppression to class exploitation but with African Americans significantly in the lead, doing much to shape the struggle and, indeed, providing some of the most glorious episodes of that struggle from the slave era to rise of the Congress of Industrial Organizations."[72]

Tracking the blues moments in *Don't You Want to Be Free*, we see not only the music's emergence as an American art but also the concomitant first stirrings of an interracial Socialist movement. In a 1941 *Phylon* article, Hughes identified the music with Black America, just as he did in many of his other writings. The blues, he wrote, are sung "out of black, beaten, but unbeatable throats."[73] But, in the same article, he foresaw the creation of "Great American [blues] dances containing all the laughter and pain, hunger and heartaches, search and reality of the contemporary scenes—for the Blues have something that goes beyond race or sectional limits, that appeals to the ear and heart of people everywhere." The beginnings of such dances, Hughes thought, could be found in the recent work of the white dancer-choreographer Felicia Sorel.[74] She had taken part in HST's November 17, 1938, multidisciplinary "Evening of the Blues."[75] In *Don't*'s twentieth-century moments, the exclamation "Colored folks made the blues!" becomes a refrain. "We made 'em," the Young Man says, "out of being poor and lonely. And homes busted up, and desperate and broke." But he also realizes that "now everybody sings 'em," for others have shared some of this experience.[76] This new embrace of a Black-authored art coincides with the rise of an interracial, revolutionary, working-class struggle, whose beginnings (for example, the advent of the "Colored and white [CIO] unions") the Black characters perceive as they await an answer from white America at the play's conclusion.[77] If the multitudinous "I" of "Let America Be America Again" speaks from three hundred years in the life of an interracial, multiethnic American people, the central characters in *Don't You Want to Be Free* traverse a long Black past leading to the Popular Front present, the first real chance for Socialism and cultural democracy.

Whereas *Don't You Want to Be Free* centers Black cultural expression, the Suitcase skits are more concerned with showing how it has been decentered. The HST brochure introduced the company as an answer to an American theater that had generally "given no place to the Negro" or else assigned the Black actor "a comic or servile role."[78] Like "Democracy and Me," Hughes's skits depict Black people's marginal relation to the nation's Jim-Crow cultural apparatus. The satires *Colonel Tom's Cabin*, *Limitations of Life*, and *Scarlet Sister Barry* expropriate and transform canonical literary and Hollywood representations of Blackness: Harriet Beecher Stowe's *Uncle Tom's Cabin* (1852), the 1934 film adaptation of Fannie Hurst's *Imitation of Life* (1933), and Ethel Barrymore's blackface performance in the 1930 Broadway adaptation of Julia Peterkin's *Scarlet Sister Mary* (1928). *Young as We Is*, a portrayal of racialized underemployment and unemployment, focuses in large part on Black people's exclusion from mainstream media and arts economies. The main characters are three Black boys: a shoeshine boy, a newsboy, and a busking dancer. All three try unsuccessfully to find work in a white New York City neighborhood whose residents object to their presence. When the shoeshine boy asks the newsboy why he is trying to sell the *Amsterdam News* in this area, he replies, "Why not? Colored folks reads white papers. How come white folks ought'n ter read colored papers?"[79] Even the dancer, Bo, cannot get paid to "jangle"—there can be only one Bojangles. An Irish police officer finally drives the boys off, and they return to Harlem.[80] A character called the "Negro American" is likewise driven from the sidewalk public square in *Hurrah, America!* Here the setting is a fascist Jersey City, in whose real-life counterpart Mayor Frank Hague was then waging a war on the CIO. Hughes's Negro American is denied even patriotic speech, though the "German-American" can wear a swastika pin and the "Italian-American" a fasces pin. After these white ethnics beat him, the Negro American is carried away by a police officer (who "*might be Irish*").[81] In this Jersey City, as in the New York of *Young as We Is*, "Nordic and non-Nordic" whites are aligned against their Black neighbors and interracial cultural democracy. Hughes's memories of Central High School notwithstanding, white ethnics could not be presumed to be "more democratic" and "less anti-Negro," especially now, a generation later in their Americanization, and especially outside of the sort of left subculture in which he had moved in Cleveland.

The Em-Fuehrer Jones, though, imagines a Popular Front metropolis with a Black culture worker at its center. Another send-up of prevailing mass-cultural representations of Blackness, this playlet takes aim at Eugene O'Neill's *The Emperor Jones* (1920), which was produced on Broadway in 1920 and 1921 and adapted as a feature film (starring Robeson) in 1933. Set in a Caribbean island nation evocative of Haiti, O'Neill's Expressionist drama and the film adaptation are about a Black American Pullman porter who declares himself emperor of the Black nation but is incapable even of self-mastery. Before being assassinated by rebels, he is returned in waking dream visions to his personal and racial pasts, indeed to Africa, and he devolves into barbarism. In Hughes's script, the emperor is Hitler, and the island is the "Black Forest" of New York. There he gropes his way through a menacing phantasmagoria of Ethiopians (whose nation was occupied by fascist Italy in 1936), "Gefullterfish!"-chanting Jews, Hail-Mary-ing Catholics, Bolsheviks, and the Black athletes Jesse Owens and Joe Louis, the last of whom vanquishes the Em-Fuehrer in the skit's final moment.[82] This conclusion recalls the heavyweight boxer Louis's victory over Germany's Max Schmeling at Yankee Stadium in June 1938, an event that challenged Nazi claims to racial superiority and lifted Louis to the pinnacle of anti-fascist celebrity. Seizing a microphone to address the spectators, the fighter exults, "Ah guess it was dat punch to de ribs dat got him!"[83] The triumph over fascism and reigning conceptions of Blackness is complete when the Black vernacular culture hero can claim a role in the cultural apparatus.

Hughes's association with the IWO continued through much of the 1940s. The Order published more of his work, including a one-dollar edition of *The Sun Do Move* (1942), a Black vernacular drama similar to *Don't You Want to*

Be Free. Hughes and Emerson Harper's new Double-V anthem "Freedom Road" was featured in a 1942 "international night of the dances and songs of many nations" sponsored by the IWO's Center in the Loop in Chicago.[84] In the fairly elaborate instructional bulletin that the IWO prepared for its annual Negro History Week celebrations, the section on literature directed readers to the work of Hughes, Margaret Walker (also on the Communist left), and Black writers of previous eras.[85] As the keynote speaker at the New York District's October 10, 1943, City-Wide Cultural Conference, Hughes again worked as a Popular Front coalition-builder, helping to establish a War Council of Cultural Groups that would coordinate the win-the-war efforts of IWO arts units across disciplinary lines and ethnic boundaries.[86] The brochure for the IWO's "Call to a Cultural Conference" promotes cultural work as critical to the war effort: "'No culture, no history, Heil Hitler!' is the slogan of death raised with the swastika.... In this global war against fascism, the music, songs, drama, dances of the people are mighty weapons. Let's use them for victory!"[87]

By the end of the decade, though, Hughes was no longer publicly identified with the Communist left, and he would soon publicly repudiate it. As scholars have long noted, he generally sidestepped his radical 1930s and 1940s works when he compiled such Cold War–era collections as *The Langston Hughes Reader* (1958) and his *Selected Poems* (1959). But, even in these volumes, as in his 1953 Senate testimony, one hears echoes of the longings whose origins he traced back to his Cleveland adolescence, the same yearnings that stimulated his IWO projects. Among the "18 Poems for Children" included in the *Reader* is "Little Song," which was first published in this volume. At first glance, the poem appears to be a liberal affirmation of international or cross-ethnic friendship. The first quatrain announces,

> Carmencita loves Patrick.
> Patrick loves Si Lan Chen.
> Xenophon loves Mary Jane.
> Hildegarde loves Ben.

The poem becomes a good deal more provocative in a final pair of these opening clauses, one of a number of homoerotic significations to be found in Hughes's writings: "Natasha loves Miguelito— / And Miguelito loves me."[88] This queer "me" indeed defines a radical social nexus, for, as we soon learn, all of these lovers have assembled for May Day. Hughes's *A New Song* had included two poems about May Day parades, events in which the IWO and its ethnic societies had figured prominently. And the poet was surely one of the celebrants described in Haverty-Stacke's account of the holiday's 1930s heyday: "Many [CPUSA] members and supporters had sincerely expressed the harmony they believed existed between their radical political aspirations and their democratic and pluralist heritage as Americans."[89] Appearing in the waning hours of labor's May Day, "Little Song" evoked a maypole and colored ribbons, the trappings of the older holiday with the same name, but the poem memorialized the dual struggle for Socialism and cultural democracy in which Hughes and the IWO had taken part. Much like Hughes's Senate testimony, "Little Song" revisited youth to confront the Cold War present with the memory of interethnic radical solidarity.

NOTES

1. Hughes appeared before the McCarthy committee on two days: March 24 and 26, 1953. The March 24 testimony would not be made available to the public until 2003, but the March 26 hearing was televised (see US Congress, Senate, Permanent Subcommittee on Investigations of the Committee on Government Operations, *Hearing on State Department Information Program—Information Centers*, 83rd Cong., 1st sess., 1953). On that day, Hughes stated that from the late 1920s or early 1930s until the mid- or late 1940s he had been involved in the Communist movement and had admired the USSR but that he had since lost faith in both and left the movement.

2. US Congress, *Executive Sessions*.

3. Langston Hughes, "Langston Hughes Speaks," *The Crisis*, May 1953, 279.

4. US Congress, *Executive Sessions*.

5. In 1940, Louise Thompson married CPUSA organizer William L. Patterson, and she is now most often known as Louise Thompson Patterson.

6. Roger Keeran, "National Groups and the Popular Front: The Case of the International Workers Order," *Journal of American Ethnic History* 14, no. 3 (Spring 1995): 38.

7. Langston Hughes, *The Big Sea: An Autobiography* (Knopf, 1940), 30.

8. Hughes, *Big Sea*, 31.

9. Hughes, *Big Sea*, 31, 34.

10. Hughes, *Big Sea*, 32.

11. Hughes, *Big Sea*, 32.

12. For more detailed accounts of Hughes's and Patterson's often intersecting lives, see Faith Berry, *Langston Hughes: Before and Beyond Harlem* (Lawrence Hill, 1983); Anne Donlon, "Langston Hughes and Louise Thompson," in *Poetry, Politics, and Friendship in the Spanish Civil War: Langston Hughes, Nancy Cunard, and Louise Thompson*, ed. Anne Donlon (Center for the Humanities, Graduate Center, City University of New York, 2012); Keith Gilyard, *Louise Thompson Patterson: A Life of Struggle for Justice* (Duke University Press, 2017); Joseph McLaren, *Langston Hughes: Folk Dramatist in the Protest Tradition, 1921–1943* (Greenwood, 1997); Arnold Rampersad, *The Life of Langston Hughes*, 2 vols. (Oxford University Press, 1986–88); and Robert M. Zecker, *"A Road to Peace and Freedom": The International Workers Order and the Struggle for Economic Justice and Civil Rights, 1930–1954* (Temple University Press, 2018).

13. In her testimony on the IWO's behalf in the case in which New York State sought to liquidate the Order, Patterson recalled that for most of the white members whose aid she sought, "it did not seem unnatural that a Negro woman should be sent out by the national office to assume this responsibility." See Bohlinger v. International Workers Order, 305 N.Y. 258 (NY Supreme Ct., 1953), 3793. Decades later, she remembered that "women played a large role in the organization itself, in the [IWO] community centers and some of them ran the individual sections." See interview with Louise Thompson Patterson, May 14, 1987, Louise Thompson Patterson Papers, MSS 869, box 27, folder 7, Rose Library, Emory

University, Atlanta, Georgia (hereafter Louise Thompson Patterson Papers). I thank the Patterson Estate for permission to quote from this collection.

14. Gilyard, *Louise Thompson Patterson*, 130.

15. Langston Hughes, *Letters from Langston: From the Harlem Renaissance to the Red Scare and Beyond*, ed. Evelyn Louise Crawford and MaryLouise Patterson (University of California Press, 2016), 136.

16. Michael Denning, *The Cultural Front: The Laboring of American Culture in the Twentieth Century* (Verso, 1996), 98.

17. League of Professional Groups for Foster and Ford, *Culture and the Crisis: An Open Letter to the Writers, Artists, Teachers, Physicians, Engineers, Scientists and Other Professional Workers of America* (Workers Library, 1932), 11.

18. Langston Hughes, "Democracy and Me," in *Good Morning Revolution: Uncollected Social Protest Writings*, ed. Faith Berry (Lawrence Hill, 1973), 127.

19. Langston Hughes and Carl Van Vechten, *Remember Me to Harlem: The Letters of Langston Hughes and Carl Van Vechten, 1925–1964*, ed. Emily Bernard (Knopf, 2001), 122–23.

20. Hughes, "Democracy and Me," 128.

21. Hughes, "Democracy and Me," 128, 129.

22. Hughes, "Democracy and Me," 128.

23. C. Wright Mills, "The Cultural Apparatus," in *Power, Politics, and People: The Collected Essays of C. Wright Mills*, ed. Irving Louis Horowitz (Ballantine, 1963), 406.

24. Zecker, "A Road to Peace and Freedom," 155.

25. Interview with Louise Thompson Patterson, August 12, 1984, MSS 869, box 27, folder 3, Louise Thompson Patterson Papers.

26. For a more thorough account of the IWO's cultural work, see Zecker, "A Road to Peace and Freedom."

27. *Bohlinger v. International Workers Order*, 3795.

28. *Bohlinger v. International Workers Order*, 3778.

29. Louise Thompson Patterson, "The Paris Conference and the Harlem Suitcase Theatre," n.d., MSS 869, box 20, folder 7, Louise Thompson Patterson Papers.

30. *Bohlinger v. International Workers Order*, 3800.

31. Hughes, *Letters from Langston*, 132.

32. Hughes and Van Vechten, *Remember Me to Harlem*, 123.

33. Langston Hughes, *A New Song* (International Workers Order, 1938).

34. "Langston's Hughes's *A New Song*," advertisement, *New Order*, April 1938.

35. Hughes, *A New Song*, 8.

36. Langston Hughes, introduction to *I Hear the People Singing: Selected Poems of Walt Whitman*, by Walt Whitman (International Publishers, 1946), 9, 8.

37. Langston Hughes, "I, Too," *Survey Graphic*, March 1, 1925, 683.

38. Hughes, *A New Song*, 26.

39. Robert Shulman, *The Power of Political Art: The 1930s Literary Left Reconsidered* (University of North Carolina Press, 2000), 296.

40. Donna T. Haverty-Stacke, *America's Forgotten Holiday: May Day and Nationalism, 1867–1960* (New York University Press, 2009), 163, 157. The first celebration of labor's May Day, also known as International Workers' Day, is generally dated to May 1, 1886, when workers in cities across the United States went on strike for an eight-hour workday. But the holiday emerged as a retrospective construction following the events of the next several days. On May 3, police fired into a crowd of striking workers, killing two, at Chicago's McCormick Harvesting Works. A day later, workers gathered in the city's Haymarket Square to protest this violence and to sustain the demand for an eight-hour workday. As the demonstration was coming to an end, a bomb was thrown into a large column of police officers, and a deadly confrontation between police and

protestors ensued. Eight anarchists faced charges in connection with the violence; all of the men were convicted at the end of a tainted trial and four of them were executed. For anarchists and socialists, these events dramatized the need for anti-capitalist struggle, and for many years thereafter, American radicals annually reaffirmed their collective commitment on the first of May, the date on which the present era in this struggle seemed to have begun.

41. Rampersad, *The Life of Langston Hughes*, 1:29, 37.

42. Barbara Foley, *Spectres of 1919: Class and Nation in the Making of the New Negro* (University of Illinois Press, 2003), 45.

43. Foley, *Spectres of 1919*, 175.

44. Foley, *Spectres of 1919*, 160.

45. Hughes, *A New Song*, 9.

46. Hughes, *A New Song*, 10.

47. Hughes, *A New Song*, 9.

48. Anthony Dawahare, "Langston Hughes's Radical Poetry and the 'End of Race,'" *MELUS 23*, no. 3 (Fall 1998): 34. For other arguments along these lines, see Shulman, *The Power of Political Art*, and Eric Schocket, *Vanishing Moments: Class and American Literature* (University of Michigan Press, 2006).

49. Rampersad, *The Life of Langston Hughes*, 1:320.

50. Hughes, *A New Song*, 11.

51. "Announcing the Seminar in Negro History," brochure, 1938, Langston Hughes Ephemera Collection, MSS 0567, box 1, folder 1, Special Collections, University of Delaware Library, University of Delaware, Newark, Delaware (hereafter Langston Hughes Ephemera Collection), http://udspace.udel.edu/handle/19716/23688. When Hughes was in Spain, he asked Patterson about the possibility of the Order's publishing *Negroes in Spain*, a collection of his Spanish Civil War articles, but this idea did not come to fruition. See Donlon, "Langston Hughes and Louise Thompson," 36; Gilyard, *Louise Thompson Patterson*, 130; and Rampersad, *The Life of Langston Hughes*, 1:351.

52. *Bohlinger v. International Workers Order*, 3797.

53. In the 1940s, Gordon married IWO organizer June Croll, who became, around the same time, the executive director of the Emma Lazarus Women's Division of the IWO's Jewish Peoples Fraternal Order. See Donna Halper, "Eugene F. Gordon," in *Harlem Renaissance Lives from the African American National Biography*, ed. Henry Louis Gates Jr. and Evelyn Brooks Higginbotham (Oxford University Press, 2009), 224–25.

54. "Announcing the Seminar in Negro History"; "Seminar in Negro History," flyer, 1938, MSS 869, box 8, folder 9, Louise Thompson Patterson Papers; interview with Louise Thompson Patterson, May 14, 1987, MSS 869, box 27, folder 7, Louise Thompson Patterson Papers.

55. Langston Hughes, letter to the Harlem Suitcase Theatre, June 14, 1939, Langston Hughes Papers, JWJ MSS 26, box 74, folder 1430, James Weldon Johnson Collection in the Yale Collection of American Literature, Beinecke Rare Book and Manuscript Library, Yale University, New Haven, Connecticut (hereafter Langston Hughes Papers).

56. Rampersad, *The Life of Langston Hughes*, 1:356, 358.

57. Hughes, *Letters from Langston*, 150. Clipping from July 5, 1939, *New York Times*, MSS 869, box 7, folder 5, Louise Thompson Patterson Papers.

58. Rampersad, *The Life of Langston Hughes*, 1:356.

59. Patterson, "The Paris Conference."

60. For accounts of HST's demise, see Rampersad, *The Life of Langston Hughes*, vol. 1, and McLaren, *Langston Hughes*.

61. Langston Hughes, *The Collected Works of Langston Hughes*, vol. 5, *The Plays to 1942: Mulatto to the Sun Do Move*, ed. Leslie Catherine Sanders and Nancy Johnston (University of Missouri Press, 2002), 570.

62. "Langston Hughes and Suitcase Theatre Actors," n.d., JWJ MSS 26, box 512, folder 12718, Langston Hughes Papers.
63. "Langston Hughes and Suitcase Theatre Actors"; "The Harlem Suitcase Theatre," brochure, n.d., JWJ MSS 26, box 536, folder 13158, Langston Hughes Papers.
64. Edward Lawson, "Theatre in a Suitcase," *Opportunity*, December 1938, 361.
65. Lawson, "Theatre in a Suitcase," 360. For more extensive discussions of HST, see McLaren, *Langston Hughes*; Rampersad, *The Life of Langston Hughes*, vol. 1; and Leslie Catherine Sanders, *The Development of Black Theater in America: From Shadows to Selves* (Louisiana State University Press, 1988).
66. Alain Locke, "The Negro: 'New' or Newer?: A Retrospective Review of the Literature of the Negro for 1938," *Opportunity*, January–February 1939, 10.
67. See Free Southern Theater, *The Free Southern Theater Records, 1963–1978: Register* (Amistad Research Center, 1985), 5.
68. "Harlem Suitcase Theatre Constitution," MSS 869, box 7, folder 4, Louise Thompson Patterson Papers.
69. Interview with Patterson, August 12, 1984.
70. Hughes, *The Collected Works*, 5:573.
71. Hughes, *The Collected Works*, 5:540.
72. James Smethurst, "Remembering Nat Turner: Black Artists, Radical History, and Radical Historiography, 1930–55," in *Lineages of the Literary Left: Essays in Honor of Alan M. Wald*, ed. Howard Brick et al. (University of Michigan Library, 2015), http://dx.doi.org/10.3998/maize.13545968.0001.001.
73. Langston Hughes, "Songs Called the Blues," *Phylon* 2, no. 2 (Second Quarter 1941): 143.
74. Hughes, "Songs Called the Blues," 145.
75. "Harlem Suitcase Theatre Presents an Evening of the Blues," palm card, 1938, MSS 0567, box 1, folder 1, Langston Hughes Ephemera Collection.
76. Hughes, *The Collected Works*, 5:557.
77. Hughes, *The Collected Works*, 5:568.
78. "The Harlem Suitcase Theatre," brochure.
79. Hughes, *The Collected Works*, 5:587.
80. Hughes, *Collected Works*, 589.
81. Hughes, *Collected Works*, 580.
82. Hughes, *Collected Works*, 577.
83. Hughes, *Collected Works*, 579–80.
84. Hughes, *Letters from Langston*, 229.
85. *Negro History Week Bulletin*, pamphlet, February 1945, International Workers Order (IWO) Records #5276, box 19, folder 12a, Kheel Center for Labor-Management Documentation and Archives, Catherwood Library, Cornell University, Ithaca, New York (hereafter Kheel), https://digital.library.cornell.edu/catalog/ss:20631816.
86. "Call to a Cultural Conference," brochure, 1943, box 49, folder 6, Kheel, https://digital.library.cornell.edu/catalog/ss:19043101.
87. "Call to a Cultural Conference."
88. Langston Hughes, "Little Song," in *The Langston Hughes Reader* (George Braziller, 1958), 154.
89. Haverty-Stacke, *America's Forgotten Holiday*, 173.

6

STAGING THE INTERRACIAL LEFT
Paul Robeson, Black Artistry, and the International Workers Order

Felicia Bevel

In Port Murray, New Jersey in 1940, Paul Robeson stood on a makeshift stage in front of a diverse group of children and sang to them in a deep, soothing voice. The children, sitting close together on the ground with wide, open grins—with one child half-sitting on the stage just inches from Robeson's feet—gazed up at his tall frame in awe, mesmerized by his presence. Robeson looked down upon the smiling children. He stood diagonally across from two life-size murals—one of a group of three Black men carrying a long piece of wood in an open field, the other of Paul Robeson himself, which the children had created in his honor. As he smiled down at the children and stood across from his own smiling face, the actor relayed a powerful message, one inscribed on a sign hanging above his head that read "freedom."[1]

This is a scene from Camp Wo-Chi-Ca (Workers Children's Camp), an integrated proletarian camp in New Jersey sponsored by the International Workers Order (IWO). June Levine and Gene Gordon provide details about this performance by Paul Robeson in their 2002 memoir, *Tales of Wo-Chi-Ca: Blacks, Whites, and Reds at Camp*. Levine and Gordon, who attended the camp as children, present an in-depth view of the life at the camp, drawing from numerous interviews with other individuals who attended Camp Wo-Chi-Ca during its roughly two-decade existence. This scene is just one of many from Paul Robeson's several visits that capture his performances at the camp and interactions with its young attendees.

Paul Robeson performed several times for the International Workers Order, a leftist fraternal organization established in 1930 that provided a range of services and benefits to its diverse membership and fought against racial and class injustices. Robeson's visit to Camp Wo-Chi-Ca embodied everything that he and the IWO represented: interracial solidarity, activism against racial and class oppression, and support of the livelihoods and artistic expression of the working class and people of color. In many ways, Robeson's visit encapsulated the intersection of art and politics that defined his career.[2] In IWO spaces such as Camp Wo-Chi-Ca, the artist and activist found a home for his leftist politics and joined a host of other Black cultural producers such as Langston Hughes, Carlton Moss, and Kenneth Spencer in using performance to protest.

Robeson became a member of the IWO and participated in or attended various IWO-sponsored cultural events—such as later performances at Camp Wo-Chi-Ca and Camp Kinderland (another camp for the children of workers), IWO rallies, a festival in support of anti-fascist efforts in Spain, and performances for the Jewish Peoples Fraternal Order and other sections of the IWO.[3] However, three events in particular—his performance in 1940 at Camp Wo-Chi-Ca, his performance at the International Fiesta in February 1941, and his performance at IWO Day at the Civilian and National Defense Exposition in October 1941—featured "Ballad for Americans," a song that he either sang (sometimes accompanied by an IWO or other integrated chorus) or listened to as others sang to him. These performances occurred as the United States prepared for and then entered World War II and it served as a platform for the actor to critique the nation and its failure to live up to its inclusive rhetoric. During these performances, Robeson embodied a Black leftist politics that presented working-class experiences and racial inclusiveness as important to a present and future America. This aligned with the IWO's ethos of class-conscious resistance and investment in interracial solidarity. For Robeson, performance was an avenue through which people of all backgrounds could come together under a unifying message, something that he demonstrated time and again through his artistry.

Beyond "Ballad for Americans," Robeson also developed a broader legacy within the IWO. From the Paul Robeson Playhouse at Camp Wo-Chi-Ca to a Paul Robeson Children's Program at the Du Sable Community Center in Chicago run by IWO members, small cultural tributes to the actor happened many times. These fleeting moments do more than simply demonstrate the lasting impact of Robeson's artistry within the IWO. They also illuminate the network of Black cultural producers and production that found both temporary and permanent homes within the organization. Through Robeson, we can better understand how the IWO served as a space for other Black artists—whether well-known or obscure, professional or amateur—to share their work and, in many cases, continue the labor of challenging racism and other forms of oppression. Langston Hughes, for instance, similarly created literature in the IWO that stressed the need for Black liberation if America would ever be America, as Matthew Calihman explores in his chapter. Through their artistry, Black leftists such as Robeson and Hughes found a home in the IWO's fraternal society, showing the important role the IWO played in Black leftist history. Like Robeson's singing, their cultural work not only found an audience in the IWO but also created a genealogy of artistic expression, as IWO members performed their plays, recited their poems, and sang their songs in numerous settings.

Focusing on three of Robeson's IWO performances and the larger genealogy of Black creative expression he inspired magnifies the specific critique that Robeson and other Black artists relayed through their work. While the IWO carried out broad civil rights activism and cultural activities during its roughly twenty-four-year history, in the early 1940s Robeson's IWO performances called on Americans to complete a difficult assignment—to acknowledge the racial injustices that still plagued American society and challenge the hypocritical ideals of democracy the United States projected onto the global stage but failed to live up to at home. Robeson's influence on other artistic expression within the IWO was significant, and until it was shut down the organization continued his message of resistance even in his absence.

The International Workers Order and Its Marriage of Art and Politics

Paul Robeson's visit to Camp Wo-Chi-Ca in 1940 provides a snapshot of the full extent of his participation and cultural legacy in the IWO. He not only performed at the IWO-sponsored camp several times, but was also one its most ardent supporters—sometimes performing in other venues to raise money for the camp's operation and help children whose parents could not otherwise afford the admission fee. He was a member of the camp's board of trustees and even sent his own son, Paul Jr., to the camp. June Levine and Gene Gordon capture the powerful impact that Robeson had at the camp: "So many lofty, splendid visitors to Camp Wo-Chi-Ca! And yet one stood above all others—the tallest tree in the forest, Paul Robeson." Many other campers who shared this sentiment offered anecdotes about their interactions with Robeson, often expressing their appreciation for his talent and activism. For campers such as Steve Cogan, Robeson was both larger than life and familiar, like someone they had known for years but only at a distance. When recalling Robeson's visit to the camp, he stated, "I recall clearly his voice and how familiar a presence he seemed to me, as though he had stepped out of his phonograph record that we had in our collection at home." In a letter written to Robeson in 1950 lamenting his absence, a group of campers told him that he was "a symbol of what we Wo-Chi-Cans want to accomplish in our lives" because he had "done so much for all peoples." Even though he could not join them that year (because of increasing surveillance of his activities by the state), the children promised to "sing your songs and play your records just as though you were with us." For many campers, his use of performance to advocate for people of all backgrounds made him a hero; he demonstrated that intersection of art and politics during his performance at Camp Wo-Chi-Ca and at other IWO-sponsored spaces and events.[4]

When not performing for the IWO, Robeson organized and attended numerous IWO events. Some were intimate gatherings in the homes of IWO members and in IWO offices; a 1944 reception at a private office was one such event.[5] A much larger IWO-sponsored event was a "Chicago Salutes Paul Robeson" concert at Chicago's Civic Opera House in 1947.[6] He attended IWO events as an honored guest, including a testimonial dinner for IWO president William Weiner held in 1941 in New York.[7] He also helped organize IWO-sponsored events related to Black history and civil rights. In 1946, for instance, he organized a rally in Washington, DC, to launch a one-hundred-day anti-lynching campaign.[8] At the rally, participants attended a religious meeting and met with government officials to discuss policy initiatives to end lynching. The rally was held on the eighty-fourth anniversary of the Emancipation Proclamation, so as to demonstrate the unfinished process of Black liberation in the United States and the urgency of adopting an anti-lynching agenda.

Robeson supported the IWO's mission of service to its members and racial and ethnic diversity. The International Workers Order provided a variety of benefits to its diverse membership (including health insurance, life insurance, and burial and unemployment insurance) and services such as dental and medical care.[9] It also offered specific services for its female members, such as contraceptive care through its New York–based birth control center.[10] Insurance benefits especially helped African American members who often faced discrimination from insurance companies that refused to sell them policies or charged them higher prices. The IWO, which understood itself as a "militant lobbying organization," also worked externally to secure certain rights for workers such as union representation and fair wages.[11]

Ethnic and racial diversity defined its mission, and numerous ethnic associations like the Slovak Workers Society joined the organization during the first few years of its existence.[12] In addition to Puerto Ricans, Mexicans, Jews, Italians, Serbians, Hungarians, and Arabs, African Americans constituted a significant percentage of the Order's membership. Some held leadership roles. Louise Thompson Patterson, a friend of Paul Robeson, was a prominent Black officer who led the Harlem branch of the IWO. She was elected as its national secretary in 1935 and then served as vice president.[13] An outspoken anti-lynching advocate, she frequently expressed her anti-racist views concerning Black rights and racial segregation in the *Fraternal Outlook*, an important news organ of the Order.

IWO militancy certainly extended to its civil rights activism. It was vigilant in its grassroots organizing against lynching, housing and job discrimination, and exclusion of African Americans from public spaces. It not only fought against racism within the United States but also challenged oppression beyond national borders, showing support, for instance, for decolonization movements in Africa and Asia.[14] Its emphasis on civil rights activism and interracial solidarity within and beyond its ranks made it revolutionary, a quality that (along with its Communist origins) eventually led to its demise within the Cold War surveillance culture that erupted after World War II.

Throughout its existence, the IWO demonstrated its commitment to racial justice through both representation and practice. In addition to having a diverse membership—with people of color not only belonging to the rank and file of the organization but also occupying leadership roles—it also carved out spaces that tailored to the needs of specific communities. Spaces like the Cervantes Society for Puerto Ricans and other Latinos/as and the Frederick Douglass–Abraham Lincoln Society for African Americans rendered the IWO even more inclusive. Even lodges that did not cater to members of color supported racial justice initiatives. A North Philadelphia Ukrainian lodge, for instance, celebrated Negro History Week as part of the IWO's national educational program. The IWO also advocated for several key civil rights issues. The organization actively fought against Jim Crow structures that sought either to keep African Americans in their place (through the denial of voting rights) or punish them for committing racial transgressions (through forms of racial terror). The IWO protested the poll tax and took an active role in anti-lynching campaigns, encouraging its members, for instance, to support the 1935 Wagner Anti-Lynching Bill (to no avail). It supported high profile civil rights cases such as the Scottsboro defendants case by raising funds to support their legal defense team. Its racial justice work extended beyond the scope of fighting for the rights of Black Americans, which was evident in its public condemnation of Japanese incarceration during World War II.[15]

The strength of the IWO's civil rights activism also resulted from its collaboration with other racial justice organizations, some of which contained members who were also members of the IWO.[16] Some of these cross-pollinated entities included the Sojourners for Truth and Justice group, the National Negro Congress (NNC), and the Civil Rights Congress (CRC). The IWO supported the CRC in its efforts to help Black families facing resistance when moving into all-white neighborhoods and joined them during the mid-1940s in a campaign against the Mississippi senator Theodore Bilbo for his endorsement of segregationist policies and racist remarks. When the NNC organized a boycott against the Noxzema Cosmetics Company due to its refusal to hire Black employees, the IWO was right there ready to assist. When white trolley motormen in Philadelphia went on strike to prevent the hiring of Black workers during World War II, the IWO joined progressive national organizations in denouncing the unionized motormen's hate strike. Yet the IWO's class-based critique of American racism, along with its pro-Soviet stance, often put it into conflict with more conservative racial justice organizations such as the National Association for the Advancement of Colored People (NAACP) and the Urban League. It clashed with the NAACP's approach during the defense of the Scottsboro defendants in the 1930s and during the Ingram case in the 1940s. When it tried to join the "National Emergency Civil Rights Mobilization" in 1949, the Order received a letter from the NAACP stating that it was not welcome. Much of this conflict heightened after World War II due to the Cold War surveillance culture and the NAACP's fears about ties to left-wing organizations and thought.[17]

In addition to its civil rights activism and grassroots organizing about issues affecting working-class communities, the IWO was a natural home for Paul Robeson because it aligned with his commitment to connecting politics with art. Robeson was well known for his anti-colonial, anti-fascist, and anti-classist politics, and frequently expressed this in various public venues. In a 1937 interview published in the *Daily Worker*, the actor spoke about his decision to join Unity Theater, a leftist theater organization established in London in 1936 that catered to working-class audiences and offered plays, revues, and other productions that presented working-class experiences.[18] He stated, "When I step on to a stage in the future. . . . I go on as a representative of the working class." He went on to declare: "I shan't do any more films after the two that are being finished now. . . . Not unless I can get a cast-iron story—the kind that can't be twisted in the making."[19] An opportunity to participate in a "cast-iron story" arose in 1942 through a film about labor and civil rights organizing called *Native Land*.[20] Produced by the leftist film production company Frontier Films, the documentary "create[d] afresh those feelings of basic American patriotism" through a "deeply moving commentary" created by the poet David Wolf and narrated by Paul Robeson.[21] This was a clear departure from other films in which Robeson had recently starred such as *Sanders of the River* (1935) and *Show Boat* (1936), which glorified British colonialism in Nigeria and romanticized Black labor in the postbellum South, respectively. His commitment to anti-racist and anti-capitalist representation continued for the remainder of his career, a sentiment he expressed much later in a 1957 interview: "My labors in the future will remain the same as they have in the past. They will be based on my whole experience—in the antifascist struggle that saw its finest expression in Spain, in the worldwide struggle of working people against their oppressors."[22]

Robeson's politics placed him among a diverse network of Black leftists who understood the intricate relationship of race and class at home and abroad. Esther Cooper Jackson, A. Philip Randolph, and others believed that Black liberation could not become a reality until class oppression ended—that capitalist structures perpetuated disparity along racial lines. For people such as Randolph—who founded the all-Black Brotherhood of Sleeping Car Porters in 1925—evidence of this emerged in the workplace, where white unions refused to extend membership to and protect Black workers despite the exploitation they shared with their white counterparts.[23] Writers such as Richard Wright illuminated the experiences of working-class Blacks living in segregated Northern cities through literature.[24] African American women such as Esther Cooper Jackson believed that gender was also important to consider: that Black female domestic workers in white homes, for instance, were particularly vulnerable to multiple, intersecting forms of oppression not only because of their race and class but also due to their gender.[25] Such activists shared their beliefs publicly in *The Messenger* and similar leftist magazines.[26]

One way that some Black leftists examined this intersection of race and class was through a transnational lens. They not only centered the experiences of working-class African Americans in their critiques of the United States, but also considered the plight of working-class whites and people of color in other countries. Ending racism and class oppression was a global project, one that required solidarity across national lines. Robeson Taj Frazier argues that Afro-Asian solidarity was particularly appealing for Black leftists during the repressive anti-Communist censorship of the middle of the century.[27] China became a home for Black leftists, some of whom sought refuge after persecution for their political beliefs and others who left the United States to find new political inspiration. NAACP chapter leader Robert F. Williams and his wife Mabel Williams relocated to first Cuba and then China, where they continued to denounce not only Jim Crow segregation but also US military intervention in Vietnam.[28] The labor activist Vicki Garvin spent several years teaching in China due to attacks by the US government on leftists and leftist organizations such as the Communist Party USA (CPUSA) (of which she was a member until 1958).[29] In her teaching, Garvin used Mao Zedong's philosophy of cultivating revolutionary thought in working-class youth to teach Chinese students about the Black freedom struggle.[30] Building interracial alliances, especially with people of color who had participated in revolutionary struggle or still experienced oppression under colonial rule was thus an important facet of Black leftism during the mid-twentieth century.

The IWO demonstrated its leftist politics by welcoming Black cultural expression, specifically collaborating with Black artists to hold cultural events. An IWO lodge called Lincoln Steffens Lodge 500 in New York led efforts to institutionalize Black culture: in addition to its Negro History Week lineup, it also offered monetary prizes to Black artists.[31] It was also a space where Black artists such as actor/singer Kenneth Spencer and jazz pianist Mary Lou Williams performed.[32] Other IWO events featuring Black artists also helped fund Red camps. The IWO and other like-minded organizations wanted as many workers' children as possible to attend these camps and frequently called for donations, ran fundraising drives (sometimes organized by IWO children), and held benefit performances to raise funds to reduce the admissions price and/or send more children to camps. One such benefit performance featured jazz pianist Hazel Scott and dancer Pearl Primus, who taught dance at Camp Wo-Chi-Ca. The two Black artists performed at New York City's Webster Hall in 1944 in the Variety Musical Program and Dance hosted by the Lincoln Steffens Lodge to raise funds for renovations at Camp Wo-Chi-Ca, a cause that Pearl Primus praised, describing her artistic contribution and that of Scott as a way of "helping organizations who help children."[33] Such performances by Black artists illustrated the organization's commitment to creating an environment where children understood the importance of interracial solidarity and would emphasize this as they continued to do anti-racist work in the future.

The IWO also supported Black artists when they came under scrutiny or faced persecution. Robeson was one such artist. When concert venues banned him from performing during the late 1940s due to his outspokenness regarding civil rights, the IWO stood by his side. A 1947 *Atlanta Daily World* article quoted the IWO executive committee's public declaration of support for the actor. After condemning the attacks on Robeson, the committee stated: "We therefore call upon our societies and the 1,800 lodges of our order to intensify their efforts in behalf of the struggle for equality and for Negro rights. Our general council not long ago pledged support to Mr. Robeson's decision to devote his great talents and energies to the fight against prejudice and intolerance wherever they appear."[34] Although the state had not yet constrained his movement by taking away his passport, which it would do in 1951, the Cold War surveillance apparatus had already started to tighten its grip on the actor.

Just two years before the State Department stripped Robeson of his passport, two concerts in Peekskill, New York, vividly demonstrated the persecution the actor would face in the decade to come and the IWO's steadfast support of him. Organized by the Civil Rights Congress and fully supported by the IWO, the concerts were supposed to be an opportunity for Robeson to use the stage once more to protest ongoing forms of racial violence in the United States. The very thing that he meant to condemn, however, became a reality at Peekskill. During both concerts (the latter of which only happened because of and in resistance to the racial violence that had abruptly stopped Robeson's first concert from starting), local white residents and police officers attacked the audience. In addition to physical violence, the Black and Jewish audience members also endured racial slurs and anti-Communist language. The IWO once again defended Robeson, calling the assailants "rockthrowing fascists" and declaring the attacks to be part of the larger culture of "redbaiting" that had overwhelmed the country.[35]

During the 1950s, however, Robeson faced direct attack from the US government. Tony Perucci points to the actor's "alleged" comments at the 1949 Paris Peace Conference as the catalyst. In a clear departure from his use of the IWO stage to express patriotism during World War II, Robeson spoke out against the assumption that African Americans should support US war efforts in light of the racism they still experienced. In response, the House Un-American Activities Committee marked him as a "mad black traitor," claiming his supposedly un-American beliefs stemmed from a deeply rooted mental illness. The State Department took away his passport between 1951 and 1958, preventing him from leaving the country. Robeson resisted their claims by continuing to publicly condemn the Cold War, warning that efforts to contain Communism would actually facilitate the spread of capitalism and further exploit vulnerable nations. During his 1956 HUAC hearing, he pushed back on the committee's claims of Communist ties by revealing the real reason they targeted him: his critiques of US racism and global white supremacy. He also called the committee out on its racism by confronting specific members for sponsoring bills that sought to prevent immigrants of color from entering the country. Despite his containment, the actor remained steadfast in his political beliefs and did not hesitate to express them throughout the 1950s.[36]

Although audiences were well accustomed to Robeson's politics, the late 1940s and the 1950s were a turning point in the policing of his artistry. The very activism that made him famous and beloved around the world became the cause of his persecution by the US government and ordinary citizens. As quickly as he rose to fame because of his soothing voice and charisma, he swiftly fell from grace as the result of his critiques of the United States, support of the Soviet Union, and membership in organizations such as the IWO. While the State Department championed some Black artists and sent them abroad as official ambassadors of the nation, it policed Robeson and other artists whom it deemed subversive.[37] Yet, in spite of (and perhaps because of) this persecution, Robeson persevered, finding innovative ways to continue to share his artistry with diverse audiences around the world.

Performing in the IWO: Robeson's Critical Vision of America

From the moment Robeson arrived at Camp Wo-Chi-Ca in 1940, he immediately won the hearts of the young campers. June Levine and Eugene Gordon paint a vivid picture of his arrival:

> The mess hall bell announces his arrival. A giant of a man emerged from the camp station wagon. Raising an enormous arm, he breaks into a big wide mile.... Campers and counselors stream down the hill flourishing painted banners: PAUL ROBESON DAY. WELCOME PAUL! Kitchen workers desert their pots and pans. Kids clamor and swarm over Robeson; he scoops them up in a warm embrace. Up the dirt road they throng, children perched on Paul's broad shoulders or clinging to his massive arms.[38]

From this memory, it is clear that Robeson's visit was a powerful moment for the campers (or "Wo-Chi-Cans" as they called themselves), as his arrival literally brought all operations to a standstill. It was a highly anticipated event and the campers were as excited to see the actor as he was excited to spend the day with them. He was their hero and they were in awe of his presence. As former camper Sheila Newman remembered: "He mesmerized me with his towering presence and booming voice. He had huge, gentle hands and a magnetic smile. When he sang for us my love for opera was born."[39]

Paul Robeson spent the day with the working-class children of Camp Wo-Chi-Ca along with Dr. Max Yergan of the National Negro Congress. During Robeson's visit the children presented him with gifts, performed for him, ate lunch with him, and joined him in a game of baseball. The October 1940 issue of the IWO magazine *Fraternal Outlook* quoted ten-year-old Sheila Raffel as saying, "I don't think any camper who was here to see this marvelous sight will ever forget it." Twelve-year-old Benjamin Matheison echoed her enthusiasm: "I hope both Dr. Max Yergan and Paul Robeson will again be our guests at Camp Wo-Chi-Ca."[40] These remarks clearly indicate the campers' appreciation of the actor's visit and performance and show the lasting impact it had on the children and the IWO community. His singing, however, was the highlight of the trip. As in many of his public appearances, he used performance as a platform for political discussion, sharing his recent activism in Spain and the ongoing problem of racism in America with the campers, making sure to draw parallels between injustices at home and abroad. The camp, of course, was the perfect space for the actor to wed art and politics given its own merging of revolutionary practice and cultural/recreational activities.

Red camps such as Camp Wo-Chi-Ca centered a proletarian consciousness in several ways. First, they were less expensive to attend, making them more accessible to working-class children, and they offered scholarships. In fact, in 1931, a similar IWO camp called Camp Kinderland reduced its admission prices, charging parents who either belonged to the IWO or whose children attended one of its Jewish children's schools "$20 for two weeks, $65 for five weeks, and $130 for the whole season." At the WIR (Workers International Relief) Camp in Wingdale, New York, admission prices were based on a family's income and the children of unemployed parents could attend free of charge. Second, these proletarian camps grounded all their activities in revolutionary politics, from a morning salute of the worker's flag to an evening campfire discussion about class struggle. Red camps such as Camp Wo-Chi-Ca practiced what Robert Zecker calls "class conscious recreation," coupling leisure activities such as baseball and swimming with revolutionary thought and practice.[41]

The *Daily Worker* described Camp Wocolona in Monroe, New York, as "revolutionary entertainment." A 1934 advertisement for Camp Nitgedaiget (meaning "no worries" in Yiddish) in Beacon, New York, similarly promised: "Our camp is a worker's rest place with daily proletarian cultural activities." Red camps allowed IWO children an escape from capitalist society where they could "rehearse narratives countering the dominant society's message that free-market capitalism was the all-American way." A 1934 issue of the *Daily Worker* perfectly described this ethos when talking about Camp Wo-Chi-Ca: "To combine with the sunshine, nourishing food and play a working class education. The projects in which the children participate fuse manual labor with education. All tasks before the revolutionary movement such as Scottsboro, Angelo Herndon, Thaelmann, Unemployment and Social Insurance, War, Fascism and the defense of the Soviet Union are the base around which all activities are built."[42]

This combination of recreation and politics, of encouraging in workers' children a revolutionary praxis, was central to these proletarian camps. Awareness about current injustices and the actions of leftist organizations and activists to correct these wrongs was also important. At Camp Wo-Chi-Ca, for example, the son of Rosa Lee Ingram (whose wrongful conviction was condemned during a rally at the IWO's Paul Robeson Lodge in 1948) received a suit from his fellow campmates while attending in 1949.[43] News organs such as the Communist *Daily Worker* further instilled these values of social justice and interracial solidarity, publishing letters from children who attended the camp that discussed their experiences learning about certain issues and including cartoons showing Black and white children helping each other.[44]

Robeson's marriage of performance and politics therefore easily found a home at Camp Wo-Chi-Ca. Robeson's biggest thrill, however, happened when the campers sang one of his signature songs: "Ballad for Americans." Like the song that audiences most closely associated Robeson with throughout his career ("Ol' Man River"), "Ballad for Americans" became deeply associated with the actor. Created by composer Earl Robinson and lyricist John Latouche, "Ballad for Americans" characterized the United States as a nation where all Americans could feel at home.[45] First recorded by Robeson on the eve of World War II, its patriotic tone was of course significant: despite their differences, Americans should come together to fight the enemy abroad. The setting of its debut—a variety program called *Pursuit of Happiness* that portrayed the United States as a land of opportunity—also shaped the ballad's patriotic tone. Although the song underwent various iterations across time, when sung by Robeson accompanied with an integrated chorus comprised of working-class individuals, "Ballad for Americans" specifically placed African Americans and workers at the forefront of the nation. It became an anthem of the Popular Front and was a song that Robeson performed at countless concerts throughout his career.[46] It was also the specific anthem of his IWO performances and a song that connects his visit at Camp Wo-Chi-Ca to two other IWO events.

A year after his first visit to Camp Wo-Chi-Ca, Robeson performed "Ballad for Americans" at the IWO's International Fiesta in February and then at IWO Day at the Civilian and National Defense Exposition in October. At each performance, the ballad took on a specific meaning given the context. Organized by the IWO's New York City Central Committee, the International Fiesta occurred on February 23, 1941, at the Manhattan Center in New York City. It was a much-anticipated event within the IWO spring lineup, which included a membership drive, a women's conference, and a People's Lobby for Peace demonstration in Washington, DC. The IWO women's director, Rose Nelson, encouraged the organization's women's clubs to promote and attend the International Fiesta. The event showcased a broad array of Black talent and displayed the IWO's commitment to interracial solidarity. The April 1941 issue of *Fraternal Outlook* emphasized this by titling the article (as the subtitle) an "International Fiesta Contribution to Inter-Racial Unity."[47]

Sam Pevzner (IWO national education secretary) recalled the event in vivid detail. Robeson's presence on stage was especially moving for both actor and audience. Thousands showed up that winter day to see Robeson perform, so many that the announcement, "No more room! Sorry! No more room!" greeted some of the guests who came after the venue had reached capacity. He performed "Negro spirituals and Jewish, Spanish and Russian folk songs [that were] brimming with love for his audience" and when talking about the importance of interracial solidarity, "tears welled up in his eyes." For audiences who loved Robeson's artistry and activism, few things could have made them happier than seeing him perform live, hearing the emotion in his voice, and witnessing his steadfast commitment to racial justice. For Robeson, the event reinforced the importance of Black history and culture and the IWO's investment in these narratives, specifically through its feature program—a play called *The Negro in American Life*, written by Carlton Moss, with music by the composer Al Moss, and directed by Hillary Phillips. The pageant featured important historical figures such as Harriet Tubman and Frederick Douglass, who emerged against the backdrop of the "tragic story of Negro slavery and the inspiring record of the men and women who fought against this system."[48]

This display of Black artistry solidified the message of resistance and critique that structured the fiesta and demonstrated the network of Black artists with whom the IWO often collaborated. In addition to the IWO Junior Band and the Radischev Group (a Russian troupe that danced in honor of the Soviet Union), a range of Black cultural producers appeared on stage. They included Dean Dixon (conductor), Al Moss (composer), Richard Huey (actor), the Harlem Players (theater group), Calvin Jackson (jazz pianist), Laura Duncan (jazz singer), Carlton Moss (playwright), and Hillary Phillips (theater director). As Black artists participating in or directing this production about Black life in the US, the Harlem Players, Carlton Moss, and Hillary Phillips continued the legacy of the Harlem Renaissance of the 1920s and 1930s.

As the cultural arm of the New Negro movement, the Harlem Renaissance was heralded as the intellectual and cultural rebirth of Black Americans. Cheryl A. Wall defines it as "not just a time when the Negro was in vogue. . . . [It] was also a time when black people redefined themselves and announced their entrance into modernity."[49] It was an opportunity and desire to correct the image of Black people, to "overcome the prevailing theme, in more mainstream culture, that African Americans were inferior and unassimilable in American 'civilization,'" according to the scholar Gene Andrew Jarrett.[50] From Alain Locke and Richard Wright to Nella Larsen and Langston Hughes, Black artists presented nuanced portrayals of Black life that challenged the one-dimensional depictions of Blackness saturating American culture, critiqued the relationship between Black people and the nation, and situated Blackness within a global context.

These cultural producers understood, however, that class also structured Black experiences. During the 1920s, Black labor activists in Harlem helped establish the Trade Union Committee for the Organization for Negro Workers. Black leftists A. Philip Randolph and Chandler Owen created a leftist magazine called *The Messenger* that featured a range of essays critiquing issues such as US imperialism, African Americans' position during wartime, and lynching, and "cast the New Negro racial militancy of the Harlem Renaissance in a broader class-conscious frame." Paul Robeson in fact contributed to *The Messenger*, writing a short piece in 1924 reflecting on his burgeoning acting career and highlighting the role of Black art in society. "Above all things," he wrote, "we boast that the only true artistic contributions of America are Negro in origin." The production and content of artistic work also illustrated the intersection of labor politics and Black artistry. The visual artist Charles White, who also taught art at Camp Wo-Chi-Ca, demonstrated this in his work, which consisted of portraits and other artwork that appeared in settings accessible to working-class Black people and depicted ordinary Black people and Black leftists (like our very own Paul Robeson). Jacob Lawrence and his wife, artist Gwendolyn Knight, also taught art at Camp Wo-Chi-Ca.[51]

The IWO's own cultural apparatus aligned with this Harlem Renaissance ethos. In addition to holding political discussions in her Harlem home, IWO vice president Louise Thompson also had connections to Zora Neale Hurston, Marion Cuthbert, and other Black writers and artists.[52] The organization supported and indirectly connected itself to theater productions that portrayed Black working-class experiences and the effects of racism on Black Americans' everyday lives. One such theater was the Harlem Suitcase Theatre (HST)—aptly named because it was a traveling theater for working-class audiences.[53] Founded in 1938 through the collaborative efforts of Langston Hughes and Louise Thompson, the theater put on numerous plays by Hughes such as *Don't You Want to Be Free* and *Blues to Now—and Then Some!* The HST existed alongside other theater groups such as the Rose McClendon Players and within a longer genealogy of Black theater groups.[54] Hillary Phillips (former director of HST) and Carlton Moss (previously involved in New York's Negro Progressive Theater) thus brought the tradition of Black progressive theater to this IWO event.

Al Moss's and Laura Duncan's presence on stage shows how critiques of the nation often emerged within Black cultural production, both within and outside IWO spaces. When announcing the upcoming fiesta, the January 1941 issue of the *Fraternal Outlook* mentioned Al Moss in connection with his "special arrangement of 'Strange Fruit.'"[55] Often associated with jazz singer Billie Holiday, "Strange Fruit," written by Abel Meeropol, uncovered the violent contradictions at the heart of Jim Crow society.[56] It expressed the anger and sorrow of Black people facing lynching and other forms of racial terror (which took on a particular urgency during World War II). "In 'Strange Fruit,'" writes Farah Jasmine Griffin, "Holiday left us a powerful and enduring song of protest against racial violence" that galvanized a postwar civil rights movement in which singers such as Nina Simone took the song up as protest once more.[57] Although a number of singers performed "Strange Fruit" as a song of protest, Paul Robeson in fact did not particularly care for the song because he thought it did not portray African Americans as having the power to change the racial violence they experienced.[58]

Nevertheless, "Strange Fruit" sent a powerful message that day when jazz singer Laura Duncan sang it during the pageant. "As the shadow of the lyncher's noose swayed over the stage," wrote Sam Pevzner in *Fraternal Outlook*, "Laura Duncan sang 'Strange Fruit,' the haunting cry of protest against mob violence."[59] By itself, "Strange Fruit" challenged the five thousand audience members to reckon with the continued racial terror that plagued the United States, but coupled with "Ballad for Americans," the songs laid bare the deep contradictions at the nation's foundation, now even further exposed as the United States entered World War II espousing ideals of democracy and freedom. Led by Black conductor Dean Dixon, Robeson and the IWO's American People's Chorus sang "Ballad for Americans." This time, however, "Ballad for Americans" appeared in a play written by Black writers, featuring Black actors, and relaying the troubling history of Black life in the United States. Like his commentary on American racism during his visit to Camp Wo-Chi-Ca, Robeson again attached a critique of anti-Black practices to his performance—one that not only encouraged interracial solidarity but also called out the United States for its treatment of Black communities.

When Robeson concluded the fiesta by urging "all minorities to unite in making 'America a real land of freedom and democracy,'" he reinforced the message that American democracy could only be true and real once marginalized communities united and overcame their oppression.[60] Robeson, too, was an American (as he once again announced through the final lyrics of the ballad) but he was an American whose skin color bore witness to multiple layers of violence. He too was an American who both contributed to the cultural and political fabric of the nation and was vulnerable to the racial violence at its core. Although he possessed certain privileges as a celebrated and internationally acclaimed actor, as a Black man he could go on stage and sing to thousands of people one day and fear for his life the next. The "shadow of the lyncher's noose" that "swayed on the stage" while Laura Duncan sang "Strange Fruit" was a shadow that followed Robeson and the other Black artists at the International Fiesta every day of their lives.[61]

Later that fall, Robeson once again performed "Ballad for Americans" at an IWO event, this time during IWO Day at the Civilian and National Defense Exposition, held on October 12, 1941, just prior to the US entrance into the war following the bombing of Pearl Harbor. The Order's participation in the exposition was the result of its larger campaign to promote "national defense and national unity."[62] It was one of three initiatives the IWO had put together to support the nation's move to a wartime footing, including "the authorization of the purchase of $50,000 in United States Defense bonds and the passage of a resolution urging President Roosevelt to free Earl Browder," the Communist Party leader who was serving time in prison for alleged passport fraud.[63] Robeson was the featured soloist for IWO Day and advertisements for his performance appeared in newspapers such as the Boston-based *Guardian* leading up to the exposition.[64]

IWO Day included two points of access, a live concert at New York's Grand Central Palace and a radio broadcast of the event. In addition to Robeson, the general program included the American People's Chorus, the Radischev Russian folk dancers, the Al Moss Singers, and the IWO Junior Band. Listeners tuning in to the radio heard a segment on the "IWO in Civilian and National Defense," "Ballad for Americans" (sung by Robeson and the chorus), and the "Al Moss Singers in 'Songs for Democracy.'"[65] Zecker argues that the IWO demonstrated its commitment to the incipient national war effort and support for defense industries by holding this event: "The Order endeavored to place itself firmly in the mainstream of national defense efforts." He also notes that "thousands of members were registering for civilian defense and buying defense bonds."[66] Given the working-class makeup of the organization, the IWO's national defense campaign was patriotic yet still aligned with its mission of advocating for workers' rights. Perhaps most importantly, the IWO's staunch support for the Soviet Union after Operation Barbarossa—Hitler's invasion of the USSR in June 1941—was seen as aligned with US national defense goals.

On stage next to the IWO's American People's Chorus in 1941, Robeson fought white supremacy once again, this time within the context of World War II and calls for Americans to unite against a common enemy. African Americans were joining the war effort at home and abroad and witnessing the paradox of American democracy unfold as they fought racist ideologies abroad only to return home to the all-too-familiar American version of white supremacy. This period "threw African Americans' longstanding struggle to reconcile their black identity with their American identity into sharp relief."[67] It came on the heels of Black activists and artists such as W. E. B. Du Bois, Langston Hughes, and James Weldon Johnson figuratively and literally crossing the Pacific to exchange ideas and build alliances with Chinese and Japanese leftists. Robeson, of course, claimed membership in this transnational group of Black artists and activists, and like his peers, understood the obliteration of global white supremacy as the basis for Black freedom in the United States.

By singing the already popular "Ballad for Americans" at the 1941 exposition, then, Robeson became the face of a nation with deep contradictions at its core, contradictions that a decade later would result in his own persecution for standing up for civil rights. As he would do in later performances of the song, he sang the refrain "You Know Who I Am" as he and the IWO's American People's Chorus narrated Lincoln's role in ending slavery and other important historical moments in US history.[68] The scholar John B. Jones contends that the ballad that Robeson sang "details what makes the United States a democracy for everyone—the little guy as well as the big shot—but even more, it extols America for its racial, ethnic, and religious diversity."[69] Robeson and the integrated IWO American People's Chorus exemplified this message on stage. Ending the song by announcing that he was "America! America!," Robeson demanded that he too was an American, a sentiment he expressed in a 1949 issue of the London publication *Reynolds News* as he described the contributions of his family and his people to the United States and his continued feeling of belonging despite his persecution as "un-American."[70] His deep baritone voice marked Black and working-class Americans as equal members of the nation and signaled the urgency with which the nation should secure their rights and livelihood.

The wartime context amplified the complicated position in which African Americans found themselves: defenders of the nation on the one hand and victims of its racist policies and practices on the other. This exemplified the "Double-V Campaign" of the 1940s, whereby African Americans called for "victory at home and abroad." For proponents of the Double V-Campaign, US victory against fascist Germany and its allies was not enough; the United States must also fight its own racial inequality at home. In fact, this wartime moment was the perfect opportunity for the United States to reassess its treatment of African Americans as second-class citizens. If African Americans were going to fight abroad for the freedom of others, their own freedom should be guaranteed as well. A. Philip Randolph most notably put this campaign into action during his march on Washington movement. Throughout the 1940s, he (along with other members of a March on Washington Committee) called on the Roosevelt and Truman administrations to end racial discrimination in the defense industries and desegregate the military, or face tens of thousands of Black citizens marching outside the capitol. Randolph was successful in his efforts and strategically forced both presidents to acquiesce to his demands.[71]

Robeson also urged African Americans to think about World War II through the lens of their own experiences at home. For example, in a 1943 *People's Voice* article, he stated, "The Negro must view the domestic scene in its relation to the global struggle against fascism." He understood the parallels between what was happening to people of color abroad living under colonial regimes and African Americans at home experiencing Jim Crow segregation. When condemning the 1935 Italian invasion of Ethiopia during his remarks about civil rights at the Twelfth Annual Herald-Tribune Forum in 1944, he spoke of the "parallel between his [African American] own interests and those of oppressed people abroad." At the 1943 Free People's Dinner in his honor, he began his remarks by declaring the true purpose of the war, stating, "The triumphant end of this war must bring a world where there can be no question of a colored people or a white people." For Robeson, World War II was an opportunity for the United States to live up to the democratic ideals it projected on the international stage by securing the rights of its own marginalized citizens. "Let us make sure," he said when concluding his remarks, "that the victory that follows will be one that assures full freedom for all people in this world regardless of race or color." Black liberation meant the end of oppression for people suffering in distant lands; until everyone was free, Black people were still in chains.[72]

Just as he called on Black Americans to see themselves in the struggles of African and Asian peoples all over the world, he encouraged this audience at the exposition to see themselves in him. As his voice rang out across the Grand Central Palace, he invited audience members to see him and the working-class chorus with whom he shared the stage as equal citizens. The true victory at the close of the war would be the ability of white Americans to see him, too, as fully American, as someone deserving of all the rights afforded to him under the Constitution.

Whether or not audience members at the exposition understood this message from Robeson is unclear. Although IWO Day included Black artists such as Al Moss among its performers, its setting primarily conveyed a patriotic message. If the audience picked up on a Black critique of American democracy, they perhaps only found it in the lyrics that Robeson sang or by seeing a Black performer singing alongside a mainly white and working-class chorus. "Ballad for Americans" appeared in numerous iterations and took on different meanings as amateur and professional singers performed it in various settings. While it may have symbolized American patriotism within the context of the exposition, "the song fell into disfavor during the late 1940s with the coming of the second Red Scare."[73] In other words, the context in many ways shaped its reception. What is clear, however, is that Robeson's performance of "Ballad for Americans" resonated with many working-class Americans and many children embraced it, as was evident during his visit to Camp Wo-Chi-Ca.

In *Tales of Wo-Chi-Ca*, former camp attendee Ronnie Gilbert, who would later carry forward Robeson's artistic and activist legacy by singing with Pete Seeger in the Weavers, sets the stage for the reader:

> The camp chorus is rehearsing in The Barn, a cool, dark refuge from the heat. We are learning John Latouche and Earl Robinson's "Ballad for Americans." . . . The barn door swings open. Yes! There he stands, framed black in the doorway, and I swear, the light dancing on his shoulders like little flames. Then comes the deep voice, rolling into our camp, into our Barn, into our lives: "Old Sam put on a three cornered hat / And in a Richmond church he sat / And Patrick Henry told him that / While America drew breath / It was Liberty or Death!"[74]

This vivid recounting of the "Ballad for Americans" performance clearly illustrates Gilbert's enthusiasm at meeting and singing with Robeson. Having rehearsed the song in the days leading up to and in anticipation of his visit, campers such as Gilbert stood in awe as their hero sang the powerful lyrics about the American Revolution and the birth of the nation back to them. "At one point in the performance," recounts camper Sy Rosen, "he let loose and sang along with us (What a voice, I can still feel the vibrations!)."[75] These detailed descriptions of the actor's voice and presence echoed other campers' positive memories of his performance.

In this moment, Robeson became both performer and audience, first listening to the children singing to him and then joining in with them. Within the setting of this proletarian camp, the message of inclusion underlining the ballad took on a specific meaning. With its integrated educational and recreational activities and overall accessibility to working-class children, the camp served as a microcosm of the type of America that the ballad portrayed. As the children sang to Robeson, they showed him that such a democratic and inclusive society was possible, even if it still seemed a long way from becoming a reality. In fact, he reportedly told them, "When I look at you, I know the future is safe."[76] He saw that children like the ones with whom he interacted at Camp Wo-Chi-Ca would continue anti-oppression activism and that what they were fighting for could become a reality. If Robeson's performance of the ballad at the 1941 exposition called on Americans to create an inclusive nation, the children at Camp Wo-Chi-Ca in 1940 embodied it. "Ballad for Americans" had indeed become, as Michael Denning contends and Lisa Barg reiterates, the "unofficial anthem" of the Popular Front, so much so that only a year after its first recording, working-class children knew it and sang it to its original performer.[77] Robeson's work within the IWO was thus a dialogue mediated by performance, one in which he spoke but also listened, and served as a catalyst for future radical work within the fraternal order.

Robeson's Legacy: A Genealogy of Black Cultural Production in the IWO

Paul Robeson's visit that day at Camp Wo-Chi-Ca does not simply highlight the actor's use of song as protest during his performances at IWO events. It also provides a glimpse of the cultural imprint he left behind at the camp and within the fraternal order more broadly.[78] When reminiscing about his visit, several campers referenced "the barn" that served as the site of Robeson's performance and also housed a mural of him that the campers had painted. Before his arrival and long after his departure, the mural remained on the barn wall, freezing in time his smile and presence for future campers. During one of his last visits to the camp in 1948, the campers presented him with another symbol in his honor, a hut-like structure that they named the Paul Robeson Playhouse.[79]

Other IWO spaces arose in his honor as well. One such space was the Paul Robeson Lodge in Newark, New Jersey, which organized demonstrations and fundraised in support of various civil rights causes. In 1948 it sponsored a rally for the wrongfully convicted Mrs. Rosa Lee Ingram and her two sons, who were framed for murder in Georgia and initially sentenced to death, although their sentence was reduced to life imprisonment following widespread outrage.[80] Also to aid the Ingram family, the lodge sent $255 to the Philadelphia Committee to Save the Ingram Family in 1949.[81] Fundraising efforts and demonstrations such as this continued Robeson's legacy of fighting for racial justice.

At a May 1947 fundraising event in Chicago for the Abraham Lincoln School, which involved the Du Sable Lodge and Community Center—a space established by IWO leader Louise Thompson—the actress and singer Lena Horne spoke of Robeson as her inspiration. A *Chicago Star* article did not provide further details about whether—like the children at Camp Wo-Chi-Ca—she sang any of the songs that had become synonymous with Robeson. Nevertheless, her praise of him demonstrated how his Black leftist artistic work reverberated throughout the fraternal order, sometimes through the actions of other artists and IWO members, and how his work became institutionalized within the IWO. Another speaker at this event was Mrs. Agnes L. Dorsey who had held a Paul Robeson Children's Program at the Du Sable Community Center a month prior.[82] This program was fitting—Robeson enjoyed and prioritized performing and interacting with children. Robeson's appeal to children was well-known and he often made it a point to perform for children during his domestic and international travels—whether at Camp Wo-Chi-Ca or at a Christmas performance for a group of Chinese, Indigenous, and white children during his 1960 Australia and New Zealand concert tour.[83]

The Paul Robeson Playhouse at Camp Wo-Chi-Ca also sheds light on other Black cultural producers whose creative work found a home in the IWO. Another Black singer visited the camp in 1947: Kenneth Spencer. Born in Los Angeles in 1913, Spencer shared several similarities with Robeson. An actor and baritone singer, he appeared in the 1933 and 1946 stage adaptations of *Show Boat* as the character Joe—a role with which Robeson is most famously associated.[84] Audiences in fact called him "another Paul Robeson."[85] He, too, was an IWO member and performed at IWO-sponsored events. An early 1940s issue of *Fraternal Outlook* includes a spotlight on the actor, not only calling him "one of the best musical prospects of the season," but also praising his efforts to "lead Juniors of his lodge in community singing at a Junior Peace Rally."[86] His visit to Camp Wo-Chi-Ca in 1947 demonstrated his larger commitment to youth mentorship and engagement.

Like Robeson's visit in 1940, Spencer's visit seven years later was a memorable moment for the actor and the children for whom he sang. Despite bad acoustics and a faulty microphone, Spencer delivered a star performance: "The acoustics were terrible, children would overflow their hard wooden benches and spill onto the splintery floor, the microphone frequently failed. Still, no plush concert hall or Broadway theater could provide Kenneth the comradeship he felt at Camp Wo-Chi-Ca." Through the performance, campers encountered another, slightly younger version of their beloved Robeson. Like his predecessor, Spencer found hope in Camp Wo-Chi-Ca, declaring it "wonderful to see here in Wo-Chi-Ca how the spirit of America is being carried out, the spirit that the men in the Revolutionary War fought for and that all true Americans wish for their children to have. That kind of America is here in Wo-Chi-Ca." Spencer saw a glimpse of the inclusive nation for which Robeson and so many other Black artists fought during this visit. However, Spencer did not just follow in Robeson's footsteps but also helped support the institutionalization of his legacy within the IWO. The construction of the Paul Robeson Playhouse—dedicated to its namesake the following year—in part resulted from the fundraising efforts of Kenneth Spencer, who held a concert at Carnegie Hall to raise money for the structure.[87]

Another artist who emerges in relation to the playhouse is Langston Hughes. According to Levine and Gordon: "They say if you put your ear to a certain corner of the Paul Robeson Playhouse, you can hear a poem of Langston Hughes." There is nostalgia for their days at camp expressed in that statement, for the days when they met Black performers such as Robeson and Spencer and recited poetry by Black poets such as Hughes. They feature a poem by Hughes called "Merry Go Round," which includes lines like "White and colored can't sit side by side," referencing the "Jim Crow section" on public transport. The reciting of this poem would not have been unusual for children at Camp Wo-Chi-Ca, for the IWO also served as a space where Hughes shared his artistic work. In addition, IWO vice president Louise Thompson featured some of his plays in the Harlem Suitcase Theatre, and the IWO also sponsored a lecture tour for Hughes called "The Negro Poet Looks at a Troubled World."[88]

Like Robeson's, Hughes's work appeared through the creative expression of other performers working within the IWO and by IWO members. For instance, a woman named Edith Benjamin—who occupied the secretarial role at IWO Lodge 691 in New York City and served as the editor of the lodge's monthly newsletter *Solidarity*—continued Hughes's legacy in the IWO by performing at a conference held by the IWO's Commission on Negro Work on October 19,

1940.[89] After a program that called on IWO members to participate in racial justice efforts to improve the lives of African Americans, Benjamin sang a few songs by Langston Hughes.[90] Benjamin used Hughes's work to drive home the importance of participating in civil rights activism, and showed how such activism emerged not only through demonstrations and rallies but also through song.

Hughes's work also resonated with IWO youth. Sheila Newman reminisced about her time at Camp Wo-Chi-Ca as a child, recalling how "it was a great thrill to perform a dance choreographed to a Langston Hughes poem in his honor."[91] Even more demonstrative of Hughes's legacy, however, was the fact that Newman and other campers performed this dance for Robeson. The children as performers and Robeson as audience connected in this moment through the creative work of Hughes.

Paul Robeson's performative work within the IWO demonstrates how Black artists not only found a home within the fraternal order but also inspired others to take up their creative work to advance the organization's mission. As both performer and audience, Robeson continued the organization's tradition of interracial solidarity and support of Black culture despite the Cold War and the toll it took upon him and his family. Throughout the 1940s, '50s, and early '60s, Robeson traveled around the world—sometimes literally, sometimes by sending recordings of himself singing to events in other countries—and called for the end of fascist and colonialist regimes, often drawing parallels between the oppression of other workers and people of color and the plight of his own people at home. Robeson went to the US and Canadian border for the second time in 1953 to critique his own containment and celebrate the recently formed People's Republic of China; he went to Australia in 1960 to condemn settler colonialism against Aboriginal Australians. During these performances, he used song (specifically revised versions of songs such as "Ol' Man River") as a platform for fighting white supremacy in its myriad forms and to forge global alliances with marginalized communities who shared experiences of racism with African Americans.[92]

The three performances discussed here—the Camp Wo-Chi-Ca visit in 1940 and the International Fiesta and IWO Day at the Civilian and National Defense Exposition in 1941—demonstrate how Robeson used song, specifically "Ballad for Americans," to protest injustices at home and abroad. "Ballad for Americans" served as a focal point around which Robeson performed a Black leftist politics within the IWO. Through the ballad, Robeson put forth a vision of American democracy that afforded Black Americans their due rights as citizens and as contributors to America's founding.

These IWO performances also show how Robeson connected art and politics throughout his career. Sometimes his politics surfaced explicitly in speeches and other remarks he gave during concerts; at other times his politics appeared in subtle changes to a song's lyrics or pacing. On some occasions, his decision to perform at all was itself a protest, as when he chose to defy his bodily containment and send recordings of himself singing to events such as the 1955 Bandung Conference, a gathering of African and Asian nations combating colonialism.[93] The power in his message, however, sometimes also surfaced when he simply listened. His 1940 visit to Camp Wo-Chi-Ca is evidence of this, as he saw himself and his years of activism reflected in the children smiling back at him and saw the embodiment of a truly democratic America.

His marriage of artistry and activism also sheds light on other Black cultural producers who worked within and alongside the IWO. Langston Hughes, Carlton Moss, Kenneth Spencer, and Laura Duncan are just four of the numerous poets, singers, actors, playwrights, and musicians who saw the IWO as a welcoming space and used their creative expression to fight for racial justice. Like Robeson, these artists left their mark on the organization, evident in IWO members—both young and old—who took up their work in various settings. Black culture and history were fundamental parts of the IWO and its mission, and its members made sure to keep that legacy alive.

In the years following the IWO's demise in 1954, Paul Robeson continued performing in the spirit of interracial solidarity and coalition-building. Despite his containment by the US government, Robeson used his performances during the 1950s and 1960s to call for people of color and working-class whites to rise up together and combat racial and class injustices. Some of his signature songs—including "Ol' Man River"—became vehicles for his activism around the world. He continued his role as both creative artist and critic, as someone who simultaneously performed and protested, who laid bare the nation's deepest divisions and greatest accomplishments. Audiences came to his concerts to hear his deep, mesmerizing voice, which time and time again shook them into action.

NOTES

I would like to express my sincerest gratitude to Robert Zecker and Elissa J. Sampson, who graciously invited me to contribute this chapter. I also thank Rhaisa Williams and Stacie McCormick for commenting on a draft of this chapter. Thank you as well to Alison Bruey, David Jaffee, and their international studies class at the University of North Florida for listening to an oral presentation of part of this chapter. I am grateful to The American Council of Learned Societies and the Florida Education Fund, who provided funding to complete archival research for this chapter. Finally, I would like to thank Cornell University Press and the anonymous reviewers for their valuable feedback throughout this process.

1. June Levine and Gene Gordon, *Tales of Wo-Chi-Ca: Blacks, Whites, and Reds at Camp* (Avon Springs Press, 2002), 1. See, too, Paul Mishler, *Raising Reds: The Young Pioneers, Radical Summer Camps, and Communist Political Culture in the United States* (Columbia University Press, 1999).

2. For biographies of the actor with special attention to his marriage of art and politics, see Gerald Horne, *Paul Robeson: The Artist as Revolutionary* (Pluto Press, 2016) and Lindsey R. Swindall, *Paul Robeson: A Life of Activism and Art* (Rowman & Littlefield, 2013).

3. Robert M. Zecker, *"A Road to Peace and Freedom": The International Workers Order and the Struggle for Economic Justice and Civil Rights, 1930–1954* (Temple University Press, 2018), 14, 119, 159. See Elissa Sampson, "Yiddish Leftists as Early Inter-Ethniks," in *Beyond Whiteness: Revisiting Jews in Ethnic America*, ed. Jonathan Karp (Purdue University Press, 2023).

4. Levine and Gordon, *Tales of Wo-Chi-Ca*, 8, 65, 62, 55, 63, 177.

5. "Our Town," *Guardian* (Boston), February 5, 1944, 2.

6. "Chicago Salutes Paul Robeson," *Chicago Star*, April 12, 1947, 13. See poster advertising this benefit performance for the IWO-adjacent Abraham Lincoln School, International Workers Order (IWO) Records, KCL05276, box 57, folder 11, Kheel Center for Labor-Management Documentation and Archives, Catherwood Library, Cornell University, Ithaca, New York. Henceforth Kheel.

7. "Labor Honors IWO Pres. with Dinner," *Omaha Guide*, June 14, 1941, 7.

8. "Rally will Launch 100-Day Campaign Against Lynching," *Evening Star* (Washington), September 11, 1946, 22.

9. Zecker, *"A Road to Peace and Freedom,"* 1.

10. Elizabeth Temkin, "Contraceptive Equity: The Birth Control Center of the International Workers Order," *American Journal of Public Health* 97, no. 10 (2007): 1740.

11. Zecker, *"A Road to Peace and Freedom,"* 3.

12. Roger Keeran, "National Groups and the Popular Front: The Case of the International Workers Order," *Journal of American Ethnic History* 14, no. 3 (Spring 1995): 26.

13. Zecker, *"A Road to Peace and Freedom,"* 103.

14. Zecker, *"A Road to Peace and Freedom,"* 4.

15. Zecker, *"A Road to Peace and Freedom,"* 101, 119, 97, 110, 103, 120.

16. Paul Robeson, for example, was a member of the CRC's Prisoners Relief Committee. See Zecker, *"A Road to Peace and Freedom,"* 119.

17. Zecker, *"A Road to Peace and Freedom,"* 113, 115, 125, 118, 97, 107, 132.

18. Cathy Brigden and Lisa Milner, "Radical Theatre Mobility: Unity Theatre, UK, and the New Theatre, Australia," *New Theatre Quarterly* 31, no. 4 (2015): 328–29.

19. "Why I Joined Labor Theatre," *Daily Worker*, November 24, 1937, in *Paul Robeson Speaks: Writings, Speeches, Interviews, 1918–1974*, ed. Philip S. Foner (Brunner/Mazel, 1978), 119–20.

20. Swindall, *Paul Robeson*, 92.

21. "Frontier Films," *The Wrangell Sentinel* (Wrangell, AK), November 23, 1951, 1.

22. "My Labors in the Future Will Remain the Same as They Have in the Past," *Daily Worker*, August 15, 1957, in Foner, *Paul Robeson Speaks*, 441.

23. Cornelius L. Bynum, *A. Philip Randolph and the Struggle for Civil Rights* (University of Illinois Press, 2010), 119.

24. See Richard Wright, *Native Son* (Harper & Row, 1940).

25. Erik S. McDuffie, "'No Small Amount of Change Could Do': Esther Cooper Jackson and the Making of a Black Left Feminist," in *Want to Start a Revolution?: Radical Women in the Black Freedom Struggle*, ed. Dayo F. Gore et al. (New York University Press, 2009), 25–46.

26. Bynum, *A. Philip Randolph*, 85.

27. Robeson Taj Frazier, *The East Is Black: Cold War China in the Black Radical Imagination* (Duke University Press, 2015).

28. Frazier, *The East Is Black*, 146–47.

29. Frazier, *The East Is Black*, 161.
30. Frazier, *The East Is Black*, 168–72.
31. "Award to Be Made to Negro Artist," *Daily Bulletin* (Dayton, OH), December 29, 1944, 4.
32. "Originator of Negro History Week Cites IWO's Activities," *New York Age*, February 2, 1946, 2.
33. "Artists Foster Camp for Worker's Youngsters; Hazel Scott and Pearl Primus Give Benefit for IWO," *Guardian*, January 29, 1944, 2.
34. "IWO Backs Robeson," *Atlanta Daily World*, May 2, 1947, 2.
35. Appeal to the American Jewish Congress Convention, November 4, 1949, KCL05276, box 53, folder 1, Kheel, https://digital.library.cornell.edu/catalog/ss:19043852.
36. Tony Perucci, *Paul Robeson and the Cold War Performance Complex: Race, Madness, Activism* (University of Michigan Press, 2012), 2, 11, 18, 34, 15, 39, 51, 60.
37. The State Department and United States Information Agency (USIA) sent the cast of *Porgy and Bess* on tour abroad just as the State Department was restricting Robeson's movement. Similarly, the State Department sent Dizzy Gillespie, Louis Armstrong, and other jazz musicians to perform around the world to promote a positive image of the United States during the Cold War. These musicians, however, challenged that image and instead used the international stage to protest ongoing racism in the United States. See Kate A. Baldwin, *Beyond the Color Line and the Iron Curtain: Reading Encounters Between Black and Red, 1922–1963* (Duke University Press, 2002); Penny von Eschen, *Satchmo Blows Up the World: Jazz Ambassadors Play the Cold War* (Harvard University Press, 2006).
38. Levine and Gordon, *Tales of Wo-Chi-Ca*, 62.
39. Levine and Gordon, *Tales of Wo-Chi-Ca*, 62.
40. "Spotlight on Juniors," *Fraternal Outlook*, October 1940, 21.
41. "Registration Open for Camp Kinderland," *Daily Worker*, May 19, 1931, 2; "WIR Camp Committee Meets Tonight; Make Ready Camp Opening," *Daily Worker*, June 10, 1931, 2; "Workers' Children Find Refuge from Sweltering Heat in Camp Wo-Chi-Ca," *Daily Worker*, July 9, 1934, 5; Zecker, "A Road to Peace and Freedom," 146.
42. "Proletarian Camps," *Daily Worker*, June 13, 1931, 2; "Camp Nitgedaiget," *Daily Worker*, April 28, 1934, 8; Zecker, "A Road to Peace and Freedom," 145; "Workers' Children Find Refuge," *Daily Worker*, July 9, 1934, 5.
43. "A New Suit for the New Year," *Guardian*, January 15, 1949, 1.
44. "With Our Young Readers," *Daily Worker*, July 28, 1934, 6.
45. Lisa Barg, "Paul Robeson's Ballad for Americans: Race and the Cultural Politics of 'People's Music,'" *Journal of the Society for American Music* 2, no. 1 (2008): 27.
46. Michael Denning, *The Cultural Front: The Laboring of American Culture in the Twentieth Century* (Verso, 1998), 115.
47. "Paul Robeson to Appear at I.W.O Fiesta," *Fraternal Outlook*, January 1941, 29.
48. Sam Pevzner, "The Negro in American Life," *Fraternal Outlook*, April 1941, 5.
49. Cheryl A. Wall, *The Harlem Renaissance: A Very Short Introduction* (Oxford University Press, 2016), 3.
50. Gene Andrew Jarrett, *Representing the Race: A New Political History of African American Literature* (New York University Press, 2011), 74.
51. Shannon King, *Whose Harlem Is This, Anyway?: Community Politics and Grassroots Activism During the New Negro Era* (New York University Press, 2015), 54; Bynum, *A. Philip Randolph*, xvii; "An Actor's Wanderings and Hopes," *Messenger* 7, no. 1 (January 1925); Mary Helen Washington, *The Other Blacklist: The African American Literary and Cultural Left of the 1950s* (Columbia University Press, 2014), 73.
52. Erik S. McDuffie, *Sojourning for Freedom: Black Women, American Communism, and the Making of Black Left Feminism* (Duke University Press, 2011), 64–66.

53. Zecker, "A Road to Peace and Freedom," 151.

54. Adrienne M. Braconi, *Harlem's Theaters: A Staging Ground for Community, Class, and Contradiction, 1923–1939* (Northwestern University Press, 2015), 11. That history dated back to William Alexander Brown's African Theater during the 1820s and extended forward to the American Negro Theater of the 1940s.

55. "Paul Robeson to Appear at I.W.O. Fiesta," *Fraternal Outlook*, January 1941, 29.

56. CPUSA member Abel Meeropol first wrote "Strange Fruit" as a poem. In 1939 he adapted it into a song. Other artists had already started performing the song at various clubs before Billie Holiday sang it at the integrated jazz club Café Society in New York. The Meeropols, both of whom were involved in music, adopted the orphaned Rosenberg sons and sent them to Camp Wo-Chi-Ca.

57. Farah Jasmine Griffin, *If You Can't Be Free, Be A Mystery: In Search of Billie Holiday* (Free Press, 2001), 131.

58. For more on Robeson's critiques of the song, see David Margolick, *Strange Fruit: Billie Holiday and the Biography of a Song* (Ecco Press, 2001), 27, 74, 76.

59. Pevzner, "The Negro in American Life."

60. Martin Duberman, *Paul Robeson* (Alfred A. Knopf, 1988), 250.

61. Pevzner, "The Negro in American Life."

62. "IWO Enlarges Campaigns for Defense," *People's Voice*, September 24, 1941, 3.

63. "IWO Enlarges Campaigns for Defense," 3. CPUSA chairman Earl Browder had been convicted of passport fraud.

64. "Paul Robeson," *Guardian*, October 11, 1941, 3.

65. "Paul Robeson Sings for I.W.O. Day at the Civilian and National Defense Exposition," flyer, 1941, KCL05276, box 49, folder 16, Kheel, https://digital.library.cornell.edu/catalog/ss:19043801.

66. Zecker, "A Road to Peace and Freedom," 191.

67. Chris Dixon, *African Americans and the Pacific War, 1941–1945: Race, Nationality, and the Fight for Freedom* (Cambridge University Press, 2018), 7.

68. Earl Robinson and Paul Robeson, "Ballad for Americans," *Carnegie Hall Concert*, vol. 2, track 1, 1965, Vanguard VSD-79193, 33⅓ rpm.

69. John Bush Jones, *The Songs That Fought the War: Popular Music and the Home Front, 1939–1945* (Brandeis University Press, 2006), 67.

70. "I, Too, Am American," *Reynolds News*, February 27, 1949, in Foner, *Paul Robeson Speaks*, 191–93. Philip Foner taught history classes for the JPFO, other IWO societies, and the Party's Jefferson School in the 1940s.

71. Neil A. Wynn, *The African American Experience During World War II* (Rowman & Littlefield, 2010), 40, 33–35, 95.

72. "'Democracy's Voice' Speaks," *People's Voice*, May 22, 1943, in Foner, *Paul Robeson Speaks*, 144; "American Negroes in the War," in Foner, *Paul Robeson Speaks*, 147; "A Victorious War Must Free All," *People's Voice*, August 4, 1943, in Foner, *Paul Robeson Speaks*, 144, 145.

73. Peter Gough and Peggy Seeger, *Sounds of the New Deal: The Federal Music Project in the West* (University of Illinois Press, 2015), 160.

74. Levine and Gordon, *Tales of Wo-Chi-Ca*, 227.

75. Levine and Gordon, *Tales of Wo-Chi-Ca*, 63.

76. "These Days," *Daily Alaska Empire*, January 20, 1950, 4.

77. Barg, "Paul Robeson's Ballad," 32; Denning, *The Cultural Front*, 115.

78. Although I focus on Black artists at Wo-Chi-Ca, other activists of color also visited the camp. One activist named Liu Liangmo—a friend of Robeson—visited the camp several times and also sent his son there. During his visits he taught Chinese songs to the children and watched them perform a play about Chinese-Indian solidarity. Liangmo's

visits to the camp not only illustrate Robeson's genealogy of resistance but also his commitment to interracial and transpacific solidarity. See Gao Yunxiang, *Arise Africa!, Roar China!: Black and Chinese Citizens of the World in the Twentieth Century* (University of North Carolina Press, 2021), 140–41.

79. Levine and Gordon, *Tales of Wo-Chi-Ca*, 65.

80. "Mother Speaks at Ingram Rally," *Guardian*, May 8, 1948, 2.

81. Philadelphia Committee to Save the Ingram Family, receipt, 1949, KCL05276, box 17, folder 7, Kheel, https://digital.library.cornell.edu/catalog/ss:20631705.

82. "Lena Horne Honored at DuSable Fund Meet," *Chicago Star*, May 24, 1947, 15.

83. "Christmas Treat," *Australian Women's Weekly*, December 28, 1960, 46.

84. Arnold Rampersad and David Roessel, eds., *Selected Letters of Langston Hughes* (Knopf, 2015), 140.

85. Mark D. Naison et al., *A Dancer in the Revolution: Stretch Johnson, Harlem Communist at the Cotton Club* (Fordham University Press, 2014), 109.

86. "A New Voice," *Fraternal Outlook*, November 1942.

87. Levine and Gordon, *Tales of Wo-Chi-Ca*, 48–49.

88. Levine and Gordon, *Tales of Wo-Chi-Ca*, 25; the Harlem Suitcase Theatre presented several of Langston Hughes's plays, such as *Don't You Want to Be Free* and *Blues to Now!—And Then Some*. See Zecker, "A Road to Peace and Freedom," 151–52, and Matthew Calihman's chapter in this book.

89. "Back in New York—Same Day," *Fraternal Outlook*, February 1941, 28.

90. "Commission on Negro Work Holds Conference," *Fraternal Outlook*, November 1940, 25.

91. Levine and Gordon, *Tales of Wo-Chi-Ca*, 115.

92. See Gao Yunxiang, *Arise Africa!*, 89; Ann Curthoys, "Paul Robeson's Visit to Australia and Aboriginal Activism, 1960," in *Passionate Histories: Myth, Memory and Indigenous Australia*, ed. Frances Peters-Little et al. (ANU Press, 2010), 163–84.

93. See chapter 3 in Shana L. Redmond, *Anthem: Social Movements and the Sound of Solidarity in the African Diaspora* (New York University Press, 2013).

7

FIGHTING FOR BLACK RIGHTS THROUGH THE FRATERNAL ARENA

Louise Thompson Patterson in the International Workers Order

Elissa Sampson and Robert M. Zecker

To paraphrase Karl Marx, American Communists forcefully battled anti-Black racism, but they did not always do so under circumstances of their own choosing, or to the complete satisfaction of their Black comrades. The career of Louise Thompson Patterson, vice president of the International Workers Order (IWO) and African American Communist, offers glimpses into the tensions and possibilities percolating in the Communist Party USA (CPUSA) and its affiliated circles during the existence of the IWO and how they affected Black nationalists who were negotiating theory and praxis amid the geopolitics of racism. The IWO (1930–54) was an unusual interracial, multiethnic, and pro-Soviet fraternal order initially composed of "national" sections. Its Jewish immigrant founders rapidly added sections that eventually included Slovaks, Hungarians, Poles, Russians, Italians, Croatians, Finns, and other white ethnics. Founded during the Comintern's militant Third Period, the IWO also reached out to Black and Latino/a working people. Thompson's work in the IWO brings to the fore questions about how to forge solidarity between ethnic "white progressives" and people of color, while shaping shared interracial as well as distinctively Black communal spaces, institutions, and politics. The IWO uniquely labored to create a multiethnic and interracial working-class radicalism within a fraternal cultural arena that could simultaneously meet the needs of its members for insurance and other benefits.

All of this transpired in the wake of two Comintern "Black Belt" resolutions, and the Southern Black Belt theses that propelled them in the late 1920s and 1930s. These resolutions played out in CPUSA and Comintern circles in a variety of ways that needed negotiation as people toed—and/or contested—the zigzagging Party line. While the CPUSA initially offered up the slogan "Self-Determination for the Black Belt" in response to these resolutions, it eventually promoted in its place various renditions of the interracial slogan "White and Negro Unity, together" (although with perhaps somewhat more vigor during the Popular Front period).[1] In all of these choices there was a good dose of enlightened self-interest in response to the considerable pressure that the CPUSA was under given Comintern concerns, some of which reflect the active presence of US Black nationalists at the 1928 Sixth Party Congress in Moscow at a time of growing anti-colonial movements in Africa and the Caribbean.[2]

The relatively newly minted CPUSA, much like its predecessors in earlier versions of the Socialist Party, attracted Black members and recruited them, but was often reluctant to pay much attention to their particular historical situation or respond to demands that it consider an analysis of both race and class that highlighted national groups' aspirations for self-determination. Indeed, the CPUSA could be overly eager to lump more radical tendencies into the dreaded category of bourgeois nationalism from which it needed to be distinguished.[3] Nonetheless, the persistent activism of Caribbean- and American-born Black militants in the Party and the initial support they garnered from the Comintern eventually led the CPUSA to conclude that racial oppression and imperialism needed to be foregrounded in the fight against capitalism. The career of Louise Thompson Patterson, a Communist who for almost twenty years sought to build a space within the IWO for militant Black nationalism even as she committed to the Order's brand of interracial activism, offers an opportunity to fruitfully interrogate these tensions. Her career raises the question of how and why a left immigrant fraternal benefits society was a good fit for Black radicals.

Background/Black Ground

The Black affinity for involvement in the Party has been well noted: William (Pat) Patterson, Louise Thompson (Patterson), Claudia Jones, Walter Garland, Benjamin Davis Jr., Cyril Briggs, Harry Haywood, Claude McKay, Lovett Fort-Whiteman, Otto Huiswoud, Grace Campbell, Queen Mother Audley Moore, Maude White (Katz), Eugene Gordon, and James Ford are just a few of the names associated with earlier CPUSA membership and sometimes its leadership.[4] Hence it is interesting to think through what happened in broader CPUSA circles as Black nationalism took off in the late 1920s and the Comintern proposed a Black nation thesis in two Comintern resolutions (1928, 1930) that supported self-determination for the Southern Black Belt.[5]

These resolutions wrestle with the criteria Stalin articulated in *Marxism and the National Question* (1913) and their adoption coincided with the rise of theories of Black revolutionary transnationalism, which came into play with the advent of anti-colonial and national movements that reflected prior Marxist debates on "the Colonial Question," "the Negro Question," "the Woman Question," and the "Jewish Question."[6] In the Black Belt thesis, the Party asserted that Black Americans in the parts of South where they constituted a majority formed a distinct nation that could potentially engage in a national liberation struggle. Should Black Belt African Americans desire it, they had the right to self-determination and to create an autonomous nation. Indeed, similar ideas and Pan-Africanist ferment had already been percolating outside the Party's orbit; as early as 1900, W. E. B. Du Bois and others had founded the anti-colonialist Pan-African Conference, where linkages between campaigns against Jim Crow in the United States and against the imperialism abroad that subjugated Africans were pressed and likely later came to the Comintern's notice courtesy of Black Comintern attendees including McKay and Briggs. The Party's anti-colonial campaigns would also soon be embraced by the IWO's Spanish-language Cervantes Society. Headed by Afro–Puerto Rican nationalist Jesús Colón, it enrolled Mexican, Cuban, and Guatemalan members as well, who chafed at US dominance of their homelands. The Comintern's expectation of a short-lived period of American exceptionalism that would move into revolutionary action also came into play here, especially at the start of the Depression.

Although the Southern Black Belt was the focus of Comintern resolutions, the Great Migration had already created an urban Black Belt in the North and Midwest; the resolutions and debates in Moscow suggest that the Comintern recognized that the Black Belt nation was not a solution to the plight of these urban African Americans. Despite ensuing debates about these resolutions while the CPUSA and International Labor Defense (ILD) were organizing around the Scottsboro case and recruiting sharecroppers in Georgia, Alabama, and Mississippi, the CPUSA arguably was not terribly interested in Black nationalism in the United States per se, most especially if Black nationalism included the right to self-determination in the South. Still, some stalwart Black Communists were indeed interested, especially in exploring transnational connections. In 1930, Harlem Party leader James Ford had penned "World Problems of the Negro People," which linked anti-lynching battles at home to anti-colonial struggles from the Caribbean to Africa. In 1929, too, Harlem Communists held a "Toussaint L'overture [*sic*] mass meeting" at which the 1804 Haitian Revolution was held up as an exemplar for ongoing anti-colonial, anti-racist struggles. African American Communist Williana Burroughs of the Party's American Negro Labor Congress was one of the speakers; attendees were urged to "honor your working-class heroes," a bit of a stretch since L'Ouverture made a better revolutionary than he did a working-class figure.[7] What was clear was that the use of the term nation, however defined, as well as the term people, as in the "Negro people" was in play.

When the Depression combined with the Popular Front period in the mid-1930s, in which the CPUSA in alignment with the Comintern altered course in response to the rise of European fascism to work with progressive organizations to combat the right, the stress on the achievement of equal rights became far more compelling for those working in CPUSA circles. Campaigns in alliance with non-Marxists in organizations such as the National Negro Congress as well as with Black churches necessitated greater focus on racial equality. The move to support "Negro Work" pushed unions to admit Black members, and radical activists attracted new levels of support for legal and political initiatives affecting income, safety, food security, voting, housing, integration, labor organizing, and, of course, anti-lynching campaigns and legislation. The IWO was an arena in which these agendas were promoted and also shaped in unexpected ways, which suggests that attention to earlier debates ensuing from the Black Belt resolutions lingered.

Internationalism and the Proletariat

As lynching, mob riots, and Jim Crow became increasingly entrenched realities after World War I, it became apparent that a half-hearted attempt to formulate or echo a Party line would not suffice for discussions of self-determination, race, and nation in the Southern United States. Extant terms that describe agrarian societies, such as feudalism and color "caste," were used and stretched to explain the persistence of racism in the aftermath of chattel slavery and its relation to monopoly capitalism, thus helping to retrofit the African diaspora into existing and evolving Marxist theory and connect what was formulated as a US national question to anti-colonial, revolutionary activity in Africa.[8]

In theory, the proponents of the Black Belt resolutions assumed the revolutionary potential of Southern Black people and envisioned Black ownership and control of contiguous Southern agrarian land as well as of industry, and a communal national structure tied into a classless society. The Party asserted Black Americans' right to self-determination, but assumed that when this occurred it would do so in a Marxist manner. Communist doctrine in the early 1930s attempted to articulate what constituted a nation—or a nation within a nation, or an oppressed nation—whether in debates in Moscow, New York City, or elsewhere. These debates also addressed questions of the pertinence of a majority or minority policy when remedying racial oppression in relation to Communist theory, as in how best to deal with white workers and ensure a Black presence in CPUSA institutions.

While anti-Communists derided the Black Belt thesis as implausible and irrelevant to African Americans' realities, Black intellectuals such as Du Bois remembered the unfulfilled promise of land reform and "forty acres and a mule" offered during Reconstruction. Some Black radicals may have recalled, too, that ex-slaves in the 1890s organized to lobby for federal pensions, to no avail. In such contexts, Communist support for Black control of contiguous Southern land may not have seemed so quixotic.[9] The Comintern's 1928 resolution called for self-determination; the 1930 resolution explicitly used the term oppressed nation:

> In the interest of the utmost clarity of ideas on this question the Negro Question in the United States must be viewed from the standpoint of its peculiarity, namely as the question of an oppressed nation, which is in a peculiar and extraordinarily distressing situation of national oppression not only in view of the prominent racial distinctions (marked difference in the colour of skin, etc.), but above all because of considerable social antagonism (remnants of slavery).[10]

In the visual repertoire supporting these resolutions, the Bolshevik Revolution was represented by the image of the liberated Black peasant (emancipated serf) joining the industrial worker. In an age of colonial revolt and revolution, Marxist Black nationalists worked to define the proletariat suffering from racial capitalism; the Black Belt resolutions tied that struggle to the national fight against US racial oppression and its persistence in the agrarian South. In a 1932 publication, the IWO echoed this cause, twinning Black and working-class liberation, in an image in which a rural black sharecropper is joined with a white factory worker in clasping Communist symbols (see figure 7.1).

In regard to Black Marxist thought, Minkah Makalani has argued that "the purchase in continuing to plumb this history is not merely to recoup a lost or obscured past. The historical value in such work is what it might reveal about the black radical imagination, the processes of rethinking and reshaping radical politics."[11] Despite their mixed reception in CPUSA circles, the Black Belt resolutions generated a heady ferment for redefining the boundaries of that radical imagination over time. Indeed, when working for the IWO in Alabama, Thompson penned an essay describing her 1934 arrest that uses the term "oppressed nation."[12] In her highly pragmatic world, one in which praxis was not always neatly separated from theory, a Black radical imagination can be seen in her organizing, writing, and cultural work. Some historians also understand figures such as Louise Thompson Patterson as building on aspects of the Marxist-Leninist vision to articulate a broader notion of a Black proletariat and vanguard, one that

FIGURE 7.1. *New Order Magazine*, October 1932, vol. 1, no. 7, cover image. Publication of the IWO Youth Section. Courtesy of the Kheel Center.

prioritized Black women by seeing them as the key to that revolutionary struggle.¹³ Her identification of the term triple exploitation as early as 1936 suggests that those at the very bottom must lead the way in changing society "as workers, as women, and as Negroes." While she operated within constraints engendered by Party loyalty, she was committed to creating Black space, however defined politically and culturally, that was tied to transnational formations, artistic expression, and interracial working-class solidarity.

Louise Thompson Patterson

Louise Thompson, a gifted organizer, a Berkeley graduate who first met Du Bois when he lectured there, a Black nationalist, and a member of the CPUSA, spent fifteen years on the IWO's payroll and moved up rapidly in its ranks. She migrated into the IWO after teaching at Black colleges, moving in artistic circles in Harlem, and visiting the Soviet Union as part of an all-Black cast contracted to make a Soviet film about US race relations. After working on Scottsboro organizing in Harlem, she started in the IWO as an insurance clerk, a position that some of her friends in the CPUSA derided as insufficiently militant, but she quickly became an organizer in the South and was arrested in Birmingham, Alabama. Thompson then went on to become the national secretary of the IWO's English Section, eventually becoming an IWO vice president as well as president of its Illinois District, "the first woman and the first Negro to have this honor."[14] By 1940, Thompson had married William Patterson, the lawyer who headed the ILD and its successor, the Civil Rights Congress (CRC), and henceforth she was known as both Louise Thompson and Louise Thompson Patterson. The couple moved to Chicago, where Louise began to work on Midwest labor and Black community organizing.

Thompson (1901–99), whose work is regarded today as prefiguring Black feminism, helped establish the radical civil rights organization Sojourners for Truth and Justice in 1951, along with Beulah Richardson, Shirley Graham Du Bois, Charlotta Bass, Lorraine Hansberry, and Queen Mother Audley Moore.[15] As Carole Boyce Davies and others have noted, like Claudia Jones, Thompson has been associated with early formulations of intersectionality or triple oppression: that of class, race, and gender.[16] In 1936 while working for the IWO, Thompson wrote: "Over the whole land, Negro women meet this triple exploitation—as workers, as women, and as Negroes. About 85 per cent of all Negro women workers are domestics, two-thirds of the two million domestic workers in the United States."[17] In denouncing the exploitation of Black female domestic workers hired in the Bronx's notorious "slave market," Thompson was the first writer to explicitly link class, racial, and gender oppression. Her early articulation of triple exploitation broadened critical theoretical understandings of the proletariat as primarily the industrial working class, focusing on the colonized, agrarian exploited workers and toilers in urban domestic spaces. Her work and that of other Black feminists shifted understandings of the Party's vanguard in ways that prefigured contemporary analyses of intersectionality. Countless less celebrated women of the IWO and Sojourners for Truth and Justice who combined anti-racism and anti-colonial activism with class-based activism and advocacy of a peace-oriented foreign policy echoed Thompson's example. Pauline Taylor of the Youngstown, Ohio lodge of the IWO, for example, was one of nineteen African Americans who followed Thompson's much earlier footsteps in touring the Soviet Union in 1951; that same year Taylor delivered an affidavit to the New York court overseeing the IWO's liquidation proceedings, extolling the IWO's work combating racial discrimination.[18]

Recent interest in Thompson has grown: Keith Gilyard describes her life as one of "Communist-inflected advocacy for labor, radical culture, and black freedom" with an acute awareness of "superexploitation."[19] As the chapters in this book show, her long-term friendships with Du Bois, June Gordon, Paul Robeson, and Langston Hughes (the latter two of whom she brought into the IWO's sphere) have garnered attention, as have her social and political ties to the Harlem Renaissance. Not least, as Charisse Burden-Stelly and Jodi Dean have recently argued, the theorizing of early Black feminist organizers such as Thompson deserves further attention; Erik McDuffie's earlier comparison of Thompson to Claudia Jones and others bears this out.[20]

For Black nationalists in CPUSA circles, choosing between the different renditions of what was worth fighting for—and with whom as an ally—required a theorization of praxis. If the construction of racial capitalism and its entwined offshoots, fascism and colonialism, are the cause of the color line, then pulling down capitalism becomes more theoretically compelling and would require a praxis in which the Black national minority had white workers as allies. The choice of many IWO Black activists to support actual revolutionary, anti-colonial movements abroad and support the ostensibly revolutionary CPUSA within the United States posed a quandary. It meant choosing to prioritize "Negro Work" along with anti-lynching bills and educational programs, all of which required theoretical Marxist articulations of how this might aid the transformation of the "Negro masses." It also required the skills to navigate what was possible in the United States given what was being promoted by the USSR.[21]

Pivotal moments stand out in Thompson's early political development that helped shape her political consciousness and connections to Black Communist women and other female Black activists in the United States, Soviet Union, and elsewhere. Her simultaneous pursuit of Black nationalism and Soviet policy in 1932 earned her the sobriquet "Madame Moscow" after she famously organized a US Black delegation, including Hughes, to visit the Soviet Union to make a film about Black America. The film featured a script that Hughes and Thompson found tin-eared and ultimately it was never made, but her visit to the Soviet Union nonetheless garnered much attention.[22] Once she returned to America, she successfully worked with church and other community groups as the organizer of the CPUSA's and ILD's 1933 "Free the Scottsboro Boys" march on Washington. Shortly thereafter she joined the IWO, where her first organizing assignments were in the South among Black workers. During a 1934 IWO recruiting tour, Black members in New Orleans, Atlanta, and Birmingham dropped out due to negative press coverage of the group's Communist links and police raids on IWO meetings, but Thompson continued and was jailed in Birmingham, Alabama. She was interrogated by Eugene "Bull" Connor thirty years before he gained notoriety for brutalizing civil rights activists; she emerged from Connor's jail unscathed, but not before the light-skinned activist (whom Connor apparently believed was white) was lectured on the dangers of race-mixing.[23]

In her work for the Order Thompson also recruited miners and steelworkers in Pennsylvania, West Virginia, and Ohio and campaigned on behalf of unionization drives.[24] After she was promoted to the Order's leadership ranks to organize "concentration lodges" such as Harlem's Solidarity Lodge, she traveled to Spain in 1937 as part of the IWO's support for the anti-fascist Loyalist government. In addition to solidifying ties with the Soviet Union, travel for Thompson, as it was for Du Bois (see Ratskoff's chapter), was critical to building networks and obtaining a broader global perspective on related struggles: in describing the 1932 film trip, Thompson later testified that "we did have an opportunity of traveling, and because as Negroes we were interested in the question of the national groups, we traveled primarily in and among the national minorities of the Soviet Union."[25]

The IWO Years

When Thompson transferred to Chicago after having married ILD head William Patterson in September 1940, she had been working for the IWO for seven years. By 1936, she had become the IWO's national recording secretary while spending five overlapping years as its secretary of general lodges, and then had moved up the ranks yet again in 1940. As a vice president and recording secretary, she found herself in good company with its president, artist Rockwell Kent (previously the IWO's vice president), vice president and congressman Vito Marcantonio, and Rubin Saltzman, vice president as well as the Jewish Peoples Fraternal Order's (JPFO) general secretary and IWO's founder.[26] By 1949, she had moved back to Harlem, primarily to work for the Council on African Affairs (CAA).

The IWO's purpose was to provide nondiscriminatory, low-cost health and life insurance to working people, the vast majority of whom were not members of the CPUSA. From its founding as an immigrant fraternal society, it uniquely combined mutual aid and insurance benefits with a platform stressing the need to combat racism, antisemitism, and anti-immigrant sentiment as well as class-based oppression through support of labor causes. African Americans, Thompson later recalled, in particular appreciated the equitable insurance and quality medical care that the IWO afforded them. Unlike for-profit insurance companies, the IWO did not discriminate against Black policyholders, many of whom gained access to attractive medical, dental, and optometry coverage for the first time through the Order. Of course, these features were also welcomed by "white ethnics" employed in hazardous industrial professions, and the Order's rapid growth reflected its appeal to workers of many kinds across its sixteen "language divisions."

With Thompson's active support, its sections came to include the Douglass-Lincoln section for Black members in addition to the earlier Spanish-language Cervantes Society catering to Latinos/as. The Cervantes was a pan-Latino/a society; although in East Harlem and Brooklyn members were primarily Puerto Rican, in Tampa, Florida, Cuban cigar-makers also organized lodges, while in Texas, California, and elsewhere Mexican and even Guatemalan migrants enrolled in Cervantes.

In a fraternal organization composed of "national" groups, how the logic of a Black section was framed was important especially given that English-speaking general lodges were always racially integrated.[27] Thompson noted: "It's Douglass-Lincoln, . . . so that it is, I wouldn't say the Negro society of the IWO, but I would say the international society of the IWO as contrasted to the national group societies where the Negro people have the greatest opportunity for giving and sharing their leadership and their experiences with the whole Order."[28]

Thompson was needed and wanted by the IWO to attract Black fraternal members. This work was vital, she noted, since the IWO insurance coverage was superior to the "nickel and dime" policies offered by for-profit insurance companies, which discriminated against Black customers.[29] An African American member of the IWO from New Haven, as well as an African American minister in the Order, would later extol the better treatment received within the IWO when compared to the rough justice of corporate America. The IWO's motto—"No Jim Crow in the IWO!"—was a welcome calling card in Black America, the *Baltimore Afro-American* editorialized. The ongoing fight for "Negro Work" was taken seriously; by the time the IWO was shut down, a third of its headquarters staff was Black or Puerto Rican.

In doing her work in the Order, Thompson negotiated the tension surrounding the creation of a uniquely "Black space" in the IWO—one that could ostensibly be understood as an expression of Black nationalism—as opposed to an integrated interracial space. This was an especially acute problem given the CPUSA's ambivalence and often hostile attitude to such exclusively Black initiatives.[30] She was also aware of the CPUSA's varying messages on "women's work" and equivocation as to the evolving role of women who worked outside of the home as wage earners, including Black domestics, and its general preference for native English-speaking "Americans," even as it defended ethnic immigrants.

The challenges facing Thompson, and the IWO, in recruiting Black members were great. African Americans embracing Black liberation often looked not to white allies, but to a long tradition of communal support as well as sometimes violent resistance to slavery and Jim Crow segregation, a celebrated heritage of self-emancipation. (Alleged) white allies were often viewed warily. As Robin D. G. Kelley notes, "Stalin certainly did not invent" the concept that a "community of culture" was an oppressed nation's defining feature. African, African American, and West Indian nationalists were already asserting a Pan-African identity rooted in a common culture decades before the Comintern's Black Belt thesis. Kelley notes, too, that "many African Americans . . . showed irreverence to the Party's interracialism," perhaps understandably, since white "allies" often proved patronizing or worse when the chips were down.[31]

Within the IWO, too, Black members at times complained about the condescension that Jewish organizers in Harlem and Ukrainian comrades in Michigan showed toward them. In Harlem, Sol Winnick faced IWO discipline after a Black woman complained of his behavior, while Black organizer Eleanor Broady in Detroit had frequent run-ins with Ukrainian comrade John Mykytew. Later, in the housing crunch that ensued in the wake of World War II, Detroit Italians and some other Motor City ethnic lodges moved away from earlier commitments to civil rights.

Still, for all the challenges, the IWO pushed boundaries in promoting an integrationist model with the incorporation of female and Black members as organizers, staffers, and officers. By 1937, too, the IWO had established a birth-control clinic at its headquarters off New York's Union Square as well as other programs to ameliorate the special burdens that working women and homemakers faced. Thompson, whose sharp attire and attitude spoke to the changing times, was put in charge of the IWO's Chicago-based recruiting efforts around the same time that its Jewish American Section tasked immigrant Clara Lemlich Shavelson (who in 1909 had led the first women's garment action, known as the "Strike of the 20,000"), June Gordon, Rose Nelson, and others with running women's committees, which worked with homemakers as well as workers.[32] The organization's anti-racist, nonprofit health care and other benefit programs proved attractive to working people and were critical to recruitment in Black communities.

Much as she did in Harlem, Thompson Patterson made sure that the recruitment for Chicago Du Sable Lodge 751 included a number of events based on community work that brought together churches, a fraternity, labor, and other organizations, in addition to a workers' education program. Her community-based cultural approach made her a visible presence in the WPA-created South Side Community Art Center. She broke labor barriers in organizing a union educational vacation retreat to Madison for IWO African Americans and then ensured that the lodge's new center provided active support during the 1948 packing house strike. Ukrainian, Polish, and other white workers joined Black comrades at Du Sable events, too.[33] She also organized a 1947 gala concert in support of Robeson just as he had begun to feel the pain of being Red-baited and blacklisted. Featuring singer Lena Horne, the gala was held under the auspices of the lodge and the Abraham Lincoln School in Chicago.

7. FIGHTING FOR BLACK RIGHTS 183

FIGURE 7.2. Du Sable pamphlet, "Our Family is Protected in the IWO," cover photo. Courtesy of the Kheel Center.

Recruitment materials from the Du Sable Lodge, such as the pamphlet "Our Family Is Protected in the IWO," used sharp modern graphics (see figures 7.2 and 7.3). Showing a photo of a Black family on one leaf and a picture of Robeson standing next to Thompson Patterson and Du Sable Lodge president Dr. Luther Peck on another, the brochure reads: "Paul Robeson says: In the IWO peoples of many nationalities, Negro and white, live and work together in a true fraternal spirit in the kind of genuine democracy I would like to see practiced in ALL of America. I value my membership in the Order. We do not only talk equality—we practice it. We not only fight for Fair Employment Practice Acts (FEPC) and

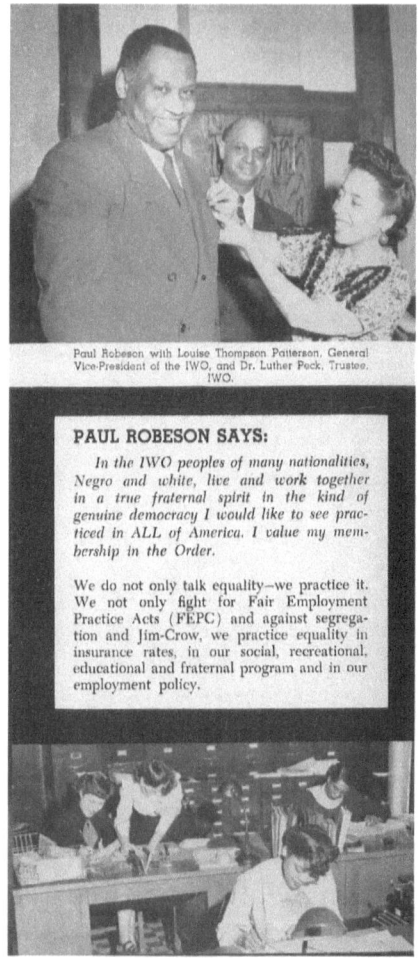

FIGURE 7.3. Du Sable pamphlet, Paul Robeson standing next to Thompson Patterson and Du Sable Lodge president Dr. Luther Peck. Courtesy of the Kheel Center.

against segregation and Jim-Crow, we practice equality in insurance rates, in our social, recreational, educational and fraternal program, and in our employment policy."[34]

In evolving into an example of broad-based, Popular Front "big-tent" progressivism, the IWO offered a broad array of programs (theater, music groups, sports leagues, and publications) that equalized and celebrated "Negro culture" and its associated arts and history as part of a panoply of ethnic cultures whose immigrant languages and folk traditions were part of the IWO's progressive brand of Americanism.[35] Such cultural organizations and events were often attended by

Order members of different races and ethnicities, as when Polish Philadelphians participated, along with Black members, in observances of Negro History Week. Yet in celebrating multiethnic, interracial models of progressive, working-class Americanism, the Order nonetheless was explicit about the distinctive history of enslavement and its ongoing violent aftermath, even as it linked the fight against Jim Crow to battles against antisemitism and anti-immigrant sentiment. The IWO's anti-racist multilingual pedagogy, too, as practiced in its extensive network of workers' schools, children's schools, and summer camps, provided a model of intersectional cultural and political activism relevant to the twenty-first century.

The IWO's fraternal program attracted many luminaries of the American progressive left during the Popular Front and war years who appreciated its anti-racist and social justice work as well as its multiethnic and multilingual approach to American life. Michigan state senator Stanley Nowak, Clara Lemlich Shavelson, Jesús Colón, Michael Salerno, and Itche Goldberg, all of whom were closely affiliated with the IWO, worked extensively in their native tongues. Some members, such as Marcantonio, Thompson Patterson, and artist Rockwell Kent, served as officers; the organization also collaborated with cultural workers, some of whom were fellow travelers. These included Pearl Primus, Howard Fast, Langston Hughes, Jules Dassin, Marc Chagall, Paul Robeson, Albert Einstein, Sholem Asch, Ruth Rubin, Earl Robinson, Hazel Scott, and Pete Seeger, who worked to advance cultural and political goals for the IWO's working-class members through artwork, literature, performance, and much more. These prominent artistic figures were complemented by myriad local theater, dance, band, and arts groups sponsored by local lodges for regular IWO members. The IWO also fostered a tight-knit multigenerational closeness that extended to the familial sphere: Robeson's son, Michael Salerno's son, and the Rosenberg (Meeropol) children attended an IWO summer camp, Wo-Chi-Ca, as did children of other activists and performers.

This unusual unity within left diversity, which proved attractive to working people, was usefully harnessed during World War II. By 1947, despite the advent of the Cold War, the IWO had enrolled 188,000 members of many political stripes and backgrounds, with more than 50,000 Jewish fraternal members as well as thousands of Slavs, Greeks, Finns, Hispanics, and Italians. The Order also began to form Douglass-Lincoln Black lodges. Unlike their leadership, relatively few IWO members belonged to the CPUSA, nor were they recruited to join its ranks. Perhaps the Order's success lay—aside from its attractive medical and insurance programs—in its active appeal to both national cultures and the interethnic, interracial celebration of culture as inherently American. At a time when antisemitism, anti-immigrant sentiment, and virulent racial segregation were prevalent, the IWO was a haven for the celebration of distinct folk cultures that deliberately fostered a relatively cosmopolitan brand of multilingual internationalism.[36]

This internationalism is evident in organizations such as Harlem's Suitcase Theatre, which was founded by Hughes with the active support of Thompson and the IWO. Described in this book by Matt Calihman, it was viewed as politically and culturally congruent with expressions of diverse cultures such as Ukrainian dance troupes and Yiddish poetry journals. At Thompson's urging, the IWO published Hughes's poetry booklet *A New Song*, featuring the poet's anthem "Let America Be America Again" (see figure 7.4). Its IWO foreword encouraged "better understanding and closer solidarity between nationalities."[37] As Felicia Bevel explains in this book, IWO performances, including sponsorship of the cantata "Ballad for Americans" with the IWO All People's Chorus and Robeson as narrator, were celebrated as a contribution to a broader, progressive coalition in multiethnic America.[38]

The Jewish left's overall focus on harnessing *Kultur-Arbet* (cultural work) for overtly political ends was shared by other IWO ethnic sections and connected to the fight for a different, fairer United States. IWO sponsorship of edgy Yiddish-speaking marionettes and Italian theater troupes paradoxically reinforced a sense of multiethnic solidarity with other marginalized groups on occasions such as Negro History Week or May Day, or in organizing around campaigns for anti-racist legislation or Congress of Industrial Organization (CIO) union drives. As such, the IWO, with its nondiscriminatory insurance policies and interracial constituency, was well situated to tackle the equal-rights end of the Black nationalist equation through agitating for anti–poll tax legislation, anti-lynching bills, voting rights, and integration, whether in New York's Stuyvesant Town housing development or in local or national sports (an African American IWO delegation including Robeson in 1943 paid a visit to baseball commissioner Kenesaw Mountain Landis demanding the integration of America's pastime; more locally, Chicago Ukrainians, Slovaks, and Lithuanians in the Order participated in campaigns to integrate bowling alleys).

The Order aligned its commitment to fighting Jim Crow laws and racist prosecutions (Ingram, Scottsboro) with its overall active support for the ILD and its successor the Civil Rights Congress, including through support for Robeson at the 1949 Peekskill riot. The civil rights work that the IWO undertook sounds more mainstream in retrospect than it then seemed in part because the organizations it supported—the National Negro Congress (NNC) and CRC—and its causes were in fact important precursors to the work of the 1960s and the development of Black nationalism.

FIGURE 7.4. Joe Jones's cover illustration for Langston Hughes's *A New Song* (International Workers Order, 1938). James Weldon Johnson Memorial Collection in the Yale Collection of American Literature, Beinecke Rare Book and Manuscript Library.

Struggles: Equal Rights, Black Internationalism/ Transnationalism

As seen in the divided response to the Black Belt resolutions, there was a palpable tension in the 1920s and '30s in CPUSA circles as to how calls for Black nationalism/internationalism should be incorporated. These debates resulted in advocacy for African or Pan-African national/international diasporic support and unity as part of a shared Black revolutionary struggle, which was sometimes articulated in combination with calls for Black and white working-class unity in the United States. Thompson, a member of the NNC and the IWO, grappled with this in representing these organizations. This debate can also be seen in the work of IWO organizer Walter Garland, who fought in Spain and was a strong voice for internationalism both in the CPUSA and the IWO, as well as that of CPUSA member Harry Haywood, a drafter of the Black Belt resolutions.

Thompson's IWO work demonstrates her successful efforts to tie together support for US Black anti-racist and anti-colonial national liberation struggles and to push the IWO's commitments to these positions. Her stances were not at variance with those of the Party; rather, they rounded out its contours. In that vein, she advocated for fighting fascism in Ethiopia and as an IWO vice president she traveled to Spain in 1937 during the Spanish Civil War after first attending the Second International Conference on Antisemitism and Racism in Paris. Like Paul and Eslanda Goode Robeson, she took a strong interest in the IWO members and Black fighters in Spain and gave a series of IWO-sponsored talks about fascism upon her return to the United States (see figure 7.5).[39]

In 1938, Thompson organized "The Seminar in Negro History" at the Harlem Community Center of the IWO Solidarity Branch 691, which she helped found (see figure 7.6). The anti-fascist spring program series included Hughes on Spain; Eugene Gordon on "A Negro Sees Russia"; a discussion of anti-lynching legislation by James Ford, the CPUSA's perennial candidate for US vice president; and Max Yergan's discussion, "A Negro Views the Tokio-Berlin-Rome Axis."[40] (The program took pains to note that Yergan "will answer the question of Japan's role in the destiny of the darker people," which was relevant at a time when the Party was working to counter Tokyo's assertions that it was the guardian of African Americans and other members of the "colored races.")[41] While there was already support within the IWO for the creation of "concentration" lodges such as the one in Harlem that could offer a space to serve as a cultural as well as political center to recruit Black members, the pace of these changes accelerated in tandem with the IWO's wartime and postwar commitments to equal rights.[42]

Less visible but also important in Thompson's IWO world was the daily work of organizing with women's and other committees that worked on rent strikes, anti-eviction actions, support for domestic workers, and food and other boycotts, often in coalition with Black churches. She joined the National Council of Negro Women, developed a friendship with its head, Mary Church Terrell, and convinced the IWO to pay for her membership and to make an organizational financial contribution. After her organizing campaigns in the South, her IWO work involved organizing in Black communities primarily in New York City (Harlem), Chicago (South Side), Detroit, and Cleveland. The approach in these first two cities was to create "concentration" lodges, which echoed urban

FIGURE 7.5. IWO meeting flyer, "We Saw Spain: Hear the News Direct from the Front" with Max Bedacht and Louise Thompson, November 2, 1937, Chicago. Courtesy of University of Pittsburgh.

Black Belt language on the need for Black self-determination and emphasis on cultural autonomy. Additionally, as head of the English-speaking lodges and then as president of the Illinois District, Thompson spent much of her time working with the IWO's "national" immigrant linguistic sections, whose younger generation wanted English-language opportunities. Her work in the English Section was a good fit, not least since African Americans were native speakers of English, and the language also served as the IWO's lingua franca (see figure 7.7).

Her impact was apparent in the February 1941 IWO executive plenary session minutes, which start by noting that "Vice President [Rockwell] Kent presented

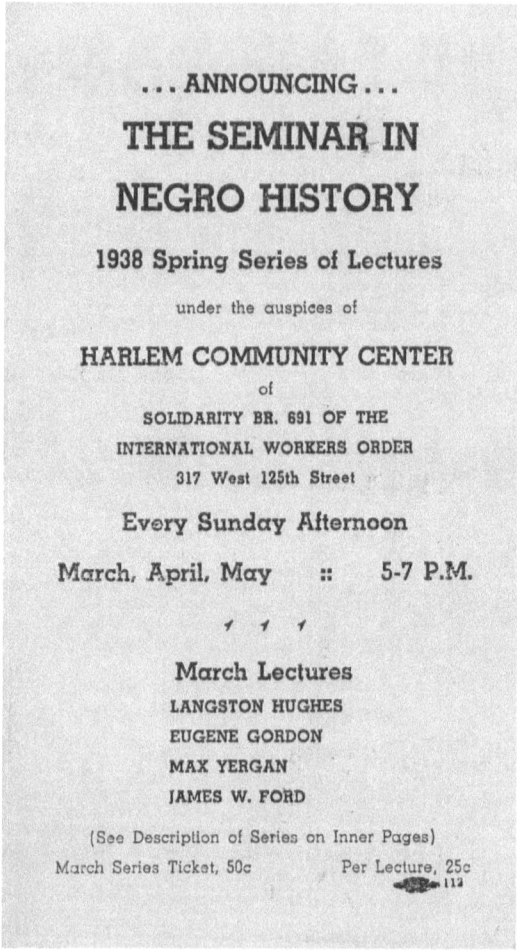

FIGURE 7.6. Program of "The Seminar in Negro History," 1938 series at the Harlem Community Center of IWO Solidarity Branch 691, which Louise Thompson helped found. Courtesy of Emory University and MaryLouise Patterson.

a distinguished guest, Paul Robeson, famous singer, who was welcomed with a rising ovation. Brother Kent then introduced Earl Robinson, noted composer and honored member, who was also greeted with applause. . . . Vice President Thompson in opening the afternoon session introduced the Rev. B.W. Harris of Norfolk who addressed the Board." The minutes finish by detailing resolutions showing that the IWO agreed to deepen commitments to "Negro work," as well as to follow the NNC's program.[43] In this respect, Thompson, as well as African American minister Harris and IWO organizer Sam Patterson, urged the Order to

National Committee of the English Section, reading left to right, front row: Nathan Polak, Dave Greene, Louise Thompson, National Secretary, Nathan Shaffer and Benjamin McLaurin. Standing, left to right: George Starr, Lester Zirin, Esther Posner, Sam Pevzner, Ernest Rymer, Emanuel Levin. Members not appearing in this picture are: George Primoff, Joseph Landy, Louis Eis and Samuel C. Patterson.

FIGURE 7.7. National Committee of the English Section photo with caption accompanying the article "With Our Lodges" by Louise Thompson, national secretary, English Section. *Fraternal Outlook*, June–July 1940, special anniversary issue, page 52. Courtesy of the Kheel Center.

pay more attention to "the problem of Negro work," particularly "jobs, insecurity and discrimination." The board recommended, too, that the IWO journal *Fraternal Outlook* "print articles about certain phases of the problem . . . such as the campaign for jobs for Negroes." At the same session the following resolution was approved: "To instruct the Organization Committee to establish a Women's Work Department, and to place a full-time director in charge of the work."[44]

Thompson's commitment to anti-colonialism remained unwavering and can be seen in her defense of the Party's abrupt and uncomfortable switch to neutrality toward Nazi Germany following the August 1939 Molotov-Ribbentrop Pact. In a 1940 speech she criticized calls to come to Great Britain's aid, noting that London's brutal rule of millions of non-white people in India, Africa, and the Caribbean made a mockery of assertions that Churchill was fighting to defend democracy. Thompson also linked anti-colonialism to the defense of African Americans at home at the IWO's 1940 convention, which passed anti-lynching, anti-poll tax, and antisemitism resolutions. During her report at the convention, Thompson noted that the IWO had recruited two thousand Black members, but needed to do better. She called this number inadequate, and "not a figure to shout about. Rather it is a reflection of the lack of country-wide attention to the job of winning large sections of the Negro people for our Order."[45]

At the same convention, Thompson also articulated the fight for Black rights and community organizing in English-speaking lodges as "the cementing of the unity of the native-born Negro and white peoples," but called for combining these issues by working with local communities in response to their needs in a unified defense of ethnic immigrants and in the fight against antisemitism:

> This means we must know our community and its social composition. If it is a Jewish community, then our emphasis must be against anti-Semitism and we should work closely with such organizations as the Jewish People's Committee. Should it be a Negro community then the fight for Negro rights, the National Negro Congress, the National Association for the Advancement of Colored People, the fight for the passage of the anti-lynch bill become our community ties. If an English lodge is located in an Italian community or a community predominately populated by any other national group, then we must know these peoples, their organizations, their special needs.[46]

Even when promoting English-language Americanization in the IWO, as a "recognition of the reality about us; that we live in a country in which the native-born population is in the majority; that our Order will function best as an American organization when it reflects in the composition of its membership, the composition of the general population in due proportion," Thompson's view was that recruitment needed to consider local ethno-racial demographics, allies, and associated communal priorities to best fight "anti-Semitic, anti-Negro, anti-alien propaganda and legislation."[47]

Thompson's pragmatic approach to theory offers a window into the large shift that can be seen from the 1930s into the 1940s when the war changed everything for the IWO. After Hitler attacked the Soviet Union in Operation Barbarossa in June 1941 and the Soviet Union obtained Allied support after Japan attacked Pearl Harbor that same year, the IWO and CPUSA enthusiastically gave their all to the war effort. In championing the "Double-V Campaign"—victory over fascism abroad and racism at home—the IWO's push intensified for "Negro Work" and "armed forces integration." Thompson Patterson gave a speech at the IWO's 1944 convention promoting a resolution to cement hard-won wartime gains by establishing a new organization, one with Black community roots and origins, within the Order. "This Convention therefore pledges renewed activity for the outlawing of Jim Crowism, and for the complete integration of the Negro people into every aspect of American life," she said. Referring to the Order, she insisted that "it should be an organization of thousands of members with its roots in the Negro community, functioning as a normal part of the life of the Negro people," and that "it will also bring the Negro people into alliance with organized white progressives, making the IWO membership and others more conscious of the relationship of the struggles of the Negro people to their own problems and struggles."[48]

In looking at Louise Thompson Patterson and other Black nationalists, we might ask why active alliance with immigrant ethnic fraternalists was attractive to advocates of a Black nationalist agenda. One answer, although it may not be entirely satisfactory, would point to the importance for Thompson and others of the unique availability in the IWO of the nondiscriminatory rates that allowed Blacks to obtain much-needed insurance benefits. Thompson said as much in her earlier writing about insurance for IWO journals and in later interviews.[49] A different, albeit not mutually exclusive answer, may come back to the combination of theory and praxis. If you do not get the less privileged white ethnic working class—most especially the part that already sees itself as progressive—to advocate for equal rights and disavow white supremacy, how are you going to overthrow the ultimate source of racism, that is to say capitalism, with its creation of class, race, and divisions of labor?

In the postwar years, it is likely that Party loyalty in advocating for equal rights based on a "Black and White unity" approach, one strongly supported by William Z. Foster in the CPUSA, played a large role in explaining the attraction of working for, and with, the IWO. William Patterson, as head of the ILD, served time in prison due to his membership in the CPUSA and was not unique in that regard; almost everyone involved in the IWO or CPUSA leadership ranks was investigated by the House Committee on Un-American Activities (HUAC) and other governmental authorities. Some, like Claudia Jones, were jailed, blacklisted, or deported as aliens as well. It is worth noting, too, that many chairmen and members of HUAC were Southern advocates of Jim Crow segregation. It is therefore not surprising that some of the most punitive Red Scare investigations involved radical Black advocates of racial equality. Paul Robeson, chair of the Council on African Affairs and IWO member, asserted in his appearance before HUAC that he needed no lectures on Americanism from segregationists. Neither did Louise Thompson Patterson's husband, William Patterson, who served time in prison for contempt of Congress in 1954–55. The charge of Communism, that one was "Red," was often lobbed most forcefully at perceived champions of Black and white unity, whether or not they were members of the CPUSA.

Robeson's rejoinder to HUAC suggests that such intimidation was not entirely successful although it exacted a high price. To be sure, many members, if not most, became disillusioned with the CPUSA either due to Stalin or Party politics or mounting Cold War pressures at home. However, not only did many others stay loyal, but some of those in Louise and William Patterson's circles became somewhat belatedly affiliated or more closely associated with the CPUSA, most famously Du Bois and Robeson.[50]

Yet another part of the answer to the question of why Black nationalists would ally themselves with immigrant ethnic fraternalists may be related to the issue of local agency as seen in organizations that moved in the CPUSA's pro-Soviet orbit. One of the IWO's strengths was its ability to see Black people and women as potential fraternalist constituencies whose issues became increasingly, if unevenly, visible in its own identity politics. These commitments in turn affected some executive committees and positions; women in leadership roles who were active in the CPUSA were critical to building ties and forging broader coalitions. Into the late 1940s Louise Thompson Patterson was respected and liked by her leadership peers despite the pressures of the postwar Red Scare and the increasing lack of interest in Black rights by some of the IWO's ethnic national sections, most especially in Detroit. There, some Italian IWO lodges fought public housing proposed for their neighborhoods, expressing fear of racial integration. This policy naturally distressed African American IWO members such as Detroit's Reverend Charles Hill. Nevertheless, the IWO continued to advocate for Black civil rights. Indeed, the last check legally written prior to the IWO's final closure by the State of New York in 1954, and signed on October 27, 1949 by IWO and JPFO founder Rubin Saltzman, was to the Civil Rights Congress's bail fund.

The civil rights message was also important during the war years, and Thompson Patterson's speech in support of the war effort at the IWO's 1944 convention compared US racial segregation and oppression to Hitlerism:

> The IWO in Convention here assembled reaffirms its conviction and position that the practice of racial segregation is the counterpart in America of Hitlerism in Europe; that all manifestations of racial and religious discrimination, all practices of segregation and oppression, are detrimental to the war effort and in direct conflict with any program for national unity, winning the war and carrying out the objectives of Teheran. This Convention therefore pledges renewed activity for the outlawing of Jim Crowism, and for the complete integration of the Negro people into every aspect of American life.[51]

Far stronger echoes of that important 1944 equation can be found in the introduction of the 1951 lawyerly petition "We Charge Genocide," which was presented to the United Nations by William Patterson and Paul Robeson.[52]

> The Hitler crimes, of awful magnitude, beginning as they did against the heroic Jewish people, finally drenched the world in blood, and left a record of maimed and tortured bodies and devastated areas such as mankind had never seen before. . . . Justice Robert H. Jackson described this holocaust to the world in the powerful language with which he opened the Nuremberg trials of the Nazi leaders. Every word he voiced against the monstrous Nazi beast applies with equal weight, we believe, to those who are guilty of the crimes herein set forth.
>
> Here we present the documented crimes of federal, state, and municipal governments in the United States of America, the dominant nation in the United Nations, against 15,000,000 of its own nationals—the Negro people of the United States. These crimes are of the gravest concern to mankind.[53]

Signatories included Haywood, one of the drafters of the original Black Belt resolutions and a strong, continuing proponent for a Black republic, as well as the Sojourners Claudia Jones, Charlotta Bass, and Louise Thompson Patterson, along with Mary Church Terrell and Albert Kahn, the head of the JPFO, the largest constituent of the IWO.

The IWO's immigrant left imagined a United States without racism and antisemitism, devoid of nativist sentiment. It navigated the tensions of celebrating particular ethnic cultures and languages while valorizing and championing cultural pluralism in the United States as integrally connected to supporting the Soviet Union's policies as an alternative to capitalism. The IWO's Douglass-Lincoln Black section members and the IWO's Black leadership, including Thompson Patterson, navigated all that and more. Reconciling the particularities of transnational diasporas; gendered organizing; and the goals of obtaining multiracial, international solidarity and self-determination were challenged by the Great Depression, the Molotov-Ribbentrop Pact, World War II, and ultimately by the Cold War's Red Scare, which shut down the IWO and most of the pro-Soviet left.

These tensions—internal and external to the organization—could be seen in the IWO's goals of "Black and white unity," which in promoting integration and racial equality did not allow for Black nationalism to become a central theoretical concern except when organizing in the Black community. Nonetheless, a "black female radical imagination" can be discerned in this earlier moment, one that evinced its disappointment with the failure of the Double-V Campaign in the war's aftermath, even as it geared up for a new, long round of making its demands heard.

While the IWO's organizational voice was silenced by government harassment and, by 1954, liquidation, Thompson Patterson's voice continued to be raised in advocating for racial justice. In the 1970s, '80s, and early '90s (when she was more than ninety years old), she continued to be an active campaigner in the civil rights struggle, most notably in working to defend and free Angela Davis, who was imprisoned in 1970 on charges of conspiracy to commit murder. Thompson Patterson's decades-long, unrepentant career as a civil rights advocate suggests that many former IWO members likely also retained their commitment to racial, gender, and class justice long after the government dismantled the Order.

Her trajectory, though, was not surprising, for the road map to activism was laid out with her comrade and spouse, William Patterson, and with others in response to the violence and race mob riots that marked the earlier part of the twentieth century. "We Charge Genocide" shows a documented postwar landscape littered with bodies along with a simultaneous insistence that demands to stop violence cannot be kept at bay forever. Among its multiple heirs are those in the early radical Civil Rights Movement who benefited from the activism of Black nationalist leftists such as Patterson, Thompson Patterson, Garland, Haywood, Robeson, Jones, and even less celebrated figures such as Youngstown's Pauline Taylor, all of whom—albeit in different ways—pressed Party leaders to confront the centrality of racism, whether they wished to or not. Something happened that can be heard in the continuing echoes of the Black Belt resolutions, as seen in Louise Thompson Patterson's attention to theory and praxis in Black organizing in forging a prefiguring that speaks directly to the importance of intersectionality and the creation of "Black space," even as it addresses the challenges of working with ethnic "white progressives."

NOTES

1. The preamble to the 1930 Comintern Resolution on the Black National Question in the United States, Sixth Party Congress, emphasized that

> the struggle of the Communists for the equal rights of the Negroes applies to all Negroes, in the North as well as in the South.... In the South,... the main Communist slogan must be: The right of self-determination of the Negroes in the Black Belt.... In the South the Negroes are suffering no less but still more than in the North from the glaring lack of all equality; for the most part the struggle for their most urgent partial demands in the Black Belt is nothing more than the struggle for their equal rights, and only the fulfilment of their main slogan, the right of self-determination in the Black Belt, can assure them of true equality.

The 1928 translated resolution apparently initially appeared in English in the *Daily Worker*, the newspaper of the Workers (Communist) Party of America, on February 12, 1929, page 3, https://www.marxists.org/history/usa/pubs/dailyworker/1929/1929-ny/v05-n347-NY-feb-12-1929-DW-LOC.pdf. For commentary, see "The 1928 Comintern Resolution and the Black National Question," in *On the Roots of Revisionism: A Political Analysis of the International Communist Movement and the CPUSA, 1919–1945* by Bay Area Study Group (April 1979), 321–51, https://www.marxists.org/history/erol/ncm-8/roots-revisionism/chapter-13.pdf.

Caveat emptor: there are differences in versions due to translation and politics. Both resolutions were reprinted in the Communist International's *The 1928 and 1930*

Comintern Resolutions on the Black National Question in the United States (Revolutionary Review Press, 1975), with an introduction by Lowell Young. They have also been published in Nelson Perry, *The Negro National Colonial Question* (Workers Press, 1972), 133–58; and *The Communist International* 8, no. 2 (February 1, 1931), a semimonthly journal defunct since 1940.

2. Mark Solomon, *The Cry Was Unity: Communists and African Americans, 1917–1936* (University Press of Mississippi, 1998), 68–92. See Oscar Berland, "The Emergence of the Communist Perspective on the 'Negro Question' in America: 1919–1931, Part Two," *Science & Society* 64, no. 2 (Summer 2000) as to the Black Belt resolutions' emphasis on the national question as providing "operational value" in elevating its salience and importance in the CPUSA. Berland suggests that "the idea of the Negro question as a national question gave the Comintern a revolutionary ground for demanding that the American party give it serious attention" (213).

3. "Always, for the Party, there was bourgeois nationalism and the 'national revolutionary movement of the Negro people.' Both were shaped and driven by social class, but the internal nature and relationship of class forces within those distinct modes were strikingly dissimilar. The two were also contradictory." Solomon, *The Cry Was Unity*, 164.

4. On the African Blood Brotherhood, see Minkah Makalani, *In the Cause of Freedom: Radical Black Internationalism from Harlem to London, 1917–1939* (University of North Carolina Press, 2011); Harry Haywood, *Black Bolshevik: Autobiography of an Afro-American Communist* (Liberator Press, 1978); on Claudia Jones, see Carole Boyce Davies, *Left of Karl Marx: The Political Life of Black Communist Claudia Jones* (Duke University Press, 2008).

5. *The 1928 and 1930 Comintern Resolutions on the Black National Question in the United States* (Revolutionary Review Press, 1975), http://www.marx2mao.com/Other/CR75.html. The 1928 resolution initially appeared in the *Daily Worker*, the newspaper of the Workers (Communist) Party of America, on February 12, 1929, page 3, https://www.marxists.org/history/usa/pubs/dailyworker/1929/1929-ny/v05-n347-NY-feb-12-1929-DW-LOC.pdf. For the 1928 resolution, see https://www.marxists.org/history/erol/ncm-8/roots-revisionism/chapter-13.pdf. The 1930 resolution was first published in *The Communist International* 8, no. 2 (February 1, 1931).

6. "Thus, a nation is not a racial or tribal, but a historically constituted community of people." Joseph Stalin, *Marxism and the National Question*, Marxists Internet Archive, 1913, https://www.marxists.org/reference/archive/stalin/works/1913/03a.htm. In full, it "is a historically constituted, stable community of people, formed on the basis of a common language, territory, economic life, and psychological make-up manifested in a common culture."

7. James W. Ford, "World Problems of the Negro People (A Refutation of George Padmore)," pamphlet, 1930, Reference Center for Marxist Studies Collection, PE043, box 5, Tamiment Library and Robert F. Wagner Labor Archives, New York University, New York, New York (hereafter Tamiment/Wagner, NYU); poster for Toussaint L'overture [sic] Memorial mass meeting, May 20, 1929, reel 139, delo 1842, Records of the Communist Party USA, Library of Congress, Washington, District of Columbia.

8. See Kate A. Baldwin, *Beyond the Color Line and the Iron Curtain: Reading Encounters Between Black and Red, 1922–1963* (Duke University Press, 2002) as to how the Comintern read the US situation through a prior Russian imperial lens on Africa and post–World War I anti-colonial activity. See J. A. Zumoff, "The American Communist Party and the 'Negro Question' from the Founding of the Party to the Fourth Congress of the Communist International," *Journal for the Study of Radicalism* 6, no. 2 (Fall 2012), as to the CPUSA's earlier stances on a Black nation. The 1930 resolution called for "a fighting alliance with the revolutionary white proletariat."

9. W. E. B. Du Bois, *Black Reconstruction in America* (1935; repr., Atheneum, 1992); Thulani Davis, *The Emancipation Circuit: Black Activism Forging a Culture of Freedom* (Duke University Press, 2022); Mary F. Berry, "Reparations for Freedmen, 1890–1916: Fraudulent Practices or Justice Deferred?," *The Journal of Negro History* 57, no. 3 (July 1972): 219–30.

10. *The 1928 and 1930 Comintern Resolutions.* See Black Belt Thesis Study Group, *The Black Belt Thesis: A Reader* (1804 Books, 2023), 12.

11. In a parallel vein, Minkah Makalani's reading of the work of Aimé Césaire documents the redefinition of the proletariat in the 1930s to include the colonized and adds those in the United States who struggled for Black nationalism in its various flavors. Makalani, *In the Cause of Freedom*, 230. Also see Robin D. G. Kelley, *Freedom Dreams: The Black Radical Imagination* (Beacon Press, 2002), 51.

12. "It is the Communist Party which has analyzed the Negro Question as that of an oppressed nation of people, defined the alignment of class forces for and against the Negro people's struggle for liberation, and begun the organization of white and Negro working masses together." Louise Thompson, "Southern Terror," *The Crisis*, November 1934. Reprinted in Black Belt Thesis Study Group, *The Black Belt Thesis*, 142.

13. Charisse Burden-Stelly and Jodi Dean, eds., *Organize, Fight, Win: Black Communist Women's Political Writing* (Verso, 2022).

14. Louise Thompson, "With Our Lodges," *Fraternal Outlook*, June–July 1940, 52; Edith Benjamin, "Louise Thompson Honored at Dinner," *Fraternal Outlook*, April 1941, 25–26.

15. Erik S. McDuffie, *Sojourning for Freedom: Black Women, American Communism, and the Making of Black Left Feminism* (Duke University Press, 2011).

16. See Boyce Davies, *Left of Karl Marx*.

17. Louise Thompson, "Toward a Brighter Dawn," *The Woman Today* 1, no. 14 (April 1936). Black female domestics could be theorized as an especially vulnerable, organizable, and critical component of a newly visible Black proletariat.

18. *We Saw for Ourselves: Report of the Nineteen Americans on Their Visit to the USSR* (New World Review, 1951).

19. Keith Gilyard, *Louise Thompson Patterson: A Life of Struggle for Justice* (Duke University Press, 2017), 145.

20. See Burden-Stelly and Dean, *Organize, Fight, Win*; and McDuffie, *Sojourning for Freedom*.

21. Gilyard, in *A Life of Struggle for Justice*, describes Thompson as moving from "embodied resistance to racial, economic, and gender exploitation, moving beyond theory to action" (2). It is hoped that overlapping framings, including ones explored here, may offer additional insight into the multidirectional movements that feed theory and praxis.

22. McDuffie writes: "No issue was more important in fostering . . . Thompson's support for the Soviet Union than its symbol as an apparent revolutionary ally and model to colonized and racially-oppressed people globally. . . . As Thompson and her comrades traveled deeper into Central Asia, they increasingly identified with an imagined, transnational, multi-racial community of people struggling against capitalism, imperialism, national oppression, poverty, women's subjugation, and archaic cultural traditions." *Sojourning for Freedom*, 71.

23. The following can be found in Louise Thompson Patterson Papers, mss. 869, box 8, folder 8, Stuart A. Rose Manuscript, Archives, and Rare Book Library, Emory University, Atlanta, Georgia (hereafter Louise Thompson Patterson Papers): letter from Sadie Doroshkin to Louise Thompson, June 4, 1934; letter from Louise Thompson to Max Bedacht, February 23, 1934; letter from Louise Thompson to Max Bedacht, February 24, 1934; Max Bedacht, "To Whom it May Concern," regarding Thompson's credentials as an IWO

organizer, February 28, 1934; Max Bedacht to name redacted, June 7, 1934; letter from Sadie Doroshkin to Louise Thompson, June 7, 1934; letter from Max Bedacht to Louise Thompson, June 9, 1934; letter from Louise Thompson to Sadie Doroshkin, June 12, 1934; letter from Sadie Doroshkin to Louise Thompson, June 20, 1934; letter from Sadie Doroshkin to Louise Thompson, June 19, 1934; letter from Louise Thompson to Sadie Doroshkin, March 9, 1934; letter from Sadie Doroshkin to Louise Thompson, May 21, 1934; letter from Louise Thompson to Birmingham attorney C. B. Powell, May 21, 1934; letter from Louise Thompson to Sadie Doroshkin, May 22, 1934; letter from C. B. Powell to Louise Thompson, May 21, 1934; letter from Louise Thompson to Joseph Brodsky, May 23, 1934; letter from Sadie Doroshkin to Louise Thompson, May 28, 1934; letter from C. B. Powell to Louise Thompson, n.d.; Thompson Patterson manuscript autobiography, chap. 6, pg. 11, box 20, folder 5, Louise Thompson Patterson Papers; transcript of interview with Louise Thompson Patterson [1950–51?], box 20, folder 5, Louise Thompson Patterson Papers. See Thompson, "Southern Terror," for a somewhat different account.

24. Gilyard in describing her labor organizing notes: "Louise spent a lot of time in saloons and poolrooms because they were the only meeting places available in many of the areas where no lodge existed yet. In these cities and towns of the Midwest and adjacent states, her focal region during this period, no one within the sphere of the IWO balked significantly at accepting leadership from an African American woman. In fact, she stayed in numerous white homes, with the families feeling it an honor to host her. In this context she began to make significant progress in conveying the IWO's political platform and getting both black and white audiences to understand the interconnectedness of the fights for labor and for African American rights" (*A Life of Struggle for Justice*, 133).

25. See Court of Appeals of the State of New York, *In the Matter of the Application of the People of the State of New York, by Alfred J. Bohlinger, Superintendent of Insurance of the State of New York, Petitioner-Respondent, for an Order Directing Him to Take Possession of the Property and to Liquidate the Business, and Dissolving the Corporate Existence, of the International Workers Order*, 1951, 3767, https://catalog.hathitrust.org/Record/005663863. Henceforth, Court of Appeals.

26. For a list of IWO officers, see State of New York Insurance Department to Superintendent of Insurance, regarding examination of IWO finances, January 1949, International Workers Order (IWO) Records #5276, box 6, folder 7, Kheel Center for Labor-Management Documentation and Archives, Catherwood Library, Cornell University, Ithaca, New York (hereafter Kheel), https://digital.library.cornell.edu/catalog/ss:21072868.

27. "The IWO also began to organize black Americans. This proved a more difficult problem than organizing any other group, and caused considerable consternation and debate among IWO leaders. 'Shouldn't blacks be organized within English-speaking lodges, on the principle of interracial unity?' some members asked. Others responded that, according to the Communist Party's 'black belt' hypothesis, blacks constituted a unique minority group and should, therefore, be accorded the status of a national section." Jennifer Young, "Fighting Anti-Semitism and Jim Crow: 'Negro-Jewish Unity' in the International Workers Order," *AJS Perspectives* (Fall 2014), https://associationforjewishstudies.org/docs/default-source/ajs-perspectives/ajsp14fa.pdf?sfvrsn=4998d906_2.

28. Patterson testified: "We came to the development of this society somewhat hesitantly, for we did not wish to have any impression that the IWO carried out in any way Jim Crow policies, so that is why I say it is the result of a culmination of our experiences. . . . It is the Negro-white society of the International Workers Order in which the Negro people have the greatest opportunity for leadership, that is the emphasis here." Court of Appeals, 3185.

29. Patterson also testified: "[The] International Workers Order was . . . a nondiscriminatory fraternal insurance society. This was very important to me, because I had

as a principle not joined insurance companies such as the Metropolitan, which every Negro knows about, because I protested against being a part of an organization which made me pay more and get less, and due to the fact that my family had no insurance, and my mother who had died that year—I had checked the last penny out of the bank in order to pay for her funeral." Court of Appeals, 3773.

30. That the CPUSA's stance provoked a gendered response is not surprising. McDuffie, *Sojourning for Freedom* (121), notes that

> the CPUSA's obsession with interracialism alienated some African Americans, women particularly, from the Party. Abner Berry recollects that this was the case: "The thing I came up against most often was that the blacks wanted to be together. They didn't mind on occasion being integrated, but in general, they wanted to be involved in something they could call their own." Party officials, however, viewed all-black gatherings as dangerous manifestations of "nationalism." The CPUSA regularly expelled blacks, even prominent officials for this apparent "crime." Given the Party's unique political and social movement culture, black women found themselves in a precarious situation. As a minority within a minority in the CPUSA, black women had fewer social and political options than their black male and white female counterparts.

31. Robin D. G. Kelley, *Race Rebels: Culture, Politics, and the Black Working Class* (Free Press, 1994), 109–10, 114–15.

32. See Jennifer Young's discussion in this book of June Croll Gordon, who was married to Black journalist Eugene Gordon, a writer for the *Saturday Evening Quill* and the *Boston Daily Post*, as well as for CPUSA-connected publications such as *New Masses*. June Gordon organized primarily Jewish homemakers in the 1930s but also Black women, and then worked in the JPFO's Women's Department, the precursor to its Emma Lazarus Division.

33. Robeson and Lena Horne performed to raise money to construct the Chicago Du Sable Community Center. Thompson testified in 1951 that "we had a real mass campaign that got into the ranks of the community . . . so we had a meeting to launch the organization of this drive, we had a dinner at which we had many of the Negro ministers and leaders of other community organizations so that in moving in a mass way into the community we had to do it with the understanding and with the approval of the leaders of that community." Court of Appeals, 3809-1310.

34. Membership recruitment pamphlet for African Americans, ca. 1945, box 6, folder 4, Kheel.

35. On the question of multilingualism, Solomon, Berland, and others have argued in their writing about the CPUSA that it was dissatisfied with the lack of native speakers of English, of "real" Americans, and tried to play down the high participation of immigrants in the Party's ranks. "Resolution on Language Work," in Central Committee Plenum, *Thesis and Resolutions for the Seventh National Convention of the Communist Party of USA, March 31–April 4, 1930* (Workers Library Publishers, 1930), 79–87, notes "the prevalence of nationalist ideology in many workers' language schools for children where the tendency of 'developing national culture' still prevails. This is connected with another tendency still existing in the language work, namely, *insufficient interest in the political and economic struggles of the working class in the United States*" (italics in original).

These tensions can be seen in the IWO, most especially in policies by Max Bedacht, Herbert Benjamin, and William Weiner that promoted English and in the pushback this incurred. Ironically, Bedacht was a German immigrant. McDuffie describes the IWO's leftist commitment to immigrant cultures and languages as fostering "an anti-racist, anti-fascism movement culture celebrating the unique national cultures of its membership while simultaneously promoting pan-ethnic working-class solidarity." *Sojourning for Freedom*, 105.

36. See Robert M. Zecker, *"A Road to Peace and Freedom": The International Workers Order and the Struggle for Economic Justice and Civil Rights, 1930–1954* (Temple University Press, 2018).

37. Langston Hughes, *A New Song* (International Workers Order, 1938), https://collections.library.yale.edu/catalog/17290814.

38. Lisa Barg, "Paul Robeson's *Ballad for Americans*: Race and the Cultural Politics of 'People's Music,'" *Journal of the Society for American Music* 2, no. 1 (2008), https://doi.org/10.1017/S1752196308080024.

39. Other Black leaders in the IWO and in the CPUSA also connected racism to fascism. "Reverend Moran Weston, as their [IWO] Director of Negro Work [in Harlem] . . . needed political changes for black Americans. In a 1941 newspaper article, Weston connected prejudice against blacks to the war in Europe, arguing that Jim Crow was a form of fascism." Young, "Fighting Anti-Semitism."

40. *Announcing the Seminar in American Negro History*, brochure, 1938, box 8, folder 9, Louise Thompson Patterson Papers, https://exhibitions.lib.udel.edu/langston-hughes/exhibition-item/langston-hughes-a-poet-looks-at-a-troubled-world-the-seminar-in-negro-history-harlem-community-center-solidarity-br-691-of-the-international-workers-order-new-york-march-6-19/.

41. "The Sino-Japanese War and the Negro Question: Material for Discussion Issued by the Organization Education Commission, Central Committee, February 3, 1938," Educational Department of the Harlem Division of the Communist Party, New York, and the Negro Commission, C.C., Matt N. and Evelyn Graves Crawford Papers, mss. 882, box 7, folder 19, Stuart A. Rose Manuscript, Archives and Rare Book Library.

42. Patterson testified in court as to whether the Solidarity Lodge had white members:

> One of our concerns, as we began to develop and get a larger membership, was to build . . . a social center for our lodge in Harlem. . . . We canvassed in Harlem together. . . . We were building an interracial society. This, of course, tied very much in with my feeling of what real interracial unity meant, a growing concept with me. . . . We were building a lodge where we wished to have the leadership coming from the community where the lodge was established. The white membership was a part, but we were never mechanical about it. (Court of Appeals, 3778–79)

43. Sam Pevzner, minutes of the plenary session of the General Executive Board, February 22–24, 1941, 4, box 1, folder 8, Kheel, https://digital.library.cornell.edu/catalog/ss:22377618.

44. Pevzner, minutes, 5.

45. Louise Thompson, "Report on the English Section," Fifth National Convention, International Workers Order, June 8–14, 1940, New York, pg. 11, box 3, folder 2, Kheel.

46. Thompson, "Report on the English Section," 21–22.

47. Thompson, "Report on the English Section," 30. Thompson also said, perhaps disingenuously, "Does this mean . . . that our General Executive Board is going to pay less attention to and minimize the importance of our national group sections? Not at all."

48. Louise Thompson Patterson, "IWO Resolution on Negro Work," resolution presented at the general executive board meeting of the Sixth National Convention of the International Workers Order, July 2–7, 1944, New York, pg. 112, box 3, folder 4, Kheel.

49. International Workers Order, *Five Years IWO*, IWO 1935 full convention souvenir journal, 1935, box 48, folder 13, Kheel. Pages 35–40 include the Louise Thompson article "Fraternalism and the Negro People."

Louise Thompson authored articles and gave talks about the economic hardship that resulted from the inability of Black people to purchase quality insurance at nondiscriminatory rates and promoted fairly priced benefits as a recruiting tool. "Fraternalism and the Negro People" (1935) includes the subheadings "Jim Crow Polices of White Insurance Companies," "Bourgeois Insurance Preaches White Chauvinism," "Negro Insurance Companies and 'The Way Out,'" "Negro Bourgeoise Helps White Master Class," "The Role of Negro Fraternal Organization in the Liberation Struggle," "Negro Fraternal Organization Were Often Misused," "The Task of the International Workers Order," and "Racial Equality Exists Within I.W.O." Also see Louise Thompson Patterson, "Excerpt from Memoirs on Scottsboro Boys Organizing," in *We Shall Be Free!: Black Communist Protests in Seven Voices*, ed. Walter T. Howard (Temple University Press, 2013), 96–108.

50. As to Robeson's politics, see Gerald Horne, *Paul Robeson: The Artist as Revolutionary* (Pluto Press, 2016).

51. Patterson, "IWO Resolution on Negro Work," 112.

52. Although the term "oppressed nation" is not used in "We Charge Genocide," by January 1945 William Patterson had already written in defense of the CPUSA: "So the Communists have fought aggressively and zealously, persistently and systematically for an equal status for Negroes. American Communists study every written word of Communists elsewhere who were or who ever had been confronted with the problem of liberating colonial peoples, national minorities, or oppressed nations. Their understanding of the Negro question has deepened and matured with their experiences, and for the first time in the history of the United States they gave the question exact definition—that of an oppressed nation." James Ford et al., *Communists in the Struggle for Negro Rights* (Workers Library Publishers, 1945), 14–15, https://digital.library.manoa.hawaii.edu/items/show/3537.

Noteworthy is that the early multiple heirs of "We Charge Genocide" include those who claimed reparations.

53. Introduction to *We Charge Genocide: The Historic Petition to the United Nations for Relief from a Crime of the United States Government Against the Negro People*, ed. William L. Patterson (Civil Rights Congress, 1951), https://depts.washington.edu/moves/images/cp/WeChargeGenocide.pdf.

Part III
A LEFT DIASPORA
Internationalism and Radicalism

As sojourners newly arrived from many lands, progressives in the immigrant Old Left were often internationalist in outlook. The IWO cooperated with Canadian and South American Communist organizations in developing workers' and children's educational institutions, supporting an autonomous Jewish homeland in the Soviet Union, and building international anti-fascist solidarity in the 1930s. This transnational solidarity was perhaps most prominently on display in IWO members' broad support for and combat in the Abraham Lincoln Brigade, part of the International Brigade defending 1930s Spain from fascist assault.

8

DI PROGRESSIVE
YKUF in Argentina and South America

Nerina Visacovsky

Between the end of the nineteenth century and World War II, numerous Yiddish-speaking Jews arrived in the Americas escaping European misery and antisemitism. Most settled in the United States: it is estimated that by 1924 two million Jews had passed through the gates of Ellis Island in New York. Argentina and Canada tied for second place, with one-tenth of that number. The Jewish communities of Mexico, Cuba, Brazil, Uruguay, and Chile were smaller still and concentrated in the capital cities.[1] The Jewish progressive (*Di progressive*) movement in Argentina and elsewhere in South America had its origins in the formation of ethnic associations that expanded at the beginning of the twentieth century.

During the 1920s, most especially in Buenos Aires, three Jewish left-wing institutional networks were organized that reflected the politics of Jewish transnational movements, whose main expression was seen in the erstwhile Yiddish press, schools, theaters, and libraries. Their Latin American establishment and institutionalization, and that of the uniquely Latin American ICUF, the Idisher Cultur Farband, reveals a Jewish immigrant context whose legacy can still be traced today.[2] Broadly speaking, the Latin American offshoots of international Yiddish movements came from the Socialists of the Bund (Algemeyner Yidisher Arbeter Bund inn Rusland, Poyln un Lite [General Union of Jewish Workers of Russia, Poland, and Lithuania]), the Socialist Zionists of Linke Poale Tsiyon (Left Zionist workers), and the Communist YKUF (Yidisher Kultur Farband [Yiddish cultural association]).

YKUF Communists had maintained an ideological and political connection with the Jewish Peoples Fraternal Order (JPFO) in the United States and the United Jewish People's Order (UJPO) in Canada, as seen in their ties to the broader International Workers Order (IWO). When ICUF was formally established as YKUF's South American branch in 1941, it took on the tasks that in North America were divided among the JPFO, UJPO, IWO, and YKUF. South Americans participated with IWO delegates in the 1930s Popular Front Paris conference that established an international YKUF, and their battles to achieve class justice in a Yiddish-speaking milieu parallel the battles of the JPFO, with whom they retained tight social, literary, and political connections. Unlike the IWO, however, many Argentine organizations participating in YKUF survived the 1950s Red Scare. Subsequently, the revolutionary and anti-imperialist Latin American politics of the 1960s and 1970s had an impact on a new Latin American–born generation that grew up in the Jewish progressive movement. This in turn led to a profound transformation that was reflected in the Yiddish leftist institutions of the Bund Socialists, the Left Socialist Zionist Workers, and the Communists.

The first among the early immigrant leftists was the Bund Jewish Workers' Party, which founded the Di Avangard (Avant-garde) group in 1908; it defended Yiddish culture and opposed both Zionist territorialism and the Bolshevik Revolution's pivot to Lenin's one-party system. Although Bundist ideology coincided with that of the Argentine Socialist Party until World War II, it responded primarily to the directives of the Bund in Poland while preserving its South American autonomy. The second group was the Linke Poale Tsiyon, the left-wing sector of the Zionist workers, supported the ideas of Dov Ber Borokhov, who believed that the Jewish people should be brought together in one territory as a preliminary step toward the proletarian revolution. Some were Socialists and others were Communists, but all were Zionists who promoted both Hebrew and Yiddish.

The third group was led by Marxist-Leninist Jews and emerged when an internationalist and pro-Bolshevik sector split from the Bund in 1918. Like other language sections promoted by the Comintern in 1919, the Yevsektsiya—the Jewish Section—was formed in several cities but focused its activities on Buenos Aires due to its relatively large Jewish community. As news spread of the success of the 1917 Russian Revolution and its later official commitment to equal rights for minorities, more Jews became sympathetic to the Bolshevik cause.

During the 1920s the Party's "ideological" supporters multiplied, but few affiliated themselves; in Argentina they were mostly sympathizers. Even so, the leadership of the Argentinian Communist Party, which was founded in 1918, claimed to be recruiting some of its members through foreign sections, especially the Italian and Jewish ones. Although very few of the Jewish communists were affiliated with the Party, the Party claimed that its Jewish section was one of its strongest sections. In the twenties, for example, it was estimated that 14 percent of its members in Buenos Aires were Jewish; the Yiddish-language press organ, *Der Roiter Shtern* (Red star) had 2,000 subscribers with print runs of 3,500 copies, constituting the largest foreign-language Communist newspaper in general circulation after *La Internacional* (International) in Spanish.[3] The Yiddish section was also the only one that managed to establish a network of Marxist-Leninist workers schools or *arbeter shules*, which functioned between 1922 and 1932. The left wing of Poale Tsiyon, some of whom were Communist, also had a network of *shules* (Yiddish schools) called Borokhov *shuln*.

From 1924 on, as was the case in North America, many leftist Jews participated in the project of promoting Jewish colonization in Soviet Russia, most especially in the region later called Birobidzhan, through the organization known as PROCOR (the Committee for Jewish Pro-Colonization in Soviet Russia), which operated in many locations throughout Argentina, Uruguay, and Brazil.[4] The Comintern's policy allowed members to participate in Yiddish as part of a transnational workers' organization, which explains why many Socialists from the Bund and Jewish anarchists who did not fully share in its political ideology joined the Yevsektsiya, because Yiddish was promoted in that environment. Jewish sympathies toward Lenin grew as he fulfilled his promise to eliminate the Black Hundreds, responsible for bloody pogroms, while ensuring that the Red Army's mission expanded to include staunching antisemitic violence. Many Jews saw the USSR as a new nation where they could integrate as first-class citizens; have free access to education, culture, and politics, and later, have Birobidzhan as a Yiddish-speaking oblast in the erstwhile land of tsarist oppression. New left-wing Jewish organizations began to support the policies of the Soviet Union during the second half of the 1930s following the international Popular Front call to unity in the struggle against fascism.

In the new Popular Front context, when the Comintern was encouraging class collaboration, Yiddish-speaking Communists promoted the integration of other leftist Jews into a broader movement, thus offering a far more comfortable space than was possible when the line was "class against class." The Argentine militants who had integrated the Yevsektsiya sought to align themselves with the Socialists of the Jewish Labor Bund and the Socialist Zionists of Linke Poale Tsiyon as well as with the "progressive Jewish bourgeoisie."[5] Whatever their aspirations, this consolidation was not easily achieved: the radicals' preexisting positions had created conflicts among those groups. These dynamics were similar around the world, and were also seen with the IWO/ JPFO and UJPO organizations in the United States and Canada.

Despite the conflicts with Socialists, anarchists, and Zionists, due in part to the direct involvement and funding of the JPFO, Communists managed to predominate with their call for unity, which seemed imperative after the Nazis' 1935 implementation of the Nuremberg Laws. Communists led the First Congress of Jewish Culture in Paris between September 17 and 21, 1937, which resulted in the founding of the YKUF.[6] The Congress, led by Communist Jews, many of them members of the JPFO and IWO who had come from the United States and Canada, was a success. The Comintern allowed the YKUF to combine their Yiddishkayt with Communist ideals and to bring writers and institutions that were not Communist-aligned under their umbrella.

The Paris Congress had twenty-three national delegations from North and South America, Europe, Australia, and the Middle East.[7] However, with the outbreak of World War II in 1939, the top-down structure of the YKUF was interrupted and the national sections gained autonomy.[8] This was the basis upon which the YKUF emerged in South America as ICUF.[9] The international YKUF group took over the responsibility of promoting left-wing Yiddish culture through important editorial work that circulated around the world. In New York and Toronto, since YKUF needed to coordinate its action with the already existing JPFO and UJPO, its power among left-wing Jewish circles was less dominant than in South America. In fact, the international YKUF had also been a creation of the JPFO.

In April 1941, in Buenos Aires, the Argentinian section of YKUF held its first congress, replicating the Paris meeting. It was there that the participants founded the Idisher Cultur Farband (Yiddish cultural organization), or ICUF, in South America. By 1946, the Argentine ICUF network counted nine thousand members and by 1955 it had almost twenty thousand participating in associated landsmanshaften, libraries, cultural centers, theaters, schools, cooperatives, youth clubs, women's circles, publishing ventures, and press activities.

While many institutions that joined ICUF had been founded in the 1910s, others were created in the 1940s and 1950s with the help of the ICUF federation. ICUF worked as a channel to enhance the relationship between left-wing secular Jews and Communists, but its institutions were autonomous in their functioning and decision-making. While ICUF's members have been identified with the Communist Party (CP) and the Soviet Union throughout its history, ICUF's activities changed over time. Initially, its Jewish immigrant founders sought to replicate the secular experiences of the Yiddish-speaking home they had left in Europe. Later, in the 1960s, with the participation of a newer generation, member activities were adapted into Spanish (or Portuguese) and ICUF's political focus increasingly shifted to Latin American issues. While in the 1950s ICUF still acted as the think tank that oriented the political shape of its affiliated institutions, its influence gradually diminished: by the 1990s it was very weak. At the beginning of the twenty-first century, ICUF Buenos Aires renewed its activism and began working on building ties to bring various South American entities together again. While its audience is very small, this initiative proved productive and continues to this day.

The Historiography of Everyday Life

Despite bilingual challenges, during the Popular Front years ICUF's network went through its most fruitful period as expressed in its institutional development; high number of members; and its outstanding educational projects, theater performances, and publishing ventures.[10] South American scholarship usually dismisses the ICUF network as an "ethnic expression" of Communist militants or, as seen from the other side, as the "radicalized sector" of the Jewish community. It is important to underline that except in Cuba, Communism was persecuted and censored in Latin American countries and that this explains the dearth of historical sources. During the 1930s, for example, Argentina's authoritarian governments utilized an earlier law to deport "undesirable" immigrants, while activists' use of foreign languages such as Yiddish was often used as a pretext to suppress left-wing organizations. The main Argentinian Jewish organizations such as the Asociación Mutual Israelita Argentina (Argentine Jewish mutual association) (AMIA) and the Delegación de Asociaciones Israelitas Argentinas (Delegation of Jewish Argentinian associations) (DAIA) also worked against ICUF by trying to persuade the public that Communist organizations could not rightfully belong to the Jewish community. In this regard, ICUF's status has parallels with the fate of the JPFO, which was ostracized after the Second World War by other left-wing Jewish organizations as well as by more conservative ones. This "truth" also influenced and directed the perspective of researchers.

However, progressive Jewish institutions began to receive more attention after the fall of the Soviet Union in the 1990s, when with the passage of time "being a Communist" or speaking frankly about Communism no longer implied risking one's safety, or one's life, and testimonies began to appear. In other words, thanks to the temporal distance from the Soviet age and the end of fascist governments in Latin American countries, research interest in ICUF started to grow, along with the "discovery" that this sector indeed constituted an important part of the Jewish community that immigrated to South America.[11]

Even though the ICUF network engaged in many activities, scholars frequently focused on its political positions. This means that the Communist leadership's speeches received more attention than the lived daily practices and experiences seen in its landsmanshaften, schools, theaters, vacation camps, youth and women's activities, and literary movements.[12] I argue that in order to explain ICUF's network in depth, the ethnic and political dimensions, so often divorced, must be considered together, which requires a meticulous review of ICUF's institutional practices and local organizations.

Certainly, ICUF's transnational linkages to organizations such as the IWO are relevant and must be deeply explored. The international atmosphere of the anti-fascist struggle and support for the Soviet Union determined its ideological lines.[13] But it is also important to explore how all this appears in the actual literature and content taught in *shules*, summer camps, and children's clubs. In studying these practices, one can see that entire generations were socialized into a left-wing Jewish culture that had many more utopian elements than simply doctrinaire Marxism. Curricula for children and teens did not include *The Communist Manifesto*, but did include *The Diary of Anne Frank* and *When I Am Little Again* by Janusz Korczak, for example. In other words, ICUF mainly provided a Jewish secular education that promoted humanist and interethnic values of solidarity among people; even Soviet topics were often not expressed as rigid Communist indoctrination. One of the main goals of ICUF's educational programs—like those of other Jewish left-wing movements—was to prepare men and women to create "a velt fun sholem un gerekhtikayt" (a world of peace and justice). Parallels might be seen in North American institutions such as the Jewish Workers University, which had earlier offered a utopian, Yiddish curriculum.

From YKUF Paris to ICUF Buenos Aires

The cultural congresses that gave rise to YKUF (Paris, 1937) and ICUF (Buenos Aires, 1941) were born out of the urgent fight against fascism but were also continuations of previous mobilizations in defense of Yiddish. The Czernowitz Conference, held in Ukraine from August 30 to September 4, 1908, was convened by some of the most renowned Jewish writers, including I. L. Peretz, Sholem Asch, and Dr. Chaim Zhitlowsky. On that occasion, Yiddish was declared *a* national language of the Jewish people if not *the* national language. Czernowitz represented the political triumph of a secularized Jewish intellectual vanguard that was influenced by the Enlightenment and aimed at the cultural development of a language of the masses. In 1908, more than five million Jews were living confined in the tsarist Russian Empire's "Pale of Settlement," an area that included parts of today's Ukraine, Poland, Russia, Belarus, and Lithuania.[14]

In the mid-1930s, just before YKUF was created, other similar demonstrations in defense of Yiddish popular culture emerged as part of the struggle against the dramatic advance of European fascism and antisemitism. Thus, Jewish writers' meetings were held, among other places, in Moscow in 1934; in New York in April 1935; and in Vilnius in August 1935. Two important international events also converged at this historical juncture. One was the First Congress of Writers in Defense of Culture, held between June 21 and 25, 1935, in Paris.[15] The second was the eighth, and last, Comintern congress, held in Moscow in August 1935, which called for unity with as many progressive institutions as possible and for the promotion of popular fronts to combat the rise of fascism.

All these events and mobilizations were part of the atmosphere while the USSR was playing a decisive role in supporting the Republicans in Spain; by mid-1936, the outbreak of the Spanish Civil War had mobilized important solidarity actions around the world. Support for the Republican government in Madrid was interpreted by leftist Jews as a first act of resistance against fascism and antisemitism.[16] As Annabel Cohen's chapter in this book demonstrates, members of the IWO answered the call and fought with the International Brigades allied with Loyalist Spain as did 911 Jewish Argentinian volunteers.

North American Yiddish Communists acting on behalf of the IWO and the JPFO in the United States and the UJPO in Canada were very active in planning and financing the YKUF Congress in 1937 along with the Europeans.[17] Paris was chosen since the French Popular Front government, led by Léon Blum, was seen as providing a more congenial political climate for promoting Yiddish unity than that which prevailed in America. The host committee was headed by the Communist writer Haim Slovès, who gave the inaugural lecture. The main lectures were given by Moissaye Olgin, Joseph Opatoshu, Moyshe-Leyb Halpern, H. Leyvick, and other renowned Jewish writers, including some associated with ProletPen's New York circles.[18] As the growing specter of National Socialism hovered, speakers offered analyses of the primary, and increasingly difficult, challenges for Jews and Yiddish culture worldwide.[19] The twenty-three national sections presented on the specific situation of Yiddish and Jewish life in each country; Menachem Kopelman spoke on behalf of Brazil and Pinie Katz addressed the situation in Argentina and Uruguay.[20]

During the four days of the congress, the delegates worked in committees addressing literature, theater, art, schools, education and sciences, mandates (commissions), and on formulating an organization that detailed YKUF's international structure. They also drafted a "YKUF Manifesto," in which they agreed to create language schools, cultural centers, and publications in Yiddish to save and reinforce the language while fighting fascism. They determined that the Central Directorate of the YKUF would be based in Paris and would have two sub-directorates: one in New York and the other in Warsaw. It was also decided to create a fund with contributions from the national sections that would allow the Central Directorate to produce Yiddish-language reading materials that it could then distribute to the sections.

Due to the war's devastation in Europe, YKUF's transnational structure was dismembered. Although the United States took over the distribution of publications to other nations, the envisioned hierarchical structure did not materialize. ICUF in South America started to grow as an autonomous organization based on its earlier antecedents and on its commitment to YKUF's 1937 program. Although the Comintern closed the language sections in 1930, Jews in Argentina continued working in the 1930s to develop educational and cultural institutions in Yiddish and to intensify the fight against fascism and antisemitism. In Buenos Aires, Pinie Katz led the Organización Popular contra el Fascismo y el Antisemitismo (Popular organization against fascism and antisemitism) (OPcFA) from 1933 to 1943 with the collaboration of Simón Gordon and Mina Fridman Ruetter in Rosario. Like other left-wing organizations from this period, OPcFA actively opposed the rise of the German National Socialists and supported the Republican struggle in Spain. OPcFA was the forerunner of ICUF and published the Yiddish magazine *Af der waj/Oif der Vakh* (On guard). In 1935, it published two books in Yiddish, *Hitler's Plan* and *The Brown Book of Fascism*, its editorial stance inspired by the national Communist-led Committee Against Racism and Antisemitism in Argentina.[21]

Throughout the thirties, some Jewish Communist and Socialist militants and sympathizers also participated in Socorro Rojo Internacional (International Red Aid, later known as Liga por los Derechos del Hombre or the Argentine league for human rights); the Agrupación Femenina Antiguerra (Feminist group against war), which would become the Unión Argentina de Mujeres, then the Junta para la Victoria, and finally the Unión de Mujeres Argentinas (Union of Argentine women); and other organizations that emerged in the 1920s and 1930s under Communist leadership. Many members were imprisoned because of their political activities, especially for organizing workers' movements or strikes. Those organizations strongly denounced the application of law 4.144, which enabled the Argentinian government to expel "undesirable" foreigners from the country; with the advent of the Russian Revolution, suspicion of a "Jewish-Bolshevik" conspiracy operating in Yiddish had firmly taken hold within the military, the Catholic Church, and the upper classes of Argentinian society.[22] (Arguably, this fascination with a particular version of *Żydokomuna* [Jewish-Bolshevik conspiracy] on the part of the military and police has continued to play a role in Argentinian politics.)

The anti-fascist struggle and the solidarity with Spanish Republicans and later with the Allies strengthened those organizations in which Yiddish-speaking Jews, especially Communists, played a leading role. The letter that arrived from Paris in 1936 inviting Argentinian Jews to be part of the YKUF Congress was addressed to the OPFA in Buenos Aires, with the expressed goal of creating a world federation of Yiddish culture. Once the date and the venue of the event was set in 1937, the expensive trip had to be financed. One of the OPFA militants, Gregorio Lerner, argued that there was no longer enough time to raise funds. Besides, the government of President Agustín P. Justo, a military man, had forbidden public events in Yiddish without prior authorization.[23] Therefore, the OPFA held a Pinie Katz "farewell" event without speakers; thanks to the attendance of six hundred people money was obtained and Katz was able travel to Paris as the delegate. He brought with him a report on the Argentine and Uruguayan situation that had been produced in 1936 by the "Preparatory Committee" composed of Samuel Glazerman, Jacobo Botoshansky, Lazaro Zhitnitzky, L. Groisman, J. Goldszer, Samson Drucaroff, Sznaier Waserman, J. Kovenski, Wolf Kuper, M. Lew, and Abraham Moshkovich.[24]

On September 17, 1937, two years before the start of World War II, YKUF's Ershter Alveltlekher Idisher Kultur Kongres (First International Congress of Jewish Culture) opened at the prestigious Salle Wagram in Paris, with sessions continuing at the Palais de la Mutualité. Katz was there at the inaugural event along with four thousand others: the 104 registered delegates represented 23 nations and 677 organizations. The US delegation was the largest, although its leader, Chaim Zhitlowsky, was absent due to illness. Its eleven delegates, mostly from New York, represented 442 organizations, primarily small Yiddish-oriented cultural and labor groups. From Latin America, there were four delegates from Mexico, Cuba, and Brazil, as well as Pinie Katz on behalf of twenty-two Argentinian and five Uruguayan organizations.[25]

The Soviet delegation, an important promoter of this meeting, was surprisingly absent. Some participants accurately attributed the situation to Stalin's purges and persecutions. In fact, the Bund in Paris had boycotted the event because of this news. Others preferred to remain silent, and some others, those most radicalized and committed to the USSR such as Pinie Katz, completely disregarded these complaints, which they considered fallacious. The radical Communists were convinced that these were lies meant to discredit Stalin, or that it was their duty to protect the Socialist system through keeping silent.[26] They were encouraged by the recent establishment in 1934 of the remote Birobidzhan Oblast on the banks of the Amur River, a Jewish region with Yiddish as its official language—an unprecedented achievement of which Communists were very proud. The radical Jewish contingent also highlighted the great flowering of Yiddish-Soviet literature that emerged after the 1917 revolution. In April 1941, four years after Paris but before Operation Barbarossa, Katz explained the Soviet absence at the ICUF Buenos Aires congress:

> The picture of the Paris Congress was not complete. The fertile Jewish culture of the Soviet Union, with its thousands of schools and institutes of higher education, with its magazines and publishing houses, with its libraries and theaters, with its great Jewish writers, was missing in Paris. It was lacking because, on the one hand, in the U.S.S.R. Yiddish already possessed the status of a state culture and, therefore, did not need any longer to be defended. On the other hand, its determined status and

socialist leadership, made it impossible to have it submit to the resolutions of a World Congress. Besides, the Soviets did not wish to influence or impose their own orientation, perhaps inadequate in the conjunctures of our time and for the great part of the Jewish organizations in occidental countries.[27]

Katz was in effect saying that the Soviet Union's progressive Jews had to do what the Soviet government said, not what a world congress might declare. That is to say that they could not be "subsumed," or reduced to the lesser authority of what a congress proposed or dictated.

Prominent writers, such as Opatoshu and Leyvick, gave challenging talks that generated the initial discussions at the 1937 Congress in Paris. They moved beyond their political differences in agreeing that the preservation of Yiddish was at stake and that their beloved mother tongue had to be defended. Subsequently, the national delegates presented on the Yiddish language and its institutional development even as they diagnosed the levels of fascism and antisemitism in their respective countries.

Under the encroaching shadow of World War II, they also worked on seven thematic commissions. The commissions' main resolutions set the agenda that was subsequently adopted by ICUF in South America. The Literature Commission resolved to create a publishing house for Yiddish books based on the contributions of fifty thousand worldwide subscribers; the US delegation undertook to obtain thirty thousand of them. The Literature Commission also organized ways to disseminate Yiddish literature through presentations, readers' circles, conferences, and literary discussion days. Books and magazines were to be sent from headquarters to all YKUF movement libraries.

The Theatre Commission agreed to organize a theatrical center to promote youth groups and help professionalize existing drama groups, stimulate the exchange of directors, musicians, and scenographers, and encourage the creation of new plays. The commission also decided to create a magazine exclusively for theater and agreed that each country should have the autonomy to manage its theaters on a partnership and cooperative basis.

The School Commission proposed that YKUF should accept Yiddish-speaking secular schools regardless of ideological orientation and develop its work by taking into consideration the particular circumstances of each national educational system. The YKUF would coordinate existing *shules* and schools and help create new ones; it would be central to supporting the growth of kindergartens, children's homes, supplementary schools, teachers' schools, adult night schools, and popular workers' universities. It would collaborate with the creation of textbooks, teach literature, support school journalism, and create a Yiddish encyclopedia. To professionalize teaching, it would organize a world congresses of secular Jewish teachers, aspiring to create a Jewish teaching profession responsive to the needs of various countries. The Science Commission suggested measures aimed at the use and inclusion of Yiddish in national universities.

The Art Commission encouraged exhibitions and exchanges between artists from different cities and planned to begin with an event in Paris and London in 1938, to be repeated in New York in 1939. It suggested that books on Jewish artists be published in tandem with the creation of museums of Jewish art in each country. The Mandates Commission proposed to oversee the records as well as census data. Finally, the Structural Commission of the Congress decided that the new Popular Front umbrella organization would be called the Yidisher Kultur Farband (YKUF), an organization to which all institutions that agreed with the YKUF manifesto could belong.[28]

Upon returning from the 1937 conference, Pinie Katz reported to his comrades in Buenos Aires, who decided to begin immediately to follow the YKUF agenda. In November, they invited all Yiddish-speaking secular Argentinian Jewish entities from different localities and orientations to a conference. At that first meeting Katz and his comrades proposed that all attendees work together under the Argentinian YKUF's section guidelines. They also established communication with "sister" institutions in Uruguay, Chile, and Brazil. Consequently, throughout 1938 and 1939, many meetings were held in Buenos Aires under the leadership of Pinie Katz and other prominent Communist Jews. Yiddish speakers with different ideas were invited and participated in debates resonant of those heard in Paris.

The first big shock for the new organization came in August 1939, following the signing of the Molotov-Ribbentrop Pact with Nazi Germany. Several adherents resigned and two opposing tendencies emerged within left Jewish circles: one side blindly supported Stalin and the other gave some credence to Bundist and Zionist accusations that half of Poland's Jews were betrayed to Nazi occupying forces.[29] As a result, recognized intellectuals from Buenos Aires such as Jaim Finkelstein and Jacobo Botoshansky moved away from ICUF, and more radicalized militants began displaying their leadership.[30] Nevertheless, in 1939–1940, in the wake of the Nazi invasion, leftists gained supporters in the Jewish Street. Still, among the *linke* (the left) there were different positions with respect to the Communist Party and the USSR. Some agreed with the creation of a federation of secular institutions defending Yiddish but did not trust Communists; they specifically did not believe that YKUF/ICUF would respect the "ideological pluralism" promised within the Popular Front framework.[31]

Given the growth of the Yiddish-speaking left, the Argentinian section called for convening a Yiddish culture congress in South America. Thus, in April 1941, the Yiddish Culture Congress in Buenos Aires gathered 113 delegates from 57 entities representing 8,655 associates from Argentina, Uruguay, Brazil, and Chile, and declared Pinie Katz its honorary president.[32] The Congress was a success; sympathy for Communism had already been growing in the Jewish community even prior to Operation Barbarossa, which began in June 1941. Shortly after the Congress, the combination of support from Soviet Yiddish writers taken together with the development of Birobidzhan that accompanied the increasing Jewish integration into the highest spheres of Soviet society allowed ICUF's leadership to declare that the right paths for human progress and the new man had indeed been established.

In the wake of Operation Barbarossa, Soviet Yiddish intellectuals formed the Jewish Anti-Fascist Committee (JAC) and began publishing *Eynikayt* (Unity), a journal sent to Jewish leftists worldwide. With the approval of the Soviet authorities, this committee was dedicated to seeking international support against Nazi Germany. Yiddish theater director Shloyme Mikhoels was its general secretary and its members included Itzik Fefer, Ilya Ehrenburg, Leib Kvitko, Vasily Grossman, Peretz Markish, Dovid Bergelson, Dovid Hofshteyn, Benjamin Zuskin, and Lina Shtern. In 1943, Mikhoels and Fefer began a seven-month tour in the United States, Mexico, Canada, and the United Kingdom that the JPFO helped organize. The JAC succeeded in raising 16 million dollars, as well as acquiring medicines, ambulances, and clothing for the Soviet people and the Red Army. During the wartime tour, which they undertook with the help of the US-based IWO, they also emphasized the need to open a western front. At the end of the war, the JAC undertook collaborative work with American Jewish organizations, including the JPFO, to document and publicize Nazi atrocities and the heroism of the Partisan resistance. This work was documented in the *Black Book* (*Dos shvartse bukh*), which was edited in the United States but censored in the Stalinist USSR.

During the years that followed, most JAC figures were accused by the Soviet government of being involved in Zionist-Trotskyist conspiracies and killed due to these false accusations. August 12, 1952, is remembered as the Night of the Murdered Poets, since on that day, thirteen of those prominent writers were tragically executed. Many Jewish anti-fascist organizations that had worked with the JAC directorate, such as ICUF in Argentina, were shocked by these developments, which generated a crisis of great magnitude in left-wing Jewish institutional networks.

However, even as the Argentinian Yiddishist Bund sharpened its anti-Communist stance, ICUF continued to support Soviet policies. Its main leaders refused to accept the fact of the purges and denied their veracity. They eventually did so after 1956, when the truth came to light with Nikita Khrushchev's "secret" speech denouncing the killings engendered by Stalin's "cult of personality." By 1952, the main Jewish organizations, AMIA and DAIA, had already expelled ICUF from their boards of directors, which represented the "official" Jewish community. That expulsion, the *kherem* as it was known in Yiddish, originated with a DAIA proclamation condemning the USSR for antisemitic trials in Prague. In the AMIA assembly of December 18, 1952, ICUF leaders Ioel Linkovsky and Mikhl Raizman refused to sign that condemnation. As a result, AMIA's leaders withdrew their subsidies to seven ICUF schools and disseminated intense propaganda against the "Jewish schools identified with Soviet policy."[33] The disagreement of 1952 was the straw that broke the camel's back when combined with the competition for Yiddish schools, control over the funds collected by the Keren Kayemet LeIsrael (Jewish National Fund) (KKL), and the increasing international presence of Zionist ideology. Similar developments occurred within the progressive Jewish sectors and main Jewish organizations in many other countries. In the United States, JPFO schools were denied the use of public-school facilities in New York; Chelsea, Massachusetts; Philadelphia; and elsewhere, and the JPFO was expelled from Jewish umbrella organizations.

In short, South American communities mirrored the battles of the international left in the second half of the 1950s, placing themselves on either side of the Iron Curtain. As the Cold War entered a deep freeze, institutional circuits became more irreconcilable. Zionists, from left to right, aligned with the policies of the State of Israel and its alliance with the United States, while the progressives of the ICUF remained faithful to the Communist Party and to the USSR. Although some activists withdrew after the revelation of the Soviet purges in 1956, the ICUF networks in South America did not lose people rapidly. Amid this ideological readjustment, its second and third generations were integrating renewed activities in Spanish. Thanks to the success of its schools, theaters, cooperatives, and clubs, the movement remained healthy at least until the end of the sixties, although it had begun to move away from Yiddish, including in its schools. In the meantime, its immigrant worker founders and their offspring had largely become middle class and socially upwardly mobile. The organization's economic growth was reflected in its institutional development: new buildings were constructed with more activities and athletic facilities. The "educational proposition" was excellent in Rio de Janeiro, São Paulo, Montevideo, Buenos Aires, and other Argentine cities; the ICUF approach incorporated Jewish elements, including the teaching of Yiddish, without fostering a ghetto-like environment, and the movement was kept alive because the bonds of socialization resisted those of partisan dissidence.

South American Culture, Education, and Integration: A Collective Desire

Many of the issues addressed in Paris in 1937 were not new for Yiddish leaders who had settled in South America. In Argentina, one of their first actions was to set up a local institutional network in defense of Yiddish. The First Israelite Convention of Culture was held in November 1915 at La Plata's Max Nordau Center. On that occasion, inspired by the 1908 Czernowitz congress, Yiddish authors and others gathered at the convention representing fourteen associations from Buenos Aires, Santa Fe, Córdoba, Santiago del Estero, Tucumán, and La Pampa. Leftwing radicals were the leaders of that meeting: the main speakers, Pinie Wald and Maximo Rozen, were from the Bund.[34] They agreed to defend Yiddish but also to promote immigrant integration into Argentina through creating Yiddish schools and children's libraries while also organizing evening Spanish courses for adults. Adult students were required to learn politics, history, economy, and the Argentinian Constitution.[35] Subsequently, these initiatives were combined with the educational impulses of the Yevsektsiya during the 1920s. Well before the YKUF/ICUF congresses were held there had already been significant actions taken to create a modern Yiddish institutional network; the adverse context of the early thirties in effect accelerated this process.

In an atmosphere of instability defined by the Wall Street crisis of 1929 and the growth of European fascism, liberal democracies were challenged and attacked. In Argentina, a coup d'état headed by José F. Uriburu on September 6, 1930, was supported by the most conservative nationalist sectors: the armed forces and the Catholic Church. These sectors continued in power during the pseudo-democratic mandate of Agustín P. Justo (1932–38), which reached its apex with a new coup d'état (1943–45). Throughout this period, Communism was outlawed, many workers' organizations were repressed, and Yiddish workers' schools of all leftist orientations were censored and closed. Later, a more favorable if contradictory social environment began for the working class. It was during Juan D. Perón's governments (1946–55) that many immigrants became middle class and the institutional network development of the ICUF flourished.[36] Although the Peronist decade was complex and replete with nuance, the liberal sectors and the left considered its government a continuation of the authoritarianism of the previous years, as did ICUF.[37]

In the early fifties, Argentina was home to about thirty Jewish cultural organizations. There were fifteen complementary schools with 2,500 students, as well as two publishing houses, ICUF and Heimland (Homeland), which translated and published more than one hundred books, mostly in Yiddish until the 1960s and then in Spanish.[38] There was also the Zumerland Camp for children as well as many youth clubs and women's groups that worked within these organizations.[39] During the forties and fifties, with the background of the tragedy in Europe, the small and precarious *arbeter shules* (workers' schools) of the 1920s became important *veltleje shules* (secular, cultural schools), numbering fifteen at their peak. In the 1960s, ICUF's pedagogical apparatus was recognized as "avant-garde" by its contemporaries; this was also the case with Montevideo's Zhitlovsky Shule (Zhitlowsky school) and the two Brazilian *shules*, Colegio Sholem Aleijem de Rio de Janeiro (Sholem Aleichem school of Rio de Janiero) and Escola Sholem Aleijem de São Paulo (Sholem Aleichem school of São Paulo).

In Brazil, the Jewish community was only one-third the size of the Argentinian one.[40] Due to the repressive policies of the Estado Novo and the prohibition of "foreign activities," ICUF did not play an important role there until 1945; by that time many earlier institutions from the 1920s and 1930s were reduced or had simply disappeared.[41] But at the end of the war, the movement gained great popularity in the *rua judaica* (Jewish Street). New institutions were created, mainly in São Paulo and Rio de Janeiro, but also in Niteroi, Porto Alegre, Curitiba, and Minas Gerais. In São Paulo, the Casa do Povo (People's house), part of the Instituto Cultural Israelita Brasileiro (Brazilian Jewish cultural institute) (ICIB), was a "Culture Palace" built in 1948 with an important school, *kinder club* (children's club), and prominent theater. In Rio de Janeiro, the Biblioteca Israelita Brasileira Sholem Aleikhem (Sholem Aleichem Jewish Brazilian library) (BIBSA), founded in the 1920s, was transformed into the Associação Sholem Aleikhem (Sholem Aleichem association) (ASA) in 1964, also with a school and many sports and cultural activities. Both ICIB and ASA are still open, but their schools closed in the 1980s and 1990s. The children's camp, Kinderland, is still active in Rio de Janeiro. In Porto Alegre, the Clube de Cultura (Culture club) was an important center, dedicated especially to theater activity.

Early leaders of these organizations were Yiddish-speaking immigrants, mostly workers or peddlers, and were very active in the press, trade unions, and landsmanshaften. As Lida Kinoshita argues, in those years it was not possible to distinguish between those who were Communist Party militants and those who were exclusively acting within the Jewish milieu. These institutions had a double function: to spread Jewish progressive culture in their community and, at the same time, to constitute a legal arena for the development of left-wing militants.[42]

Once the United Nations voted in favor of the State of Israel's creation in November 1947, the Yiddish schools and other small organizations in Montevideo, Uruguay, joined behind a new project: the Asociación Cultural Israelita Zhitlovsky (Zhitlowsky Jewish cultural association) (ACIZ), which inaugurated a new building in 1950 containing a Yiddish children's *shule*, library, gymnasium, and a five-hundred-seat theater. Due to its geographical and cultural proximity,

ACIZ often functioned as another entity with organizational ties to ICUF in Buenos Aires.[43] Santiago de Chile also had a small group linked with ICUF called the Sociedad Progresista Israelita (Progressive Jewish society) that was active from 1938 into the sixties. In 1951 the Sociedad moved and renamed itself the Centro Cultural Scholem Aleichem (Sholem Aleichem cultural center). We know based on testimonies and memories that its former president, Jacobo Pilowsky, participated in the 1941 ICUF congress in Buenos Aires. The Chilean Yiddishists were also very close with the Argentinian Idisher Folk Teater (Jewish people's theater, also known as Teatro IFT) and its company inspired them to develop their own Yiddish theater.[44]

In Buenos Aires, São Paulo, Río de Janeiro, and Montevideo, Jewish amateur dramatic groups were the seedbed of independent and popular theater, and many well-known artists started their careers on these stages. The Idisher Folk Teater, situated in the neighborhood of "Once" in Buenos Aires, the Theatre de la Casa do Povo (TAIB) in the Brazilian neighborhood of "Bom Retiro," and the Theatre Zhitlovsky in Montevideo's city center were all well attended in the fifties and sixties.[45] These institutions changed during the twentieth century, but at least until the long seventies they were a recognizable and important part of a Latin American Jewish milieu that also worked with Yiddish theater groups and actors in New York. The linguistic political divides that arose in the 1960s and 1970s played out most especially in the IFT but also in Yiddish theater more broadly.

As they did in the *shules* and with other cultural activities, the second generation, which was comprised of young people born in South America, demanded the transition from Yiddish to Spanish and Portuguese in theatrical productions so that plays could be understood by a wider audience. Some members of the Communist Party in Argentina demanded the same, urging its militants and sympathizers to put an end to "language sectarianism" in order to communicate with the masses and win them over politically.

In the sixties, especially in sports facilities and kindergartens, ICUF institutions did something characteristic of progressive institutions that was not typical of Jewish ones: they opened their doors to non-Jews. By the 1990s, however, many had ceased to function, as had most other neighborhood-based clubs and schools. The history of the Centro Cultural Israelita Isaac León Peretz of Villa Lynch (The I. L. Peretz Jewish cultural center of Villa Lynch) (1940–96), for example, clearly shows this development.[46] The postwar expansion of Brazilian institutions was interrupted by the 1964 dictatorship; gradually, ICUF groups were considerably reduced in both Brazil and Argentina. The Villa Lynch Institution, which had three thousand active members in 1977, no longer exists. A second case is the Casa do Povo (ICIB) in São Paulo, which had six thousand members in the fifties, but by 1982 had just 150 members.[47] The Zhitlovsky institution in Montevideo is still open and offers a *kinder* club and familial cultural activities, but as an institution, it has lost the importance it had in the fifties.

From the very beginning, sociocultural and sports institutions constituted the vital force of ICUF as a federation. There are few entities left, but they continue to act under its orbit in the provinces of Buenos Aires, Santa Fe, Córdoba, and Mendoza.[48] Their "sister" institutions in Montevideo, São Paulo, and Rio de Janeiro also participate in some ICUF events. Although they were once characterized by a left-wing Jewish milieu, they have become increasingly similar to neighborhood clubs, camps, theaters, or schools, with mostly Jewish members, but accessible to everyone.

In the 1920s the number of Communism's adherents in the Jewish Street grew despite the illegal status of the Communist Party in South America, which was combined with deadly workers' persecutions, repression, and expulsion, most especially in the thirties and then again from the fifties onward due to the McCarthyist influence on Latin American goverments. This happened for several reasons. First, when the immigrants arrived, the Comintern allowed its militants to use Yiddish, and recognized them as part of an internationalist movement. Second, the growth of the Birobidzhan project was accompanied by the sense that equal rights for minorities existed in the USSR; the founding of the Jewish region was experienced as a type of historical reparation after so much suffering in Poland and the Pale of Settlement. Third, for native-born generations, the possibility of being part of a Jewish institution but at the same time feeling deeply integrated with a broader swath of society was important. In the periods of armed struggle and military dictatorships, during the 1960s and 1970s, ICUF centers functioned as educational and cultural refuges from authoritarian governments, fearful societies, and the censorship of free expression.

From its initial creation, the ICUF federation's activists were mainly loyal to the USSR. During World War II, when the Soviet Union was perceived as saving the Jews and all of humanity from the "clutches of Nazism," being a Yiddishist and a Communist seemed to be a natural condition for many of ICUF's members. This unquestionable truth began to crumble when news of Soviet antisemitism and the damning statements of Nikita Khrushchev at the Twentieth Congress of the Communist Party of the USSR in 1956 were revealed.

The reasons explaining the broader loss of Yiddish go beyond these pages but the main points are worth mentioning: the inevitable language assimilation of the third and fourth generations in the Americas; the genocide of six million Jews in Europe; and the language policy of the State of Israel that gave exclusivity to Hebrew. When Hebrew became the official language of Israel, most Jewish diasporic institutions changed their school programs, abandoning Yiddish as they started to teach Hebrew while incorporating new curricular content about the

Middle East's history and geography. The ICUF schools, which did not perceive themselves as diasporic in the way the term is often used, saw themselves as fully Argentinian, Uruguayan, or Brazilian, and taught Yiddish until their complementary *shules* definitively closed in the sixties and early seventies. At that point, only educational-recreational activities remained.

While in the 1960s and 1970s the fight against antisemitism and for anti-fascist causes continued to animate the movement, it no longer carried the same meaning as it had for an earlier generation that had lived through World War II. A Yiddish school teacher from the sixties, Aida, remembered that the headmaster of the *shule*, the engineer Samuel Kogan (known as Tzalel Blitz), was very committed to ICUF but lacked "psychology." On one occasion, he started to run across the schoolyard chasing a student who had escaped from the classroom, shouting after him in Yiddish: "Fascist, fascist!" She recalled, "For Blitz it was a terrible insult, but for the boy it meant absolutely nothing!"[49] This anecdote shows that the passage of time not only eroded the language but also the meanings of the political-cultural world that immigration and world events had brought with it.

Second-generation youth around 1955 became interested and participated in other social and political environments and slowly became integrated into political parties and social movements, including those at universities. Some of them became involved with left-wing political parties, most especially the Federación Juvenil Comunista (Communist youth federation) (*la Fede*), which was influenced by the Cuban Revolution of 1959 and then by the 1970s Chilean Socialism of Salvador Allende. The revolutionary and anti-imperialist processes of the sixties and seventies had an impact on the Jewish community and ICUF's activities reflected these transformations.

The political context of the second part of the 1960s and the 1970s in South America was marked by youth political radicalization and the disastrous appearance of military dictatorships to combat them. Under the guise of recovering social order, military governments promoted state terrorism against civilian populations. In Chile this occurred between 1973 and 1990; in Brazil between 1964 and 1985; in Uruguay between 1973 and 1985; and twice in Argentina, first between 1966 and 1973, and later with the most genocidal stage occurring between 1976 and 1983 during the last military junta government.

Several of the young people linked to ICUF and to the Jewish left in general participated in organizations of armed struggle. In Argentina, the brutal dictatorship left thirty thousand people "disappeared," among whom an estimated 10 percent were Jews. In those years, many human rights associations also emerged to denounce the atrocities and search for missing children and grandchildren. It is estimated that about five hundred babies were born in captivity and given to other families by the abductors; these children grew up with false identities. The

Mothers of Plaza de Mayo was, and still is, among the most prominent of the organizations seeking truth and justice. The ICUF institutions, like other organizations linked to left-wing and human-rights causes in Argentina and Latin America, continue to express their support and commitment to memory and the search for truth and justice.

On March 17, 1992, during the neoliberal government of Carlos Saúl Menem, there was a terrorist attack on the Israeli Embassy in Buenos Aires that left twenty-two dead and more than two hundred wounded. But two years later, on July 18, 1994, the biggest terrorist attack in the history of the country took place. A car bomb exploded at the Asociación Mutual Israelita Argentina (AMIA), killing eighty-five people. Even today, after three decades, the investigations of these cases remain unresolved, and sadly, used for political ends.

In retrospect, tracing the history of *Di progressive*, the Jewish left, shows their impact as part of the Jewish community in responding to the circumstances of their day and to changing times. The priorities and possibilities of progressive Jewish organizations in Argentina and South America more generally changed over the course of the twentieth century. During the time of the Comintern's Popular Front, its leadership faithfully acted according to the proposals established at the Paris Congress of 1937. The tragedy caused by Nazism motivated ICUF's postwar international responsibility to protect Yiddish culture and language even as it built upon the prior institutionalization of its earlier immigrant foundations. A new generation born in Latin America reflected ICUF's earlier sense of values and institutional presence even as it committed to its own search for political and social justice in ways that the immigrants could not have imagined. The YKUF/ICUF entities expanded within the Parisian framework and even today, after eight decades, their formal principles remain unchanged: a commitment to educate future generations to fight against fascism and antisemitism, and to build a world of peace and social justice.

NOTES

1. For Jewish immigration statistics, see Sergio Della Pergola, "World Jewish Population, 2019," in *American Jewish Year Book 2019*, ed. Arnold Dashefsky and Ira Sheskin (Springer, 2020), 263–53. Regarding immigration to Argentina, see Fernando Devoto, *Historia de la inmigración en la Argentina* [History of immigration in Argentina] (Sudamericana, 2004). For information on specific Jewish groups, see Haim Avni, *Argentina y la historia de la inmigración judía, 1810–1950* [Argentina and the history of Jewish immigration, 1810–1950] (Universitaria Magnes y Universidad Hebrea de Jerusalén, 1983).

2. Some Yiddish transliterations are rendered as seen in Spanish or Portuguese.

3. More in Hernán Camarero, *A la conquista de la clase obrera: Los comunistas y el mundo del trabajo en la Argentina, 1920–1935* [To the conquest of the working class: The Communists and the world of labor in Argentina 1920–1935] (Buenos Aires: Siglo XXI, 2007), 297–311.

4. PROCOR, "Cinco años de PROCOR, 1924–1929," *Der Idisher Poier* 2 (1929): 3–4, Procor Collection, Centro Documental y Biblioteca Pinie Katz (hereafter CeDoB Pinie Katz), Buenos Aires. See Henry Srebrnik's chapter in this book on ICOR in Canada, a Birobidzhan settlement organization that was also strongly supported by the JPFO in the United States.

5. The Yiddish-speaking language section of the Comintern acted on an international scale from 1918 until 1930, when it was dissolved. Its main national branches were in the USSR, Poland, the United States, France, and Argentina. In the Soviet Union and other countries, it was known as Yevreyskaya Sektsiya or Yevsektsiya. In South America it was known as the Ídishe Sektzie fun der Komunistishe Partei or by its abbreviation: Idsektzie. Its militants continued their activism beyond the Yevsektsiya's formal dissolution. After setting up the ICUF in Argentina, in 1941 they formed the Comisión Israelita del Partido Comunista Argentino (Jewish commission of the Argentinian Communist Party).

The complete name of the Bund is the Algemeyner Yidisher Arbeter Bund inn Rusland, Poyln un Lite (General Union of Jewish Workers of Russia, Poland, and Lithuania). Founded in Lithuania in 1897, it was the first Jewish workers' party. It acted as the main force in the formation of the Russian Social Democratic Workers' Party, but later confronted the Bolshevik current. Sections of the Bund were active in several Latin American cities, most especially in Argentina and Mexico.

6. See Cornell's Kheel Center holdings on YKUF's founding in its digital collection: https://digital.library.cornell.edu/collections/iwo-jpfo, particularly the correspondence with the head of the Jewish American Section of the IWO (JPFO), Rubin Saltzman, and with Henri Slovès and others. Materials of particular interest can be found in International Workers Order (IWO) Records #5276, box 53, folder 7; box 29, folder 4; box 63, folder 8; Kheel Center for Labor-Management Documentation and Archives, Catherwood Library, Cornell University, Ithaca, New York.

7. Comité Central del YKUF, *Ershter Alveltlekher Yidisher Kultur Kongres* (Alveltlekhn Yidishn kultur-farband, 1937). Thanks is due to Isaac Rapaport of CeDoB Pinie Katz for translation into Spanish.

8. Dina Lida Kinoshita, "Judíos progresistas en São Paulo y la Casa do Povo" [Jewish progressives in São Paulo and the Workers House], in *Cultura judeo-progresista en las Américas* [The Culture of Jewish progressives in the Americas], ed. Nerina Visacovsky (Imago Mundi-CEHTI-ICUF, 2022), 147–70.

9. The Yidisher Kultur Farband (YKUF) established in Paris in 1937 was replicated in New York in 1938 and in Buenos Aires in 1941. In Argentina, it was transliterated as Idisher Cultur Farband (ICUF) and exercised considerable autonomy.

10. Nerina Visacovsky, "La izquierda judeo-progresista en Sudamérica" [The Jewish progressive left in South America], *Archivos de historia del Movimiento obrero y la izquierda* 8, no. 15 (September 2019): 7–15.

11. See Visacovsky, *Cultura judeo-progresista*. This book presents and analyzes the experiences of the non-Zionist Jewish leftist movement in Canada, the United States, Mexico, Cuba, Brazil, Chile, Uruguay, and Argentina throughout the twentieth century, reflecting the collaboration of a group of specialists: Ester Reiter from Canada; Paul C. Mishler, Elissa Sampson, and Edna Nahshon from the United States; Daniela Gleizer from Mexico; Maritza Corrales Capestany from Cuba; Esther Kuperman, Dina Lida Kinoshita, Airan Milititsky Aguiar, Monique Sochaczewski Goldfeld, and Lilian Starobinas from Brazil; Valeria Navarro-Rosenblatt from Chile; Gabriel Slepac Grudzien from Uruguay; and Carolina Kaufmann, Paula Ansaldo, and Nerina Visacovsky from Argentina.

12. Visacovsky, *Cultura judeo-progresista*, 24–25.

13. See Gennady Estraikh, "A Quest for Yiddishland: The 1937 World Yiddish Cultural Congress," *Quest: Issues in Contemporary Jewish History*, no. 17 (September 2020): 96–117, https://doi.org/10.48248/issn.2037-741X/2947.

14. These 5 million Jews were mainly impoverished, not allowed to buy land, and were often victims of violent pogroms. This relative isolation generated a vast cultural and educational development of its own, primarily in Yiddish. More in Martin Gilbert, *Los judíos de la URSS: Su historia en mapas y fotografías*, a translation of his *The Jews of Russia: Their History in Maps and Photographs* (La Semana Publicaciones, 1978).

15. There, 230 delegates from 38 countries participated in and founded the International Federation of Writers in Defense of Culture. The French anti-fascist intelligentsia led by Romain Rolland, André Gide, André Malraux, and Henri Barbusse, among others, received figures such as Sinclair Lewis, Upton Sinclair, Heinrich Heine, Thomas Mann, Bertolt Brecht, George Bernard Shaw, Selma Lagerlöf, Ilya Ehrenburg, and Maxim Gorky. Among the Latin Americans attending were Raúl González Tuñón and Pablo Neruda. As the story goes, it was Ilya Ehrenburg and other Jewish writers participating in that Congress who, at the end, resolved that it was imperative to hold a similar event, but exclusively with Yiddish-speaking writers, whose identification with the USSR was at its peak at least partly because Yiddish had been established as the official language of the Birobidzhan Autonomous Region. See Visacovsky, "La izquierda judeo-progresista," 9–10.

16. It is estimated that about thirty-five thousand volunteers from more than fifty countries participated in the International Brigades in Spain through April 1939. Socialist Jews from Poland formed the Naftali Botwin Company, created as a Jewish unit in the Palafox Thirteenth Battalion of the Dombrowsky Brigade. The United States was represented in the Abraham Lincoln Brigades, which included CPUSA members as well as members of the IWO. The high proportion of Jewish volunteers in Spain may be accounted for by the fact that Jews went not only to fight Franco, but also Franco's allies Hitler and Mussolini, and that this was the first act of Jewish resistance. This interpretation, moreover, demystifies a supposed "Jewish passivity" in the face of the Nazi genocide. See Gerben Zaagsma, *Jewish Volunteers: The International Brigades and the Spanish Civil War* (Bloomsbury Academic, 2017), 2.

17. See Paul Buhle, "Jews and American Communism: The Cultural Question," *Radical History Review* 23 (Spring 1980): 9–33. In Visacovsky, *Cultura judeo-progresista*, see the following: Elissa Sampson, "El Archivo de Jewish Peoples Fraternal Order: Recuperando voces de la izquierda judía estadounidense" [The Jewish Peoples Fraternal Order archive: Revisiting voices of the American Jewish left], 49–78; Ester Reiter, "La izquierda judía canadiense y el sueño de un mundo mejor" [The Canadian Jewish left and the dream of a better world], 3–26; and Paul Mishler, "De varias raíces, un árbol: Los judíos y el origen del comunismo multiétnico en Estados Unidos (1921–1972)" [From many roots, one tree: Jews and the origin of multiethnic communism in the United States (1921–1972)], 27–48, which is an earlier version of his chapter in this book.

18. ProletPen (Proletarian pen) was an organization of Yiddish-language writers founded in 1929 in New York City that addressed radical social issues, most especially poverty, labor, and racism. In 1938 their members became part of the Yidisher Kultur Farband (YKUF) and they were dissolved.

19. Comité Central del YKUF, *Ershter Alveltlekher Yidisher Kultur Kongres*.

20. Pinie Katz (b. 1881, Ukraine; d. 1959, Buenos Aires) was a political leader in the Yiddish cultural milieu in Buenos Aires. A writer, journalist, and prolific translator, he arrived in Argentina in 1906 and quickly joined the labor movement. He created the newspaper *Di Presse* in 1918 and served as its editor in chief. Throughout his career, he participated in numerous Yiddish-speaking Communist and anti-fascist organizations,

most especially the Committee for Jewish Pro-Colonization in Soviet Russia (and later, Birobidzhan), or PROCOR; International Red Aid; and the Popular Organization Against Fascism and Anti-Semitism. He was a delegate at the Paris Conference (1937) and the first president of ICUF Argentina (1941), and his *Geklibene Schriftn* [Collected writings] were published in 1946 in nine volumes by Editorial ICUF of Buenos Aires. His works include a 1929 complete history of Jewish journalism in Argentina. Thanks to his translations into Yiddish, many immigrants were able to know great works of world, Spanish, and Argentinian literature. Katz translated *Don Quixote* by Miguel de Cervantes Saavedra into Yiddish (1950); *Idn Gautchen* by Alberto Gerchunoff (1952); and *Espartacus* [*Spartacus*] by Howard Fast (1955). Most of these works were published by the ICUF *Farlag* (publishing house).

21. This non-Jewish organization was founded by prominent leaders, including Emilio Troise (Communist Party); Américo Ghioldi (Socialist Party), Ricardo Balbín (Radical Party leader), Arturo Frondizi (Argentinian president, 1958–62), and Arturo Illia (Argentine president, 1963–66), among others. See Ricardo Pasolini, *Los marxistas liberales: Antifascismo y cultura comunista en la Argentina del siglo XX* [The Marxist liberals: Antifascism and Communist culture in twentieth-century Argentina] (Sudamericana, 2013).

22. The Residence Law of 1902, in combination with the 1910 Social Defense Law, allowed the government to expel foreigners from the country "who disturbed the social order."

23. Interview with Gregorio Lerner by Efraim Zadoff, Buenos Aires, 1986, interview number 53 in Archive of the Word, Archivo del Centro de Documentación e Información Marc Turkow, Asociación Mutual Israelita Argentina (AMIA), Buenos Aires.

24. Nerina Visacovsky and Gabriela Horestein, *La tribuna icufista: Tiempo de Aportes* (Astier Libros-CeDoB Pinie Katz, 2021), 13.

25. See Gennady Estraikh, "A Quest for Yiddishland: The 1937 World Yiddish Cultural Congress," *Quest: Issues in Contemporary Jewish History*, no. 17 (September 2020): 10, https://doi.org/10.48248/issn.2037-741X/2947. For South America, see Visacovsky, "La izquierda judeo-progresista," 11.

26. Paul Buhle, "Jews and American Communism"; Alain Brossat and Sylvie Klingberg, *Revolutionary Yiddishland: A History of Jewish Radicalism* (Verso, 2016), 65; Zaagsma, *Jewish Volunteers*, 35.

27. Visacovsky and Horestein, *La tribuna icufista*, 38.

28. Comité Central del YKUF, *Ershter Alveltlekher Yidisher Kultur Kongres*.

29. The dispute would last until June 1941, when due to the Nazi invasion of the USSR, some reconsidered, accepting ICUF again as part of the community. However, this was not enough to allow the rivals to create schools, theaters, or libraries together. Both groups, Bundists and leftist Zionists, formed their own institutional networks, which is why in the forties there were three secular left-wing Yiddish groups in Argentina, culturally very similar, but ideologically opposed. See more in Efraim Zadoff, *Historia de la educación judía en Buenos Aires, 1935–1957* [The history of Jewish education in Buenos Aires, 1935–1957] (Milá, 1994).

30. Isaac Rapaport, *Actas del Comité Preparatorio de la Federación ICUF en Argentina (1937–1940)* (Centro Documental y Biblioteca [CeDob] Pinie Katz, 2019). Thanks is due to Isaac Rapaport of CeDoB Pinie Katz for translation into Spanish.

31. To express that spirit of unity, in April 1940, Communist Jews in Buenos Aires created the first issue of the ICUF monthly journal: ICUF: Khoydesh Shifrt far literatur un kritik (Revista Mensual Israelita de Literatura y Arte ICUF). Published for almost three decades, it was similar to *Yidishe kultur*, the YKUF monthly journal edited in New York until the beginning of the twenty-first century.

32. The 1941 Yiddish Culture Congress in Buenos Aires formed a Committee for a Yiddish Cultural Federation. Its leadership comprised Pinie Katz, Sznaier Waserman, Elias

Shmerkovich, and R. Rozen, and its organizing committee was composed of Lazaro Zhitnitzky, I. Epelboim, and Lili Katz. Of the 113 delegates, nine were women. The committee included three journalists and publicists; three teachers; five doctors; one dentist; seven students; ten white-collar employees; fifty-one workers and craftsmen; five industrialists; twenty-five peddlers; three homemakers; one farmer; and one pharmacist. Forty of them were under thirty years of age. There were sixty-eight delegates whose ages ranged from thirty to fifty years, and only four were over fifty. This indicates that the great majority were young men, workers, and artisans. In *ICUF: Revista Mensual Israelita de Literatura y Arte* 2, no. 7 (May 1941): 41–44. See Visacovsky and Horestein, *La tribuna icufista*, 29–33.

33. Zadoff, *Historia de la educación*, 412–14.
34. Benito Sak, *Toda una historia* (Mimeo, 2000), 107.
35. Comisión Directiva, *Max Nordau: Publicación 80 Aniversario* (Comité editor, 1992), 2–4.
36. Unlike the oscillating and shifting positions that the Communist Party in Argentina held with respect to President Juan Domingo Perón and his policies that favored workers, the ICUF did not cease to denounce Perón as a "reactionary" and "Nazi-fascist" leader. This position had its roots in Perón's membership in the Group of United Officers (GOU), who were responsible for the 1943 coup d'état that had dissolved political parties, decreed Catholic education in the schools, sympathized with the Axis countries, and formed a government that included antisemitic officials. In addition, the entry of Nazi criminals into Argentina since 1946 and the political concessions that Perón had given to xenophobic nationalists and the Catholic Church in the field of education made the negative view that ICUF already had of Perón unalterable. Therefore, unlike the initial "neutralism" of the Party, the ICUF was emphatically opposed to Perón. During Perón's second government, which began in 1952 in a climate of growing political and economic instability, Communists were persecuted and many ICUF activities were forbidden. At this stage, ICUF members suffered police arrests, censorship, and surveillance. Especially problematic was the case of the Idisher Folk Teater (IFT), a theater affiliated with the ICUF.
37. See Carlos Altamirano, *Bajo el signo de las masas (1943–1973)* (Ariel, 2001); Cristián Buchrucker, *Nacionalismo y Peronism: La Argentina en la crisis ideológica mundial (1927–1955)* (Sudamericana, 1987).
38. Arguably the most important postwar Yiddish publishing was done by the Tsentral Farband far poylishe yidn in Argentine (Central union of Polish Jews in Argentina).
39. The most important organizations were the Organización Femenina del ICUF-OFI and the Federación de Instituciones Juveniles Israelitas Argentinas [Federation of Argentine Jewish youth institutions] (FIJIA).
40. All statistics on Jewish populations are estimated. Approximately 310,000 Jews lived in Argentina in 1960, while about 90,000 lived in Brazil and about 30,000 in Uruguay. See Sergio Della Pergola and Uriel Schmeltz, "La demografía de judíos de Latinoamérica," *Rumbos en el judaísmo, el Sionismo e Israel*, no. 15 (1986): 17–38. Obviously, if the percentage of Jews is considered in relation to the total population of the country, in the Brazilian case the Jewish community is smaller, and in the Uruguayan, proportionately larger than the Argentinian.
41. "Estado Novo" means "New State," which was the name by which Getúlio Vargas's authoritarian regime was known. He was elected at the beginning of the decade but organized a coup d'état on November 10, 1937, and remained in power until October 29, 1945. He had a second term in office from 1951 to 1954. Vargas was inspired by the regime implemented in Portugal by António de Oliveira Salazar, also called Estado Novo. Both regimes were characterized by the centralization of power, nationalism, anti-Communism, and an authoritarian system of government.
42. See the following in Visacovsky, *Cultura judeo-progresista*: Esther Kuperman, "Roite idn: Izquierda judía en Río de Janeiro," 125–46; Dina Lida Kinoshita, "Judíos progresistas

en São Paulo y la Casa do Povo," 147–70; Airan Militistki Aguiar, "Clube de Cultura de Porto Alegre: Una colectividad judía para la sociedad gaúcha brasileña," 171–90; Lilian Starobinas, "TAIB: Un escenario para el teatro judeo-progresista de São Paulo," 327–38.

43. Gabriel Slepac Grudzien, "'¡Como el Uruguay no hay!': Judeo-progresismo en Montevideo," in Visacovsky, *Cultura judeo-progresista*, 211–34.

44. Valeria Navarro-Rosenblatt, "Fragmentos olvidados del judaísmo chileno: La Sociedad Progresista Israelita y el Centro Cultural Sholem Aleichem (1938-1964)," in Visacovsky, *Cultura judeo-progresista*, 191–210.

45. Starobinas, "TAIB," 327–38; Paula Ansaldo, "Por un teatro popular judío en Argentina: Una aproximación al Idisher Folks Teater (IFT)," 349–58; Gabriel Slepac Grudzein, "Teatro y música en Montevideo: Tras las huellas de los pioneros," 339–48; all in Visacovsky, *Cultura judeo-progresista*.

46. Nerina Visacovsky, "La utopía de los textiles de Villa Lynch: El club I. L. Peretz," in *El hilo rojo: Palabras y prácticas de la utopía en América Latina*, comp. Marisa González de Oleaga and Ernesto Lázaro Bohoslavsky (Paidós, 2009), 135–50.

47. Dina Lida Kinoshita, "O ICUF como uma rede de intelectuais," *Revista Universum*, no. 15 (2000): 392.

48. In Buenos Aires, most ICUF activities are concentrated in "Sholem Buenos Aires," created in 2007. This institution is today the outcome of the fusion of the many parts associated with the ICUF movement. There is a primary Spanish school, the IFT theater, the Zumerland camp, as well as many educational, cultural, and sports activities.

49. Interview with Aída Rotbart (an ICUF teacher active in the Villa Lynch I. L. Peretz School in the 1960s), Buenos Aires, May 2008, Oral Archive, CeDoB Pinie Katz, Buenos Aires.

9

A CONSTELLATION OF ONE'S OWN
Canadian Jewish Communists and Their Mass Organizations

Henry Srebrnik

When the Soviet state emerged out of the ruins of the tsarist empire following the 1917 revolution, Socialists throughout the world hailed it as the beginning of a new age. For many Jewish radicals, it also heralded the approaching end of some two millennia of persecution and marginalization. In Canada, many Jews became involved, either as members or sympathizers, with the Communist Party of Canada (CP). Founded in 1921, the CP by 1927 had formed a national Jewish Bureau, a subcommittee of the party's central committee, with members in Montreal, Toronto, and Winnipeg.[1] Erna Paris quotes a CP official as stating that in 1929, some 20 percent of the members of the Communist Party were Jewish. In the 1940s, some 30 percent of the CP membership in Toronto was Jewish, according to Sam Lipshitz, a Communist functionary, while Harry Binder, then a leading Quebec Communist, related that in Montreal it may have been as high as 70 percent.[2] Historian David Rome asserted that the Jewish group was the most vital faction in the Canadian Communist movement: "It was a total society with its own political and cultural institutes."[3]

Much has been written about radical politics in Winnipeg, site of Canada's most famous labor upheaval, the general strike of 1919. Jews such as Shloime Almazov, later a militant in the United States, played a major role in the turmoil. Winnipeg's North End, home to most of that city's fifteen thousand Jews, was an especial hotbed of radical politics, and its Jewish cultural life was dominated by secular Yiddishists, to the extent that "the strongest of Winnipeg's Jewish political organizations . . . were leftist."[4] This was the neighborhood where a Yiddish-speaking Communist, Joe Zuken, would be elected to the Winnipeg

School Board in 1941 and would serve twenty years on the board and another twenty-two on the Winnipeg City Council.[5]

The Jewish Communists saw themselves as part of a larger movement, active not just in Canada, but also in the United States, Mexico, Argentina, Great Britain, France, South Africa, and even Palestine itself, all working for Socialism in the interests of the Jews as a people.[6] Yiddish-language pro-Soviet groups, comprised mainly of eastern European working-class immigrants, were in particular concerned with Soviet treatment of the Jewish population.

They were also embedded in a larger left movement. In Canada, ethnic federations, such as the Finnish Organization of Canada (FOC) and the Ukrainian Labour Farmer Temple Association (ULFTA), were formally recognized in 1922 as language sections of the Communist Party. In Winnipeg, Ukrainian-born W. M. Kolisnyk was elected to the city council in 1926, the first Communist elected anywhere in North America. Jewish radicals often joined forces with Ukrainians, Finns, and others during strikes and demonstrations. In Toronto, the connection between the city's immigrant ethnic minorities, in particular the Jews, Finns, and Ukrainians, was so pronounced that in 1928 a special police edict attempted to curtail left-wing organizing by prohibiting the use of any language other than English in any public gathering.[7]

In 1923 the Jewish Communists in Toronto opened a Frayhayt (Freedom) Club and organized the Jewish Women's Labour League (Yidishe Arbayter Froyen Farayn). One year later, the Communists in Toronto broke away from the Workmen's Circle (Arbeter Ring) and formed the Labour League (Arbeter Farband). The Morris Winchevsky Shule was created in 1928 by the League.[8] In Winnipeg, the Jewish Workers' Cultural League (Yidisher Arbeter Kultur Farband), and in Montreal, the Canadian Labour Circle (Kanader Arbeter Ring), were founded at the same time. Winnipeg leftists in 1932 managed to keep control of the Liberty Temple, renamed the Arbeter Frayhayt Temple, in the North End after a split with the non-Communists. Radical Jewish women in Winnipeg also formed the Muter Farayn, or Mother's League, in 1919.[9] The Jewish Communists founded a weekly newspaper, *Der Kamf* (Struggle) in November 1924. Joshua ("Joe") Gershman assumed the editorship in 1935 and would remain at the helm of *Der Kamf* and its successor, the *Vochenblat-Canadian Jewish Weekly*, until it ceased publication in 1978.[10]

Jewish Communists began to propagandize on behalf of the new Jewish Autonomous Region (JAR) in Birobidzhan, which the Soviets established in 1928 as a territorial home for Soviet Jewry in the far east of the USSR, and among the various pro-Soviet groups were two left-of-center organizations whose specific aim was to provide support for the Soviet project. One was the Organization for Jewish Colonization in Russia (Yidishe Kolonizatsye Organizatsye in Ratn-Farband), known by its Yiddish acronym, ICOR or IKOR, founded in the United States in 1924 and active within the immigrant, working-class milieu. Its Canadian branches became a separate Canadian organization in 1935. The second was the American Committee for the Settlement of Jews in Birobidjan (Ambijan), a group for English-speaking, middle-class Jews. Ambijan was founded in 1934 during the Popular Front, a period when the Communists were seeking alliances against the increasing menace of Nazism and fascism. Its Canadian counterpart, the Canadian Birobidjan Committee, did not operate in Canada to any extent until after World War II.[11]

The Popular Front years of the 1930s were the heyday of cultural creativity and activism for the Jewish left. These left organizations supported the establishment of Jewish workers cultural centers as well as groups such as the YKUF, the Yidisher Kultur Farband (Yiddish Cultural Association). They also supported choruses, sports leagues, dance and drama groups, reading circles, mandolin orchestras, Jewish schools, and summer camps, and provided members with mutual aid in the form of life insurance, health and medical care, credit unions, unemployment benefits, and funeral facilities.

The first of the Jewish summer camps, called Kindervelt (children's world), was started in 1925 in Long Branch, near Lake Ontario in Toronto. The Montrealers opened their children's camp, Kinderland, in 1927 on Fourteen Island Lake three miles from Shawbridge in the Laurentians. (Kinderland was given the same name as the New York state camp founded in 1923.) In 1936, the Toronto camp moved to Eldorado Park in Brampton and was renamed Naivelt (New world). International Workers Order members from Michigan also attended the Kindervelt camp.

Naivelt was visited by thousands of people. Morris Biderman, a prominent activist, described these visits in his memoirs. "In the early years," he said, "people would gather at 7 Brunswick Ave. on Sunday morning to take a truck ride to the camp for 35 cents. (There were not too many car owners among the members and friends in the Labour League in those years.)"[12] His son, Ron Biderman, who spent summers at the camp from the age of six until his teenage years, nurtured fond memories: "Younger people especially remember the summers they spent there. The intensity, which grew out of the concentration of so many young, dedicated, energetic and enthusiastic people in their teens, twenties and thirties was remarkable."[13]

By 1937 the Spanish Civil War had taken center stage in the Communist movement, and the International Brigades, organized by various national Communist parties, had entered the war on the Republican side. "The branches across the country have taken a very lively part in the work of raising aid for the Spanish people's government," reported Herman Abramovitch at the December 1937

ICOR conference in Toronto, an enthusiastic response entirely consistent with that of the IWO in the United States. (See Annabel Cohen's chapter.) He was certain that they would continue to "do their share in the struggle against fascism."[14] In Montreal, the ICOR had already taken the initiative in convening a committee comprising over eighty other Jewish organizations to raise money for Dr. Norman Bethune's medical unit in Spain. A Toronto conference later that year decided to mount a campaign to help the Mackenzie-Papineau Battalion, formed in July 1937 as a unit of the International Brigades.[15] The three Toronto ICOR branches united under an umbrella Toronto City Committee and held special meetings to organize the campaign successfully. The campaign culminated in a mass meeting and concert on February 6, 1938, in the Strand Theatre. The fourteen Toronto branches of the Labour League also resolved to support the ICOR's campaign on behalf of the Spanish Republicans. The total collected amounted to $244.45 from the three Toronto ICOR branches; $158.10 from the Labour League; and another $70 from various societies.[16]

Perhaps partly due to such social and political activities, the Labour League, unlike many other CP-led groups, managed to survive the hiatus of 1939–41, the period of the Molotov-Ribbentrop Pact, almost undiminished.[17] After 1941, as Morris Biderman would recall in his autobiography, the League "became acceptable in the community" as "Toronto's outspoken Jewish pro-Soviet organization."[18] After all, as Ben Lappin, a Canadian Jewish Congress functionary, later recalled, "The summer of 1943 was no time to cast aspersions on the Soviet Union."[19]

In 1944–45, the various pro-Soviet groups in Montreal, Toronto, Winnipeg, Calgary, Windsor, Hamilton, Niagara Falls, and Vancouver came together to form the United Jewish People's Order (UJPO) to supersede the Labour League in Toronto and similar front organizations elsewhere in the country. They had many cross-border connections with their sister organizations, especially the Jewish Peoples Fraternal Organization (JPFO), the Jewish section of the International Workers Order (IWO) in the United States.[20]

The formation of the UJPO was to some extent an acknowledgment that the Jewish movement was a legitimate yet separate component of the Canadian Communist world. Most of the leaders of the organization were Communists, although Morris Biderman, the national secretary until he left in 1959, estimated that only 5 per cent of the membership were CP members or even self-identified as Communists.[21] Biderman had been a member of the CP since 1927; manager of *Der Kamf*, the Communist Yiddish newspaper, between 1937 and 1939; and a member of the Labour League since 1937. He was the league's president after 1942. Dr. Sam Sniderman of Hamilton was the national president. Others in the leadership included Sam Lipshitz, Sol Shek, Charles Starkman, Sholem Shtern,

J. B. Salsberg, Alfred Rosenberg, Abraham Nisnevitz, Joseph Zuken, Sam Carr, Fred Rose, and A. B. (Archie) Bennett.

With its network of schools, cultural centers, choirs, and camps already in existence under the Labour League, the UJPO hoped to become a major presence in the Canadian Jewish community. The Order sponsored fundraising dinners that included guests such as Toronto alderman Nathan Phillips, a future mayor of Toronto; and Abraham Feinberg, rabbi of Toronto's then preeminent synagogue, the Reform denomination Holy Blossom Temple.[22] By January 1948 the UJPO counted 1,368 members in Toronto alone. The *Vochenblat*, successor to *Der Kamf*, became its de facto press organ. Joshua Gershman became the general secretary, and Harry Guralnick the executive secretary, of the Canadian Jewish Weekly Association, the paper's publisher.ABe Arnold, in later years a well-regarded president of the Canadian Jewish Historical Society, was the editor of its English section from mid-1947 to 1948, when he moved to Vancouver.[23]

The decade between 1941 and 1951 was a time of significant left-wing influence in the Canadian Jewish community. In 1943 Fred Rose was elected to the Canadian parliament from the very Jewish riding of Cartier in Montreal and a year later J. B. Salsberg won election to the Ontario legislature in the heavily Jewish constituency of Saint Andrew in Toronto; both ran for the Labor-Progressive Party (LPP), the Communists' legal party.[24] Rose and Salsberg were prominent Jewish Communists, trade union leaders, and UJPO members. No assimilationist, Salsberg emphasized his Jewishness in his political and trade union activities. The Communist Party was, for him, "a vehicle for celebrating secular Judaism and cultural nationalism expressed through the medium of Yiddish."[25]

Once the war was over, Abraham Jenofsky, the national secretary of the ICOR in the United States, complained that not enough was being done for Birobidzhan in Canada.[26] Many Canadian landsmanshaften and fraternal groups, heeding Ambijan's call, asked Jews to respond to the campaign.[27] In 1945, Canadian supporters of the Jewish Autonomous Region, including the UJPO, began efforts to develop a Canadian-wide organization to aid this work and organized the Birobidjan Appeal to Aid Jewish War Orphans in the USSR.

On November 19 and 20, 1945, representatives of various Jewish organizations agreed to form a provisional Canadian Birobidjan Committee; on February 17, 1946, the Committee held its first meeting in Montreal. More than two hundred delegates, including MP Fred Rose, attended the conference, which was presided over by Max Bailey, president of the Montreal UJPO, and Joseph Yass. J. M. Budish, chair of the American Birobidjan Committee's administrative committee and its executive vice president, traveled to Montreal from New York to report to the conference on recent developments in Birobidzhan and on the activities of Ambijan.[28]

On March 8, 1946, Joshua Gershman wrote to Joe Zuken, a Winnipeg school board trustee for Ward 3, where the overwhelming majority of Winnipeg Jews lived, that steps should be taken to strengthen the Committee and "plan together with the Jewish People's Committee of Winnipeg and the various Russian-Ukrainian Farbands [leagues] in the east, a national conference for the official inauguration of a Canadian Birobidjan Committee." Gershman suggested Charles Rosen as national director, and Winnipeg UJPO activist Louie (Vasil) Guberman as organizer for Winnipeg and points west.[29]

The Communists began a Dominion-wide fundraising campaign to help in the building of Birobidzhan and, in particular, to raise money for the resettlement of one thousand orphans there. In early May, the 106-member Toronto Jewish Folk Choir, under the direction of Emil Gartner, gave a performance at Massey Hall, Toronto, of the oratorio "Biro Bidjan," which was, in the words of Sam Carr, "a rhapsody of gratitude by Jacob Schaefer to the Jewish Autonomous Region of the Soviet Union." The Birobidjan Committee held its first Canada-wide conference on May 26, 1946, at the B'nai Jacob Shul in Montreal. The following day, a "mass meeting" and concert took place at the Folks Shule. At that second event, the Montreal Jewish Folk Choir, accompanied by a mandolin orchestra, sang Birobidzhaner songs and the cantata "Der mogen dovid bagrist dem roytn shtern" (The shield of David salutes the red star). The two keynote speakers were Dr. Benjamin A. Victor of Winnipeg and Rabbi Abraham J. Bick of the Warsaw Center in New York, president of the Union of American Jews of Ukrainian Descent and a member of the New York–based Jewish Peoples Fraternal Order (JPFO) section of the IWO as well as of Ambijan's national committee in the United States.

Irving J. Myers, who was elected executive director of the Birobidjan Committee, praised Montreal for being the first community to engage in pro-Birobidzhan work after the end of the war. Montreal activists had sent a transport of clothing for 3,500 orphans and had also been involved in many other activities, he stated. Dr. Victor gave a speech drawing on his personal experiences in Birobidzhan, which he had visited in 1936. Gershman, national organizer for the recently formed National Jewish Committee of the LPP (the CP's name after 1943), also spoke; he underscored the great significance of the new organization. A message of greetings from the Soviet embassy was read out, praising the committee for its efforts.

The Committee also issued a manifesto describing the tragic conditions in which European Jews found themselves following the Holocaust. "In the present gloomy circumstances in which our people find themselves," stated the manifesto, "the Jewish Autonomous Region in Birobidzhan shines like a bright beam.... We do not see a conflict between Biro-Bidzhan and Palestine.... There is room for

[both] Zionists and non-Zionists in the aid work on behalf of Biro-Bidzhan. Just as all Jews are interested in helping with the construction of Palestine, and in aiding those Jews who wish to settle there, so too should the work on behalf of Biro-Bidzhan and the Soviet solution of the Jewish question be evaluated by all Jews, without regard to party affiliation."[30]

Jewish communities throughout Canada held meetings and raised money to help war orphans and refugees in Birobidzhan. The New York journalist and fellow traveler B. Z. Goldberg spoke in Toronto on December 1, 1946, and in Montreal a day later on behalf of the Canadian Birobidjan Committee and the Russian-Ukrainian Farband. Irving J. Myers told Dr. Victor that the Canadian Birobidjan Committee wanted to raise $50,000 to ship vehicles and medical supplies to Birobidzhan, though Gershman suggested to Victor that the movement broaden its aims beyond aid to orphans to support the overall direction of Birobidzhan toward becoming a full-fledged Soviet republic.[31]

Victor's 1936 trip to the USSR, his work with the YKUF, and his numerous talks and articles about Jewish life in the Soviet Union, in particular Birobidzhan, "have made him popular and well-regarded not only in Winnipeg but throughout western and eastern Canada," wrote Labl Basman, principal of the YKUF-affiliated Sholem Aleichem School. There were very few like him, "who work[ed] together with the people, rather than looking down on them," and "volunteered their strength in helping to renew Jewish social and cultural life."

Elia Trepel of Winnipeg, president of the YKUF-related Professional and Businessmen's Group, in a letter dated February 19, 1947, assured Fred Donner, the executive secretary of the city's pro-Soviet Jewish People's Committee, that the Winnipeg Biro-Bidjan Committee's effort to raise $50,000 to rehabilitate war orphans was "of the utmost importance." A day earlier, a successful fundraising dinner toward that goal had been held at the Marlborough Hotel. Victor chastised Jewish progressives for having "seriously neglected our obligation to the Jewish settlement." It was important that all Canadian Jews help "to settle Jewish orphans in a Jewish land ... so that they build the first and only Jewish republic—where our very essence of culture and language will find itself." The work "can also contribute much to friendship between the Canadian people and the peoples of the Soviet Union." The Winnipeg YKUF sent greetings "to our sisters and brothers, the builders of the future Jewish Soviet Republic in Biro-Bidzhan." The local UJPO and other progressive organizations, as well as landsmanshaften, the LPP, and garment unions, were also working for Birobidzhan relief.[32]

The UJPO gave increasing support to the Canadian Birobidjan Committee, and Toronto became the site of the second national conference of the Committee from March 8 to 9, 1947. On April 20 a mass meeting held at the Metro Theatre heard Max Levin, chair of the newly united American Birobidjan Committee's national board of directors; he also addressed a gathering of local businessmen and professionals. The Toronto branch of the Canadian Birobidjan Committee was engaged in a campaign to raise $10,000 on behalf of Jewish orphans and immigrants to Birobidzhan. Joseph Morgenstern, chair of the Ambijan Committee of Cleveland and a prominent figure in Ambijan, traveled to Detroit in April to help organize an Ambijan Committee there, but on April 24 he addressed the one across the river in Windsor that already existed. The Windsor branch of the UJPO reported in 1947 that it had succeeded in persuading the Windsor Jewish Community Council to donate $2,500 to the Canadian Birobidjan Committee. The UJPO sponsored a western Canadian lecture tour by Rabbi Abraham J. Bick. He was so well received, stated the Calgary branch, "It was too bad that he could only be with us for two days. When will you send him here again?" they asked.

"Ever since the Canadian Biro-Bidjan Committee was organized, all the branches and sections of the Order have taken an active interest in the work of the Committee," national secretary Morris Biderman told the second national convention of the UJPO, held in Montreal from June 20 to 22, 1947. "The Order last year made a considerable contribution to the financial campaign of the committee. We regard the financial campaign as not only a question of providing concrete help to the Jews of Biro-Bidjan but as a means of binding the friendship of the Jews of Canada and the Jews of the Soviet Union. It brings closer the day when world Jewish unity will be attained." The convention resolved "to give our full moral and financial help to the Jews of Biro-Bidjan and to the new immigrants who help to hasten the day when the Jewish Autonomous Region will be transformed into a Soviet Jewish Republic."[33]

Abraham Nisnevitz, chair of the Toronto YKUF and part of the national leadership of the UJPO, noted that 1947 was the year of Birobidzhan's "bar mitzvah" and wished it "long and fortune years!" Birobidzhan was becoming a new Jewish nation living in fraternal partnership with the other peoples of the Soviet Union and "building its own, new, free and healthy Jewish life." Thousands of refugees from war-torn areas were now moving to the region. Soviet Jews were a free people "among equal, free and brave peoples." Birobidzhan was proof of the possibility of national equality in a Socialist system and this was the reason the freedom-loving masses "cast their eyes towards the Soviet Union as a guide in the march forward to a prettier, richer and freer world." The Soviet Union had fulfilled the dream of the Jewish prophets: "Nation shall not lift sword against nation."[34] During 1947 the Committee sent transports of clothing, medicine, trucks, and tractors to the JAR. Thousands of Canadian Jews had donated to the cause "with love and joy, in the knowledge that their gifts would lighten the burden of those building the Jewish autonomous region, and would help resettle Jewish refugees and Jewish orphans."[35]

Immediately following the war, the *Vochenblat* advocated for an independent Palestine in which Arabs and Jews would coexist, and it ran stories describing the cooperation between the workers of both ethnic groups, who, in seeking a better life in the country, rejected the nationalistic chauvinism of both the feudalistic Arab and Zionist Jewish leaders.[36] Gershman undertook a five-week Canadian tour in which he addressed large public meetings, putting forward the LPP proposal for an independent Arab-Jewish Palestine.[37]

Yet internal documents of the LPP's Jewish leadership show that the Communist attitude toward a Jewish homeland in Palestine had begun to change. In April and in September 1945, the National Jewish Committee had recommended support for the right of the Jewish population in Palestine to self-government. This, it declared, would help, rather than hinder, the economic and political progress of all of the Semitic peoples in the Middle East. Soon afterward, Gershman wrote a thirteen-page report titled "The Attitude of the Communists to the *Erets Yisroel* Problem," explaining that the Party's position on Palestine had altered "due to the tremendous changes in the political world." The victory over fascism by the United Nations had created a situation where Jewish aspirations in *Erets Yisroel* (the Land of Israel) could not be slighted. The Jewish people in *Erets Yisroel* were living under colonial rule and, in the spirit of the postwar world, were entitled to self-determination and the full status of a modern nation. Gershman pointed out that even in the Soviet Union, where Jews had full rights, they were nonetheless granted Birobidzhan in order to become a full nationality. In Palestine, as well, the *Yishuv* (Jewish community) had now met the conditions for full nationhood. Gershman, in this document, seemed to have thought he was making a Marxist, rather than Zionist, case for legitimizing a Jewish state in Palestine by pointing to Soviet nationality policy in regard to Birobidzhan as a precedent. Not wanting to sound too much like a Zionist, Gershman concluded that, while the Jewish *Yishuv* had earned the right to nationhood in Palestine, "the final solution to the Jewish question will come about only through socialism."[38]

Indeed, as early as March 24, 1945, Fred Rose, in a speech in the House of Commons, had said that he hoped "the Arab leaders will understand that mass migration of Jewish people into Palestine is essential and is not a menace to a prosperous future of the Arab people." A Jewish state would be "a constructive factor in the development of the Near East."[39] That autumn, he had spoken at a Zionist mass meeting in Winnipeg and, according to Joe Zuken, "his talk made a good impression on those responsible for arranging the meeting and on the audience generally." Zuken suggested to Gershman that Rose bring out in parliament "the party position on Palestine and European Jewry." Tim Buck, leader of the LPP, had also spoken to a Jewish meeting on October 14, denouncing the British "White Paper" limiting Jewish immigration to Palestine.[40]

Clearly, there were tensions between support for Socialism, class solidarity, and ethno-nationalism in the Jewish Communist movement that would later come to the fore. Activists such as Rose did not work to reconcile these political contradictions. For such people, Communism retained an ethical core and remained a noble endeavor; if they had doubts, they kept these to themselves, and when that became untenable, they quit the left-Jewish movements. In 1947–48, the Communist attitude toward Zionism underwent a further shift that corresponded to the Soviet Union's decision to support a Jewish state in Palestine. On November 29, 1947, the Soviets and their eastern European allies voted in support of UN General Assembly Resolution 181, to partition Palestine into Arab and Jewish states.

In order to explain the new Soviet line, Morris Biderman was sent on a six-week voyage across western Canada at the end of 1947. He took pains to show that the Soviet position had not been "a reversal from a pro-Arab to a pro-Jewish role" but was rather "based on the consistent Soviet policy on the national question and the self-determination of minorities" as practiced in the USSR itself. "This policy, as applied to the Palestine question, is obviously neither pro-Jewish nor pro-Arab, but pro-democratic."[41] Joshua Gershman in February 1948 declared that the *Yishuv* in *Erets Yisroel* was entitled to "the most complete moral, financial and political help."[42] His comments were echoed by the national executive of the UJPO, which at a special session called on Canadian Jews to provide support for the Jewish community in Palestine.[43] "The Jewish Nation Must and Can Be Saved!" screamed a front-page headline in the *Vochenblat* of April 8.[44]

By 1948 the UJPO and other mass organizations were fully behind the newly formed State of Israel. The *Vochenblat* on its front page of May 20 reproduced the text of the Soviet government's recognition of the new state, while its editorial castigated Canada for not doing the same.[45] The UJPO and the Jewish pro-Soviet movement were organizing demonstrations on behalf of the new state and calling upon the Western democracies to grant it recognition. By this time the cause of Birobidzhan had meshed with support for Holocaust survivors, Israel, and the "new democracies" in eastern Europe. When J. B. Salsberg addressed a Jewish conference in Winnipeg on May 2, he asked those in attendance to raise $3,500 on behalf of an orphanage in France, a trade school for youths in Poland, a children's home in Belgium, a lending bank for tradespeople and workers in Tel Aviv, and a school for mechanical trades in Birobidzhan.[46] Salsberg went on to defeat Tory candidate Nathan Phillips (a future mayor of Toronto) in his Saint Andrew riding in the Ontario provincial election held that June. Truly, the Communists seemed to be on the side of the angels.

On November 28, 1948, the Council of Jewish Progressive Organizations, the umbrella group of pro-Soviet organizations in Canada headed by Joe Gershman, held a rally and concert at the Toronto UJPO Centre at 83 Christie Street to observe the first anniversary of the UN plan partitioning Palestine. "The new democracies of Eastern Europe under the leadership of the Soviet Union have played a very great role, in contributing to the victory of the yishuv and the Jewish State," asserted a pamphlet announcing the event.[47] On March 27, 1949, the Toronto Committee organized a program at the UJPO Centre to celebrate twenty-one years of Birobidzhan's progress and the twenty-fifth anniversary of its designation as a Jewish region.[48]

If it is possible to pinpoint with precision the exact moment when a movement has reached its apogee, its high-water mark, that instant when all of its political planets were in alignment and the ideological gods had smiled down upon it, then for the Canadian Jewish Communists that historical conjuncture was the period between 1947 and 1949. The Soviet Union had fathered one Jewish state, Birobidzhan, which was celebrating its second decade, and by its support of the *Yishuv* in the UN, had been midwife to the birth of a second one, Israel. The new eastern European "people's democracies" had provided the military arms that enabled the Jewish state to fend off the invading Arab armies. This had followed upon the Soviet role in defeating Hitler and liberating the remnant of European Jewry in 1945, and, by establishing Socialist governments in eastern European nations such as Hungary, Poland, and Romania, seemingly putting an end to the antisemitism and reaction rife in that region for centuries. The USSR and its allies would now foster and protect the individual and national rights of Jews, within the Socialist bloc's own borders (which included Birobidzhan) as well as in Israel. Small wonder that the Jewish Communists could confidently bask in the reflected glory of this great union of Socialist republics! No one—certainly no Jewish Communist—could as yet conceive that the Soviet Union itself would soon become a center of virulent antisemitism.

But this was quickly to change. The death in January 1948 of Shloyme Mikhoels, director of the Moscow State Jewish Theater and chair of the Jewish Anti-Fascist Committee (JAC), who during the war had visited Canada on their behalf, brought forth an outpouring of grief among the Jewish Communists. Messages of condolence were sent to the JAC by the *Vochenblat* editorial board, the UJPO, the National Jewish Committee of the LPP, the Canadian Birobidjan Committee, the YKUF, and many other local organizations.

A memorial meeting attended by a very large crowd was held at the UJPO Centre in Toronto on February 1. Speakers included Sam Lipshitz, national secretary of the National Jewish Committee of the LPP; Morris Biderman, national secretary of the UJPO; Labl Basman, now principal of the Morris Winchevsky School in Toronto; A. B. Bennett; Gershon Pomerantz, the prominent Yiddish journalist and communal worker; and Leslie Morris, editor of the *Canadian*

Tribune, the Communist Party organ. In Montreal, a February 15 memorial organized by the UJPO and the Birobidjan Committee attracted four hundred people, who heard from the poets Melekh Ravitch and Sholem Shtern; Montreal city councillor Max Bailey; and Irving J. Myers, who recounted Mikhoels's life and times, including his 1943 visit to Montreal along with the poet Itzik Fefer. Ravitch declared that Mikhoels's trip had been a seminal event in the life of North American Jews; Shtern suggested that Mikhoels was a product of the Soviet revolution. This "great Jewish artist and fighter . . . was the prototype of a new type of Jew," said Myers.

The Birobidjan Committee in Winnipeg held a Mikhoels memorial on February 29 with Sam Lipshitz, who was in the city as part of a western tour, as guest speaker. Lipshitz asked the Jewish community to honor the memory of this "radiant personality" who had worked long and hard to bring Soviet Jews closer to their compatriots in Canada and the United States by continuing to cooperate with Soviet Jewry. Councillor Joe Zuken, then chair of the Winnipeg Jewish Committee of the LPP, paid tribute to "Mikhoels, the Jew, Mikhoels the *mensh*, Mikhoels the anti-fascist fighter" and Dr. Benjamin Victor recalled his own meetings with Mikhoels in 1943, when the Soviet artist, unable to visit Winnipeg in person, produced a recording of his speech in Ottawa to send to the Jewish community. Muni Taub spoke about the present division of the world into two camps, one reactionary and the other progressive, and called upon Jews to tie their future to the camp of progress and do battle against reaction, antisemitism, imperialism, and "new Treblinkas." Yet we know that Mikhoels was killed by the Soviet secret police on the orders of Stalin, his murder masked as a traffic accident—although Jewish Communists in later years claimed that they were unaware of the true facts of Mikhoels's execution until after Stalin's death. But why then did the *Vochenblat* of January 22, 1948, reporting the story, make no mention whatsoever of the way in which Mikhoels died? Why did not a single one of the many notices printed in the paper on January 29 give readers the details of where and how his life ended? Sholem Shtern's eulogy, in which he reminded readers of the historic visit to Canada, stated only that Mikhoels "died suddenly" and "fell while on duty!" Is it possible that Shtern and the others knew more than they indicated, and perhaps, by omission, were sending a signal that something was wrong with the official story?[49]

For those still unaware that there had been a major ideological shift, though, an article translated from Russian into Yiddish that appeared in the *Vochenblat* on April 28, 1949, would enlighten the Jewish Communists. Titled "Why Cosmopolitanism Is Being Fought in the Soviet Union," it was the signal that all manifestations of Jewish "bourgeois nationalism" were now to be rooted out.[50] The "dark years" of Soviet Jewry had begun in earnest.

The Canadian Jewish Communist organizations had also begun to collapse with the intensification of the Cold War. Following the disclosure in September 1945 by Igor Gouzenko, a clerk in the Soviet embassy in Ottawa, of a Soviet spy ring operating in Canada during the war, the Royal Commission on Espionage was formed in early February 1946, headed by two Supreme Court justices, Robert Taschereau and R. L. Kellock. Ten days later, the Royal Canadian Mounted Police (RCMP) detained thirteen people who were held without charges and were not allowed to see their families or have access to lawyers; the detainees were forced to testify against themselves.[51] Following the publication of several of the Commission's interim reports in March 1946, Fred Rose, Sam Carr, and other Jewish Communists were charged with various crimes. Rose was convicted of espionage in June and was sentenced to six years in jail. His Cartier seat was declared vacant by a unanimous vote of the House of Commons on January 30, 1947; Prime Minister William Lyon Mackenzie King himself introduced the resolution.[52] Carr had fled to the United States after Rose's arrest but was caught by the FBI in 1949 and deported to Canada; charged with passport violations, he served six years in prison.[53]

By this point only the most committed of Communists "remained willing to defend an ideology that the Canadian state was clearly prepared to fight and vilify with all means at its disposal."[54] A Fred Rose defense committee was formed in Montreal in 1946, after Rose had been refused bail while appealing his verdict, with Alex Gauld as chair and Michael Buhay as secretary-treasurer.[55] But even handing out its literature proved dangerous work: A McGill University student distributing a pamphlet titled "The Defence of Fred Rose," which included a petition requesting the release of Rose on bail, was arrested by the "anti-subversive" squad of the Montreal police.[56]

Given this climate of opinion, even people on the fringes of the movement saw their livelihoods threatened and their mobility circumscribed. When Sam Lipshitz returned from a Yiddish cultural conference in Poland in 1949 and went on a speaking tour during which he solicited contributions for the *Vochenblat*, he was told by a shopkeeper in Edmonton, "a very loyal supporter for many years," to leave his shop immediately. Lipshitz was told by another merchant that the RCMP "had come into a number of stores and warned them about [him]."[57] Biderman wrote Gershman about disarray in the Winnipeg UJPO, where "the situation is getting not better but worse," with much infighting, animosity, and pressures from without.[58]

On June 6, 1950, one of the stalwarts of the Jewish Communist movement in Winnipeg, Dr. B. A. Victor, died. This news, wrote Zuken, "brought deep sorrow to all parts of the Jewish community." His death was a great loss for the Jewish community in Canada and for the "progressive forces in the country."[59] Later that year, the Korean War began, and the Communists found themselves accused of supporting Canada's enemies. In the November 1951 Ontario provincial election, J. B. Salsberg hung on to his seat, although the other LPP member of the legislature, A. A. MacLeod, was defeated in a nearby constituency with fewer Jews.[60] Despite this, the UJPO remained involved in campaigns such as the one mounted in defense of Ethel and Julius Rosenberg in the United States, with picket lines and protests in Montreal, Ottawa, and Toronto.[61]

The Soviet Union also ceased to allow continued aid to Birobidzhan from abroad. In April 1951, Gershman wrote to Dr. Rose Bronstein, a member of the national executive of the Canadian Birobidjan Committee and secretary of its Toronto Committee, informing her that he had returned from a tour in which he addressed a number of gatherings regarding the work and canvassed individual members. They had all "expressed the opinion that a decision to discontinue the further activities of the Canadian Birobidjan Committee would be quite in order." Therefore, Gershman told Bronstein, "because of the changed situation, there is really no further need for continuing the relief and educational activities of our committee."[62]

It was not until 1956, however, that the Jewish Communist movement received its mortal blow in the form of the "secret speech" by Nikita Khrushchev at the Twentieth Congress of the Communist Party of the Soviet Union, in which Khrushchev exposed the murderous deeds of Stalin and his henchmen. Hersh Smolar, the Polish Jewish editor of the Warsaw *Folks-Shtime*, wrote an article soon after revealing the extent of the suppression of Soviet Jewish culture in the USSR. Published on April 4, 1956, it was reprinted in the *Vochenblat*, the Canadian Yiddish Communist newspaper; the *Morgn Frayhayt* (Morning freedom), the organ of the American Jewish Communists; and elsewhere, including in English in *Jewish Life*, which had been associated with the JPFO. Yiddish-speaking Communists now learned about the execution of the leaders of the wartime JAC.

Nowhere was the crisis of faith more profound than among the Jewish Communists. They had defended the USSR for so many decades. But in 1956, when the depth of Soviet antisemitism and the forced assimilation policies directed at Soviet Jews under Stalin became clear, it was too powerful a contradiction to ignore or rationalize. This was indeed a watershed, and after 1956 the contours of Jewish and non-Jewish Communism would speedily diverge, even among those who did not immediately quit the Communist Party and renounce Communism altogether.

Although at conferences in Toronto and Montreal at the end of December 1956 the UJPO defined itself as an independent organization unaffiliated with any political party, most of the membership knew better.[63] Salsberg had returned from a fact-finding mission to the Soviet Union and reported that Jewish culture was being suppressed and that antisemitism was state policy. Several prominent members, including Biderman, Lipshitz, and Salsberg, struggled for a few years to save the organization by freeing it from Communist domination. But by 1959, he and the others were gone. Biderman, in his statement of resignation, spoke of the "strife and inner struggle" and the "long and bitter debates" that had wracked the organization. By October 1959 the total UJPO membership had declined to 872.[64]

At that point Sam Carr took over the presidency of the UJPO and steered it once again in a pro-Soviet direction. The organization's new national executive in April 1960 declared that it did not want to be a "base for political struggles against the Soviet Union and the Communist Party of Canada."[65] Those who remained were mainly Communists like Labl Basman, Rose Bronstein, and Joshua Gershman. Still, in 1960, the UJPO managed to build a new home in Toronto, named the Winchevsky Centre, at 585 Cranbrooke Avenue, where it still exists.

After three decades as an organizer, trade unionist, and elected official, J. B. Salsberg left the Communist Party in 1957, denounced and vilified by Tim Buck and the other leadership for daring to question Soviet policies. "The Jewish question had broken Salsberg's faith," wrote his biographer, Gerald Tulchinsky. Now referring to the party as a "straightjacket," Salsberg would eventually reengage with the mainstream Jewish community.[66] Sam Lipshitz, who also left the CP in 1957 after being a member of its central committee from 1943 to 1956, acknowledged that "the political line" of the ICOR had been "dominated by the Communist Party." By virtue of his position as a high-ranking CP official, he said, "I was involved in the ICOR. I made it my business to in some way supervise their activities. At one point in the early 1930s, during the very deep economic crisis, when a lot of people were leaning towards the left-wing movement, and out of sympathy for the Soviet Union, the ICOR had a good following."[67]

Morris Biderman, who also quit the CP in 1957, maintained that "the [Communist] Party was arrogant and dictatorial towards the UJPO and its leadership." It interfered in UJPO affairs to make certain that the UJPO followed Communist policy and the "Party line."[68] He remarked: "We in the Labour League and the UJPO believed that Jewish colonization in the Soviet Union, and the idea of a Jewish homeland, was a good thing. We had doubts before 1956, but we held our doubts until we realized what had happened. The whole idea of Birobidzhan, in retrospect, I don't think it was a genuine attempt to provide a homeland for Jews. The idea was more to get rid of the Jews who thought of settling in the Crimea."[69]

Biderman, however, differentiated between "two kinds of Communists among Jews—Communist Jews and Jewish Communists. The former happened to be born to Jewish parents but had nothing in common with Jewish consciousness." The latter, however, were involved in movements such as the ICOR and UJPO because they were "genuinely interested and concerned with the creation of a Jewish territory in the Soviet Union with its own language, culture and economy: In other words, a Jewish homeland."[70]

Biderman was right. The longing for a Jewish homeland was indeed very strong. Jewish Communism was a combination of Socialism and secular Jewish nationalism; these two ideas meshed and sought to liberate Jews from the oppressive aspects of diasporic exile, which was felt as a dialectical antithesis to "homeland" and redemption via Socialism. For the Jewish Communists, that "homeland" was Birobidzhan, because of the successful Bolshevik Revolution that had made antisemitism a crime and had liberated Russian Jewry. The idea of a separate geopolitical space that would serve as a shield from oppression and make possible the creation of a Socialist Jewish society was a goal that inspired the membership. Birobidzhan would mesh nicely with the subterranean but very powerful secular nationalist sentiments of the Jewish Communist movement.

The demise of the ICOR and the Canadian Birobidjan Committee was a part of the passing of an entire era in Jewish life and with it Birobidzhan receded into the mists of memory. The Jewish Communists, for all of their ideals, their polemical cleverness, and their efforts, were never able to prove that a Soviet Jewish republic had actually emerged in the far east. The Birobidzhan project was always a "sandcastle," a "Potemkin country," the product of the misplaced hopes of desperate people.

Yet some of the Jewish Communists would continue their pro-Soviet activities. Years of pro-Soviet politics, plus the image of the USSR as the country that vanquished Nazi Germany, made it difficult to leave. They "belonged to a party that was stronger than any religion," explained Biderman. "To betray it was a sin."[71] Joshua Gershman was one example: Though he acknowledged "the monstrous crimes committed against Jewish cultural workers and institutions in the Soviet Union," the pain of which had "grown and intensified," he refused to follow people such as Biderman, Lipshitz, and Salsberg out of the CP.[72] "The Party is my life, without it I am nothing," he told Morris Biderman. "What will I do, where can I be active?" Gershman finally left, due to his differences with Soviet policy toward Israel and toward its own Soviet Jewish population, in 1977.[73] The *Vochenblat* expired in 1978. Gershman died a decade later, on April 30, 1988.[74] The UJPO, though today a marginal force in the Canadian Jewish community, soldiers on.

NOTES

Unless otherwise indicated, all translations are my own.

1. Norman Penner, *Canadian Communism: The Stalin Years and Beyond* (Methuen, 1988), 273; Gerald Tulchinsky, *Branching Out: The Transformation of the Canadian Jewish Community* (Stoddart, 1998), 119–22.

2. Erna Paris, *Jews: An Account of Their Experience in Canada* (Macmillian, 1980), 145–46.

3. Rome was interviewed January 22, 1983 by Lewis Levendel; see Levendel, *A Century of the Canadian Jewish Press: 1880s–1980s* (Borealis Press, 1989), 151.

4. Tulchinsky, *Branching Out*, 9.

5. See the biography by Doug Smith, *Joe Zuken: Citizen and Socialist* (James Lorimer, 1990). Zuken died in 1986. At the time of his retirement in 1983, he was the last elected Communist on the North American continent.

6. Matthew Hoffman and Henry Srebrnik, eds., *A Vanished Ideology: Essays on the Jewish Communist Movement in the English-Speaking World in the Twentieth Century* (State University of New York Press, 2016). Referring to the various CP-organized groups as "pro-Soviet" or "Communist" is a distinction without a difference because by the 1930s the Communist parties themselves were to a large extent doing Moscow's bidding.

7. Rosemary Donegan, *Spadina Avenue* (Toronto: Douglas & McIntyre, 1985), 156.

8. Ruth A. Frager, "Politicized Housewives in the Jewish Communist Movement of Toronto 1923–1933," in *Beyond the Vote: Canadian Women and Politics*, ed. Linda Kealey and Joan Sangster (University of Toronto Press, 1989), 267–68; Michelle Cohen and Ester Reiter, "Women, Culture, Politics, Yiddishkayt and the Yiddish *Arbeiter Froyen Farein*," *Outlook* 33, no. 2 (1995): 9–11; Stephen A. Speisman, *The Jews of Toronto: A History to 1937* (McClelland and Stewart, 1979), 316–17.

9. Roz Usiskin, "Winnipeg's Jewish Women of the Left: Radical and Traditional," in *Jewish Radicalism in Winnipeg, 1905–1960*, ed. Daniel Stone, Jewish Life and Times 8 (Jewish Heritage Centre of Western Canada, 2003), 112.

10. Michael Buhay, in later years a Montreal city councillor, was editor for the first two years. He was succeeded in 1926 by Philip Halperin, who died in 1932. Ber Green of New York temporarily succeeded him, followed by Harry Guralnick until 1935. In the mid-1930s, *Der Kamf* had a circulation of about three thousand. During World War II, the *Vochenblat-Canadian Jewish Weekly* had a print run of between four thousand and five thousand copies. Levendel, *A Century of the Canadian Jewish Press*, 130–35.

11. Henry Srebrnik, *Jerusalem on the Amur: Birobidzhan and the Canadian Jewish Communist Movement, 1924–1951* (McGill-Queen's University Press, 2008); Henry Srebrnik, *Dreams of Nationhood: American Jewish Communists and the Soviet Birobidzhan Project, 1924–1951* (Academic Studies Press, 2010).

12. Morris Biderman, *A Life on the Jewish Left: An Immigrant's Experience* (Onward, 2000), 70.

13. Ron Biderman, quoted in Biderman, *A Life on the Jewish Left*, 71. Of all the various camps supported by the pro-Soviet left, only Naivelt still exists.

14. Herman Abramovitch speech, December 19, 1937, undated typewritten manuscript, 25–26, Bronfman Collection of Jewish Canadiana, Institutions—Yidishe Kolonizatsye Organizatsye in Rusland (ICOR), Jewish Public Library Archives, Montreal, Quebec.

15. Upwards of 1,600 Canadians were part of the Fifteenth Brigade, which also included English-speaking British and American volunteers. There is a very large literature on this. See Mark Zuehlke, *The Gallant Cause: Canadians in the Spanish Civil War, 1936–1939* (Whitecap Books, 1996).

16. "In kanader 'icor,'" [In Canadian "Icor"], *Nailebn-New Life* 12, no. 2 (February 1938): 35–36 (Yiddish section); "In kanader 'icor,'" [In Canadian "Icor"], *Nailebn-New Life* 12, no. 3 (March 1938): 35 (Yiddish section); F. Golfman, "Montreal 'icor'-taytikayt in 1937" [Montreal "Icor" efforts in 1937], *Nailebn-New Life* 12, no. 3 (March 1938): 36.

17. M. Feldman, "Der labor lig hot zikh derhoyben tsu di foderungen fun der tsayt" [The Labor League has risen to meet the demands of the time], *Kanader Yidishe Vochenblat*, January 8, 1942, 5. Since the Communists opposed Canada's declaration of war

against Germany, the CP and many of its fronts were declared illegal in June 1940 under the War Measures Act and many Communists were arrested under its provisions.

18. Biderman, *A Life on the Jewish Left*, 60.

19. Ben Lappin, "When Michoels and Feffer Came to Toronto," *Viewpoints* 7, no. 2 (1972): 45.

20. There is a large body of work relating to the IWO. A recent addition is Robert Zecker, *"A Road to Peace and Freedom": The International Workers Order and the Struggle for Economic Justice and Civil Rights, 1930–1954* (Temple University Press, 2018).

21. Biderman, *A Life on the Jewish Left*, 60.

22. Tulchinsky, *Branching Out*, 129–32; Levendel, *A Century of the Canadian Jewish Press*, 137; Irving Abella, "Portrait of a Jewish Professional Revolutionary: The Recollections of Joshua Gershman," *Labour/Le Travailleur* 2 (1977): 208.

23. Arnold was appointed editor of the *Jewish Western Bulletin* in February 1949. Abraham J. Arnold, *Judaism: Myth, Legend, History, and Custom, from the Religious to the Secular* (Robert Davies, 1995), 17; Abe Arnold, email correspondence with author, Winnipeg, February 2, 2001. Guralnick was also teaching at the Morris Winchevsky Shule in Toronto at this time. He died in 1972, at age seventy-two.

24. The Communist Party had become illegal in 1940 and was reconstituted under the LPP banner as a legal front in 1943. It reverted to its former name in 1959. Salsberg won reelection in 1945, 1948, and 1951. Salsberg's victory "was very much an ethnic phenomenon," Tulchinsky writes, because most of the city's Jews lived in "the Spadina-College nexus" and Salsberg won some 90 percent of their votes. Gerald Tulchinsky, *Joe Salsberg: A Life of Commitment* (University of Toronto Press, 2013), 68.

25. Tulchinsky, *Joe Salsberg*, 25.

26. A. Jenofsky, "Biro-bidzhan hot gemakht groysn forshrit di letste por yor" [Birobidzhan has made great strides these last few years], *Morgn Frayhayt*, July 20, 1945, 3.

27. See, for instance, the undated, circa 1945 pamphlet, "Mir muzen entferen dem ruf!" [We must answer the call!], issued by the Russian-Ukrainian Jewish Farband (Der farband fun rusish-ukrainishe yidn) in Toronto. This group had been founded in 1943 and was sympathetic to the Jewish Communist movement. Moray Nesbitt (Abraham Nisnevitz) Papers, Multicultural History Society of Ontario, series 85, Jewish Canadian Papers, F1405, file 085-015, MU 9003.02, Archives of Ontario, Toronto, Ontario (hereafter AO).

28. Alef Raysh [Alfred Rosenberg], "Biro-bidzhan konferents bashlist oysshtaten a fakh-shul far yidishe yesoymim in biro-bidzhan" [Birobidzhan conference decides to establish a trade school for Jewish orphans in Birobidzhan], *Vochenblat*, February 21, 1946, 1–2; "Canadian Birobidjan Committee," *Ambijan Bulletin* 5, no. 1 (1946): 7–8.

29. Letter from Joshua Gershman to Joseph Zuken, Toronto, March 8, 1946, Joshua Gershman Papers, F1412-1, box 2, file 9, AO. Gershman said that the NJC would help cover Guberman's salary to the extent of $500 per year.

30. S. C., "Classic, Say Critics Hailing New Concert by Jewish Folk Choir," *Canadian Jewish Weekly*, May 9, 1946, English page 8 of the *Vochenblat*; "Groyse delegatsye kumt tsu birobidzhan konferents, zuntik, may 26-tn in montreal" [Large delegation comes to the Birobidzhan conference, Sunday, May 26 in Montreal], *Vochenblat*, May 16, 1946, 1; H. Abramovitch, "Kanader biro-bidzhan komitayt bashlist ayntsuordinen toyzent yidishe yesoymim" [Canadian Birobidzhan committee decides to settle thousand Jewish orphans], *Vochenblat*, May 30, 1946, 1; "Ruf fun biro-bidzhan komitayt tsu di yidn fun kanada [Call from Birobidzhan committee to the Jews of Canada], *Vochenblat*, June 6, 1946, 3.

31. Letter from Joshua Gershman to B. Z. Goldberg, Toronto, November 5, 1946; letter from Joshua Gershman to B. A. Victor, Toronto, November 13, 1946; letter from Irving Myers to B. A. Victor, n.d. [mid-November 1946?]; all in Joshua Gershman Papers, F1412-1, box 2, file 10, AO.

32. "Carnival and Bazaar for the Jewish War Orphans and Refugees in the Jewish Autonomous Region Biro-bidjan, U.S.S.R.," pamphlet advertising the event, unpaginated and undated manuscript, mid-February 1947, Donner book box, Jewish Heritage Centre of Western Canada, Winnipeg.

33. *20 Years Progressive Fraternalism in Canada: Main Reports and Resolutions of the 2nd National Convention of the United Jewish Peoples Order, Held in Montreal, June 20th, 21st and 22nd, 1947* (National Executive, U.J.P.O., 1947), 7, 22–23, 52–23.

34. A. Nisnevitz, "Biro-bidzhan—A fraydiker onzog fur ale yidn iber gor der velt" [Birobidzhan—a joyful message for Jews all over the whole world], in *United Jewish People's Order Second National Convention Montreal, Que., June 20, 21, 22, Nineteen Hundred Forty Seven* (UJPO, 1947), 19–20.

35. Alef Raysh [Alfred Rosenberg], "Kanader biro-bidzhan komitayt vet oysbraytern zayne taytikayten ibern gantsn land" [Canadian Birobidzhan committee will broaden its efforts throughout the entire country], *Vochenblat*, January 29, 1948, 1; "Biro-bidzhan komitayt vet durkhfiren groyse fayerungen fun 20 yor yidishe autonomye teritorye" [Birobidzhan committee will conduct large festivities for the twentieth anniversary of the Jewish Autonomous Region], *Vochenblat*, February 5, 1948, 1.

36. See, for example, an article by A. Pik, from Tel Aviv, "Yidish-arabishe aynikayt is meglekh" [Jewish-Arab unity is possible], describing joint Arab-Jewish cooperation in a general strike of thirty-five thousand government employees. *Vochenblat*, May 16, 1946, 4, 6.

37. "Independence Only Way Out," *Canadian Jewish Weekly*, October 17, 1946, English page 8 of the *Vochenblat*.

38. J. Gershman, "Di shtelung fun di komunistn tsu der erets yisroel problem" [The Communist position on the Land of Israel issue], typewritten, n.d. [October 1945?], Joshua Gershman Papers, F1412-7-3-1, box 67, AO.

39. "Palestine Jewish State Can be Achieved in New World Order F. Rose M. P. Tells Parliament," *Der yidisher zhurnal—Daily Hebrew Journal* (Toronto), March 25, 1945, 1.

40. Letter from Joseph Zuken to Joshua Gershman, Winnipeg, November 5, 1945, Joshua Gershman Papers, F1412-1, box 1, file 7, AO.

41. "Palestine Plan Not Fully Understood," *Canadian Jewish Weekly*, January 1, 1948, English page 8 of the *Vochenblat*.

42. J. Gershman, "Mir muzn gebn dem yishuv in erets-yisroel fulshtendike moralishe, finantsyele un politishe hilf" [We must provide the Jewish community in the Land of Israel with comprehensive moral, financial and political backing], *Vochenblat*, February 12, 1948, 4.

43. "Natsoyonale eksecutive fun yid. folks ordn ruft shtitsen kampanye far yishuv in erets-yisroel" [National executive of the Jew. People's Order calls for a fundraising campaign for the Jewish community in the Land of Israel], *Vochenblat*, February 26, 1948, 1.

44. "Di yidishe melikhe muz un ken geratevet vern!" [The Jewish nation must and can be saved!], *Vochenblat*, April 8, 1948, 1.

45. "Tekst fun sovyetisher anerkenung fun der medineh yisroel" [Text of Soviet recognition of the State of Israel], *Vochenblat*, May 20, 1948, 1; "Kanada muz anerkenen di medineh yisroel! [Canada must recognize the State of Israel!], *Vochenblat*, May 20, 1948, 4.

46. L. Guberman, "Vinipeger yidn hobn mit groys interes oyfgenumen grus fun j. b. salsberg vegn der lage fun di yidn in europa un erets-yisroel" [Winnipeg Jews have shown great interest in J. B. Salsberg's report on the situation of the Jews in Europe and the Land of Israel], *Vochenblat*, May 20, 1948, 3. These were JPFO projects for their Million Dollar Aufbau Rehabilitation and Rebuilding Campaign.

47. "Need Greater Understanding of the Soviet Union," *Canadian Jewish Weekly*, May 27, 1948, English page 8 of the *Vochenblat*; "Forthcoming Events," *Ambijan Bulletin* 7, no. 3

(May 1948): 2; "Organizational Activities," *Ambijan Bulletin* 7, no. 4 (June–July 1948): 15; Council of Progressive Jewish Organizations pamphlet, Joshua Gershman Papers, F1412-7-4, box 71, file 3, AO.

48. "Groyse biro-bidzhan fayerung zuntik marts 27-tn, in toronto" [Large Birobidzhan celebration Sunday, March 27th in Toronto], *Vochenblat*, March 17, 1949, 2; "Dr. I. zhitnitzky fun argentina in reikhe muzikalishe program bu biro-bidzhan fayerung zuntik" [Dr. I. Zhitnitsky from Argentina in a rich musical program at the Birobidzhan celebration Sunday], *Vochenblat*, March 24, 1949.

49. "'Vochenblat' shikt iber troyer-oysdruk oyf toyt fun profesor shloime mikhoels" ["Vochenblat" sends condolences on the death of Professor Shloyme Mikhoels], *Vochenblat*, January 22, 1948, 2; Sholem Shtern, "A groyser mentsh is gefaln oyf zayn postn!" [An important man has fallen at his post!], *Vochenblat*, January 22, 1948, 4; "Biografishe shtrikhen fun sh. mikhoels-vofsi" [Biographical notes on Sh. Mikhoels-Vofski], *Vochenblat*, January 22, 1948, 7; David D. Spigler, "Jewry Mourns Mikhoels; Was Greatest Exponent of Jewish Culture," *Canadian Jewish Weekly*, January 22, 1948, English page 8 of the *Vochenblat*; "Groyser memorial-miting nokh sh. mikhoels zuntik in toronto" [Large memorial meeting for Sh. Mikhoels Sunday in Toronto], *Vochenblat*, January 29, 1948, 1; "Troyer-oysdruken oyf dem plutsimdikn toyt fun prof. shloime mikhoels" [Sorrowful expressions on the sudden death of Prof. Shloyme Mikhoels], *Vochenblat*, January 29, 1948, 3; "Impozanter memorial-miting nokh sh. mikhoels durkhgefirt in toronto" [Impressive memorial-meeting regarding Sh. Mikhoels held in Toronto], *Vochenblat*, February 5, 1948, 1; "Montrealer yidn veln ern dem ondenk fun prof. shloime mikhoels" [Montreal Jews will honor the memory of Prof. Shloyme Mikhoels], *Vochenblat*, February 12, 1948, 1; "Mikhoels-memorial in vinipeg" [Mikhoels-memorial in Winnipeg], *Vochenblat*, February 19, 1948, 1; Alef Raysh [Alfred Rosenberg] and Y. Halper, "Impozunte mikhoels memorial in montreal un in vinipeg" [Impressive Mikhoels memorial in Montreal and in Winnipeg], *Vochenblat*, March 11, 1948, 7.

50. "Farvos bakemft men kozmopolitizm in sovyetn-farband" [Why cosmopolitanism is fought in the Soviet Union], *Vochenblat*, April 28, 1949, 3.

51. For an overview of its draconian powers and methods, see Dominique Clément, "Spies, Lies and a Commission: A Case Study in the Mobilization of the Canadian Civil Liberties Movement," *Left History* 7, no. 2 (2000): 53–79; and Clement, "The Royal Commission on Espionage and the Spy Trials of 1946-9: A Case Study in Parliamentary Supremacy," *Journal of the Canadian Historical Association*, n.s., vol. 11 (2000): 151–72.

52. Rose, born in Lublin, Poland in 1907, came to Montreal in 1920. He joined the Young Communist League and was elected national secretary in 1929. After being released from prison in 1951, Rose and his wife Fanny moved first to Czechoslovakia, then to Poland, where he worked as an editor in Warsaw for an English-language publication, *Poland*. He died in 1983 at the age of seventy-six. See David Levy, *Stalin's Man in Canada: Fred Rose and Soviet Espionage* (Enigma Books, 2011) for an unflattering biography.

53. Carr, born Shloime Kogan in 1906 in Kharkov, Ukraine, came to Canada in 1924. In 1927 he joined the CP and studied at the Comintern's Lenin School in Moscow for two years. He was by 1930 the party's national organizer. He helped recruit volunteers for the Loyalists in the Spanish Civil War in the 1930s. Carr became head of the UJPO in 1960. He died in 1989. For more on this committed Communist and, according to some, the "real brains" of the party, see "Sam Carr Remembered," *Outlook* (formerly *Canadian Jewish Outlook*) 27, no. 6 (1989): 10–11; Paris, *Jews*, 167–74, 176.

54. Alvin Finkel, "The Decline of Jewish Radicalism in Winnipeg After 1945," in Stone, *Jewish Radicalism*, 198.

55. See the circular letter from the committee, signed by Alex Gauld and dated November 11, 1946, soliciting funds *and* urging readers to protest "the persecution exemplified

in this refusal." Canadian Jewish Congress Collection, series ZB, box 1, "Fred Rose," file 7, "Varia," National Archives and Reference Centre, Canadian Jewish Congress, Montreal, Quebec.

56. "Reds Here Raided, Student Held, as Fred Rose Leaflet Distributed," *Montreal Gazette*, December 9, 1946, 13. For more on this period, see J. L. Black and Martin Rudner, eds., *The Gouzenko Affair: Canada and the Beginnings of Cold War Counter-Espionage* (Penumbra Press, 2006); J. L. Granatstein and David Stafford, *Spy Wars: Espionage and Canada from Gouzenko to Glasnost* (Key Porter Books, 1990); Amy Knight, *How the Cold War Began: The Gouzenko Affair and the Hunt for Soviet Spies* (McClelland and Stewart, 2005); Ross Lambertson, *Repression and Resistance: Canadian Human Rights Activists, 1930–1960* (University of Toronto Press, 2005); Merrily Weisbord, *The Strangest Dream: Canadian Communists, the Spy Trials, and the Cold War* (Véhicule Press, 1994); and Reg Whitaker and Gary Marcuse, *Cold War Canada: The Making of a National Insecurity State, 1945–1957* (University of Toronto Press, 1994). These books contain much information on the arrest and trials of Carr, Rose, and others. There was similar official harassment of the IWO in the postwar United States, as noted in Robert Zecker's chapter, and it was much harsher.

57. Sam Lipshitz, "Followed by the RCMP," in *The Un-Canadians: True Stories of the Blacklist Era*, ed. Len Scher (Lester Publishing, 1992), 123–24.

58. Letter from Morris Biderman to Joshua Gershman, Winnipeg, November 7, 1949, Joshua Gershman Papers, F1412-1, box 2, file 19, AO.

59. Joseph Zuken, "Dr. B. A. Victor, prominenter gezelshaflekher tuer geshtorben in elter fun 58 yor" [Dr. B. A. Victor, prominent community activist dead at age 58], *Vochenblat*, June 8, 1950, 1; Y. Halper, "Riziker oylem baglayt Dr. b.a. victor tsu zayn aybiker ru" [Large crowd escorts Dr. B. A. Victor to his eternal rest], *Vochenblat*, June 15, 1950, 3. Yitzkhok Halper was principal of the Sholem Aleichem School in Winnipeg from 1947 until 1951.

60. S. Lipshitz, "Ontario Election—Some Lessons," *Canadian Jewish Weekly*, December 6, 1951, 2. Salsberg lost his seat in 1955, in no small part due to the ill-advised eulogy he delivered in the Ontario legislature two years earlier when Stalin died. Sam Lipshitz, who ran his campaigns, later would claim that Salsberg was pressured by the CP to make the speech. Sam Lipshitz, interview by the author, Toronto, June 9, 1998. MacLeod's riding, Bellwoods, was also demographically a largely immigrant, working-class area.

61. A. Rosenberg, "Der Ordn in Montreal" [The Order in Montreal], in *United Jewish People's Order Fourth National Convention Book* (UJPO, 1954). The convention was held in May 1954 in Toronto.

62. Letter from Joshua Gershman to Dr. Rose Bronstein, Toronto, April 6, 1951, Joshua Gershman Papers, F1412-1, box 3, file 22, AO.

63. "The UJPO Redefines Its Aims and Purposes," *Canadian Jewish Weekly*, December 20, 1956, English pages 1–2 of the *Vochenblat*.

64. "Report to the Annual Conference, December 5–6, 1959, by the Executive Director, M. Biderman," 1–2, 15, typescript, Joshua Gershman Papers, F1412-7-4, box 72, file 11, AO.

65. "Report to the 5th National Convention of the U.J.P.O.—April 1960," 3, typescript, Joshua Gershman Papers, F1412-7-4, box 72, file 11, AO.

66. Tulchinsky, *Joe Salsberg*, 113–14, 121. Salsberg, a cap-maker by trade, was born in Lagov, Poland, in 1902 and had immigrated with his parents to Canada in 1913. He joined the Communist Party in 1926 and visited the Soviet Union in 1939 but despite some misgivings about Birobidzhan he remained a committed Communist and into the mid-1950s continued to toe the Party line. After leaving the CP, he went into the insurance business. He died in 1998. Cynthia Gasner, "J. B. Salsberg 'a Unique Personality,'" *Canadian Jewish*

News (Toronto), February 19, 1998, 3; Ron Csillag, "Lives Lived: Joseph Baruch Salsberg," *Globe and Mail* (Toronto), March 6, 1998, A22.

67. Sam Lipshitz, interview by the author, Toronto, June 9, 1998. For more on Lipshitz, who was born in Radom, Poland, in 1910, came to Canada at age seventeen, and sat on the LPP's central committee from 1943 until 1956, see Levendel, *A Century of the Canadian Jewish Press*, 130–43, and Paris, *Jews*, 154–57, 193–98. After leaving the Communist movement, he opened a typesetting business. He died in Toronto at age ninety in 2000. Ben Rose, "Sam Lipshitz: Champion of the Yiddish Language," *Canadian Jewish News* (Toronto), September 28, 2000, 35.

68. Biderman, *A Life on the Jewish Left*, 84–85, 218.

69. Morris Biderman, interview by the author, Toronto, June 9, 1998.

70. Letter from Morris Biderman to the author, Toronto, January 27, 1999.

71. Biderman, *A Life on the Jewish Left*, 230. Biderman died in 2013, aged 105. Bill Gladstone, "Eye on Arts," *Canadian Jewish News*, Toronto, October 31, 2013, 36.

72. J. Gershman, "We Cannot Agree With You, Madame Furtseva!," *Canadian Jewish Weekly*, June 28, 1956, English page 3 of the *Vochenblat*.

73. Joshua Gershman, interview by the author, Toronto, September 5, 1978; Biderman, *A Life on the Jewish Left*, 163; Abella, "Portrait of a Jewish Professional Revolutionary," 212–13; "A Letter from Joshua Gershman to the C.C. of the Communist Party of Canada," in which he announced he was withdrawing from the party, was published in the *Canadian Jewish Outlook* 15, no. 10 (1977): 10. See also the tribute to him by Sholem Shtern, "Y. Gershman—tsu zayne 75 yor," *Vochenblat*, September 13, 1978, 5.

74. "UJPO Activist Dead at 84," *Canadian Jewish News* (Toronto), May 19, 1988, 29.

10

"DANCING AT TWO WEDDINGS"
Radical Jewish Artists and Their Relationship to Yiddishkeit, from the Popular Front to the Postwar Era

Lauren B. Strauss

In January 1933, left-wing writer William Abrams engaged in a heated debate current among leftist American Jews: how "Jewish" should a "Jewish Communist" be? Jumping into the fray, Abrams issued some cautionary advice laced with irony: a Jewish writer must write about the condition of the Jewish worker but, he declared, the writer must not be—"God forbid—national."[1] Abrams's rhetoric resonates here: by evoking God as arbiter, he used the language of Jewish culture to reinforce a radical left-wing directive. The irony of his colloquialism epitomizes a debate that raged across several decades: what should be the role of Yiddishkeit—Jewishness—in reaching out to the Jewish masses and inculcating them with a progressive message?

While this question furrowed brows from right (the so-called "right-wing" Socialists and labor activists, *di rekhte* in Yiddish) to left (radical Communists and their allies, known as *di linke*), it was thrown into sharp relief during the years immediately before, during, and after World War II. The creative voices in this debate were not limited to writers: Jewish Communist attitudes toward ethnic identification were also present in the work of visual artists—in fact, some of the most memorable and even scandalous moments were immortalized by the hands of paintbrush-wielding comrades. The artists' indelible images in response to current events reflected the left's head-spinning shifts in its attitude toward compromise and conciliation. This journey can be traced, in particular, through the activities of the International Workers Order. The approach to ethnic identification of the Jewish Peoples Fraternal Order (JPFO), the largest and founding section of the many "ethnic" sections of the International Workers Order (IWO), offers a revealing look at the interplay between progressive culture and American Jewish artists, and illuminates the unique role of ethnic factors in the lives of Jewish progressives.[2]

The best-known platform for American Communist Party (CPUSA)-affiliated cultural production in the years leading up to the war was the English-language *New Masses*, founded in 1926. The magazine devoted an unusual amount of space to the visual art supplementing its revolutionary message.[3] But the Party also recognized the need to expand beyond English-language media in America after the explosive growth in the number of subscribers to left-wing Yiddish publications convinced them to target Jewish followers with more culturally specific content.[4] This mitigated against the Party's usual reluctance to encourage ethnic affiliations, but such a large Yiddish-speaking leftist audience had too much potential to ignore. The relationship of *di linke*'s publications to its readers became even more complex during the short-lived policy of coexistence during the Popular Front era (1935–39), when liberal and progressive activists of varying stripes seemed to unify against the spread of fascism. Although their message of consensus barely masked some deep cracks in leftist circles even during this era, it was most obviously disrupted by the Molotov-Ribbentrop Pact (or Hitler-Stalin Pact) from August 1939 to June 1941—and then followed by yet another reversal after the ill-advised Nazi invasion of the USSR destroyed the pact.

Despite almost two years spent justifying Stalin's strategy and opposing American military buildups, after Hitler's invasion American Jewish Communists quickly embraced militarization. By the time the United States declared war in December 1941, its Jewish community—despite deep differences—was virtually unanimous in supporting the war effort. This was, of course, influenced by the growing threat to their families and communities that remained in Europe. With increasing revelations of atrocities against European Jews, Yiddish-speaking artists, writers, and political leaders in America embraced a two-pronged approach. Even those on the far left recast themselves as stalwart champions of democracy and Americanism, meanwhile engaging in sentimental, agonized tributes to their martyred brethren across the ocean.

Although it was not part of the Communist Party and the vast majority of its members did not belong to the CPUSA, the Yiddishist Jewish Peoples Fraternal Order was in the Party's broader orbit, participating with Slavic, Italian, and Black art, music, and theater troupes in the multiethnic Order. The JPFO's affiliated artists were central to its journey toward pro-war sentiments and toward more open identification with Jewish culture. Their winding trajectory from general progressivism to radical dogma to particularistic concern for Jews followed the changing fortunes of Jews with the rise of their fascist adversaries. This evolution by no means suggests that the artists discarded their belief in Marxism as a way to confront society's ills. Artist-activists such as cartoonist William Gropper, sculptors Aaron Goodelman and Minna Harkavy, and graphic artists Louis Lozowick and Hugo Gellert, among dozens of others, adopted a variety of approaches to Jewish—especially Yiddish—cultural identification while remaining dedicated to a progressive agenda. (Gellert's family had converted to Catholicism prior to his birth, but his Jewish roots, immigrant status, and the inclusion of his art in leftist Yiddish-language magazines often resulted in him being grouped with Jewish artists with similar political and ethnic backgrounds.) But by the end of the 1940s the answer to the conundrum raised by William Abrams and his ironic turn of phrase was clear, at least temporarily. Jewish ethnicity—and Jewish survival—was fundamental to the worldview of even the most radical American Yiddish leftists, including the artists among them.

For all these individuals, dedication to a progressive agenda meant a sometimes rapidly shifting approach to their own Jewish ethnicity, depending on current Communist Party policies.[5] It was not as simple as wholesale Communist rejection of Jewish identity, as is often assumed. At different times, ethnic signifiers and especially traditional (or "national") languages were either viewed by the Party positively, as useful tools for reaching certain constituencies, or negatively, as factors that undermined universalism. Complicating matters, the American leftist scene diverged from Soviet Party directives depending on current realities in the United States. On the language question and many other matters, Communists of various ethnicities often ignored Party directives that they did not find relevant to their needs, despite what Party higher-ups may have hoped. Yiddish-speaking Communists were different still, since they were also attuned to the needs of a large immigrant community with its own agenda.[6] The shifting relations between liberals, Socialists, and radicals working together to fight fascism yet unwilling to cede their authority to others made it difficult to define progressive art and culture. How could each artist and writer give voice (or canvas) to their individual expression, reflect the priorities of the radical groups to which they bore allegiance, and "speak the language" of their ethnic cohort to inspire and educate them?[7] Adding to the confusion was the fact that these artists expressed themselves differently in different languages and venues. The same artist who may have inked a lithograph with universalist themes in response to the Spanish Civil War or prioritized the plight of Black Americans in the pages of the *New Masses* might begin openly advocating in Yiddish forums for Jewish victims of Nazi persecution as the war progressed.

This cast of characters included such ideologically committed figures as radical cartoonist William Gropper, lithographer Louis Lozowick, painters Moses and Raphael Soyer, and others. They had all been immersed in Jewish and Yiddish culture since their youth, but they pursued professional and political connections in other realms as well, becoming quite cosmopolitan in the process. Lozowick, who had immigrated to New York from Russia as a teen after the turn of the century, returned to Europe in the 1920s. He spent several years circulating among the most innovative modern artists and intellectuals in Paris, Moscow, and Berlin and writing about the art scene for a host of English and Yiddish publications. Moses Soyer won a scholarship from the Educational Alliance Art School in 1926 and spent a year studying in Europe. Sculptors Aaron Goodelman and Minna Harkavy, who came from Russia and Estonia, respectively, and studied at classical art schools and ateliers in Western Europe, became paragons of the bicultural activist in America. They assumed leadership roles in Yiddish-language forums while immersing themselves in urban cultural politics, from the 1934 effort to establish an artist-run municipal art center in Manhattan to Depression-era rent strikes in the Bronx.

The majority of these artists were immigrants from eastern Europe. Almost all were native Yiddish speakers, though some were more comfortable speaking English—including the American-born Gropper, and even some of those who were born in Europe but arrived in the United States as small children. Still, they saw Yiddish as a necessary tool for their activism and for their employment in Yiddish-language media. Working together and as individuals, they founded and guided a series of organizations, schools, cultural centers, journals, and artist advocacy groups.[8] They forcefully superimposed visual art onto the radical progressive map, illustrating the narratives of both the Jewish left and the general progressive community.

Many of them began as students or teachers in the art school of the Educational Alliance Settlement House on New York's East Broadway. The school had existed in an earlier incarnation from the 1890s to World War I, when it closed due to lack of funds. It reopened in 1917 under the direction of Abbo Ostrowsky, an etcher and painter who had immigrated to the United States from Ukraine in 1908. Ostrowsky, an idealist and a gifted educator, was better known for running the art school and for mentoring an extraordinary number of American modern artists than for his own artwork. He believed that art should spring from a socially conscious perspective, reflecting its surroundings, and that artists could create positive change in the world. In this, he and many of his students were directly influenced by the so-called Ashcan artists, including Robert Henri, George Bellows, and John Sloan, whose subject matter focused on the city streets and the conditions of working people's lives.

The Educational Alliance Art School was also directly tied to several community and leftist organizations that viewed art education as essential to the holistic development of the successful worker. Labor unionists such as Fannia Cohn, the education pioneer and vice president of the International Ladies Garment

Workers Union (ILGWU), saw art education as another opportunity to elevate workers' lives and to demonstrate that social justice ideas belong in every arena.[9] As a result, Cohn and leaders of the Socialist, Yiddishist mutual aid society Der Arbeter Ring (Workmen's Circle) and several downtown settlement houses organized weekend museum trips for workers, publicized "downtown" art shows held in accessible locations such as schools and restaurants, and raised funds for a Workers' Art Scholarship in the mid-1920s.[10] (Recipients of the scholarship included the Social Realist painter Moses Soyer and the sculptor Dina Melicov.) Despite her Socialist bona fides and devotion to the general labor movement, Cohn also attracted criticism from some other union leaders for her willingness to work with Communists on cultural programs.

Similarly, Ostrowsky's sympathies lay somewhere between the poles of leftist activism that are so often portrayed as being immutably divided during the 1920s and early 1930s. His goal was the furtherance of a social sensibility and the continued activism of organized Jewish and artistic groups, whether or not they promoted a particular ideological orthodoxy. It was this type of transitional figure—Ostrowsky, Cohn, the Ashcan artists (who were not Jewish), and other cultural activists—that created a milieu of progressive art activism that transcended partisan infighting. This ecumenical activism receded into the background in the strident culture wars of the late twenties and early thirties. But the ties born in those early years—and the secular Jewish worldview that drew strength from combining ethnic roots (usually in Yiddish) with progressive values—would surface again as the Second World War drew near.

If one figure were chosen to represent the vicissitudes of the Jewish left in visual form, it would undoubtedly be William Gropper, the most consistently outspoken of the radical artists. The evolving trajectory of Gropper's attitude toward militarization during and after World War II was as dramatic as his black strokes of ink on white paper. Gropper was a native New Yorker, born in the teeming tenements of the Lower East Side to parents who worked day and night as laborers in the garment industry. Their toil left the young artist with indelible impressions of material inequality and social injustice—first as it applied to his own family, and then, increasingly, with regard to others. Gropper's mother did piecework, bringing home garments from the sweatshop and only being paid for each one that she completed—which meant that in theory, her work was never done. Her son Bill (William) painted and drew her many times, emphasizing the weariness of her face and body. The artist also later wrote about the "deep impression" created by his father's belief that the *goldene medine* (the "golden land") had betrayed their family through class-based exploitation. This impression was compounded by tragedy when his mother's sister, his favorite aunt, perished in the Triangle Shirtwaist Factory Fire in 1911.[11] Gropper's family situation reinforced the message conveyed by his surroundings that there was great injustice in the world, and that it was partly up to him to remedy it.

As a teenager, Gropper attended art classes at the anarchist Ferrer School in downtown Manhattan, where he studied with Robert Henri and other unconventional and idealistic teachers.[12] Hungry for money and recognition and unwilling to be pigeonholed into a single publication, genre, or medium, Gropper contributed to a host of publications. He crafted pointed political cartoons inspired by the likes of Honoré Daumier, the nineteenth-century French artist viewed by many as the first political cartoonist, and by the early twentieth-century German graphic artist Käthe Kollwitz. (Kollwitz was not Jewish but the Nazis expelled her from the Prussian Academy of Art because of her liberal political views and the modern techniques that she favored, which were considered "degenerate" under the Third Reich.)[13] Influenced by the Ashcan artist John Sloan, who frequented downtown immigrant neighborhoods to create what he and Robert Henri termed "life documents," Gropper also drew evocative scenes detailing the daily life of the neighborhood's denizens.[14] Given his interest in political cartoons and the working class, it was only natural that he would become a contributor to the *Morgn Frayhayt* (Morning freedom), the American Yiddish Communist daily paper founded in 1922, which was known in its early years for its discerning literary taste.[15] Indeed, Gropper became the artist most identified with the *Morgn Frayhayt* for much of its existence. But the paper would also be the source of his greatest controversy, at least in the eyes of the Jewish community. And although he long denied holding Communist Party membership, his role in the discord exemplifies the image of the loyal functionary, doggedly following Party directives.

Gropper's route to controversy began with events occurring thousands of miles away. In 1929, riots broke out in Palestine between Arabs, Jews, and British soldiers. Approximately 133 Jews (many of whom were women, children, and students) were murdered and well over 300 were wounded. Most of the casualties, which occurred in Jerusalem and Hebron with some in Tiberias and Safed, were perpetrated by local Muslim residents. They were reportedly angered by rumors that Orthodox Jews had erected a partition at the Kotel, the Western Wall in Jerusalem, to separate genders for prayer on the Jewish holy day of Yom Kippur. In the eyes of some local Arab leaders, the gender partition was proof of the Jews' intent to take over the entire holy site, including the Al-Aqsa Mosque. Such plans seemed to these leaders to be emblematic of the Zionist project to settle Palestine with European Jewish newcomers and take over Muslim and Arab land in the process. Ironically, most of the Jewish victims, especially in Hebron, had lived in the region for generations and were quite disconnected from the Russian Socialist newcomers who formed the "New *Yishuv*," the ideological Zionist community.

Some Jews engaged in the fighting and were killed by British soldiers, who were in the region administering their mandate from the League of Nations. During the riots 116 Arabs were killed and more than 200 wounded, mostly by British soldiers (and some by armed Jewish residents). In the wake of the disturbances, the British appointed a committee of inquiry, the Shaw Commission, which concluded that most of the responsibility for the current violence lay with Arab reactions to the perceived Jewish plans for the Western Wall. But they added a more comprehensive analysis that pointed to swelling Jewish immigration and land purchases as the cause of Arab antipathy toward Jewish residents—even toward longtime Jewish natives of Palestine who were not directly involved with the Zionist project.[16] The resulting fallout from the riots and the contrasting responses from Jewish Communists and other Jews underscores the importance of media—including the visual arts—in identifying and cementing these positions.

The *Morgn Frayhayt*, helmed by its editor Moissaye Olgin, initially portrayed the massacred Jews as the riots' primary victims. But, in a vertiginous reversal, within days of its early coverage the paper received directives from the Party that ran counter to its initial response. Arabs were to be lionized as simple workers, defending themselves against exploitation by the colonialist British and subjugation to a medieval Jewish religious cabal. The paper quickly turned against the Jewish inhabitants of the land, linking them with the British military and administration. While Arabs were portrayed as a native working class whose stories belonged with those of other laborers around the world, Jews were cast either as lackeys for the imperialist British or as avaricious capitalists and religious hypocrites, poised to exploit the native population.

Gropper's cartoons, which presented Palestine's traditional Jews and Zionists in the most negative light possible, were among the most memorable features of this conflict. Although invoking stereotypical ethnic images was common in cartoons of the era, his drawings crossed a line: they were peopled with beady-eyed, hook-nosed Jews wearing religious garb emblazoned with dollar signs, their fingers dripping with the blood of their victims. Indeed, Gropper's illustrations were so divisive that they helped to create a final wedge sundering radical Jewish Party loyalists, who defended the *Morgn Frayhayt*'s stance, from others in their milieu. Almost immediately, copies of the paper began to disappear from newsstands as sellers pulled them, and some subscribers canceled their accounts. A group of literary luminaries who had published in the *Morgn Frayhayt*'s pages united behind a new—albeit short-lived—weekly called *Vokh* (Folk). Decades later, stalwarts of the Yiddish left still took sides in the matter, often referencing Gropper's cartoons as the coup de grâce in their relationship with the *Morgn Frayhayt*.[17]

In addition to its daily paper, in 1926 the Frayhayt Farband (Frayhayt organization), the umbrella organization that ultimately included the newspaper, a children's paper, a theater group, summer camps, and a constellation of other cultural groups, founded a monthly journal called *Der hamer* (Hammer). *Der hamer*'s illustrated covers—often printed in vivid colors, especially in the magazine's early years—were brashly symbolist and underscored the devotion of the leftist community toward the Party.[18] Again, Gropper became the most frequent contributor to this medium, in which his typical covers often included strong, satisfied workers, contrasting the glory of work in the Soviet Union with the experience of New York's sweatshop denizens suffering in their capitalist hell. On other covers, he sketched a phalanx of imaginary marchers stretching into the distance while inflated figures of Lenin or Marx towered over them. His images extolled the glories of industrialization in factory and field. And, in the vibrant colors of the earlier magazine covers (often in revolutionary black and red), artists such as Gropper, Lozowick, Gellert, and humorist and leftist puppeteer Yosl Kutler frequently showcased the hammer of the magazine's name enmeshed with the sickle, in a Marxist marriage of iconography and aesthetics.

Practitioners of other art forms such as sculpture and mural painting did not lend themselves quite as much to magazine covers, but they found other ways to reach the masses. Aaron Goodelman and Minna Harkavy, for instance, took a variety of paths to political engagement. Goodelman was a mild-mannered figure, deeply immersed in secular Jewish and Yiddish culture. His wife Sarah was a longtime Yiddish educator and the couple lived for decades in the culturally active Sholem Aleichem cooperative apartment complex in the Bronx. The Goodelmans were dedicated Communists, remaining loyal to the ideals of the movement through some of the most fraught periods for *di linke*. But their worldview, and that of many others, saw no dichotomy between collective action to change the world through Communism and their love of Yiddish culture.

Aaron Goodelman was involved in leftist education well before the creation of the IWO, illustrating the covers and much of the inside content for *Kinderland* (Children's land), the Arbeter Ring's Yiddish-language children's magazine, in the early 1920s.[19] (*Kinderland* was not as radical left as the IWO would become, being more a product of the Socialist movement.) Goodelman's whimsical animals, tree houses, story characters, and elaborately calligraphed lettering blended with the magazine's realistic photos of striking miners and other workers, and with illustrations by other left-leaning artists such as Zuni Maud (see figure 10.1).

In 1925, Goodelman also illustrated the two-volume *Mayselakh*—children's stories by popular Yiddish writer Chaver Paver (Gershon Einbinder), who was also involved with IWO cultural activities.[20] This balance of creativity and conviction in educational settings would characterize Goodelman's projects throughout the coming decades. He taught in venues whose politics ranged from labor to far left, including the Communist-backed Jefferson School of Social Science in the

FIGURE 10.1. Goodelman's cover art for the left-wing Yiddish children's magazine, *Kinderland*. February 1923. Courtesy of the Kheel Center.

1940s and '50s, and at events organized by the Yiddish left at his housing complex in the Bronx. Goodelman's intimate acquaintance with prominent Yiddish cultural figures under JPFO auspices ran deep. Among other examples, the group chose him to fashion a memorial headstone for Dr. Chaim Zhitlowsky's grave after the great Yiddish theorist died in 1943 while on a speaking tour sponsored by the IWO.[21]

In accordance with Party policy, Goodelman was outspoken in condemning anti-immigrant bias (in cases such as the trial of the Italian American anarchists Nicola Sacco and Bartolomeo Vanzetti) and anti-Black racism. This was searingly illustrated in his response to the trial of the so-called Scottsboro Boys in the early 1930s. In a case that galvanized advocates around the country, nine young Black men were arrested on spurious charges of raping two white women on a train in Alabama and were initially sentenced to death. After many trials (and mistrials) and international outrage, the defendants were ultimately freed—but some of them had been imprisoned for nearly two decades. Their trial brought issues of mob justice, kangaroo courts, and racial violence—especially the scourge of lynching—to the fore. Goodelman was far from alone in responding artistically to the Scottsboro case, but his offering is one of the most hauntingly beautiful tributes created at the time. Called *The Necklace*, the subject of the small bronze sculpture (under two feet), stands tall but with head bowed, a thick manacle around the figure's neck.[22]

Most of the progressive Jewish artists in this orbit participated in one of two major art shows in 1935 and 1936 that focused on racism in general and lynching in particular. Sculptors, painters, lithographers, and others approached the difficult subject from a multiplicity of perspectives, from subtle allusions that portrayed victims as Christian martyrs, to raw and gruesome depictions of the actual crime.[23] The JPFO and other IWO societies such as the Slovak Workers Society, the American Russian Fraternal Society, the Hungarian Sick and Death Benefit Society, and the Ukrainian Society were outspoken in their support for the Scottsboro defendants. Activities stretched across the country, from the art galleries of New York City to rallies in Cleveland and Chicago to a West Coast institution known as the Cooperative Center. This center, founded in 1923 at the corner of Brooklyn and Mott Streets in Los Angeles, hosted a smorgasbord of left-leaning programs during the twenties and thirties. Some of these included a secular Yiddish school for children, IWO/JPFO-sponsored rallies for Sacco and Vanzetti and the Scottsboro Nine, and events welcoming Communist Party leaders William Z. Foster and Moissaye Olgin to Los Angeles. Irish IWO lodges in Brooklyn and Jersey City also passed resolutions demanding that the Scottsboro defendants be freed.[24]

Like Goodelman, Minna Rothenberg Harkavy was an accomplished sculptor, an advocate for Yiddish culture, and a dedicated Communist. Harkavy's name can be found on countless organizational boards and in exhibition catalogs beginning in the late 1910s. In almost every case, she is the only woman or one of two women out of twenty men or more on a list of board members. Despite being outnumbered in a field that exhibited a great deal of gender bias, Harkavy often took leadership positions in these organizations. She was a founder of the New York Society of Women Artists in 1920, and the American Artists' Congress and the Sculptors' Guild, both in the 1930s. She also participated in a variety of group exhibitions, from shows at the Jewish Art Center in the 1920s and the Communist Party's John Reed Club in the 1930s to more mainstream art shows at the Whitney Studio Club (later, the Whitney Museum), from the 1920s to the '50s.[25]

Although she was married to Yiddish writer Louis Harkavy, Minna Harkavy simultaneously had other romantic relationships. One was with the prominent Yiddish Communist Moissaye Olgin, which lasted until his death in 1939, and another with the Italian anti-fascist journalist Carlo Tresca, who was murdered in New York in 1943 (reportedly by Mafia figures linked to Mussolini).[26] Harkavy's personal, political, and cultural lives were intertwined, and often balanced seeming contradictions that were as wide-ranging as her romantic partnerships. She participated in cultural groups through Jewish community channels and negotiated with government officials on behalf of the Federal Art Project (FAP), the artists' branch of the New Deal Works Progress Administration programs, later renamed the Works Projects Administration, or WPA, and she successfully lobbied New York's mayor Fiorello LaGuardia to use public spaces for outdoor sculpture shows. Yet she also attended a 1932 conference of the Communist-backed John Reed Clubs in Amsterdam and was a delegate in 1937 to the heavily Communist founding meeting of the Yidisher Kultur Farband (Yiddish Culture Association, or YKUF) at the World Congress of Yiddish Culture in Paris. (The JPFO organized the American delegation to the conference and was involved with YKUF's founding and funding, while Latin American Jewish Communists were also well-represented at YKUF.)

Thus, over the years from the teens to the late thirties, artist-activists such as Harkavy, Goodelman, Lozowick, Gropper, and their comrades rode fluctuating waves of affiliation between the Yiddish-speaking immigrant community and the international left, often balancing between the two. But as the specter of fascism grew in Europe and produced its own xenophobic and antisemitic offshoots in the United States, liberal and progressive groups no longer had the luxury of internecine fighting given the threat of a common enemy. Knitting together advocates of Socialism, Communism, liberalism, big unions, and even New Deal Democrats, the Popular Front in the United States sought to address the twin perils of the Depression and right-wing extremism, at home and abroad. As part of this double-headed approach, artists and writers on the Yiddish far left transitioned from a stance that put liberalism in the same boat as capitalist imperialism to one that celebrated American patriotism and—after Pearl Harbor—that avidly supported joining the Allied war effort.

Even Gropper's cartoons and other mass-produced line drawings evolved as the political winds shifted. Almost until the very start of the Popular Front in 1935, the artist's acid pen took aim at the US government and the armed forces that, in his view, privileged weapons over workers and war over peace. Two *Morgn Frayhayt* cartoons from 1934 sum up Gropper's (and the Party's) outlook toward military preparedness at the time. In one, a gargantuan, anthropomorphized tank with large fangs and cannon-eyes dominates the skyline and devours bags of money. Fighter planes fly overhead and humble workers march below, their placards ignored. The caption reads, "For the Unemployed—a Sigh; For War—Billions." The other cartoon's caption announces the creation of "A Two-Sided Machine," explaining that "from the front, peace is flying; from the rear, battleships are being baked." Meanwhile, a sweating president Franklin D.

FIGURE 10.2. Gropper's tanks personify Jewish heroes fighting the Nazis. Courtesy of the Kheel Center.

Roosevelt pumps money into a machine that spits battleships out its rear while distressed angels flutter out of the front.[27]

Switching tacks entirely after Hitler invaded the USSR, the Gropper of the joint US-Soviet war effort seems to have forgotten his earlier tendency toward cynical anti-militarism. In a reversal of his anti-war stance, the artist and his comrades at the *Morgn Frayhayt* now acted in sync with the new united front of liberal-left support for the war effort. They joined efforts to raise funds for the Russian army as the most direct way of vanquishing fascists, with Gropper enthusiastically touting the importance of large armaments in fighting Hitler. Moreover, he advocated waging the fight from an openly Jewish perspective. In a 1942 cartoon that was also used for an IWO ad, Gropper's armaments become animate beings, their "heads" and "snouts" pointed menacingly at a cowering Hitler, who quakes on the ground (see figure 10.2).

Significantly, the tanks have uniquely Jewish names splashed across their armored shells, evoking Jewish historical figures whose legacy might seem incongruous in a Communist-led effort. The anti-Roman Judean rebel leader Bar

Kokhba, the anti-Assyrian Greek leader Judah Maccabee, and even the American Revolutionary War financier Hayim Solomon are all honored. (The names were part of the general campaign, not initiated by Gropper.)[28] In a pro-military era, these Jewish heroes are transformed into standard-bearers for the left by virtue of their leadership during a moment of life-or-death conflict against ruthless authoritarianism. Other names require less justification in the JPFO orbit: tanks named for Yiddish literary giants Sholem Aleichem and I. L. Peretz show that Jews can fight with more than words, while a Baruch Spinoza tank acknowledges the seventeenth-century rationalist philosopher—a natural fit for a crowd that, while newly pro-war, remained staunchly anti-religious.[29]

This campaign was part of a larger, related effort that was not only a reversal of earlier sentiments but that would seem inconceivable only a few years later, during the Red Scare of the late 1940s and '50s. The Jewish Council for Russian War Relief (part of the larger Council for Russian War Relief) assembled a surprisingly diverse group of leaders from 1942 to 1946 to create a coalition ranging from far left to liberal. With figures such as American Jewish Congress leader Rabbi Stephen S. Wise and Albert Einstein as honorary cochairs, the council brought together thousands of delegates for its annual meetings. Attendees representing a panoply of Jewish organizations applauded speeches about the importance of supporting Russia in the war and listened to addresses by the likes of US senator James E. Murray (D-MT) and New York's mayor LaGuardia.[30] The Council launched a public fundraising campaign with a goal of raising a million dollars for tanks and other weapons for the Red Army. (In the end, this plan did not come to fruition.) The Council's Yiddish-language monthly newsletter *Far Sovet Rusland* (For Soviet Russia) featured Gropper's illustrations of a Soviet soldier using his gun to bash in the head of a Nazi (see figure 10.3).

The newsletter's masthead, drawn by Zuni Maud, evoked a more peaceful form of aid: two wings protectively curl around a collection of medicine bottles and supplies. But this was 1942, and there was no room for subtlety in the all-hands-on-deck drive to crush the enemy and save European Jewry. The newsletter's headline blares: "Yidn fun der velt—nemt nekome farn folk!" (Jews of the world—take revenge for [your] people!) In a related piece of publicity for the campaign, a JPFO brochure titled "A matone fun yidishn folk tsu roiter armei" (A gift from the Jewish people to the Red Army) boasts drawings of tanks and bomber planes and is signed by more than two hundred labor leaders, calling on their members to send a thousand tanks and five hundred bombers to Russia.[31]

This turn by leftists toward American symbolism and patriotic shows of strength was not limited to an embrace of military might. Images of classical American folk heroes were also burnished with a pro-labor veneer and an outsider image in music, art, and literature. Perhaps the most evocative tale told

FIGURE 10.3. Gropper's image of a Soviet soldier beating a Nazi. Courtesy of the Kheel Center.

by these artists that depicted the woes of both workers and outsiders—in this case, African Americans—drew on the folk song "John Henry." The tragic song tells the story of John Henry, a "steel drivin' man" whose commitment to laying pieces of the American railroad never wavered, even as his heart burst with the effort. The tune was already well-known when it became a favorite of the radical leftist songbook in the mid-thirties. Though its heartrending message was hitched to the Communist wagon by Workers Music League pioneer Charles Seeger (father of the famous folk revivalist Pete Seeger), it was a group of visual artists including Thomas Hart Benton, Hugo Gellert, and later, William Gropper, who immortalized the doomed railroad builder in all his physical glory.[32] Their artwork underscored the point that this martyr to American progress was a Black man—even portrayed by some as a Jesus figure. The racial element was not only key to the Party's program of equality and integration, but it also aligned with the sympathies of left-wing Jewish artists toward the plight of Black Americans.[33] This new angle, though, combined social justice and labor sympathies into one macho, heroic package that emerged from the American heartland.

While it may appear strange or even inappropriate in retrospect for activists who were not Black to employ an African American folk hero as their ideal, since they did not share his tenuous fate in America, the use of John Henry as a recurring image is consistent with the tenor of these activists' lives. As immigrants and as religious minorities who, in the early twentieth century, were not considered unequivocally white in the United States, Jewish artists and their comrades identified strongly with the plight of Black Americans. They identified not out of a patronizing sense of noblesse oblige, but in an act of empathy for the population that most closely echoed their own history of vulnerability, marginalization, and suffering in Russia and other countries from which their families had fled.[34]

The inclusion of Henry's powerful hammer in their pictures—a not-so-subtle nod to Communist sympathies—was an added bonus for Gellert and Gropper. Not content with creating only one image of John Henry, Gellert used the character (both identified as such and more generally, as a "type") as a recurring theme in his artwork for the progressive movement. His John Henry–like figures graced the cover of *Negro Songs of Protest*, collected and published in 1936 by Lawrence Gellert, Hugo's younger brother (a left-wing musicologist whose work is now controversial as its authenticity has been disputed). Similar figures appeared on posters at political rallies and were used as something of a "mascot" for radical magazines such as the *New Masses*, the *Daily Worker*, and the Yiddish-language *Der hamer*.[35] Even an Abe Lincoln look-alike was transformed into a manly sledgehammer-wielding giant on the cover of the IWO's English-language magazine *Fraternal Outlook* in March 1939, in an issue that emphasized the anti-lynching song "Strange Fruit," popularized by Billie Holiday (see figure 10.4). (The lyrics and music were written by Jewish Communist and IWO member Abel Meeropol, under the pseudonym Lewis Allen.)

Beginning in 1939, Gropper created his own pantheon of classic American figures in a series called *American Folk Heroes*, which featured, among many others, the giant Paul Bunyan and John Henry. This culminated in his famous *American Folklore Map*, a color lithograph that was made into a poster at the federal government's initiative. It was distributed to thousands of public schools and libraries until it became a casualty of the 1950s Red Scare; its association with the radical artist made it a target of the House Committee on Un-American

FIGURE 10.4. *Fraternal Outlook*, magazine cover, March 1939. Courtesy of the Kheel Center.

Activities (HUAC). Following a 1953 appearance before HUAC, Gropper became one of the first artists to be blacklisted, and hundreds of copies of his folklore map were destroyed by the government. But, as was often the case with the irrepressible Gropper, he had the last word. He created a popular series of fifty lithographs called *The Capriccios*, which pilloried the forces controlling public discourse in America at the time: Congress, the media, and big business. (The series title is a nod to the work of one of Gropper's artistic role models, eighteenth- and nineteenth-century Spanish artist Francisco de Goya, whose series *Los caprichos—The Caprices—*mocked Spanish society of his day.)[36]

This drive to create works of Americana that meshed with their worldview emerged from the artists' genuine interest, but it was also born out of necessity. As was the case with almost all fine artists of their circle, Gropper, Gellert, Lozowick, Harkavy, Moses and Raphael Soyer, and many others sought commissions from the art section of the WPA to alleviate the privations of the Great Depression. Gropper's largest project of this type was a mural for the Department of the Interior in Washington, DC, that he began painting in 1937 and that was installed in 1940. Ever the champion of the worker, Gropper's enormous, three-panel mural titled *Construction of the Dam* highlights the muscular, straining forms of the workers carrying out their demanding jobs, while the massive concrete dam recedes into the distance—clearly of less importance than the humans struggling to erect it. Similarly, Goodelman revealed his own background as a machinist in a series of metal sculptures depicting laborers wielding heavy mechanical equipment to construct the edifices of capitalism.[37]

As the war proceeded and the world became more aware of the genocidal consequences of the conflict for European Jews, the JPFO and its associated Jewish artists became more overtly ethnic in some of their work. Even classically religious themes (not only Jewish or Yiddish cultural references) appeared with greater frequency in their sculptures, sketches, and paintings. After stories of Jewish armed resistance began to circulate in 1943, the artists also emphasized the theme of self-defense, celebrating and glorifying those who fought the Nazis specifically on behalf of Jews. These shifts indicate that the artists, realizing the scope of the catastrophe, were responding on a deep, familial level.

This connection is evident even in works that predate the beginning of the war, long before the Soviet Union joined the Allied effort. In 1938, Harkavy fashioned an all-too-prescient response to the fascist threat dominating the headlines. Her massive stone carving, featured at the 1939 Sculptors' Guild outdoor show in New York, evokes the peril facing her people in the most classical religious terms. The rough-hewn sculpture shows a mother protectively embracing her child and is captioned "Lamentations: My children are desolate because the enemy prevailed."[38] In choosing her title, Harkavy reached back to the religious upbringing of her childhood in Estonia to reference the biblical book of Lamentations (Eicha).[39] As the artist knew, Jews read Lamentations every year on Tishah B'Av, the Jewish day of mourning, to commemorate a string of calamities that befell the Jewish people on that day.

While remaining deeply immersed in her Communist-leaning social circles and in the left-wing Yiddishist YKUF organization (as well as a string of other groups), during these years Harkavy produced other works memorializing the traditional community that was quickly being lost. Two bronze heads sum up the artist's deep understanding that the world she had left behind in her youth was no more. In the first, a gaunt-faced figure titled *Martyr* (c. 1940) manifests fear in its eyes, its mouth slightly open—perhaps calling for help—while in 1941, Harkavy forged a figure who bore little resemblance to the American miners and the New England woman of her earlier, more famous works. In garb that came straight out of the artist's childhood memories, a bearded Jewish man wears a prayer shawl covering the back of his head and tefillin on his brow. His eyes are nearly closed. He looks down—not out at humanity in the direction that Harkavy and her comrades had faced for the past two decades, but inward—toward his own mortality. No explanation is necessary: the figure is simply titled *In Memoriam*.[40]

Goodelman, meanwhile, shifted his usual focus on laborers to a different kind of physical prowess: Immediately after the war he created an imposing bronze called *The Partisan* (1946). With a menacing expression and holding a bayonet next to his head, the figure (shown from his torso upward) commemorates the thousands of guerilla fighters living in the woods throughout Poland, Hungary, and other occupied countries.[41]

By the end of the war, works by some of the most fiercely doctrinaire universalists and leftists in the Yiddishist milieu demonstrated that they had been profoundly affected by the destruction of European Jewry. Joining establishment Jewish organizations to lobby world governments on behalf of the survivors, the artists led commemorations to the dead, wholeheartedly memorializing even those Jews whom they had pilloried only a few short years before. More than any other event, the Warsaw Ghetto Uprising in April and May of 1943—which followed the "Great Deportation" of three hundred thousand Jews from the ghetto to the death camps in the summer of 1942—galvanized Jews of all political stripes. With its reported images of the doomed, heroic "Davids" and their determined stand for an entire month against the Nazi "Goliath," Jews around the world committed themselves even more fully to defeating the Axis powers.

Leftist Jewish artists fully embraced this effort along with their brethren. In October 1943, the JPFO organized a "War Council of Cultural Groups" with the express purpose of using dramatists, music and dance groups, and fine artists to publicize anti-Nazi and pro-war sentiment in the press and throughout society.[42] Other IWO ethnic societies pitched in for Russian war relief, as when "a carnival of fun and frolic," sponsored by the Massachusetts Committee for Russian Relief, featured "Ukrainian, Latvian, Estonian, Lithuanian, Armenian, Russian and Jewish" musical and dance groups. Singers from Polish IWO lodges graced a Detroit blood drive and fundraising concert on behalf of the same cause. For Jewish organizations, though, the creative energies that had sustained entities such as the Frayhayt Farband dance group, its professional theater (the ARTEF theater), periodicals, rallies, and more for the past two decades were now redirected. It was not enough for them to be anti-Nazi and pro-war, like the other ethnic IWO groups. They did not reject their Communist associations, but the activists drew on them to focus attention on a different mission: memorializing Jews and saving Jewish culture.

The JPFO, with the support of the general IWO apparatus, took a lead role in these activities. Especially after the extent of the devastation was revealed at war's end, their focus turned to helping survivors and memorializing the dead. The Warsaw Ghetto Uprising and other stories of armed resistance appealed to many Jews who had been supportive of radical action in other arenas. Celebrated American Jewish author Howard Fast, himself a member of the Party, wrote an elegy to the rebels and published it with Gropper's powerful illustrations.[43] The book, *Never to Forget: The Battle of the Warsaw Ghetto*, is a lengthy, dramatic prose poem that pits a noble, pure, martyred Jewish people against the bestial rage of the Nazi monster. Fast's rhetoric is suffused with a blend of Jewish references and Marxist messaging, combining Jewish history, Socialist universalism, and the words of the Shema, the traditional Jewish testament of faith: "From the time we faced the Roman on the walls of our holy city / Hear O Israel, the Lord is our God, the Lord is One, to the time we faced the Nazi on the streets of Warsaw / Hear, oh Mankind, men are brothers, Humanity is One. . . . With a six-pointed star on my arm, and a five-pointed star on my cap, I died on the streets of Warsaw. Comrade, take the weapon I hand you and use it well!"[44]

Though he highlights figures of Red Army soldiers toward the end of the book, Gropper's illustrations include several traditional Jewish references. His indelible images are not only peopled with Warsaw's contemporary martyrs—murdered Jewish fighters dangling from gallows above jeering Nazi soldiers and women and children rounded up with bayonets and rifle butts—but also with scenes drawn from ancient Jewish history. Piles of bodies lay beside smoke circling to the sky as Nazis loot the community's treasures in an eerie déjà vu: the giant menorah over one soldier's shoulder echoes the pillaging of Jerusalem's Holy Temple by the Romans, referencing the looted menorah famously etched onto the Arch of Titus in Rome (see figure 10.5). With a few simple strokes, Gropper telescopes Jewish history—the destruction of Jerusalem is now evoked in the shadow of Treblinka's gas chambers; the road of Jewish exile has led to this time and place. His mocking depictions of religious Jews in Palestine after the 1929 riots are gone; instead, the artist would continue his lifelong dedication to social justice through his Warsaw Ghetto commemorations.

A 1948 visit to the ghetto's ruins further inspired Gropper: Standing in the rubble, he committed to creating a visual memorial to the Warsaw Ghetto fighters and victims every year for the rest of his life. Even though he did not quite accomplish this goal each year, he completed a number of important single pieces and illustrations.[45] Some of these works appeared as graphics in mass media and

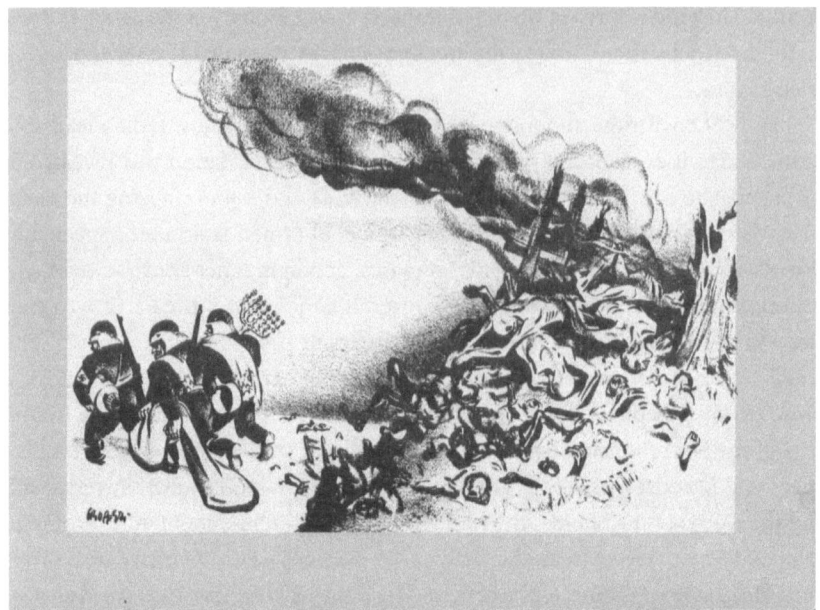

FIGURE 10.5. Gropper illustration from Howard Fast's *Battle of the Warsaw Ghetto*. Courtesy of Cornell University Library, Division of Rare and Manuscript Collections.

some as oil paintings shown in galleries. Several of his subjects are dressed in traditional religious garb—as with Harkavy's *In Memoriam* bronze, Gropper employs Jewish prayer shawls and phylacteries. He occasionally portrays his figures surrounded by Hebrew text, appealing to God in a mixture of supplication and righteous anger. A man at prayer raises his face to the heavens in Gropper's *De Profundis* (1942) pleading with God for protection, in the words of the Psalms: "Out of the depths I call to you."[46] It is almost inconceivable to imagine this reverence emanating from the same pen that had dispensed such antireligious ire only thirteen years earlier.

Not content to promote only his own Holocaust-related work, in 1949 Gropper and Herman Baron, founder of the progressive ACA Art Gallery, joined with JPFO general secretary Rubin Saltzman to launch a major show in New York.[47] Called *The Jew in Poland: From Ruins to a New Life*, the show exhibited actual ghetto and concentration camp materials shipped from the Central Committee of Jews in Poland, which were bilingually displayed, curated, and interpreted by JPFO artist Seymour Schwartz. Unlike the gallery's usual fare of leftist Social Realist art, the materials from Poland also represented the organizers' strong desire to show that this incomparable community, so decimated by the Holocaust, still held the seeds of Jewish cultural rebirth—if only the world would support its surviving, renewed remnants.

In 1948 the JPFO sponsored a major gathering in the Bronx, billed as a "Week of Jewish Culture."[48] A bilingual brochure announced the daily themes and the individuals who would lead workshops and events in both English and Yiddish. Goodelman taught sessions and showed his work, while Harkavy lectured on "Women in Art." They also mounted a special art show along with Moses Soyer, Lozowick, Gropper, and dozens of others. The names of sessions held throughout the week are revealing: "Art," "Theater," "Song," "Shule" (which focused on the Yiddish educational system in the United States), "Music," "Press," "Books"—and "Warsaw Ghetto." This curious list sent a clarion call: it declared that positive cultural content is important, but in a world that allowed the ghetto to become a reality, it does not stand alone on its own merits. After the catastrophe, the organizers felt, all other aspects of Yiddish culture existed to educate the people about their heritage, lest it disappear completely. Images of Warsaw's rubble had become as ubiquitous in this community as the hammer and sickle once were.

The artists and their cultural comrades had not abandoned their hopes for a better world, but in gathering for a week of Jewish culture in America—and mourning the loss of that culture in Europe—they revealed a new search for a world in which their people could march for universal values under the banner of their national heritage. Gropper would later attest to this transformation in his own life, reflecting on his Warsaw Ghetto commemorations: "This is my *yahrzeit*," he said, using the traditional Yiddish term for a memorial anniversary—"Hitler and fascism made me aware that I was a Jew."[49]

The case of the IWO—and in particular its Jewish section, the JPFO—illustrates the labyrinthine path taken by its leaders through a changing landscape of rising fascism, world war, and the postwar traumatic reckoning for Jewish leftists. The unique perspective of far-left Jewish visual artists paints these dilemmas in vivid colors. Unlike their writer colleagues whose usefulness in rousing political support for progressive causes was limited to those who read Yiddish, visual artists were not bound by the linguistic barriers of language activists. Yet they remained intimately connected with the tribulations and concerns of their community. In recounting their stories, we encounter more than just another example of the vicissitudes of Communist policy toward its "ethnic" members. Through their lives and works, we confront the complicated and often poignant task of defining Jewishness in a world where ideals and reality meet and evolve in an enduring—yet creative—tension.

NOTES

1. William Abrams, "Literatur in *Hamer* faren yahr 1932," *Der hamer* [Hammer], January 1933, 63. Quote translated in Bat-Ami Zucker, "American Jewish Communists and Jewish Culture in the 1930s," *Modern Judaism* 14, no. 2 (May 1994): 175.

2. Although the name "Jewish Peoples Fraternal Order" was not adopted to describe the Jewish section of the IWO until 1944, I use the acronym JPFO to describe projects of the Yiddish-speaking section of the IWO from its inception, since the newer name is generally used to refer to its earlier activities. For a detailed explanation of the group's founding, see the introduction to the International Workers Order (IWO) collection at the Kheel Center for Labor-Management Documentation and Archives, Catherwood Library, Cornell University, Ithaca, New York (henceforth Kheel): https://digital.library.cornell.edu/collections/iwo-jpfo.

3. Helen Langa, "'At least half the pages will consist of pictures': New Masses and Politicized Visual Art," *American Periodicals* 21, no. 1 (2011): 24–49. Also see Virginia Hagelstein Marquardt, "*New Masses* and John Reed Club Artists, 1929–1936," *Journal of Decorative and Propaganda Arts* 12 (Spring 1989): 56–75.

4. Arthur Liebman, "The Ties That Bind: Jewish Support for the Left in the United States," in *Essential Papers on Jews and the Left*, ed. Ezra Mendelsohn (New York University Press, 1997), 336–37.

5. "Progressive" in this era is a term associated with far-left politics and often the CPUSA itself, or so-called "fellow travelers" who may never have joined the Party but attended its events and were in sympathy with its views.

6. Note the discussions about shifting Party policies toward ethnicity in Zucker, "American Jewish Communists," and Liebman, "The Ties That Bind." Also see Matthew Hoffman's exploration of the fascinating ways that these policies played out in the left-wing Yiddish press. Hoffman, "The Red Divide: The Conflict Between Communists and Their Opponents in the American Yiddish Press," *American Jewish History* 96, no. 1 (March 2010), especially 4–5.

7. On the importance of using Yiddish as a tool of the left to reach the masses even before the advent of the Communist Party, see Tony Michels, *A Fire in Their Hearts: Yiddish Socialists in New York* (Harvard University Press, 2009), especially chapter 2: "Speaking to 'Moyshe': Socialists Create a Yiddish Public Culture."

8. I cover these institutions extensively in my forthcoming book, Lauren B. Strauss, *Painting the Town Red: Jewish Visual Artists, Yiddish Culture, and Radical Politics in Interwar New York*. There is also an excellent overview of several Jewish art institutions in the Jewish Museum catalog *Painting a Place in America: Jewish Artists in New York, 1900–1945*, ed. Norman L. Kleeblatt and Susan Chevlowe (The Jewish Museum, 1991).

9. For more on Cohn, see Annelise Orleck, *Common Sense and a Little Fire: Women and Working-Class Politics in the United States, 1900–1965*, 2nd ed. (University of North Carolina Press, 2017).

10. The Arbeter Ring, whose English name "Workmen's Circle" was changed to "Workers Circle" in 2019, was founded in 1892 as a Yiddish-speaking Socialist mutual aid society.

11. Patricia Phagan, "William Gropper and 'Freiheit': A Study of His Political Cartoons, 1924–1935" (master's thesis, City University of New York, 2000), 20–24.

12. For more on the atmosphere surrounding the Ferrer School, see Mark Bray and Robert H. Haworth, eds., *Anarchist Education and the Modern School: A Francisco Ferrer Reader* (PM Press, 2019).

13. A catalogue published by the Museum of Modern Art in 1939, *Art in Our Time*, describes the artist thus: "Käthe Kollwitz. German, born 1867. First woman elected to Prussian Academy, 1918, but lost this position under the Third Reich.

Lives in Berlin. Generally considered the greatest living woman graphic artist." https://www.moma.org/documents/moma_catalogue_2743_300061940.pdf?_ga= 2.98473439.17964022.1690776856-1201880034.1690776856, p. 221, catalogue item 252.

14. Peter Conrad, *The Art of the City: Views and Versions of New York* (Oxford University Press, 1984), 180.

15. The newspaper was first called the *Frayhayt* (Freedom) from 1922 to 1927, before it became a morning paper and thus added the word *Morgn* to its name. The umbrella organization that encompassed several different cultural and political entities in the Yiddish Communist sphere retained the name Frayhayt Farband (Frayhayt association).

16. There are extensive scholarly resources that discuss the causes and effects of the 1929 riots. Some books that focus on it and the British Mandate era specifically include Hillel Cohen, *Year Zero of the Arab-Israeli Conflict: 1929* (Brandeis University Press, 2015) and Naomi W. Cohen, *The Year After the Riots: American Responses to the Palestine Crisis of 1929-30* (Wayne State University Press, 1988). For another perspective, see Baruch Kimmerling and Joel S. Migdal, *The Palestinian People: A History* (Harvard University Press, 2003), 91-92.

17. For an in-depth exploration of the controversy illustrated through Gropper's cartoons, see Lauren B. Strauss, "*Kulturkamph* [sic] on the American Jewish Left: Progressive Artists React to Events in the 1920s and 1930s," *American Communist History* 15, no. 3 (December 2016): 263-82, https://www.tandfonline.com/doi/full/10.1080/14743892.2016.1270055. Also see Ezra Mendelsohn, "Jews, Communism, and Art in Interwar America," in *Dark Times, Dire Decisions: Jews and Communism*, ed. Jonathan Frankel (Oxford University Press, 2005), 99-132. On the creation of the weekly *Vokh*, see Ruth R. Wisse, "Drowning in the Red Sea," *Jewish Review of Books*, Fall 2011, 190-92.

18. Several of these magazine covers can be viewed and are discussed in Strauss, "Kulturkamph."

19. *Kinderland* 3, no. 3, International Workers Order (IWO) Records #5276, box 50, folder 1, https://digital.library.cornell.edu/catalog/ss:21796688.

20. Chaver-Paver, *Mayselakh* (National Yiddish Book Center, n.d.), https://www.yiddishbookcenter.org/collections/yiddish-books/spb-nybc200916/chaver-paver-gudlman-aharon-khaver-pavers-mayselakh-vol-1.

21. As seen in Cornell's Kheel Center's archives, the JPFO's dedication to Yiddish culture was underscored by its support for Zhitlowsky's burial in an IWO-sponsored section of a larger Jewish cemetery. The JPFO members viewed themselves as heirs to his legacy; although Zhitlowsky was not a member of the Communist Party and played a prominent role in advocating for diaspora nationalism and other programs of Jewish territorialism, he became pro-Soviet, worked with the JPFO, and died on a wartime fundraising tour that the JPFO sponsored. Goodelman's invoice and note to Rubin Saltzman, head of the JPFO, reminds Saltzman that he owes the sculptor a (delayed) balance for the monument. The tone of the letter is cordial, and Goodelman signs it "Fraternally Yours"—a reminder of their shared worldview even in the smallest rhetorical details. Letter from Aaron Goodelman to Rubin Saltzman, November 1, 1944, box 29, folder 6, Kheel, https://digital.library.cornell.edu/catalog/ss:20632058.

22. See Kleeblatt and Chevlowe, *Painting a Place in America*, 59.

23. For a detailed study of these two art exhibits, see Helen Langa, "Two Antilynching Art Exhibitions: Politicized Viewpoints, Racial Perspectives, Gendered Constraints," *American Art* 13, no. 1 (Spring 1999): 10-39.

24. Caroline Luce, "The Cooperative Center," UCLA Alan D. Leve Center for Jewish Studies, updated May 4, 2021, www.levecenter.ucla.edu.

25. See her obituary: "Minna Harkavy, 101, Sculptor and Teacher," *New York Times*, August 5, 1987, Y14; Moshe Nadir, "Minna Harkavy un Aaron Goodelman," *Morgn*

Frayhayt, July 9, 1939 (clipping in Goodelman Papers, reel 4936, frame 101, Smithsonian Archives of American Art [hereafter AAA], Washington, District of Columbia); and Lauren B. Strauss on Minna R. Harkavy in Fred Skolnik and Michael Berenbaum, eds., *Encyclopedia Judaica*, 2nd ed. (Keter Publishing, 2007).

26. Arguably, simultaneously maintaining multiple romances reflects Harkavy's willingness to defy convention and withstand social pressures, an attitude that would enable her consistently to be one of the only female leaders in Yiddishist leftist cultural circles. For more on Tresca, see Nunzio Pernicone, *Carlo Tresca: Portrait of a Rebel* (Palgrave Macmillan, 2005).

27. Both translations of the cartoon captions are from Phagan, "William Gropper," 529–30. The first cartoon I describe, with the money-eating tanks, is from the *Morgn Frayhayt* on January 6, 1934. The second one, with FDR and his war machine, is from January 10, 1934.

28. A South Philadelphia JPFO lodge was also named in honor of Solomon, and he was emphasized as a patriotic Jewish American in children's educational materials.

29. William Gropper, cartoon with tanks and Jewish heroes, 1942, box 45a, folder 9, Kheel, https://digital.library.cornell.edu/catalog/ss:21072643.

30. See articles in the Jewish Telegraphic Agency (JTA) from February 28, 1944, and April 30, 1945, on the annual meetings of the Jewish Council for Russian War Relief. There is a brief description of the group on the website of the Institute for the Study of Rescue and Altruism in the Holocaust (ISRAH): https://www.holocaustrescue.org/american-jewish-rescue-groups, accessed July 19, 2023. Also see relevant items in Cornell's Kheel Center IWO/JPFO collection, including a speech by Albert Einstein (in English with Yiddish translation) from October 25, 1942, titled "What Russia Means to Us" ("Vos Rusland maint far unze"), box 45a, folder 9, Kheel, https://digital.library.cornell.edu/catalog/ss:21072640.

31. Artist not identified for this brochure's illustrations. *A Gift from the Jewish People to the Red Army*, 1942, box 45a, folder 9, Kheel, https://digital.library.cornell.edu/catalog/ss:21072638.

32. Scott Reynolds Nelson, *Steel Drivin' Man: John Henry, the Untold Story of an American Legend* (Oxford University Press, 2006).

33. See earlier discussion in this chapter regarding Jewish artists' support for the Scottsboro defendants and lynching victims.

34. See Matthew Frye Jacobson, *Whiteness of a Different Color: European Immigrants and the Alchemy of Race* (Harvard University Press, 1999) on the ambiguous racial status of "New Immigrants," most particularly eastern European Jews and southern Italians.

35. Nelson, *Steel Drivin' Man*, 143–51.

36. Gropper's HUAC experience is detailed in Cécile Whiting, "William Gropper (1897–1977)," in *Encyclopedia of the American Left*, ed. Mari Jo Buhle et al. (Garland, 1990), 283.

37. See, for instance, the collection of sculptures at "Aaron J. Goodelman," Smithsonian American Art Museum, accessed July 19, 2023, https://americanart.si.edu/artist/aaron-j-goodelman-1865. During the New Deal, African American, Japanese American, and Latino artists such as Aaron Douglas, Jacob Lawrence, Charles White, Hale Woodruff, Eitarō Ishigaki, and Diego Rivera similarly celebrated the muscular achievements of Black Americans and other people of color confronting oppression—including portrayals of the Amistad Revolt—on canvases and the walls of public buildings. For Black, Japanese, and Latino, as well as Jewish muralists active during the New Deal era, see *Vida Americana: Mexican Muralists Remake American Art, 1925–1945*, ed. Barbara Haskell (Whitney Museum of American Art, 2020), including the chapter, "Migration and Muralism: New Negro Artists and Socialist Art," by Gwendolyn Dubois Shaw, 220–25.

38. "Nudes and Scrubwomen Seen at Outdoor Sculptors' Show," *New York World Telegram*, Saturday, April 15, 1939. Clipping from Goodelman Papers, reel 4936, frame 97, AAA.

39. Eicha (Lamentations) 1:16: "My children are desolate because the enemy has prevailed." The book (or scroll) of Lamentations specifically memorializes the destruction of the First Temple in Jerusalem by Babylonia in 586 BCE. Harkavy was one of ten siblings from a traditional Jewish family in Estonia, who would have been exposed to such customs as reading Eicha on the ninth of the month of Av.

40. Images of both bronzes can be found on auction house websites. The bronze titled "In Memoriam" is also owned by the Whitney Museum, listed under a different name: "The Last Prayer." Minna Harkavy, "Bronze 'Martyr,'" Invaluable, accessed August 10, 2023, https://www.invaluable.com/auction-lot/minna-rothenberg-harkavy-bronze-martyr-1218-c-ec94c86ad7; and Harkavy, "Large Minna Harkavy Bronze Sculpture," Invaluable, accessed August 10, 2023, https://www.invaluable.com/auction-lot/large-minna-harkavy-bronze-sculpture-391-c-c604dcdb04.

41. "Partisan" was exhibited, along with other Goodelman pieces, at the ACA Gallery in 1946 and was widely reviewed, according to the Magnes Collection (which received the works from the artist's widow). See image at Magnes Collections Online, accessed August 8, 2023, http://magnesalm.org/notebook_fext.asp?site=magnes&book=12454.

42. *Call to a Cultural Conference*, brochure, 1943, box 49, folder 6, Kheel, https://digital.library.cornell.edu/catalog/ss:19043101.

43. See interview with Fast in 1990 about the recent publication of his memoir, *Being Red*, in which he explains to a Soviet diplomat why his once-popular works were now unknown in the Soviet Union: "'You're too young. . . . In the 1940s, there were millions of my books in Russia. I wasn't eliminated until '56. I ceased to exist in every way.' 'Why was that?' Kirdyanov asked. 'Because I left the Communist Party.'" Susan Rubinowitz, "Author Reflects on Years as a Communist," *Greenwich Times*, November 14, 1990, https://www.trussel.com/hf/plots/t696.htm.

44. This refers to the six-pointed Jewish Star of David, and the five-pointed star of the Red Army. Howard Fast and William Gropper, *Never to Forget: The Battle of the Warsaw Ghetto* (Book League of the JPFO, 1946). Complete digitized version found at https://babel.hathitrust.org/cgi/pt?id=mdp.39015010570417&view=1up&seq=9.

45. See quotes from a later interview at "Focus In/On—William Gropper," *Gustavus Quarterly*, accessed August 15, 2023, https://gustavus.edu/quarterly/focus/gropper/gropper6.php.

46. Psalm 129 in the Book of Psalms (or Tehilim) in the Hebrew Bible, which is the same as Psalm 130 in the New Testament. Gropper's painting *De Profundis* is part of the Sandra and Bram Dijkstra Collection, San Diego. Images of the painting may be found on the worldwide web.

47. See description of the show "The Jew in Poland: An Exhibit, From Ruins to a New Life, May 1949," sponsored by the IWO and the JPFO, 1949, box 53, folder 18, Kheel, https://digital.library.cornell.edu/catalog/ss:19043947.

48. *Week of Jewish Culture in the Bronx*, program, 1948, International Workers Order (IWO) and Jewish Peoples Fraternal Order, box 35, folder 1, Kheel, https://digital.library.cornell.edu/catalog/ss:20632747.

49. Quoted in Andrew Weinstein, "From International Socialism to Jewish Nationalism: The John Reed Club Gift to Birobidzhan," in *Complex Identities: Jewish Consciousness and Modern Art*, ed. Milly Heyd and Matthew Baigell (Rutgers University Press, 2001), 156.

11
"WE'LL STAY HERE 'TIL THE FASCIST TOMB IS MADE"
The IWO and the International Brigades

Annabel Gottfried Cohen

On July 3, 1936, ten amateur athletes set sail from New York for Barcelona to compete in the "People's Olympics," an anti-fascist alternative to that year's infamous games in Nazi Germany. Among them were three International Workers Order (IWO) members: team trainer Alfred "Chick" Chakin; track runner and IWO basketball captain Myron Dickes, and Frank Payton, the African American "star athlete" of the Order's International Youth Section.[1] Interviewing the athletes at the port, the Communist *Daily Worker* reported, "Frank Payton and Al Chakin wouldn't go to the Berlin Olympics no matter who sent them . . . even if it meant lots of glory and easy jobs as their reward. They wouldn't go to Berlin because they know they could never get a break there. Frank is a Negro, and Al is Jewish."[2]

Hosted in Catalonia by the recently elected Popular Front government, the "Olimpiada Popular" was to be everything the Berlin games was not—a celebration of the internationalism and interracialism that the IWO also embodied. The participation of "races who are being outlawed or discriminated against, such as Negroes, Jews and Arabs" was actively encouraged, and the *Daily Worker* presented the games as a stand against both European fascism and the Jim Crow racial segregation that still prevailed in American sports—both issues at the heart of the IWO's program.[3] The IWO, meanwhile, was one of the most vocal organizations in the call for an anti-Nazi boycott that accompanied the alternative olympiad. The previous year, Black IWO activists in particular had helped lead the US protest movement against Mussolini's invasion of Ethiopia. A multiracial fraternal society founded by Jewish immigrants and connected to the

Communist Party of the United States (CPUSA), the IWO was at the forefront of an anti-fascist protest movement that would soon intensify around events in Spain.

In the early hours of July 19, four days after their arrival, the American athletes were awakened by "the rumbling of cannons, several thousand machine guns and rifles and the sound of marching feet." From their hotel window, they watched as armed civilians fought back against soldiers who, "led by their Fascist officers[,] had rebelled against the Republic." Willi Rapaport, a medic with the Paris *Arbeter Ordn* (Workers' order), the IWO's sister organization, quickly found himself traveling all over the city, tending not to the bruises and sprains of athletes, but to gunshot wounds. An American athlete later described how his experience of the crowds on the New York subway helped him herd civilians away from a burning building.[4]

Within a few days, the rebellion had been crushed in Barcelona, which was now largely controlled by anti-fascist workers' organizations. Some of the Americans wanted to join the militias being raised to fight the rebels in nearby Aragon but were "prohibited from doing so" by their delegation leaders. Yet within a few months, some three thousand Americans—among them Al Chakin and hundreds of other IWO members—would return to Spain to do just that. They would do so as part of an international "people's army," presented to the world as the shining example of the "brotherhood between races and peoples" that both the Order and the canceled olympiad strove to build.[5] Tens of thousands more would take part in fundraising campaigns, protests, and other demonstrations of solidarity with a cause that dominated the attention of the American Communist left until the outbreak of World War II and arguably represented the IWO's most forceful expression of its anti-fascist beliefs.

"Fight On, Heroic Brothers and Sisters of Spain!"

Stopping in Paris on their way home, the athletes learned that Hitler and Mussolini were arming the Spanish rebels. Meanwhile, Western democracies, including the United States, left the Spanish republic's desperate appeals for aid unanswered. Despite and partly because of this policy of "non-intervention," the Spanish Loyalists soon attracted huge support from the international left—particularly the Communist Party and its affiliated organizations such as the IWO, which was already mobilizing in support of the Spanish Loyalists. Within days of his return to New York, Payton found himself addressing a "mammoth meeting" in Madison Square Garden. Chakin meanwhile took the stage in Cleveland, where

IWO Branch 189 was the first to donate to a newly established aid fund. Two days later, the Italian members of Branch 2530, in Jessup, Pennsylvania, followed suit. Their "United Front Anti-Fascist Committee," formed with other organizations "in support of the Spanish people," advertised its first fundraiser dance.[6]

Encouraging the formation of these local committees, IWO leaders also renewed their efforts to form a national united anti-fascist committee of fraternal organizations. They also played a key role in other Communist-led collaborative initiatives, such as the American Society for Technical Aid to Spanish Democracy and the Joint North American Committee to Aid Spanish Democracy (NAC), an umbrella organization founded to coordinate humanitarian aid. An affiliate of the NAC, the IWO was, despite the Depression, also one its biggest donors. On August 28, 1936, the Order sent a check for $2,500, collected from members "from all parts of the country" who were "digging deep into their own meagre earnings to contribute to the aid of their Spanish brothers and sisters," prompting a message of thanks from Spanish president Manuel Azaña. Presenting a second check two months later, the IWO pledged that "as you lay down your lives on the battlefront for democracy and liberty, the 100,000 members of the International Workers Order are with you."[7]

Meanwhile, German and Italian planes were bombing the suburbs of Madrid. With Hitler and Mussolini using Spain as a testing ground for new forms of modern warfare, by the end of October 1936 the Republican government estimated that fifty thousand civilians had already been killed. "Fascism," said Spanish prime minister Francisco Llargo Caballero, was "turning Spain into a cemetery." Arriving in Madrid in early 1937, the first team of American medical volunteers—sent by the NAC and partially funded by the IWO—reported a desperate situation. "There were only about 60 ambulances.... They need at least 500.... The wounded men lay in the mud fields ... 50% of them died because of the improper conveyances."[8]

In a cause close to the heart of its own work, the IWO was soon fundraising for four ambulances (see figure 11.1), a mobile operating room, and the "Washington Friends of Spanish Democracy—International Workers Order Children's Home" in Villagorde. As early as January 1937, plans were made to name a ward of a new American hospital in Spain after the Order in recognition of its members' contributions, which had already reached $29,000.[9] German-born IWO general secretary Max Bedacht estimated that over the course of the war the Order had raised at least $40,000 for the NAC, alongside another $20,000 for other organizations—activity that repeatedly attracted government scrutiny.[10]

As Bedacht noted, these national figures did not include the "considerable sums" donated by local branches or in the cross-party efforts in which IWO members were remarkably active. In 1938, members of the IWO's Harlem

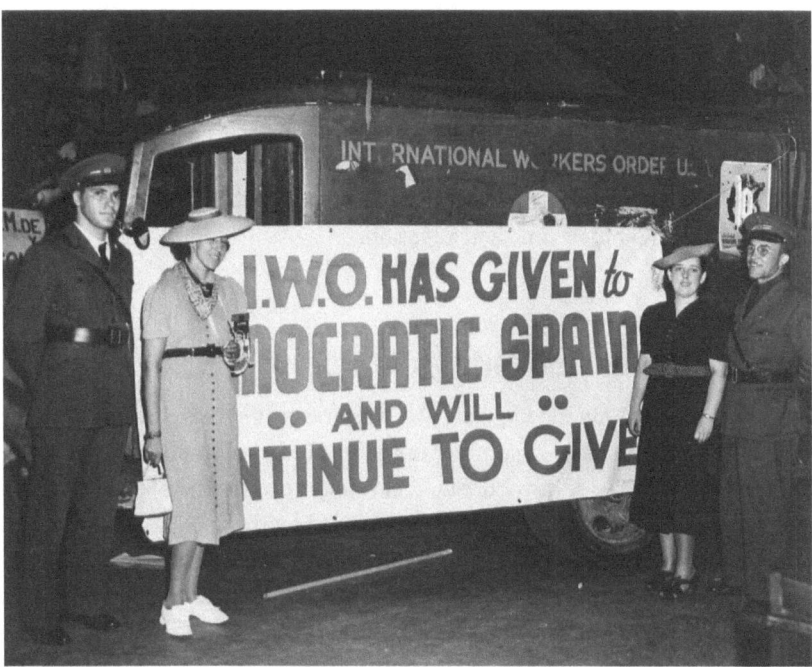

FIGURE 11.1. *Left to right*: Laboratory technician Morris Kornblum (Balter), nurse Helen Freeman, nurse Anne Shuldiner, and engineer Ives Delvaville Jacquier pose by an IWO ambulance after its return from Spain. SRRAR, box 169, folder 8.

Division sent an ambulance to Spain as part of the Negro People's Committee, which had been founded at a dinner to honor IWO leader Louise Thompson the previous year. A permanent IWO delegate supported the committee, and the Harlem Suitcase Theatre, connected with Thompson's Solidarity Lodge, helped with fundraising activities. IWO activists in Chicago also hoped to send their own medical unit, while children at the city's Slovak Workers Society school raised funds for "the working people ... fighting fiercely against the fascist murderers ... who drop bombs on the workers' apartments in Madrid, killing women and children." Onni Kaartinen, national secretary of the IWO-affiliated Finnish American Mutual Aid Society (FAMAS), reported in August 1937 that his branch alone had raised more than $5,000, describing this as "one of the most important things we have done."[11]

The scale of fundraising alone demonstrates the widespread sympathy felt by IWO members for the Spanish republic and the anti-fascist struggle. Like other Communist-led Popular Front organizations, by early 1937, the IWO's membership had also grown substantially—by 37,700 members—something Bedacht credited in part to their "anti-fascist program." Indeed, IWO leaders hoped to use the strength of feeling around Spain to galvanize existing members into more active participation, planning an "anti-fascist month" of activities focused on Spain. Of course, their concern with "inertia" reminds us not to exaggerate the extent to which IWO members really engaged with events in Spain, or indeed in the life of the movement.[12] Yet for the activists and local leaders who organized such activities—many of them also affiliated with the CPUSA—Spain soon dominated much of their time and attention.

"Every Discussion Brings in Spain"

In the summer of 1936, Irving Goff was working as athletics director at Camp Nitgedaiget (No worries)—a summer camp for needle trade workers run by the IWO and the CPUSA's Jewish Bureau. Following the uprising in Spain, Goff and other members of the camp's CPUSA group—led by the cook, a Spanish Communist named Martinez—quickly organized activities in support of the Loyalists. Returning to New York already immersed in the cause, Goff began collecting money for the NAC on the subway. Other IWO members volunteered in the NAC's warehouses and offices. In December 1936 a request for volunteers was sent to all New York City Order branches. Photographs of members of the Manhattan IWO's Spanish Workers' Club volunteering "to aid the heroic defenders of democracy and the brave victims of fascism in Spain" soon appeared "not only in American papers but also in . . . France, Spain and the Soviet Union."[13]

Writing to Patrick Roe McLaughlin, an organizer with the IWO's Irish Workers' Club, New York activist Sylvia Sadkin related how "many times during each day" she encountered "people soliciting aid in ways that I, myself, often do." She added, "So many people are eager to give their large or small shares for the cause." Excitedly describing a gathering of "3,500 people" at Mecca Temple, Sadkin reported that "$5,000 and an ambulance were collected." Meanwhile, a recent "tag day" on which collection boxes were placed in all IWO centers had raised $11,000.[14] In their own tag day—dubbed "Movieless Day"—IWO Juniors used their movie money to buy colorful tags labeled "I Gave for Liberty in Spain," presenting the NAC with "hundreds of pennies, nickels and dimes."[15]

Almost a year into the war, Sadkin still attended events in aid of the Spanish republic every week. So did the Halpern family, all of whom seem to have been Order members. Telling McLaughlin that "last Saturday night we gave a party in our home for Spain and raised some money," Clara Halpern added, "No matter what games we play, the winner always has to toss in his winnings to Spain." Meanwhile, "Mother is working towards an ambulance." Like Goff and Sadkin, Halpern portrayed Spain as something of an obsession: "Every discussion brings in Spain, almost no matter what it is." Fervent believers in Communist doctrine, these activists saw the war in Spain as the latest—perhaps the final—stage in a war against, in Sadkin's words, "the forces that enslave us." The actions of Spanish workers in taking up arms against their oppressors was proof of their movement's "inevitable" victory.[16] Armed with this conviction and organized by the Communist Party, many of the young men in these activist circles—among them Goff and McLaughlin—were soon traveling to Spain to fight.

The International Brigades

In November 1936, IWO members in New York marched toward the German Consulate chanting "Hands off Spain!" Meanwhile, the first International Brigades (IBs)—founded by the Comintern in September and October—were already fighting in Madrid.[17] While McLaughlin set sail from New York to join the Connolly Column being organized from Ireland, IWO leaders were helping the CPUSA to recruit an American IB contingent. In charge of the "recruitment committee" was future IWO national organizational director Sam (Shimshon) Milgrom, a full-time CPUSA organizer assisted by other functionaries connected to the Party's immigrant language bureaus.[18] When the first American volunteers set sail on December 26, 1936, they gathered at the Yiddish Arts Theater on Second Avenue, which was used as offices and a school by the IWO's Jewish American Section, its largest and founding section.[19]

Members of "language organizations" such as the IWO were also among those "especially" targeted for recruitment.[20] IWO National Committee member George Powers later admitted during New York State's prosecution of the Order that he and other IWO leaders had helped the CPUSA to recruit IWO members. Another state witness, Maxwell Wallach, claimed that his son, Albert, had been recruited directly by the Order, which had also given him $3,000 to take with him to Spain to cover volunteers' expenses.[21] By late September 1937, there were an estimated two hundred IWO members fighting in Spain. This does not include those who would volunteer after that date, or—following a brutal summer—the many who had already lost their lives.[22]

The role played by IWO leaders in the mobilization of American IB volunteers is illustrative of their well-documented close connection with the CPUSA. Yet the stories of IWO IB volunteers remind us it was not only the senior leadership that connected the Order to the Party. Of the fifty IWO-affiliated brigaders I have been able to identify in the volunteer lists, at least forty-three were CPUSA members, many of them long-term activists with organizational roles in the Party, the Order, or both. One story that stands out is that of a group of mostly Jewish organizers in the Young Communist League (YCL), who, having grown up in the movement, were now leaders of the IWO's Junior Section and cultural programs. Their story provides insight into the role played by the IWO not only in the IBs, but also in the wider movement of which both the Order and the brigades were part.

Spain "Gets a Taste" of IWO Antics

On August 14, 1936, Goff and his comrades at Camp Nitgedaiget were preparing for a Friday night "Franco Burns" bonfire. Meanwhile, the IWO Jewish Section's Camp Kinderland had three nights of theater in store, culminating in a performance of a new anti-capitalist musical comedy, *Let's Get Together*, composed by former camper Harry Meloff (Harold Malofsky). A photo taken by camp photographer Ben Itzkowitz a week later and subsequently printed on postcards shows members of the Kinderland YCL group posing as a Spanish militia, brandishing weapons and a flag bearing the words "Spanish People's Front" (see figure 11.2).[23] Among them appear to be several members of Meloff's popular IWO-YCL

FIGURE 11.2. Members of the Kinderland Young Communist League pose as a Spanish militia. Photo by Ben Itzkowitz, August 22, 1936, appears to include Bernard Abramofsky (*third from left on ground*), Miriam Sigel (*center back, holding banner*), Ernest Arion (*fourth from right, kneeling*), Harry Meloff (*sitting second from right*), and Paul Sigel (*right, on ground*). Courtesy of the Kheel Center.

comedy troupe "The Convulsionaries"—some of whom, including Meloff himself, would soon sacrifice their lives on the real Spanish battlefields.

A member of the IWO Junior Section since its founding, Meloff was now coleader of the IWO Youth Theatre of New York (IWOYT). Following his death in Spain, he would be memorialized in a theater festival celebrating him as the "first organizer of dramatic groups in the IWO."[24] A YCL branch was also named after him. His letters home illustrate how the IWO's program of mutual aid and proletarian culture fit into a cause that had now reached its boiling point in Spain.

Meloff left New York on the *Isle de France* on February 20, 1937, with a contingent of 107 new volunteers—the largest group so far. He was accompanied by his "closest comrade," fellow Convulsionary and Kinderlandnik Ernest "Ernie" Arion; his young cousin, IWOYT performer Bernard "Bernie" Abramofsky (Abrams); and Vaughn Love, the African American secretary of the IWO's Solidarity Lodge and a fellow organizer of left-wing, interracial theater.[25] Goff, who had recruited ten to fifteen members of his "mostly Jewish" Coney Island youth club, was also on the ship.[26] So were at least two other IWO cultural activists: the Cypriot John Demas and the Greek Al Alexander, whose "rich heritage of cultural activity" would later be memorialized in the names of both an IWO library and a youth chapter.[27] Following their predecessors' deaths in Spain, the Brooklyn Contemporary Players of the Al Alexander Youth Chapter would compete in the Harry Meloff Theatre Festival for the Harry Meloff Award.

IB volunteer lists show that these young men were among several IWO and YCL youth leaders and branch organizers who sailed for Spain in early 1937, when, following some initial difficulties, the CPUSA was beginning to rethink its recruitment strategy. Sent into action for the first time in February at Jarama, the newly formed and barely prepared American Lincoln Battalion had been all but decimated, with more than a hundred of its 263 volunteers killed in a single day.[28] With discontent among the American volunteers threatening to turn into outright insurrection, former IWO recruiter Steve Nelson was sent to Spain to help restore morale as Lincoln Battalion commissar. Other newly arrived IWO and YCL activists also turned their attention to morale-boosting activities. Arion, Meloff, and Abramofsky were "selected head of the committee" in charge of cultural activities at the IB base in Albacete. A "troupe" assembled by Harry, which included Arion, Abramofsky, and Love, was soon performing regularly for the other volunteers and the residents of the nearby towns in which they were stationed. "Spain," wrote Meloff, "is getting a taste of the Convulsionary antics."[29]

Other volunteers remembered these antics fondly. Future battalion commander Milton Wolff later recalled how the IWO comics had everyone in stitches by crouching on the floor pretending to be chickens. Harold Smith, an acquaintance of Meloff's and organizer of the YCL's Queens Astoria Branch, seemed delighted to find himself in the same company as the famous Convulsionaries and working with them as one of the "Solidarity and Cultural Directors." Writing to his co-organizer and girlfriend Jeannette, Smith boasted: "We've put on some stuff that the Brigadiers of every language and the townspeople ate up." Emphasizing the "utmost political importance" of "learning a common language," Smith described one of their "assignments"—"a 30-minute play which would dramatize one of our main slogans—'Learn Spanish.'" Probably referring to the same play, a show about "the language problem here," Meloff boasted that "the effect was so tremendously put across that our commandante is still laughing."[30]

As in the IWO, entertainment in the IBs served an important educational purpose. Recounting all his cultural activities to fellow Convulsionary and IWOYT leader Miriam Sigel, Meloff insisted, "Military activity isn't enough. Education must be combined with it." Echoing Smith, he wrote that "our major political task now is to learn the Spanish language." Another letter, describing how "everyone walks around with Spanish Dictionaries and phrase books and annoy one another to death with an unintelligible gibberish," suggests their success remained limited. Yet by using mime, hand gestures, and songs, the Convulsionaries and their comrades were already helping to forge solidarities across cultural and linguistic boundaries. Several accounts suggest that their performances also helped to "break down the barriers" with the Spanish locals, who, according to Arion, had been "very cold" when the volunteers arrived.[31]

In mid-May 1937 Abe Harris—a veteran Jewish CPUSA activist and organizer with the IWO's Educational Department, Junior Section, and New York City Central Committee—was moved to tears when he happened upon Meloff's "glee club" singing the Internationale. Known by almost all volunteers in their own languages, the Soviet-Communist anthem often produced such emotional responses. The older activist may have also been reacting to the sight of his young protégés acting as leaders in this internationalist people's army. In Spain both as an IB volunteer and a representative of the IWO's Junior Section surveying the crisis facing orphaned and displaced Spanish children, Harris was, according to Meloff, also doing "important political work."[32]

As Lisa Kirschenbaum notes, group singing was an important linguistic bridge, used to "forge and mark solidarity across national lines" in this multilingual army.[33] For Miriam Sigel's brother Paul, songs exemplified "the international aspects of our brigade." Singing was "an international language and believe me it's well-spoken here." Meloff contributed greatly to this. Writing English lyrics to the songs sung by Spanish and Italian volunteers, he also tried to get the IWO Youth Theatre's mass chant "Spain" translated into Spanish, so that this song of American solidarity might be shared on the front. Smith sent one Meloff original back to his YCL branch; another—Meloff's "Song of the International Brigade"—was sent back to New York for publication. Pledging, "We'll stay here 'til the fascist tomb is made," the song added "and when we get home once more, we'll do the same thing there."[34]

The IWO's "people's pianist" turned "battalion singing master" thus played an important part in what became one of the most celebrated symbols of the IBs.[35] Writing to Miriam after Harry's death, Paul Sigel tried to comfort his sister with the knowledge that Meloff had "continued the swell work of the Convulsionaries," writing some of "the theme songs of our IB." So popular that they were even picked up by Spanish children, Paul was certain that Harry's anthems of "spirit and courage" would be "heard throughout America and Canada and Europe." At the front, Meloff's songs kept up morale, "emphasizing the spirit of comradeship that brought them together and causing the fascist many a headache." Even following the trauma of his first battle and Arion's death, Harry had remained determined "to get everyone singing" and awaken "the old-time rookie spirit."[36]

In an army of volunteers fighting against enormous odds, the education, ideological motivation, and "rookie spirit" provided by social and cultural activities were vital. Yet the letters exchanged between these volunteers and their comrades at home also reveal a bigger picture. Frequently expressing their desire to, in Meloff's words, "bring the spirit of Madrid to N.Y.," they seem to have seen Spain as a cultural as well as a military front—a center of real, popular struggle that they hoped would have global influence. The dedication of these young activists to their work both on the Spanish front and at home in New York, which they inquired about almost obsessively, is striking. Their letters serve as a reminder that the celebrated revolutionary, internationalist culture of the IBs was not simply a propaganda tactic imposed by Communist leaders. It was also fostered on the ground by volunteers themselves for whom this leftist culture was, in the words of another IWOYT performer turned IB volunteer, Joseph Azar, "a way of life."[37]

Writing from a reserve position, Paul described a campfire at which volunteers exchanged revolutionary stories and songs from their various countries. "Stories of union life back in the old countries, tales of outwitting the bosses, the police" and of events in Spain were followed by "a German revolutionary marching song, a negro spiritual, a British cockney tune, an old Irish wooing song, an Italian antifascist hymn, . . . American revolutionary songs, Russian, Slav, Canadian" until "the whole group break into El Joven Guardia, Spain's youth's fiery anthem of victory." For Sigel, this "good, dear comradeship," this lived internationalism, was a taste of "life, friendship such as the people of the future, new world will enjoy— not master + slave, but comrade & comrade, from each as he can do, to each as he needs." Sending his comrades at home a copy of the IB journal *Volunteer for Liberty* and urging them to send news of their work, he wrote, "We'll build it on this front, you on another, working together, widening our support, enlargening [*sic*] our movement, winning our first victory."[38]

Our Boys in Spain

Taken together, the letters written to and by the "Lincolns"—as the American volunteers came to be collectively known—paint a picture of an activist community whose center, manned by some of its most militant young men, was now in Spain. In March 1937, Sadkin was sure that McLaughlin "must have met many people that I know, for I have heard of so many people, familiar to me who have left to join you." Volunteer letters are indeed full of encounters with familiar faces. Not only the IWO and YCL, but even the IWOYT was "well represented."[39] So was the IWO's Jewish Section, and its Camp Kinderland.

Finding himself bunked with Smith, Arion, Abramofsky, and another YCL comrade, Ricco Rusciano, Meloff described feeling like he was back at the IWO summer camp. Even just behind the front, Meloff was so surrounded by comrades that "if it weren't for the fact that we can distinctly hear the firing going on, one would think we were spending a vacation at Camp Kinderland." Describing how his commandante began orders with a Yiddish "nu," he added, "Lord knows there are plenty of brother Jews around." An estimated one-third of American volunteers were of Jewish origin; Meloff's letters suggest that a large number of them were affiliated with the IWO.[40]

By the time Paul Sigel arrived in July 1937, many of his friends were already in Spain. Before "Mim [Miriam]," "Bert," and "the Gang"—now all working as counselors at the Communist Camp Unity—had time to write him a letter, he had already received their "personal regards," delivered by George Watt, another former Kinderlandnik who had "just arrived."[41] The strength of activist friendships is tangible in volunteer letters, particularly in the frequent complaints that comrades at home were not writing often enough. Discussing the recent death of Bert's brother, Chicago CPUSA activist Art Witt, Paul wrote like a member of an extended family. For Meloff, who, like many Lincolns, came from something of a "broken home," the IWO and YCL seem indeed to have become his family.[42] He often expressed his gratitude for Miriam's friendship, and in the wake of Arion's death he told her, "Now more than ever I yearn for New York + I.W.O + Youth Theatre and the comrades who make life easier with their letters."[43]

Back home, the IB volunteers were a source of huge pride and excitement. According to Clara Halpern, "everyone" wanted a copy of McLaughlin's letter from Spain, which she was having printed in the *Irish Democrat* and a "very popular labor paper." She had hung the bulletin he enclosed "in a very important place, a meeting hall of workers." Sadkin, meanwhile, carried McLaughlin's letters around "almost constantly." Writing, "Believe me, they are widely read," she added, "People whom I know well and those who are just my casual acquaintances ask me constantly whether I have had further word from Spain. . . . They are greedy for all you can tell."[44]

The volunteers quickly became an important focal point for further fundraising and solidarity activity. Listed among the suggested activities for the IWO's November 1937 "anti-fascist month" were "house parties with reading of letters from fighters in Spain, . . . memorials for those who have fallen in the fight in Spain," and "women's knitting circles to produce stockings for the soldiers in Spain."[45] (Similar "care packages" would later be shipped to American, British, and Soviet soldiers during World War II by the IWO's Front Line Fighters Fund.) Back in May, an editorial in the *Daily Worker*—printed alongside volunteer letters, including one of McLaughlin's to Sadkin—had urged readers to "show them that our thoughts, our hopes are with them" by sending "gifts or funds" toward shipments of "cigarettes, medical supplies, chocolates, books, sweaters and such things" to be dispatched by the Friends of the Abraham Lincoln Brigade (FALB).[46] By October 1937, the IWO had already donated $5,273.[47] Individual branches and sections also sent money and supplies to their boys in Spain. "A major portion" of the funds raised by the Finnish Section had "gone directly to the friends of the Lincoln Battalion and through them . . . to you boys over there."[48]

In May 1937, Meloff received twenty-five dollars from the IWO in a letter from Sigel. "A good start," he wrote, adding, "Keep after them." He wouldn't be disappointed. Two months later, returning from three grueling weeks at the front, Meloff was awakened from a nap by Max Bedacht, who had arrived with an NAC delegation and "eight tons of cigarettes and chocolates." Delighted to see the IWO general secretary, Meloff boasted: "We had a swell time talking and questioning each other. . . . He's had a big fondness for me ever since the old days when I was a courtin' his Elsie (or something like it) and I used to praise his fried chicken of a Sunday dinner."[49] Personal ties also cut through movement hierarchies.

Bringing "greetings from his organization to the government forces" and presenting "the American volunteers with eleven truckloads of cigarettes, candies, gums, canned goods, and writing paper," Bedacht specifically sought out IWO members on the front. Returning to New York in October, he brought their "personal regards" to a mass meeting at the Royal Windsor Hotel. Meanwhile, a representative of the Spanish government expressed "the condolences of Spain to the relatives of the I.W.O. members who died in the struggle against the Fascists."[50] This now included Arion and Meloff.

Attended by district secretaries from across the country and New York City branches "en masse, with their branch banners," the meeting was also addressed by Louise Thompson and IWO president William Weiner, who, along with a representative of FAMAS, had joined the NAC delegation.[51] Representing the IWO's Black and Jewish members respectively, Thompson and Weiner also reported from the Second World Congress Against Racism and Anti-Semitism in Paris, reminding the crowd what the fight in Spain represented. In contrast to the fascist white supremacy that threatened their members, the meeting, which featured performances from African American and Spanish groups, was a characteristic show of the "celebratory interracialism" of both the IWO and the IBs.[52] Following this event, both Bedacht and Thompson embarked on national speaking tours for the Spanish Loyalist cause, during which time they also announced the Order's national convention, which, in a historic stand against Jim Crow, would house Black and white delegates together in the same hotel. Four months later, this gathering in Pittsburgh would receive a telegram from Russian American, Ukrainian American, Croatian American, Jewish American, and African American IWO members fighting side by side in Spain, which, read aloud, inspired "a standing ovation."[53]

"We Had Representatives from Every Race, Creed and Ethnic Origin"

For the many IWO members from countries menaced or already overtaken by fascism, the war in Spain was no abstract threat. Among the first to donate their time and money to the Loyalist cause were members of the IWO's Hispanic Section, noting the links between fascist movements in Spain and South America. By March 1937, the section was fundraising for its own ambulance to send to "the intrepid Spanish militias... in the name of our section." Calling for a "day of work on the part of every member and sympathizer," a special appeal proclaimed, "LET US MOBILIZE THE VANGUARD OF THE SPANISH PEOPLE IN THE UNITED STATES."[54]

With Mussolini supporting the rebels, the IBs offered Italian American volunteers—at least 20 percent of whom were IWO members—an opportunity to fight back against the forces that had compelled them to flee Italy.[55] Among the first to donate to the Solidarity Fund, Italian IWO members were also among the first to volunteer to fight in Spain with a contingent "sent by the Italian Bureau of the Party" in January 1937, which certain IWO leaders also seem to have had a hand in organizing.[56] So significant was the IWO presence in the Italian Garibaldi Battalion that a New York mass meeting in October 1937 celebrated them alongside the American Lincoln Battalion.[57] Like the Order's similarly named Garibaldi Society, the Italian IB unit strove to contrast their pluralistic vision of

Italian national identity with that represented by the Italian fascist troops on the other side of the battlefield.

IB propaganda, carefully tailored for each of its constituent national and ethnic groups, exemplified the proletarian national-cultural pride that, particularly during the Popular Front era, was embraced—if ambivalently—by the Communist movement. For the IWO's immigrant leadership, the IBs in many ways represented the zenith of the multinational, internationalist ideal they had long advocated. Agitating against right-wing or apathetic attitudes within their respective communities, the Order's national sections sought to advance alternative, progressive versions of their respective national cultures and histories, each of which was portrayed as part of an internationalist whole. IB propaganda—which presented each national contingent as the "best sons" of their people or nation, fighting together in an international people's army—epitomized this approach to national identity.[58]

Like other Communists involved in so-called language work, activists in the IWO's national sections actively promoted the stories of "their" volunteers, hoping to inspire their compatriots to join the anti-fascist cause. While McLaughlin's news that "the Irish are holding their own in Spain" inspired pride among Irish immigrants, branches of the IWO's Slovak Workers Society (SWS) in New York, Chicago, Cleveland, and Milwaukee raised funds to "help our Slovak Janošíks in Spain, who were wounded in battle while defending the poor Spanish people massacred by Mussolini, Hitler and Franco."[59] Meanwhile, the multiracial, predominantly immigrant American Lincoln and Washington Battalions were upheld as the symbol of the true America: the defenders of real, pluralistic American values. In the era of Jim Crow, when the US Army was segregated and would remain so for more than a decade, this was particularly significant for Black volunteers.

A Multiracial Army "to Defeat Hitler's Racial Theories"

For the first time in US history, in the International Brigades African Americans not only fought alongside white Americans as equals, they also commanded them. Fervently committed to racial equality, the Communist organizers of the IBs made a conscious effort both to recruit Black volunteers and to promote them to leadership positions. Vaughn Love, one of several African Americans selected for officer school, was made a group leader, later a sergeant. When the brigades were decommissioned in November 1938, Love was one of the four Americans chosen to represent the Fifteenth Brigade at an official farewell dinner organized by the Spanish Communist Party.[60] In June 1937, Oliver Law was appointed commander of the Lincoln Battalion, becoming "the first black officer to command white troops in any American army."[61] Walter Garland, another Black CPUSA member, was made battalion commander and joined Louise Thompson on speaking tours and radio broadcasts in Spain. He would later be promoted to IWO national organizer.

Although in reality they were only a small contingent of around eighty individuals, the majority of them CPUSA members, Black volunteers and their contributions were greatly celebrated—even exaggerated—in IB and CPUSA propaganda. With white supremacist racial theories still dominant in the United States, CPUSA and IWO activists enthusiastically advertised the heroism of the Black IB volunteers to combat such prejudice. Thompson, who had visited the African American volunteers on the front, became a leading voice in their promotion on her return from Spain. In the words of an attendee at one of her speeches, the IBs "prove the theory that if the colored race be given an equal chance they will come out on top."[62]

The preferential advancement of Black volunteers in both the ranks and in the press has sometimes been treated cynically, seen as an attempt by the CPUSA to enhance its anti-racist reputation rather than as evidence of a genuine commitment to Black liberation. Certainly, propaganda celebrating the anti-racism of the IBs often glossed over and sometimes outright denied the racism that still existed in Loyalist Spain and even in the brigades themselves. At the same time, it was this persistent and pervasive racism that the conscious promotion of Black volunteers sought to address.

Vaughn Love, who experienced racism from an IB commissar, took a pragmatic, pedagogic approach to racist incidents. Recognizing the depth of racial prejudice in American society, Love saw the experience of being commanded by African Americans as part of a necessary education for white volunteers, and some resistance to it as inevitable. Describing the IWO with "white members and Black members in the branch" as "the training ground" for a future interracial society, Love described the IBs in similar terms.[63] He also noted that in the American IB units, unlike in other American institutions, incidents of racism were strictly punished.

For Love, the brigades epitomized the pioneering role of the Communist movement in the fight for civil rights. It was this that had attracted him to the League of Struggle for Negro Rights (LSNR) and the IWO in the early 1930s and that kept him supporting the movement and even the USSR long after the war. His time in Spain confirmed his convictions. Remembering the admiration and respect shown to Black political leaders by their white comrades, he wrote, "I was in good company indeed."[64] Other African American IB veterans echoed these sentiments. "I felt like a human being, like a man," remembered Crawford Morgan. "I was treated like all the rest of the people were treated, and when you have been in the world for quite a long time and have been treated worse than people treat their dogs, it is quite a nice feeling."[65]

Love's experience of radical inclusion in the IBs seems to have consolidated his belief that the Communist movement and its "battle against Fascism" was where African Americans "belonged."[66] Rejecting the Pan-Africanism and Black separatism advocated by some civil rights activists, African American Communists such as Love and Thompson saw the way to Black liberation in the "common struggle" alongside other "minority peoples . . . victimized by Fascism."[67] This belief was clearly articulated by spokespeople such as Thompson and Langston Hughes when grappling with the uncomfortable reality that found African American IB volunteers fighting African soldiers in Franco's army. In one of his poems from Spain, Hughes used a fictional encounter between a Black Lincoln and a mercenary "Moor" to express his certainty that the fight for a "free Spain" was also a fight against colonialism and thus for a free Africa.[68] Although pushing back against the racist tropes of a "Moroccan invasion" that permeated Loyalist propaganda, Hughes, like Thompson, portrayed the Moors as "dupes" fighting for the very forces that sought to oppress them. Juxtaposing their use as "cannon fodder" with the respect shown to Black IB volunteers, he echoed Love's conviction that the latter were on the right side of Black history.[69]

In an open letter published on Abraham Lincoln Day 1938, Love and four other Black volunteers reiterated the claim that a victory in Spain would "result in the liberation of Ethiopia . . . the symbol of freedom for the Negro peoples of the world." Addressing African Americans who, concerned with racism at home, did not see the war in Spain as their battle, the Black Lincolns insisted otherwise. Comparing Hitler, Mussolini, and Franco—now pursuing the "enslavement" of Ethiopia and Spain—to American slaveowners, they presented the war in Spain as a chance to fight back against these forces. In the IBs, Black Americans were doing so as equals and as leaders, under the banner of Lincoln, "the great liberator."[70]

The battle against "the forces that enslave us" thus took on special meaning for Black volunteers who, as was the case with other ethnic and national IB contingents, were portrayed as fighting a dual battle in Spain—for their own liberation and for that of all humanity. Indeed, the IBs were upheld as proof of the Communist doctrine that national and international liberation were inextricably linked, and that the route to any people's freedom lay in their participation as equals in the common struggle—a struggle whose current priority was the defeat of fascism. Love, who worked particularly closely with Jewish IWO comrades, believed this doctrine fervently. "I had read Hitler's book . . . and I knew that if the Jews weren't going to be allowed to live . . . the Negroes would not escape. . . . We would be at the top of the list." Like many other IB veterans, Love would later serve in the US army, where he delivered political lectures to Black troops "to awaken black pride" and counter their prevailing sentiment that this "was not our war."[71] Echoing a central feature of "Lincoln Brigade" propaganda, Love continued to hold up a mirror between American racism and that of their enemy, calling publicly for mixed Black and white regiments "to defeat Hitler's racial theories."[72]

"'Nu' (as Our Commandante Says)"

While Black volunteers fought to defend Spain from "enslavement," propaganda celebrating Jewish volunteers compared the fascist onslaught to the Spanish inquisition. A book about the Jewish Lincolns, *Lebns farn lebn* ([They gave their] lives for life) produced in 1939 by the graduating class of an IWO *shule* (children's Yiddish supplementary school) in the Bronx, opened with the following words from FALB chairman David McKelvey-White: "During the 15th century the over-civilized barbarians of Spain—far ahead of Hitler . . . drove the Jews from this country with fire and violence. . . . They little thought that five centuries later Jews would return from a continent as yet unknown to help defend Spain from a fresh outburst of the old terror."[73]

Like similar appeals to Black national sentiment, such invocations of Jewish history were aimed at winning wider Jewish support at a time when, despite widespread concern for what was happening in Europe, many American Jews were still reluctant to join the anti-fascist cause. While Love argued that, as victims of racism, African Americans "belonged" in the anti-fascist movement, McKelvey-White insisted that, as the "scapegoats" of fascism, it was incumbent on "the Jewish people" to "firmly challenge" it, alongside "all who hate hatred and bitterness, who love liberty and justice."[74] For volunteers who had grown up within the milieu of the CPUSA and IWO Jewish Sections, this belief was at the core of their Jewish identities. Paul Sigel, for example, described his shock at learning from a group of volunteers from Palestine that in the *Yishuv*, "chauvinism towards the Arabs is even greater than that of Hitler's Germany toward the Jews." "It seems inconceivable to me," he continued, "that the Jews who are experiencing such terrific chauvinism in Germany, Poland, etc., should not see how such actions split and disrupt the power of the working class especially when fighting such a powerful enemy as fascism or British imperialism."[75] Like Love, Sigel saw the proletarian struggle, and not any national movement, as the natural home of oppressed minorities.

Yet while this activist understanding of Jewishness may have informed the actions of Jewish Communists—including that of volunteering—contemporary sources suggest that most American Jewish volunteers did not see themselves as fighting a *Jewish* battle in Spain. George Watt (Israel Kwatt) helped rally support for the Spanish Loyalists at Camp Kinderland, yet made no mention of his Jewishness in his many letters from Spain. Meloff, proud to see so many "brother Jews around," also did not express specifically Jewish motivations. Even in a propagandistic Yiddish postcard, stating the volunteers' readiness "to deliver the enemy a blow he won't recover from," Meloff did not mention the particular threat posed by that enemy to Jews. The same is true of camp leader and lifeguard Ephraim Bromberg's Yiddish note from the front, sent back to Kinderland on a handkerchief.[76]

When these Jewish volunteers did mention the specific antisemitic threat, it was usually—as in Sigel's remarks above—in a context of criticizing other Jews who were seemingly turning a blind eye. Indeed, in contradiction to postwar attempts to incorporate the Jewish IB volunteers into a national narrative of Jewish resistance to the Holocaust, evidence shows that the Jewish "Lincolns" often felt themselves at odds with other Jews outside of the Communist milieu. Echoing Sigel, Howard Smith described his outrage at the apparent apathy of diners in a Jewish restaurant in Barcelona: "Spain is at war with exactly those people who have and are persecuting Jews. But do you think these bastards would do what one would expect any man to do—join in the fight?" For Smith this "disgusting lot" had failed "their duty only as Jews if nothing else." While Love and Thompson drew a distinction between the Black brigaders and the mercenary "Moors" who had been "duped" to fight for Franco, Smith differentiated between different "types" of Jews. He was glad to be among the "type . . . who have proven themselves in the IB."[77]

As Gerben Zaagsma underlines in his history of the Jewish-Polish Botwin Company, the motivations and experiences of Jewish IB volunteers should be considered in the context of the leftist movements of which they were part and of the pre-Holocaust era in which they fought.[78] While propaganda aimed at a wider Jewish audience may have emphasized Jewish concerns, within the movement, Jewish and proletarian identities were so inextricably linked that it seems that no such emphasis was necessary. In contrast to McKelvey-White's English-language introduction, in his Yiddish introduction to *Lebns farn lebn*, IWO *shules* secretary Itche Goldberg did not present the Jewish volunteers as fighting a Jewish battle against their people's enemies, but as part of an international, internationalist struggle.

Describing the great pride of the Bronx's Allerton Avenue Coop in "the sons that it had raised," who were sacrificing their lives "for human freedom,"

Goldberg stressed not the volunteers' Jewishness, but their generational place in the movement. Class teacher and director of the book project Bezalel Freedman, while excited about the anti-fascist war's potential to inspire Yiddish creativity, described the Jewish volunteers quite simply as his students' "older brothers and sisters."[79] Like the volunteers' letters, *Lebns farn lebn* reveals the importance of the IWO as a community. It is also an example of the powerful role played by the IB volunteers in inspiring the following generation of activists.

It is this picture of an activist community and Jewish identity rooted in activism that shines from Meloff's affectionate references to Camp Kinderland, as well as in the limited camp records from this period. Presenting the summer camp and its milieu as something of a training ground, Meloff joked that the "Kinderland in his blood" gave him the courage to lead a "ghoulish raiding party" behind enemy lines. Meanwhile, across the Atlantic, the Kinderland bunks were divided into "loyalist" versus "fascist" for a special Spain-themed game of capture the flag. With the "fascist" bunk unwilling either to win or concede, the game ended with the flag in Lake Sylvan.[80] Following the news of Arion's death in July 1937, a small memorial was built at Kinderland by Swedish camp worker Nils Berg, who had fought alongside the Convulsionaries but was repatriated after "he had his fingers shot off."[81] Pictures of the memorial—a model cannon bearing the flags of the Spanish Popular Front—show no hint of Jewish iconography (see figure 11.3).

For many Jewish American volunteers, the war in Spain—where they witnessed the terrors that the fascist powers were willing to unleash on civilians, and fought alongside self-identifying, Yiddish-speaking Jewish volunteers from eastern Europe—did prompt reflection about their position as Jews in the struggle against fascism. We see this in Harold Smith's letter about the Jewish restaurant in Barcelona, written in 1938, as well as in certain elements of *Lebns farn lebn*, published in 1939. For those who survived, their actions in Spain would naturally take on new significance when they looked back after the Holocaust. George Watt admitted, "When we went to Spain we saw ourselves primarily as internationalists. . . . Not Jews, primarily." Nonetheless, he saw his Jewishness as a fundamental influence on the politics and values that had led him to Spain.[82]

Perhaps the question of "whether we all fought out of our Jewishness" is, as Watt argued, less important than the fact that "Jews did fight against Hitler . . . even before the general threat of Hitlerism was understood." For our purposes, evidence suggests most Jewish Lincolns volunteered primarily as committed Communists, anti-fascists, and internationalists. The Jewish identities of those studied here seem to have been almost inseparable from their political values. While many ethnic groups celebrated "their" volunteers in quasi-national terms, it has also been argued that, with the CPUSA using the multiethnic Lincolns as a symbol of its claim that "Communism is the Americanism of the 20th century," the IBs offered volunteers the chance to cast off their ethnic origins and assert

FIGURE 11.3. Members of the Kinderland Young Communist League group pose around a monument dedicated to Ernest Arion, built by IB veteran Nils Waldemar Berg. Photo by Ben Itzkowitz, August 7, 1937. ALBA.439, box 19, folder 1.

their identity as Americans.[83] In the letters under study here, a different assimilatory aim stands out: the desire to become good Bolsheviks.

"A Marvelous Experience for a Bolshevik"

A recurring theme in the letters of the Convulsionaries and their comrades presents Spain as a site of "real" Bolshevik activity and an opportunity for Communist self-improvement. While McLaughlin was congratulated for having "gone the way of all good Bolsheviks," Smith expressed his hope that with this "invaluable" training and experience, "I'll have built the foundation of a good Communist." Meloff, who confessed his longing "for a job like Bedacht's," wrote: "This army does straighten you out.... I'll be able to tackle and <u>finish</u> much greater problems than ever confronted me before." For Paul Sigel, the IBs offered "a chance to prove (especially to myself) my own capabilities.... The chance I was looking for." In Spain, he felt that "all of me, all of my actions are keeping in step with the progress of the world towards a new civilization, towards a decent social order and my one aim is to keep constantly in step until (and long after) that end has been attained." Watt—who, already working for the Party, was made a political commissar in Spain—saw himself facing "the test which [Comintern general secretary Georgi] Dimitrov spoke of when he laid down certain principles of Bolshevik leadership—the test of fire—of suffering—jail—war. The Bolshevik who has shown his steel in the bitterest and hardest struggles of all."[84]

Revealing the ambition of these young men and their dedication to the movement, these proclamations illustrate the extent to which Communists viewed Spain as the "battlefront of the world," and the IB volunteers as a vanguard within a vanguard. Reading these sentiments in letters sent home, often to female comrades, it is hard to ignore the hierarchy this created, nor its gendered dimension. As Sadkin put it, while Pat was in the front lines taking "a good solid crack" at "the hideous aims of Fascism . . . we, on this end, can combat it only in slower, milder ways. When one's blood boils with hatred of Fascism, these mild ways seem insufficient." Feeling her own work was "not nearly as important," Sadkin admitted, "I realize how envious I am of all of you." "A marvelous experience for a Bolshevik," the Spanish experience was mostly reserved for Communist men.[85]

As in Smith's above-cited letter, volunteering was an opportunity to prove oneself as "a real Communist man."[86] Meloff's macho posturing is particularly striking, often descending into outright misogyny and homophobia. Complaining frequently about what he referred to as the "No Fuckeran" policy of the American IB leadership, on one occasion he even made an inappropriate request of Sigel, which she evidently refused. Begging her not to "underestimate him," he blamed his fear of "going 'fruit,'" adding with alarm that some of the boys, including Arion, were "beginning to ogle eyes at each other." Associating "going fruit" with certain "feminine" activities such as "washing our clothes, and yes, even sewing buttons on our underwear," Meloff boasted, "Rather than do that, I threw them away and go around without."[87] He joked that Sigel might sew his buttons for him when he returned—a suggestion he seemed to know would not be greeted favorably.

Meloff's misogyny is even starker in his letters to a male comrade, Kinderlandnik Julius Blickstein. "I call my gun 'Lil' Liza the whore,'" he joked, "as she already seems to have been used by other men." Later, on leave in Madrid, he boasted that he "got drunk and vicious and beat up the whore who spent the night with me at the hotel." Adding, "She deserved it, the bitch, charging me 150 pesetas!" he continued, cheerfully, "I came back still soused, and went to bed singing."[88] It is worth noting that Meloff wrote these last comments after his first experience of battle and Arion's traumatic death. Read against the helplessness of a previous letter, it seems that such expressions of what Kirschenbaum describes as "rough masculinity" helped this young man reassert a sense of power.[89] Especially when combined with the rigid and increasingly paranoid expectations of correct Communist behavior, this could have dreadful results.

"The Old God-Damn Trotsky Menace"

If outbursts of misogyny and homophobia are a jarring reminder of "the limits of the communist commitment to emancipation," so too are references to the "Trotsky menace," which, common in volunteer letters and frequently blamed for military failures, illustrate the perniciousness of Stalinist paranoia.[90] The belief in a Trotskyist-fascist conspiracy to defeat the republic and the anti-fascist movement from within was widespread. Deviation from expected Communist behavior—including ideals of masculinity—could quickly lead to suspicion of "Trotskyism" and, by extension, even fascist sympathies. Believing that "anybody who tries to break the wonderful unity of the Popular Front here is a member of Franco's fifth column," Meloff wrote, "It's absolutely essential to get rid of the bastard Trotskyites who tried to disrupt this unity."[91] He could not have suspected that such ruthless suspicion, combined with the exhaustion and violence of war, would lead to the death of his cousin Bernie.

According to IB records, Bernie Abramofsky—who Harry joked "had to travel to Spain to be permitted as a full-fledged 'Convulsionary'"—was only seventeen years old when he volunteered. A member of the Communist Party since the age of sixteen, he was, like his cousin, an active member of the IWO and its Youth Theater. His experience in the Reserve Officers Training Corps soon earned him a promotion in Spain, prompting Meloff to quip that "the bastard will probably wind up a major-general." Yet things quickly changed once the group entered combat on July 7, 1937. Ernie Arion was manning a machine gun during one of the first charges when, according to Love, "The top of his head was blown off by an anti-tank round." Describing the battle as "nothing but a continuous nightmare," Meloff was haunted by "that look of surprise in his eyes, as the bullet penetrated."[92] Abramofsky, meanwhile, collapsed, and had to be carried away on a stretcher.

One report states he suffered a concussion, another, "shell-shock." Another document, revealing that Abramofsky had requested and been denied repatriation to the United States, claims that after one "day in the lines" he was "so much affected" by the "death of a close friend" that he "became a nuisance" and "requires stabilization."[93] Some of his comrades, including Battalion Commander Milton Wolff, observing that "not a single bullet had hit him," suspected that he was "pretending."[94] Struggling under the scorching sun and with bullets and shells raining around them, his fellow brigaders quickly became resentful of what they saw as weak, uncomradely, and even effeminate behavior, which was also sometimes seen as an indication of Trotskyist and fascist tendencies.

After a period in hospital, Bernie was returned to the IB base at Albacete. Paul Sigel, meeting him there in late July, reassured Miriam that "he had been bruised a little while at the front with the Washington Battalion but he's perfectly o.k. now." Meloff, though, was worried. "Cousin Bernie has disappeared and I don't know where the hell he is. . . . I hope he doesn't get into any trouble." Even after Bedacht's reassurance that "Bernie was not wounded" but "was 'cooling his heels' in Albacete," Meloff remained concerned, apparently aware of the rumors about his cousin's un-Communist behavior. In late August, he finally received a note from Bernie, "which said not to believe any [redacted by censor] rumors. . . . They are all lies and . . . he is sick and expects to go home soon." Meloff continued, "I'm not sore at him anyway. I appreciate now, what war can do to a guy, and Bernie was nothing compared to the others. He still has qualities that are good, and they must be brought out."[95] A demonstration that personal ties could temper the expectations of the movement, Meloff's words also reveal just how high those expectations were.

This was one of Meloff's last letters. On September 15, 1937, he was killed in action at Belchite. In mid-November, Bernie Abramofsky deserted. Along with two others—Jacob Rotter (Philip Conway) and Albert Wallach, who was also associated with the IWO—he presented himself to the US consul in Valencia asking to be repatriated. Complaining, as many deserters did, that the volunteers had been wrongfully told they were signing up for only six months, they offered to cooperate with the US government "to stop other American boys from coming over here to be slaughtered." In a story that remains unsubstantiated, they also claimed that twenty-five other Americans who had demanded repatriation on the same grounds had recently been executed. Wallach—whose father later charged the IWO with recruiting his son—claimed that he had come to Spain "primarily to do investigative work regarding the Communist Party."[96] Unfortunately for the young volunteers, following testimony that was sure to earn the ire of IB leadership, the consular officials did not help them.

Traveling to Barcelona, they were also dismissed by the unsympathetic US military attaché, who, echoing the militarism of some IB leaders, described them as "typical cowards fleeing from danger."[97] With few options, they turned to "elements in the shadows" for help to get across the French border. According to Russian-born American volunteer turned Military Intelligence Service (SIM) agent Conrad Kaye, these "elements" were part of a foreign spy network working against the republic with connections to the Gestapo.[98] This suspicion is repeated in Abramofsky's file, which claims that the young Jew from Brooklyn had formed "relationships with Gestapo agents." On December 10, 1937, Kaye arrested the three deserters. In January they were sent to prison in Albacete. Another IWO member, Jewish theater activist and occasional Convulsionary, Milton White, who went AWOL in December 1937, seems to have been implicated with Abramofsky but was sentenced only to a labor battalion.[99]

Returned to the lines in late February or early March, when the brigades were severely depleted, Bernie deserted again. Presenting himself to IB authorities in Barcelona in April 1938 with concerns about a wound, he deserted a third time and was again arrested. Sent back under guard to his battalion, now stationed on the north bank of the Ebro, he arrived following some of the worst months for the exhausted Lincolns. For those who had remained at their posts without sleep, food, ammunition, or toilet paper, "deserters were not very much appreciated." For the battalion commanders, Abramofsky was, quite simply, a problem. Having now deserted three times and suspected—however questionably—of links with Gestapo agents, he needed constant guarding at a time when they were already short of men. At "a simple meeting between commissars and officers," the decision was taken to execute him.[100] Late one night, Bernie was shot in the back of the head by an American volunteer.

Volunteers for Liberty?

Unsurprisingly, Bernie's death caused great unease in the battalion. At least three Lincolns—Harry Fisher, John Murra, and Paul Blake—refused to take part in the execution when asked, expressing their outrage to Political Commissar John Gates, who Fisher continued to blame for years to come.[101] Yet the matter has never been brought to light, and it is still not known who pulled the trigger. Perhaps if it had not been for the postwar Red Scare and the dissolution of the IWO in the 1950s, the celebration of Meloff as a hero would have prompted an investigation into what happened to his cousin.

Stories such as Bernie's unavoidably undermine the IBs' reputation as "volunteers for liberty." Indeed, some volunteers—such as William Herrick, who grew up in the same Jewish-Communist New York milieu as the Convulsionaries—left the Party after witnessing its repressive actions against the anti-Stalinist left in Spain, claiming, as did other leftists, that the Communists had betrayed the Spanish revolution. The signing of the Molotov-Ribbentrop Pact just months after Franco's victory would prompt another wave of defections, including from within the ranks of the IWO.

Yet even for many ex-Communists, the Spanish experience remained sacred—the last great stand not only against fascism but of their own cause before it became fully corrupted by Stalinism. For Vaughn Love, the Party's crucial role in Spain and his own experience of its commitment to anti-racism convinced him to remain loyal through the years of the Soviet-Nazi pact and even later. The radical solidarity of life at the front, of singing revolutionary songs simultaneously in multiple languages, of Black and Jewish Americans fighting alongside each other against an enemy that represented the epitome of antisemitic white supremacy, stand in uneasy contrast with stories such as Bernie Abramofsky's.

Since their creation, the nature of the International Brigades and Soviet-Comintern aid to Republican Spain have been hotly contested. While some have seen the IBs as a "Comintern Army" of brainwashed Stalinists, others still celebrate them as the heroic "defenders of democracy," the "premature anti-fascists" who stood up to the threat posed by Hitler and Mussolini while Western governments were still appeasing them.[102] The story of these young volunteers demonstrates that there are elements of truth in both these narratives.

While the revolution may have been temporarily subordinated to the need, in Meloff's words, "to make the world safe for democracy," it remained the ultimate aim. The "final victory" envisioned by the activists was not that of liberal democracy, which, in the era of the Depression, had failed them. Neither was it, as anti-Communist scholars have claimed, the installation of a Soviet puppet regime in Spain. It was, in their own words "a new world and a better civilization," a society not of "master + slave, but comrade & comrade, from each as he can do, to each as he needs."[103] To them, the Communist movement represented the vanguard in the fight for such a world, and the IBs the vanguard within that vanguard.

To be sure, this commitment to a better world was greatly undermined by its limitations. It was also ultimately betrayed by Soviet-Communist leaders. It is precisely these contradictions that make the volunteers' story so interesting, so important, and, at times, so tragic. Acting during a key turning point in its history, the International Brigades and wider Aid Spain campaign offer an essential case study through which to understand the complexities of the formidable movement that was international Communism.

NOTES

1. "Anti-Fascist Athletes Condemn Nazi Games," *Daily Worker* (henceforth *DW*), July 3, 1936, 5; "American Team for Olimpiada Popular," n.d., Bernard Danchik Papers, ALBA.033, box 1, folder 8, Abraham Lincoln Brigade Archives, Tamiment Library and Robert F. Wagner Archives, New York University, New York, New York (hereafter Tamiment/Wagner, NYU).
2. "Anti-Fascist Athletes Condemn Nazi Games."
3. Telegram from Olimpopular to Fair Play, June 27, 1936, Danchik Papers, ALBA.033, box 1, folder 3; "Answering Hitler's Olympics," *DW*, July 8, 1936.
4. "20,000 Hear Hathaway at Garden Meeting to Aid Spain," *DW*, August 20, 1936, 2; "How Workers Fought in Barcelona," *DW*, August 8, 1936, 7; "A lebediker grus fun bartselone" [A merry greeting from Barcelona], *Naye Prese* [New press], July 26, 1936, 2; "How Workers Fought in Barcelona," *DW*, August 8, 1936, 7.
5. "Athletes Spike Horror Stories," *DW*, August 4, 1936, 2; Olimpopular to Fair Play, June 27, 1936.
6. Quotation from heading comes from "IWO Gives $2,500 Check at Spain Rally," *DW*, October 28, 1936, 2; "Rally at Garden to Aid Spain," *DW*, August 17, 1936, 1; "Anti-Fascists in East and Midwest Build Fund to Support Struggle of Spanish Government," *DW*, August 25, 1936, 6; "Protest Today at Consulates," *DW*, August 19, 1936, 1–2.
7. "Aid Spain: IWO Renews Proposal to Workmen's Circle for Joint Action," *DW*, August 13, 1936, 8; "Society to Aid Loyalists," *New York Times*, December 27, 1936, 25; "I.W.O Sends $2,500 to Spanish Defense," *DW*, August 28, 1936, 6; "IWO gives $2,500," *DW*, October 28, 1936, 2.
8. "Caballero Asks Americans Aid Defend Spain," *DW*, October 27, 1936, 1, 4 (quote on 4); letter from Dr. H. Feltenstein to Anna Louise Strong, February 11, 1937, Spanish Refugee Relief Association Records (henceforth SRRAR), box 84, Columbia University Rare Book and Manuscript Library, Columbia University, New York, New York.
9. Letter from Col. Frank T. Woodberry to David Green, October 8, 1937, box 83, SRRAR; letter from Russell Thayer to Max Bedacht, December 16, 1937, box 83, SRRAR.
10. House Special Committee on Un-American Activities, *Investigation of Un-American Propaganda Activities in the United States*, vol. 1, *August 12–23, 1938*, appendix part 9, Communist Front Organizations (US GPO, 1938), 856; Robert M. Zecker, *"A Road to Peace and Freedom": The International Workers Order and the Struggle for Economic Justice and Civil Rights, 1930–1954* (Temple University Press, 2018).
11. Letter from Max Bedacht to Herman F. Reissig, January 21, 1937, box 83, SRRAR; Negro People's Committee meeting minutes, December 19, 1938, box 75, folder 4, SRRAR; letter from John Sherman to IWO, April 23, 1937, box 83, SRRAR; "Na IWO ambulanc pre Španielskych Bojovníkov" [IWO sends ambulance to Spanish fighters], *Ľudový denník* [People's daily], May 22, 1937, 1; "Diety Slov. Rob. Školy na Pomoc Španielsku" [Slovak workers' children's school aids Spanish Loyalists], *Ľudový denník*, January 8, 1937, 6; letter from Onni Kaartinen to Comrade Vernon, August 10, 1937, fond 545, inventory 3, file 437, pages 106–7 (106), Russian State Archive of Socio-Political History (henceforth, RGASPI), Moscow.
12. Letter from Max Bedacht to Roger Baldwin, January 8, 1937, box 83, SRRAR; "Our Coming Campaigns," [1937?], International Workers Order (IWO) Records #5276, box 49, folder 16, Kheel Center for Labor-Management Documentation and Archives, Catherwood Library, Cornell University, Ithaca, New York (henceforth Kheel), https://digital.library.cornell.edu/catalog/ss:19043966. The document is undated and has been catalogued alongside others from 1939; however, its contents, referring to the volunteers still in Spain, and the Order's third national convention, indicate that it is from 1937.

13. Quotation in heading letter from the Halpern family (Clara) to Patrick Roe McLaughlin, April 2, 1937, fond 545, inventory 3, file 437, document 32, RGASPI; Irving Goff interviewed by John Gerassi, August 24, 1980, audio file, John Gerassi Oral History Collection, ALBA.AUDIO.018, https://hdl.handle.net/2333.1/4j0zpps7; A. L. Harris to Bernie Danchik, January 4, 1937, box 83, SRRAR; Allan Chase to Spanish Workers Club, December 24, 1936, box 79, folder 1, SRRAR.

14. Letter from Sylvia Sadkin to Patrick Roe McLaughlin, May 31, 1937, fond 545, inventory 3, file 437, pages 69–74, RGASPI; letter from Sylvia Sadkin to Patrick Roe McLaughlin, March 26, 1937, fond 545, inventory 3, file 437, pages 19–22, RGASPI.

15. "Kids in I.W.O. Give for Spain," *DW*, March 6, 1937, 4; letter from William Crookston to Ernest Rymer, March 23, 1937, box 83, SRRAR.

16. Halpern to McLaughlin, April 2, 1937, 32; Sadkin to McLaughlin, May 31, 1937, 72.

17. "Reds Here Protest Nazis' Aid in Spain," *New York Times*, November 29, 1936, 32.

18. Peter N. Carroll, *The Odyssey of the Abraham Lincoln Brigade: Americans in the Spanish Civil War* (Stanford University Press, 1994), 9–10.

19. William Herrick, *Jumping the Line: The Adventures and Misadventures of an American Radical* (University of Wisconsin Press, 1998), 133.

20. Report on political activities of Felix Kusman, fond 545, inventory 3, file 453, pages 136–37, RGASPI. "Language organizations" and "language bureaus" were terms used by Communist Parties to designate Party subsections and affiliated organizations established to agitate within immigrant communities in their native languages.

21. Zecker, "A Road to Peace and Freedom," 180; House Special Committee, *Investigation*, vol. 13, *April 11–May 21, 1940* (US GPO, 1940), 7730.

22. "Bedacht, IWO Head, Returns from Spain," *DW*, September 20, 1937, 2.

23. Spanish People's Front postcard, Camp Kinderland Records, TAM.439, box 18, folder 5, Tamiment/Wagner, NYU.

24. Advertisements in *DW*, August 14, 1936, 4; press release, Al Alexander Youth Chapter IWO Brooklyn Contemporary Theater (BCT), n.d., New Theater League Records (NTL), box 7, New York Public Library Archives, New York, New York; Harry Meloff Theater Festival program, Miriam Sigel Friedlander Papers, ALBA.192, box 1, folder 12.

25. Letter from Harry Meloff to Miriam Sigel, July 16, 1937, Miriam Sigel Friedlander Papers, ALBA.192, box 1, folder 5.

26. Irving Goff, interview by John Gerassi, August 24, 1980.

27. Press release, BCT, NTL.

28. Giles Tremlett, *The International Brigades: Fascism, Freedom and the Spanish Civil War* (Bloomsbury, 2021), 315.

29. Letter from Ernest Arion to Miriam Sigel, March 20, 1937, Miriam Sigel Friedlander Papers, ALBA.192, box 1, folder 1; letter from Harry Meloff to Miriam Sigel, April 11, 1937, Miriam Sigel Friedlander Papers, ALBA.192, box 1, folder 4.

30. Email from Peter Carroll to Annabel Gottfried Cohen, June 7, 2023; letter from Harold Smith to Jeannette, n.d., Harold Smith Papers, ALBA.99, box 1, folder 22; letter from Meloff to Miriam Sigel, May 2, 1937, Miriam Sigel Friedlander Papers, ALBA 192, box 1, folder 4.

31. Letter from Harry Meloff to Miriam Sigel, May 16, 1937, Miriam Sigel Friedlander Papers, ALBA.192, box 1, folder 4; Meloff to Sigel, May 2, 1937; Meloff to Miriam Sigel, April 11, 1937; letter from Ernest Arion to Miriam Sigel, May 15, 1937, Miriam Sigel Friedlander Papers, box 1, folder 1.

32. Letter from Harry Meloff to Miriam Sigel, May 16, 1937, Miriam Sigel Friedlander Papers, ALBA.192, box 1, folder 4.

33. Lisa Kirschenbaum, *International Communism and the Spanish Civil War: Solidarity and Suspicion* (Cambridge University Press, 2015), 96.

34. Letter from Paul Sigel to Miriam Sigel, September 23, 1937, Miriam Sigel Friedlander Papers, ALBA.192, box 1, folder 6, ALBA; letter from Harry Meloff to Miriam Sigel, May 6, 1937, Miriam Sigel Friedlander Papers, ALBA.192, folder 4; letter from Harry Meloff to Miriam Sigel, August 16, 1937, Miriam Sigel Friedlander Papers, ALBA.192, folder 5; letter from Harold Smith to Jeanette, June 11, 1937, Harold Smith Papers, ALBA.099, folder 5; letter from Harold Smith to Jeanette, June 18, 1938, Harold Smith Papers, ALBA.99, folder 15; Harry Meloff, "Song of the I.B.," Miriam Sigel Friedlander Papers, ALBA.192, box 1, folder 13.

35. "Belchite 1937, Killed in Action, Harry Meloff," clipping from unknown publication, October 15, 1937, Miriam Sigel Friedlander Papers, ALBA.192, box 1, folder 12; Harry Meloff to Miriam Sigel, May 16, 1937, Miriam Sigel Friedlander papers, ALBA.192, box 1, folder 4.

36. Paul Sigel to Miriam Sigel, October 3, 1937, Miriam Sigel Friedlander Papers, ALBA.192, box 1, folder 6; Meloff to Sigel, August 16, 1937.

37. Meloff to Sigel, August 16, 1937; Joseph Azar interview, January 24, 1987, Manny Harriman Video Oral History Collection, ALBA.048, box 1, item ALBA V 48-009.

38. Paul Sigel to Miriam Sigel, September 23, 1937.

39. Sadkin to McLaughlin, March 26, 1937; Meloff to Miriam Sigel, May 16, 1937.

40. Sadkin to McLaughlin, March 26, 1937; Meloff to Sigel, May 16, 1937; Meloff to Sigel, May 6, 1937; letter from Harry Meloff to Julius Blickstein, July 26, 1937, Miriam Sigel Friedlander Papers, ALBA.192, box 1, folder 3.

41. Paul Sigel to Mim [Sigel] and Gang, July 24, 1937; August 3, 1937; August 10, 1937, all in Miriam Sigel Friedlander Papers, ALBA.192, box 1, folder 6.

42. Carroll, *Odyssey*, 17.

43. Meloff to Sigel, August 16, 1937.

44. Halpern to McLaughlin, April 2, 1937; Sadkin to McLaughlin, May 31, 1937.

45. "Our Coming Campaigns."

46. "Don't Fail Them," *DW*, May 24, 1937, 7.

47. House Special Committee, *Investigation*, appendix 9, 1:856.

48. Kaartinen to Vernon, August 10, 1937, 106.

49. Meloff to Sigel, May 16, 1937; Harry Meloff to Miriam Sigel, August 4, 1937, Miriam Sigel Friedlander Papers, ALBA.192, box 1, folder 5.

50. "Bedacht, IWO Head, Returns from Spain," *DW*, September 20, 1937, 2; "IWO to Hold Meeting for Spain," *DW*, September 8, 1937, 2.

51. "IWO to Hold Meeting for Spain."

52. Zecker, *"A Road to Peace and Freedom,"* 161.

53. "IWO Leaders to Speak at Rallies in Chicago Area," *DW*, October 30, 1937, 3; "I.W.O. Bars Jim Crow," *DW*, January 22, 1938, 5; "IWO Hears Pleas for Peace Through Collective Action," *DW*, April 26, 1938, 6.

54. Quotation in heading from Vaughn Love, unpublished postwar memoir, 57, Vaughn Love Papers, ALBA.243; Cesar Fuentes, Sección Hispana [Hispanic Section], "Extra—A todos los ramales y miembros de la I.W.O." [Extra—to all the branches and members of the IWO], box 83, SRRAR.

55. Fraser Ottanelli, "Anti-Fascism and the Shaping of National and Ethnic Identity: Italian American Volunteers in the Spanish Civil War," *Journal of American Ethnic History* 27, no. 1 (2007): 9–31.

56. "'Americans with the Garibaldi'—an interview with John Landy," October 29, 1937, fond 545, inventory 6, file 31, pages 26–28, RGASPI.

57. Zecker, *"A Road to Peace and Freedom,"* 179.

58. Comisariado de las Brigadas Internacionales [International brigades commissariat], *Nuestros Espagnoles* [Our Spaniards] (Madrid, 1937). Quoted in Gerben Zaagsma,

Jewish Volunteers: The International Brigades and the Spanish Civil War (Bloomsbury, 2017), 180.

59. Letter from Naomi to Patrick Roe McLaughlin, August 24, 1937, fond 545, inventory 3, file 437, pages 112–13, RGASPI; "Slovenskí Drotári na Pomoc Španielsku za Práva Chudoby" [Slovak tinkers aid the poor in Spain's war], *Ľudový denník*, April 23, 1937, 1, 5 (quote on 5); see also: "Chicagsky drotár je dnes na Prvej Linii" [Chicago tinkers today are on the front line], *Ľudový denník*, April 23, 1937, 1; "Odpoveď navýzvuslovenských drotárov v Chicagu" [Answer of the Slovak tinkers of Chicago to the provocation], *Ľudový denník*, May 21, 1937, 5; "Slovenskí drotári dobre zastúpeni v Španielsku" [Slovak tinkers well represented in Spain], *Ľudový denník*, May 22, 1937, 1. Janošík was the legendary eighteenth-century Slovak "Robin Hood."

60. "Bombs Fail to Halt Barcelona Fetes for Lincoln Boys," *DW*, November 3, 1938, 2.
61. Carroll, *Odyssey*, 135.
62. "Letters from Our Readers," *DW*, November 9, 1937, 6.
63. Vaughn Love interviewed by John Gerassi, 1980, audio file, John Gerassi Oral History Collection, ALBA.AUDIO.018, https://hdl.handle.net/2333.1/63xsjfcg.
64. Vaughn Love, unpublished memoir, 128.
65. Crawford Morgan interviewed by Peter Carroll, quoted in Carroll, *Odyssey*, 134.
66. Vaughn Love, unpublished memoir, 56.
67. Louise Thompson quoted in Zecker, "A Road to Peace and Freedom," 181.
68. Langston Hughes, "Letter from Spain Addressed to Alabama" (poem), *Volunteer for Liberty*, November 1937, quoted in Sarah Sackman, "The Identity Politics of Jews and African-Americans in the Spanish Civil War" (master's thesis, Cambridge University, 2006), 43.
69. "Hughes Finds Moors Being Used as Pawns by Fascists in Spain," *The Afro-American* (Baltimore), October 30, 1937, 1; Sackman, "Identity Politics," 42–43.
70. "Negroes at Teruel Hail Lincoln Day," *DW*, February 12, 1938, 4; Sadkin to Pat, May 31, 1937.
71. Vaughn Love, interview by Peter Carroll, quoted in Carroll, *Odyssey*, 30, 262.
72. "Calls for Mixed Brigade to Defy Nazi Racism," *DW*, June 8, 1942.
73. David McKelvey-White, introduction to *Lebns farn lebn: Vegn di yidishe voluntirn in shpanye* [Lives for life: About the Jewish volunteers in Spain], ed. Bezalel Friedman (Bronkser mitlshul fun internatsyonaln arbeter ordn, 1939), 4. *Shules* were Yiddish supplementary schools run by the Jewish American Section of the IWO.
74. Vaughn Love, unpublished memoir, 56; McKelvey-White, introduction to *Lebns farn lebn*.
75. Paul Sigel to Mrs. Sigel (mother), July 18, 1937, Miriam Sigel Friedlander Papers, ALBA.192, box 1, folder 7.
76. Letter from Harry Meloff to Julius Blickstein, June 17, 1937, Miriam Sigel Friedlander Papers, ALBA.192, box 1, folder 3; photo in *From Generation to Generation, 75 Years of Camp Kinderland* (Camp Kinderland, May 15, 1999), 14.
77. Letter from Harold Smith to Jeanette, July 22, 1938, Harold Smith Papers, ALBA.099, box 1, folder 17.
78. Zaagsma, *Jewish Volunteers*.
79. Itche Goldberg, "Kedey nit tsu fargesn" [Lest we forget], in Friedman, *Lebns farn lebn*, 5; Bezalel Friedman, "Mir shtoltsirn mit aykh" [We are proud of you], in Friedman, *Lebns farn lebn*, 6.
80. Meloff to Sigel, August 4, 1937; "Spanish Civil War and Peace Olympics at Kinderland" (Pauline Katz interviewed by Lesley Yalen, May 16, 2011), YouTube, 2 min., 12 sec., Wexler Oral History Project, Yiddish Book Center, Amherst, Massachusetts, https://www.yiddishbookcenter.org/collections/oral-histories/excerpts/woh-ex-0000222/spanish-civil-war-and-peace-olympics-kinderland.

81. "Dedication of Ernie Norris [sic] Memorial," August 1937, annotated loose scrapbook page with photos, Camp Kinderland Records, TAM.439, box 19, folder 1. From other photos and the date it is clear that this photo is of the monument built to Ernest Arion and that "Norris" was an error. Letter from Harry Meloff to Sigel, June 19, 1937, ALBA.192, box 1, folder 5.

82. Kara Schoonmaker, "Salud y Shalom: American Jews in the Spanish Civil War; George Watt," *Stroum Center for Jewish Studies, University of Washington* (blog), accessed August 21, 2023, https://jewishstudies.washington.edu/american-jews-spanish-civil-war/george-watt/.

83. Schoonmaker, "Salud y Shalom"; Ottanelli, "Anti-Fascism"; Sackman, "Identity Politics."

84. Naomi to McLaughlin, August 24, 1937, 112; letter from Harold Smith to Jeanette, December 13, 1937, ALBA.099, box 1, folder 10; Meloff to Sigel, May 2, 1937, his emphasis; Paul to Mim and Gang, August 19, 1937; letter from Paul to Mim (Miriam Sigel), Bert and Gang, August 29, 1937, Miriam Sigel Friedlander Papers, ALBA.192, box 1, folder 6; letter from George Watt to Ruth Watt, September 27, 1937, Watt Family Papers, ALBA.193, box 4, folder 1.

85. Langston Hughes, quoted in Sackman, "Identity Politics," 5; Sadkin to McLaughlin, May 31, 1937; letter from Harry Meloff to Julius Blickstein, May 26, 1937, Miriam Sigel Friedlander Papers, ALBA.192, box 1, folder 3.

86. Kirschenbaum, *International Communism*, 170.

87. Meloff to Sigel, May 6, 1937.

88. Letter from Harry Meloff to Julius Blickstein, June 26, 1937, Miriam Sigel Friedlander Papers, ALBA.192, box 1, folder 3; letter from Harry Meloff to Julius Blickstein, August 29, 1937, Miriam Sigel Friedlander Papers, ALBA.192, box 1, folder 3.

89. Kirschenbaum, *International Communism*, 168.

90. Quote in heading from Meloff to Sigel, May 2, 1937; Kirschenbaum, *International Communism*, 152.

91. Meloff to Blickstein, August 29, 1937.

92. Letter from Harry Meloff to Sigel, March 22, 1937, Miriam Sigel Friedlander Papers, ALBA 192, box 1, folder 4; Vaughn Love, unpublished memoir, 63; letter from Harry Meloff to Miriam Sigel, August 28, 1937, Miriam Sigel Friedlander Papers, ALBA.192, box 1, folder 5.

93. Conrad Kaye report on the arrest of Bernard Abramofsky, Albert Wallach, and Jacob Ritter, fond 545, inventory 6, file 1008, page 58, RGASPI; report in Bernard Abramofsky/Abramowski [sic] personnel file, January 16, 1938, fond 545, inventory 6, file 855, page 29, RGASPI; "List of Repatriated Comrades up to July 1st," fond 543, inventory 6, file 53; see also: Alfonso López Borgoñoz, *Rasgando la niebla: El caso de los brigadistas Albert Wallach y Anthony de Maio; Castelldefels ante el Comité de Actividades Antiestadounidenses* [Tearing through the fog: The case of the brigadistas Albert Wallach and Anthony de Maio; Castelldefels before the Committee of Un-American Activities] (Albedo Fulldome, 2019), 2:80.

94. Carroll, *Odyssey*, 186.

95. Paul Sigel to Mim and Gang, July 24, 1937; Meloff to Blickstein, July 30, 1937, Miriam Sigel Friedlander Papers, box 1, folder 3; Meloff to Sigel, August 4, 1937; Meloff to Sigel, August 16, 1937.

96. Carroll, *Odyssey*, 184.

97. Carroll, *Odyssey*, 185.

98. Kaye report, 58, 64.

99. Abramofsky personnel file, 28, 29; White personnel file, fond 545, inventory 6, file 1012, page 47, RGASPI.

100. Borgoñoz, *Rasgando la niebla*, 140.
101. Borgoñoz, *Rasgando la niebla*, 142.
102. R. Dan Richardson, *Comintern Army: The International Brigades and the Spanish Civil War* (University Press of Kentucky, 1982).
103. Letter from Meloff to Blickstein, April 1, 1937, Miriam Sigel Friedlander Papers, ALBA.192, box 1, folder 3; letter from Patrick Roe McLaughlin to Sylvia Sadkin, published under the heading "We March Shoulder to Shoulder," *DW*, May 24, 1937, 7; Paul to Miriam, September 23, 1937.

Part IV
ENDINGS
Persecution and Legacies—The Shift from the Old to the New Left

The achievements of the IWO and its Old Left allies were impressive, and the interracial solidarities built among white ethnic, Black, Asian, and Latin American comrades show a model of coalition and community-building that speaks to our own tempestuous times. Unsurprisingly, the IWO was regarded with hostility by conservative politicians, not least because of its stress on racial equality. In the end, a Cold War coterie of actors from the House Un-American Activities Committee, the federal Department of Justice, and the New York State Insurance Department dismembered the IWO. Still, as the late Paul Mishler perceptively observed, progressive activism persisted for decades among former members and their ideological heirs.

12

"A FRATERNAL ORDER SENTENCED TO DEATH"

The Legal Persecution of the International Workers Order

Robert M. Zecker

At its height, the International Workers Order (IWO) was a thriving, interracial fraternal-insurance society, providing material aid, emotional and recreational support, and an activist home to more than 188,000 members. The IWO lobbied for humane social legislation such as the Social Security and National Labor Relations Acts, militantly campaigned for racial justice, and enriched members' cultural life. As the Second World War came to an end, members of the Jewish Peoples Fraternal Order (JPFO) living along the Bronx River Parkway were confident their organization was part of the social-democratic coalition working to make Roosevelt's Four Freedoms a reality. African American "concentration lodges" in New York's Harlem and Chicago's South Side expanded as the result of concerted cultural and political community-based organizing. In steel-mill and mining towns, too, Polish and Italian lodges, among other lodges of the IWO's sixteen language societies, served as vibrant community hubs, with one Slavic lodge secretary calling the Order "the head of a big family."[1] From such vantage points it seemed the IWO's position was secure.

Even at the Order's height, however, members were vulnerable to the machinations of anti-Communist politicians who took special pains to target interracial and immigrant rights organizations as "Red." The Party membership of some IWO officers, including general secretary Max Bedacht and Black vice president Louise Thompson, caused officials to bring action against the Order and its members as early as the 1930s. It is perhaps a testament to the dedication of the Order's progressive members that the organization lasted twenty-four years. But by 1954 the actions of conservative state and federal officials had doomed the IWO, subjecting the society to a process of "liquidation" (the Stalinist subtext of New York's term for the IWO's dismemberment was likely unintentional). During the Cold War, an escalating series of government restrictions uniquely hobbled the IWO, rendering it "a fraternal order sentenced to death!"[2]

From the start of the organization, foreign-born members were vulnerable to government suppression. In 1932 Rubin Saltzman of the Jewish section warned members that the Dies Bill stipulated deportation of a foreign-born resident who "believes in, advises, advocates or teaches the overthrow by force or violence the Government of the United States." Saltzman saw this measure as "the highest mark of vicious anti-foreign born legislation." He urged IWO members to act to defeat this "white terror legislation" sponsored by Texas congressman Martin Dies, later chair of the House Un-American Activities Committee.[3]

Saltzman was right to worry. Deportation proceedings were begun against Communist IWO leaders such as Bolesław Gebert, later leader of the Polonia Society, and Sam Milgrom, later Order general secretary. Gebert had already been given a deportation order in 1931 for alleged syndicalist activity in a coal miners' strike, while Milgrom's expulsion was ordered in 1935. Both cases were held in abeyance, in Milgrom's case because his home country declined to accept him. Following World War II, deportation files on the pair were reopened.[4]

As Rachel Buff and Daniel Kanstroom have documented, the Immigration and Naturalization Service (INS) was given wide latitude to act against foreign-born labor activists, which served to suppress the efficacy of unions, IWO labor activists, and members of other organizations aiding workers.[5] In a foreshadowing of twenty-first-century raids on workplaces, in 1932 the American Committee for Protection of Foreign Born (ACPFB), which often worked closely with the IWO, warned that deportation raids had been deployed to break up strikes and the Dies Bill might further criminalize strike activity. The IWO's ethnic societies were urged to pressure legislators for the defeat of anti-immigrant measures inimical to the interests of all workers.[6] And unlike Gebert and Milgrom, not every internee had their cases deferred. The ACPFB, established to advocate on behalf of immigrants, many of them IWO members, also shared officers with the Order, including luminaries such as Vito Marcantonio, Rockwell Kent, Paul Robeson, and Stanley Nowak (of the American-Polish Committee for Protection of Foreign Born).

The threat to radical immigrants was significant. In 1934 the ACPFB publicized the case of John Ujich, detained at Ellis Island subject to deportation to Mussolini's Italy, following arrest "because of his activities in [sic] behalf of the unemployed." Ujich wrote, "When I first saw the Statue of Liberty with her flaming torch I was filled with hope and enthusiasm. Need I tell you how I feel now when I look at the same statue from the prison of Ellis Island, after 25 years of toil and five years of misery and starvation?" The Committee appealed Ujich's deportation in court and urged workers to donate to his defense fund.[7]

Similarly, Slovak IWO member Albert Fenely in 1936 recounted deportation threats leveled at union organizers in Wendel, West Virginia. Fenely lamented cases in which fathers had been deported while American-born wives and children remained behind, stories of family separation later reprised in postwar America. "Is that a humanity?" Fenely asked. "That's monstrous hell." Fenely sent a check in aid of the Slovak Workers Society, as well as taking a subscription to its newspaper, *Ľudový denník* (People's daily), but asked the paper be sent to another town, far from the coal company's prying eyes. Foreign-born IWO members faced a panopticon of repression, even during the New Deal.[8]

A more existential threat to the IWO soon emerged. In 1938 the Massachusetts Insurance Department sought to strip the Order of its license to conduct business. Bedacht warned that "reaction threatens our Order," characterizing the plan as "a foul blow at our Order; . . . a murderous stab at democracy and its principles." Bedacht, as well as general counsel Joseph Brodsky, cautioned that "we must find ways to avoid supplying" insurance departments "formal excuses for such attacks." The action of the Massachusetts Insurance Department came after a legislative committee alleged that "the activities of the International Workers Order have definitely been of a Communistic nature." The insurance department reminded IWO president William Weiner that when it granted the charter, he was told it was "with the understanding that neither the national organization nor any of its branches in Massachusetts will take part in Communistic activities and this shall be the ground of revoking the Order's license if it found that the Order indulges in such activities." The commissioner alleged, Brodsky reported, that "we had used money of the Order to support the Loyalist Government of Spain, to support political parties in Massachusetts, and that our 'New Order' was not an educational or a fraternal organ but was a political publication." Actionable, too, the state argued, was the IWO's support of the Southern Negro Congress. As it would be on the national stage a decade later, the IWO's commitment to racial equality was a red flag to conservatives.[9]

Brodsky appealed the revocation, arguing that publications such as the *New Order* were not political but for the "educational, intellectual, moral, social and religious advantages of its members." He was happy to report that he had convinced the court that no insurance funds had been used for support of Loyalist Spain or any political campaign or organization. In addition, Brodsky reported that the state's high court had ruled that the political beliefs of IWO officers were immaterial, something that would not be the case twelve years later.[10]

Although Bedacht gratefully reported that a similar investigation by the State of New York had been deflected, Brodsky was more cautious. He noted: "Some of the criticisms leveled against us by the examiner in New York are well founded. He says our sick benefit department is very sick; he says we are not charging enough to meet the demands upon it. That constitutes a good reason for any insurance commissioner stepping in." Although the IWO would continue to be rated actuarially sound by New York into the 1950s, Brodsky was already warning in 1938 that it had to be scrupulous in its finances, which also meant fully separating them from its politics. He was gratified when New York accepted his argument that the IWO had the "right to interest ourselves in those issues which face all the people of this country—social security, a health program, etc." Still, the IWO's lawyer warned, other states were scrutinizing them: "Fundamentally, . . . we must realize that we are attacked because we are the organization that we are. Since it is clear that we do not intend to stop our activity as a workers' fraternal organization, it becomes equally clear that we must learn to carry on in a manner least harmful to ourselves." Brodsky cautioned, "Our organization, like Caesar's wife, must be above all suspicion," adding, "Danger signals . . . have been hoisted; let us pay attention to them."[11]

Conservatives' hostility to the Order soon resurfaced. Dies's Un-American Activities Committee in 1939 issued a report condemning the IWO as "possibly one of the most effective and closely knitted organizations among the Communist 'front' organizations." Support for Communist candidates for office (including Bedacht, who in 1934 ran for Senate in New York), participation in "leftwing strikes" and its "foreign and radical elements" were held to prove the IWO's menace to society.[12] In response, the IWO came out swinging. Rallies from Detroit to Harlem heard IWO officials counter: "We are the real patriots and the real Americans." An East Harlem Italian lodge cheered their own congressman Vito Marcantonio's denunciation of Red-baiting when he joined a mass rally, "Against the Dies Committee, for the New Deal." As historian Gerald Meyer noted, "Marc," who was president of the IWO's Garibaldi Society and an Order vice president, remained overwhelmingly popular among his poorer district's Italians and Puerto Ricans; his attacks on HUAC, the House Un-American Activities Committee headed by Dies, only honed his appeal.[13]

Fraternal Outlook, the Order's multilingual monthly magazine, promptly labeled Dies one of the "aspiring tin-horn fascists" seeking "to abridge the Bill of Rights." Bedacht testified before HUAC, revealing nothing more sinister than "that the I.W.O. was a progressive, fraternal organization which welcomes all people into its membership regardless of their race, political creed or color." For the arch-segregationist Dies, this perhaps was subversive enough, for adherents of racial equality were often suspected of Communist leanings by HUAC's segregationist Southern members. The magazine's subscribers, though, were sympathetic to the William Gropper cartoon accompanying the article. A diabolical, top-hatted millionaire tears a copy of the Bill of Rights. "Speaking of 'Un-American Activities,'" ran the caption. The following year a Slovak-language article in the magazine presciently warned of the perils posed to progressive organizations by the Smith Act's overly broad interpretation in criminalizing advocacy of forceful overthrow of the government.[14]

While defiant in public, privately officers were worried. Bedacht confided to an IWO board meeting that the Dies Committee was becoming a fascist fourth branch of government "silencing and hogtying the American public into helplessness."[15] When committee agents raided IWO Philadelphia headquarters, it seemed Bedacht's warnings were coming true. Fortunately, a judge ruled that the raid had violated the organization's rights, although he reserved judgment on whether its material, stored in a government warehouse, had to be returned. While the matter was under deliberation, a series of "Stop Dies" rallies occurred. In Bensonhurst, Brooklyn, a lodge heard Vice President Thompson and speakers from the American Civil Liberties Union, International Labor Defense, and leftist Fur Workers Union decry attacks on the IWO.[16]

In 1939 the IWO was successful in regaining its Philadelphia material, although Dies mused to the *New York Sun*: "If the International Workers Order has nothing to hide, then they will come in now and surrender those records and invite their publication." Bedacht replied, "We will never help you to persecute, to hound and to blacklist innocent people by volunteering to turn over names to your committee," accurately forecasting HUAC's postwar demand that witnesses name names.[17] While the IWO successfully fended off suppression, at the local level intimidation exacted a heavy toll. At a Detroit "Stop Dies" rally, Thompson urged lodge members have their group photo taken for publication in *Fraternal Outlook*, a suggestion that elicited members' alarm. That the lodge meeting was reported by an undercover agent to the Detroit Police's "Red Squad" suggests members had good reason to worry.[18]

Throughout 1941 multiple lodge secretaries feared that being branded Communist had caused trouble in retaining or recruiting members. Sam Klezmer of Indianapolis attributed loss of members to "the reactionary drive against the progressive movement," a view echoed by Joseph Sweedock, secretary of a lodge with Russian but also Spanish-speaking members in Mahanoy City, Pennsylvania. In coal patches, Sweedock reported, "Most members who dropped the IWO quit because of it being too well branded as being red." (Sweedock, though, made no secret of his Party membership.) Likewise, the secretary of a Black lodge in Aliquippa, Pennsylvania, noted that after members signed a petition circulated by headquarters, some lost their jobs, while "some had to face court." "[The] situation is growing worse," the secretary added. "The faithful few needs protection."[19]

Throughout World War II the Dies Committee pressured state insurance departments to bring proceedings against the IWO; in April 1941 Michigan's insurance commissioner demanded "membership lists of that state, which have been requested by the Dies Committee." The Order replied that their membership lists were open to inspection, but would not be turned over to Dies, who, they alleged, was cooperating with the anti-union Ford Motor Company to blacklist IWO members.[20] The following year Bedacht noted "the demand of the Dies Committee that we turn over membership lists and [its] attempt to deprive us of our license in some states." He also complained that some Justice Department officials were preventing IWO members from becoming naturalized, a problem that would reach critical intensity following the war.[21]

While the IWO ardently supported the Second World War, it expressed ambivalence toward government surveillance. The Order worried that the "continued activities of the FBI . . . seem to be guided by the fascist-like mentality of Martin Dies," but nevertheless cheered when the bureau turned its attention to "dealing vigorously with fifth columnists." They likewise approved of the investigation of "fascist" Ukrainian and Polish Americans that the Order labeled "Pilsudski-ites," connecting them to the former right-wing Polish chief of state Józef Piłsudski. As Donna Haverty-Stacke has documented, Communist-affiliated organizations cheered rather than criticized the government when it prosecuted Minneapolis Teamsters in the Trotskyite Socialist Workers Party. Lauding government prosecution of one's enemies, or those whom the IWO perceived as insufficiently loyal to Roosevelt's "win-the-war" administration, set a bad precedent when suppression of the Order later escalated.[22]

During the war, however, Order officials felt they were on the side of the progressive angels in an administration fighting fascism abroad and hunger and need at home. For all his demonization of Dies, in 1943 Bedacht joked the Order should wear its membership on HUAC's "index expurgatoris" as a badge of honor, since it proved the Order deserved a place on "the roll of honor of American anti-fascist organizations."[23] The American Slav Congress, a left-wing, win-the-war consortium of progressive organizations in which the Polonia Society, Slovak Workers Society, and other IWO Slavic nationality branches avidly participated, boasted that the majority of workers in steel, coal, and other essential war industries were Slavic Americans, a claim that would in a few years be cited by a young HUAC member—Richard Nixon—as proof that the Slav Congress was a threat to military readiness! During World War II, however, the Slav Congress and its IWO affiliates publicized congratulatory letters and appearances at conventions by Secretary of the Interior Harold Ickes and Paul McNutt, director of the War Manpower Office. Even Roosevelt lauded the Slav Congress for its patriotic war work. The mayors of Cleveland and Pittsburgh also appeared at wartime IWO rallies to bless the Order.[24]

Although the Office of Strategic Services' Foreign Nationalities Branch (FNB) scrupulously reported on the Polonia Society and other IWO societies, it did not find them overly supportive of or reliant on the Soviet Union. Rather, the FNB regarded Polish American supporters of the Polish Government-in-Exile, who were receiving funds to disseminate conservative propaganda, as more of an impediment to the war effort. During the war, the IWO and its progressive allies seemed on firm political footing.[25]

By 1944, officials of the IWO were confident that the Red-baiting storm had passed. Marcantonio delivered a rousing speech to the Order's national convention: "I hope that the day is not far off when I will not be the only member of Congress who is a member of the International Workers Order. In fact, I am confident. . . . Very soon there will be less Dieses, less Rankins, and more members of the IWO in the halls of Congress!" He added that in 1939, "the Dies Committee was going to destroy the International Workers Order." But "in 1944 . . . the Dies Committee runs to cover, the Dies Committee is dying, and the International Workers Order is growing."[26] The cheering delegates, who had just endorsed Roosevelt's reelection, were confident that reactionaries were on the way out.

They were quickly proven wrong. Attorney General Tom Clark in December 1947 released a list of organizations deemed subversive, with the IWO and all of its nationalities societies included. Of the IWO's 188,000 members, only approximately 10 percent also belonged to the Party, but in the incipient Red Scare, any association with Communists was suspect. While Clark avowed his "Red List" was solely to be used to ascertain the loyalty of government employees, placement on the list soon led to punitive actions. City councils, school boards, the Federal Housing Administration, the Internal Revenue Service—and, for the IWO, most ominously, state insurance departments—used the list to act against the Order, whose existence was predicated on being able to sell insurance. The subversive listing was only the beginning of a seven-year-long death by a thousand cuts.[27]

Judging from meeting minutes and private letters, banishment from the New Deal coalition came as a shock to IWO officers, but they quickly rallied to fight the listing. General Secretary Milgrom, Treasurer Peter Shipka, and President Rockwell Kent sent a letter to all members, alerting them that "the Attorney-General committed an act that might well be considered a new Pearl Harbor against the civil rights of the American people." Members were assured legal action would be taken to lift the subversive designation, which came "without hearing or warning." Lodges were urged to adopt resolutions against the list and send these to congressmen.[28]

Românul American (Romanian American), the newspaper of the IWO's Romanian society, reiterated the condemnation of Clark's "Pearl Harbor against the liberties of the American people," while the Polonia Society paper, *Głos Ludowy* (People's voice), branded Clark's action "despotic and scandalous" and publicized "Protection of American Liberties" rallies held in various cities. The Slovak Workers Society engaged in similar actions, while the Garibaldi Society's Marcantonio railed against Clark's listing, which "denies every element of democratic procedure and fair play." "The IWO has proven its loyalty with deeds," he declared.[29]

Locally, similar actions were taken. The vice president of a JPFO branch sent a letter to Clark condemning his "violation of the constitutional rights of all free peoples" and his "attempt to eliminate all democratic principles." He asserted that the IWO represented "all creeds, races, colors, religions and nationalities" working "to help create a better world to live in" and cited its wartime record. "We do not expect medals for our deeds," the writer added, for "these things were done, because we are, and shall always be in the midst of the fight, to preserve our Democratic Ideals, which you have seen fit to abuse." The petitioner urged Clark to live up to the ideals of Lincoln, Jefferson, and Roosevelt, the Constitution, and the Bill of Rights, and become a good American.[30]

The IWO published a speakers' guide similarly stressing the organization's fealty to the principles of Lincoln, Jefferson, and Frederick Douglass; "Who can question the loyalty of leaders who teach the children these things?" the Junior Branch guide asked. They publicized speeches by Paul Robeson and Idaho senator Glen Taylor, who was running for vice president on the Progressive Party ticket, that opposed the subversive list. The Idaho firebrand declared, "The Constitution of the United States doesn't provide for any Lord High Executioner of the people's liberties and we don't intend to have one sneak up on us behind our back." Robeson proclaimed that he was proud of his IWO membership, saying the "blacklists are aimed at the people's organizations fighting Jim Crow and segregation, fighting American-style fascism, fighting for peace." Again, Southern segregationists' hostility to civil rights advocates who were rapidly also tarred as Communists did not escape condemnation as the Order fought the Texas-born attorney general's diktat.[31]

In June 1948 the IWO filed suit to have the subversive list declared unconstitutional.[32] Clark rejoined that placement on the list had not harmed the organization, claiming that "there is no controversy between the IWO and the defendants, including the Attorney General and the members of the President's Loyalty Board." He argued that the IWO itself had no standing to file suit, but only individual members in the civil service who might be dismissed. Any other governmental action that may have harmed the IWO was, in Clark's telling, "indirect and incidental." The court agreed with Clark, ruling no deprivation of free speech or association had occurred.[33]

But the harm was already substantial. Although ostensibly only government employees were required to take a loyalty oath, the list opened the door to attacks on members of organizations that were branded political pariahs. The federal Loyalty Board hounded IWO members who were in the Marine auxiliaries, but even those employed by the post office were grilled to make sure they delivered mail in a non-subversive way. In November 1948 a postman from Harlem had to answer a slew of "interrogatories" regarding his activities in the IWO, Artkino Films, and the Communist Party. He was required to "give a complete explanation of your membership" in the IWO, including "whether you subscribe to the *Fraternal Outlook*, whether you agree with the policies expressed by the *Fraternal Outlook* with respect to Communism and Soviet Russia, and such other facts as may be pertinent."[34] Arthur Drayton, a Black postman who had been active in union and civil rights causes in addition to the IWO, was suspended.[35] As with more famous activists such as IWO member Paul Robeson, his championing of racial equality was what had led to his harassment. A postman in Hammond, Indiana, faced similar grilling and asked the IWO to stop sending *Fraternal Outlook* to his home, writing, "One of these days the hysteria will die down and light will appear again."[36]

For foreign-born members, a high percentage of the Order's Italian, Greek, Romanian, and Slavic societies, the hysteria escalated. In 1947, Milgrom warned of INS "terrorization of the Yugoslav-American community of Farrell, Pennsylvania," where IWO members were threatened with denaturalization and deportation. Other members in Gary, Indiana, were threatened with deportation for IWO membership and singing from the *Little Red Songbook* in the city's Croatian Glee Club. Serbian Society leader Nick Baltich alerted headquarters that member Ljubice Pribicevich had been told by the INS that she could not get her citizenship papers until she resigned from the IWO. A Slovak in Passaic, New Jersey, was similarly threatened, and his alarmed wife burned their policies and dues books. In Farrell, one woman facing deportation had arrived in America in 1908, as a three-year-old; her subversive IWO membership evidently counted more than her two sons in the Marine Corps. As in the twenty-first century, the surreality of the hysteria around deportation was outweighed by the gravity of the dilemma for those targeted.[37]

Some unrepentant members remained lyrically defiant. "One thing they don't understand—our stubbornness. We are fearless people," a Carpatho-Russian member wrote to his society's president. "Even if they deport me to the North Pole, among the Eskimoes [sic], I shall show, by gesticulation, if needs be, to these Eskimoes the wrong we are being done by Capitalism. There too I shall prepare for the day of the overthrow of the oppressors of the working people. They will not get rid of us, no matter where they deport us!"[38]

Leaders were often targeted for deportation. Proceedings were reopened against Milgrom, who was held in detention on Ellis Island—"already a concentration camp," as the general secretary termed it. His deteriorating health in December 1952 prompted his removal to Mount Sinai Hospital, although he was still under guard there nine months later.[39] The government likewise sought to strip Detroit's Stanley Nowak of citizenship and send him back to Poland, in spite of (or perhaps because of) the fact that he had served as a progressive Michigan state senator and leader of that state's IWO. "An American family faces separation or exile," pamphlets defending Nowak declared; photos of the former senator and his American-born wife and daughter played up Cold War images of domesticity, noting: "The family is one of the most sacred of institutions, but many forces tend to break up families in America today." Here the draconian INS and anti-radical McCarran-Walter Act were the family destroyers. The pro-Nowak pamphlet also featured the endorsement of the United Auto Workers' Walter Reuther, who urged, "Repeal the McCarran-Walter Act or tear down the Statue of Liberty, because the two simply don't go together."[40] The 1952 McCarran-Walter Act particularly targeted foreign-born leftists, and Red-listed organizations were required to register with the Subversive Activities Control Board.

Many IWO officials lost their bouts with the INS and were expelled from the country. Such was the fate of Henry Podolski, who had taken the helm at the Polonia Society after Bolesław Gebert resigned and returned to Poland after a thirty years absence, one step ahead of deportation. The IWO noted Podolski was targeted for removal even as the government welcomed eastern European "displaced persons" with records of wartime fascist collaboration. The Statue of Liberty was once again enlisted, with the Committee in Defense of Henry Podolski asking, "Shall we tear down the Statue of Liberty and build concentration camps?" The Order labeled Podolski a victim of the "deportation delirium" and "a fearless fighter for democratic rights." If Podolski were removed from the country, the IWO suggested, the equally subversive Declaration of Independence should be shredded.[41] Andrew Dmytryshyn, vice president of the Ukrainian Society, was also deported in a "mass murder of civil liberties."[42]

In January 1950, the *Jewish Fraternalist* featured the plight of the hundreds of noncitizens facing a "deportation hysteria," including Peter Harisiades, head of the IWO's Greek Society, who faced separation from his American citizen wife and children due to his previous Communist Party membership. The IWO again enlisted the Statue of Liberty to come to its aid. "Should Miss Liberty be deported?" an IWO-issued pamphlet wanted to know. As another immigrant with suspect ideas of freedom and democracy, the statue should be in the boat with Harisiades if the Red Scare witch hunt continued. In a solidarity-building bit of agitprop, IWO members were reminded they were working in an all-American heritage of progressivism.[43]

Sadly, the Justice Department did not see it the IWO's way, and Harisiades was deported in 1952, even though he had been brought to America at age nine and lived there for almost forty years. Fearing his life would be in peril from the Greek regime, Harisiades opted to relocate to Poland, even though he spoke not a word of Polish. There he joined several thousand Greek partisans who had been defeated in the recent civil war by the US-backed authoritarian government.[44]

Under such circumstances IWO headquarters received a slew of resignations from members fearing punishment. The secretary of an Italian lodge reported the resignation of two leaders. Even a "fervent anti-fascist" reader of the *Daily Worker* and *L'unita del Popolo* (Unity of the people) quit, saying, "It is a matter of our bread and of our future." Polish, Slovak, Jewish, and Hispanic members facing government harassment quit. A government employee from the Bronx wrote, "I'm sorry that I have to do this, as I have no alternative in this matter."[45] Others were angrier as they left. "Sorry I ever paid a damned cent into your organization," E. T. Besenyodi of Akron wrote on his way out the door.[46]

School boards contributed to the IWO's harassment: in New York and elsewhere the JPFO and other IWO societies were barred from using public schools for meetings, children's programs, and events. The JPFO noted that New York was basing its ban on the attorney general's list, which would "deprive thousands of Jewish families in the City of New York the right to supplement the general education of their children with an after-school secular, progressive Jewish education." Pointing out that the superintendent of after-school programs himself admitted that there had never been any reports of JPFO schools teaching anything subversive, and that the board of education's president had defended "traditional civil freedoms" in rejecting an earlier attempt to ban the schools, the Order urged Mayor William O'Dwyer and the board to continue standing up to the Red-baiting "hysteria." JPFO president Saltzman argued that the textbooks used in schools as well as the children's magazine *Jungvar* (Youth) "offer concrete evidence and proof of the healthy spirit and program of our schools," and urged the board to defend "the principle of freedom of education" and not "fall victim to slanders and the spirit of Inquisition." When the city nevertheless banned the JPFO from using public schools, the JPFO's National School Committee appealed to the state commissioner of education, again noting that its classes had always been inspected by the city and no complaint of anything "subversive" had ever been received. The ban was attributed to a professional anti-Communist "scandal-monger," a disgraced former rabbi. Such appeals were unavailing.[47]

In smaller cities the fight was even more bitter. Chelsea, Massachusetts, expelled the JPFO *shule* (after-school program), tarred as the "little red schoolhouse" by the local paper after "defrocked" anti-Communist rabbi Benjamin Schultz denounced its pedagogy. Schultz and an unnamed "Negro investigator" linked the Chelsea Jewish Children's School to a "deliberate Communist conspiracy to inflame racial and religious minorities here against the United States." Paul Robeson's activism was mentioned by the rabbi in this regard, too. In testimony before HUAC as well as in letters to the *Chelsea Record*, officials of the school denied it was Communist, but was rather "non-political and interested solely in giving its pupils a knowledge of Yiddish and Jewish history and culture." While the JPFO was disingenuous in backpedaling from its Communist links, in 1949 they had few other options as they fought for survival. A teacher at the school wrote to the paper that the only time he had sought to overthrow a government by violent means was when he was in the army fighting the Nazis, summoning the IWO's wartime bona fides. As for the Chelsea school, he said he saw nothing nefarious in teaching a Yiddish poem that "praises the ideal of racial brotherhood." However, in 1949, when segregationist Southern congressmen chaired HUAC, interracial activism was one of the many strikes against the IWO. Other letter writers stressed the IWO's subversive listing and noted that the *shule* critiqued public schools, where workers' children were "educated in a spirit of loyalty to all the institutions of capitalist society... that oppresses them." By 1949 such proletarian rhetoric was anathema; the Chelsea school was ordered closed.[48]

Shules were likewise ejected from schools and community centers in suburban Philadelphia and Petaluma, California.[49] By 1950, JPFO schools director Itche Goldberg was appealing for funds to save beleaguered *shules*.[50] Red-baiters, though, continued to patrol for any hint of IWO infiltration. In May 1951 the *New York World-Telegram and Sun* reported that the American Jewish League Against Communism had alerted New York's Board of Education to a "Jewish Youth Festival" that the JPFO had reportedly held at Washington Irving High School, and to *shule* graduation ceremonies at another high school.[51]

Some cities sought to bar not just schools but the very presence of "subversive" people. Erie, Pennsylvania, and Jacksonville, Florida, both passed ordinances barring members of designated organizations from living in their cities. Russian IWO members in Erie felt particularly threatened, despite reassurance from their society's president, who exclaimed: "It must be believed that progress still is moving forward!" A judge struck down the Pennsylvania ordinance. But in Florida, a distraught IWO member attempted suicide by stabbing himself in the chest with an ice pick after being sentenced to ninety days at the state prison farm for violating Jacksonville's anti-Red ordinance. The correspondence from Jacksonville makes palpable the emotional toll taken on members, many of whom suffered destroyed careers or witnessed the crumbling of progressive friends' lives.[52]

Public-housing residents, too, were told to quit the Order or pack up and move. In 1952 the Gwinn Amendment excluded from public housing any member of a "subversive" organization. A lawsuit testing the government's right to scrutinize tenants' beliefs concerned IWO members living in Brooklyn's Williamsburg Houses; the IWO won a temporary injunction prohibiting enforcement of the oath, and *Głos Ludowy* hailed successful campaigns to "halt evictions." In the escalating Red Scare, the IWO made alliances with former enemies when it backed a lawsuit challenging the loyalty oath in Newark's housing projects. There a legless veteran faced eviction from Seth Boyden Terrace due to membership in the Socialist Workers Party. In a time of acute government suppression, the IWO forgave James Kutcher's Trotskyist heresy. A court cited "the present-day context of world crisis after crisis" as justifying the Gwinn Amendment; only "loyal" tenants need apply. Although the US Supreme Court later rejected the oath, this victory came too late for the IWO, for the ultimate dagger was about to be unsheathed.[53]

In the end, prosaic insurance law did in the IWO. As early as 1938 Massachusetts had sought to revoke the Order's license to write policies; following publication of the subversive list the IRS revoked the organization's tax-exempt status (a ploy similarly used to punish the ACPFB and currently leveled at Palestinian charities). States such as Pennsylvania consulted with Attorney General Clark as to whether placement on the list warranted removal of the IWO's insurance license.[54] For a few years states demurred, but in 1951, New York deployed insurance regulations and compliant courts to destroy the IWO. The state insurance department warped the actuarial term "hazard"—a financially unsound insurance society—to encompass the novel legal understanding that the IWO was a moral and political hazard for advocating unpalatable ideas, even though its finances were impeccable. For twenty-one years the IWO had scrupulously followed auditing and other insurance-law requirements, and officers pointed out that New York's auditors had consistently praised their finances, a fact reiterated by a Newark accountant in the Order who averred that the organization had "restricted its investments to municipal, state and Government bonds because as a group, such securities offer greater safety." New York now argued that the political beliefs of IWO officers such as Saltzman or Thompson *might* constitute a moral and political hazard (again, twisting this actuarial term out of shape) and moved to declare the liquidation of the IWO. Order treasurer Shipka declared this elastic "interpretation of 'public hazard' . . . the grossest violation of . . . the Constitution, [and] . . . a grand political frame-up." The move against members' assets was denounced as "the greatest insurance grab in the history of our country" and the real hazard to all Americans.[55]

The Polonia Society pointed out that the imposition of a political litmus test was lopsided. While their organization was targeted for liquidation, "no insurance commissioners attack the Polish National Alliance because their leaders publicly . . . indorsed [sic] the Republican candidate to the Presidency in 1948."

The IWO's lawyers likewise noted that the donations that for-profit insurance corporations made to the Republican Party incurred no legal crackdown.[56] IWO officers Saltzman and Shipka ripped into the Knights of Columbus's embrace of the "cannibalistic ideology" of Spain's fascist leader Francisco Franco and wondered why it was not permitted for a fraternal organization to oppose fascism.[57]

The IWO organized a Policyholders Protective Committee to fight the state diktat and raise funds for appeals.[58] The Committee issued a "statement to Governor Thomas E. Dewey," stressing that his state's insurance examiners had for twenty years found the Order to be "sound and solvent." Only a "politically motivated" and "spurious" assault on the Order accounted for the liquidation. Beyond that, the Committee emphasized that the Order "has provided insurance and protection for all, Negro and white, Christian and Jew, . . . on the basis of equality." It highlighted their commitment to racial equality and noted that any for-profit insurance company assigned the assets of a liquidated IWO would make no such commitment to nondiscriminatory rates and benefits. The preaching of brotherhood is a common thing," they told the governor. "But is the practice of brotherhood to be forbidden?"[59]

Lodges were now severely restricted in their activities. In upholding the state's liquidation decree, courts froze all IWO funds, save those used for legal defense. State administrators were placed in supervision of the IWO, and its correspondence and records were shared with the very department seeking the Order's liquidation. Slovak officers wisely told distant branches not to send letters to the IWO's Fifth Avenue headquarters, now overseen by New York state's watchdogs. The IWO was placed under state receivership and prohibited from enrolling new members; the Order's membership, already dwindling, now plummeted. Likewise, the state prevented the IWO from holding its annual convention, a decree in violation of the insurance department's own regulations governing mutual benefit societies. The department feared the IWO would elect new, non-Communist officers at its meeting, thus camouflaging its real ideology—Marcantonio and others "could therefore serve as 'window dressing,' a familiar Commie trick," the *New York World-Telegram and Sun* charged. The *New York Herald Tribune* agreed, declaring in a more genteel fashion that "it is clear that the sole function of the convention will be to carry out the instructions of the Communist Party. It may also be assumed that the entire aim of the convention will be to whitewash the International Workers Order." There was no way for the Order to win if even non-Communist officers were proof of subversive chicanery.[60]

Policyholders cited the Constitution's right of free association in asking Judge Henry Clay Greenberg to lift the liquidation order. Rallying IWO members declared New York insurance superintendent Alfred Bohlinger the real moral hazard, decrying the liquidation as "Hitlerism with an insurance twist."[61]

Hundreds of IWO members from across the country offered affidavits attesting to the interracial fellowship of the Order, its progressive value to the country through its civil rights and social policy activism, its outstanding support of World War II, and, most important, the nonideological, non-Communist nature of their lodges. "Whoever says that the IWO is a political party or supports a political party does not know anything about the life of the IWO," a Polish member from the Bronx said, adding, "the Court must prevent anyone from prying into our private opinions."[62]

Greenberg, however, thought otherwise. In June 1951 he upheld New York's ruling, and the IWO was ordered liquidated, even though both the insurance department and court acknowledged its finances and reserves were excellent and its insurance-policy business actuarially sound. In a Kafkaesque twist, the state alleged that the IWO was *too* solvent, hence funds might easily be transferred to Moscow. No proof that any such action had ever occurred or been contemplated was offered; the Communist affiliation of some IWO officers was "hazard" enough. Greenberg accepted the argument that the IWO was closely tied to the CPUSA, noting the proletarian militancy of Order publications from the early 1930s as evidence of this. The judge also agreed that some hypothetical future conflict with the Soviets made it too risky for the IWO to continue in business. Greenberg ruled, "If the time arrives when there is a conflict between the interests of this country and the world of Communism, it is not beyond the realm of reasonable probability that the funds of this Order will be expropriated." To forestall that hypothetical, Greenberg confirmed the confiscation of millions of dollars in assets from some 160,000 members.[63] Some IWO members might have reflected on the irony of an ostensibly Communist-controlled organization fighting to retain its private property against state seizure.

While Greenberg declared policyholders' interests would be protected pending appeal, he directed the Order to turn over all papers, books, and documents to the New York State Department of Insurance. Administrator William Karlin zealously followed through on this decree, demanding the Order deliver "all [its] books, work papers, other papers, accounting reports . . . , tax reports . . . , documents, pamphlets, publications, accounts, files and other records" as well as records from medical departments, schools, cemetery departments, camps, the Front Line Fighters Fund, the JPFO Book Fund, and the Franklin D. Roosevelt Hospital Fund. This list suggested the breadth of the organization's good works, but Karlin was more interested in the Order's speedy liquidation.[64]

In demanding a rehearing, lawyers argued that the concept "moral hazard" had no basis in insurance law or regulations, and liquidation amounted to a state seizure of millions of dollars of policyholders' assets. New York once again insisted the Order posed a moral and political hazard. The state's move to liquidate, it argued, was brought on by the "Communist and hence seditious activity" of the IWO. In the state's petition, the economic hazard of a potential funneling of IWO funds to Communists abroad—although again no evidence of such a scheme was presented—was conflated with a broad moral hazard.[65]

In a political milieu in which Julius and Ethel Rosenberg were convicted of conspiracy to commit espionage and had been unmasked at their nearby trial as IWO members, it was difficult for the Order to prevail, and in April 1953 the appellate court let the liquidation stand. As lawyers petitioned the US Supreme Court to consider the IWO's appeal, the Policyholders Protective Committee issued a pamphlet stating its case: "A fraternal order sentenced to death!"[66] Indeed, by September 1954, when the Supreme Court refused the Order's final appeal even though it had just affirmed that the IWO should be dropped from the Red List, the Order was declared both subversive and liquidated, its assets scattered to for-profit insurance corporations, its members stripped of their fraternal "big family."[67]

The Order's policyholders were given the option of cashing in their policies or having them assigned to the Continental Assurance Company of Illinois. But in his letter explaining members' insurance options, Bohlinger also warned that "joining or maintaining any connection with any fraternal, cultural, social or other group which has been organized or which may be organized by former officers or leaders of the former IWO . . . may well be considered to be membership in a subversive or a Communist-front organization." *Jewish Life*, a magazine closely associated with the late JPFO, decried this "fascist piece of impudence." Nineteen former IWO officers blasted Bohlinger's "crassest example of thought control."[68] Many recent IWO members ignored Bohlinger's advice; Stanley Nowak and Conrad Komorowski, former Polonia Society members, had already founded a new Polish Political Club in Detroit in 1954.[69] After the liquidation, the Order's accomplishments were catalogued by *Głos Ludowy*. "IWO helped blaze trail in fight for democracy," the paper declared, perhaps the final verdict on the International Workers Order.[70]

Such defiant progressivism by ex-members in some cases lasted for decades. Herbert Aptheker in 1966 spoke against the Vietnam War in Detroit before former Order members, while the Detroit Police Intelligence Division in 1973 reported on a leftist "International Bazaar for Peace and Freedom" taking place at the same address that the 1936 "Red Squad" flagged as hosting an IWO lodge.[71] Dick and Mickey Flacks had been teen members of the IWO Juniors, activism they carried forward in helping lead the Students for a Democratic Society.[72] After the dissolution of the Cervantes Society, Jesús Colón continued advocating for racial justice for Black and Latino/a citizens, as well as for Puerto Rican independence, until his death in 1974. IWO member Paul Robeson continued to speak out and perform where possible. Louise Thompson Patterson founded Sojourners for Truth and Justice with other like-minded female Black activists. Throughout the 1980s and early 1990s, Patterson continued her social-justice and anti-war activism. Stanley Nowak edited the leftist *Głos Ludowy* into the 1970s, and Ed Falkowski wrote columns for the paper that in the 1960s and early '70s took the government to task for the shallowness of its commitment to racial equality (although he also opposed the use of affirmative action by universities, perhaps indicating that not every leftist kept pace with all of the positions of the New Left). Still, former IWO member and executive secretary of the eastern Pennsylvania IWO, Sol Rotenberg, as treasurer of the Delaware Valley Committee for Democratic Rights, hosted an address by Communist Party stalwart Elizabeth Gurley Flynn on "The McCarran Act and American Liberties" in 1963.[73] Commitment to racial and class justice persisted among countless former members.

This is not to discount the devastation the Order's persecution wrought on the movement for social justice. The liquidation of the IWO remains the only time a court has ruled that the political beliefs of its members or officers constituted a "hazard" as defined in insurance law, a sobering reminder of the lengths to which the government went during the Red Scare to rout out those whose political beliefs were considered beyond the norm. Just as non-Communist IWO members were stripped of their right to belong to the fraternal society of their choosing, the government's actions also stifled the civil liberties and freedom of thought of non-Communist liberals, who were cowed into silence for fear of being branded "Red."[74] Similarly, in the twenty-first century all manner of pressure has been brought to bear against Muslim charities and nonprofits that have earned the wrath of conservative politicians, and student demonstrators have recently learned how tenuous their free-speech rights are on Ivy League and other campuses. The ease, too, with which demonstrators against corporate interests and environmental activists have recently been stigmatized as "terrorist" bears a striking resemblance to the case of the International Workers Order, "a fraternal order sentenced to death."[75] The narrow parameters within which charities, nonprofits, or any citizen, may exercise their free speech and free association rights were set in quite limited ways in the liquidation of the International Workers Order and other prosecutions of the Red Scare era.

NOTES

1. Letter from Joseph Petercsak to US Supreme Court, October 23, 1953, International Workers Order (IWO) Supplemental Records #5940, box 3, Kheel Center for Labor-Management Documentation and Archives, Catherwood Library, Cornell University, Ithaca, New York. Henceforth Kheel Supplemental.

2. "A Fraternal Organization Sentenced to Death! The Strange Case of the IWO Now Before the U.S. Supreme Court," pamphlet, 1953, International Workers Order (IWO)

Records #5276, box 16, folder 13, Kheel Center for Labor-Management Documentation and Archives, Catherwood Library, Cornell University, Ithaca, New York. Henceforth Kheel.

3. Letter from Rubin Saltzman to "Dear Comrade," June 20, 1932, Records of the Communist Party USA, reel 234, delo 3037, Library of Congress, Washington, District of Columbia. Henceforth, CPUSA, LC.

4. Bill Gebert biography, sent by Gebert to the executive committee, Communist International, April 15, 1932, Don Binkowski Papers, box 4, folder 4-14, Reuther Library, Wayne State University, Detroit, Michigan (hereafter Binkowski); "Bolesław K. Gebert, Bolshevik Agitator," Bureau of Investigation report, July 25, 1919, box 4, folder 4-22, Binkowski; Bureau of Investigation reports on Gebert, July 10, 1919 and July 8, 1919, box 4, folder 4-22, Binkowski; affidavit (1919) by witness in Gebert deportation hearing, box 4, folder 4-22, Binkowski; memorandum on Gebert deportation proceedings, November 4, 1919, box 4, folder 4-22, Binkowski; letter from commissioner general of immigration, October 13, 1919, box 4, folder 4-23, Binkowski; memorandum on Gebert attached to deportation proceedings, October 13, 1919, box 4, folder 4-23, Binkowski; J. S. Apelman, Bureau of Investigation affidavit, January 19, 1920, box 4, folder 4-22, Binkowski; letter from William Burns, director, Bureau of Investigation, to secretary of labor, April 21, 1922, box 4, folder 4-23, Binkowski; "Brief by Alien" in Gebert's deportation proceeding, n.d. [1931?], box 4, folder 4-14, Binkowski; hearing on deportation of Gebert, November 18, 1931, box 4, folder 4-23, Binkowski; letter from Roger Baldwin to Daniel MacCormack, commissioner general of immigration, November 28, 1934, box 4, folder 4-23, Binkowski; letter from W. W. Brown, assistant to MacCormack, to Baldwin, January 17, 1935, box 4, folder 4-23, Binkowski; letter from David Bentall to Department of Labor, January 26, 1937, box 4, folder 4-23, Binkowski; letter from J. R. Espinosa, chief supervisor of special inspections, Department of Justice, to "Mr. Brown" of the Immigration Service, October 20, 1941, box 4, folder 4-23, Binkowski; "Bon Voyage, Bill," *Fraternal Outlook* 18, n.d. [1947?], box 4, folder 4-14, Binkowski; Bolesław K. Gebert, resignation letter, August 11, 1947, box 5, folder 12, Kheel; Arthur Sabin, *Red Scare in Court: New York Versus the International Workers Order* (University of Pennsylvania Press, 1993), 280–81.

5. Rachel Buff, *Against the Deportation Terror: Organizing for Immigrant Rights in the Twentieth Century* (Temple University Press, 2018); Daniel Kanstroom, *Deportation Nation: Outsiders in American History* (Harvard University Press, 2007).

6. Letter from National Provisional Committee for Protection of Foreign Born to "Dear Friends," n.d. [1932?], reel 260, delo 3380, CPUSA, LC.

7. John Ujich, "A Letter from a Prisoner at Ellis Island," December 16, 1934, issued by the Committee for Protection of Foreign Born, reel 287, delo 3716, CPUSA, LC; letter from Christ Popoff, Ray Carlson, Paul Kettunen, and Oscar Mannisto, Ellis Island, to American Committee for Protection of Foreign Born (ACPFB), December 30, 1934, reel 287, delo 3716, CPUSA, LC.

8. Letter from Albert Fenely to "Dear Comrade Browder and all," May 5, 1936, reel 305, delo 4034, CPUSA, LC.

9. Minutes, general executive board (GEB), IWO, September 10–11, 1938, Bedacht and Brodsky, reports delivered to GEB meeting, box 1, folder 5, Kheel.

10. Brodsky report to GEB, IWO, September 10–11, 1938, box 1, folder 5, Kheel; decision, Commonwealth of Massachusetts, Suffolk County, Supreme Judicial Court, "International Workers Order, Inc., v. Commissioner of Insurance of the Commonwealth, Findings, Ruling and Order," March 6, 1939, box 5, folder 2, Kheel.

11. Brodsky report to GEB, IWO, September 10–11, 1938, box 1, folder 5, Kheel; "Proposal for the Establishment of an Official Organ," spring 1938, box 2, folder 2, Kheel.

12. "Dies Demands 'Alien' Groups be Prosecuted: Note to Hull Claims Registration Law Violated," *Milwaukee Sentinel*, November 28, 1938, 3; FBI report on Detroit division IWO, December 31, 1946, citing report of Special Sub-Committee on Un-American Activities, January 3, 1939, box 16, folder 16–37, Binkowski.

13. FBI report, Detroit division IWO, December 31, 1946, citing January 16, 1939, Detroit meeting, box 16, folder 16–37, Binkowski; telegram from International Workers Order Lodge 2501, La Progressiva, January 24, 1939, box 47, Vito Marcantonio Papers, New York Public Library, New York, New York (hereafter Marcantonio Papers); flyer for mass meeting against Dies Committee, in English and Italian, January 29, 1939, box 47, Marcantonio Papers; letter in Italian, n.d. [January 1939], box 47, Marcantonio Papers; petition against Dies Un-American Activities Committee from the IWO Dante Alighieri Lodge 2579, January 1939, box 47, Marcantonio Papers; Gerald Meyer, *Vito Marcantonio: Radical Politician, 1902–1954* (State University of New York Press, 1989).

14. Peter Morell, "The Threat to Civil Liberties," *Fraternal Outlook*, November 1939, 3–5, 28, box 48, Kheel; "Koncentračné Tábory v Amerike? Výpad reakčných Kongressmanov proti 'Bill of Rights'" [Concentration camps in America? Reactionary congressman's attack on the "Bill of Rights"], *Fraternal Outlook*, December 1939, 33, box 48, Kheel.

15. Max Bedacht, report to GEB, January 27, 1940, 16–17, box 2, folder 4, Kheel.

16. "IWO National 'Stop Dies' Drive Gets Mass Support," *Daily Worker*, May 15, 1940, 5, reel 318, delo 4243, CPUSA, LC; "IWO Calls an Anti-Dies Rally in Brooklyn," *Daily Worker*, May 18, 1940, 5, reel 318, delo 4243, CPUSA, LC; Sabin, *Red Scare in Court*, 167.

17. "Court Allows I.W.O. to Inspect Seized Files," *Daily Worker*, May 17, 1940, 5, reel 318, delo 4243, CPUSA, LC; Max Bedacht to Vito Marcantonio, "Copy of following telegram sent to Martin Dies, Chairman, Investigating Un-American Activities," n.d [May 1940], box 47, Marcantonio Papers.

18. Detroit Police Department, Special Investigation Squad, report on IWO Lodge 747 meeting, March 10, 1940, box 5, folder 5-30, Binkowski.

19. Questionnaires for lodges from IWO headquarters with replies from Sam Klezmer, Indianapolis (April 15, 1941); Joseph Sweedock, Mahanoy City, Pennsylvania (May 1, 1941); Jerry Knox, Aliquippa, Pennsylvania (April 5, 1941), box 18, folder 13, Kheel.

20. Minutes of the IWO Executive Committee, April 11, 1941, box 1, folder 8, Kheel; Karen Miller, *Managing Inequality: Northern Racial Liberalism in Interwar Detroit* (New York University Press, 2017); Beth Tompkins Bates, *The Making of Black Detroit in the Age of Henry Ford* (University of North Carolina Press, 2012); Nelson Lichtenstein, *The Most Dangerous Man in Detroit: Walter Reuther and the Fate of American Labor* (Basic Books, 1996).

21. Report, Max Bedacht to GEB, February 7–8, 1942, box 2, folder 6, Kheel.

22. Minutes of the general executive board, February 7–8, 1942, including "Resolution on Government Policy Toward Aliens and Foreign Born," box 1, folder 9, Kheel; Herbert Benjamin, "Unity for Victory" report to GEB, February 7, 1942, 6–8, box 1, folder 9, Kheel; Max Bedacht, "Our Civic and Organizational Problems," report to GEB, February 26, 1943, box 2, folder 9, Kheel; Donna Haverty-Stacke, *Trotskyists on Trial: Free Speech and Political Persecution Since the Age of FDR* (New York University Press, 2015).

23. Bedacht, "Our Civic and Organizational Problems."

24. Testimony of George Pirinsky, hearings of the Senate Subcommittee on Immigration and Naturalization, June 8, 1949, box 2, folder 2-19, Binkowski; "Young Slavs in U.S. to be Wooed by Reds," *New York World-Telegram*, September 10, 1946, box 1, folder 1-19, Binkowski; Archibald McLeish to "Dear Steve" [Steve Early?], April 22, 1942, box 1, folder 1-17, Binkowski; telegram from President Franklin Roosevelt to American Slav Congress, April 25, 1942, box 1, folder 1-17, Binkowski; "The American Slav Congress Will Convene Saturday April 25th and Sunday April 26th," *Národné noviny* [National news], April 22,

1942, 5; "An Address by Paul V. McNutt, Chairman of the War Manpower Commission and Federal Security Administrator, at the American Slav Congress, April 26, 1942," *Národné noviny*, May 6, 1942, 5; Committee on Un-American Activities, *Report on the American Slav Congress and Associated Organizations* (US GPO, 1950), https://archive.org/details/reportonamerican00unit/page/n3/mode/2up. On the ASC, see Robert Szymczak, "From Popular Front to Communist Front: The American Slav Congress in War and Cold War, 1941–1951" (PhD diss., Lancaster University, 2006).

25. "BUTTS 899," "Views and Actions of Left-Wing IWO Leaders and Editors," and "Vive Le Russe," reports of the Office of Strategic Services/Foreign Nationalities Branch (OSS/FNB), January 6, 1945, box 4, folder 4-29, Binkowski; "The Polish American Left," report of the OSS/FNB, June 16, 1944, box 2, folder 2-53, Binkowski; Robert Szymczak, "Uneasy Observers: The OSS Foreign Nationalities Branch and Perceptions of Polish Nationalism in the United States During World War II," *Polish American Studies* 56, no. 1 (Spring 1999): 7–73.

26. Vito Marcantonio, speech, in *Proceedings of National Convention, IWO*, July 2–7, 1944, 10–12, box 3, folder 4, Kheel; telegram from IWO to Marcantonio, February 4, 1943, and letter from Marcantonio to IWO, February 9, 1943, box 47, Marcantonio Papers; letter from Dave Greene to Marcantonio, March 11, 1942, and letter from Marcantonio to Greene, March 12, 1942, box 47, Marcantonio Papers.

27. Sabin, *Red Scare in Court*, 36, 51, 61; David Caute, *The Great Fear: The Anti-Communist Purge Under Truman and Eisenhower* (Simon and Schuster, 1978); Eleanor W. Schrecker, *Many Are the Crimes: McCarthyism in America* (Princeton University Press, 1998); Alan Barth, *The Loyalty of Free Men* (Viking Press, 1951); Robert Justin Goldstein, *American Blacklist: The Attorney General's List of Subversive Organizations* (University Press of Kansas, 2008).

28. Letter from Rockwell Kent, Sam Milgrom, and Peter Shipka to "Brothers and Sisters," n.d. [December 1947], IWO Collection, folder 6, Tamiment Library and Robert F. Wagner Labor Archives, New York University, New York, New York (hereafter IWO, NYU); minutes of executive committee meeting, "Action re: Clark's Attack," December 8, 1947, box 1, folder 13, Kheel; "IWO Challenges Constitutionality of Attorney General Clark's Report; Plans Legal Action," press release, December 5, 1947, box 31, IWO, NYU.

29. "Reaction to Subversive Listing," FBI report on IWO Detroit division, November 20, 1953, 18, and citing *Românul American*, January 3 and 10, 1948, and "Protection of American Liberties, Theme of IWO Call in Ten Cities," *Głos Ludowy*, June 19, 1948, box 16, folder 16-38, Binkowski; letter from Sam Milgrom to "Brother [Charles] Korenič" of Slovak Workers Society, December 16, 1947, box 5, folder 1, Kheel. Similar letters went out to other ethnic society leaders. Remarks of Congressman Vito Marcantonio, *Congressional Record*, December 17, 1947, box 5, folder 2, Kheel. See, too, letter of New York City councilman Stanley Isaacs to Attorney General Tom Clark, January 6, 1948, folder 31, IWO, NYU.

30. Letter and petition from M. Rosenblatt, corresponding secretary, Branch 2360, Jewish Peoples Fraternal Order, to Tom Clark, February 7, 1948, box 17, file 15, Kheel.

31. "Notes and Materials for Speakers on Attorney General Clark's Report to the Loyalty Board," n.d. [1947?], box 17, folder 14, Kheel; *The IWO Builds for Tomorrow: Leader's Guide for IWO Junior Leaders* 2, no. 2 (March–April 1948), box 5, folder 2, Kheel; IWO news release condemning the subversive listing, July 8, 1948, folder 31, IWO, NYU.

32. "IWO Files Suit Against Attorney General Clark," news release, June 7, 1948, folder 31, IWO, NYU.

33. Memorandum, "Attorney General Clark's answer to IWO lawsuit," n.d. [1948?], box 3, folder 8, Kheel; IWO Executive Committee minutes, September 14, 1948, box 1, folder 14, Kheel.

34. Letter from Dave Greene to Mary Samsonick, November 6, 1947, box 4, folder 4, Kheel; letter from N. Chalpin to Gedalia Sandler, March 10, 1947, and letter from Sandler to Chalpin, March 26, 1947, box 25, folder 9, Kheel; "Interrogatories" from Post Office Department to Seymour Goldman, November 30, 1948, box 32, folder 31, Kheel; report of Lee Pressman on "the legal problems we have faced in the past few years," minutes of JPFO National Board meeting, November 19, 1949, box 27, folder 2, Kheel.

35. Letter from Abraham Chapman to Lee Pressman, January 16, 1950, box 1, Kheel Supplemental; "Arthur L. Drayton Fights 'Loyalty' Suspension," *Fraternal Outlook* draft article, January 1950, box 1, Kheel Supplemental.

36. Letter from Seymour Press to Sylvia Rigel, January 10, 1950, box 32, folder 24, Kheel.

37. Sam Milgrom, "Yugoslav-American Community Terrorized by Naturalization Officials," press release on behalf of ACPFB, April 14, 1947, box 4, folder 2, Kheel; "IWO Urges Investigation of Immigration Office in Youngstown, Ohio," press release, April 25, 1947, folder 31, IWO, NYU; FBI report on American Slav Congress, January 26, 1944, in author's possession courtesy of Freedom of Information Act request and generosity of John Enyeart; letter from Nick Baltich to Dave Greene, August 30, 1948, box 4, folder 4, Kheel; Slovak Workers Society, letter to "Dear Brother" (name blacked out), October 2, 1950, folder 42, IWO, NYU.

38. Letter from a Carpatho-Russian member to "Michael" [Michael Logoyda], February 9, 1947, box 25, folder 2, Kheel.

39. Warrant for arrest of alien Sam Milgrom, May 9, 1950, box 1, Kheel Supplemental; letter from Rockwell Kent to Milgrom, May 13, 1950, box 3, folder 10, Kheel; letter from Kent to Molly Tallentire, May 13, 1950, box 3, folder 10, Kheel; letter from Milgrom to Kent, May 26, 1950, box 3, folder 10, Kheel; letter from Milgrom to Kent, June 20, 1950, box 3, folder 10, Kheel; letter from Dave Greene to Peter Shipka, n.d., box 4, folder 6, Kheel; Committee for the Freedom of Sam Milgrom, letter "To My Fellow Members of the IWO" from "Sam Milgrom, Ellis Island, N.Y.," n.d., box 16, folder 11, Kheel; Committee for the Freedom of Sam Milgrom, news release, February 18, 1953, box 16, folder 11, Kheel; "Rally Organized to Demand Milgrom's Release on Bail," news release, February 4, 1953, box 16, folder 11, Kheel; letter from Committee for the Freedom of Sam Milgrom to "Dear Friend," November 2, 1952, box 16, folder 11, Kheel.

40. Stanley Nowak Defense Committee, *An American Family Faces Separation or Exile*, pamphlet, April 1956, box 7, folder 7-48, Binkowski; FBI report, Stanley Nowak Defense Committee (1953), citing defenses of Nowak in *Głos Ludowy*, January 17 and 31, 1953, box 7, folder 7-49, Binkowski.

41. Committee in Defense of Henry Podolski, "Shall We Destroy the Statue of Liberty and Build Concentration Camps?," flyer, n.d. [1949?], box 8, folder 8-42, Binkowski; "IWO Condemns Deportation Arrest of Henry Podolski," news release, August 16, 1949, box 48, Kheel.

42. Fred Winter, "Deporters on Merry-Go-Round," typescript, July 14, 1950, box 17, folder 14, Kheel; Fred Winter, "Sponsored by the U.S. Government: 'Mr. and Mrs. Informer,'" typescript, July 21, 1950, box 17, folder 14, Kheel; news release on Andrew Dymytryshyn deportation, May 9, 1950, box 48, Kheel; Arthur Kinoy, memorandum in re: Dmytrysh [sic] decision, box 1, Kheel Supplemental; minutes, IWO Executive Committee, October 21, 1952, box 3, Kheel Supplemental.

43. "Should Miss Liberty Be Deported? The Case of Peter Harisiades," flyer, 1950, box 46, Marcantonio Papers; draft resolution, IWO, on Peter Harisiades, n.d., box 13, folder 11, Kheel; minutes, Chicago Council meeting, February 10, 1947, box 6, folder 13, Kheel; "Memorandum re: 'The Attacks on the Order,'" June 13, 1950, box 10, folder 10, Kheel; letter from Stanley Nowak to Serbian American Federation, IWO, June 10, 1947, box 13,

folder 11, Kheel; resolution on McCarran-Walter Law passed at general council meeting (IWO), September 13, 1952, box 3, Kheel Supplemental; Earl Browder, *Who Are the Americans?* (Workers Library, 1936).

44. "Should Miss Liberty Be Deported?"; "Greek, Here Since 1916, Finally Deported as Red," *New York Herald Tribune*, November 13, 1952, box 2, Kheel Supplemental. Thanks to David Ost for information on the Greek exile community in Poland.

45. Letter from Fabio Ligi to "Dear Secretary," May 26, 1947, box 25, folder 5, Kheel; letter from Math. Polanka to Joseph Schiffel, October 30, 1950, box 26, folder 5, Kheel; Polish letter from Mary Zbrzyszny to secretary, Polonia Society branch 3548, Neffs, Ohio, March 15, 1953, box 21, folder 40, Kheel; letter from Benjamin Elian to Frances Shifrin, March 24, 1950, box 32, folder 35, Kheel; letter from Manuel del Pozo to Dave Greene, September 26, 1949, box 26, folder 6, Kheel.

46. Letter from E. T. Besenyodi to IWO, May 17, 1948, box 8, folder 8, Kheel.

47. "To Mayor O'Dwyer and the New York Board of Education," flyer, reprinted from *New York Star*, January 19, 1949, folder 30, IWO, NYU; statement from the Jewish Peoples Fraternal Order to members of the Board of Education (New York City), January 12, 1949, box 40.1, folder 1, Kheel; letter from Sam Rothberg and Samuel Davis, National Committee of the JPFO, "to the Hon. Francis Spaulding, Commissioner of the State of New York," February 18, 1949, box 40.1, folder 1, Kheel.

48. Letter from Itche Goldberg to Lew Marks, July 20, 1949, box 38, folder 8, Kheel; "Rabbi Names Local Jewish School as Communist Front," *Chelsea Record*, July 14, 1949, box 38, folder 8, Kheel; "Jewish School Officials Deny It Is Communist," *Chelsea Record*, July 15, 1949, box 38, folder 8, Kheel; Rubin Saltzman, letter to the editor, "Jewish Children's School Defended Against Charges," *Chelsea Record*, August 27, 1949, box 38, folder 8, Kheel; Jack Weinman, teacher, Chelsea Jewish Children's School, letter to editor, *Chelsea Record*, July 20, 1949, box 38, folder 9, Kheel; letter from Itche Goldberg to Dr. H. B. Steller, August 24, 1949, box 38, folder 9, Kheel; letter from Steller to "Comrade Davidovitch," August 24, 1949, box 38, folder 9, Kheel; letter to the editor, "Says Jewish Children's School Affiliated with Known Communist Group," *Chelsea Record*, August 13, 1949, box 38, folder 9, Kheel; Saltzman, letter to editor, *Chelsea Record*, August 1949, box 38, folder 9, Kheel.

49. Letter from Sol Rotenberg to Rubin Saltzman, December 1, 1949, box 8, folder 11, Kheel; letter from Sol Rotenberg to Sam Milgrom and Rubin Saltzman, December 27, 1949, box 8, folder 11, Kheel.

50. Letter from Itche Goldberg to "Dear Friend," April 18, 1950, box 38, folder 3, Kheel; letter from Ann Bailes, secretary of Jewish Community Center, Petaluma, California, to JPFO, October 3, 1950, box 30, folder 17, Kheel. The JPFO *shules*, like the Emma Lazarus Division and Camp Kinderland, were legally spun off before the IWO was dissolved. The Cemetery Society survived since it had remained a separate legal entity. A different story explains how *Jewish Life* became *Jewish Currents* in 1956.

51. "Charges Groups Labeled Pro-Red Still Use Schools," *New York World-Telegram and Sun*, May 23, 1951, box 2, Kheel Supplemental.

52. Letter from Daniel Kasustchik to Ya. Peters, N. Daneyko, and M. Burenko, September 20, 1950, box 25, folder 1, Kheel; letter from S. Nowacki to "Dear" (named blacked out), September 26, 1950, box 26, folder 3, Kheel; letter from Ossip Blachnic to Kasustchik, October 9, 1950, box 25, folder 1, Kheel; letter from Kasustchik to Blachnic, October 11, 1950, box 25, folder 1, Kheel; monthly letter of the IWO Garibaldi Society, November 1950, box 10, folder 10, Kheel; "Anti-Red Law Effect Halted," *Milwaukee Journal*, October 27, 1950, 6; letter from B. Klein to George Starr, JPFO, September 14, 1950, and letter from Starr to Klein, September 22, 1950, box 32, folder 11, Kheel. Klein's letter was accompanied by September 13, 1950, clippings: "Stab Wound, Fall Imperil Life of Red," *Florida*

Times-Union, and "Trainor Still Reported on Critical List," from a second, unidentified newspaper.

53. Letter from Dave Greene to Rockwell Kent, January 14, 1953, box 4, folder 6, Kheel; letter from Greene to "Dear Brother or Sister," January 22, 1953, box 17, folder 14, Kheel; letter from Greene to "Dear Brother or Sister," January 29, 1953, box 4, folder 8, Kheel; letter from Kent to Greene, January 30, 1953, box 4, folder 6, Kheel; "The Order Obtains Temporary Injunction," *Morgn Frayhayt* (Morning freedom), January 30, 1953, 1, box 2, Kheel Supplemental; "Newark Housing Authority Called to Court on Tenant's Loyalty Oath," *New York Times*, February 3, 1953, box 2, Kheel Supplemental; letter from Greene to "Dear Brothers and Sisters," February 10, 1953, box 4, folder 8, Kheel; "State Supreme Court Rules Against Tenant Oath," news release, July 9, 1953, box 17, folder 14, Kheel; "Loyalty Question to Tenant Upheld," *New York Times*, March 9, 1954, 19, box 3, Kheel Supplemental; "Turning Searchlight on Reds," *National Republic*, March 1953, in FBI file on IWO's Polonia Society, box 5, folder 5-29, Binkowski; "IWO Secures Injunction to Halt Evictions Under Gwinn Law," *Głos Ludowy*, February 7, 1953, 4, sect. 2; "IWO Wins Halt to Evictions," *Głos Ludowy*, February 28, 1953, 1, sect. 2.

54. IWO Executive Committee minutes, April 20, 1948 and June 4, 1948, box 1, folder 14, Kheel; letter from Dave Greene to "Dear Editor" of foreign-language newspapers, June 11, 1948, box 5, folder 3, Kheel.

55. Speech by Peter Shipka to IWO general council, February 3-4, 1951, folder 18, IWO, NYU.

56. Polonia Society, "From Organization Bulletin for December, 1950," box 26, folder 3, Kheel; "Haley Report for Purposes of Cross-Examination," n.d. [1950], box 23, folder 6, Kheel.

57. R. Saltzman, "Did the Order Violate Its Own Constitution?," *Morgn Frayhayt*, September 27, 1951, 5, box 2, Kheel Supplemental; Peter Shipka speech, February 3-4, 1951; report by Shipka to IWO general council, November 12-13, 1949, box 2, folder 17, Kheel.

58. Letter from Shipka to "Lodge Financial Secretaries," December 28, 1950, box 5, folder 16, Kheel; "IWO Policyholders Form Protective Committee, Plan Albany Gathering and Visit to Gov. Dewey," news release, December 28, 1950, box 16, folder 13, Kheel.

59. Statement to Governor Dewey by a delegation of the IWO Policyholders Protective Committee, Albany, February 19, 1952, box 16, folder 13, Kheel; "An Open Letter to the N.Y. Superintendent of Insurance from IWO Policyholders Protective Committee," *Compass*, April 22, 1951, box 23, folder 5, Kheel.

60. "Among Reddest Red Nests," *New York World-Telegram and Sun*, January 20, 1951, box 2, Kheel Supplemental; Sabin, *Red Scare in Court*, 97–98, citing *New York Herald Tribune*, January 11, 1951, 3; "Medzinárodný Robotnícky Spolok nazvaný nástrojom Komunistov" [The International Workers Order called a tool of the Communists], *New Yorkský denník* [New York daily], January 10, 1951, 1; "Súd zakázal konvenciu Medzinárod. Robotníckeho Spolku v New Yorku" [Judge forbids New York convention of the International Workers Order], *New Yorkský denník*, January 12, 1951, 1; "Šesť úradníkov Medzinárodného Spolku považovaní za Komunistov" [Six officers of the International Workers Order exposed as Communists], *New Yorkský denník*, February 1, 1951, 1.

61. "Answer to Superintendent of Insurance Bohlinger Adopted at Membership Meeting of the International Workers Order—Saint Nicholas Arena, March 7, 1951," box 23, folder 4, Kheel; letter of D. Fedonik of Boston "to the Plenum of the IWO Committee," translation from Russian, January 24, 1951, box 25, folder 1, Kheel.

62. John Hinkelman, affidavit, April 24, 1951, box 3, Kheel Supplemental.

63. Sabin, *Red Scare in Court*, 299–396.

64. Sabin, *Red Scare in Court*, 306; letter from "Alfred J. Bohlinger, Superintendent of Insurance, by William Karlin, senior Insurance Examiner" to Morris Greenbaum,

March 25, 1952, box 1, Kheel Supplemental; letter from Eve Reidelman, secretary, Detroit JPFO, to Donner & Kinoy, December 21, 1951, box 1, Kheel Supplemental.

65. Petition for rehearing, superintendent of insurance of the State of New York, September 11, 1952, box 3, Kheel Supplemental; memorandum to Supreme Court of NY State from Paul Williams and James Henry, special assistant attorneys general of NY State, September 16, 1952, box 3, Kheel Supplemental; Arthur Kinoy, preliminary notes on NY State Appellate Court case, re: liquidation of the IWO, July 8, 1952, box 1, Kheel Supplemental.

66. "A Fraternal Organization Sentenced to Death!"

67. "Statement of the Policyholders Committee on U.S. Supreme Court Denial of Review of IWO Case," news release, October 20, 1953, box 16, folder 13, Kheel; "IWO Demands Re-Hearing of Supreme Court Denial to Hear Its Case," news release, 1953, box 23, folder 7, Kheel; IWO petitions for rehearing, October 23 and November 4, 1953, box 4, Kheel Supplemental; "Supreme Court Rejects Second Appeal of Order to Consider Appeal Against Liquidation Order," *Morgn Frayhayt*, December 5, 1953, 1, and "The Answer of the Members of the Order to the Dewey-Brownell Pogrom," *Morgn Frayhayt*, editorial, December 9, 1953, 4, box 2, Kheel Supplemental; letter to all policyholders from New York State Insurance Department, November 18, 1953, box 23, folder 3, Kheel; letter from Alfred Bohlinger to "All Policyholders and Certificate Holders of the International Workers Order," September 1, 1954, box 2, Kheel Supplemental. See, too, "Right to Belong to Fraternal Group Strangled by Gov't. Attack on IWO," *Daily Worker*, n.d. [1953?], box 53, Kheel; transcript of the Subversive Activities Control Board hearing for IWO, December 16, 1953, box 1, Kheel Supplemental; order and report of the Subversive Activities Control Board, re: IWO, January 14, 1954, box 1, Kheel Supplemental; letter from insurance superintendent of New York to Kinoy, November 30, 1953, box 2, Kheel Supplemental; "Statement of the Former Officers of the Order Concerning the Order of the McCarran Board," *Morgn Frayhayt*, January 16, 1954, 2; letter from Joseph Petercsak, secretary, Lodge 1007, to US Supreme Court, October 23, 1953, box 3, Kheel Supplemental.

68. "New Violation of Free Association," *Jewish Life*, March 1954, 30, box 53, Kheel.

69. Conrad Komorowski FBI file 100-1886, box 7, folder 7-49, Binkowski.

70. "IWO Helped Blaze Trail in Fight for Democracy," *Głos Ludowy*, March 12, 1955, 16.

71. Detroit Police Criminal Intelligence Bureau report, February 16, 1966, box 2, folder 2-55, Binkowski; "International Bazaar for Peace and Freedom," Detroit Police Intelligence Section report, March 8, 1973, box 2, folder 2-55, Binkowski; "The Communist Party in Detroit," Detroit Police report, October 21, 1936, box 2, folder 2-55, Binkowski.

72. Dick and Mickey Flacks, *Making History, Making Blintzes: How Two Red Diaper Babies Found Each Other and Discovered America* (Rutgers University Press, 2024).

73. Flyer, Delaware Valley Committee for Democratic Rights, June 8, 1963, Communist Party USA Papers, box 297, folder 1, Tamiment Library and Robert F. Wagner Labor Archives, Elmer Holmes Bobst Library, New York University, New York, New York.

74. See Landon Storrs, *The Second Red Scare and the Unmaking of the New Deal Left* (Princeton University Press, 2013), and "Liberals! Where Are You?," *New York Post (and Bronx Home News)*, editorial, April 29, 1948, box 19, folder 7, Kheel.

75. Thanks to David Ost for noting the Muslim charities parallel.

13

FROM MANY ROOTS, ONE TREE
Jews and the Origins of Multiethnic Communism in the United States, 1921–1972

Paul C. Mishler

When the Communist Party of the United States (CPUSA) was organized in 1919, the vast majority of its supporters were working-class immigrants. Most of these radical immigrants had come from the vast eastern European Russian and Austro-Hungarian empires where ethnic and national oppression was combined with economic exploitation and poverty. Immigrant Jews, who had come from communities facing additional discrimination, economic exclusion, and antisemitic massacres, made up a large bloc within US radicalism, including Communism, and became the voice associated with working-class radicalism in New York City. Jews were not alone in this regard: there was also significant participation in radical movements from Ukrainians, South Slavs, Finns, and Hungarians, among other smaller groups.[1] Most of these Jewish immigrants worked in the burgeoning ready-made garment industry and became the organizers and members of the large garment trade unions—the International Ladies Garment Workers Union (ILGWU) and the Amalgamated Clothing Workers of America (ACWA)—as well as of the smaller Fur Workers Union, which was led by Communists and remained independent throughout its existence.

The Jewish working class, because of its urban concentration and because of the role of radicals within it, exerted an important influence on the social, cultural, and political development of New York City. The continuing importance of the children, grandchildren, and even great-grandchildren of these working-class radicals in the numerically small left in the United States speaks to the continued salience of the cultural strength of this tradition.[2]

The Jewish left, and especially the Jews who were active in the Communist movement, influenced the politics of what is now called "multiculturalism." The word currently suggests a positive conception of a society made up of a multiplicity of ethnic and racial cultures, rather than the narrow ethnic particularism that sees white, primarily English-speaking immigrants as the basis of US culture. Indeed, multiculturalists argue that this view never reflected the reality of a nation that had always included African Americans, Native Americans, and non-Anglophone immigrants. Multiculturalism remains a controversial issue in US society. Conservative commentators believe that the embrace of ethnic and racial diversity is inherently radical and a challenge to the national cohesiveness of the country. The proponents of multiculturalism, by contrast, claim for themselves a new, more inclusive patriotism. Ironically, while multiculturalists often root their claims in the Civil Rights Movement, certain conservatives are much more likely to see the entire project as rooted in the left and traced back to Marx.[3]

However, the Marxist tradition was generally hostile to ethnic culture and identity, seeing it as a diversion from the necessity for an international, working-class consciousness. Marx's followers expected the cultural and linguistic assimilation of immigrant workers into the general workers' movements in the countries to which they migrated. Friedrich Engels, for example, argued that the German immigrants who brought Marxism to the United States needed to give up their language and culture in order to have an influence on the US working class. He wrote about the predominantly German immigrant Socialist Labor Party that "they will have to doff every remnant of their foreign garb. They will have to become out and out American. They cannot expect the Americans to come to them; they, the minority and the immigrants, must go to the Americans, who are the vast majority and the natives. And to do that, they must above all things learn English."[4]

American Marxists, including most Socialists and the Communist Party at its inception, shared Engels's belief that immigrants who brought their radicalism from Europe would have to shed their "foreign garb" if Marxism were ever to find a true home in the United States. This kind of universalism did *not* mean that these radicals were unsympathetic to issues of racism or ethnic exclusion as is sometimes maintained by young radicals today.[5] German Socialists, for example, expressed solidarity with the immigrant Chinese workers so often maligned by labor activists, even though they did so mostly in German-language publications.[6]

Nonetheless, immigrant workers, even if only to continue to organize and communicate with their fellow immigrants from their home countries, built and maintained ethnic/language institutions and sections within the Socialist movement. What was different about the radical Jewish immigrants is that they truly had no nation. In no country was their language, Yiddish, the national language (although it is worth noting that, prior to 1918, Poles, Serbs, Croats, Slovaks, Lithuanians, and Ukrainians had no nation or language rights within the Austro-Hungarian and Russian empires, either). Scholars such as W. E .B. Du Bois similarly noted that Southern Blacks had been rendered effectively stateless due to the white terrorism that shut down Reconstruction, and the CPUSA agreed to adopt the Comintern's 1930 Black Belt thesis that described African Americans as an "oppressed nation." Indeed, the left in eastern Europe, primarily within the Jewish Labor Bund, developed a diasporic conception of the relationship between nationality and Socialism based on what they called "cultural-national autonomy"—that is, wherever Yiddish was spoken, that was their homeland.

The historical literature about Jewish radicalism and its Communist component is quite extensive.[7] This literature generally follows one of two paths. Some historians have examined the Jewish left in the United States as a subculture in itself, while others have looked at Jewish radicalism in its relationship to US Jewish history. Both these approaches remain insular. They consist of Jews talking to and about Jews. The issue of the relationship between the Yiddish-speaking labor movement and the development of a "multicultural" perspective within the Jewish community has been most saliently addressed by Daniel Katz, who focuses on the work of the Education Department of the ILGWU as it attempted to reach out to non-Jewish workers in the garment industry, both in New York and increasingly throughout the United States.[8] Jewish radicals with roots in the Yiddish-speaking immigrant community directed the Education Department of the ILGWU. These members of the non-Communist left worked to develop a "multicultural" educational program for members, which shows that some Jewish immigrant leftists had begun to conceive of belonging to a very multiethnic working class. The garment union also contained two Italian local chapters, which similarly offered an array of musical, theatrical, and other social programs for their members, many of whom joined the Garibaldi Society of the pro-Soviet International Workers Order (IWO) as well. The difference between the approach of the ILGWU and the Communists during the 1920s was that while the ILGWU's contribution remained primarily *within* the ranks of union members, the Communists' efforts were directed at the working class as a whole. Other leftist unions developed similar, multiethnic educational institutions.

While they may have directed their efforts at the working class as a whole, the ethnic particularities of the Jewish left, especially those within the Communist Party, influenced the left in the United States and through them US society in general. The CPUSA developed a Marxist *and* a broadly democratic perspective (if often contested) on the relationship between people of different ethnic or ethnic/racial backgrounds and on the political and ideological relationships between movements mobilized to challenge discrimination and marginalization.

This perspective was unique in the overall history of the left internationally and played a significant role in formulating a vision of American society that remains significant (even if its roots in the radical movement are only recognized by the conservative adversaries of this vision). At the center of this process were left-wing Jewish immigrants in New York City but also in other large urban areas such as Chicago, Los Angeles, and San Francisco.[9] Again, by way of contrast, a later appraisal of the ethnic aspects of the Socialist and Communist left can be felt in newer critiques of multiculturalism that address its celebratory "leveling" function, which among other things ignores structural inequalities and racial hierarchies.

There were four historical moments in which Jewish Communists played a significant role in defining this new Marxist approach to multiethnic politics. The first was the 1930 formation of the Yiddish-speaking International Workers Order out of a split within the Arbeter Ring/Workmen's Circle, the Socialist Jewish fraternal organization. As the Order conceived of it, the cultural traditions and historical heritage of various ethnic groups were to be recovered and transformed as forces for workers' progress and unity as well as celebration. These Jewish leftists chose to grow the IWO by intentionally welcoming and working with other groups that had their own progressive heritage and who, like them, had welcomed the Soviet state. Italian IWO members, for example, linked Garibaldi, hero of the nineteenth-century Risorgimento, to struggles for social democracy for all people in Depression-wracked America. Each group within the IWO similarly valorized its heritage while simultaneously working, playing, and celebrating with other Order members across ethnic and racial lines, forging a vision of a progressive multiethnic movement, of unity within diversity.

The second historical moment was when the CPUSA, in dialogue with the Communist International, recognized that the struggle against racism directed primarily against African Americans was central to the workers' struggle in the United States. For Jewish Communists this was especially important because it decentered the Jewish experience in eastern Europe and helped Jewish immigrant Communists confront the centrality of racism and other forms of chauvinism and oppression to the struggle in the United States. Rather than seeing others' experience as "like" antisemitism, they came to see antisemitism as a related form of racism.

Third, during the period in the 1930s when the Communists were committed to the development of a "Popular Front Against Fascism," Jewish Communists, like other members of the Party, became partisans in the struggle to democratize America, not simply to overthrow its capitalist form. Finally, during the 1950s and 1960s, the children and grandchildren of these Jewish Communists further developed these ideas and came to see that as the direct struggle for Socialism receded, due to repression and other factors, what brought all those decades' struggles together were battles for an anti-fascist "democracy." While this anti-fascist democracy was rooted in the Popular Front, it was divorced from the Socialist and Communist traditions and came to include reinvigorated trends from the past and to incorporate new struggles against marginalization and oppression.

The Immigrant Jewish Left

The Arbeter Ring or Workmen's Circle (AR) was founded in 1892 in the tradition of workers' mutual aid societies that had been among the first working-class organizations in the industrial era. These organizations provided collective types of assistance such as death benefits and modest health care in an era when only the best-paid workers had access to them. As they developed, the level of benefits increased. Initially these organizations had provided the basis for trade-union organization and were the sites for the development of Socialist culture. The AR was explicitly Socialist and explicitly Yiddishist, and so its educational component came to include an extensive network of leftist Yiddish schools for children that carried through into the summer by means of summer camps.

The battle between Socialists and Communists in the aftermath of the Russian Revolution and the formation of the Communist Party was especially fierce in New York City's Jewish left. By the 1930s the Socialist movement had come to speak for the Jewish working class of the city, so struggle was carried out over the course of the decade in every social and political institution of the Jewish immigrant working class, including the *Forward* newspaper and the Workmen's Circle. Yiddish-speaking Communists broke away from the Arbeter Ring in 1930 and created the International Workers Order with its founding Yiddish section, which eventually became known as the Jewish Peoples Fraternal Order (JPFO). *Di linke* (the left) had previously supported the founding of the newspaper *Morgn Frayhayt* (Morning freedom) to compete with the Socialist *Forward*.[10]

The IWO drew on the traditions and practices of the Arbeter Ring with one significant difference: they envisioned the inclusion of other ethnic societies that had existed alongside the Socialist Party (SP) or had been organized independently. Some had been part of the "foreign-language federations" directly affiliated with the Socialist Party, and others had existed on the fringes of the SP as independent organizations. Most of these societies, such as the Finnish Socialist Federation, had undergone divisions between Communists and Socialists similar to what had occurred in the Workmen's Circle. In due course, along with the JPFO, the IWO included Slovak, Hungarian, Russian, Ukrainian, Polish, Finnish, and Croatian organizations or sections, among others.[11]

The formation of the IWO in 1930 seemed to be a Communist version of the Arbeter Ring or the Socialist foreign-language federations. There was one significant difference. While the previous left-wing ethnic societies were imagined as being temporary way stations for immigrant workers until they and their families learned English, the IWO saw fraternal ethnic identification as a road to radicalism, rather than a hindrance to it. The IWO became a federated order with its own approach to the role of ethnic identification within larger struggles. Even though it had always been led by figures identified with Communism, its members were typically not Party members, nor was the IWO institutionally affiliated with the CPUSA. The IWO defended its vision of "multiculturalism" against fellow Communists who desired to "Americanize" the Order. Indeed, after World War II, the CPUSA sent Steve Nelson to discuss adding an English page to the Finnish-language CP paper *Työmies* (Worker). The Finns refused.

Despite the fact that the children, and especially the grandchildren of radical immigrants would be English-speaking, the IWO schools and newspapers endeavored to keep the old languages and cultures alive in a secular leftist milieu while at the same time maintaining the loyalty of English-speaking offspring. In this scenario, ethnic culture was celebrated as harmonious with radicalism, not its antithesis. During the Popular Front, schools also celebrated the progressive strains of American culture, aiming to instill in pupils a concept of patriotic, leftist, and *ethnicized* Americanism. IWO sections, and the CPUSA, were deeply committed to maintaining the idea that they were the legitimate heirs of tradition even as they transformed it in offering a tamed critique of the melting pot.

Although the JPFO was always the largest section of the IWO, the organization was deeply committed to the idea that the IWO, as a federation of ethnic fraternal societies, should reflect *all* the ethnic groups under its umbrella. This is most clearly seen in the creation of English-speaking African American and general lodges during the 1930s.[12] What the JPFO brought to this multiethnic mélange was the belief that ethnic immigrant culture could stand against the conservatism of American culture. This issue had been part of the discussion among eastern European Jewish radicals both organizationally and theoretically. In essence, the IWO's position was an expansion of the Bundist view of the role of ethnic autonomy to non-Jewish ethnic communities within the larger struggle for Socialism.

Jewish Communists and the Struggles of African Americans

As these ideological and practical developments were taking place among Jewish immigrant Communists and their allies, another discussion was emerging in the Communist movement that also distinguished the Communist approach to ethnicity, race, and nationality from their Socialist forebears. While Jewish immigrant radicals were debating their role in the United States, the worldwide Communist movement was addressing an issue seemingly quite far from these discussions: the relationship between the Communist movement and the struggles for national liberation in the colonized and newly independent countries of Asia, Africa, and Latin America. The Communist perspective on the role of African Americans in the United States and the importance of the struggle against racism more clearly differentiated them from their Socialist rivals than the debates inside of the Jewish radical movement. As far from the debates over the "Jewish Question" as these seemed to be, they would have a major impact on the development of Jewish Communism in the United States.

Lenin and the Communist International made a sharp break with earlier Socialist approaches to the question of European colonialism. For Lenin and his supporters one of the significant betrayals of the Socialist International in not opposing World War I was that it illustrated the Socialist neglect of the struggles against colonialism emerging in the "Third World." When the Communist International (Comintern) formed, there were twenty-nine conditions for membership. Number 8, written by Lenin, committed the Communist International to supporting the struggles for independence in Europe's colonies.[13] Most of the discussion regarding the fight against colonialism in the Communist movement until today concerns combating Western imperialism and supporting national liberation.

The anti-colonial stance of the Comintern was met with great sympathy by a group of West Indian immigrants and African Americans in the United States who were active in and around the Garveyite movement. Organized into the African Blood Brotherhood, they merged with what became the CPUSA as Marcus Garvey moved right.[14] During the 1930s both Black and white Communists organizing in Northern and Southern Black communities distinguished themselves as fierce anti-racist activists and as supporters of emerging radical Black cultural activists.

Most of this discussion and activity was directed toward encouraging Communist participation in the Black freedom struggles, challenging the racist exclusionary policies of the traditional trade unions, and building the CPUSA among African Americans. Jewish Communists came to play a significant role in these developments. The relationship between Black and Jewish Communists not only affected the development of the Black radical movement(s) but also played a significant role in the development of a particularly American Jewish radicalism as well.[15]

Both sympathizers with and adversaries of Jews and Jewish Communists have noted the early involvement of Jews in the struggles of African Americans in the

United States. Commentators such as Harold Cruse have argued that Jews distorted that struggle, while those on the far right have noted the alliance between Jewish and African American radicals as "proof" of a nefarious conspiracy.[16] What has been little noted is the impact of this involvement on the development of Jewish radicalism, especially in the CPUSA and its broader orbit.

Perhaps more than any other group of white Communists, Jewish Communists came to see the African American struggle as their own. This is first apparent in the campaign to free the Scottsboro defendants, nine young African American men from Alabama who were falsely accused of rape in 1931. Similar cases had happened before in the South and were quite well known due to the anti-lynching campaigns of the early 1900s. The CPUSA undertook to make this case a national issue, the first time that a majority-white organization would campaign against racist terror in the South. Jewish Communists participated in the campaign from the beginning. Articles, including poetry, about Scottsboro appeared in the *Frayhayt* and other Yiddish Communist publications. Other radical ethnic communities also quickly denounced "the lynch verdict in Scottsboro," with Slovak and Latvian Communist newspapers offering defenses of the nine young men as early as May 1931, and the IWO's Slovak Workers Society consistently orchestrating fundraising for their appeals.[17]

The case was first brought to the attention of the CPUSA by James Allen, the editor of the *Southern Worker*. Allen, whose birth name was Sol Auerbach, was born to immigrant Jewish parents in Philadelphia. Upon joining the CPUSA he was sent to edit the *Southern Worker*, based in Chattanooga, Tennessee, and he alerted the International Labor Defense (ILD) and the CP about the Scottsboro defendants.[18] Through the prodding of William Patterson, who was head of the International Labor Defense, the CPUSA's legal defense organization hired Jewish lawyer Samuel Leibowitz to defend the accused.[19] After Scottsboro the Jewish left continued its engagement with the African American struggle. Jewish Communist historians Herbert Aptheker, Philip Foner, and James Allen were the first white historians to highlight the history of African American resistance and to celebrate anti-racism, notably teaching or documenting Black history at IWO schools and the CPUSA's Jefferson School for Social Science. Communist labor organizers brought interracial unionism into the South, and many of them were Jewish. In Chicago, where efforts to unionize the meatpacking industry floundered in the face of racism and employer terror, Jewish Communist Herb March led union organization during the 1930s on an explicitly anti-racist basis. Leon Davis, another Jewish Communist, led the largely Jewish Pharmacist Union, Local 1199, to organize the mainly Black and Latino workers in the private hospitals of New York City. The 1962 strike brought support from across the Civil Rights Movement, including from Martin Luther

King Jr., Malcolm X, and A. Philip Randolph.[20] Martin Luther King called 1199 his "favorite union."[21]

Jewish participation in the African American struggle has been explored extensively, but much of this research is oriented toward looking at the Jewish impact on the Black freedom movement. What has been neglected are the questions of how the Black freedom struggle affected Jewish radicalism, and the related question of how this relationship influenced the development of American radicalism in general. Hasia Diner has argued that Jewish support for African American rights was part of the immigrant Jewish efforts toward "Americanization and acculturation."[22] R. J. Uhlmann points out that the role of Jewish radicals is deliberately obscured in Diner's work, but there is room for Jewish radicals in this analysis. While many southeastern European migrants returned to Europe after short stays in America, undoubtedly many other European immigrants who arrived during the first part of the twentieth century wanted to be "Americans" and faced obstacles in pursuit of that tension-ridden quest. The difference for immigrant radicals in general and for Jewish radicals in particular is that Jewish radicals wished to become "Americans" in the country as it might be, not as it was. The role the Black freedom struggle played in the consciousness of Jewish Communists was that it offered a direction toward what their America might look like.

The Popular Front

In 1935, with Nazis in power in Germany and Mussolini's fascists in power in Italy, the Communist International (Comintern) shifted significantly in their political approach. From the formation of the Comintern in the aftermath of the Bolshevik Revolution, among the most important aspects of the Communist perspective had been their critique of the Socialists and other radicals as being, essentially, traitors to the Socialist cause. In part, this came from the struggle between the Bolsheviks and Mensheviks during the Russian Revolution and from the suppression of the German revolutionary attempt of 1919 by Social Democrats. The deaths of revolutionaries Karl Liebknecht and Rosa Luxemburg at the hands of reformist Socialists cemented this inter-left hostility.

However, at the Seventh Congress of the Communist International, the general secretary, the Bulgarian Georgi Dimitrov, called for Communists to help form a "United Front" against fascism. While still criticizing the Socialists, he also criticized fellow Communists for underestimating the danger of fascism. He called for Communists and Socialists to unite in opposition to fascism and to reach out to *all* workers in defense of bourgeois democracy.[23]

For Communists in the United States this shift in approach had implications in every arena of Communist activity. However, Dimitrov's approach to the development of ethnic/national culture in particular in the context of his call for a united front against fascism influenced the CPUSA's view of the multiethnic character of the US working class, one that drew on the efforts of Jewish Communists in the JPFO, as well as the members of the various language federations of the IWO such as the Polonia Society and the Italian Garibaldi Society. Dimitrov directly challenged the "universalism" that had been characteristic of radical movements since the nineteenth century. He recognized that one of the attractions of fascism was its appeal to national and ethnic pride. He wrote, "The fascists are rummaging through the entire history of every nation so as to be able to pose as the heirs and continuators of all that was exalted in its past, while all that was degrading or offensive to the national sentiments of the people they make use of as weapons against the enemies of fascism. . . . Communists who suppose that all this has nothing to do with the cause of the working class, who do nothing to enlighten the masses on the past of their people, . . . who do nothing to *link up the present struggle with the people's revolutionary traditions and past*—voluntarily hand over to the fascist falsifiers all that is valuable in the historical past of the nation, that the fascists may bamboozle the masses" (italics mine).[24] Following from Dimitrov's speech, most of the discussion of the relationship of Communists to the national past of their countries at the Seventh Congress concerned the ways that fascist movements claimed legitimacy from the national histories of European countries. However, Dimitrov's address was a significant challenge to Communists elsewhere, especially in the colonized nations of Asia and Africa, the countries of Latin America, and in the United States.

In the United States, the Popular Front idea led to the Communist creation and embrace of a "democratic" anti-fascist tradition that had two significant characteristics. First, it legitimized the practice of radical immigrants forming their own organizations for propagandizing and organizing in the languages that were spoken in their own communities. No longer viewed as temporary way stations for immigrants as they became acculturated to "American" life, these organizations were now valued as constituent to the development of anti-fascist culture. Second, it led to Communist engagement in the creation of an alternative American history, one that included stories of African Americans, labor unions, and radical activists. This emphasis on progressive Americanism led to some unintended ironies, such as the Popular Front's celebration of both Thomas Jefferson and "Negro slave revolts" as progressive American icons.[25]

In the United States the shift in perspective promoted by the adoption of the Popular Front validated practices that had long been characteristic of the Jewish Communist movement. This is not to neglect the Jewish engagement with internal factional struggles, which were fought not only with militancy, but also with a kind of glee.[26] But the creation of mass Jewish cultural organizations; the maintenance of Yiddish theater, poetry, and literature; and the organization of Jewish choruses and mandolin orchestras, among other institutions, marked the Jewish Communist left as a distinctive part of the Communist movement and as a legitimate and popular participant in Jewish life in the United States (the JPFO alone had more than fifty thousand members by 1944). A joke from that period illustrates this approach.

> On a Saturday morning little Hymie is watching his father put on his best suit. He asks, "Papa, why are you dressing up today?" His father answers, "I am going to *shul*." "But Papa, why are you going to *shul*? We are Communists." "Hymie," his father says, "my good friend Moishe goes to *shul* to talk to G-d. I go to *shul* to talk to Moishe."

The practices of the Jewish Communists in the creation of a radical Jewish culture influenced the non-Jewish Communist ethnics through the formation of the International Workers Order, where the JPFO remained its largest section. Other immigrant radicals, Communists or not, participated in cultural activities that were dedicated to the creation of an ethnically specific radical culture. While pre-existing radical Slovak, Hungarian, and Russian fraternal societies, for example, amalgamated with the IWO beginning in the early 1930s, the Jewish Communist experience, because it had been one of the most successful, sometimes became a model for the functioning of other organizations.[27] Of particular significance, as Zecker and Keeran both note, was the creation of African American IWO lodges. In this case the Communists in the IWO wanted to use a model developed among immigrants to create an organization for African Americans in order to incorporate them into an overall multiethnic conception of American society, one that asserted the necessary ties between the fight against antisemitism and anti-immigrant prejudice and the fight against Jim Crow. Members of the IWO pointed out repeatedly that the same people who enforced Jim Crow racial segregation were often virulently antisemitic and dismissive of immigrants, as when Mississippi senator Theodore Bilbo hurled a vicious anti-Italian slur at a Brooklyn IWO member who was lobbying for enactment of the Fair Employment Practices bill. In defending workers of all backgrounds against America's reactionaries, the Order forged a progressive brand of working-class interracialism that came out of its interethnicism.

The role of individuals in left-wing politics from the 1960s through to the present has been the subject of numerous historical studies and memoirs.[28] Indeed, since the 1990s more than five hundred articles, books, and films have traced how activists linked their political engagement to the influence of Jewish

Communists during the 1930s and 1940s.[29] The predominantly Yiddish-speaking Jewish Communist left of the 1920s through 1940s had influenced a conception of multiethnic radicalism that saw ethnicity as a strength in the working-class movement, not simply as something to bear with while immigrant workers and their children learned English. Yet by the late 1930s and 1940s, the Communists who had been known for the celebration of ethnic particularism and Communists who had committed to maintaining customs and languages brought from Europe were increasingly Anglophone and Americanized. In fact, the children of the immigrant Communists *did* grow up speaking English, and by the third generation many did not speak the Yiddish, Italian, or Polish of the immigrant generation, even if some words and phrases remained—especially in the English spoken in New York City. Even the fiercely ironic sense of humor nurtured in the shtetls of eastern Europe became a part of American urban sensibility.

Within the Jewish Communist world the political beliefs, values, and activities that had been expressed in Yiddish were translated into English. Although this may be seen as a "natural" process, it was rarer among Communists of other ethnic groups. For example, Finns, who had made up one of the largest ethnic groups within the Communist orbit and were concentrated in Minnesota, Wisconsin, and Michigan, did not reproduce their politics in the next generation.[30] While individual Communists of other ethnicities did find their way into the radical movement, no other ethnic group made as significant a contribution to subsequent generations.

The main exception to this lack of intergenerational transmission were the African American and Latin American Communists. Those who grew up among Black Communists were much more likely to join the mass organizations of the Civil Rights Movement than those who did not. Angela Davis is a good example of someone whose family knew and were friends with Communists, Black and white, and who then became a prominent Communist herself. A similar dynamic prevailed among Cuban and Puerto Rican Communists who remained tied to mass revolutionary movements in their home countries. After the Cuban Revolution there was a significant return migration to Cuba on the part of Cuban American Communists (a phenomenon that remains understudied), while the children of Puerto Rican Communists in the United States became activists in the Puerto Rican Socialist Party, which saw itself as heir to the traditions of both the Communist and the Nationalist parties, both on the island and on the mainland during the 1970s.

Jewish Socialism and then Communism were at their greatest strength from the end of the nineteenth century through the 1950s. Born from the experiences of oppression in the tsarist empire, the Jewish left transformed itself from being simply a radical voice within a non-English-speaking immigrant community into a force within the larger American left. These activists advocated a framework that recognized the importance of the specific and particular historical and cultural experiences of different communities, be it Jews and other European immigrant groups, African Americans and Latin Americans, or Appalachians (often coal miners or steelworkers.) While it is a matter of active debate, some recent historians have shown that this model was also adopted (if somewhat unevenly) for women and gay people far earlier than has been generally realized.[31] This remained unique even within the US Marxist left. Neither the Socialist Party nor the Trotskyist movement, in all their forms, developed perspectives about these issues until the 1960s. Socialists retained their view that all forms of oppression could be subsumed into the general struggle of the working class, while Trotskyism, in its hostility to the Popular Front, saw support for sectoral liberation struggles as simply another example of Communist opportunism.

The Decline of *Jewish* Communism and the Rebirth of a Jewish Left

Jewish immigrant radicalism remained a significant presence in the CPUSA through the 1960s. In 1972, however, Paul Novick, the venerable and well-loved editor of the pro-Communist Yiddish daily newspaper, the New York City–based *Morgn Frayhayt*, was expelled from the Communist Party.[32] Novick and the *Frayhayt* had been increasingly alienated from the CPUSA over issues such as the existence of continued antisemitism in the Soviet Union, and most importantly, over how Communists and others on the left should see Israel. His expulsion was due to differences between Novick and the CPUSA regarding Israel that were also reflected in the concurrent split within the Israeli Communist Party over similar issues.[33]

The final split between the *Frayhayt* and the CPUSA represented the end of a significant period in the histories of the Jewish community, especially in New York City, and the CPUSA itself. Mass immigration of Jews from the Russian Empire beginning in the 1880s had transformed New York into a city with a strong Jewish flavor, even though the city had large numbers of non-Jewish immigrants as well. Eastern European Jews' immigration was severely restricted by the federal government in 1924, along with that of other "New Immigrants," at the same time that Asian immigration was completely banned. Even with the decline of mass migration, however, eastern European Jews remained influential because of their radicalism. Like others who came to the United States in this period, these Jews were fleeing poverty, political repression, and ethnic oppression. These racialized Jewish immigrants also brought with them experience in mass left-wing politics and a conception of the role of a minority ethnic culture in the struggles for revolutionary change.[34] However, ideological and generational shifts eventually made the split between the *Frayhayt* and the CPUSA inevitable. The people who had created and maintained this particular form of ethnic Communism were dying. Their children often spoke English, along with Yiddish, but their grandchildren were quite removed from the social and historical experiences that had given birth to the tradition.

Many of these children and grandchildren came to be at the center of the emerging New Left of the 1960s. Within the movement, these connections were often kept private. Many activists felt that emphasizing these connections would give strength to the right wing, which already believed that Jewish Communism was at the root of all pro–civil rights and student activism.[35] For many Jewish activists in the movements of the 1960s and 1970s, even "red diaper babies," their relationship to the tradition of the Jewish left was not as important as their response to their current concerns: the Civil Rights Movement and ensuing urban riots and strife, the struggle against the war in Vietnam, and the diverse movements that came out of those struggles. To the extent that there was a particular *Jewish* left during this period it came from religious Jews who were responding to the same issues as their non-Jewish contemporaries.

The signal event of this era's Jewish left was the Freedom Seder organized by historian and future rabbi Arthur Waskow in Washington, DC, on the third night of Passover—April 4, 1969—the one-year anniversary of the assassination of Martin Luther King Jr. Waskow's parents were pre–World War II Jewish leftists. Raised in Baltimore, he had previously published on the 1919 race massacres and on the then-contemporary Civil Rights Movement response. Held in the basement of an African American church on a burnt-out block, the Freedom Seder was attended by eight hundred people. The updated Passover Freedom Haggadah text had been published in the left-wing magazine *Ramparts* the previous February and incorporated elements from contemporary social justice writers into the traditional text. It has since become the basis of thousands of self-created Haggadahs for radical seders throughout the country.[36]

During the 1960s Jewish radicals were typically more concerned with the problem of being white than with the particulars of the Jewish left experience. Often, they shared in a national liberal consensus about the role of Israel and the progressive nature of Israeli society that was based on a myth promoted by the still–Socialist identified Israeli Labor Party and its supporters in the United States: that Israel was a society based on European social democratic ideals and that the kibbutzim (the collective farms built by left-wing Zionists) were the central institution of Israeli society. The 1967 Six Day War changed this. For the first time American Jews were exposed to the existence of a subordinated

Palestinian people who had been forced from their land and were now living in "refugee camps" in marginal communities inside Israel and dispersed throughout the Arab world. It was in this period that the Palestine Liberation Organization (PLO) emerged as a public voice for the Palestinian struggle and gained the support of the Soviet Union and its allies internationally. While the Jewish left in the United States was struggling with being "white," the struggle for Palestinian rights showed Israel as a "white" country internationally. While Jewish left activists, especially those from left-wing backgrounds, often expressed only nominal support for Israel, many others came to believe that defending Israel was the essence of being Jewish. Ironically, other left-wing Jews came to reidentify with their *Jewishness* by representing Jewish tradition within the small Palestine solidarity movements.[37]

This began to change with the Palestinian intifadas, the first in 1987 and the second in 2002. It became clear that the Israeli government, especially under the right-wing Likud Party, was not interested in resolving the conflict between Israel and Palestine and met every expression of popular Palestinian resistance with increasing military repression. This struck a chord among young Jews who began to organize specifically Jewish sites of Palestinian solidarity. Beginning with the Second Intifada, organizations such as Jews Against the Occupation (JTO), Jewish Voice for Peace (JVP) and #IfNotNow emerged among young Jewish activists. Interestingly, the activists in these organizations tended to have grown up in generally liberal, somewhat religious families. They had gone to synagogue and been B'nai Mitzvahed. They identified as Jews, but in a Reform Jewish suburban way. Jewish leftists with roots in the Communist tradition joined and participated in this work but were not a significant force.[38]

Between 1900 and the end of the 1950s Jewish radicalism in all its forms—Socialism, Communism, anarchism—were recognized parts of the overall Jewish community. All of these political perspectives were rooted in the experiences of oppression in Europe and in the struggles of the immigrant Jewish working class. Jewish Communists brought a sensitivity to ethnic oppression and a conscious connection to the communities in which they lived to the broader Communist movement. This changed as the immigrant generation underwent the Red Scare, started dying out, and their children and grandchildren became beneficiaries of the opportunities opened up by the New Deal and the GI Bill and moved from working-class communities into the new suburbs. Even with this change, many kept their radical sensibilities if not the complete ideologies of the Jewish immigrant left. Struggles over the relationship between African Americans and Jews during the 1968 New York City teachers strike that pitted predominantly Jewish teachers against African American parents and the emerging consciousness of the rights of Palestinians pushed these traditional leftists further from their roots in the Jewish communities. When a particularly Jewish form of radicalism was reborn in the Jewish movements in solidarity with Palestinians, it would be among those who did not come from this tradition or were very far removed from it.

But it was the election of Donald Trump as president of the United States in 2016 that truly mobilized a new Jewish left. Trump's election unleashed political forces that had been mainly submerged since the Second World War: an overtly antisemitic, pro-Nazi right wing. This newly emergent fascist right united racism and anti-immigrant agitation with a virulent and explicit antisemitism that had not been seen in the United States since the 1930s. A *New York Times* article titled, "Mazel Tov, Trump: You Have Revived the Jewish Left," detailed the mobilizations in the Jewish community in response to the new public antisemitism associated with Trump's supporters.[39]

And what of the Jewish Communist tradition? It lives on in two sometimes contradictory tendencies. The Communist approach that recognized the importance of sectoral oppression of Jews, African Americans, and women has been expanded in significant ways. Today all ways that individuals face inequality are included, and LGBTQ+ people and people with disabilities now have public voices that they did not have before. Often the ideology that drives these new forms of "multiculturalism" is quite removed from the vision expressed in the Communist movement. For Communists these oppressions were linked because the individuals were part of the working class. Today the struggle against these oppressions are often about differential access out of the working class.

But the older tradition has also returned in other ways through institutions that played an important role for the left-wing movements in immigrant communities even as those institutions that survived have transformed generationally. Camp Kinderland just celebrated its centennial; *Jewish Currents* (formerly *Jewish Life*) is far more popular now than it ever was. Somewhat similarly and surprisingly, descendants of Finnish leftists continue to operate Mesaba Coop Park, a cooperative camp and school in Minnesota's Iron Range. More generally, institutions were spaces for the transmission of ethnic cultures—especially languages—from immigrants to their American-born children; they made possible immersive spaces where their left-wing political ideals were not stigmatized or marginalized, and they represented the spirit of utopian or prefigurative radicalism through which activists could envision what it would be like to live in the kind of society they hoped for. These institutions emerged at a time when children growing up in working-class families did not need to go to work for wages and their parents could afford to spend some money to provide special activities for them on school holidays.

Arguably, on the Jewish left, a type of continuity can be seen in the campaigns of Vermont senator Bernie Sanders for president. Sanders was born in Brooklyn and grew up in the New York Jewish community that was the site of Jewish leftism. He is an open Socialist (although, unlike in the past, the *kind* of Socialism he supports is quite vague). He is getting support far beyond the Jewish radical milieu from which he comes, and in a pattern that might have been familiar to members of the multicultural IWO, Sanders has made alliances on the left with Muslim congresswomen Rashida Tlaib and Somali immigrant Ilhan Omar. Sanders, too, has drawn thousands to his anti-Trump rallies, speaking alongside Latina congresswoman Alexandria Ocasio-Cortez. Perhaps this example of a contemporary "multicultural" defense of immigrant and other cultures, tinged with the Popular Front understandings that Jewish Communists embraced, is the future of that immigrant radical tradition for Jews and non-Jews alike?

NOTES

1. The new Communist Party's initial base of support was in ethnic communities of immigrants who had left the tsarist empire and for whom the overthrow of the tsar made it possible for them to combine their leftist outlook with the general national aspirations they had brought with them from Europe. In the Socialist Party, they were organized as foreign-language federations that had a semiautonomous relationship within the English-speaking Socialist Party. Along with the Jewish immigrants, Slavs, Ukrainians, Finns, Latvians, and Lithuanians all had significant Socialist blocs, including newspapers, cultural centers, and fraternal organizations.

2. Left-wing activists were never the only, or even the largest of groups within the immigrant Jewish community in New York. Religious, Zionist, and political conservatives played significant roles in the Jewish community, and still do. Yet, of all ethnic communities that contained a significant left wing, the Jewish leftists were the most successful in creating a transgenerational left-wing tradition. See Paul C. Mishler, "Red Finns, Red Jews: Ethnic Variation in Communist Political Culture during the 1920s and 1930s," *YIVO Annual of Jewish Social Science* 22 (Spring 1995):142–47; and Judy Kaplan and Linn Shapiro, eds., *Red Diaper Babies: Growing Up in the Communist Left* (University of Illinois Press, 1998).

3. See Cyril Levitt, review of *The Menace of Multiculturalism: Trojan Horse in America*, by Alvin J. Schmidt, *The Canadian Journal of Sociology/Cahiers canadiens de sociologie* 24, no. 2 (Spring 1999): 321–23.

4. Fredrick Engels, preface to the English edition of *The Condition of the Working-Class in England* (John W. Lovell Company, 1887).

5. Adolph Reed Jr., "The Myth of Class Reductionism," *The New Republic*, September 25, 2019, https://newrepublic.com/article/154996/myth-class-reductionism.

6. This is not to argue that all Socialists had given up the racist and ethnic prejudices they brought with them. Rather, even within class-based universalism, there was a tradition that took notice of ethnic differences. Marx and Engels understood that British imperialism in Ireland created English working-class chauvinism against the Irish workers in England. Some workers, though, could overcome ethnic or racial prejudices in heartening ways. There is new research being conducted on nineteenth-century German-language Socialist publications that shows a greater sympathy for Chinese workers on the West

Coast than has been generally understood. Lorenzo Costaguta, "Must They Go? American Socialism and the Racialization of Chinese Immigrants," 1876–1890," in *Workers of All Colors Unite: Race and the Origins of American Socialism* (University of Illinois Press, 2023).

7. Examples of this literature include Irving Howe, *World of Our Fathers: The Journey of East European Jews to America and the Life They Found and Made* (Simon and Schuster 1976; repr., New York University Press, 2005) and Arthur Liebman, *Jews and the Left* (Wiley, 1979). While Howe's book is magisterial and sympathetic to the left in general, it also is a clear expression of Social Democratic anti-Communism. Morris Schappes, a Communist historian and writer, and JPFO leader, wrote a rejoinder to Howe, "Irving Howe's 'The World of Our Fathers': A Critical Analysis," *Jewish Currents*, September 1977, 3–31. Indeed, a recent analysis of the role of Jews in the Communist movement sees an ongoing conflict between "Communist Jews" who were Communists first and Jews second, and "Jewish Communists" who were the reverse. See Matthew Hoffman, "'At What Cost, Comrades'? Exploring the Jewishness of Yiddish-Speaking Communists in the United States," in *A Vanished Ideology: Essays on the Jewish Communist Movement in the English-Speaking World in the Twentieth Century*, ed. Matthew Hoffman and Henry Srebrnik (State University of New York Press, 2016), 19–45.

8. Daniel Katz, *All Together Different: Yiddish Socialists, Garment Workers, and the Labor Roots of Multiculturalism* (New York University Press, 2011).

9. For an analysis of the cultural strength of radicalism in the Jewish community during this period, see Paul Buhle, "Jews and American Communism: The Cultural Question," *Radical History Review* 23 (1980): 9–33.

10. In the United States, Jewish radicals allied themselves with different sectors of the movement, each with their own Yiddish newspaper(s). The first and most influential was the *Forverts* (Forward), which was the voice of Socialism allied with European Social Democracy. It continues to be published, although no longer in Yiddish (except for a Yiddish online version). Anarchists published and read the *Freie Arbeiter Stimme* (Free voice of labor).

11. The historical treatment of the IWO has been sparse, and in some early cases it was framed as simply another organization manipulated by the CPUSA. Most recently Robert M. Zecker's *"A Road to Peace and Freedom": The International Workers Order and the Struggle for Economic Justice and Civil Rights, 1930–1954* (Temple University Press, 2018), approached the IWO with a more social historical perspective. Earlier treatments are Arthur Sabin, *Red Scare in Court: New York Versus the International Workers Order* (University of Pennsylvania Press, 1993); Roger Keeran, "National Groups and the Popular Front: The Case of the International Workers Order," *Journal of American Ethnic History* 14, no. 3 (Spring 1995): 23–51; and Paul C. Mishler, *Raising Reds: The Young Pioneers, Radical Summer Camps, and Communist Political Culture in the United States* (Columbia University Press, 1999), chap. 2, "Americans All! Immigrants All!," 64–82.

12. Zecker, *"A Road to Peace and Freedom,"* 34–35.

13. Vijay Prashad, introduction to *Liberate the Colonies: Communism and Colonial Freedom, 1917–1924*, ed. John Riddell et al. (LeftWord Books, 2019), 19.

14. See Mark Naison, *Communists in Harlem During the Great Depression* (University of Illinois Press, 1983), 6–8. The history of the Communist Party's approach to and relationship with the struggles of African Americans has been quite well researched. Among the significant studies include Cedric J. Robinson, *Black Marxism: The Making of the Black Radical Tradition* (University of North Carolina Press, 2000); Mark Solomon, *The Cry Was Unity: Communists and African Americans, 1917–36* (University Press of Mississippi, 1998); Robin D. G. Kelley, *Hammer and Hoe: Alabama Communists During the Great*

Depression (University of North Carolina Press, 1990); Carolyn Boyce Davies, *Left of Karl Marx: The Political Life of Black Communist Claudia Jones* (Duke University Press, 2008).

15. For a particularly hostile discussion of this relationship, see Harold Cruse, *The Crisis of the Negro Intellectual: A Historical Analysis of the Failure of Black Leadership* (Morrow, 1967). Cruse, an ex-Communist, saw Jewish influence in the Black freedom struggle as essentially negative. His book continues to be the subject of fierce debates among Black radicals.

16. Cruse, *The Crisis of the Negro Intellectual*.

17. Letter from John Mackovich to central committee, CPUSA, May 6, 1932, Communist Party USA files, reel 214, delo 2766, Library of Congress, Washington, District of Columbia (henceforth CPUSA, LC); minutes, language department meeting, CPUSA, May 11, 1931, reel 177, delo 2332, CPUSA, LC; letter from Charles Dirba of the Lettish bureau to language department, CPUSA, May 6, 1931, reel 177, delo 2336, CPUSA, LC; letter from Czecho Slovakian buro, CPUSA, to John Mackovich, May 7, 1931, reel 177, delo 2336, CPUSA, LC.

18. See James Allen, *Organizing in the Depression South: A Communist's Memoir* (MEP Publications, 20001).

19. The best account of Jewish participation in the Scottsboro defense campaign is an Australian master's thesis, R. J. Uhlmann, "A Bunch of Jews Defending Them Damned Ni**ers" (Australian National University, 1997).

20. All three of these leaders were scheduled to speak at a rally supporting Local 1199 along with Dorothy Height of the National Council of Negro Women. King was called away to deal with a crisis in Albany, Georgia. If King had stayed, it would have been the only time that all three leaders of these different tendencies in the Black freedom struggle had been on the same platform. Malcolm X expressed admiration for Leon Davis, then sitting in jail for leading an illegal strike. This was two years before he openly broke with the generally anti-white nationalism of the Nation of Islam. Leon Fink and Brian Greenberg, *Upheaval in the Quiet Zone: A History of Hospital Workers' Union, Local 1199* (University of Illinois Press, 1989), 109.

21. Greenberg, *Upheaval in the Quiet Zone*. Local 1199 joined the Service Employees International Union (SEIU) to help form the SEIU National Health Care Union, the largest union for hospital workers in the United States.

22. Hasia Diner, *In the Almost Promised Land: American Jews and Blacks, 1915–1935* (Johns Hopkins University Press, 1995), cited in Uhlmann, "A Bunch of Jews," 6. Uhlmann critiques Diner for her overly cynical account of Jewish motives and for her focus on Jews active in such mainstream organizations as the National Association for the Advancement of Colored People (NAACP), which continues the general neglect of radicals in the historiography of Black-Jewish relations in the United States.

23. Dimitrov wrote, "Joint action by the parties of both Internationals against fascism, however, would not be confined in its effects to influencing its present adherents, the Communists and the Social Democrats; it would also exert a powerful influence on the ranks of *Catholic, Anarchist, and unorganized workers, even upon those who had temporarily become victims of fascist demagogy*." Georgi Dimitrov, *The Fascist Offensive and the Tasks of the Communist International in the Struggle of the Working Class Against Fascism*, in *Selected Works*, vol. 2 (Sofia Press, 1972), https://www.marxists.org/reference/archive/dimitrov/works/1935/08_02.htm#s2.

24. Dimitrov, *The Fascist Offensive*.

25. The best analysis of Communist cultural activism during this period is in Michael Denning, *The Cultural Front: The Laboring of American Culture in the Twentieth Century* (Verso, 1996).

26. For a wonderful description of how Jewish radicals enjoyed a good factional fight, see John Sayles's short story, "The Anarchists' Convention," in *The Anarchists' Convention and Other Stories* (Nation Books, 2005), 23–35.

27. See Zecker, *"A Road to Peace and Freedom,"* and Keeran "National Groups."

28. While the CPUSA continues to exist and its activists continue to play significant roles in the broader left, neither it nor any other explicitly Marxist organization has the kind of hegemony that the CPUSA had in the left until the 1950s. The "Red Scare" of that period was certainly a major cause of the decline of Communist influence, but it accelerated due to a series of internal crises culminating in the 1991 split that reflected internal dissatisfaction with the leadership and the reaction to the end of the Soviet Union and the Socialist countries of Eastern Europe. It is important to note that former Communists most often remained activists, contrary to the narrative that was common during the 1950s.

29. I have compiled a bibliography of writings about children and families in the Communist world in the United States that contains more than five hundred entries since 1985. Paul C. Mishler, "Bibliography: Children, Socialist Education, and the Radical Family," unpublished manuscript, 2019. The relationship between young activists and their Communist forebears began informally early in the New Left, where the term "red diaper baby" came to refer to those who grew up in Communist families. Among the early contributions to this discussion were Kaplan and Shapiro, *Red Diaper Babies*, and Mishler, *Raising Reds*.

30. See Mishler, "Red Finns, Red Jews."

31. See Kate Weigand, *Red Feminism: American Communism and the Making of Women's Liberation* (Johns Hopkins University Press, 2002). For early CPUSA support for gay rights, see the public presentation by Alan Bérubé, "No Red-Baiting! No Race-Baiting! No Queen-Baiting!," OutHistory, 2016, https://outhistory.org/exhibits/show/no-baiting/red-race-queen, which details the ways that the West Coast Marine Cooks and Stewards Union, a branch of the Communist-led National Maritime Union, fought for the rights of their gay members. Harry Hay, the founder of the first gay rights organization in the United States in the 1950s, the Mattachine Society, had been a Communist member of this union.

32. At its height during the 1920s, the *Frayhayt* had a circulation of more than twenty thousand. The newspaper lasted until 1988, serving an ever-smaller community.

33. In 1975, the Communist Party of Israel (CPI) split between the "Mikunis-Sneh" group that advocated accommodation with Israeli Zionism and "Rakah" (now Maki, the original Hebrew name of the CPI), which became a significant representative of the Arab population within Israel and closely aligned with the Palestine liberation movement. See Joel Beinin, *Was the Red Flag Flying There: Marxist Politics and the Arab-Israeli Conflict in Egypt and Israel, 1948–1965* (University of California Press, 1990), 251. The CPI remained committed to welcoming both Arabs and Jews, and until recently one of its elected Knesset members was Dov Khenin, an Israeli Jewish Communist. See an interview with Khenin by Mairav Zonszein, *Jewish Currents*, July 5, 2019, https://jewishcurrents.org/one-of-us/.

34. The Jewish Labor Bund was founded in 1897. Dedicated to organizing *within* the Jewish community, the Bund developed a perspective opposed to both Zionism, which they thought of as being both utopian and escapist, and the assimilationist tradition characteristic of the Socialist and later Communist movement. Their view was that Jews were an ethnic culture that should have a kind of autonomy based not on land but in the common use of the Yiddish language. The Bund did not initially have branches outside of eastern Europe, and many Bundists joined the radical organizations of the United States upon immigration.

35. The far right was attentive to the role of second- and third-generation Jewish radicals in the New Left. In 1965, the *Young Guard*, a publication of the far-right John Birch Society, published the names of activists in the Berkeley free speech movement who were "red diaper babies." "Red Diaper Babies Grow Up," *Young Guard* (September 1965), 11.

36. Arthur Waskow, "The Original Freedom Seder," https://web.archive.org/web/20210511200943/https://theshalomcenter.org/sites/default/files/freedomseder.pdf. Waskow later went on to become a rabbi. See the online Freedom Seder exhibit based on the Shalom Center files: "Freedom Seder: American Judaism and Social Justice," Innovations in Jewish Life Collections, University of Colorado Boulder, accessed May 26, 2025, https://embodiedjudaism.omeka.net/exhibits/show/freedomseder/exhibitxredits.

37. This was my experience.

38. At the national Jewish Voice for Peace (JVP) convention in Chicago in 2017, I and some members of my family attempted a workshop on the history of the Jewish left and there was very little interest.

39. Michelle Goldberg, "Mazel Tov Trump: You've Revived the Jewish Left," *New York Times*, August 24, 2019, https://www.nytimes.com/2019/08/24/opinion/sunday/trump-jews.html.

CODA
"The Melting Pot Has a Scorched Base"

Paul Buhle

It should not be a surprise for an oral historian or a scholar of any kind to revisit something from forty years earlier, especially if the subject has been, for the scholar, almost life-defining. But it surprised me when I reexamined an essay from 1980 in the *Radical History Review* titled, "Jews and American Communism, the Cultural Question." The essay was written between visits on my road tour of interviews, when I was spending lots of time in various locations with Yiddish speakers that included former members of the International Workers Order (IWO) and its associated Jewish Peoples Fraternal Order (JPFO).[1] I was also then reading the Yiddish volumes that they gave me, or in one notable case, that I plucked from an apartment in the Allerton Avenue co-ops from which humorist Sam Liptzin had departed in every sense a few days earlier.[2] Most of the volumes went on to the Yiddish Book Center, eventually. A couple dozen are precious volumes in my personal library.[3]

The essay explored the background of the issue through a handful of leftist ethnic communities, including Finns, Slovenians, Italians, and Hungarians, with the Germans in the distant, nineteenth-century background. The Jewish experience was unique, but hardly idiosyncratic. The experience of mostly but not entirely blue-collar immigrant communities adapting to life in the United States, creating cultural and benefit societies, responding first to capitalism and then to the First World War, the Russian Revolution, fascism, and the Popular Front carried the story along.

Within this larger story, I came quickly back to a smaller and more intimate one, very close to the subject of our online conference on *di linke* (the Yiddish left) hosted by Cornell University, in December 2020. Itche Goldberg—teacher, mentor, exemplar—was my friend and mentor even if I was never fortunate enough to take a course from him or to contribute to *Yidishe kultur*, the journal he edited in its final decades.[4] The Zhitlowsky Foundation, which published *Yidishe kultur*, sent me on my first trip to Miami Beach in 1978 and in that way propelled me into a two-year National Endowment for the Humanities grant, where I managed to do a lot of other fieldwork in oral history with Yiddish speakers, now gathered into an archive at Tamiment Library, New York University, as "The Oral History of the American Left."[5]

I have a small secret from this period in my life. I had already published two left-wing, mainly historical and cultural journals on thin budgets between 1967 and 1980. On one of my visits to his office, Itche hinted that, if anyone could, I might manage somehow to keep *Yidishe kultur* going, an impossible idea for many reasons. It was, nevertheless, one of the most flattering offers ever made to me. I was probably not the only one to receive it.

It was hopeless, even apart from my fumbling fluency in Yiddish. The readers were in the last years of their long lives. And the end was near.

But a decade later, I thought I should have proposed a bilingual journal and found someone to help me do it. And who knows? At any rate, what Itche sought to explain in 1942 by saying that America's melting pot had a scorched bottom was that the purported option of assimilation into the American Dream and its hollow identity actually deprived immigrant cultures of their sources of nourishment. These remarks were a Jewish-Yiddish articulation of the very best pious spirit of the Popular Front.

An IWO leader, Ernie Rymer, had explained to me that he had organized, around 1938, a demonstration in Washington, DC, where a dozen ethnic and racial groups in their costumes marched together, expressing their profoundly democratic and radical idea of the United States as a nation of nations in which its parts would not have to give up their own identities.[6] Linked to anti-fascism, it was a far more socialistic version of multiculturalism than the one we see in the twenty-first century, eight decades later. It assumed that the New Deal was a sort of transition to a higher form of cooperative society in the United States, a transition that never took place.

Behind and beneath the various communal expressions of the immigrant left—the choruses, the schools, and the language groups—was a collective memory reaching back centuries, recuperating the precious legacies of earlier times. The Guyanese novelist Wilson Harris once explained that these buried memories are always with us.[7] They are in us but must be recovered because we desperately need them against the terrors of our own time.

I say, in my 1980 essay, that Cold War biases blinded Irving Howe, among others, from seeing the Yiddish left in its richness.[8] This was also the moment in time when Howe's *World of Our Fathers* appeared and I was asked to be on a panel of the Organization of American Historians assessing the book. I had real quarrels about his treatment or lack of treatment of the Jewish Communist left. For example, he declined to acknowledge the *Morgn Frayhayt* (Morning freedom) as a daily paper . . . because it had no Sunday edition. But I was reminded in my dialogue with Howe at that panel of *World of Our Fathers* that like political views, the aesthetic biases of modernism could weigh heavily.[9]

We split a lance on another issue, seemingly unrelated but actually related in a fundamental way. As a modernist, he disdained the "Teardrop Millionaires," the Yiddish poets of the 1890s like Morris Rosenfeld, who were said to be paid in the tears shed for their poems by workers in the sweatshops who experienced the poets in newspapers and books but also suffering with their devoted readership on picket lines and at rallies.[10] Their poems, some of them adopted by choral groups and still sung in 1980, offended or repelled him, as they would any modernist. This poetry was direct. It was didactic, in the ways that the creation of modern, poetic art cannot possibly be. In *Partisan Review* language, it somehow smelled of kitsch.

For me, of course, this poetry was appealing for the same reasons that the songs of Paul Robeson were appealing, or the dozens of the best films scripted by future Hollywood blacklistees.[11] For many of my generation of the New Left, the culture of the Popular Front years is the greatest of legacies. And for me, this legacy cannot be understood without an immersion in Yidishkayt (Yiddish culture).

A famed radio example during wartime, the sweeping poem "Lonesome Train" is about the travel of Abraham Lincoln's body from Washington, city by city, to its destination in Springfield, Illinois. It was written by another Jewish blacklistee that I interviewed, Millard Lampell, who had been a member of the Almanac Singers and a sometime roommate of Woody Guthrie.[12] All of this straightforward, emotive sensibility was undesirable for political reasons, but also in part because an older group of left writers and artists, many of them in a kind of lifelong dialogue with popular culture or folk culture, was about to be discredited in order for a newer group to take hold, a newer group known in part as the New York intellectuals.

Actually, I think Howe understood this. Beneath the revival of old quarrels, as much against the generational conflict of the 1960s as against the Stalin-Trotsky conflict of the 1930s, he was happy to hear that Yiddish was studied again, and even eager to reconcile. After all, 1982 brought the Democratic Socialists of America into being, with Dorothy Healey and Irving Howe at the same figurative table.¹³ In the Yiddish world, too, the healing had begun, and Itche Goldberg played an important role there, too.

I was doing some more research and writing about comic strips and comic books at this time, and I came across an essay by Irving Howe from 1949 saying that comic books were among the most degrading form of culture that had ever existed, and warning parents to keep their children away from them.

This was the high modern attack on popular culture, with nearly all popular cultures being degraded. But also, in my mind, it was an attack on the WPA-style art and New Deal sentiment of finding things in life around you, finding things in communities around you, which was, by the 1950s, something that was no longer to be seen, heard, or really appreciated. We, historically interested people in the New Left, had to rediscover this part of American history. Labor history walking tours are a tiny part of it, but they are representative of the search to recuperate it.

And I would say that this volume is another element in this search to recuperate a past that was taken away, but seems more and more precious now that we're decades away from it.

There were other types of reconciliation of time and memory as well. In 1980, I interviewed half a dozen or so Emmas at the Emma Lazarus Clubhouse in New York, many of whom had been JPFO members. The main rule was that if you wouldn't leave for Co-op City or wherever it was and get all the way to a meeting, you were out.¹⁴ They were very determined that everyone be active until they literally were ready for an IWO funeral ceremony.

Memory poem: This is a little something that came from going to an apartment in Miami Beach in one of those big buildings. And I think there were six ladies who were in their mid-eighties. And before they began, I turned to the host closest to me.

And she said, pointing to a photograph next to her chair, "Take a look at that photograph over there—our convention, 1931. We had a needle trade union of our own and it was Red. But we had to go back to the ILGWU with our heads down. We have one rule in our book circle—you have to say something new, and do not talk about your aches and operations."¹⁵

But as I said, the Emma Lazarus League was seen as a place for Americanized leftist Jewish women and other women they could recruit. And as a very special place in which they knew what they did and could do things that were crucial. And my belief is, from interviewing the elderly ladies in Miami Beach, that their wartime activity organizing to raise money became viewed as the most critical women's activity since the Depression rent strikes. Women were again at the very center of activities. And this elevated them in ways they had not been elevated within the broad Popular Front milieu.

Why, then, do we reach back now? There are very good scholarly reasons within Jewish American life and beyond. Of all the fuller history of the Jewish left, the JPFO and the IWO remain the most neglected and, at the same time, are among the richest historical probes.

Why? Because the activity in and around the JPFO was more popular and more neighborhood-like than activities in and around the political movement as such. It was more tied to everyday life, more tied to family life, more tied to cultural memories, more tied to anti-racist work even as it fought antisemitism.

And there, we really hit some kind of *Amerikanski* bullseye where children could be told about race relations and the situation of Black people in the United States by their parents, read about them, and as little Jews think about what persecution meant, means, and identify in some vital way so that when Paul Robeson or someone like him visits, it's not an abstraction. It's a very real thing. And the joining of these people into some kind of global anti-fascist movement achieved a solidity and reality that an earlier primitivist Sovietist something or other could not achieve, but that gave Camp Kinderland and Yiddish a kind of vitality during the Popular Front even as most Yiddish speakers in the world were about to be destroyed.[16]

We can see this in Ben Katchor's art and his understanding of 1930s leftist children's art; Ben's immigrant father not coincidentally was an IWO supporter.[17] Ben's cartoons bring back vanished worlds. And in my mind, his art always speaks to that sense of loss, the same sense of loss that he's written about in prose, of walking around New York City and seeing all the vernacular architecture that's disappeared and been replaced by essentially a big shopping center across large parts of the city.

Why is this so terribly important to remember now? Partly because it's disappearing with such incredible speed, partly because it speaks to those things in our collective memory that are of a different way of seeing life, a more collective—if not always more cooperative—way of seeing life, but one that was at the human scale of the small merchant and the sidewalk stroller, rather than the scale of the enormous buildings and the wealthy people who own these fabulously priced condominium units.

Ben's work has done this repeatedly, and if only a wider audience would look at this, glance at it, not merely as being entertainment and enjoyable and so forth, but read deeper and deeper into Ben's work—something we all should encourage—they would find a great deal more for themselves, but also something to trouble them in a highly useful way, and to understand that very particular thing in Yiddish culture, which seems now, perhaps, more important than it's ever been.

NOTES

1. The IWO (International Workers Order) was founded in 1930 as an immigrant fraternal order that provided high-quality, low-cost health and burial insurance and other benefits for members. Founded by Yiddish-speaking immigrants who eventually became known in 1944 as the JPFO (Jewish Peoples Fraternal Order), the IWO (the *Ordn*) rapidly grew to encompass sixteen distinct "national/ethnic/linguistic" sections. For those familiar with the Yiddish-speaking immigrant left, the JPFO was often referred to as *di linke* (the left). Its origins arose from a decade of splits (1920–30) concerning the USSR, the Bolshevik Revolution, and Communism that consumed the Jewish Federation of Socialists and Arbeter Ring (Workmen's Circle) groups associated with Eugene V. Debs's Socialist Party. While the vast majority of the IWO's members—almost two hundred thousand at its peak right after World War II—did not belong to the Communist Party of the United States of America (CPUSA), the IWO's politics and leadership were largely aligned with those of the Party, although its emphasis on immigrant interethnicity and efforts to fight antisemitism and "Jim Crow" racism distinguished it in many regards. The IWO was legally disbanded by the State of New York in 1954 due to the Cold War Red Scare. Without its critical mutual benefit insurance component, the JPFO reconstituted itself in a much-weakened form as the Jewish Cultural Clubs and Societies.

2. Sam Liptzin (1893–80)—"Uncle Sam"—was a Yiddish humorist and songwriter who wrote primarily for the Yiddish leftist press, including the *Morgn Frayhayt*, which was associated with the CPUSA. See Yiddish lexicon (Leksikon Fun Der Nayer Yidisher Literatur), Congress for Jewish Culture, for a list of his publications, accessed April 1, 2025, http://yleksikon.blogspot.com/2017/04/sam-liptzin-shepsl-sem-liptsin.html.

The Bronx Allerton Avenue co-ops, known as the "Coops," were built by the United Workers Coop Organization in 1927 in two major phases. The Coops were run cooperatively and to some degree were financed internally by initial investments. As part of *di linke's* overlapping organizational world that connected to the JPFO, they represented a new type of living arrangement for Yiddish-speaking immigrant garment trade workers, most especially for those who had previously lived in the world's densest urban area, the Lower East Side. Distinctive characteristics of Coop life included welcome proximity to Bronx River Park, basement space for WPA-supported arts programs and for children's science and arts clubs, a large multilingual library, and much more. Yiddish-oriented leftist institutions such as the JPFO's largest *shule* thrived in this world. Arguably it was an ideological disregard for financial management that eventually resulted in the complex unnecessarily being sold off to a private landlord. See Michal Goldman and Ellen Brodsky, prods., *At Home in Utopia*, 57 mins., Michal Goldman and Independent Television Service, 2008.

3. The Yiddish Book Center, located on the campus of Hampshire College in Amherst, Massachusetts, is dedicated to the preservation of Yiddish literature. It is the largest repository of Yiddish books in the world and offers many of the resources associated with Yiddish culture in all its fullness.

4. Itche Goldberg was head of the JPFO's *shule* (Yiddish after-school) program, the cultural director of its Camp Kinderland, and served broadly as the JPFO's cultural and educational director. The longtime editor of YKUF's journal *Yidishe kultur*, Goldberg also edited a pedagogical journal, *Proletarishe dertsiung* (Proletarian education) (later known as *Heym un dertsiung* [Home and education]), and *Yungvarg* (Youth), a monthly children's magazine. When the JPFO legally spun off its departments into independent organizations, Goldberg pulled the JPFO's schools into the Independent Service Bureau for Jewish Education. The Jewish Cultural Clubs also obtained separate legal identities for Camp Kinderland, the IWO Cemetery Department, and the journal *Yidishe kultur*. IKUF, *Yidishe Kultur*, ed. Itche Goldberg and Nakhmen Mayzil, 57 vols. (Alveltlekher Yidisher Kultur Farband, 1938–95). See Itche Goldberg, "Di Yidishe kultur un di yidishe shuln in

amerike" [Yiddish culture and schools in America], in *In dinst fun folk: Almanakh fun Yidishn Folks-Ordn* [In service to the people: Almanac of the Jewish Peoples Order], ed. Y.A. Rontsh, Itche Goldberg, and Rubin Saltzman (New York: Book League of the Jewish People's Fraternal Order, 1947), 29.

5. The Zhitlowsky Foundation was established after the death in 1943 of Dr. Chaim Zhitlowsky, a famous writer and theorist who fused Marxist thought with that of secular Yiddishism. Zhitlowsky, whose political stances varied over the years, died on a wartime fundraising tour for the IWO. The foundation, with which Itche Goldberg was deeply involved, funded some of the Yiddish educational, cultural, and political work that could no longer take place under the JPFO name once the IWO was forcibly dissolved by the State of New York in 1954.

6. Ernie Rymer was an active JPFO leader who after the war became its national director of youth and veterans activities, which sponsored its Jewish Young Fraternalists group. He also taught "shop" for the WPA (Works Progress Administration) at the Allerton Avenue Coops.

7. Wilson Harris, a prolific Guyanese poet and writer, wrote about memory, diaspora, landscapes, history, and empire.

8. Irving Howe was a well-known New York Jewish literary intellectual whose original leftist leanings veered toward Trotskyism and eventually toward social democracy. Irving Howe, with the assistance of Kenneth Libo, *World of Our Fathers* (Harcourt Brace Jovanovich, 1976).

9. The *Morgn Frayhayt* was a New York City–based Yiddish-language newspaper affiliated with the Communist Party.

10. Morris (Moshe) Rosenfeld was the best known of the "Sweatshop Poets" who documented the deplorable conditions under which they labored in the Lower East Side's needle trades. Their poems were published by leading Yiddish newspapers; some were turned into songs that are still sung today as klezmer classics, the most famous being Rosenfeld's "Mayn rue plats."

11. Paul Robeson was arguably the most famous singer of his generation, but this hardly describes his diverse talents, which encompassed theatrical performances, academic success as a Rhodes scholar and lawyer, and athletic prowess. His left-wing politics, which put Blackness squarely into view, were aligned with those of the Civil Rights Congress (CRC) and other organizations within the IWO's orbit. Among other connections, he sent his son to the IWO's Camp Wo-Chi-Ca and held benefit concerts for the CRC at Peekskill, New York, in 1949, as well as for the IWO. He was connected to the IWO's leadership and became a member.

12. Millard Lampell was a Hollywood blacklistee whose myriad accomplishments included being one of the founders of the Almanac Singers, a left-wing folk group branded as seditious by the FBI. He was a playwright; novelist; TV, radio, and movie scriptwriter; and much more. Composer Earl Robinson set Lampell's words to "Lonesome Train" into a musical cantata that was performed on television and released as an album.

13. Dorothy Rosenblum Healey was an early Communist leader and famous union organizer in the 1930s known as an active supporter of Black and Chicano workers in California. Disillusioned with the CPUSA, most especially after the 1968 Soviet invasion of Czechoslovakia, by 1982 she had joined with the Democratic Socialists of America.

14. Emmas were members of the feisty Emma Lazarus Federation (ELF), which became its own legal entity in 1951. Its earlier incarnation, the Emma Lazarus Division of the JPFO, was founded in 1944 to encourage women's organizing. As per the American Jewish Archives, ELF worked primarily in English on "(1) Jewish culture and education, (2) child welfare and education, (3) antisemitism and discrimination, (4) aid to Jews in other lands, and (5) civic action in interests of home and family. . . . Popular projects

included donations to libraries of books pertaining to Jewish and African-American subjects." The federation's namesake, Emma Lazarus, was a nineteenth-century Sephardic Jewish poet whose famous words, "Give me your tired, your poor, your huddled masses yearning to breathe free" are inscribed at the base of the Statue of Liberty. Co-op City is a Mitchell-Lama cooperative housing development that was built between 1966 and 1973 in the northeastern Bronx.

15. The International Ladies' Garment Workers' Union (ILGWU) was the main union for the needle trades when it was founded in 1900. In its earlier incarnations, it was famously associated with JPFO founder Clara Lemlich (Shavelson), who led the 1909 Uprising of the 20,000 and organized against the Triangle Shirtwaist Factory, where 146 workers, primarily young immigrant women, tragically died in 1911 when fire doors were locked. In later years, the ILGWU was primarily associated with David Dubinsky and its politics veered away from any association with Socialism although it kept the memory of the Triangle fire alive not least through the efforts of Leon Stein, Rose Pesotta, Rose Schneiderman, and Pauline Newman.

16. Camp Kinderland was founded in 1923 on Sylvan Lake (Hopewell Junction, near Beacon, New York) as an overtly leftist Yiddishist camp for workers' children, many of whom attended *shules* that aligned with *di linke*. (Its rapid success then spurred the Arbeter Ring to found Camp Kinder Ring on the other side of the lake.) Its pro-Soviet campers, counselors, and alumni, and those of Lakeland, its associated adult camp, engaged in deep cultural programs providing top-notch access to the dramatic and musical arts. ARTEF troupe actor Jules Dassin staged two Yiddish productions there before being blacklisted after producing *The Naked City*; Dassin subsequently left the United States to become a famous film director in France. Despite the Cold War, Kinderland had a resurgence in the 1960s and continues to promulgate its political and cultural values as it has now marked its centennial.

17. Ben Katchor (1951–) is a cartoonist and illustrator best known for his satirical strip, *Julius Knipfl, Real Estate Photographer*. Katchor teaches illustration at the Parsons School of Design, the New School, and has given presentations on leftist children's art as seen in Camp Kinderland in the 1930s.

Appendix

The materials listed here are primarily from the Kheel Center's archival holdings on the International Workers Order. They were chosen to convey through original documents the topics covered in this book and reflect the range of source materials used. Readers can access selected documents from the IWO archive through Cornell University Press's "Supplementary Book Materials" collection in Cornell University Library's eCommons repository and from other digital repositories. Each item includes a URL where the documents may be found and downloaded.

Dittmer, Dean W. "16 in Army Cited as 'Communists.'" *The Philadelphia Daily News*, July 18, 1945. Box 45, folder 1, clipping, Kheel Center, 5276b45f01_03.pdf, https://digital.library.cornell.edu/catalog/ss:21072656.

Federal Bureau of Investigation. Vito Marcantonio, part 11 of 12, file number 100-281261. Vito Marcantonio part 22 of 25, 1951–52. FBI Records: The Vault, https://vault.fbi.gov/Vito%20Marcantonio/Vito%20Marcantonio%20Part%2022/view.

Harap, Louis. Letter from *Jewish Life* to W. E. B. Du Bois, February 13, 1952. W. E. B. Du Bois Papers, MS 312, Special Collections and University Archives, University of Massachusetts Amherst Libraries, https://credo.library.umass.edu/view/full/mums312-b137-i103.

International Workers Order. *Call to a Cultural Conference*. Brochure, 1943. IWO Records #5276, box 49, folder 6, Kheel Center, 5276b49f06_01.pdf, https://digital.library.cornell.edu/catalog/ss:19043101.

International Workers Order. *Five Years of International Workers Order: 1930-1935*. Full convention book souvenir journal. Box 48, folder 13, Kheel Center, 5276b48f13_01.pdf. Pages 35–40 include the Louise Thompson article "Fraternalism and the Negro People." https://resolver.library.cornell.edu/misc/ss:40523820.

International Workers Order. "June Gordon and the Emma Lazarus Division, Statement of the Jewish Fraternal Order on Behalf of the FEPC." Press release, July 9, 1945. Box 28, folder 2, Kheel Center, 5276b28f02_24.pdf. https://resolver.library.cornell.edu/misc/ss:40523816.

International Workers Order. *Our Family Is Protected in the IWO*. Brochure featuring Paul Robeson, Louise Thompson, and Dr. Luther Peck, circa 1945. Box 6, folder 4, Kheel Center, 5276b06f04_01.pdf. https://resolver.library.cornell.edu/misc/ss:40523804.

International Workers Order. "Rockwell Kent Peekskill, N.Y., Paul Robeson Concert." Press release, September 26, 1949. Box 48, folder 28, Kheel Center, 5276b48f28_12.pdf.

International Workers Order. *Week of Jewish Culture in the Bronx*. Pamphlet, 1948. Box 34, folder 1, Kheel Center, 5276b35f01_07.pdf, https://digital.library.cornell.edu/catalog/ss:20632747.

International Workers Order Policyholders Protective Committee. *A Fraternal Order Sentenced to Death: The Strange Case of the International Workers Order Now Before the U.S. Supreme Court*. Brochure, 1953. Box 16, folder 13, Kheel Center, 5276b16f13-001.pdf. https://resolver.library.cornell.edu/misc/ss:40523827.

Mikhoels, Solomon, and Itzik Feffer. "Solomon Mikhoels and Itzik Feffer to Rubin Saltzman in Thanks." Telegram, October 1943. Box 29, folder 5, Kheel Center, 5276b29f05_14.pdf, https://digital.library.cornell.edu/catalog/ss:20631978.

Morell, Peter. "The Threat to Civil Liberties." In *Fraternal Outlook*, November 1939, 3–5, 28. Includes a William Gropper cartoon of a millionaire shredding the Constitution. Box 48, folder 17, file 1, Kheel Center, 5276b48f17001.pdf. https://resolver.library.cornell.edu/misc/ss:40523826.

Schaeffer, Jacob. *Mit Gezang tzum Kamf* [With song to the struggle]: *Songs for Voice and Piano*. New York: International Workers Order, 1932. Box 49, folder 11, Kheel Center, 5276b49f11_01.pdf, https://digital.library.cornell.edu/catalog/ss:19043111.

Contributors

Felicia Bevel is an assistant professor of history at the University of North Florida, where she serves on the Africana Studies and the Digital Humanities Institute advisory boards and is a faculty contributor on the Red Hill Cemetery Project. Her research and teaching interests include African American history, transnational cultural history, and Southern Studies. She is currently working on a book project that examines twentieth-century American culture that romanticized the Old South and circulated within the larger Pacific world. Her work has been supported by the Ford Foundation, the American Council of Learned Societies, and the Florida Education Fund.

Paul Buhle is a longtime scholar of the Jewish left in the United States and an editor and creator of graphic novels. Among his forty-some books are *Tender Comrades: A Backstory of the Hollywood Blacklist* (University of Minnesota, 1997) and *Jews and American Popular Culture* in three volumes (Praeger Publishers, 2006), followed by a robust series of graphic novels on the American left (*Yiddishkeit: Jewish Vernacular and the New Land* with Harvey Pekar, 2011), including most recently on Paul Robeson, and on the Bund. He is also coeditor of the *Encyclopedia of the American Left*.

Matthew Calihman is a professor of English at Missouri State University. He has published articles and book chapters on Amiri Baraka, Ralph Ellison, and John A. Williams. His most recent publication is the chapter titled "African American Political Poetries," in *The Cambridge Companion to American Poetry and Politics Since 1900* (ed. Daniel Morris [Cambridge University Press, 2023]). Calihman is the coeditor, with Gerald Early, of *Approaches to Teaching Baraka's Dutchman* (MLA, 2018) and the coeditor, with Tracy Floreani and A Yẹmisi Jimoh, of the Ralph Ellison special issue of *American Studies* (vol. 54, no. 3 [2015]).

Annabel (Annie) **Gottfried Cohen** is a PhD student in history at the University of Edinburgh, researching Communist activists centered in and around Barcelona during the 1936–39 Civil War. She has a master's (MRes) in history with distinction from the University of London, for which she was also awarded best overall performance at master's level and best dissertation for her thesis on grassroots Communist activists and the origins of the International Brigades.

CONTRIBUTORS

Ben Katchor is a cartoonist, writer, librettist, and illustrator who teaches at the New School, where he is an associate professor at Parsons. His picture-stories have been collected in a number of books: *Cheap Novelties: The Pleasures of Urban Decay* (Penguin, 1991); *Julius Knipßel, Real Estate Photographer: Stories* (Little, Brown, 1996); *The Cardboard Valise* (Pantheon, 2011); *The Jew of New York* (Pantheon, 1999); *The Jew of New York* (Pantheon, 1999); *Hand Drying in America and Other Stories* (Pantheon, 2013), *The Dairy Restaurant* (Pantheon, 2020), and *Hotel & Farm* (Pantheon, forthcoming). Katchor has collaborated with composer Mark Mulcahy on six musical theater shows, most recently *The Imaginary War Crimes Tribunal*. He has been the recipient of a MacArthur Foundation Fellowship, a Guggenheim Fellowship, and a fellowship at the American Academy in Berlin. Katchor's father was a Polish Jewish immigrant and reader of the *Morgn Frayhayt*.

Dylan Kaufman-Obstler holds a PhD in history from the University of Wisconsin–Madison (class of 2021). Her dissertation, "Language for a Revolution: Yiddish Schools in the United States and the Making of Jewish Proletarian Culture," explores Yiddish education in the Communist movement and its significance in the history of the Old Left. Kaufman-Obstler lives in the Eastern Sierra region of California and works as adjunct faculty in history at Cerro Coso Community College.

Paul Mishler (d. 2024) was an associate professor of labor studies at Indiana University. His book, *Raising Reds: Young Pioneers, Radical Summer Camps, and Communist Political Culture*, was published by Columbia University Press in 1999. His most recent publications included "Respectability and Its Discontents: Sexuality and Marginalisation in the Marxist Tradition in the United States," *Twentieth Century Communism* 20 (2021). He was a proud grandson of IWO members who carried on the Jewish radical tradition.

Ben Ratskoff is an assistant professor in the Department of Critical Theory and Social Justice at Occidental College. He received his doctorate in comparative literature from the University of California–Los Angeles in 2021.

Elissa Sampson is an urban geographer who has worked extensively with Cornell University's Kheel Center archives on the International Workers Order (IWO). Along with her spouse, Professor Jonathan Boyarin, Sampson is responsible for the partial digitization of the archive. Based largely on holdings related to the Jewish Peoples Fraternal Order (JPFO) of the IWO, she organized a public, online academic conference, "Di Linke," whose weeklong series of webcasts in December 2020 attracted more than six hundred attendees. A Research Associate, she was a lecturer in Cornell's Jewish Studies Program, where she taught labor and gender history, including the 1911 Triangle Shirtwaist Fire, its memorialization, and its relationship to current activism. She has published in the fields of urban geography and memory studies as well as on the IWO.

Henry Srebrnik is a professor of comparative politics in the Department of Political Science at the University of Prince Edward Island and in his research examines the impact of nationalism and ethnically based political conflict on societies. He has written or coedited four books on the subject of Jewish communities and Communist movements, including one on the United Kingdom.

Lauren B. Strauss is a professor of Jewish history and culture at the American University in Washington, DC, where she also serves as director of undergraduate studies for the Jewish Studies Program. A scholar of American Jewish political and cultural history, her forthcoming book is *Painting the Town Red: Jewish Visual Artists, Yiddish Culture, and Radical Politics in Interwar New York.*

Nerina Visacovsky has a PhD in history and education from the University of Buenos Aires (UBA). She is an investigador de carrera at the National Council for Scientific and Technical Research (CONICET) and a professor at the School of Politics and Government at San Martin University (UNSAM). She has published several articles and book chapters on the identity and culture of left-wing Jews in Argentina and Latin America. Additionally, Visacovsky is the editor of *Cultura Judeo-progresista en las Américas* (Progressive Jewish culture in the Americas) (Imago Mundi, CEHTI, 2022) and the author of *Argentinos, judíos y camaradas: Tras la utopía socialista* (Argentinians, Jews and comrades: Beyond the socialist utopia) (Biblos, 2015). She is the founder and director of the Pinie Katz Documentation Center and Library (CeDoB) of ICUF (YKUF) in Buenos Aires.

Jennifer Young is a public historian who is the education program manager at the Yiddish Book Center. She is the author of "The Scorched Melting Pot: The Jewish Peoples Fraternal Order and the Making of American Jewish Communism, 1930–1950," in *A Vanished Ideology: Essays on the Jewish Communist Movement*, ed. Matthew Hoffman and Henry Srebrnik (State University of New York Press, 2016); and "A Shprakh iz vi a Gortn: Shloyme Davidman and the Role of Children's Literature in American Yiddish Communist Culture," in *Children and Yiddish Literature from Early Modernity to Post-Modernity*, ed. Gennady Estraikh et al. (Legenda Press, 2015); as well as "Beyond the Color Line: Yiddish Ethnography and the Politics of Race," in *Choosing Yiddish: New Frontiers of Language and Culture*, ed. Lara Rabinovitch et al. (Wayne State University Press, 2013).

Robert M. Zecker is a professor of history at Saint Francis Xavier University, Nova Scotia, Canada, where he teaches courses in race, immigration, social movements, and US history. His research includes immigration, radicalism, and the popular culture of immigrants on the left. He is the author of many articles in journals such as the *Journal of American Ethnic History*, *American Communist History*, the *Journal of Popular Culture*, and the *Journal of Transnational American Studies*. He is the author of four books, most recently *"A Road to Peace and Freedom": The International Workers Order and the Struggle for Economic Justice and Civil Rights, 1930–1954* (Temple University Press, 2018). He is currently writing a history of the workers' schools of the CPUSA.

Index

Abraham Lincoln Brigade, 14, 225n16, 283, 286–94, 299
Abraham Lincoln School, 164, 182
Abramofsky, Bernard, 283, 286, 297–300
Abramovitch, Herman, 231
Abrams, William, 251, 253
Achdus (Wartime Jewish Unity), 23–24, 27–28, 31–32, 34, 37–38, 45n9
African Blood Brotherhood, 339
Aleichem, Sholem, 263
Alexander, Al, 283
Allen, James, 340
Allen, Lewis. *See* Meeropol, Abel
Allende, Salvador, 222
Almanac Singers, 356
Almazov, Shloime, 229
Alter, Wiktor, 29
Amalgamated Clothing Workers of America, 333
American Artists' Congress, 260
American Civil Liberties Union, 313
American Committee for Protection of Foreign Born, 88, 310, 321
American Committee for the Settlement of Jews in Birobidjan (Ambijan), 231, 233–36
American Committee of Jewish Writers, Artists and Scientists, 34
"American Folklore Map," 265
American Hellenic Brotherhood, 115, 318
American Jewish Conference, 24, 28, 31–32, 34–37, 39, 42, 44n3
American Jewish Congress, 36, 37, 38, 42, 48n31, 263
American Jewish League Against Communism, 320
American Labor Party, 100, 116
American Nazi Party, 91
American Negro Academy, 100, 101, 111
American Negro Labor Congress, 174
American People's Chorus, IWO, 159–61
American-Polish Committee for Protection of Foreign Born, 310
American Russian Fraternal Society, IWO, 7, 16, 17n3, 260
American Slav Congress, 7, 26, 31, 314

American Society for Technical Aid to Spanish Democracy, 278
Americanization, 13, 44, 52, 54, 55, 57, 139, 184–85, 192, 338, 341, 344, 357
Amsterdam News, 138
anti-colonialism, 6, 12, 129, 149, 175, 179, 202n52, 291, 339; *Głos Ludowy* and, 15; Robeson and, 161, 166–67; Soviet Union and, 77, 173–74; Thompson Patterson and, 188, 191
anti-Communism, 10, 15, 151, 193, 309, 311–13, 315–16, 320–21, 324, 325; Canada and, 241; deportations and, 88, 115, 317–19; Du Bois and, 115–16; Gropper and, 265–66; JPFO and, 42–43; Latin America and, 209, 218, 221; Robeson and, 153, 193–94
anti-eviction campaigns, 6, 9, 10, 188, 321
anti-lynching campaigns, 5, 6, 7, 18n9, 24, 44n1, 135, 148–49, 157, 174, 175, 179, 186, 188, 191, 192, 340
anti-poll tax campaigns, 24, 44n1, 91, 149, 186, 192
antisemitism, 23, 29–31, 40–41, 73, 90, 102, 111, 115, 192, 210, 217, 293, 333, 348; Latin America and, 212, 223; Nazi Germany and, 51, 61, 104, 195; Soviet Union and, 42–43, 207, 221, 239–40, 242–43, 345
Anvil, 126
Aptheker, Herbert, 18n9, 112, 113, 114, 115, 324, 340
Arbeter Frayhayt Temple, 230
Arbeter Ring. *See* Workmen's Circle
Argentina, 13–14, 34, 205–8, 211–12, 215–18, 223
Argentine Communist Party, 206–7
Argentine Socialist Party, 206
Arion, Ernest, 283–87, 294–97
Arnold, Abe, 233
Arow Farm, 16
art, 13, 158, 185, 211, 215, 251–58, 260–71, 357, 358
ARTEF (Arbeter Teater Farband), 29, 268
Artkino Films, 317
Asch, Sholem, 25, 34, 185, 210
Ashcan artists, 254, 255, 256

assimilation, 3, 52, 57, 86, 218, 221, 242, 295, 334, 355
Asociación Mutual Israelita Argentina (Argentine Jewish Mutual Association) (AMIA), 209, 217, 223
Association for the Study of Negro Life and History, 135
Atlanta Daily World, 152
Attorney General's List of Subversive Organizations, 42, 315–17, 319–21
Auerbach, Sol. *See* Allen, James
Di Avangard, 206
Azaña, Manuel, 278
Azar, Joseph, 285

Bailey, Max, 233, 240
Baker, Ella, 7
"Ballad for Americans," 12, 133, 146, 156, 159, 160, 162–63, 166, 186
Baltich, Nick, 317
Baltimore Afro-American, 126, 181
Bandung Conference, 167
Bar Kokhba, 32–33, 262–63
Bardi, Gino, 14
Baron, Herman, 270
baseball, 5, 7, 154, 155, 186
basketball, 7, 124, 276
Basman, Labl, 235, 239, 243
Bass, Charlotta, 178, 195
The Battle of Russia, 42
Bedacht, Max, 5, 8, 14, 37, 47n28, 189, 278, 279, 287, 288, 296, 298, 309, 311–14
Bennett, A. B., 233, 239
Bennett, Gwendolyn, 135
Berg, Nils, 294, 295
Bethune, Norman, 232
Bick, Abraham, 234, 236
Biderman, Morris, 231, 232, 236, 238, 239, 241, 243–44
The Big Sea, 124, 128
Bilbo, Theodore, 19–20n23, 149, 343
Binder, Harry, 229
Birobidjan Appeal to Aid Jewish War Orphans, 233
Birobidzhan, 14, 207, 213, 216, 221, 230, 233–39, 242–44
birth control, 2, 10, 129, 148, 182
Black Belt thesis, 77–78, 172–76, 182, 187–88, 195, 196, 335
Black Book, 42, 216
"Black Hundreds," 207
#BlackLivesMatter, 5, 11, 16
Blitz, Tzalel. *See* Kogan, Samuel

Bloor, Ella Reeve, 75–76, 82
B'nai B'rith, 26, 34, 35, 37, 39
Board of Immigration Appeals, 88, 91
Bohlinger, Alfred, 322, 324
Bohlinger v. International Workers Order, 129, 130
Bolshevik Revolution, 2, 6, 27–28, 45n10, 53, 75, 125, 176, 206, 212, 244, 337, 341, 354
Bolshevization, 2, 51, 55–57, 59, 61
Borokhov, Dov Ber, 206
Boston Daily Post, 80–81
Botoshansky, Jacobo, 213, 215
Botwin Company, 293
Bridges, Harry, 80
Briggs, Cyril, 173, 174
Broady, Eleanor, 182
Brodsky, Joseph, 311–12
Bronstein, Rose, 242, 243
Brooklyn Contemporary Players, 283
Brotherhood Month, 90
Browder, Earl, 159
The Brown Book of Fascism, 212
Brown, John, 123
Buck, Tim, 237, 243
Budish, J. M., 233
Buhay, Michael, 241
Bund (Jewish Labor Bund), 28, 29, 45n10, 52, 205–7, 213, 215, 216, 218, 335, 352n34
Burroughs, Williana, 174

Caballero Llargo, Francisco, 278
Cahan, Abraham, 29
Calmenson, Jesse, 35
Camp Kinderland, 15, 34–35, 40, 50, 63, 87, 146, 155, 231, 282, 283, 286, 293, 294, 348, 358
Camp Kinderland (Canada), 231
Camp Kindervelt (Naivelt), 231
Camp Nitgedaiget, 155, 280, 282
Camp Unity, 286
Camp Wo-Chi-Ca, 12, 87, 145–48, 152, 154–56, 158–59, 162–67, 185
Camp Wocolona, 155
Canada, 14, 74–75, 166, 205, 206, 207–8, 211, 229–31, 235, 236, 238–42
Canadian Birobidjan Committee, 231, 233–36, 239, 240, 242, 244
Canadian Jewish Congress, 232
Canadian Jewish Historical Society, 233
Canadian Jewish Weekly Association, 233
Canadian Labour Circle, 230
Canadian Tribune, 239–40
Cannon, James P., 56

Capra, Frank, 42
"The Capriccios," 266
Carr, Sam, 233, 234, 241, 243
Casa do Povo (People's House), 219–20
Cervantes Society, IWO, 4, 5, 13, 38, 129, 149, 174, 181, 324
Chagall, Marc, 25, 42, 185
Chakin, Alfred, 276, 277
Chelsea Jewish Children's School (Massachusetts), 320
Chinese Exclusion Act, 80
choirs, 27, 29, 50, 129, 130, 146, 156, 159–63, 186, 231, 233, 234, 317, 343, 355
Civil Rights Congress, 87, 149, 152, 178, 186, 194
Civilian and National Defense Exposition, 146, 156, 159–60, 162, 166
Clark, Tom, 42, 315–16, 321
Cohn, Fannia, 254–55
Cohn, Roy, 122
Colón, Jesús, 4, 129, 174, 185, 324
Colonel Tom's Cabin, 136, 138
Comintern (Communist International), 60, 75, 134, 339; Black Belt thesis and, 77, 172–76, 182, 335; Popular Front and, 175, 207, 210, 341; Spanish Civil War and, 281; Yevsektsiya and, 206–8, 211, 221
Commission on Negro Work, IWO, 165
Committee against Racism and Antisemitism in Argentina, 212
Committee for Jewish Pro-Colonization in Soviet Russia (PROCOR), 207
Communist Party of Canada, 75, 229–30, 233, 243, 244
Communist Party USA (CPUSA), 2, 3, 5, 6, 8, 28, 41, 79, 82, 192–93, 333, 342, 345; African Americans and, 78, 103, 172–79, 181, 187–88, 290, 339; Americanization and, 55; Molotov-Ribbentrop Pact and, 15; Spanish Civil War and, 281, 283, 290, 294; women and, 75–76, 84, 85, 194; Workers Schools and, 12–13, 50, 55–58, 181
Communist University of the Toilers of the East, 76–78
Communist Youth Federation, 222
Congregational Education Society, 125
Congress of Industrial Organizations (CIO), 1, 3, 11, 15, 129, 137, 139, 186
Congress of Jewish Culture, 208
Congress of Racial Equality (CORE), 7
Connolly Column, 281
Connor, Eugene, 179–80
Construction of the Dam, 267

consumer boycotts, 9, 10, 82–84, 188
Continental Assurance Company of Illinois, 324
"The Convulsionaries," 283–85, 294, 295, 297, 299, 300
Co-op City, 357
Cooperative Center (Los Angeles), 260
Council of Jewish Progressive Organizations, 238
Council on African Affairs, 135, 180, 193
Council for Russian War Relief, 263
The Crisis, 103, 123
Croatian Glee Club (Gary, Indiana), 317
Cuban Revolution, 222, 344
Culture and the Crisis, 127, 128
Cuney, Waring, 135
Cuthbert, Marion, 158
Czernowitz Conference, 210, 218

Daily Worker, 13, 150, 155, 265, 276, 287, 319
dance, 129, 130, 135, 138, 140, 152, 157, 160, 166, 186, 231, 268
Davis, Angela, 92, 196, 344
Davis, Leon, 340
Debs, Eugene, 123, 125
Delaware Valley Committee for Democratic Rights, 16, 325
Delegación de Asociaciones Israelitas Argentinas (Delegation of Jewish Argentinian Associations), 209, 217
Demas, John, 283
"Democracy and Me," 128–29, 138
Democratic Socialists of America, 356
deportations, 11, 79–80, 88–89, 91, 115, 193, 209, 212, 241, 310–11, 317–19
Detroit Police Intelligence Division ("Red Squad"), 16, 313, 324
Dewey, Thomas E., 322
Dies Bill, 310
Dies, Martin, 310, 312–15
Dimitrov, Georgi, 296, 341–42
displaced persons, 39, 42, 48n35, 318
Dixon, Dean, 157, 159
Dmytryshyn, Andrew, 318
Donner, Fred, 235
Don't You Want to Be Free?, 136–40, 158
Dorsey, Agnes L., 164
"Double V Campaign," 140, 161, 192, 195
Douglass, Frederick, 157, 316
Douglass-Lincoln Society, IWO, 1, 2, 149, 181, 185, 195
Dreyfus Affair, 101, 111–12
Du Bois, Shirley Graham, 87, 100, 115, 178

INDEX

Du Bois, W. E. B., 13, 18n9, 99–116, 160, 174, 176, 177, 179, 180, 194, 335
Duncan, Laura, 24, 157–59, 167
Du Sable Community Center (Chicago), 4, 146, 164
Du Sable Lodge 751, IWO (Chicago), 182–84

Educational Alliance Art School, 254
Einbinder, Gershon. *See* Paver, Chaver
Einstein, Albert, 25, 32, 34–35, 185, 263
Ellis Island, 88, 205, 310
Emancipation Proclamation, 80, 148
The Em-Fuehrer Jones, 136, 139
Emma Lazarus Division of Jewish Clubs, 12, 72–74, 76, 81, 85–86, 89–92, 357
The Emperor Jones, 139
Engels, Friedrich, 334
English lodges, IWO, 5, 38, 40, 60, 126, 178, 181, 189, 192, 338
Epshtein, Shakne, 29, 59
Erlich, Henryk, 29
Estado Novo (New State), 219, 227n41
Estreicher, Stanisław, 106–7, 108, 109, 111
Ethiopia, 15, 25, 139, 161, 188, 276, 291
Eynikayt (Unity), 27, 216

Fair Employment Practices Committee, 5, 183, 343
Falkowski, Ed, 15, 325
Far Sovet Rusland, 263
fascism, 9, 40, 51, 60, 61, 124, 127, 210, 252, 261–62, 276, 318, 341–42; African Americans and, 161, 175, 188, 288, 291–92; Latin America and, 212, 218; Spain and, 14, 134, 188, 211–12, 232, 277–78, 280, 288, 291, 294, 296, 322
Fast, Howard, 25, 185, 269
Federal Art Project, 261
Federal Bureau of Investigation (FBI), 10, 78–79, 88, 91, 241, 314
Federal Housing Administration, 315
Fefer, Itzik, 34–35, 216, 240
Feminist Group Against War, 212
Fenely, Albert, 311
Ferrer School, 256
Fight Against War and Fascism, 131
film, 138, 139, 150, 179–80, 356
Fine, Fred, 16
Finnish American Mutual Aid Society, 279, 287, 288
Finnish Organization of Canada, 230
Finnish Socialist Federation, 337
Finnish Work People's College, 55

First Congress of Writers in Defense of Culture, 210
First International Congress of Jewish Culture, 213
First Israelite Convention of Culture, 218
Flacks, Dick and Mickey, 324
Flynn, Elizabeth Gurley, 16, 325
Folks-Shtime (Warsaw), 43, 242
Foner, Philip, 340
Ford, James W., 135, 173, 174, 188
Forverts (Forward), 29, 34, 337
Foster, William Z., 193, 260
Four Freedoms, 7, 309
Franco, Francisco, 14, 134, 282, 289, 291, 293, 297, 300, 322
Franklin D. Roosevelt Hospital Fund, 323
Fraternal Outlook, 6, 24, 126, 149, 154, 156, 158, 159, 164, 191, 265, 312, 313, 317
Frayhayt Club, 230
Frayhayt Farband, 257, 268
Free Southern Theater, 136
Freedman, Bezalel, 294
Freedman, Blanch, 92
Freedom Seder, 346
Friends of the Abraham Lincoln Brigade, 287, 292
Front Line Fighters Fund, IWO, 85, 287, 323
Frontier Films, 150

Garibaldi Battalion, 288
Garibaldi Society, IWO, 5, 8, 31, 38, 99, 288, 312, 316, 335, 342
Garland, Walter, 173, 188, 196, 290
Garrison, William Lloyd, 123
Gartner, Emil, 234
Garvey, Marcus, 339
Garvin, Vicki, 151
Gates, John, 299
Gauld, Alex, 241
Gebert, Bolesław, 80, 88–89, 310, 318
Gellert, Hugo, 253, 258, 264, 265, 267
Gellert, Lawrence, 265
Gershman, Joshua (Joe), 230, 233–35, 237, 238, 241–44
GI Bill, 347
Gilbert, Ronnie, 162–63
Gitlow, Kate, 81
Głos Ludowy, 9, 15, 321, 324, 325
Goff, Irving, 280, 281, 283
Gold, Mike, 130
Goldberg, B. Z., 25, 34, 235
Goldberg, Itche, 35, 62, 67, 68, 185, 293–94, 320, 355, 357

INDEX

Goodelman, Aaron, 253–54, 258–61, 267, 268, 271, 273n21
Gordon, Eugene, 80–81, 90, 92, 135, 173, 188
Gordon, Gene, 145, 147, 154, 165
Gordon, June, 12, 21, 72–82, 85–86, 89–92, 179, 182
GOSET. *See* Moscow State Jewish Theater
Gouzenko, Igor, 241
Great Depression, 2, 8–9, 60, 73, 79, 82, 126, 127, 132, 174–75, 195, 218, 254, 261, 267, 278, 300, 336
Great Migration, 174
Greenberg, Henry Clay, 322, 323
Gropper, William, 13, 32, 253–58, 261–67, 269–71, 312
Guberman, Louis, 234
Guralnick, Harry, 233
Guthrie, Woody, 356
Gwinn Amendment, 320, 321

Hadassah, 39, 73
Hague, Frank, 139
Haitian Revolution, 174
Halevi, Judah, 32
Halpern, Clara, 280, 286
Halpern, Moyshe-Leyb, 211
Der hamer, 55–57, 258, 265
Harap, Louis, 99
Harisiades, Peter, 89, 115, 318–19
Harkavy, Minna, 13, 253–54, 258, 260–61, 267–68, 270, 271
Harlem Community Center, 135, 188
Harlem Federal Theatre Project, 136
Harlem Players, 157
Harlem Renaissance, 132, 157, 158, 179
Harlem Suitcase Theatre, 11, 12, 130, 135–39, 158, 165, 186, 279
Harris, Abe, 284
Harris, B. W., 190
Haymarket Riot, 131, 142–43n40
Haywood, Harry, 173, 188, 195, 196
Healey, Dorothy, 356
health clinics, 2, 8, 129
Henri, Robert, 254, 256
Herndon, Angelo, 155
Herrick, William, 300
Heym un dertsiung. See *Proletarishe dertsiung*
Hitler, Adolf, 15, 25, 29, 32, 40, 41, 139, 160, 192, 252, 262; Spain and, 277, 278, 289, 291, 292, 300
Hitler's Plan, 212
Holiday, Billie, 24, 158, 265

Holocaust, 13, 29–30, 38, 41, 42, 92, 101, 195, 221, 234, 238, 267–71, 293, 294
Holodomor, 43
Home Relief Bureau, 82
homophobia, 296–97
Hoover, J. Edgar, 78, 91
Horne, Lena, 164, 182
hospitals, 39, 91, 278, 318, 323, 340
House Un-American Activities Committee, 10, 15, 153, 193–94, 265–66, 307, 310, 312–15, 320
Huey, Richard, 157
Hughes, Langston, 1, 12, 25, 122–41, 146–47, 157, 158, 160, 165–67, 179, 185–88, 291
Hungarian Workingmen's Sick and Benefit Society, 7, 260
Hurrah, America!, 136, 139
Hurston, Zora Neale, 127, 158

Ickes, Harold, 314
Idisher Folk Teater (Yiddish Folk Theater) (IFT), 220
#IfNotNow, 347
Immigration and Naturalization Service, 88, 310, 317, 318
immigration restriction, 2, 7, 80, 124, 345
Ingram Children's Education and Welfare Fund, 87
Ingram, Rosa Lee, 2, 87, 88, 90, 92, 150, 155, 164, 186
Instituto Cultural Israelita Brasileiro (Brazilian Jewish Cultural Institute) (ICIB), 219
insurance, 5, 26, 178, 311–12, 314, 315; African Americans and, 129, 148, 181, 183–84, 186, 193, 199–200n29, 202n49; liquidation and, 43, 321–24
Internal Revenue Service, 315, 321
International Bazaar for Peace and Freedom (Detroit), 16, 324
International Brigades, 14, 134, 211, 225n16, 231–32, 281–84, 286, 288–94, 296–300
International Committee on African Affairs, 134
International Conference on Antisemitism and Racism, 188
International Fiesta, 146, 156, 158–59
International Labor Defense, 79, 174, 179, 180, 186, 193, 313, 340
International Ladies Garment Workers Union, 55, 254–55, 333, 335, 357
International Red Aid, 212
International Youth Section, IWO, 276

interracial solidarity, 5, 6, 7, 8, 60, 123, 124, 129, 146, 149, 156, 159, 167, 172, 177, 185, 186, 195, 201n42, 288, 323; camps and, 152, 155, 166; difficulty achieving, 182; Emma Lazarus Clubs and, 74, 89; English lodges, IWO, and, 40, 126; Jewish-American Section, IWO, and, 23
intifadas, 347
Irish Democrat, 286
Irish Workers' Club, IWO, 280
Israel, 39, 42, 217, 219, 221, 237–39, 244, 345, 346, 347
Israeli Communist Party, 345
Israeli Labor Party, 346
IWO Junior Band, 157, 160
IWO Youth Theatre (New York), 283–86, 297

Jackson, Calvin, 157
Jackson, Esther Cooper, 151
Janošík, 289, 304n59
Jefferson School of Social Science, 67, 71n43, 116, 258, 340
Jefferson, Thomas, 13, 33, 316, 342
Jenofsky, Abraham, 233
Jewish-American Section, IWO, 11, 12, 21, 23, 25–26, 29–32, 34–38, 81, 182, 281. *See also* Jewish Peoples Fraternal Order
Jewish Anti-Fascist Committee, 11, 24–25, 27–28, 31–34, 38, 42, 43, 216, 239, 242
Jewish Art Center, 260
Jewish Council for Russian War Relief, 32, 34, 263
Jewish Currents, 15, 43, 348
Jewish Educational Institute, 67
Jewish Folk Choir, 234
Jewish Fraternalist, 318
Jewish Life, 15, 43, 99, 100, 104, 108, 109, 110, 113, 242, 324
Jewish Peoples Fraternal Order (JPFO), 1, 4, 26, 72, 117n5, 194, 232, 234, 251, 252, 259, 260, 337, 338, 343, 357, 358; anti-Communism and, 42–43, 99, 209, 217, 319; Palestine and, 39, 42; World War II and, 23–25, 27–28, 31, 32, 37–38, 40–41, 67, 216, 263, 268–71; YKUF and, 205–8, 211, 261
Jewish Peoples Fraternal Order Book Fund, 323
Jewish Peoples Fraternal Order National School Committee, 319
Jewish Socialist Federation, 27, 57
Jewish Voice for Peace, 347
Jewish Women's Labour League, 230
Jewish Workers' Cultural League, 230
Jewish Workers' Party, 206
Jewish Workers University, 13, 21, 28, 29, 50–52, 54–63, 67, 210
Jews Against the Occupation, 347
Jews Without Money, 130
"John Henry," 264–65
John Reed Clubs, 126, 260, 261
Johnson-Reed Act, 2, 7
Joint Distribution Committee, 34
Jones, Claudia, 87, 88, 90, 115, 173, 179, 193, 195, 196
Jones, Robert Earl, 135

Kaartinen, Onni, 279
Kahn, Albert, 19n23, 195
Der Kamf, 230, 232, 233
Karlin, William, 323
Katz, Pinie, 211–16, 225–26n20
Kaye, Conrad, 299
Kennedy, Robert, 15
Kent, Rockwell, 5, 25, 44n5, 180, 185, 189–90, 310, 315
Keren Kayemet LeIsrael (The Jewish National Fund) (KKL), 217
Khrushchev, Nikita, 217, 221, 242
kibbutzim, 346
Kinderland, 258–59
King, Martin Luther, 7, 91, 340–41, 346
King, William Lyon Mackenzie, 241
Knight, Gwendolyn, 158
Knights of Columbus, 322
Knopf, Blanche, 128, 130
Kogan, Samuel, 222
Kolisnyk, W. M., 230
Kollwitz, Käthe, 256
Komorowski, Conrad, 15, 324
Kopelman, Menachem, 211
Korean War, 242
Kosciuszko, Tadeusz, 33
Kronstadt Uprising, 53
Krzycki, Leo, 31
Ku Klux Klan, 104
Kutcher, James, 321
Kutler, Yosl, 258

La Guardia, Fiorello, 34, 261, 263
La Internacional (The International), 207
Labor-Progressive Party (Canada), 233–35, 237, 240, 242
Labour League, 230, 243
Lamentations, 267
The Lamp, 89, 90

Lampell, Millard, 356
Landis, Kenesaw Mountain, 186
Landsmanshaften, 27, 208, 219, 233, 235
Langston, John M., 123
Lappin, Ben, 232
Larsen, Nella, 157
Latouche, John, 133, 156, 162
Law Oliver, 290
Lawrence, Jacob, 158
Lawson, Edward, 136
Lazarus, Emma, 72–74, 89
League Against Fascism and Dictatorship, 30
League of American Writers, 126, 127, 128
League of Nations, 257
League of Professional Groups for Foster and Ford, 127
League of Struggle for Negro Rights, 126, 290
Lebns farn Lebn, 292–94
Leibowitz, Samuel, 340
Lenin School (Moscow), 76
Lenin, Vladimir, 50, 125, 206, 258, 339
Lerner, Gregorio, 212
"Let America Be America Again," 132–34, 138, 186
Let's Get Together, 282
Levin, Max, 235
Levine, June, 145, 147, 154, 165
Leyvick, H., 211, 214
Liberia, 80
libraries, 135, 205, 208, 213, 218, 219, 265, 283
Liebknecht, Karl, 341
Likud Party (Israel), 347
Limitations of Life, 136, 138
Lincoln, Abraham, 13, 80, 123, 160, 265, 291, 316
Linke Poale Tsiyon (Left Zionist Workers), 54, 205–7
Lipshitz, Sam, 229, 232, 239, 240, 241, 243, 244
Liptzin, Sam, 354
liquidation, 10, 16, 89, 99, 100, 126, 178, 194, 195, 310, 321–25
Locke, Alain, 136, 157
"Lonesome Train," 356
Louverture, Toussaint, 174–75
Love, Vaughn, 283, 289–93, 297, 300
Loyalty Board, 316–17
Lozowick, Louis, 253–54, 258, 261, 267, 271
Ľudové noviny, 16
Ľudový denník, 311
L'unita del Popolo, 115, 319
Luxemburg, Rosa, 341

Maccabee, Judah, 32–33, 263
MacCormack, Daniel, 80

Mackenzie-Papineau Battalion, 232
MacLeod, A. A., 242
Malcolm X, 341
Marcantonio, Vito, 4, 5, 9, 12, 25, 99, 100, 180, 185, 310, 312, 315, 316, 322
March on Washington for Jobs and Freedom, 91
March on Washington Movement, 161
Markoff, Abraham, 56
Marmor, Kalman, 58, 61
Martyr, 268
Marx, Karl, 172, 258, 334
Marxism, 54, 58, 62, 68, 76, 79, 103, 114, 174–76, 179, 206, 207, 210, 237, 252, 258, 269, 334, 335
Marxism and the National Question, 45, 174
masculinity, 76, 265, 267, 274n37, 296–97
Mason, Charlotte Osgood, 126–27
Massachusetts Committee for Russian Relief, 268
Massachusetts Department of Insurance, 311
Maud, Zuni, 258, 263
May Day, 131, 140–41, 142–43n40, 186
McCarthy, Joseph, 122, 124
McCarran Act, 16, 88, 325
McCarran-Walter Act, 318
McKay, Claude, 173, 174
McKelvey-White, David, 292, 293
McLaughlin, Patrick Roe, 280, 281, 286, 287, 289, 295, 296
McNutt, Paul, 314
medical care, 5, 8, 30, 39, 129, 148, 180, 182, 185, 231, 278, 287, 288
Meeropol, Abel, 24, 158, 185, 265
Meloff, Harry, 282–87, 293, 294, 296–300
Mesaba Coop Park, 348
The Messenger, 151, 157
Metropolitan Life Insurance Company, 9, 19n20
Meyerhold, Vsevolod, 135
Michigan Department of Insurance, 314
Mikhoels, Shloyme, 32, 34–35, 43, 47n21, 216, 239–40
Milgrom, Sam, 281, 310, 315, 317, 318
Military Intelligence Service, 299
Mindel, Jacob, 57
misogyny, 296–97
Molotov-Ribbentrop Pact, 3, 15, 25, 29, 43, 63, 191, 195, 215, 232, 252, 300
Montgomery Improvement Association, 91
Montreal Labor College, 75, 79
Moore, Queen Mother Audley, 173, 178
Morgan, Crawford, 291
Morgenstern, Joseph, 236

Morgn Frayhayt, 29, 43, 82, 242, 256, 261, 262, 337, 340, 345–46, 356; workers schools and, 57, 58, 71n43; World War II and, 30, 34; Zionism and, 39, 257
Morris, Leslie, 239
Morris Winchevsky Shule, 230, 239
Moscow State Jewish Theater (GOSET), 34, 239
Moss, Al, 157, 158, 160, 162
Moss, Carlton, 146, 157, 158, 167
Mother's League, 230
Mothers of Plaza de Mayo, 223
multiculturalism, 334–36, 338, 342, 348, 349, 355
Murray, James, 41–42, 263
Mussolini, Benito, 31, 32, 260, 276, 277, 278, 288, 289, 291, 300, 310, 341
Myers, Irving J., 234, 235, 240
Mykytew, John, 182

Nadir, Moshe, 29
National Association for the Advancement of Colored People, 87, 91, 99, 103, 113, 123, 150, 151, 192
National Committee for the Defense of Political Prisoners, 126
National Committee to Free the Ingram Family, 87, 88
National Council of Negro Women, 188
National Education Department, IWO, 130
National Emergency Civil Rights Mobilization, 150
National Jewish Committee of the Labor-Progressive Party, 234, 237, 239
National Labor Relations Act, 309
National Miners Union, 80
National Negro Congress, 149–50, 154, 175, 186, 188, 190, 192
National Negro Department, CPUSA, 78
National Textile Workers Union, 79
National Urban League, 136, 150
National Women's Commission, CPUSA, 76
Nazism, 3, 13, 30, 32, 38, 41, 42, 61, 104, 113, 139, 195, 207, 216, 231, 253, 256, 263, 268–69, 276, 341; Molotov-Ribbentrop Pact and, 191, 215; Spain and, 14
Nearing, Scott, 77
The Necklace, 260
Needle Trades Workers Industrial Union, 79
"The Negro and the Warsaw Ghetto," 100, 101, 110, 115, 116
Negro Caravan, 134
Negro Experimental Theater, 135

Negro History Week, 18n9, 24, 90, 135, 140, 149, 152, 185, 186
The Negro in American Life, 157
Negro Progressive Theater, 158
Negro Songs of Protest, 265
Negro Worker, 126
Nelson, Edward, 3
Nelson, Rose, 82, 84, 88, 91, 156, 182
Nelson, Steve, 283, 338
Never to Forget: The Battle of the Warsaw Ghetto, 269
New Deal, 3, 8, 41, 261, 310, 312, 315, 347, 355, 357
New Masses, 126, 130, 252, 253, 265
New Order, 126, 130, 311
A New Song, 1, 130–34, 140, 186–87
New York City Board of Education, 320
New York Herald Tribune, 322
New York Society of Women Artists, 260
New York State Department of Insurance, 10, 24, 43, 307, 321–23
New York Sun, 313
New York Times, 348
New York Workers School, 56–59, 61–63, 67
New York World-Telegram and Sun, 320, 322
Night of the Murdered Poets, 43, 216
Nisnevitz, Abraham, 233, 236
Nixon, Richard, 314
North American Committee to Aid Spanish Democracy, 126, 278, 280, 287
Novick, Paul, 345
Nowak, Stanley, 15, 185, 310, 318, 324, 325

Ocasio-Cortez, Alexandria, 349
O'Dwyer, William, 319
Office of Strategic Service, Foreign Nationalities Branch, 10, 315
Okhlopkov, Nikolay, 135
"Ol' Man River," 156, 166, 167
Olgin, Moissaye, 29, 45n8, 58, 211, 257, 260
Omar, Ilhan, 349
O'Neill, Eugene, 139
Opatoshu, Joseph, 211, 214
Operation Barbarossa, 25, 160, 192, 213, 216
Organización Popular contra el Fascismo y el Antisemitismo (Popular Organization Against Fascism and Antisemitism) (OPFA), 212
Organization for Jewish Colonization in Russia (ICOR), 230–33, 243, 244
Ostrowsky, Abbo, 254, 255
"Our Plan for Plenty," 8
Owen, Chandler, 157
Owens, Jesse, 139

INDEX

"Pale of Settlement," 210
Palestine, 38–39, 42, 44n3, 48n31, 85, 234–35, 237–39, 256–57, 269, 292, 321, 347–48
Palestinian Liberation Organization, 347
Pan-African Conference, 100, 174
Parkchester houses, 9, 19n20
Parsons, Lucy, 78
The Partisan, 268
Partisan Review, 356
patriotism, 31, 38, 150, 153, 156, 160, 162, 252, 261, 263, 288–89, 294–95, 312, 314, 334, 338, 342
Patterson, Louise Thompson, 3, 10, 12, 92, 148–49, 164, 176–78, 180–86, 188–96, 313; CPUSA and, 8, 309; Hughes and, 123, 125–27, 130, 135, 137, 158, 165, 186; interracial solidarity and, 40, 129–30, 172–73; Sojourners for Truth and Justice and, 89, 100, 178, 325; Spanish Civil War and, 279, 288, 290, 291, 293; "Triple Oppression" and, 1, 81, 90, 178
Patterson, Sam, 190
Patterson, William L., 12, 115, 173, 178, 180, 193–95, 340
Paul Robeson Playhouse (Camp Wo-Chi-Ca), 164–65
Payton, Frank, 276, 277
Paver, Chaver, 258
Peace Information Center, 99
Pearl Harbor, 30, 159, 192, 261
Peck, Luther, 183–84
Peekskill, NY, riot, 9, 86, 152–53, 186
People's Lobby for Peace, 156
"People's Olympics," 276
People's Voice, 161
Peretz Jewish Cultural Center of Villa Lynch, 220
Peretz, Y. L., 210, 263
Perkins, Frances, 80
Perón, Juan, 218, 227n36
Peterson, Dorothy, 135
Pevzner, Sam, 156, 159
Pharmacist Union, 340
Philadelphia Committee to Save the Ingram Family, 164
Phillips, Hillary, 157, 158
Phillips, Nathan, 233, 238
Phillips, Wendell, 123
Phylon, 138
Pilowsky, Jaccobo, 220
Piłsudski, Józef, 314
Pittsburgh Courier, 105, 113
Podolski, Henry, 89, 115, 318

Policyholder Protective Committee, IWO, 322, 324
Polish Home Army, 104
Polish National Alliance, 321
Polish Political Club (Detroit), 324
Polonia Society, IWO, 15, 16, 26, 33, 38, 115, 310, 314, 315, 316, 318, 321, 324, 342
Popular Front, 3, 60–61, 84, 124, 131–34, 139, 156, 163, 173, 175, 184, 185, 207, 252, 261, 279, 289, 336, 341–42, 356; Workers Schools and, 51, 56, 60–63, 67, 68, 338; World War II and, 7, 25, 140; YKUF and, 14, 27, 209, 215, 231
Powers, George, 281
Primus, Pearl, 152, 185
Progressive Jewish Society, 220
Progressive Party, 7, 316
Progressive Women's Council. *See* United Council of Working Class Women
Proletarishe dertsiung, 67
ProletPen, 211
Prussian Academy of Art, 256
public housing, 9, 19, 194, 320–21
Puerto Rican Socialist Party, 344
Pulaski, Casimir, 33
Pursuit of Happiness, 156

Race riots, 9, 104, 175, 196, 346
"Racism—Enemy of the Jewish People," 89–90
Radischev Russian Dancers, 157, 160
Rand School of Social Science, 55, 56, 75
Randolph, A. Philip, 91, 151, 157, 161, 341
Rankin, John, 19n23, 315
Rapaport, Willi, 277
Rapoport, Nathan, 100, 117n5
Ravitch, Melekh, 240
Reconstruction, 112–15, 123, 176, 335
"Red Diaper Babies," 346
Reeve, Carl, 75, 76, 91
rent strikes, 82, 188, 254, 357
Reserve Officer Training Corps, 297
Reuther, Walter, 318
Risorgimento, 336
Robeson, Eslanda, 87, 188
Robeson, Paul, 12, 35, 115, 133, 139, 150–51, 158, 160, 182–84, 186, 188, 190, 310, 356; anti-Communism and, 153, 193–94, 316, 320; camps and, 145–48, 154–57, 159, 162–67; Peekskill riot and, 9, 86, 152–53, 186
Robinson, Earl, 156, 162, 185, 190
Rockwell, George Lincoln, 91
Roiter Shtern (Red Star), 207

Romanian society, IWO, 315
Românul American, 315
Roosevelt, Eleanor, 73
Roosevelt, Franklin, 3, 7, 15, 31, 41, 80, 159, 161, 261–62, 309, 314, 315, 316
Rose, Fred, 233, 237, 238, 241
Rose McClendon Players, 158
Rosen, Charles, 234
Rosenberg, Julius and Ethel, 24, 43, 115, 185, 242, 324
Rosenfeld, Morris, 356
Ross, Edward Alsworth, 3
Rotenberg, Sol, 16, 325
Rovnosť ľudu, 6
Royal Canadian Mounted Police, 241
Rozetski, Ruth, 67
Rusciano, Ricco, 286
Russian Revolution. *See* Bolshevik Revolution
Rymer, Ernie, 355

Sacco and Vanzetti, 259, 260
Sachsenhausen concentration camp, 106
Sadkin, Sylvia, 280, 281, 286, 287, 296
Salerno, Michael, 115, 185
Salsberg, J. B., 233, 238, 242, 243, 244
Saltzman, Rubin, 34, 38, 39, 45n8, 48n31, 53, 68, 180, 194, 270, 273n21, 310, 319, 321, 322
Sanders, Bernie, 349
Savage, Augusta, 127
Scarlet Sister Barry, 136, 138
Schaefer, Jacob, 234
Scheibenreif, Frank, 16
School of Jewish Studies, 68, 71n43
Schultz, Benjamin, 320
Schwartz, Seymour, 270
Scott, Hazel, 152, 185
Scottsboro defendants, 2, 9, 87, 89, 103–4, 126, 129, 149, 150, 155, 174, 179, 186, 259–60, 340
Sculptors' Guild, 260, 267
Second Front, 31, 38, 216
Second World Congress Against Racism and Anti-Semitism, 288
Sedition Act, 125
Seeger, Charles, 264
Seeger, Pete, 162, 185, 264
segregation, 9, 15, 91, 110, 122, 149, 151, 161, 184, 186, 193, 194, 276, 289, 312, 316, 320, 343
Seminar in Negro History, 135, 188, 190
Senate Permanent Subcommittee on Investigations, 122
Serbian Society, IWO, 317

Seth Boyden Terrace (Newark, New Jersey), 321
Shavelson, Clara Lemlich, 10, 25, 84, 85, 182, 185
Shaw Commission, 257
Shipka, Peter, 6, 315, 321, 322
Shockley, William, 16
Sholem Aleichem Cultural Center, 220
Sholem Aleichem Institute's People's University, 58, 59
Sholem Aleichem Jewish Brazilian Library, 219
Sholem Aleichem School (Canada), 235
Sholem Aleichem School of Rio de Janeiro, 219
Sholem Aleichem School of São Paulo, 219
Show Boat, 150, 164
Shtern, Sholem, 232, 240
Shules, 39, 47n21, 53, 62, 67, 207, 210, 214, 219, 220, 222, 230, 234, 271, 292, 293, 319–20
Sigel, Miriam, 284–87, 296, 298
Sigel, Paul, 284–86, 292, 293, 296, 298
Simone, Nina, 158
Six Day War, 346
Sloan, John, 254, 256
Slovak Workers Society, 3, 6, 7, 8, 16, 67, 85, 148, 260, 279, 289, 311, 314, 340
Slovès, Haim, 45n8, 211
Smith Act, 313
Smith, Harold, 283, 284, 286, 293–96
Smolar, Hersh, 43, 242
Sniderman, Sam, 232
Social Security, 2, 5, 8, 38, 129, 155, 309, 312
Socialist International, 339
Socialist Labor Party, 334
Socialist Party, 6, 34, 56, 173, 337, 345
Socialist Workers Party, 314, 321
Sojourner Truth housing project riot, 9
Sojourners for Truth and Justice, 10, 89, 100, 149, 178, 195, 325
Solidarity, 165
Solidarity Lodge, IWO (Harlem), 130, 135, 180, 188, 201n42, 279
Solomon, Hayim, 33, 263
Sons of Italy, 31
Sorel, Felicia, 138
The Souls of Black Folk, 102, 103, 107, 111–14, 116
South Side Community Arts Center (Chicago), 182
Southern Christian Leadership Conference, 7
Southern Negro Congress, 311
Southern Worker, 340

Soviet Union, 6, 28, 39, 52, 55, 76–77, 126, 135, 177, 179, 180, 209, 213–14; antisemitism and, 42, 43, 239, 242–44; Birobidzhan and, 207, 216, 221, 230, 235–37, 239, 242; Israel and, 238–39; Molotov-Ribbentrop Pact and, 29–30; Spanish Civil War and, 211; World War II and, 3, 7, 23–25, 27, 30–34, 42, 160, 192, 221
Soyer, Moses, 253–54, 255, 267, 271
Soyer, Raphael, 253, 267
Spanish Civil War, 14, 211, 225n16, 231–32, 278, 281, 283, 284, 287, 297–99; Hughes and, 126, 134; Thompson Patterson and, 126, 134, 180, 188, 288, 291
Spanish Workers Club, IWO, 280
Spencer, Kenneth, 146, 152, 164–65, 167
Spinoza, Baruch, 33, 263
Stalin, Joseph, 25, 29, 31, 34, 42, 43, 45n10, 55, 174, 181, 194, 213, 215, 217, 240, 242, 252
Starr, George, 35, 40
Statue of Liberty, 72, 310, 318
"Strange Fruit," 24, 158–59, 265
"Strike of the 20,000," 10, 182
Students for a Democratic Society, 324
Stuyvesant Town houses, 9, 19n20, 186
Subversive Activities Control Act. *See* McCarran Act
Subversive Activities Control Board, 318
The Sun Do Move, 139

"Talented Tenth," 116
Tate, Carroll, 137
Taub, Muni, 240
Taylor, Glen, 316
Taylor, Pauline, 178, 196
Teheran Conference, 38, 194
Terrell, Mary Church, 188, 195
Thaelmann, Ernst, 155
Theatre de la Casa do Povo (TAIB), 220
Theatre Zhitlovsky, 220
"Third Period," 2, 51, 62, 78, 134, 172
Thompson, Louise. *See* Patterson, Louise Thompson
Tlaib, Rashida, 349
Trade Union Committee for the Organization for Negro Workers, 157
Trade Union Unity League, 79
Treblinka, 240, 269
Trepel, Elia, 235
Tresca, Carlo, 260
Triangle Shirtwaist Fire, 26, 255
"Tribute to the Warsaw Ghetto Fighters," 99
"Triple oppression," 1, 81, 90, 177, 178

Trotskyism, 297–98, 314, 321, 345
Truchman, Jennie, 89, 90
Truman, Harry S, 15, 39, 88, 161
Trump, Donald, 348
Truth, Sojourner, 89
Tubman, Harriet, 89, 157
Työmies, 7, 16, 338

Ujich, John, 310–11
Ukrainian Labour Farmer Temple Association, 230
Ukrainian People's Auditorium (Chicago), 16
Ukrainian Society, IWO, 149, 260, 318
Unemployed Councils, 82
Union of American Jews of Ukrainian Descent, 234
Union of Argentine Women. *See* Feminist Group Against War
United Action Committee Against the High Cost of Living, 83
United Auto Workers, 318
United Council of Working Class Women, 81–84
United Jewish People's Order, 75, 206–8, 211, 232–36, 238–44
United Nations, 12, 39, 48n31, 115, 194–95, 219, 238, 239
United States Holocaust Memorial Museum, 101
United Workers Cooperative Colony, 51, 53, 55, 69, 258, 293, 354
Unity Theater, 150
universal health care, 2, 7, 8, 38

Vanguard Club, 127
vanguardism, 176–77, 296, 300
Victor, Benjamin, 234, 235, 240, 241
Vietnam, 15, 92, 151, 324, 346
Vochenblat-Canadian Jewish Weekly, 230, 233, 237, 238, 239, 240, 241, 242, 244
Vokh, 257
Volunteer for Liberty, 285
Vrábel, Helen, 10, 85

Wallach, Albert, 281, 298
War Council of Cultural Groups, 268
War Manpower Office, 314
Warsaw Ghetto, 13, 100, 101, 104, 113, 116, 117n5, 269, 271
Warsaw Ghetto Uprising, 100, 102, 104, 117n5, 268, 269
Washington Battalion, 289, 298
Washington, Harold, 16

Waskow, Arthur, 346
Watt, George, 286, 293, 294, 296
"We Charge Genocide," 12, 115, 194–96, 202n52
The Weary Blues, 125
The Weavers, 162
Weiner, William, 148, 288, 311
White, Charles, 158
White, Maude, 77–80, 87, 89, 173
White, Milton, 299
"White Paper" (Palestine), 237
whiteness, 265, 346, 347
Whitman, Walt, 130–31, 133
Whitney Studio Club, 260
Williams, Bonita, 83–84
Williams, Mary Lou, 152
Williams, Robert F., 151
Williamsburg Houses (Brooklyn), 321
Win the Peace Conference, 12
Winchevsky Centre, 243
Winnick, Sol, 182
Wise, Louise Waterman, 73
Wise, Stephen, 34, 36, 38, 263
Witt, Art, 286
Wolfe, Bertram, 56
Wolff, Milton, 283, 298
Women's Committees, IWO, 10, 81–84, 191
Woodson, Carter G., 135
Workers' Art Scholarship, 255
Workers International Relief Camp, 155
Workers Monthly, 126, 132
Workers Music League, 264
Workers Schools, 12–13, 56, 58, 59, 61–63, 67, 70n16, 116, 129, 207, 214, 218–19, 258
Working Woman, 79, 81, 84

Workmen's Circle, 2, 4, 6, 26–27, 53, 54, 58, 59, 230, 255, 258, 336, 337, 338
Works Progress Administration, 182, 261, 267, 357
World Jewish Congress, 34
World War I, 2, 28, 75, 124, 339, 354
World War II, 3, 11, 23, 27, 29–31, 34, 85, 221, 262, 287, 314–15; African Americans and, 149–50, 160–61, 192
Wright, Richard, 151, 157

Yergan, Max, 135, 154, 188
Yevsektsiya (Yiddish section of the Comintern), 206–7, 218
Yiddish Book Center, 354
Yiddish Cultural Association (Yidisher Kultur Farband, YKUF), 14, 27, 45n8, 205–6, 208, 210–15, 231, 235, 236, 239, 261, 267
Yiddish Cultural Association, South America (ICUF), 205–6, 208–12, 214–23
Yiddish Culture Congress, 216
Yishuv, 38–39, 42, 237, 238, 239, 256, 292
Young As We Is, 136, 138–39
Young Communist League, 282–84, 286, 295
Young Workers League, 57
Youth March for Integrated Schools Committee, 91

Zhitlowsky, Chaim, 35, 210, 213, 259, 273n21
Zhitlowsky Foundation, 355
Zhitlowsky Jewish Cultural Association, 219–20
Zhitlowsky School (Montevideo), 219
Zionism, 37, 38, 42, 54, 205–7, 215, 217, 235, 237–38, 256–57, 346
Zionist Organization of America, 37
Zuken, Joseph, 229–30, 233, 234, 237, 240, 241

www.ingramcontent.com/pod-product-compliance
Lightning Source LLC
Chambersburg PA
CBHW031414230426
43668CB00007B/305

www.ingramcontent.com/pod-product-compliance
Lightning Source LLC
Chambersburg PA
CBHW031414230426
43668CB00007B/305